D1306415

ATTENTION and PERFORMANCE VIII

Proceedings of the Eighth International Symposium on Attention and Performance
Princeton, New Jersey, USA, August 20–25, 1978

ATTENTION and PERFORMANCE VIII

Edited by

Raymond S. Nickerson

Bolt Beranek and Newman Inc.
Cambridge, Massachusetts, USA

LEA LAWRENCE ERLBAUM ASSOCIATES, PUBLISHERS

1980   Hillsdale, New Jersey

Lawrence Erlbaum Associates, Inc., Publishers
365 Broadway
Hillsdale, New Jersey 07642

Library of Congress Cataloging in Publication Data

International Symposium on Attention and Performance,
  8th, Princeton, N.J., 1978.
  Attention and Performance VIII.

  Includes bibliographies and indexes.
  1. Attention--Congresses. 2. Performance--Con-
gresses. I. Nickerson, Raymond S. II. Title.
BF321.I57 1978   155.7'33   80-23850
ISBN 0-89859-038-8

Printed in the United States of America

Contents

PART VIII: REASONING, PROBLEM SOLVING, AND DECISION PROCESSES

Contributors and Participants

The names of conference participants who did not contribute to this volume are preceded by an asterisk (*). The names of contributors who did not participate in the conference are preceded by a dagger (†). The list of contributors includes coauthors.

Marilyn J. Adams, Bolt Beranek and Newman Inc., 50 Moulton Street, Cambridge, Massachusetts 02138, USA

Alan Baddeley, Medical Research Council, MRC Applied Psychology Unit, 15 Chaucer Road, Cambridge CB2 2EF, England

†**Susan D. Baillet,** University of Denver, Denver, Colorado 80210, USA

Jonathan Baron, Department of Psychology, University of Pennsylvania, Philadelphia, Pennsylvania 19104, USA

Donald E. Broadbent, Department of Experimental Psychology, University of Oxford, Oxford OX1 3UD, England

†**Margaret Broadbent,** Department of Experimental Psychology, University of Oxford, Oxford OX1 3UD, England

Ronald Cole, Department of Psychology, Carnegie-Mellon University, Pittsburgh, Pennsylvania 15213, USA

***Charles E. Collyer,** Department of Psychology, University of Rhode Island, Kingston, Rhode Island 02881, USA

Lynn Cooper, Department of Psychology, Cornell University, Ithaca, New York 14853, USA

Diana Deutsch, Center for Human Information Processing, University of California, San Diego, La Jolla, California 92093, USA

*Stanislav Dornic, Department of Psychology, University of Stockholm, S-113 85 Stockholm, Sweden

*Marshall Farr, Personnel and Training Programs, Department of the Navy, Office of Naval Research, Arlington, Virginia 22217, USA

Baruch Fischhoff, Decision Research, A Branch of Perceptronics, 1201 Oak Street, Eugene, Oregon 97401, USA

†Jennifer Freyd, Department of Psychology, University of Pennsylvania, Philadelphia, Pennsylvania 19104, USA

Anthony W. K. Gaillard, Institute for Perception, TNO, Kampweg 5, Postbus 23, Soesterberg, The Netherlands

Wendell R. Garner, Department of Psychology, Yale University, New Haven, Connecticut 06520, USA

†S. Garrod, Department of Psychology, University of Glasgow, Glasgow, G12 8RT, Scotland

David J. Getty, Bolt Beranek and Newman Inc., 50 Moulton Street, Cambridge, Massachusetts 02138, USA

Denis J. Glencross, The Flinders University of South Australia, Bedford Park, South Australia 5042

*Sam Glucksberg, Department of Psychology, Princeton University, Princeton, New Jersey 08540, USA

†Daniel Gopher, Technion-Israel, Institute of Technology, Haifa, Israel

†Carol Harris, Massachusetts Institute of Technology, Cambridge, MA 02139, USA

†William E. Hockley, University of Toronto, Toronto M5S 1A1, Canada

James E. Hoffman, Department of Psychology, University of Delaware, Newark, Delaware 19711, USA

Tarow Indow, School of Social Sciences, University of California, Irvine, Irvine, California 82717, USA

Gregory Jones, Department of Psychology, University of Bristol, Bristol BS8 1HH, England

*Michael Kaplan, U.S. Army Research Institute for the Behavioral and Social Sciences, 5001 Eisenhower Avenue, Alexandria, Virginia 22333, USA

Janice Keenan, Department of Psychology, University of Denver, Denver, Colorado 80208, USA

†Julia Kinchla, Rutgers University, New Brunswick, New Jersey 08903, USA

Ronald Kinchla, Department of Psychology, Princeton University, Princeton, New Jersey 08540, USA

Walter Kintsch, Department of Psychology, University of Colorado, Boulder, Colorado 80309, USA

*Stuart Klapp, Department of Psychology, California State University, Hayward, California 94542, USA

Raymond Klein, Department of Psychology, Dalhousie University, Halifax, Nova Scotia B3H 4J1, Canada

V. K. Kool, Humanities and Social Science Department, Indian Institute of Technology, Powai, Bombay 400 076, India

*Sylvan Kornblum, Mental Health Research Institute, University of Michigan, Ann Arbor, Michigan 48109, USA

Judith Kroll, Institute for Cognitive Studies, Rutgers—The State University, New Brunswick, New Jersey 08903, USA

Michael Kubovy, Psychology Department, Yale University, New Haven, Connecticut 06520, USA

*Elsie Leavitt, Bolt Beranek and Newman Inc., 50 Moulton Street, Cambridge, Massachusetts 02138, USA

Pekka K. Lehtiö, Department of General Psychology, University of Helsinki, Ritarikatu 5, SF-00170 Helsinki 17, Finland

†**K. Lieberman,** Department of Psychology, Stirling University, Stirling, Scotland

John B. Long, Ergonomics Unit, University College London, London WC1H 0AP, England

Christie L. MacKenzie, University of Waterloo, Department of Kinesiology, Waterloo, Ontario N2L 3G1, Canada

Tony J. Marcel, Medical Research Council, MRC Applied Psychology Unit, 15 Chaucer Road, Cambridge CB2 2EF, England

Ronald G. Marteniuk, Department of Kinesiology, University of Waterloo, Waterloo, Ontario N2L 3G1, Canada

*Florence T. Maurer, Bolt Beranek and Newman Inc., 50 Moulton Street, Cambridge, Massachusetts 02138, USA

*Gail McKoon, Dartmouth College, Hanover, New Hampshire 03755, USA

Donald McNicol, School of Psychology, University of New South Wales, Kensington, New South Wales 2033, Australia

Bennet B. Murdock, Jr., Department of Psychology, University of Toronto, Toronto M5S 1A1, Canada

David Navon, Department of Psychology, University of Haifa, Mount Carmel, Haifa 31 999, Israel

Allen Newell, Department of Computer Science, Carnegie-Mellon University, Pittsburgh, Pennsylvania 15213, USA

*Raymond S. Nickerson, Bolt Beranek and Newman Inc., 50 Moulton Street, Cambridge, Massachusetts 02138, USA

*Robert Ollman, Bell Laboratories, 600 Mountain Avenue, Murray Hill, New Jersey 07974, USA

†**Oren Patashnik,** Bell Laboratories, 600 Mountain Avenue, Murray Hill, New Jersey 07974, USA

†**Laila Poikonen,** University of Turku, Finland

*James Pomerantz, Department of Psychology, State University of New York, Buffalo, New York 14214, USA

Mary Potter, Department of Psychology, Massachusetts Institute of Technology, Cambridge, Massachusetts 02139, USA

Wolfgang Prinz, Abteilung Psychologie, Universitat Bielefeld, 48 Bielefeld, Postfach 8640, West Germany

Roger Ratcliff, Department of Psychology, Dartmouth College, Hanover, New Hampshire 03755, USA

†**Adam Reeves,** Institute fur Arbeitsphysiologie, Universitat Dortmund, West Germany

Jean Requin, Institut de Neurophysiologie et Psychophysiologie, Department de Psychobiologie Experimentale, 13274 Marseille Cedex 2, France

David Rosenbaum, Bell Laboratories, 600 Mountain Avenue, Murray Hill, New Jersey 07974, USA

Andries F. Sanders, Institute for Perception, TNO, Kampweg 5, Postbus 23, Soesterberg, The Netherlands

Anthony J. Sanford, Department of Psychology, University of Glasgow, Glasgow, G12 8RT, Scotland

*Walter Schneider, Department of Psychology, University of Illinois, Champaign, Illinois 61820, USA

Marilyn Shaw, Department of Psychology, Douglass College, Rutgers—The State University, New Brunswick, New Jersey 08903, USA

*Carl E. Sherrick, Department of Psychology, Princeton University, Princeton, New Jersey 08540, USA

†Paul Slovic, Decision Research, A Branch of Perceptronics, 1201 Oak Street, Eugene, Oregon 97401, USA

J. E. Keith Smith, Human Performance Center, University of Michigan, Ann Arbor, Michigan 48104, USA

*Joan Gay Snodgrass, Department of Psychology, New York University, New York, New York 10003, USA

George Sperling, New York University, New York and Bell Laboratories, Murray Hill, New Jersey 07974, USA

Robert Sternberg, Department of Psychology, Yale University, Box 11A Yale Station, New Haven, Connecticut 06520, USA

*Saul Sternberg, Bell Laboratories, 600 Mountain Avenue, Murray Hill, New Jersey 07974, USA

†Judith Stewart, Department of Psychology, University of Pennsylvania, Philadelphia, Pennsylvania 19104, USA

John A. Swets, Bolt Beranek and Newman Inc., 50 Moulton Street, Cambridge, Massachusetts 02138, USA

†Joel B. Swets, Bolt Beranek and Newman Inc., 50 Moulton Street, Cambridge, Massachusetts 02138, USA

*Rebecca Treiman, Department of Psychology, University of Pennsylvania, Philadelphia, Pennsylvania 19104, USA

†Kirsti Tuuainen, University of Turku, Finland

*William R. Uttal, Institute of Social Research, University of Michigan, Ann Arbor, Michigan 48106, USA

*Alan T. Welford, Department of Psychology, University of Adelaide, G.P.O. Box 498, Adelaide, South Australia

Christopher D. Wickens, Department of Psychology, University of Illinois at Urbana-Champaign, Champaign, Illinois 61820, USA

Michael Williams, Navy Personnel Research and Development Center, San Diego, California 92152, USA

†Stephanie Santos-Williams, Navy Personnel Research and Development Center, San Diego, California 92152, USA

*Joseph Young, National Science Foundation, 1800 G Street, N.W., Washington, D.C. 20550, USA

†Victor Zue, Research Laboratory of Electronics, Massachusetts Institute of Technology, Cambridge, Massachusetts 02139, USA

Preface

It is my very good fortune to have been associated with Attention and Performance since the first symposium of the series was held under Andries Sanders' able leadership in Soesterberg in 1966. I have enjoyed these meetings immensely, have learned much from them, and have come to think of them as exemplifying what scientific symposia should be: quality presentations of timely research, lively discussions and debates, and several days of intellectual and social interaction among colleagues whose paths too infrequently cross.

It was, however, with mixed feelings that I accepted the invitation of the Executive Committee to organize Attention and Performance VIII. I was pleased and honored to have been asked, but somewhat intimidated by the model established by the organizers of the preceding symposia. In accepting the invitation my hope was to match that model.

One of the traditions that was carried over from earlier symposia to Attention and Performance VIII was that of interpreting "attention and performance" broadly to incorporate most of what is usually included today under the rubric of human information processing. Another was the policy of flexible structure, or, if you prefer, structured flexibility: While several themes were selected around which to organize the papers, invitees were chosen less on the basis of how neatly they could be mapped onto this thematic organization than on their ability to contribute interesting ideas and research findings in the broadly defined domain of interest. The topical organization of the chapters in the book is a reasonable reflection of content but is not completely free of arbitrariness and forced fitting.

Also, as in some preceding Attention and Performance symposia, the intent in the present case was for each session to be introduced by an overview paper. The writers of these papers were not asked to produce comprehensive reviews of their respective areas but were encouraged to focus on a few key issues that they considered to be particularly timely and significant. As it turned out, the session on Language Comprehension did not include an overview paper because the invitee who was to prepare this paper was unable to participate.

The main departure from tradition in Attention and Performance VIII was the inclusion of the first of what is intended to be a series of Association Lectures. The Association Lecturer is chosen by the Executive Committee in recognition of outstanding past contributions to the study of attention and performance and in anticipation of a singular contribution to the planned symposium. The Committee's choice for the first Association Lecturer was Professor Wendell Garner. Professor Garner's talk was a highlight of the symposium and his chapter sets a superb standard for Association Lectures of the future. It is a special pleasure to have that chapter in this volume.

The planning and running of an international symposium and the preparation of the symposium proceedings require assistance and cooperation from many quarters. Attention and Performance VIII was no exception in this regard. I sought and received help from several people, and wish to acknowledge explicitly those contributions that were most influential in shaping the meeting and this book.

The selection of invitees and the structuring of the symposium sessions were done in consultation with my friend and colleague, Richard Pew, whose help I am most pleased to acknowledge. It had been my hope that Dick would serve as co-organizer of the symposium and co-editor of the proceedings, but his work responsibilities, which involved a one-year relocation, precluded this. His inability to participate was a loss to both the symposium and the proceedings.

Our planning was at once complicated and simplified by the superb response of the members of the Attention and Performance Advisory Council to a request for names of possible contributors. The complication resulted from the fact that the Council produced several times as many candidates as the number of papers permitted by the Association Bylaws. Without doubt, the most unpleasant task that an organizer of a symposium has is that of deciding, if only by default, who shall not be invited; and a long list of qualified candidates makes the choices that much more difficult. In another sense, however, the Council's response greatly simplified the selection task, inasmuch as all of the suggestions were attractive, and the choice conflicts involved were "approach-approach" in kind.

Each of the chapters in this volume was reviewed by two individuals; in most cases one of the reviewers was another participant in the symposium and one was not. Both the contributors to, and the readers of, the volume are indebted to these reviewers, whose comments were extremely helpful. I am particularly appreciative of the time spent by people who did not contribute chapters to the volume in reviewing the manuscripts of those who did. The names of these reviewers are listed below.

Special thanks also go to Elsie Leavitt and Florence Maurer, for coordinating the logistics of the meeting, and to Florence Maurer and Anne Kerwin for managing correspondence and the processing of the manuscripts.

Funding for the symposium was obtained from three sources: the U.S. Army Research Institute, the National Science Foundation, and the U.S. Office of Naval Research. The project managers for the three agencies were, respectively, Robert Sasmor, Joseph Young, and John O'Hare. Without the support provided by these agencies, the symposium could not have been held.

As organizer of the symposium and editor of the proceedings, I am, of course, most indebted to the symposium participants themselves. It was their efforts that made the symposium the intellectually stimulating event that it was, and whatever is of lasting value in this book is a consequence of the quality and significance of the work and ideas it records.

Raymond S. Nickerson

Attention and Performance reviewers who did not contribute to proceedings:

John R. Anderson	R. Duncan Luce
Edward C. Carterette	David Meyer
Herbert H. Clark	Lloyd H. Nakatani
Allan M. Collins	Robert G. Pachella
Michael C. Corballis	Allan Paivio
Jerry G. Ells	Stephen E. Palmer
Bert Forrin	Charles A. Perfetti
John Frederiksen	Gordon Pitz
David M. Green	James Pomerantz
Susan Haviland	Michael Posner
James E. Hoffman	George R. Potts
Daniel Kahneman	Keith Rayner
Barry H. Kantowitz	Tim Shallice
Daniel P. Keating	Joan Gay Snodgrass
William J. Kelly	George E. Stelmach
J. A. Scott Kelso	Saul Sternberg
Marcel Kinsbourne	Kenneth N. Stevens
Stuart Klapp	John Theios
Paul A. Kolers	Anne Treisman
Sylvan Kornblum	Charles S. Watson
Michael Kubovy	Daniel L. Weber
Alvin M. Liberman	Alan T. Welford
Robert S. Lockhart	Arthur Wingfield
Norman Loveless	

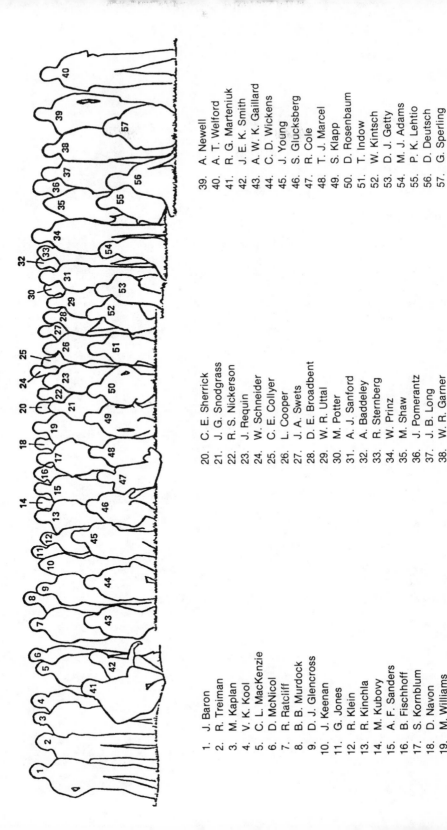

1. J. Baron
2. R. Treiman
3. M. Kaplan
4. V. K. Kool
5. C. L. MacKenzie
6. D. McNicol
7. R. Ratcliff
8. B. B. Murdock
9. D. J. Glencross
10. J. Keenan
11. G. Jones
12. R. Klein
13. R. Kinchla
14. M. Kubovy
15. A. F. Sanders
16. B. Fischhoff
17. S. Kornblum
18. D. Navon
19. M. Williams
20. C. E. Sherrick
21. J. G. Snodgrass
22. R. S. Nickerson
23. J. Requin
24. W. Schneider
25. C. E. Collyer
26. L. Cooper
27. J. A. Swets
28. D. E. Broadbent
29. W. R. Uttal
30. M. Potter
31. A. J. Sanford
32. A. Baddeley
33. R. Sternberg
34. W. Prinz
35. M. Shaw
36. J. Pomerantz
37. J. B. Long
38. W. R. Garner
39. A. Newell
40. A. T. Welford
41. R. G. Marteniuk
42. J. E. K. Smith
43. A. W. K. Gaillard
44. C. D. Wickens
45. J. Young
46. S. Glucksberg
47. R. Cole
48. T. J. Marcel
49. S. Klapp
50. D. Rosenbaum
51. T. Indow
52. W. Kintsch
53. D. J. Getty
54. M. J. Adams
55. P. K. Lehtio
56. D. Deutsch
57. G. Sperling

1

Association Lecture: Functional Aspects of Information Processing

W. R. Garner
Yale University
New Haven, Connecticut
United States

ABSTRACT

Functional aspects of information processing are discussed, with function having three different but related meanings. First, function is contrasted with structure, and such functional properties as expectancy, attention, effort, and state and process limitation are shown to differ from the primary structural construct of information processing stages. Second, function is a presuppositional aspect of information processing experiments, and these presuppositions, while keeping the experimental effort within bounds, must be considered as operations that converge to theoretical constructs as much as the experiments themselves do. Third, functional measurement decreases the importance of time as an absolute metric, thus exchanging for the power of absolute time a flexibility of interpretation which will allow methodological constructs such as additive and subtractive factors logic to survive experimental inconsistencies.

INTRODUCTION

In this chapter I discuss several substantive and methodological issues that I see as important in the study of human information processing, and these all relate to the idea of function in information-processing research. At Attention and Performance VI, A. F. Sanders (1977) spoke on structural and functional aspects of the reaction process, and some of the things I mention fit comfortably onto the ideas he expressed in distinguishing these two aspects of the reaction process. Stages constitute the primary structural aspect of information processing, but I want to expand the concept of function and to elaborate some very specific issues concerning functional aspects of information processing. Three different ways in which the idea of function enters into information processing research are described. To anticipate, there is function as contrasted with stages, function as presupposition in experimental design, and function as a guideline for measurement.

FUNCTIONAL PROCESSING

One specific article served as the immediate impetus for what I have to discuss because it involves all three of these issues in information processing. The article is by Shwartz, Pomerantz, and Egeth (1977), and we might look at some of their data to start this discussion. Figure 1.1 shows the data outcome for just part of one of the two separate experiments they reported, but it is enough to introduce the issues. The subject's task was to identify with a vocal response either the letter A or the letter H, displayed on a cathode-ray tube. Reaction time was, of course, the primary measure of performance. The experimental design followed the additive factors logic introduced by Sternberg (1969), and the total experiment involved three factors (although, for present purposes, discussion of just the two illustrated in Fig. 1.1 is sufficient). These two factors were whether a mask of dots was present or not and whether the two letters were physically similar or dissimilar. The additive factors logic says that if two factors have additive effects, which is to say that they do not produce interaction in an analysis-of-variance sense, then we can conclude that the two factors influence separate processing stages. Given this beautiful noninteractive outcome, that is what the authors of this article concluded. Furthermore, I have no quarrel with this conclusion as long as it is

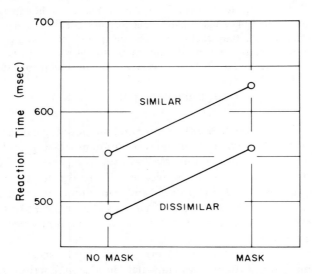

FIG. 1.1.   Discrimination time for the letters A and H, similar and dissimilar, masked or unmasked (after Shwartz, Pomerantz, & Egeth, 1977).

restricted to the specific experimental manipulations they used, that is, to the particular type of mask and the particular method of producing a difference in similarity.

State and Process as a Functional Distinction

However, the reason for choosing these particular factors or variables to manipulate was based on the constructs of state and process limitation that I have developed over the years, and they considered the use of masking to produce a state limitation and the use of low similarity to produce process limitation. Now the problem is that I have never considered the distinction between state and process, whether used as a concept of limitation or as a concept of perceptual independence, to involve stages or structure at all. Quite the contrary, I have considered the distinction to be a functional one (Garner, 1970, 1972, 1974). So, lest all functional distinctions become inadvertently reduced or translated to stage distinctions, I would like to elaborate on the role of function in information processing, with particular emphasis for the moment on the state–process distinction.

State and Process Independence. I first used the terms *state* and *process* in 1969 in an article published with John Morton concerned with concepts of perceptual independence rather than perceptual or processing limitation. The ideas we were trying to develop were concerned with the different ways in which information-processing psychologists were using the idea of perceptual independence (although the same problems existed in other psychological realms, such as memory). We felt in particular that two quite distinct ideas were being given a common designation, to the detriment of both. One of these ideas had to do with whether processes directly interacted, and the other had to do with whether the efficiencies of two processes were correlated. Although the full elaboration of this difference can become quite complicated, the distinction at a basic level is really quite straightforward, simply involving two kinds of data analysis required for the two types of independence or correlation. Table 1.1 illustrates, with hypothetical data, the type of analysis required if we want to ask whether two separate processes interact. These processes may be channels, variables, dimensions, or any other distinction that portrays concurrent ongoing processes, processes that can function at any stage. In the table I have simply used the general term *process,* although in the original article we referred to *attributes.*

The important point about this table is how the rows and columns are defined, because they must be defined in terms appropriate to the nature of the processing itself. In this particular illustration we are looking at two possible responses (1 and 2) to two possible processes (A and B), and you can see that there is a correlation, thus nonindependence, between these two processes. If we know that the inputs appropriate to each of these responses or

TABLE 1.1
A Table of Data Analyzing One
Form of Process Interdependence[a]

		Response to Process A		
		1	2	Σ
Response to	1	30	20	50
Process B	2	20	30	50
	Σ	50	50	100

[a]After Garner and Morton, 1969.

outputs are uncorrelated, then the existence of a correlation between the responses shows that there is interaction between the two processes. Many other tables could be constructed to show the exact nature of the interaction, tables that would portray data necessarily spanning several stages of information processing. One such table, for example, would show rows as input for process B, with columns being response or output for process A; and if such a data matrix showed a correlation, it would indicate that the output for process A is responsive to input for process B, at some unknown stage of processing. Thus this concept of process independence or correlation is simply not a stage concept at all but a functional concept that can span several processing stages.

Table 1.2 shows data in a different form, appropriate now for asking about state independence. Notice the different form in which the rows and columns are defined from those of Table 1.1 Now columns still refer to performance on process A and rows to performance on process B, but the separate columns or rows indicate whether performance was right or wrong. Once again there is correlation in this set of hypothetical data, but now there is no indication of a direct interaction between the two processes, only that performance on the two processes is better or worse together. It is the kind of outcome that would occur if there were fluctuations in alertness, attention, effort level, and other

TABLE 1.2
A Table of Data Analyzing State Interdependence[a]

		Process A		
		Right	Wrong	Σ
Process B	Right	44	16	60
	Wrong	16	24	40
	Σ	60	40	100

[a]After Garner and Morton, 1969.

such functional factors, factors that could and would operate at any stage of processing.

So Morton and I intended the distinction between state and process independence to be applicable to any or all stages of processing, with the concepts of state and process themselves being orthogonal to each other. The distinction between the two was unequivocally a distinction of function and not a distinction of structure or stages. With this particular distinction, the term *function* actually has two possible meanings. It can imply function in the sense that Sanders distinguished function from structure, and of course I am discussing stages because that is the major structure notion having currency now. But function can also imply the way data are treated, and in that sense the difference between state and process is almost a simple operational distinction.

State and Process Limitation.   I later (Garner, 1970) extended the concepts of state and process to involve limitation, not just interaction. Norman and Bobrow (1975) also explored distinctions between types of limitation, differentiating in particular between data and resource limitations; although their distinctions are related to those I have made between state and process, they are far from identical and are actually more in line with stage distinctions than with functional distinctions. In my own case, even while shifting from ideas of independence to those of limitation, I clearly intended the distinction to be functional and not structural.

The best way I know of differentiating between state and process limitations is shown in Fig. 1.2. At the top I have indicated the minimum sequence of events that can be involved in an information-processing act: an input stage, an internal-processing stage, and an output stage. It is this sequence which directly involves the processing of information, and any limitation which directly affects the processing of information as specified by the task requirements is a process limitation. Such limitations might be inadequate stimulus differentiation if at the input side of the sequence or an undifferen-

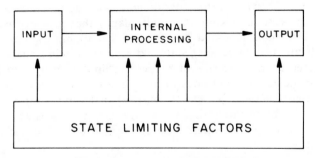

FIG. 1.2.   The relation between process and stage limiting factors.

tiated response system if at the output end, or any limitation on encoding, memory, retrieval, comparison, or other internal-processing stage.

State limiting factors are any factors that affect the ability of the organism to carry out the specified information-processing task but are not themselves directly relevant to that task. Thus if the organism is asleep, that is a state limiting factor; so also would be inadequate energy at the input end or weak fingers at the output end if the output is to be a lever push.

The point that must be understood is that process limitations can occur at any stage in processing and so also can state limitations. What differentiates the two is not stages but function with respect to the task as defined by the experimenter for the particular experiment. Thus when a stimulus has inadequate energy, a state limitation is produced if the task is one of discriminating between two letters, as in the experiment by Shwartz et al. (1977). If, however, the task requires discrimination of a stimulus with some energy from one with no energy, then energy or its lack would be a process limiting factor. Process limitation and state limitation are orthogonal functional concepts, and if a particular experimental outcome justifiably seems to imply stage differentiation, then that is because by chance or otherwise one type of limitation was applied to one stage and another type of limitation was applied to another stage. An outcome indicating stage differences should not be used to imply that there are not very important functional differences to be considered, and it is important not to lose sight of these functional differences. In other words, we should continue to ask not only the when of stages but also the what and how of functions.

Because I have written on the functional role of state versus process limitation before (Garner, 1970, 1972, 1974), I do not attempt an extended treatment of the problem here. However, I shall note that my original and later uses of the distinction between state and process limitation had to do largely with the function of different types of redundancy in coping with inadequate information processing. If the inadequacy was due to a state limitation, then I argued and showed experimentally (see Garner, 1974, for a review) that some form of redundancy that repeated the stimulus in time or place would be effective. On the other hand, if the inadequate performance was due to a process limitation, then redundancy that provided correlated dimensional information would be effective. So to me the emphasis on function in distinguishing between state and process both in terms of perceptual independence and in terms of processing limitation has always been there, and for the distinction to be interpreted as one of stages is to lose the basic conceptual meaning. Stages do exist, of that I am comfortably convinced, but information processing also concerns functions as well as stages, and a great deal of our research should continue to be focused on these functional differences.

Functional Masking.   Let me continue this emphasis on function a bit further by considering that even the nature of masking or other forms of stimulus degradation should be investigated in terms of the functional role of the degradation rather than simply looking for stage differences. For quite a few years now various investigators have been aware that different types of visual mask produce different effects, depending on the specific nature of the stimuli and on the specific task. Haber (1970), fairly early, simply noted that in the use of poststimulus masks the noise should somehow be appropriate to the nature of the stimulus. Johnston and McClelland (1973) showed quite specifically that the use of a plain white field rather than a mask of high-contrast random contours had a very different effect in an investigation of the word–letter effect, in which letters within words are perceived more accurately than letters within nonwords or even single letters. They showed that the word–letter advantage occurred only when the pattern mask was used.

Much of Donald Broadbent's recent research has been concerned with the effect of different types of stimulus degradation on word perception, and Broadbent and Broadbent (1977) have even showed in a recent article a fascinating interaction in the correct perception of words between their commonness and their emotional tone. Broadbent and Broadbent have stated so clearly the point I want to make that I shall simply quote their conclusion rather than describe the experiments in detail. They state that "... different frequencies of masking noise produce different results, and that therefore some important information is based on relations between widely spaced events in the visual field such as word shape, while other information comes from concentrated detail." And still further, "our evidence is that techniques involving loss of the broad or shape information make it easier to demonstrate the puzzling effect of word emotionality." In other words, word stimuli have different informational properties, including both local detail and overall configuration, and these different properties may contribute to performance with some words but not with others. Then whether a particular form of mask or degradation will interfere with performance depends on what stimulus properties are involved in a particular task. Thus once again, in order to understand information processing, we have to ask the what of function rather than the when of stages.

Let me carry this point, and its complexities, a step further by reference to some of my own research. Forrest Haun and I (Garner & Haun, 1978) investigated the role of state and process limitation on the perception of letters presented tachistoscopically. The two types of degradation we used were short duration, which we considered to produce state limitation, and a form of pattern masking or distortion, which we considered to produce process limitation. We had a specific hypothesis to test, and because the results completely supported the hypothesis, I shall simply summarize the results. When a letter set differs in attributes that can be described dimension-ally in terms of up–down and right–left locations of properties, such as the block lowercase p, d, q, b set we used, both forms of degradation produced much the same effect on the error distributions. When, however, a letter set differs in attributes that can be described in terms of presence or absence of specific features, such as the block uppercase letters I, L, T, and C (with the left bar missing on the T to make the set of letters completely definable by simple features), then there is an asymmetric distribution of errors from letters with more features to letters with fewer features, but this asymmetry existed only with short duration and not with pattern distortion.

Consider how to interpret this result in terms of stages. If we want to say that process limitation affects a later stage than state limitation, we would then also have to say that the stage difference is true only when the letters are formed from features and not when they are formed from dimensions. That doesn't seem very reasonable at all. But when we consider that state limitation produces the loss of something, then there should be an asymmetry of errors if the alternative letters differ in the amount of something but not when the letters do not differ in the amount of something. And I would be willing to argue that this loss of something need not occur at an input stage, or even at an early stage of encoding, but could occur at any stage of processing. I would, in other words, maintain my argument that state and process limita-tions are functional and not stage differences.

Expectancy as Function

The question of whether a particular process or process distinction is better considered as a structural or as a functional question is, of course, not at all limited to the distinction between state and process. Processing factors of effort, attention, stress, and even encoding, such as emphasized by Broadbent (1971) and Kahneman (1973), are all primarily concerned with functional rather than stage distinctions and, I would even argue, are appropriate at many if not all stages of processing. Let me describe, however, some research related to one such factor, that of expectancy, which is functional and can be operative at any stage of processing. Sanders (1977), in discussing these issues, has reviewed much research done in the stage tradition with the additive factors logic, and I shall not attempt a further review here. Two more recent articles are enough to establish the nature of the issue. Both of these articles were concerned with the effects of unequal probability of occurrence of stimulus items, a factor that I would suggest should be considered on a priori grounds to induce a differential expectancy. Biederman and Stacey (1974) concluded that the total number of items affects the memorial compar-ison stage, whereas the probability of items within the set affects the response selection stage. Miller and Pachella (1976), following some earlier work of their own on this topic, concluded that stimulus probability affects an encoding stage, but only when the stimuli are familiar numbers and not when they are visual forms without names. So just from these two reports, we have expectancy operating at four different stages, which is a very confusing state of affairs if we consider our primary task to be the location of stages. From some work in my own laboratory, I argue that expectancy is a function, not a stage, and that it can easily and directly be demonstrated to operate at least at both the input and output ends of the processing sequence.

The research I describe is from Donna Sutliff Ruth's doctoral dissertation (1976). Some stimuli she used, and her experimental paradigm, are illustrated in Fig. 1.3. The basic task for the subject was simply a two-response classification, with a four-to-two stimuli-to-responses mapping. Two dot patterns were assigned to each of two keys as responses, with reaction time measured. One of the patterns for each response had a good configuration and one had a poor configuration. Before each stimulus presentation, a cuing stimulus occurred that gave probabilistic information about what the stimulus would be, following the technique of LaBerge, Van Gelder, and Yellott (1970). Cuing was done either for the response or for the goodness of the stimulus pattern. If the response was cued, then the indicated response occurred on 75% of the trials, with the other response occurring on 25% of the trials. In similar fashion, if goodness was cued, then the indicated goodness level occurred on 75% of the trials. The property not relevant to cuing occurred at each of its two levels half of the time.

The question for us right now is whether the expectancy induced by the cuing stimulus could function equally effectively for either the response or the stimulus property. Figure 1.4 shows the effect of cuing the response. The results are quite clean and even fit comfortably into the additive factors logic:

RESPONSE :

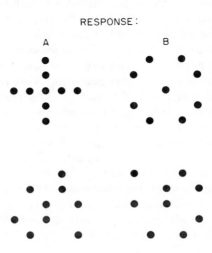

FIG. 1.3.   Some stimulus patterns and response assignments used by Sutliff Ruth (1976). Each of two responses was made to one good and one poor pattern.

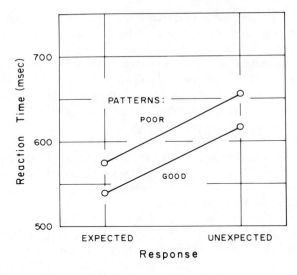

FIG. 1.4.   Reaction time to good and poor patterns with expected and unexpected responses (data from Sutliff Ruth, 1976).

The expected response was given 79 msec faster on the average than the unexpected response, and although good stimuli were responded to faster than poor ones, by 37 msec, there is no discernible interaction between these two factors. We can even accept the interpretation that goodness and *response* expectancy operate at different stages, although my personal conviction is based far more on the rationale of the experimental manipulations than on the arithmetic of the outcome.

Figure 1.5 shows how induced expectancy operates when the goodness of the stimuli is expected rather than the response. This graph is not completely the complement of the last one because, other than a slight bias for right-hand responses, the nature of the response is uninteresting. What is shown is the actual goodness of the pattern as a parameter. The results can be summarized by noting that the expected patterns are responded to faster than the unexpected patterns, by 78 msec on the average. Thus inducing expectancy for pattern goodness is just as effective as inducing expectancy for a response and is the reason for my argument that expectancy is not to be located in a stage but can operate at any stage. It is function, not structure.

When the results are scanned for the effect of actual pattern goodness, there is no loss of the expectancy effect, because expectancy improves performance for both configurally good and poor patterns. But there is a slight interaction in this case, and if interactions are what you look for to determine that a single stage of information processing is operating, then at least this one-stage interpretation makes sense in terms of the rationale of the experimental

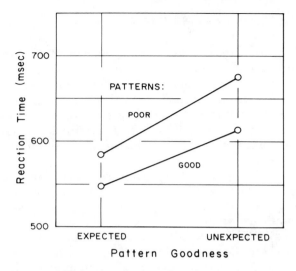

FIG. 1.5.   Reaction time to good and poor patterns with expected and unexpected pattern goodness (data from Sutliff Ruth, 1976).

manipulations because both expectancy and goodness are now relevant to the stimulus as input rather than to the response. However, even in this case I prefer a functional interpretation of the interaction, one which is concerned with what produces this particular form of interaction. I think it is due to the nature of the expectancy process with respect specifically to the role of pattern goodness. Good patterns, if left to their own devices, imply themselves or other good patterns, whereas poor patterns imply themselves and also good patterns. Thus the induction of a specific expectancy for a poor pattern has a greater effect than for a good pattern, because good patterns already have some degree of built-in expectancy. This argument is advanced further in Garner (1974).

I might just add here that the specific problem of the role of goodness in information processing has given the same frequently erratic picture that has the research on the effects of stimulus probability. Checkosky and Whitlock (1973) had argued that goodness operated at a memory-comparison stage. With some reanalysis of their data, I (1974) argued that it also affected an encoding stage. Later Sutliff and I (Garner & Sutliff, 1974) showed goodness to affect an encoding stage in simple discrimination, but then Pomerantz (1977) argued that his results showed the influence of goodness to be primarily in memory. I think now that probably all the interpretations are true, that goodness itself, as well as expectancy, influences many stages of processing and that we need to seek the specific function of goodness more than stages of processing.

FUNCTION AS EXPERIMENTAL PRESUPPOSITION

Now I want to turn to the second idea of function in information processing, that of function as presupposition in experimental design. My use of the term *function* in this respect refers quite specifically to the function of experimental factors in our research, but function of experimental factors is closely allied to our functional constructs and even, as I shall show, to structural stage constructs as well. So although I am shifting the term *function* from processing construct to experimental factor, the two senses of function are indeed closely tied together.

In the fall of 1977 I gave a talk at a symposium on perceptual organization (Garner, 1980) in which I stated that someday when presumably I would have more leisure at hand I intended to write a book. This book, however, was not to be based on all that we know from the experiments we have done but rather was to be based on all that we know from the experiments that we know better than to do. The specific example I gave there concerned an investigation of mine about whether letters or word configurations served as the primary perceptual factor in word perception. The point I made was that I had made two presuppositions that restricted the range of my investigation: One presupposition was that at large sizes of print only the individual letters could provide the information basis, and the other presupposition was that at small sizes only the word configuration could do so. I then had used an intermediate size at which presumably either outcome was possible. But the point I was making is that I really knew, or at least presupposed, much more about the nature of word perception from what I did not do experimentally than I expected to learn from what I did do.

Presupposition of Processing Function

Although in that example I deliberately chose conditions where more than a single result could happen, in the present context I want to discuss the extent to which our choice of experimental factors is based on such strong presuppositions that the interpreted outcome is severely limited. And to forewarn you, I am not about to argue that these presuppositions should not be involved in our research but only that we should be very self-conscious about their operation and even include them in our interpretation of results.

Let me return to the article that was the immediate impetus for this discussion. Figure 1.6 shows four stimuli used by Shwartz et al. (1977). These were the two dissimilar letters, in the masked and the unmasked condition, and although I have allowed myself some slight liberties in reproducing these stimuli, they are functionally accurate representations. Now we can look at these four stimuli and immediately recognize that there are two experimental factors represented in them: which letter and whether masking was present or

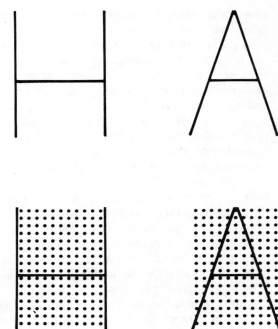

FIG. 1.6.   The two dissimilar letters used by Shwartz et al. (1977) in the unmasked and masked condition.

not. But that is not at all the way the experiment was run, nor is it the way the data demonstrating the lack of interaction were portrayed in Fig. 1.1. The experiment was actually run with two-choice reactions involving the top two stimuli and in other blocks of the experiment with two-choice reactions involving the bottom two stimuli. In other words, of the six possible pairs of stimuli that could have been used in a choice reaction task, only two of the pairs were in fact used. Now this experimental paradigm illustrates what I mean by presupposition concerning the function of experimental factors. The presupposition here is that the appropriate information-processing factor is only discrimination between letters and that the mask serves the function of making the processing variable more or less difficult. And, incidentally, this relative role of the two variables is exactly what I mean in differentiating state from process variables. In this case, pattern discrimination is the information process, whereas masking is a state variable that presumably can influence the efficiency with which the information processing is carried out.

But to have run the experiment this way is to accept so completely the presupposition of which role each variable should play that the experiment is quite unable to demonstrate that these two variables might actually operate at a single processing stage or even perform a single function. On a purely logical basis, these same four stimuli could have been used in such a way that one two-choice reaction involved the masked and the unmasked H, whereas the other two-choice reaction involved the masked and the unmasked A. In this case, the functional roles of the two variables would have been reversed, and the function of the configuration would have been to make available the existence of masking; thus it would have been the state variable and the existence of masking would have been the process variable. I agree with you, and presumably with the authors of the experimental report as well, that such a presupposition is not very reasonable. But it was nevertheless a presupposition that determined how the experiment was run by determining which factor would play which role in the experiment, and it was not a construct whose validity was determined from the experimental outcome.

To illustrate still further the extent to which presuppositions determined the experimental design and thus the outcome constructs, consider four other stimuli used by these authors, shown in Fig. 1.7. These stimuli consist of two similar letters, still the A and H, and once again the experimental factor of masking. Here again, choice reactions between masked and unmasked letters were never required but only reactions between the two pairs of differing letters. But note that presuppositions were also operating for the use of stimuli from these two figures. At no time, for instance, were two-choice reactions required between the ordinary H of Fig. 1.6 and the distorted H of Fig. 1.7 or between the two different A's or between any pair of letters with one letter masked and the other unmasked.

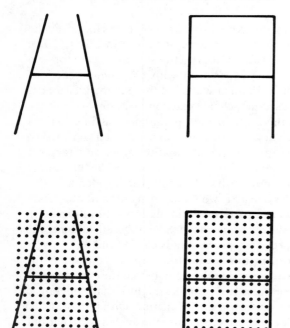

FIG. 1.7.   The two similar letters used by Shwartz et al. (1977) in the unmasked and masked condition.

To summarize the amount of presupposition in this experiment as outlined here, there were eight different stimuli used altogether. There are, of course, 28 pairs of these eight stimuli that could have been used in two-choice discrimination tasks, but in fact only four pairs were ever actually used. The nonuse of 24 of these pairs was based entirely on the presupposition that the function of the masking variable was to make discrimination more or less difficult and that the function of the similarity variable was also to make discrimination of the process or information variable to be more or less difficult but that neither the similarity nor the masking variables were to be considered as process variables themselves. Figure 1.1, which is what started my discourse, shows the lack of interaction between the masking and the similarity variables, but the structure of this experiment was based entirely on presuppositions concerning the functions of these variables, presuppositions that also excluded the possibility that similarity and form (the actual letters, that is) would have given the same lack of interaction if allowed to by the experimental design. Now my personal presuppositions are that masking has a different function in processing than does the figural differentiation, but I would be most uncomfortable if it turned out that the particular letter and the degree of similarity did not function at the same processing stage. In other words, the four different letters are simply four forms, and whatever processes operate in discrimination, they truly should be similar in function and in stage for these two variables.

I hope I do not appear to be complaining about these particular authors. I am not; I am simply using their very complete experimental design for purposes of illustration. I could easily use other authors to illustrate. For example, Flowers and Garner (1971) carried out a logically similar experimental task in an investigation of the effects of redundancy on speeded classification. Dots were placed to the left or to the right of the center of a card and then repeated to provide redundancy. In one condition the dots were far apart and in another, close, to give a factor of similarity. Still another experimental factor was whether the dots were light or dark, to provide what we considered to be state limitation. Did we ever require discrimination of dark dots from light dots? The answer is no, because we presupposed that the function of contrast was to make the information-processing variable available, just as Shwartz et al. (1977) did. In other words, we considered it to be a state limiting variable. The use of presupposition is not at all uncommon, but its role in prejudging an experimental outcome is often forgotten.

Presupposition of Processing Stage

In some experiments it seems less appropriate to consider the presuppositions as related to function in information processing than to consider them as related to stages. This type of presupposition is more apt to occur when the experimental design involves some control over temporal relations between

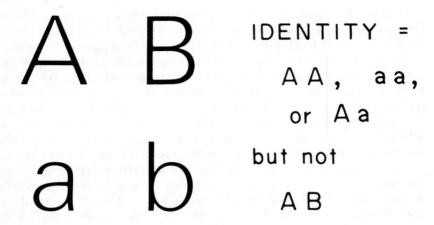

FIG. 1.8.   Schema of experiment by Posner and Mitchell (1967) showing two rules for identity used and one rule not used.

stimuli, but such a design is not at all necessary. Let me illustrate this time with some research of Posner's, specifically Posner and Mitchell (1967). Their experiments are already classic, so I can prototypify their experimental design for purposes of expositional simplicity without doing them an injustice. Four stimuli of the sort they used are shown in Fig. 1.8. These four stimuli can also be described in terms of two attributes or dimensions: the specific letter, A or B, and the case, upper or lower. The experimental procedure Posner and Mitchell used was a same–different task, with different pairs of these stimuli being presented simultaneously. The logic of the experimental design, of course, is not different if they are presented sequentially.

These authors used two different definitions for sameness: In one case, sameness meant physical identity; that is, any of the four stimuli was to be considered the same as another only if the two stimuli were exactly the same. In the second case, sameness meant the same letter (or letter name), although the case of the letter could be different. Thus a pair of letters such as uppercase and lowercase A's were to be responded to as same even though they were not physically identical.

The presupposition that enters into this experimental paradigm is that there is a logical hierarchy in processing, presumably in terms of stages, whereby letters can be responded to as same on the basis of physical properties at an early stage but that response to the letters in terms of their name could occur only after a verbal encoding stage. The results showed that on the average the same response was faster if physical identity was the rule rather than name identity, and many additional analyses in general supported the presupposition. To use just one example, if the rule for sameness was name identity, then stimuli that were in fact physically identical were responded to faster than if they were in fact identical in name but differed in case. Not at all an unreasonable outcome, although it possibly seems more reasonable a decade later than it did at the time.

But sameness could also have been defined in terms of same case, so that, for example, same could be the uppercase A and B or the lowercase a and b; yet that condition was never used in the experiment, just as Shwartz et al. (1977) never required discrimination of masked from unmasked letters or discrimination of an ordinary A from a distorted A. In other words, the presuppositions about stages of processing determined the nature of the experimental design, and although the presuppositions may be entirely reasonable, they do determine the function of the experimental factors in the design and thus limit ultimate construct interpretation. I have made this particular point before (Garner, 1974) but am making it again because of the context of functional aspects of information processing that I am emphasizing here.

Such presuppositions that determine the role of factors in the experimental design are extremely common, and although they often seem reasonable, they do not always seem so. To illustrate, Larsen and Bundesen (1978) used a sequential same–different task, with stimuli that were either letters or random geometric forms. Thus form was one experimental variable. But size was another variable, and the specific purpose of these authors was to determine whether reaction time was greater when two identical letters, to illustrate, differed in size than when the two letters were the same size. They found that reaction time was greater, the greater the difference in size. But once again, note the presupposition: Only form was considered as a relevant, i.e., process, variable, and the only function of size was as an irrelevant variable. But their entire experiment could have been run with size as the variable relevant for sameness, with form as an irrelevant variable. I cannot know, but I strongly suspect, that size judgments would be interfered with if form is varied irrelevantly, and such a result would have considerably complicated the construct interpretation for Larsen and Bundesen.

Are Presuppositions Necessary?

In the light of this discussion, we might well ask whether presuppositions that define the function of experimental factors are necessary at all. My answer is an unequivocal yes, just as with Hake and Eriksen (1956) I had argued that no particular experiment should try to carry out all the converging operations for a given construct. The reason is simply that not to use presuppositions would overly burden the experimental enterprise, making it unwieldy and inefficient. I would like, however, to see all of us be self-conscious about our use of functional presuppositions and to enter them into our construct development in a more explicit fashion than has been customary. Too often the presuppositions play their role in determining the function of experimental factors but then cease to have any further role. A presupposition is a converging operation every bit as much as an experimental outcome is. And then, of course, there are the occasions when we turn out to restrict the function of experimental factors inappropriately or prematurely, and some other scientist with better judgment or intuition does the experiment differently to the mutual benefit of us all. Let me give two examples.

First is an experiment by Robert Schroeder that is reported by Posner (1979). I had myself (1974) suggested, within the context of separability or integrality of stimulus dimensions, that color and form might have an asymmetric relationship. Schroeder directly tested this idea, using both the classification paradigm that I have so frequently used and also the same–different procedure with simultaneous presentation. He used nine stimuli generated by three forms times three colors, but rather than presupposing the functions of the two variables he used both color and form in a completely balanced experimental design. Figure 1.9 shows some results he obtained with the same–different procedure, for same responses only. If identity was defined with color as the dimension relevant for sameness, then there was no difference in reaction time when form differed in the pair of stimuli presented and when it was the same. If, however, identity was defined as the same form, then when the two colors differed, reaction time was much greater than when the stimuli were the same in both form and color. Other analyses with both procedures gave the same basic result that color seems to be necessary for the judgment of form, but form does not seem to be necessary for the judgment of

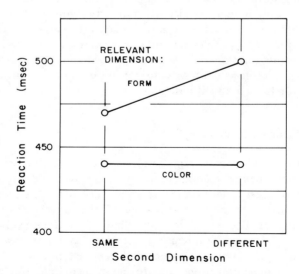

FIG. 1.9.   Reaction time for identity response to relevant dimensions of color and form when the second (irrelevant) dimension was the same or different (data from Schroeder, cited in Posner, 1979).

color. This is the result that I (1974) termed *asymmetric integrality*, and it easily leads to a quite sensible interpretation in terms of stages, with color being processed at an earlier stage than form. Thus in this case if color had been presupposed to be a necessary defining condition for form perception, it would have been correct. I rather suspect, however, that few of us would have felt very sure about this particular presupposition.

The second example concerns the role of two successive stimuli in the experimental paradigm commonly considered to provide evidence of backward masking. The experiment is by Bernstein, Smith, and Adey (1977) and in it they used the letters B or D as two successive stimuli, in all four possible sequences. Rather than simply presupposing that the function of the second stimulus was to mask the first, they required reports of both the first and second stimuli. They then did an analysis of these reports as though each was the relevant stimulus, using the analytic techniques that Morton and I (1969) had proposed for determining whether there was process interaction. I shall not present detailed results here but report simply that each stimulus interacted with the other such that both stimuli tended to be perceived as the same letter. Thus the sequence B–D would be reported as B–B or D–D. (This outcome, incidentally, is unequivocally what I would call *process* rather than *state* interaction.) So in this case a considerable amount was learned by not presupposing that the function of the second stimulus is to be the mask, whereas the function of the first stimulus is to be the process variable.

FUNCTIONAL MEASUREMENT

The last aspect of function in information processing I discuss, and that only briefly, concerns the nature of measurement. For quite a while now, many areas of experimental psychology that are concerned with quantitative measurement have been exploring the consequences of loosening the metric assumptions involved in measurement. Although some of the issues involved go back to Thurstonian scaling methods, and more recently to signal-detection theory, both of which use a derived metric, most specifically the introduction of nonmetric measurement models comes from the work of Roger Shepard (1962), with his introduction of the methods of nonmetric multidimensional scaling of similarities. The basic idea, of course, is very simple. Rather than using the metric of the experimentally obtained numbers as they come from the laboratory, numbers such as direct similarity judgments or distributions of errors, the assumption that the numbers mean what they imply up to interval or possible ratio properties is relaxed to the simpler assumption that only the ordinal properties are pertinent. There is, of course, an exchange for other assumptions, for example, solutions with fixed dimensionality or a specified multidimensional metric such as the Euclidean or city block.

Of more immediate interest to the present discussion is the work of Norman Anderson (1970, 1977) who has used the term *functional measurement* to describe his feeling that it is more important to make assumptions about the proper metric to use from a specific theoretical base than it is to stick to the apparent metric of the numbers as given. And he has made quite explicit one point of concern in information-processing work, namely, that the parsimony of assuming no interaction between experimental variables is often preferable to accepting the numbers as given and then having to live with the often awkward consequences of an interaction whose interpretation is difficult if not impossible.

The Tyranny of Absolute Time

Why has this influence not penetrated the study of information processing? And in my opinion, it has not done so sufficiently. I believe the answer is as simple as that time, in the sense of duration, is so easily considered to be an absolute metric that we have been seduced into making the metric properties of time dominate both our experimenting and our theoretical construct making. The idea of absolute time has become a tyranny in our lives.

We have shifted, presumably, away from the use of Donders' subtractive technique, for reasons that have been stated by many. Usually, however, these stated reasons have to do with the inadequacy of the construct conceptualization, constructs that could allow one to subtract one reaction time from another to determine just how long one stage or process took. I would like to suggest that the fundamental difficulty with the use of the subtractive procedure lies not in the inadequacy of our constructs but in the metric assumption that times are to be taken seriously as having not only interval or ratio properties but even of having absolute properties.

Today we have shifted to the additive factors logic, introduced by Sternberg (1969). But with it we have accepted once again the tyranny of absolute time and have made it the unique consideration in our theoretical constructing. I am not about to suggest that we drop the additive factors logic or even the subtractive logic of Donders. On the contrary, the idea of stages is an extremely important and useful conception, one that we cannot afford to lose. But I think it could be an even more powerful constructual tool if we did not insist that time had to be an absolute.

There seems little reason to me why time should be considered an inviolate absolute in our research and theorizing. It has no more special status than do many other things we measure that have absolute measurement properties if we choose to take that fact seriously. Consider some data of mine from some years ago, shown in Fig. 1.10. The experimental task was to discriminate the right or left location of dots on cards, sorting a deck of cards as fast as possible. Different decks had smaller or larger differences in the positions of

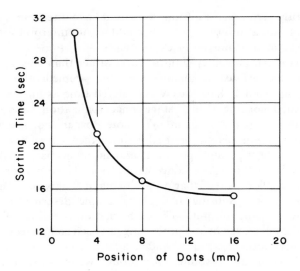

FIG. 1.10. Time required to sort a deck of 32 cards with dot stimuli positioned to the left or right of center as indicated (data from Garner, 1969).

the dots, that is, different discriminabilities. As the figure shows, there is a nonlinear relation between the absolute, physical measure of position and the absolute measure of time. I am sure that you all recognize the naturalness of this relation and that as discriminability becomes zero, time logically has to go to infinity. But why, with such relations, should I take the absolute measurement of time so seriously? It is every bit as rational to argue that the absolute measure of distance should be taken seriously and then to transform the time measures (logarithms would probably do fine) so as to demonstrate a linear relation between reaction time and discriminability. But why should I be required to do either? Functional measurement would say that we can transform either measure (monotonically only, of course) in any way that provides us with a parsimonious explanation consonant with some theoretical expectation.

Time as a Sloppy Absolute

There is plenty of evidence that we should not take time seriously as an absolute, that perhaps we should consider it only as a somewhat sloppy absolute. Consider the work of Pachella and his colleagues (Pachella, 1974), showing that speed and accuracy are used in a tradeoff relation in many tasks, or the work of Lappin and his associates (Lappin & Disch, 1972) showing the same kind of relationship. There simply is no evidence that reaction time is not so responsive to criterial shifts as errors are and that if any subject ever accepted a truly zero-error criterion, we would have utterly uninterpretable reaction times—all at infinity. Not only could we not interpret such data, we would never be able to finish our experiments.

When we concern ourselves with function rather than stages, we are less likely to take time seriously as an absolute. Thus people like Broadbent and Kahneman, and even I, have rarely considered time as an absolute. And Posner, although working within a stage conceptualization, has preferred not to use time as an absolute measure. To quote Posner and Mitchell (1967): "The emphasis is not placed upon the times themselves but upon their relevance for understanding operations and mechanisms...." And others who want to work within a stage conceptualization of information processing often used concepts of stages that do not demand that we consider time an absolute. Norman and Bobrow (1975), for example, describe "The principle of continually available output." Thus information is continually fed from one stage to the next, even before processing has been completed. And Taylor (1976), with his excellent critique of stage analysis, assumes that processing time within stages is not absolute, even though we might want to consider processing time between stages absolute. And in a more sophisticated line of argument, Krantz (1972) notes that "One sometimes hears the argument that duration is a physical, ratio-scale measure.... This is wrong... ordinal measurement is involved."

What do we gain by allowing time to be a sloppy absolute, by allowing monotonic transformations of reaction-time data? It is to give us greater flexibility and freedom of interpretation of our data; it is to take away an unnecessary constraint on our theorizing. I can make the point very easily with a last experimental example, illustrated in Fig. 1.11. These are data from Stanovich and Pachella (1977), displayed in the way that is now customary when using the additive factors logic. There were two factors, one being high and low contrast as what I would call a *state variable* and the other being whether real or pseudoletters were used as a process variable. Reaction time for stimulus recognition was measured, and the displayed underadditive interaction was obtained. This outcome produced a problem for these authors. In the first place, by the additive factors logic, an interaction implies a single stage of processing, and for these two factors that seems quite unreasonable. In the second place, interactions are usually overadditive, and so how does one understand this underadditivity?

My answer would be that you shouldn't try. Any monotonic transformation of these data will eliminate the interaction, and there is thus a problem to be explained only if this interaction and its particular form is taken seriously. I would keep the additive factors logic but would loosen the assumption of absolute time and accept the possibility that these two factors indeed did operate at different stages. Congruence with other results, such as those of Shwartz et al. (1977), the article that provided the impetus for this discussion,

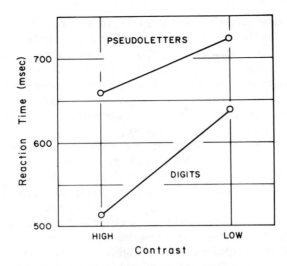

FIG. 1.11.   Reaction time in a same–different task for two types of stimuli and two contrasts (after Stanovich & Pachella, 1977).

would comfortably lead to a reasonable understanding of the outcome. In other words, experimental convergence will allow us to use the additive factors logic without being confounded by too strict an acceptance of the absolute metric of time. And I believe that unless we accept the idea of functional measurement, these apparent conflicting outcomes will lose us additive factors as a valuable tool in our logical thinking. That loss would be as great as, in my opinion, has been the loss of the subtractive factors logic. And the loss of both is unnecessary if we simply place more emphasis on experimental converging operations and less emphasis on the absolute nature of time.

CONCLUSION

In conclusion, let me briefly summarize the three aspects of function in information-processing research. First, there is function as contrasted with structure, or stages of time, and such constructs as state and process limitation, expectancy, attention, and effort can and do function at any and all stages of processing. Even at a more detailed level, such as investigations of the effect of masking, the results are more readily interpretable in terms of the specific stimulus properties and the functional relationship of masking properties to these than to ideas of stages.

A second functional aspect of information processing is in presuppositions that determine the functional role of factors in our experiments. Commonly both processing functions and processing stages are presupposed in our experimental designs. Although the interests of scientific efficiency demand that we use such presuppositions, they should be considered as operations that converge to the constructs we use just as the experimental outcomes themselves converge. And sometimes we need to learn by experimentally violating what seem like reasonable presuppositions.

A third functional aspect concerns the nature of measurement and the acceptance of time as an absolute metric. Although this acceptance does make unambiguous whether an interaction exists in the analysis-of-variance sense, it also unduly constrains us in our construct development. Acceptance of the idea of functional measurement, with permissible monotonic transformation of metrics, will lead to more interpretations of separate stages, with a greater need for further converging operations, but such acceptance will probably make the additive factors logic more viable. If so, it might well survive experimental inconsistencies and even the subtractive method might once again find utility.

ACKNOWLEDGMENTS

This research was supported by Grant MH 14229 from the National Institute of Mental Health to Yale University. Many of the ideas expressed here were sharpened by discussion with students who attended a seminar in 1977 (Forrest Haun, Peter Podgorny, and Marc Sebrechts) and with Sylvan Kornblum, who attended that seminar as a visitor during his sabbatical.

REFERENCES

Anderson, N. H. Functional measurement and psychophysical judgment. *Psychological Review*, 1970, *77*, 153–170.

Anderson, N.H. Note on functional measurement and data analysis. *Perception & Psychophysics*, 1977, *21*, 201–215.

Bernstein, I. H., Smith, D. B., & Adey, M. Perceptual and response interdependencies in visual masking. In S. Dornic (Ed.), *Attention and performance VI*. Hillsdale, N.J.: Lawrence Erlbaum Associates, 1977.

Biederman, I., & Stacey, E. W. Stimulus probability and stimulus set size in memory scanning. *Journal of Experimental Psychology*, 1974, *102*, 1100–1107.

Broadbent, D. E. *Decision and stress.* London: Academic Press, 1971.

Broadbent, D. E., & Broadbent, M. H. P. General shape and local detail in word perception. In S. Dornic (Ed.), *Attention and performance VI*. Hillsdale, N.J.: Lawrence Erlbaum Associates, 1977.

Checkosky, S. F., & Whitlock, D. The effects of pattern goodness on recognition time in a memory search task. *Journal of Experimental Psychology*, 1973, *100*, 341–348.

Flowers, J. H., & Garner, W. R. The effect of stimulus element redundancy on speed of discrimination as a function of state and process limitation. *Perception & Psychophysics,* 1971, *9,* 158–160.

Garner, W. R. Speed of discrimination with redundant stimulus attributes. *Perception & Psychophysics,* 1969, *6,* 221–224.

Garner, W. R. The stimulus in information processing. *American Psychologist,* 1970, *25,* 350–358.

Garner, W. R. Information integration and form of encoding. In A. W. Melton & E. Martin (Eds.), *Coding processes in human memory.* Washington, D.C.: Winston, 1972.

Garner, W. R. *The processing of information and structure.* Potomac City, Md.: Lawrence Erlbaum Associates, 1974.

Garner, W. R. The analysis of unanalyzed perceptions. In M. Kubovy & J. R. Pomerantz (Eds.), *Perceptual Organization.* Hillsdale, N.J.: Lawrence Erlbaum Associates, 1979, in press.

Garner, W. R., Hake, H. W., & Eriksen, C. W. Operationism and the concept of perception. *Psychological Review,* 1956, *63,* 149–159.

Garner, W. R., & Haun, F. Letter identification as a function of type of perceptual limitation and type of attribute. *Journal of Experimental Psychology: Human Perception and Performance,* 1978, *4,* 199–209.

Garner, W. R., & Morton, J. Perceptual independence: Definitions, models, and experimental paradigms. *Psychological Bulletin,* 1969, *72,* 233–259.

Garner, W. R., & Sutliff, D. The effect of goodness on encoding time in visual pattern discrimination. *Perception & Psychophysics,* 1974, *16,* 426–430.

Haber, R. N. Note on how to choose a visual noise mask. *Psychological Bulletin,* 1970, *74,* 373–376.

Johnston, J. C., and McClelland, J. L. Visual factors in word perception. *Perception & Psychophysics,* 1973, *14,* 365–370.

Kahneman, D. *Attention and effort.* Englewood Cliffs, N.J.: Prentice-Hall, 1973.

Krantz, D. H. Measurement structures and pyschological laws. *Science,* 1972, *175,* 1427–1435.

LaBerge, D., Van Gelder, P., & Yellott, J. I. A cueing technique in choice reaction time. *Perception & Psychophysics,* 1970, *7,* 57–62.

Lappin, J. S., & Disch, K. The latency operating characteristic: II. Effects of visual stimulus intensity on choice reaction time. *Journal of Experimental Psychology,* 1972, *93,* 367–372.

Larsen, A., & Bundesen, C. Size scaling in visual pattern recognition. *Journal of Experimental Psychology: Human Perception and Performance,* 1978, *4,* 1–20.

Miller, J. O., & Pachella, R. G. Encoding processes in memory scanning tasks. *Memory & Cognition,* 1976, *4,* 501–506.

Norman, D. A., & Bobrow, D. G. On data-limited and resource-limited processes. *Cognitive Psychology,* 1975, *7,* 44–64.

Pachella, R. G. The interpretation of reaction time in information-processing research. In B. Kantowitz (Ed.), *Human information processing: Tutorials in performance and cognition.* Hillsdale, N.J.: Lawrence Erlbaum Associates, 1974.

Pomerantz, J.R. Pattern goodness and speed of encoding. *Memory & Cognition,* 1977, *5,* 235–241.

Posner, M. I. *Chronometric explorations of mind.* Hillsdale, N.J.: Lawrence Erlbaum Associates, 1979.

Posner, M. I., & Mitchell, R. F. Chronometric analysis of classification. *Psychological Review,* 1967, *74,* 392–409.

Ruth, Donna Sutliff. *The effects of pattern goodness on automatic and strategy-dependent processes.* Yale Ph.D. dissertation, 1976.

Sanders, A. F. Structural and functional aspects of the reaction process. In S. Dornic (Ed.), *Attention and performance VI.* Hillsdale, N.J.: Lawrence Erlbaum Associates, 1977.

Shepard, R. N. The analysis of proximities: Multidimensional scaling with an unknown distance function. *Psychometrika,* 1962, *27,* 125–140, 219–246.

Shwartz, S. P., Pomerantz, J. R., & Egeth, H. E. State and process limitations in information processing: An additive factors analysis. *Journal of Experimental Psychology: Human Perception and Performance,* 1977, *3,* 402–410.

Stanovich, K. E., & Pachella, R. G. Encoding, stimulus-response compatibility, and stages of processing. *Journal of Experimental Psychology: Human Perception and Performance,* 1977, *3,* 411–421.

Sternberg, S. The discovery of processing stages: Extension of Donders' method. In W. G. Koster (Ed.), *Attention and performance II.* Amsterdam: North-Holland, 1969.

Taylor, D. A. Stage analysis of reaction time. *Psychological Bulletin,* 1976, *83,* 161–191.

I PREPARATORY PROCESSES AND MOTOR PROGRAMMING

2 Information Processing in Movement Organization and Execution

Ronald G. Marteniuk
Christie L. MacKenzie
Department of Kinesiology
University of Waterloo
Waterloo, Ontario, Canada

ABSTRACT

In this chapter we first selectively review literature pertinent to the concept that voluntary movement is a product of various levels of organization within the nervous system. We then use the facts from this literature review to evaluate work in experimental psychology concerned with identifying processes and codes involved in movement organization and execution.

THE IDEA OF THE "MOTOR PROGRAM" CRITIQUED

The term *motor program* has been used to describe those processes that underlie movement organization and execution, but in different ways by different investigators. Thus, definitions of a motor program range from an abstract plan of action (Bernstein, 1967; Miller, Galanter, & Pribram, 1960) to a centrally stored, prestructured set of muscle commands (Keele, 1968; Schmidt, 1976) to descending force signals from the motor cortex (Evarts, 1968).

These definitions of the motor program implicitly or explicitly restrict movement behavior to cases where peripheral feedback has little or no role. In contrast, Brooks (1979) sees movement organization and execution as depending on the integration, through feedback and feedforward, of several levels of the central nervous system that work concurrently to produce movement related to the performer's goal and the requirements of the environment. Similarly, Sternberg, Monsell, Knoll and Wright (1978) see programs, in addition to preplanning movement sequences that are then run off in open-loop fashion, as including "instructions for sensing and responding to feedback, or programs that can themselves be altered in response to feedback, or even programs that consist of ordered sets of 'response images'... to which feedback from the movement sequence is compared." This allows one to conceptualize situations where a performer's movement is delicately coordinated between organization and execution phases, where these two processes are not mutually exclusive but may overlap.

The view of *motor programming* as the central programming of a sequence of movements executed in the absence of peripheral feedback has relied heavily on studies that use deafferentation of proprioceptive input to block the use of feedback during movement or that use "ballistic" movements too fast to be altered by proprioceptive feedback (i.e., shorter than a reaction time). In deafferentation studies, the loss of "elegance" in movement is important. The assumption that feedback is not being used in movements with a duration shorter than a reaction time may be invalid in view of the accumulating research demonstrating a hierarchy of feedback loops and the presence of very fast conducting transcortical reflexes modifiable by set (Eccles, 1973; Evarts, 1972, 1975; Evarts and Tanji, 1974; Granit, 1973; Houk, 1978; Marsden, Merton, & Morton, 1972).

Kelso and Stelmach (1976) state that "it is misleading to assume that sensory feedback, important though it may be, is always necessary to elicit further motor output. Equally unrealistic is the notion that neural networks within the CNS generate stored movement patterns in total independence of peripheral feedback." In this chapter the term *motor program* is used in a way that diverges from its traditional meaning. The main emphasis, instead, is to examine those codes and processes involved in the larger concept of movement organization and execution. In this regard a code refers to an internal representation of information resulting from processing operations within the central nervous system.

NEUROPHYSIOLOGICAL CONSIDERATIONS IN MOVEMENT ORGANIZATION AND EXECUTION

Role of the Higher Centers, Especially the Cerebral Cortex

Of the various definitions of *motor programs* that we have examined, the highest level of organization in the nervous system is seen to have an abstract representation of a plan of action. This action plan (which may be seen as a supramodal, nonmotor perception/action interface), essential for goal-directed behavior, controls the order of a sequence of operations to be performed by specifying the desired environmental consequences (Miller et al., 1960). The plan is intimately related to the image [or schema (Bartlett, 1961; Pew, 1974) or cognitive map (Tolman, 1948)]. Miller et al. (1960) stress that the plan and the image are not mutually exclusive.

How is this abstract, nonmotor plan of *action* transformed into the more concrete representations necessary for *movement* organization and execution? Brooks (1974, p. 300) has proposed that we "look to the limbic system for the drive to move and thence to frontal and parietal cortex for formation of the needed associations, to be channeled by way of the cerebellum and basal ganglia through the thalamic funnel of the ventrolateral nucleus of the thalamus to the motor cortex. Thus several paths to the spinal cord are provided as well as channels for feedback between these various centers."

The Frontal-Limbic System. The frontal–limbic system is considered by many investigators to be the highest level or directive in the planning of action (Luria, 1973; Pribram, 1973; Roy, 1975; Teuber, 1972). Excluding the primary motor and premotor areas (also in the frontal lobe), there appear to be two major frontal areas partaking in the planning of action: the orbital and dorsolateral regions, together termed the *prefrontal cortex.* The prefrontal cortex is connected reciprocally with all the major sensory afferent systems, so that it not only receives information indirectly from these systems but acts back upon them as well as upon limbic, diencephalic, and mesencephalic structures (Nauta, 1972).

The orbital region, closely tied to the limbic system, must be intricately related to emotional reactivity and impulse control since orbitofrontal lesions profoundly disturb these aspects of behavior. In contrast, dorsolateral lesions generally lead to problems in the making and evaluation of plans and in the initiation and termination of action (Luria, 1973; Teuber, 1972). Whereas Luria (1966) suggests that prefrontal patients typically notice neither their mistakes in execution nor the fact that their actions do not conform to the original plan, Teuber (1972) suggests that many patients do indeed recognize their errors in action but do not utilize this knowledge in modifying the action to conform to intentions.

These observations (and many others) led Teuber (1964, 1972) to postulate that the prefrontal area of the cerebral cortex is the source of "corollary discharge" whereby a feedforward mechanism results in the prediction of the anticipated consequences of *action*. The corollary discharge notion serves not only to assess the voluntariness of the ensuing movement (as it is most commonly interpreted) but also to evaluate alternative courses of action.

Closely related to plan formation must be the contribution of spatial cues. Luria (1966) suggests that the parietal lobes contribute to the required spatial information for the planning of action and subsequent organization of movement. In monkeys with dorsolateral prefrontal, posterior parietal, and control lesions, Pohl (1973) found egocentric spatial orientation (based on body position) and allocentric spatial orientation (based on an external referent) related to frontal and parietal mechanisms, respectively (for related findings with human lesions, see Semmes, Weinstein, Ghent, & Teuber, 1963). This supports Pribram's (1973) idea that prefrontal mechanisms are crucial when environmental contingencies are incompletely specified and the plan of action depends on internal processes.

To this point then, the frontal–limbic system has been identified as containing processes relevant to the planning of action. These processes result in action plans (nonmotor in nature) being transformed into goal-directed movement patterns through the use of a spatial map. Bernstein (1967) believes the spatial map, which he describes as a topological motor image of space, produces codes that represent both the relative position of the body parts and the position of the body to external environmental referents. This means, therefore, that this stage must be concerned with codes for movement organization that are concerned with "ball park figures" for the effecting limbs and their direction as well as relative sequencing. It thus remains to determine how these rather general codes are transformed into the more specific information needed for the actual execution of movement.

The Motor Cortex.   The motor cortex has been identified as the final relay station for what has been going on in widely dispersed areas of the cerebral cortex, basal ganglia, and cerebellum (Eccles, 1973).

The giant pyramidal cells of Betz give rise to the corticobulbar and corticospinal tracts (the pyramidal system) that monosynaptically or through interneurons excite both alpha and gamma motorneurons. Electrical stimulation studies have demonstrated the motor mapping in man and found that the extent of representation is proportional to the skilled usage of a given part of the body. Thus, there is greatest representation for the face and hand (Penfield & Rasmussen, 1957). For the hands and fingers, cerebral representation is almost exclusively contralateral or crossed, whereas more proximal and axial musculature is both contralaterally and ipsilaterally represented (Brinkman & Kuypers, 1972; Muram & Carmon, 1972).

What is the output (code) from the motor cortex that is sent to the spinal cord and musculature? Evarts (1967, 1968) used microelectrode recording techniques in monkeys trained on a wrist flexion–extension task. He found relevant pyramidal tract activity preceded EMG onset by about 40 msec and that pyramidal tract neuron discharge was much less related to the extent of flexion or extension than to the *force* of flexion or extension. Further, the discharge was more related to changes in force over time than to force per se. We see later that this finding may be tied to the specification of the equilibrium point of length–tension relationship in the agonist–antagonist musculature. Evarts (1975) suggests that the activity of pyramidal tract neurons in the motor cortex is related to patterns of activity within *groups* of muscles and depends on the input from other neural structures, such as the ventrolateral nucleus (VL) of the thalamus, a relay center for afferents from the basal ganglia and cerebellum. Both the topographic relations of VL thalamus and the divergence of thalamo–cortical projections suggests that the motor effects relayed by VL thalamus are probably to groups of prime movers as well as to the appropriate axial–proximal musculature (Rispal-Padel, Massion and Grangetto, 1973). Thus, while the motor cortex is specifying output in terms of force–time characteristics, it is doing so in the manner consistent with synergistic control theory.

The Cerebral Association Areas, Basal Ganglia, and Cerebellum. The premotor area of the cerebral cortex is intimately connected with the frontal area (Nauta, 1971), the basal ganglia, and the cerebellum in the organization of the sequential and phasing aspects of movement (Allen & Tsukahara, 1974; Luria, 1966).

Kornhuber (1971) has proposed that the commands from the frontal and parietal association areas are converted by the basal ganglia and cerebellum into the required spatiotemporal motor patterns. Evidence for this viewpoint comes from patients with parietal–occipital damage that results in disturbances to movement sequencing. This is seen to result from disarranged spatial information being sent to the frontal lobe and subcortical structures (Haaxma & Kuypers, 1974; Kornhuber, 1971). This points out that all actions must be made with respect to a spatial map (Benton, 1969; Corballis and Beale, 1976; Critchley, 1953; Trevarthen, 1968). Therefore it may be concluded that these areas of the cerebral cortex, in concerted working with the basal ganglia and cerebellum, are concerned with processes involved in the production of codes relevant to the sequencing and phasing of movement.

The cerebellum consists of three anatomically (and possibly functionally) distinct divisions. The lateral hemispheres receive information almost exclusively from the cerebral cortex, especially frontal and parietal association areas via the pontine nuclei. The pars intermedia receives both cerebral and peripheral (spinal) information. The vermis receives almost exclusively spinal and vestibular input. The only output of the cerebellar cortex is the inhibitory output of the Purkinje cells, which project to the deep cerebellar nuclei. Only the vermis functions independently of the cerebral cortex and, via the reticulospinal and vestibulospinal tracts, automatically regulates body position with respect to gravity. The pars intermedia may function as a comparator for incoming feedback and a copy of efferent commands from the motor cortex; thus it appears to be most related to the ongoing regulation of evolving movement. The lateral hemispheres, in contrast, may be related to the organization and initiation of the elemental movements. Both the lateral hemispheres and the pars intermedia may exert their influence via the pyramidal tracts originating in the motor cortex, or they may bypass the motor cortex and affect/effect motor outlflow through the rubrospinal tract (Allen & Tsukahara, 1974; Eccles, 1969, 1973; Evarts & Thach, 1969).

In examining the role of the cerebellum in movement, we have discussed three descending pathways (rubrospinal, vestibulospinal, reticulospinal) distinct from the pyramidal tract. One tends to think of the pyramidal system or the final common pathway as functioning solely in bringing about muscular changes, when in fact there are a number of descending systems which, *in parallel,* are bringing about excitatory/inhibitory changes at various levels in the spinal cord. It thus seems most plausible that there is much parallel processing activity occurring in all the higher centers of the nervous system. This is of interest because higher centers are probably involved in sensitizing or biasing (tuning) the spinal apparatus toward the upcoming movement. Since the cerebellum has been implicated in adjusting body position with respect to gravity, it may possibly also produce excitatory or inhibitory effects on spinal structures that will become involved in the intended movement. This speculation is supported by the fact that not only does the cerebellum have access to lower spinal centers but also that both the cerebellum and the basal ganglia are active prior to activity in the motor cortex (Evarts & Thach, 1969; Allen & Tsukahara, 1974).

Role of Lower Centers and Their Interaction With Higher Centers

Biomechanical and Neurophysiological Analysis of Gait.   The underlying structure, processes, and codes of movement execution are perhaps best introduced with respect to gait. Grillner (1975) and Shik and Orlovski (1976) contend that force is the code used to produce gait. Biomechanical evidence for this is found when characteristics of the gait cycle are studied as a function of the velocity of gait. For this purpose gait is divided into a stance phase where the limb touches the ground and a swing phase where the limb is elevated and moved forward. As velocity of gait increases, the number of step cycles per second increases, but this reduction in the duration of the step cycle is due almost entirely to a shortening of the stance phase, whereas the swing phase remains almost constant. Since propulsive force can only be applied during the stance phase, this means that progressive increases in velocity are brought about by force being injected into progressively briefer periods of time. Thus, the code concerning the control of gait is the propulsive force or impulse generated during the stance phase.

The next question of interest is whether higher centers send force signals to individual muscles or to groups of muscles. Evidence already reviewed indicated higher centers control movement through synergies and the biomechanical evidence from gait agrees with this. In studies reviewed by Shik and Orlovski (1976) the pattern of EMG activity during the gait cycle is examined. It is found that the entire pattern EMGs in the main limb muscles can be inferred from the EMG of only one muscle. Shik and Orlovski conclude that the nervous system controls a limb as a whole rather than individual muscles or joints [compare Bernstein's (1967) observation that motor coordination involves a reduction in the number of degrees of freedom in the motor system]. Within a limb, the sequence of EMG activity varies to a greater extent than does the pattern of joint movements. The kinetic parameter of gait (e.g., muscular torque) can change within and between gait cycles according to the conditions under which gait is executed (Craik, Herman, & Finley, 1976; Herman, Wirta, Bampton, & Finely, 1976). This change in the kinetic properties of gait is seen as necessary to maintain the functional kinematics (e.g., joint displacement) of locomotion.

Although the displacement of limbs is achieved through the regulation of force to synergistic groups of muscles, there is evidence from animal work that the higher centers only indirectly control the frequency of stepping. The spinal cord contains mechanisms, called *spinal pattern generators,* that are capable of controlling not only single limbs but also interlimb coordination (Grillner, 1975; Shik and Orlovski, 1976; Stein, 1978). Grillner (1975) argues that in cats and dogs a spinal generator for each limb coordinates the muscles as a whole during gait. In turn, interneurons coordinate the four separate spinal generators.

Effector Units of Movement.   The review of gait implies that control of movement occurs through effector units (i.e., groups of muscles coordinated by a spinal pattern generator) rather than through individual muscles. However, the transition from gait, a relatively stereotyped activity, to other types of activity where movements must be correlated with rapidly changing environmental situations (e.g., catching a ball), makes it hard to argue for the existence of relatively rigid spinal generators for the control of movement, because quite distinct types of movement are required on each successive attempt at the skill. Yet, as Bernstein (1967) has maintained, the brain reduces the degrees of freedom of movement by dealing with units of effector activity rather than with individual muscles or joints. One current notion is that the central nervous system composes movements not by commanding single muscle contractions, or even joint movements, but rather by commanding *units* of motor activity of some kind. Easton (1972, 1976, 1978) suggests that central control of movement is achieved by executive centers commanding units of motor activity that take the form of reflex patterns.[1] His idea is based

---

[1]This is one version of a synergistic control theory. Note that earlier in this chapter the work of Rispal-Papel *et al.* (1973) was cited as evidence for another version. In this case synergistic control is theorized to arise from input to the motor cortex that is to groups of prime movers and related postural musculature rather than to individual muscles. Regardless of which version of synergistic control theory is considered, the end result is the same; that is, control of movement is achieved by controlling synergistic groups of muscles and not by the control of individual muscles.

on similarities between reflexes and portions of voluntary movements. Easton proposes that the central nervous system has the capability of interconnecting sets of neurons into coordinative structures. When these are appropriately activated, coordinated sequences of activity result. Similarly, Turvey (1977) argues that movements are produced by fitting together structures each of which deals relatively autonomously with specific parts of the movement. Further, because the action plan is an abstract image, what is needed is a system capable of mapping "successively larger collections of increasing smaller and less complex coordinative structures, with each representation approximating more closely the desired action [Turvey, 1977]."

Turvey (1977) then points out that in such a system there must be constant communication among the various levels of movement organization and control. As reviewed in subsection A.3, the higher association areas of the cerebral cortex, the basal ganglia, and the cerebellum are in constant communication and have close contact with the spinal mechanisms that will eventually execute the intended movement.

Coupled with this supraspinal integration is the integration, dependent initially on supraspinal process (due to tuning—to be discussed later) but during movement acting autonomously and in concert to produce the desired movement. The spinal cord acts as an executive in that specific interneurons coordinate the activities of those that they interconnect. However, these interneurons themselves communicate with both supraspinal processes and the processes that they are coordinating. The executive command does not need to provide all the details required for successful movement execution. Rather, it initiates some form of approximate command ("ball park" command) and leaves the fine structuring or modulation of the movement to the spinal levels (Greene, 1971).

Preparation of Effector Units for Movement.   Although the executive center is relatively ignorant of the microdetails of movement execution, which is consistent with the concept of economy of organization alluded to earlier, the lower levels must be informed of relevant environmental conditions and the intentions of the higher centers in order for movement to be efficient. This is termed *tuning* (see Easton, 1978, and Turvey, 1977). Tuning is a process, related directly or indirectly to commands from higher levels involved in monitoring the environment and preparing for voluntary movement, that is manifested at spinal levels as an altered state of the excitability of the motoneuron pool (Easton, 1978; Hayes, 1978). Tuning prepares the motor centers to act in accordance with the intentions of the higher centers once the trigger for movement is supplied. Turvey (1977) regards tuning as the adjustment of the behavior of selected coordinative structures by specifying parameters, relevant to the execution of movement, to coordinate structures and in turn muscles.

Evidence for the way in which higher centers prepare effector units for movement is provided in recent studies by Bizzi and his colleagues (Bizzi, Dev, Morasso, & Polit, 1978; Bizzi & Polit, 1979; Bizzi, Polit & Morasso, 1976). They looked at the ability of well-trained monkeys to make head and arm movements to brief visually presented targets (the target light was turned off before movement began and therefore the movement was made in complete darkness) both under normal and under deafferented conditions. In addition, at the beginning and during movement of the head or arm a load was sometimes unexpectedly applied to the movement. With both head and arm movements of normal monkeys, the addition of the load resulted in the movement undershooting the target but when the load was released at this position, the movement then successfully reached the target. The same happened when the monkeys were deafferented and exposed to equivalent conditions. In the experiments on arm positioning, a second way of disturbing the responding limb was studied. Just after presentation of the visual target but before activation of the motor units in the agonist muscle, the limb was displaced from its starting position. Displacement of the arm occurred in directions further away from the target position, sometimes closer to it, and at other times beyond it. Again both normal and deafferented monkeys were able to attain the intended position regardless of the starting location of the limb.

Because the monkeys were well trained and, being deafferented, there was no proprioceptive feedback to their higher control centers, Bizzi and his colleagues concluded that these animals established an equilibrium point (i.e., a specific length–tension relationship) between agonists and antagonists of the movement such that the correct position of the head or arm is reached regardless of external perturbations. These results imply that amplitude or duration of movement are not the relevant parameters or codes upon which movement is based.

Yet the role of proprioception was not completely dismissed for movement execution. First, the deafferented monkeys achieved the final position of movement in a much less smooth manner than normal monkeys. Second, when the monkeys' trained postural relationship to the apparatus was changed, the deafferented animals were very inaccurate in attaining the presented target positions. In contrast, the normal monkeys quickly adapted to the new postural setting. Thus proprioception updates and adjusts well-learned motor patterns.

The Mass–Spring Analogy of Movement Control.   Bizzi and Polit (1979) estimate that in the head movement studies, the compensation to these loads was due largely to the intrinsic mechanical properties of the neck musculature (cf. Asatryan & Fel'dman, 1965; Fel'dman, 1966a, b; and recently Houk, 1978; Fitch and Turvey, 1978; Turvey, 1977). They liken the equilibrium point of a joint–muscle system to a mass–spring system in which the initial setting of the parameters of the mass–spring system, specifically the stiffness and damping parameters, determine the equilibrium point. Thus, once the parameters of stiffness and damping are determined, the spring will always return to its resting position regardless of its initial length or the manner in which it is perturbed (resisted) as it is assuming its resting length.

It appears, then, that the higher centers are capable of preparing effector units for movement by providing them with parameters upon which movement is based. Once these parameters are established, the effector units can execute movement autonomously. Further, the mass–spring analogy of movement control is consistent with the view that the language of lower motor centers is force or, more correctly, some force–time relationship. When one describes movement in terms of a force–time relationship and the effect it has on the segmental apparatus of the spinal cord, one is explaining movement in terms of its dynamics where terms like *force, stiffness,* and *damping* are used. On the other hand, the kinematics of movement (amplitude, velocity, and acceleration) are determined by the dynamics of the system. This leads to the conclusion (Fitch & Turvey, 1978) that a system can be explained by its dynamics and there is therefore no need to look for control structures that operate on kinematic codes.

TIME DEMANDS AND INTERFERENCE EFFECTS IN MOVEMENT ORGANIZATION AND EXECUTION

Section II has outlined evidence regarding the codes that the central nervous system uses in the organization and execution of movement. The present section deals with the same issue but from a different approach. First, literature related to the time demands of movement organization and execution are reviewed. Second, studies are reviewed that try to make inferences about the underlying processes of movement organization and execution by selectively interfering with these processes.

Time Demands

Execution—The Role of Force in Movement Production.   If the control system underlying movement is best explained in terms of its dynamics, one is tempted to reinterpret past descriptions that relied on kinematics. One such example is Fitts's law (Fitts, 1954), that movement time (MT) depends on both movement distance (A) and required target width (W) as expressed in the equation: $MT = a + b \log_2 2A/W$, where a and b are constants. Whereas Fitts (1954) attempted to explain the law in terms of movement uncertainty (uncertainty in selecting movement amplitude and precision), more recent work (Crossman & Goodeve, 1963; Keele, 1968) theorizes that MT can be explained in considering the nature of feedback-based movement corrections. However, we feel that these attempts to explain the underlying mechanisms that limit MT are unsatisfactory.

Our view is that MT is only a kinematically derived result of the dynamic processes involved in movement production and the ultimate answer must involve a kinetic explanation. Schmidt, Zelaznik, and Frank (1978) review limitations of current theories involving feedback-based movement correc- tions and reconceputalize the task, experimentally manipulating MT and amplitude, using effective target width as their dependent measure. A model is proposed in which the primary determinant of end point variability is impulse variability. The model predicts that the limitations in an individual's capacity to move quickly is an indirect result of the variability produced by those central mechanisms responsible for production of force–time relation- ships. The model is believed to be applicable to movements of durations longer than 200 msec but may not apply to visual (or other modality) *guided* movements.

Next, consider the work of Brooks (1974, 1979). Monkeys were trained to make rapid elbow flexions and extensions between mechanical stops. Once this task was well learned, the mechanical stops were either singly or in combination unexpectedly moved in such a way that the flexions or extensions, or both, were shortened. Results showed that the original rhythm and hence the number of movement alternations were maintained as learned and this was caused by the monkeys continuing to exert muscular force for the usual length of time for each movement. The animal, upon hitting a block that stopped the movement short of the learned end point, would continue to exert force against the block for a duration equivalent to the time the learned movement would have taken. It was concluded that force and its timing were the parameters responsible for controlling the movements.

Further interpretation would be that the force and timing of force were commands originating in relatively high levels of the nervous system and the actual mechanism for executing the intended movements was some function- al structure interrelating the activity of the flexors and extensors of the elbow joint to the demands of the task. This effector unit would then be controlled by the higher centers supplying: (1) the parameters necessary to establish length–tension ratios that would allow the limb to assume the learned posi- tion automatically; and (2) the parameters necessary to sequence and phase the alternation between flexors and extensors of the coordinative structure. Interpreted in this way, these results are virtually identical to those found by Bizzi and his colleagues reported earlier.

Time Demands of Movement Organization. Here we review literature dealing with the manipulation of response factors (variables manipulated by the experimenter), while keeping input and decision factors constant, that influence reaction time and thus can be used to infer that the manipulated factors affect the processes concerned with the central organization of a movement.

The first relevant study was by Henry (1960). He found that simple reaction time (the interval between presentation of a stimulus and the initiation of a movement) increased with the complexity of the movement to be initiated, presumably because more time was needed for the nerve impulses to be coordinated and channeled to the appropriate output centers.

Klapp and his colleagues (Klapp, 1977a; Klapp, Wyatt, & Lingo, 1974) have suggested that the negative or contradictory findings from simple reaction time studies may merely reflect the possibility that subjects, knowing the required response before the stimulus is presented, might "program" or perform the necessary organization processes prior to the stimulus onset. To overcome this problem, Klapp et al. advocate the use of a choice reaction paradigm, keeping the number of alternatives constant, so that subjects must wait for stimulus onset before performing the necessary response selection and organization processes. When subjects are faced with only one stimulus and response, planning in advance of the presentation of the stimulus results in an underestimation or elimination of the organization time required for any particular movement. When two or more stimuli and responses are used, however, the resulting reaction times are validly measuring the organizational times.

With this distinction between the simple and choice reaction time paradigms made, we can now examine the pertinent literature. Table 2.1 shows the movement factors manipulated by the reviewed studies and whether or not different levels of these factors produce differential time demands, as reflected by reaction time, for both simple and choice paradigms. Note that some of the movement factors identified in the table may not nominally correspond with those factors as labeled by specific investigators, however, in our judgment, we have correctly identified all factors through the use of the labels in the table.

From Table 2.1 a number of pertinent discussion points are evident. The first concerns the comparison of the simple versus choice reaction time paradigms that according to Klapp (1977a), should result in the simple reaction time paradigm producing more inconsistent results than the choice one. However, this proves not to be the case. Although what Klapp has said is intuitively appealing, a number of investigators have found increases in reaction time with manipulation of some movement factors using only the simple paradigm or both simple and choice paradigms. In addition to this, Table 2.1 indicates that for some movement factors (e.g., the kinematic factors of movement extent, duration, and precision) the overall results indicate that even with using just the choice reaction time paradigm, equivocal results are obtained.

Why are we faced with the seemingly contradictory results in Table 2.1? We believe there are two issues that must be considered. The first is the nature of the factors being examined. Second, there are crucial differences between the simple and choice paradigms that must be taken into account if unequivocal results are to be obtained.

In terms of the first issue, Kerr (1978) has recently suggested that movement factors defined by external physical task dimensions are probably not what the central nervous system uses to organize the forthcoming movement. In Table 2.1, we can see that factors such as extent, movement precision, and reversals are externally defined. Similarly, kinematic measures such as absolute movement duration, velocity, and extent are merely resultant measures of the dynamics of the system as we have discussed previously.

Our analysis of Table 2.1 leads to a more coherent picture. The important internal variables are choice of effecting limbs, direction of movement, sequencing and timing of the appropriate effector units, and the specification of force–time relationships for these units. These variables are inherent in the first four factors identified in Table 2.1, the factors that have produced consistent results.

Let us continue our consideration of the relevant internal variables in examining those factors that have led to equivocal results. The discrepancies in the findings of movement reversals might be resolved by use of the concept of movement control by synergistic groups of muscles or effector units as previously defined. One might expect that a simple reversal of direction through, for example, flexion and extension of the elbow is controlled as an effector unit (Glencross, 1972, 1973). In contrast, a reversal of direction through more than one plane, requiring "nonsynergistic" muscle groups about different joints may involve more than one effector unit (Henry, 1960; Norrie, 1967). The concept of synergies, or functional muscle groupings, is an important one that must not be dismissed in examining the internal factors underlying movement organization.

At this point, we must address (and defend) the one unequivocal factor in Table 2.1 that may appear to contradict our previous discussion, that of force/ resisted force. From the few studies we reviewed, there appear to be no time demands associated with this factor. Yet here and in section II, we have identified force–time specifications as an important internal variable. Resisted force (Glencross, 1973) we do not see as a problem, because subjects do not necessarily have to organize the force for resistance until the movement is initiated. Further, examination of the one paper that examined force output (Klemmer, 1957) shows that the instructions and methodology used were not specifically designed to test the hypothesis that increases in *actual* force output would be reflected by increases in reaction time. Although this hypothesis awaits empirical test, it may be that increments in amount of force output is a low-level specification to the same effecting unit and therefore would not be reflected in additional time demands for its organization.

So much of the contradictory results we have examined are a function of selecting external or kinematic factors rather than the internal factors revealed by neurophysiological research.

TABLE 2.1
Response Factors and Initiation Time[a]

Movement Factors	Simple Reaction Time		Choice Reaction Time	
	Yes	No	Yes	No
# of anatomical units (limbs or fingers) used simultaneously in response	Glencross (1973) Klapp (1977b) Rosenbaum & Patashnik (this volume)		Klapp & Erwin (1976) Rabbitt et al. (1975)	
# of units used sequentially in response	MacKenzie & Roy (1978) Rosenbaum & Patashnik (this volume) Sternberg et al. (1978)		MacKenzie & Roy (1978)	
timing (pauses) within a response	Glencross (1972) Jagacinski et al. (1978a) Rosenbaum & Patashnik (this volume)		Jagacinski et al. (1978a) Rosenbaum (1976)	
direction uncertainty	X	X	Ells (1973) Gottsdanker (1966) Kerr (1976) Klapp (1975) Megaw (1972) Rosenbaum (in press) Zelaznik (1978)	

reversals in response	Henry (1960), Norrie (1967)	Glencross (1973)		Glencross (1972), Glencross (1973)
force/resisted force	Glencross (1973), Klemmer (1957)	Glencross (1973)		Glencross (1973)
duration/velocity	Newell (1978)	Klapp et al. (1974)	Klapp (1977b), Klapp & Erwin (1976), Klapp et al. (1974)	
precision or index of difficulty	Glencross (1976)	Glencross (1976)	Klapp (1975), Siegel (1977), Semjen & Requin (1976)	Ells (1973), Fitts & Peterson (1964), Jagacinski et al. (1978b), Semjen & Requin (1975)
extent	Fitts & Peterson (1964), Rosenbaum (in press), Williams (1971)	Brown & Slater-Hammel (1949), Glencross (1972), Lagassee & Hayes (1973)	Glencross (1973), Rosenbaum (in press), Semjen & Requin (1976)	
extent uncertainty	X	X	Kerr (1976), Rosenbaum (in press)	Megaw (1972), Megaw & Armstrong (1973), Searle & Taylor (1948)

[a] The X'd cells are undefined. The Yes columns include those studies which have demonstrated differential time demands (i.e., significant effects on reaction time) with experimental manipulation of the movement factors.

The second issue concerns the basic assumptions underlying the simple and choice reaction-time paradigms. Klapp (1977a) has contended that organization effects may be minimized or eliminated in the simple paradigm. In contrast, Sternberg et al. (1978) caution that the choice paradigm may be overestimating organization effects due to the unwanted intrusion of non-response-related processes. For example, they suggest possible inflation of "movement organization time" due to S–R compatibility and S-ensemble–R-ensemble compatibility. However, although S–R and SE–RE compatibility problems may prove to be greater in the choice paradigm than in the simple paradigm, the use of the choice paradigm has some value in examining response organization processes, in that it can provide information unavailable from the simple paradigm.

The first source of information concerns the effects observed with uncertainty regarding a movement organization factor (e.g., direction uncertainty). However, related to this type of paradigm is another compatibility problem that Sternberg et al. (1978) address, that of response–response compatibility. They suggest that "ultimately an account of the planning and execution of responses will have to explain R–R compatibility." We agree and further suggest that systematic manipulation of R–R compatibility in the choice paradigm may help to account for the processes underlying planning and execution of responses. For example, we may identify two factors, A and B, that have some theoretical basis as being important internal variables for the response organization process. In one condition we block over trials on Factor A and make Factor B the uncertain variable (i.e., choice indicates level of Factor B). In a second condition we block on Factor B and make Factor A uncertain. Using a subtractive method, if (Factor A uncertain – Factor A certain) > (Factor B uncertain – Factor B certain), then one might conclude that organization of Factor A is performed before organization of Factor B, that is, the resultion of uncertainty of Factor A has a greater effect than the resolution of uncertainty of Factor B due to the greater R–R compatibility when Factor B is uncertain. To overcome the valid criticism of spurious effects due to SE–RE compatibility, it would be necessary to replicate this effect using a different S–R ensemble.

A second source of information not available in the simple reaction time paradigm is a potentially very powerful technique in the choice paradigm involving the use of the precuing technique. This technique has been used by Rosenbaum (in press) who studied how decisions about the selection of the arm, direction, and extent of forthcoming hand movements were made by providing subjects with precues about the forthcoming movement. These precues gave partial, complete, or no information about which of the two arms, which of two directions, and which of two extents the forthcoming movement would be composed of. His results indicated that selection times were longest for arm and shortest for extent and, in addition, arm and direction were selected before extent.

As Rosenbaum points out, the movement precuing technique is valuable because it allows one to make inferences about movement organizational processes that are impossible to make with the simple reaction time paradigm or the traditional choice paradigm. Conceivably, the technique can be applied to any type of movement factor in order to solve issues of theoretical and practical concern.

Interference Effects

Thus far we have discussed those factors that we think are important in the selection and organization of movement as reflected by their time demands. However, there may be factors related to response organization and execution that do not reflect differential time demands but, nevertheless, do play an important role in these processes. For example, perhaps the reaction time for making a movement with one reversal is no different than the reaction time for making a movement with two changes of direction. But to conclude that movement reversals are not part of the premovement organization processes would be premature without first seeking additional evidence.

This additional evidence concerns the attentional demands and the central information processing structures involved in the organization and execution phases of movement. In considering attention effects first, there is a substantial theoretical framework for studying the attentional requirements of behavior, and there have been a number of applications of this framework to motor behavior (Ells, 1973; Kahneman, 1973; Keele, 1973, Kerr, 1973; and Klein, 1976). The notion is that humans possess a central system of limited capacity that is required in the performance of most voluntary acts. When a human performer is viewed as an information processing system, in which a number of information processing stages are postulated to intervene between a stimulus and response, the question of interest is what stages require attention. Although there are different theories on the nature of the limited system, the common assumption is that when two processes both require access to the limited capacity system, one or both of the processes will be interfered with.

Although most information-processing models lump response processes for movements into one component, or the two components of organization and execution, our view is that the organization of a response may entail a number of processes requiring time and perhaps attention for its successful completion. Further, there are information processing demands during movement execution that must be quantified in terms of time and attention effects.

One method of determining the attention demands of movement organization and execution is the use of the dual-task paradigm. In one version, the primary task (i.e., the task which the subject is instructed to perform to the best of his ability and of which the experimenter wishes to investigate the underlying information processes) is a discrete movement and the secondary task, a probe stimulus requiring a discrete response, must be performed simultaneously.[2]

Although lengthening of the reaction time to the probe stimulus (probe reaction time) can be interpreted as an interference effect due to the attention required by performance of the primary task (see Kantowitz & Knight, 1978; Kerr, 1973, and Klein, 1976, for appropriate methods and controls for this paradigm), a rival interpretation of these effects is sometimes possible. This concerns the possibility of structural interference effects that result from the secondary task requiring the same perceptual, memory, or response system as the primary task (Kahneman, 1973). The limitation in this case is due to structure rather than capacity. Although some investigators (Kerr, 1973; Klein, 1976) have cautioned that an experimenter must ensure that the probe task utilizes psychological structures that are independent of those used in the primary task so as to minimize the effects of structural interference on attentional limitations, this may be harder than it first appears.

The possible role that structural interference may play in any situation where an individual performs two simultaneous tasks is illustrated by the work of Kinsbourne and Hicks (1978). They suggest that except for highly overlearned tasks there will always be some structural interference from dual-task performance when the two tasks require different "motor programs" (e.g., performing movements with unrelated rhythms or hand movements with speaking). This is necessarily so because their view is based on the notion that the human performer has a limited amount of functional cerebral space and that the control centers, responsible for initiating and executing movements within this space are neurally linked, in varying degrees, into one network. When two of these control centers are simultaneously active, neural activity from each center spreads to the other center, causing interference.

McLeod (1977, 1978) has nicely demonstrated the existence of structural interference effects in the dual-task paradigm. In one study (McLeod, 1977) he used a two-choice secondary task (either manual or vocal) with a continuous manual tracking task. He found that subjects making manual responses to the probe had significantly greater tracking errors than the vocal probe group, who in turn made more errors than the no-probe control group. Note, that in determining how the secondary task affected the primary task, McLeod was in essence violating the traditional assumption for the study of

---

[2]In the movement literature there have been three major versions of the dual-task paradigm: (1) a discrete probe secondary task with a discrete primary task; (2) a discrete probe secondary task with a continuous primary task; and (3) a continuous secondary task with a continuous primary task. Although the latter two have been used to investigate specific questions about the attention demands of movement execution, we do not review this work here because our interest is primarily in studying those information processes occurring during both the latency and execution phases of movement. The advantage of using the probe during both the latency and execution phases of movement is that it allows for the assessment of any common processes that might underlie these two phases.

capacity effects, that the secondary task should not have any influence on the primary task. Nevertheless, his study points out the existence of structural interference effects in a dual-task paradigm even for two responses (manual tracking and a vocal response) that are usually thought to be relatively independent in terms of their structure.

McLeod's (1978) second study examined the assumption that if the probe task is directly measuring the capacity demands of the primary task, then similar capacity limitations should result when different secondary probe tasks are used with the same primary task. For this study he used a manual response for the primary task of same–different name matches and a probe task consisting of a discrete one-choice manual or vocal response to auditory stimuli. His results showed an interaction between type of probe response and time of probe onset in the primary task. From these results he questioned whether a single form of probe response can be used as a "pure" measure of capacity.

The work of McLeod (1977, 1978) not only demonstrates the existence of structural interference in dual-task paradigms but also leads us to an important consideration in the use of the dual-task paradigm in investigating underlying processes of movement organization and execution. Remember that we are primarily interested in those processes occurring during both the reaction time and execution phases of voluntary movement and hence the use of a discrete primary task and a discrete secondary task is appropriate. Based on McLeod's work and the framework supplied by the functional space model, this type of dual-task paradigm might be used to uncover systematically those structural processes responsible for movement organization and execution. What this entails is the analysis of the primary task in terms of the operations involved in the organization and execution phases. One or, more profitably, several secondary tasks, each relying on one specific organizational or execution process, can then be used to probe the primary task. Each secondary task would be inserted as a probe at specific times over both the reaction time and execution phases of the primary task. What would be obtained, according to this framework, is a family of curves each indicating interference effects at specific points in time of the primary task. It does not have to be assumed that the curves would be totally independent in terms of the sepcific time at which interference occurs. For example, one might predict that if the processing stages in the initaition phase of the primary task were sequential, then probe tasks specifically interfering with the processes in these stages would show interference effects at different times. However, if the manipulated factors (i.e., the probes) were nonadditive, one might expect these probes to show interference effects at the same point in time of the primary task.

Another related issue concerns the nature of performance of the primary task in the dual-task conditions. As McLeod (1977) demonstrated, there is a distinct possibility that interference in the primary task will occur simultaneously with interference in the secondary task. This emphasizes the importance, in future dual-task studies, of examining both tasks for interference effects. What this suggests, of course, is a reinterpretation of the basic assumption of what psychological processes are being investigated through the use of the dual-task paradigm. To this point in time in the movement behavior literature, it has been assumed that variability in the performance of the secondary task has been an index of the capacity demands of the primary task. This, however, may not be the case as indicated by the McLeod (1977, 1978) data and considerations of the functional space model.

Although our discussion of the dual-task paradigm has questioned whether a pure measure of capacity is possible, we believe our interpretation of the role of structural interference in dual-task performance is an important one. The utility of this approach is that it utilizes known neurological relationships among cerebral control centers responsible for the control of movement. In this respect the functional space model is consistent with the basic neurophysiological principle that there is a high degree of functional unity within the central nervous system. This is the point we have emphasized earlier when considering the structure of the central nervous system, and it is a point we make when reviewing other literature in later sections.

Interference During Initiation and Execution Phases of Movement. As mentioned previously, to look at the psychological processes underlying both the organization and execution phases of movement and to determine any relationships between these phases, one must use studies based on the dual-task paradigm where both tasks are of a discrete nature. Unfortunately we know of only two such published studies. (See also Glencross, this volume.)

One study was by Ells (1973) where subjects performed a primary task with their right arm consisting of moving a lever as rapidly as possible in one of two possible directions to targets of two possible widths. The secondary task consisted of a manual response (pushing a toggle switch forward or backward with the left hand) to a two-choice auditory stimulus (a high or low tone). The purpose of the study was to determine the time and attention demands of the possible number of movements (i.e., the number of directions) and the precision (i.e., target width) demanded of the movements.

Analysis of the results included the reaction and movement times of the primary task and the probe or secondary task reaction times. It was found that reaction time for the primary task was only influenced by the number of alternative movements and that movement time was only affected by the required precision of the movement. On the other hand, analysis of the probe reaction times, during the reaction time phase of the primary task, indicated that significant delays were associated with both the number of possible alternative movements *and* their required precision. In contrast, during the movement phase of the primary task, probe reaction time was only sensitive to target precision.

Ells' concluded from these results that organizational processes for movement are concerned with codes related to the direction of the intended movement. This was reflected by both the time (i.e., reaction time for the primary task) and the interference[3] (i.e., probe reaction time during the reaction time interval) effects. With respect to the finding that reaction time of the primary task was uninfluenced by required precision but that there were large effects of interference, represented by significant probe reaction time delays for this variable during the reaction-time interval, Ells explained these latter effects by suggesting they were caused by processes occurring during the movement phase since this is when the response to the probe actually took place. With this assumption, and in light of the time and interference effects associated with required precision during the movement phase of the primary task, Ells concluded that movement precision effects are not associated with organization of the movement but only with its execution. Finally, taking his results as a whole, he concluded that his data were support for the notion that reaction time and movement time were determined by independent processes. Thus, his final conclusion was that the number of alternative movements determined reaction time and precision of the required movement determined movement time.

We think there is room for reinterpretation of some of Ells' results, and our argument is twofold. One deals with the relationship between time and interference effects, whereas the other has to do with the issue of the independence of reaction and movement time. These issues, as we see them, are related.

In terms of the relationship between time and interference effects, one rationale for Ells' (1973) rejection of the observed interference effects, associated with movement precision during the initiation phase of the primary task, was the lack of a significant difference in the initiation times to the different-sized targets. The question was, how could different levels of a variable require differential amounts of "attention" but at the same time not have differential time effects? Any attempt at resolving this apparent paradox would run contrary to the assumptions of the large theoretical field dealing with the relationship between time and attention.[4]

---

[3]Note that we are using the term *interference* to include the possibility that interference is caused by structural and/or capacity effects.

[4]Interestingly, the only other published study that we know of that investigates time and interference effects of movement initiation and execution (Kerr, 1975) ran into a similar problem. In the initiation phase of the primary task, no time differences were obtained between two conditions of movement uncertainty but reliable interference effects were found. Although structural interference was hinted at as a possible cause of this apparent paradox, Kerr, like Ells (1973), suggested rather that the interference effects were due to processing differences during the execution phase (when the probe response was actually completed) rather than the initiation phase.

However, if one introduces the concept of structural interference, and specifically the way in which it is used by Kinsbourne and Hicks (1978) in their functional space model, it then becomes possible to speculate on the previous issue. If one takes the interference effects during the reaction time interval found by Ells (1973) and Kerr (1975) at face value (i.e., the interference is caused by processes occurring during the reaction-time phase of the primary movement and not during the execution phase), it can be predicted that two levels of a movement factor might not require more time to be organized, but if they represented different levels of complexity (i.e., result in greater spread of activation), it would be predicted that they would differentially interfere, in a structural sense, with a simultaneously performed secondary task. It would also be predicted that for some movement processes, especially those evolving late in the organization of movement, their influence would be manifest during both the initiation and execution phases of movement.

At the base of this prediction is the assumption that in some cases there is a functional relationship between processes occurring during the organization and the execution phases of movement production. We believe there is now ample evidence to support this contention. Kerr (1978) concluded that to retain the notion that initiation time and movement time are independent would be naive. Evidence comes from work such as Fitts and Peterson (1964) that showed a small but significant increase in simple reaction time as movement complexity [measured by Fitts' (1954) index of difficulty] increased. Fitts and Radford (1966) found similar effects but this time a choice reaction time paradigm was used. It is interesting to note that these studies, particularly the one by Fitts and Peterson (1964), have been used for support of the idea that processes underlying reaction time and movement time are independent. However, the facts are that not only did reaction time increase significantly with the index of difficulty (5.4 msec/bit ID) but the correlation of these two variables was significant ($r = .79$). Although the time effect is not large, it is reliable and has been ignored by subsequent investigators. Klapp (1975) and Siegel (1977) have also shown choice reaction time for short movements to be influenced by target width. In Klapp (1975), the correlation between reaction and movement times was $r = .82$.

Finally, the work of Kantowitz (1969) shows this relationship in a different way. In an S_1–R_1, S_2 paradigm (i.e., where no response was required for S_2), when S_2 was inserted during the reaction time interval, it was found that both reaction time to S_1 and movement time (R_1) were lengthened in a systematic fashion as S_2 approached S_1. This clearly demonstrates, for these conditions, the reliance of reaction time and movement time on similar processes. Whether Kantowitz's results demonstrate an attentional or structural interference effect is another question but the conclusion appears to be valid.

If, then, the processes underlying organization and execution phases (for at least some movement parameters) are similar, this opens the door for a new line of investigation. Future studies, designed after those of Ells (1973) and

Kerr (1975), might place greater emphasis on not only determining relationships between reaction and movement times but also looking for interference effects that signal common processes. Certainly, we interpret the Ells (1973) finding that required movement precision affected probe reaction time both during the reaction time and movement phases of the primary task as a demonstration of this phenomenon. In addition, one must not forget the distinct possibility that the probe reaction times may be reflecting structural interference rather than capacity interference.

Common Processes Underlying Organization and Execution Phases. Although data from the behavioral sciences establish the fact that there are, at least for some movement parameters, common processes underlying organization and execution phases, evidence from the neurosciences is also consistent with this viewpoint. Previously in this chapter, literature was reviewed suggesting that higher centers, during the organization phase of movement (i.e., the reaction time interval), might prepare the segmental apparatus for the upcoming movement by supplying parameters related to the demands of the movement. The parameters discussed in this regard were concerned with the length–tension relationships of muscles involved in the movement. If higher centers can influence the state of the musculature during the organizational phase, it can be predicted that a functional relationship between some organizational and execution processes would exist. Further, if the organizational process is interfered with (as in the Kantowitz, 1969, study), the observed decrements in this process should also be manifested in execution. The efficiency with which some movement parameters are organized at a central level would be reflected in the efficiency of the actual movement.

This last statement is also supported from the viewpoint of the functional space model (Kinsbourne & Hicks, 1978). This model would predict that control centers in the cerebral cortex exert their influence both during the reaction time and execution phases of movement. Variables that interfere with this control center would thus influence the efficiency of both the organization and execution phases of movement.

SUMMARY AND CONCLUSIONS

We have discussed literature from both the neural and behavioral sciences that bear on the processes within the central nervous system underlying the organization and execution of voluntary movement. The first issue concerned the fact that processes involved in organizing and executing movement occur within a heterarchical neurological system that is anatomically composed of multiple levels of control. At any instant in time, control of movement is realized by a tightly integrated system with communication occurring through feedback and feedforward mechanisms. These feedback and feedforward communications underly the complex, continually adapting environment–individual interface. From this viewpoint, we concluded that the concept of a "motor program," where commands are centrally organized and executed without reference to peripheral feedback, was not ecological.

Neuroscientific evidence suggested that the central representation of movement probably involves the internal representation of the relationships among the body, effecting limbs and the environment; direction of the intended action; selection, sequencing, and phasing of effector units; and force–time specifications. Evidence suggests that for many movements the basic effector units are groups of synergistic muscles controlled by higher centers as autonomous units through both feedforward and feedback. One concept of feedforward discussed was the notion that higher centers prepare effector units for movement by establishing specific length–tension relationships among the groups of agonist and antagonist muscles involved in the planned movement.

From the behavioral sciences, literature dealing with the central time demands of movement organization yielded inconclusive results about those response factors that are dealt with by the higher centers. The reason for these equivocal findings may have been the use of external physical task dimensions (e.g., precision, extent) rather than variables produced by the central nervous system (e.g., force–time, direction). Related is the use, by many studies, of dependent variables related to the kinematics of movement (extent, velocity, acceleration), whereas we believe a concentration on kinetic or dynamic variables (e.g., force, force–time) is more appropriate because the kinematics of a system are determined by its kinetics.

Another confounding issue in the measurement of the time demands of central processes in organizing movement concerns the use of simple and choice reaction-time paradigms. Both paradigms are capable of yielding informative, but different, types of information regarding the processes underlying movement organization.

One other way of determining the processes involved in movement organization and execution involves studying dual-task performance and systematically accounting for observed interference effects. Two types of interference were identified: (1) that due to attentional effects (capacity interference); and (2) that due to the nature of cerebral control centers (structural interference). It was concluded that in the movement behavior area it would be very difficult to assess the pure capacity demands of processes involved in movement organization and execution because of the necessary presence of structural interference whenever two movement tasks are performed simultaneously. Nevertheless, interference effects from dual-task performance, interpreted in terms of structural interference, might provide valuable knowledge about the processes underlying movement organization and execution. One application of this view, in this chapter, resulted in evidence being gained for the dependence of reaction time and movement time for some movement parameters.

This conclusion runs counter to the current opinion that the processes underlying these two measures are independent.

ACKNOWLEDGMENT

The second author wishes to acknowledge support from the National Science and Engineering Research Council of Canada.

REFERENCES

Allen, G. I., & Tsukahara, N. Cerebro-cerebellar communication systems. *Physiological Reviews,* 1974, *54,* 957–1006.

Asatryan, D. G., & Fel'dman, A. G. Functional tuning of the nervous system with control of movement or maintenance of a steady posture.I. Mechanographic analysis of the work on the joint on execution of a postural task. *Biophysics,* 1965, *10,* 925–935.

Bartlett, F. C. *Remembering: A study in experimental and social psychology.* London: Cambridge University Press, 1961.

Benton, A. L. Disorders of spatial orientation. In P. J. Vinken and G. W. Bruyn (Eds.), *Handbook of clinical neurology.* Vol. 3, New York: American Elsevier, 1969.

Bernstein, N. *The coordination and regulation of movements.* Oxford: Pergamon Press Ltd., 1967.

Bizzi, E., Dev, P., Morasso, P., & Polit, A. Effect of load disturbances during centrally initiated movements. *Journal of Neurophysiology,* 1978, *41,* 542–556.

Bizzi, E., & Polit, A. Processes controlling visually evoked movements. *Neuropsychologia,* 1979, *17,* 203–213.

Bizzi, E., Polit, A., & Morasso, P. Mechanisms underlying achievement of final head position. *Journal of Neurophysiology,* 1976, *39,* 435–444.

Brinkman, J., & Kuypers, H. Splitbrain monkeys: cerebral control of ipsilateral and contralateral arm, hand, and finger movements. *Science,* 1972, *197,* 536–539.

Brooks, V. B. Some examples of programmed limb movements. *Brain Research,* 1974, *71,* 299–308.

Brooks, V. B. Motor programs revisited in R. E. Talbot, and D. E. Humphrey, (Eds.), *Posture and movment: Perspective for integrating sensory and motor research on the mammalian nervous system.* New York: Raven Press, 1979.

Brown, J. S., & Slater-Hammel, A. T. Discrete movements in the horizontal plane as a function of their length and direction. *Journal of Applied Psychology,* 1949, *39,* 84–95.

Corballis, M. C., & Beale, I. L. *The psychology of left and right.* Hillsdale, N.J., Lawrence Erlbaum Associates, 1976.

Craik, R., Herman, R., & Finley, F. R. Human solutions for locomotion. II. Interlimb coordination. In R. M. Herman, S. Grillner, P. S. G. Stein, and D. G. Stuart (Eds.), *Neural control of locomotion.* New York: Plenum, 1976.

Critchley, M. *The parietal lobes.* London: Edward Arnold Ltd., 1953.

Crossman, E. R. F. W., & Goodeve, P. J. Feedback control of hand movements and Fitts law. In the *Proceedings of the Experimental Society,* Oxford, 1963.

Easton, T. A. On the normal use of reflexes. *American Scientist,* 1972, *60,* 591–599.

Easton, T. A. Reflexes and fatigue: New directions. In E. Simonson & P. C. Weiser (Eds.), *Psychological aspects and physiological correlates of work and fatigue.* Springfield, Ill.: Charles C. Thomas, 1976.

Easton, T. A. Coordinative structures—the basis for a motor program. In D. M. Landers & R. W. Christina (Eds.), *Psychology of motor behavior and sport.* Champaign, Ill.: Human Kinetics Pubs., 1978.

Eccles, J. C. The dynamic loop hypothesis of movement control. In K. N. Leibovic (Ed.), *Information processing in the nervous system.* New York: Springer-Verlag, 1969.

Eccles, J. C. *The understanding of the brain,* New York: McGraw-Hill, 1973.

Ells, J. G. Analysis of temporal and attentional aspects of movement control. *Journal of Experimental Psychology,* 1973, *99,* 10–21.

Evarts, E. V. Representation of movements and muscles by PTN of precentral motor cortex. In M. D. Yahr & D. P. Purpura (Eds.), *Neurophysiological basis of normal and abnormal motor activities.* New York: Raven Press, 1967.

Evarts, E. V. Relation of pyramidal tract activity to force exerted during voluntary movement. *Journal of Neurophysiology,* 1968, *31,* 14–27.

Evarts, E. V. Feedback and corollary discharge: A merging of the concepts. *Neurosciences Research Progress Bulletin.,* 1972, *9,* 86–112.

Evarts, E. V. Changing concepts in the central control of movement. *Canadian Journal of Physiology and Pharmacology,* 1975, *53,* 191–201.

Evarts, E. V., & Tanji, J. Gating of motor cortex reflexes by prior instruction. *Brain Research,* 1974, *71,* 479–494.

Evarts, E. V., & Thach, W. T. Motor mechanisms of the CNS: cerebrocerebellar interrelations. *Annual Review of Psychology,* 1969, *21,* 451–498.

Fel'dman, A. G. Functional tuning of the nervous system with control of movement or maintenance of a steady posture. II. Controllable parameters of the muscles. *Biophysics,* 1966, *11,* 565–578. (a)

Fel'dman, A. G. Functional tuning of the nervous system with control of movement or maintenance of a steady posture. III. Mechanographic analysis of the execution by man of the simplest motor tasks. *Biophysics,* 1966, *11,* 766–775. (b)

Fitch, H. L., & Turvey, M. T. On the control of activity: Some remarks from an ecological point of view. In D. M. Landers & R. W. Christina (Eds.), *Psychology of motor behavior and sport.* Champaign, Ill.: Human Kinetics Pub., 1978.

Fitts, P. M. The information capacity of the human motor system in controlling the amplitude of movement. *Journal of Experimental Psychology,* 1954, *47,* 381–391.

Fitts, P. M., & Peterson, J. R. Information capacity of discrete motor responses. *Journal of Experimental Psychology,* 1964, *67,* 103–112.

Fitts, P. M., & Radford, B. K. Information capacity of discrete motor responses under different cognitive sets. *Journal of Experimental Psychology,* 1966, *71,* 475–482.

Glencross, D. J. Latency and response complexity. *Journal of Motor Behavior,* 1972, *4,* 251–256.

Glencross, D. J. Response complexity and the latency of different movement patterns. *Journal of Motor Behavior,* 1973, *5,* 95–104.

Glencross, D. J. The latency of aiming movements. *Journal of Motor Behavior,* 1976, *8,* 27–34.

Gottsdanker, R. The effect of superseding signals. *Quarterly Journal of Experimental Psychology,* 1966, *18,* 236–249.

Granit, R. Demand and accomplishment in voluntary movement. In R. B. Stein, K. G. Pearson, R. S. Smith, & J. B. Redford (Eds.) *Control of posture and locomotion.* New York: Plenum Press, 1973.

Greene, P. H. *Problems of organization of motor systems.* Institute For Computer Research, University of Chicago, Quarterly Report No. 29, 1971.

Grillner, S. Locomotion in vertebrates: General mechanisms and reflex interaction. *Physiological Reviews,* 1975, *55,* 247–304.

Haaxma, R., & Kuypers, H. Role of occipito-frontal cortico-cortical connections in visual guidance of relatively independent hand and finger movements in Rhesus monkeys. *Brain Research,* 1974, *71,* 361–366.

Hayes, K. C. Supraspinal and spinal processes involved in the initiation of fast movement. In D. M. Landers & R. W. Christina (Eds.), *Psychology of motor behavior and sport.* Champaign, Ill.: Human Kinetics Pub., 1978.

Henry, F. M. Increased response latency for complicated movements and a "memory drum" theory of neuromotor reaction. *Research Quarterly,* 1960, *31,* 448–458.

Herman, R., Wirta, R., Bampton, S., & Finley, F. R. Human solutions for locomotion. I. Single limb analysis. In R. M. Herman, S. Grillner, P. S. G. Stein, & D. G. Stuart (Eds.), *Neural control of locomotion.* New York: Plenum, 1976.

Houk, J. C. Participation of reflex mechanisms and reaction-time processes in the compensatory adjustments to mechanical disturbances. In J. E. Desmedt (Ed.), *Cerebral motor control in man: Long loop mechanisms: progress in clinical neurophysiology.* Vol. 4, Karger, Basel, 1978.

Jagacinski, R. J., Hartzell, E. J., Ward, S., & Biship, K. Fitts' law as a function of a system dynamics and target uncertainty. *Journal of Motor Behavior,* 1978, *10,* 123–132. (a)

Jagacinski, R. J., Shulman, H. G., & Burke, M. W. *Measuring the time course of motor programming.* Paper presented at the meeting of the North American Society for the Psychology of Sport and Physical Activity. Tallahassee, Fla. 1978. (b)

Kahneman, D. *Attention and Effort.* Englewood Cliffs, N.J.: Prentice-Hall, 1973.

Kantowitz, B. H. Double stimulation with varying response information. *Journal of Experimental Psychology,* 1969, *82,* 347–352.

Kantowitz, B. H., & Knight, Jr., J. L. Testing tapping timesharing: Attention demands of movement amplitude and target width. In G. E. Stelmach (Ed.), *Information processing in motor control and learning.* New York: Academic Press, 1978.

Keele, S. W. Movement control in skilled motor performance. *Psychological Bulletin,* 1968, *70,* 387–403.

Keele, S. W. *Attention and Human Performance.* Pacific Palisades, Calif.: Goodyear Pub. Co, 1973.

Kelso, J. A. S., & Stelmach, G. E. Central and peripheral mechanisms in motor control. In G. E. Stelmach (Ed.), *Motor control: Issues and trends.* New York: Academic Press, 1976.

Kerr, B. Processing demands during mental operations. *Memory and Cognition,* 1973, *1,* 401–412.

Kerr, B. Processing demands during movement. *Journal of Motor Behavior,* 1975, *7,* 15–27.

Kerr, B. Decisions about movement direction and extent. *Journal of Human Movement Studies,* 1976, *3,* 199–213.

Kerr, B. Task factors that influence selection and preparation for voluntary movements. In G. E. Stelmach (Ed.) *Information processing in motor control and learning.* New York: Academic Press, 1978.

Kinsbourne, M. Neuropsychological analysis of cognitive deficit. In M. Kinsbourne (Ed.), *Asymmetrical function of the brain.* New York: Cambridge University Press, 1977.

Kinsbourne, M., & Hicks, R. E. Functional cerebral space: A model for overflow, transfer, and interference effects in human performance. In J. Requin (Ed.), *Attention and performance VII.* New York: Academic Press, 1978.

Klapp, S. T. Feedback versus motor programming in the control of aimed movements. *Journal of Experimental Psychology, Human Perception and Performance,* 1975, *104,* 147–153.

Klapp, S. T. Reaction time analysis of programmed control. In R. S. Hutton (Ed.), *Exercise and sport sciences reviews.* Santa Barbara, Calif.: Journal Publishing Affiliates, 1977. (a)

Klapp, S. T. *Timing of motor responses.* Paper presented at meetings of the Psychonomic Society, Washington, D.C., November, 1977. (b)

Klapp, S. T., & Erwin, C. I. Relation between programming time and duration of response being programmed. *Journal of Experimental Psychology, Human Perception and Performance,* 1976, *2,* 591–598.

Klapp, S. T., Wyatt, E. P., & Lingo, W. M. Response programming in simple and choice reactions. *Journal of Motor Behavior*, 1974, *6*, 263–271.

Klein, R. M. Attention and movement. In G. E. Stelmach (Ed.), *Motor control: Issues and trends.* New York: Academic Press, 1976.

Klemmer, E. T. Rate of force application in a simple reaction time test. *Journal of Applied Psychology*, 1957, *41*, 329–332.

Kornhuber, H. H., Motor functions of the cerebellum and basal ganglia: The cerebellocortical saccadic (ballistic) clock, the cerebellonuclear hold regulator, and the basal ganglia ramp (voluntary speed, smooth movement) generator. *Kybernetik*, 1971, *8*, 157–162.

Lagasse, P. P., & Hayes, K. C. Premotor and motor reaction time as a function of movement extent. *Journal of Motor Behavior*, 1973, *5*, 25–32.

Luria, A. R. *Higher cortical functions in man.* New York: Basic Books, 1966.

Luria, A. R. *The working brain.* London: Penguin Books, 1973.

MacKenzie, C. L., & Roy, E. A. *Handedness and response complexity in a finger sequencing task.* Presented at the meeting of the North American Society for the Psychology of Sport and Physical Activity, Tallahassee, Florida, May 1978.

Marsden, C. D., Merton, P. A., & Morton, H. B. Servo action in human voluntary movement. *Nature*, 1972, *238*, 140–143.

McLeod, P. A dual task response modality effect: Support for multiprocess models of attention. *Quarterly Journal of Experimental Psychology*, 1977, *29*, 657–667.

McLeod, P. Does probe RT measure central processing demand? *Quarterly Journal of Experimental Psychology* 1978, *30*, 83–89.

Megaw, E. D. Direction and extent uncertainty in step-input tracking. *Journal of Motor Behavior*, 1972, *4*, 171–186.

Megaw, E. D., & Armstrong, W. Individual and simultaneous tracking of a step input by the horizontal saccadic eye movement and manual control systems. *Journal of Experimental Psychology*, 1973, *100*, 18–28.

Miller, G. A., Galanter, E., & Pribram, K. H. *Plans and the structure of behavior.* New York: Henry Holt, 1960.

Muram, D., & Carmon, A. Behavioral properties of somatosensory-motor interhemispheric transfer. *Journal of Experimental Psychology*, 1972, *94*, 225–230.

Nauta, W. J. H. The problem of the frontal lobe: A reinterpretation. *Journal of Psychiatric Research*, 1971, *8*, 167–187.

Nauta, W. J. H. Neural associations of the frontal cortex. *Acta Neurobiologica Experimentalis*, 1972, *32*, 125–140.

Newell, K. Latency to movement as a function of temporal direction and velocity. In D. M. Landers & R. W. Christina (Eds.), *Psychology of motor behavior and sport.* Champaign, Ill.: Human Kinetics Pub., 1978, in press.

Norrie, M. L. Practice effects on reaction latency for simple and complex movements. *Research Quarterly*, 1967, *38*, 79–85.

Penfield, W., & Rasmussen, T. *The cerebral cortex in man.* New York: Macmillan, 1957.

Pew, R. W. Human perceptual-motor performance. In B. H. Kantowitz, (Ed.), *Human information processing: Tutorials in performance and cognition*, Hillsdale, N.J. Lawrence Erlbaum Associates, 1974.

Pohl, W. Dissociation of spatial discrimination deficits following frontal and parietal lesions in monkeys. *Journal of Comparative and Physiological Psychology*, 1973, *82*, 227–239.

Polit, A., & Bizzi, E. Characteristics of motor programs underlying arm movements in monkeys. Journal of Neurophysiology, 1979, *42*, 183–194.

Pribram, K. H. The primate frontal cortex—Executive of the brain. In K. H. Pribram & A. R. Luria (Eds.), *Psychophysiology of the frontal lobes*, New York: Academic Press, 1973.

Rabbitt, P. M. A., Vyas, S. M., & Fearnley, S. Programming sequences of complex responses. In P. M. A. Rabbit & S. Dornic (Eds.), *Attention and performance V*, New York: Academic Press, 1975.

Rispal-Padel, L., Massion, J., & Grangetto, A. Relations between the ventrolateral thalamic nucleus and motor cortex and their possible role in the central organization of motor control. *Brain Research,* 1973, *60,* 1–20.

Rosenbaum, D. A. *Mental time and real time in the production of manual responses.* Paper presented at the meeting of the Psychonomic Society, Saint Louis, Mi., November 1976.

Rosenbaum, D. A. Human movement initiation: selection of arm, direction and extent. *Journal of Experimental Psychology: General,* in press.

Roy, E. A. Towards a typology of apraxia. *Mouvement,* 1975, 29–44.

Schmidt, R. A. Control processes in motor skills. In J. Keogh & B. S. Hutton (Eds.), *Exercise and sport sciences reviews.* Santa Barbara, Calif.: Journal Publishing Affiliates, 1976, *4,* 229–261.

Schmidt, R. A., Zelaznik, H. N., & Frank, J. S. Sources of inaccuracy in rapid movement. In G. E. Stelmach (Ed.), *Information processing in motor control and learning.* New York: Academic Press, 1978.

Searle, L. V., & Taylor, F. V. Studies of tracking behavior. I. Rate and time characteristics of simple corrective movements. *Journal of Experimental Psychology,* 1948, *38,* 615–631.

Semjen, A., & Requin, J. Movement amplitude, pointing accuracy and choice-reaction time. *Perceptual and Motor Skills,* 1976, *43,* 807–812.

Semmes, J., Weinstein, S., Ghent, L., & Teuber, H. L. Correlates of impaired orientation in personal and extrapersonal space. *Brain,* 1963, *86,* 747–772.

Shik, M. L., & Orlovski, G. N. Neurophysiology of locomotor automatism. *Physiological Reviews,* 1976, *56,* 465–501.

Siegel, D. S. The effect of movement amplitude and target diameter on reaction time. *Journal of Motor Behavior,* 1977, *9,* 257–265.

Stein, P. S. G. Motor systems, with specific reference to the control of locomotion. *Annual Review of the Neurosciences,* 1978, *1,* 61–81.

Sternberg, S., Monsell, S., Knoll, R. L., & Wright, C. E. The latency and duration of rapid movement sequences: Comparisons of speech and typewriting. In G. E. Stelmach (Ed.), Information processing in motor control and learning. New York: Academic Press, 1978.

Teuber, H. L. The riddle of frontal lobe function in man. In J. M. Warren & K. Akert (Eds.), *The frontal granular cortex and behavior.* New York: McGraw-Hill, 1964.

Teuber, H. L. Unity and diversity of frontal lobe functions. *Acta Neurobiologica Experimentalis,* 1972, *32,* 615–656.

Tolman, E. C. Cognitive maps in rats and men. *Psychological Review,* 1948, *55,* 189–208.

Trevarthen, C. Two mechanisms of vision in primates. *Psychologische Forschung,* 1968, *31,* 299–337.

Turvey, M. T. Preliminaries to a theory of action with reference to vision. In R. Shaw and J. Bransford (Eds.), *Perceiving, acting and knowing: Toward an ecological psychology.* Hillsdale, N.J.: Lawrence Erlbaum Associates, 1977.

Williams, L. R. T. Reaction time and large response movements. *New Zealand Journal of Health, Physical Education and Recreation,* 1971, *4,* 46–52.

Zelaznik, H. N. *Response execution in choice reaction time: On program, parameters and muscles.* Unpublished doctoral dissertation. University of Southern California, 1978.

3 Some Effects of Instructed Muscle Tension on Choice Reaction Time and Movement Time

A. F. Sanders
Institute for Perception TNO
Soesterberg, The Netherlands

ABSTRACT

In three experiments the effects of instructed muscle tension on reaction time (RT) and movement time (MT) are explored with regard to some other variables affecting RT. Two conditions of instructed muscle tension were compared. In one subjects had to relax the relevant muscle groups fully, being taught to do so by biofeedback. In the other condition they had to strain the relevant muscles optimally. Relaxation prolonged RT by some 40–60 msec but did not affect MT. The effect interacted with that of foreperiod duration (Experiment 1), showed a second-order interaction with foreperiod duration and relative S–R frequency (Experiment 2), and was additive to those of S–R compatibility and signal degradation (Experiment 3). Application of the additive factor logic to the results suggests four processing stages, the nature of which are discussed.

INTRODUCTION

Preparatory activity in a discrete choice reaction task refers to the capability of presetting the relevant sensory, motor, and central mechanisms during the interval between a warning and an imperative signal. During the interval a subject performs "in advance what can be performed in advance" of the reaction process proper (Näätänen & Merisalo, 1977, p. 133). Presetting reduces the processing time during the reaction process, and consequently a shorter reaction time (RT) is obtained. It has been shown that optimal preparation can only be maintained for a short period of time (Gottsdanker, 1975).

Although various mechanisms are likely to play a role in preparation, one expects intuitively that patterns of motor excitation and muscular tension constitute at least one important component; witness, for example, the changes in posture of an athlete preparing for a start or of a cat preparing for a jump. Consequently there should be some inverse relation between RT and muscular activity or reactivity of the spinal reflex pathways during the preparatory interval. The most simple hypothesis suggests that it is merely a matter of the *level* of muscle tension and of spinal reflex excitability, but this fails to find support (Meyer, 1953; Requin, Bonnet, & Semjen, 1977). On the contrary, there is even evidence for a decrease of both muscle tension (Obrist, 1976) and reactivity of the spinal reflexes (Requin et al., 1977) during a 1-sec preparatory interval, which has led to a motor inhibition rather than a motor excitation hypothesis of preparation.

As Brunia (1980) has argued, however, Obrist's results have been mainly obtained with muscles that are not involved in the response (the chin electromyogram). In his own experiments Brunia found increased reflex excitability in the limb involved in the response during a 4-sec preparatory interval. In analogy with recent findings on the course of the contingent negative variation (CNV) in the EEG (Gaillard, this volume), Brunia has suggested that reflex excitability may be clouded by aftereffects of the warning signal when short foreperiods are used. Moreover, he failed to find a decrease of reflex excitability in the noninvolved limb that argues against the generality of the motor inhibition hypothesis for noninvolved muscles.

This discussion illustrates that the relations between RT and muscular activity are far from clear. RT seems not to be related at all to the level of muscle tension but rather to some complex pattern of excitation and inhibition. On the basis of the present evidence it is also not excluded that intuition is misleading in the sense that no systematic relationships exist. A preliminary answer to this last possibility may be obtained by manipulating muscle tension as an independent variable. This will be attempted in the present chapter. The effect of two instructions on RT will be compared, namely, complete relaxation (taught by means of biofeedback) and the instruction to be optimally tense. The point is that whatever the way muscular activity contributes to preparation, it will be ineffective in the relaxed and operative in the tense condition. Hence, RT is expected to be longer in the case of complete relaxation. It is realized that this manipulation does not constitute an ideal independent variable, because no circumscribed activity pattern is taught in the tense condition. The subjects' interpretation of "optimally tense" depends on their own criterion. Yet, this criterion is likely to depend on the state of other variables, affecting motor preparation, and that is worth investigating.

Two variables are interesting candidates in this respect. The first is foreperiod duration, the effect of which has been repeatedly described in terms of an intensive component of preparation (Holender & Bertelson, 1975; Näätänen & Merisalo, 1977; Posner & Boies, 1971). In accordance with this view, the effect of foreperiod duration interacts with some arousing properties of the signal (Sanders, 1977; Sanders & Andriessen, 1978). The locus of the foreperiod effect is still very much debated. In recent articles it has been ascribed to perceptual and motor as well as to central-integrative aspects of preparation (Laming, 1979; Klein & Kerr, 1974; Sanders, 1977). Yet, Frowein and Sanders (1978) found additive effects of foreperiod duration to those of S–R compatibility and signal degradation, and (following Sternberg's additive factor logic) this result supports neither a perceptual nor a central locus. An interaction between the effects of foreperiod duration and instructed muscle tension would be consistent with the hypothesis that the foreperiod effect is located near the motor side of the reaction process.

A second variable under consideration concerns relative S–R frequency, the effect of which has been mainly described in terms of selective preparation, being more directed toward the more frequent event (Holender & Bertelson, 1975). The size of the effect of this variable clearly depends on S–R compatibility (Broadbent & Gregory, 1965). Theios (1975) has even suggested that its effect is exclusively determined by the same processing stage that also underlies the effect of S–R compatibility. However, more processing stages are affected by relative S–R frequency. Thus, Pachella and co-workers are on record as arguing strongly for at least some locus of relative frequency effects as being in the encoding stage, albeit perhaps only in the case of extremely small probabilities (Stanovich & Pachella, 1977). In addition, however, it has been found that the size of the relative S–R frequency effect depends on whether the response starts with a common or a specific phoneme (e.g., *ses* or *sas* versus *es* or *as* in response to a visually presented *E* or *A*.) The effect of this variable, labeled *response specificity,* may reflect selective motor preparation.[1]

Evidence regarding the mutual relation between the effects of foreperiod duration and relative S–R frequency is conflicting. Thus, Bertelson and Barzeele (1965) found that the effect of relative S–R frequency was considerably smaller at long as compared to short foreperiods, suggesting that intensive and selective aspects of preparation are interrelated. On the other hand Holender and Bertelson (1975) were unable to replicate this result

---

[1]Hawkins, MacKay, Holley, Friedlin, and Cohen (1973) have suggested that the negligable effect of S–R frequency in Sanders' (1970) common phoneme condition might be an artefact due to a possible greater opportunity for the abortion of an incorrect response during pronouncing the common *s*. Indeed, this was a time-consuming process of about 75 msec. Yet there are arguments against Hawkins' suggestion in Sanders (1970). In addition, the S–R frequency × phoneme specificity interaction was also observed in an unpublished study where the common phoneme was a *r*, which takes about 10 msec. Hence, I am inclined to consider the effect as sufficiently reliable. Theios (1975) used a vocal digit-naming task and found virtually no effect of relative S–R frequency in his compatible condition. He failed to note, however, that his vocal responses happened to have common phonemes (digits 4 and 5). Hence his account is at least incomplete.

and found additive effects, so that this issue is far from settled. In the following, three experiments are reported, the first two of which are concerned with the mutual relations between the effects of instructed muscle tension, foreperiod duration, and relative S–R frequency. In the third study, the variables are instructed muscle tension, S–R compatibility, and signal degradation. The effects of the last two variables have been repeatedly found to be additive (Frowein & Sanders, 1978; Sternberg, 1969), and they are considered to affect, respectively, an "encoding" and a "choice" stage of the reaction process. The hypothesis is that if instructed muscle tension affects motor aspects of preparation, then its effect should be additive to those of S–R compatibility and signal degradation.

EXPERIMENT 1: INSTRUCTED MUSCLE TENSION AND FOREPERIOD DURATION

Method and Procedure

Task.   The subject was seated in a sound attenuating cubicle at a sloping desk. The task involved a visual choice reaction with RT and MT as dependent variables. The visual signals were generated on a Nixie tube (3 × 6 cm) situated at about eye level and at a distance of about 70 cm in front of the subject. The warning signal was a 500-msec flash of all elements of the Nixie tube, and the imperative signals consisted of a 500-msec flash of a diagonal and an horizontal line, joining in one of the four corners of the Nixie tube. Four round-topped buttons (diameter 15 mm) were located just outside the corners.

The index finger of the subject's preferred hand was resting on a release button located on the desk, between the Nixie tube and the subject. Upon arrival of an imperative signal the subject's task was to move his index finger from the release button to the button to which the signal was pointing. The distance between the release button and the target button was 13 cm for the two bottom target buttons and 20 cm for the two top target buttons. The subjects were instructed that the warning signal served to prepare for a fast response and that once the movement was initiated, it should be made as rapidly as possible and without hesitation about which button should be pressed. Hesitations or changes in direction could easily be noticed, because the movement time (the time between leaving the release button and arriving at the target button) was disproportionally longer in such trials. Much attention was devoted during practice toward avoiding such responses. Pre-programmed signal presentation and response registration were performed by the PSARP system (van Doorne & Sanders, 1968). Apart from the movement time (MT), this allowed the measurement of reaction time (RT), defined as the interval between the onset of the imperative stimulus and the release of the release button.

EMG Recording.   The EMG was recorded from the arm, using Beckman bipotential electrodes, filled with electrode paste; one electrode was placed at a third of the distance from the lateral numeral epicondyle to the syloid process of the ulna, and the other was approximately 5 cm in the distal direction along the same line. A second set of two electrodes was attached to the pectoralis, at the same side as the responding arm. This was done because results of pilot studies suggested that some subjects tended to prepare by stretching the pectoralis while the arm flexors were completely relaxed.

Finally, an electrode attached to the ball of the thumb served as a ground. EMG signals were amplified with a preamplifier and integrator combination. The preamplifier was set at a time constant of 0.01 sec (6 dB/octave). After rectifying, the signals were integrated using an envelope with a time constant of 250 msec. The signals were fed into a PDP lab 8 computer for further analysis.

Procedures.   The two major experimental variables were *foreperiod duration* (a constant interval of either 1 or 10 sec between the offset of the warning signal and the onset of the imperative signal) and *instructed muscle tension*. In one set of conditions subjects were instructed to stretch their muscles to the extent that would subjectively render most effective performance with regard to both speed and accuracy. In order to obtain a base-line EMG they were further instructed to relax after a response and not to stretch before the arrival of the next warning signal. It was made clear that they did not need to stretch immediately upon seeing the warning, in particular not in the case of the long foreperiod, as long as they were optimally prepared at the time that the imperative signal was presented. In the other set of conditions, subjects were instructed to relax completely throughout the test, except of course when responding.

Ten paid students from the University of Utrecht served as subjects. One subject was removed because of inability to obey the instruction to relax. A within-subjects design was used with a randomized order of conditions between blocks, with the restriction that the two relaxed conditions (foreperiods 1 and 10 sec) either preceded or followed the two tense conditions. For each condition, blocks of 17–20 trials were run. The first trials were considered as warming up and occasionally a trial was discarded in the relaxed conditions when the instructions were disobeyed. This was continually checked on the lab 8 scope display. After performing two conditions, subjects had about 20 min rest. In total they participated in three experimental sessions, each consisting of all the forementioned four conditions. Prior to the experimental sessions, subjects were thoroughly practiced. First it was assured that they had reached the criterion that, in a block of 17–20 trials, the standard deviation of both RT and MT was less than 15% of the mean. Then the electrodes were attached and subjects were taught by auditory feedback of electromyographical activity to relax the relevant limbs completely. Practice continued until subjects could either turn on or turn off the auditory signal on command.

The next practice stage concerned performance of the reaction task with special emphasis on immediate relaxation following a response. Practice continued until means and variances were comparable with those obtained prior to attaching the electrodes. Somewhere during this last procedure auditory feedback was omitted and replaced by verbal feedback when instructions were disobeyed. Experimental sessions did not start until the subjects had completely mastered these procedures. Pairs of two subjects alternated in the tests. Subjects were hired for 1.5 days.

Results

Figure 3.1 shows mean RT and MT, averaged over subjects and sessions, as a function of instructed muscle tension and foreperiod duration. An ANOVA carried out on the individual mean RT's per block showed significant main effects of instructed muscle tension ($F = 18.1$; $df = 1, 8$; $p < 0.01$) and foreperiod duration ($F = 26.1$; $df = 1, 8$; $p < 0.001$). The effect of sessions was not significant ($F = 0.07$; $df = 2, 16$;). Apart from several significant interactions with subjects, there was a significant instructed muscle tension × foreperiod duration interaction ($F = 15.8$; $df = 1, 8$; $p < 0.01$). A similar analysis on individual mean MT's showed only a significant main effect of subjects

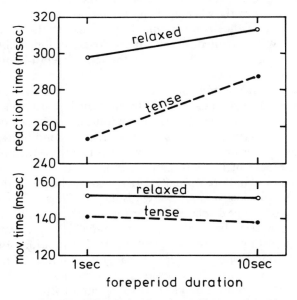

FIG. 3.1.   The effects of foreperiod duration and instructed muscle tension on RT and MT (Experiment 1).

(F = 418; df = 8, 16; $p <$ 0.001) and significant interactions between subjects and the other main variables. The error terms for the two main variables were their interactions with subjects. The highest interaction was used as error term when subjects were a factor.

The average error percentages were 2.7 (relaxed, 1 sec), 4.3 (tense, 1 sec), 3.9 (relaxed, 10 sec) and 1.9 (tense, 10 sec), which were not significantly different. These percentages include real errors as well as correct responses with long MT's ($>$ 100 ms above the mean).

EMG Recordings. In the relaxed conditions, changes with regard to base-line EMG were virtually zero. In the tense conditions, EMG amplitudes during the 250 msec preceding the arrival of the imperative signal were 32.2 μV at the 1-sec foreperiod and 28.7 μV during the 10-sec foreperiod, which implies a nonsignificant trend toward a lower amplitude at the long foreperiod (t = .88). At 1 sec, the activity reached a maximum within 500 ms after presentation of the warning, whereas a more gradual increase was observed at the long foreperiod. This gradual increase could, however, easily be an artifact of averaging.

EXPERIMENT 2: INSTRUCTED MUSCLE TENSION, FOREPERIOD DURATION, AND RELATIVE SIGNAL FREQUENCY

Method and Procedure

Task. The task was again a visual four-choice reaction task, but for reasons to be discussed later, the visual signals were lights that had been mounted on the sloping desk on the periphery of a semicircle. A release button was in the center of the circle. The lights were located in the 9, 11, 1 and 3, o'clock positions. A fifth light, positioned in front of the release button, served as warning signal. Four target buttons were positioned, one close to each light, on the radii connecting the release button with the lights. The distance between the release button and the target buttons was always 13 cm. The index finger of the subject's preferred hand was resting on the release button. Upon presentation of a light, he had to move his finger from the release button to the target button that was closest to the light presented. Subjects were instructed to fixate the warning light during the foreperiod.

All other properties of the display, the apparatus, the EMG recording, and the specific instructions, were similar to those of Experiment 1.

Procedures. The three major experimental variables were *foreperiod duration* (a constant interval of either 1 sec or 10 sec between the offset of the warning signal and the onset of the imperative signal), *instructed muscle tension* (tense versus relaxed) and *relative S–R frequency*. As to the last variable, there was always one frequently presented light (probability: .55) and three infrequently presented lights (probability: .15). The position of the frequent light was varied between subjects. Subjects were informed about the frequency imbalance and instructed to be prepared to respond to that light on all trials. Hesitations or changes in direction during the movement were again considered as errors.

Ten new students from the University of Utrecht served as subjects. A within-subjects design was used with a randomized order of conditions with the restriction that the relaxed conditions either preceded or followed all tense conditions. Obviously instructed muscle tension and foreperiod duration were varied between and relative S–R frequency within blocks of trials. A block contained 30–40 trials so as to obtain about 15 correct reactions to both the frequent and infrequent signals. As in Experiment 1 there were three replications (sessions) of all blocks.

All other properties of the method and procedure were similar to those of Experiment 1.

Results

Mean RT and MT as functions of foreperiod duration, instructed muscle tension, and relative S–R frequency—averaged over sessions and subjects—are presented in Fig. 3.2 and 3.3.

An ANOVA performed on the RT data with the individual means per session as cells showed significant main effects of relative S–R frequency ($F = 114$; $df = 1, 9$; $p < 0.001$), instructed muscle tension ($F = 15.9$; $df = 1, 9$; $p < 0.01$), foreperiod duration ($F = 45.6$; $df = 1, 9$; $p < 0.001$), and subjects. The following significant interactions were observed: Relative signal frequency × instructed muscle tension ($F = 26.1$; $df = 1, 9$; $p < 0.001$) and relative signal frequency × instructed muscular tension × foreperiod duration ($F = 11.2$; $df = 1, 9$; $p < 0.001$). In addition, various interactions with subjects were significant. There were no significant differences between sessions. A similar ANOVA carried out on the MT data showed significant main effects of relative signal frequency ($F = 7.92$; $df = 1, 9$; $p < 0.05$) and session ($F = 4.85$; $df = 2, 18$; $p < 0.05$). In addition to the usual differences due to subjects, the interaction between instructed muscle tension and relative signal frequency was significant ($F = 8.2$; $df = 1, 9$; $p < 0.05$). Average error percentages were 0.1 (frequent–tense–1 sec), 0.2 (frequent–tense–10 sec), 0.4 (frequent–relaxed–1 sec), 0.7 (frequent–relaxed–10 sec), 0.9 (infrequent–tense–1 sec), 1.1 (infrequent–tense–10 sec), 1.6 (infrequent–relaxed–1 sec), and 1.8 (infrequent–relaxed–10 sec). The EMG recordings showed a similar picture as in Experiment 1. In the relaxed conditions, the increases of EMG activity with respect to the base line were always smaller than 1 μV. In the tense conditions, the average EMG, during the 250 msec preceding the arrival of the imperative

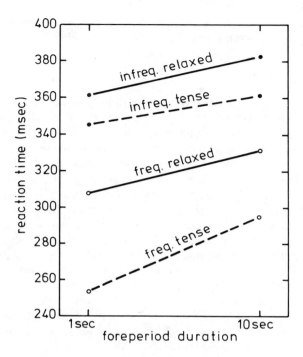

FIG. 3.2.   The effects of foreperiod duration, relative S–R frequency, and instructed muscle tension on RT (Experiment 2).

signal was 42 μV at the 1-sec foreperiod and 35 μV at the 10-sec foreperiod, which again is nonsignificant. Pooling the EMG data of Experiments 1 and 2 gives $t = 1.41$, $(0.05 < p < 0.1)$, suggesting that average muscle tension at the end of the long foreperiod may be slightly less than at the end of the short foreperiod.

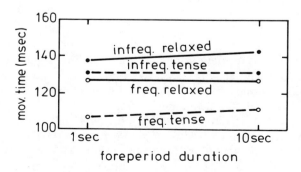

FIG. 3.3.   The effect of the same variables as mentioned in Fig. 3.2 on MT (Experiment 2).

EXPERIMENT 3: INSTRUCTED MUSCLE TENSION, S–R COMPATIBILITY, AND SIGNAL DEGRADATION

Method and Procedure

The task and the method of EMG recording were the same as in Experiment 1. The three main variables were *instructed muscle tension, S–R compatibility,* and *signal degradation.* Compatibility was varied in the following manner. The correct target button in the compatible condition was indicated by the joining point of the two lines of the Nixie tube, whereas the correct response in the incompatible condition was to press the next target button in the counter-clockwise direction. Signal degradation was achieved by superimposing a photonegative with a visual noise pattern upon the surface of the Nixie tube. The noise pattern consisted of a cluster of black nonsense shapes each averaging about 1 mm in diameter. The light to dark ratio was about 30%. To avoid differences in light intensity between the degraded and undegraded conditions a similar photonegative without visual noise was used for the undegraded conditions (Frowein & Sanders, 1978).

Nine new students from the University of Utrecht served as subjects. A within-subjects design was used with a randomized order of the eight conditions (compatibility × signal degradation × instructed muscle tension) between blocks of trials with the restriction that all four relaxed conditions always preceded or followed the tense conditions and that within a sequence of either relaxed or tense conditions the two compatible conditions preceded or followed the incompatible ones. After performing two conditions, subjects had a 20-min rest period. When testing was resumed, they practiced again prior to the start of the next experimental block. For each condition, blocks of 17–20 trials were run in which the first trials were considered as warming up. As in the previous experiments there were three replications (sessions) of all blocks of trials. The method and procedures were otherwise similar to those of Experiment 1.

Results

Mean RT and MT as a function of S–R compatibility, signal degradation, and instructed muscle tension—averaged over sessions and subjects—are presented in Fig 3.4 and 3.5. An ANOVA with the individual mean RTs per block as cells showed significant main effects of compatibility ($F = 73.2$; $df = 1, 8$; $p < 0.001$), signal degradation ($F = 59.4$; $df = 1, 8$; $p < 0.001$), instructed muscle tension ($F = 35.6$; $df = 1, 8$; $p < 0.001$), and subjects. No significant interactions were found, apart from those with subjects. A similar analysis carried out on MTs showed significant effects of compatibility ($F = 13.2$; $df = 1, 8$; $p < 0.01$), and subjects. There were no significant inter-

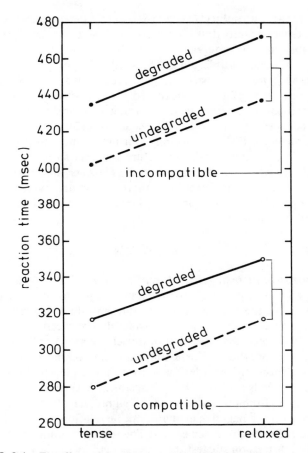

FIG. 3.4. The effects of signal degradation, S–R compatibility, and instructed muscle tension on RT (Experiment 3).

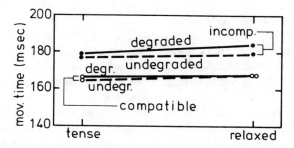

FIG. 3.5. The effects of the same variables as mentioned in Fig. 3.4 on MT.

actions other than with subjects. The average error percentages were 3.0% for compatible, tense, degraded; 0.7% for compatible, tense, undegraded; 3.2% for compatible, relaxed, degraded; 3.0% for compatible, relaxed, undegraded; 9.6% for incompatible, tense, degraded; 5.9% for incompatible, tense, undegraded; 5.9% for incompatible, relaxed, degraded, and 4.7% for incompatible, relaxed, undegraded. In degraded and incompatible conditions, errors were significantly more frequent (by a sign test). There was no significant interaction between the variables with regard to errors.

With regard to the EMG recordings, during the last 250 msec before the arrival of the imperative signal, the picture was very similar to those of the 1-sec conditions of Experiments 1 and 2. The base-line value was well-maintained in the relaxed conditions; there was strong evidence for EMG activity during the tense conditions, but this was not affected by variations in compatibility or signal degradation.

DISCUSSION

The Main Effect of Instructed Muscle Tension. The results of all three studies showed a clear effect of instructed muscle tension on RT, amounting to 40–60 msec on the average between the tense and relaxed conditions. Obviously, the EMG activity differs considerably between these conditions, but it should be noted that the level of muscle tension hardly differentiates within the tense conditions. For example, when comparing the results on short and long foreperiods under the tense condition (Experiment 1 and 2), the usual increase in RT is found but the average EMG activity, measured 250 msec in advance of the presentation of the signal, hardly differs. This result fully concurs with the negative evidence on the relation between RT and the level of muscle tension discussed earlier. The present findings on the effect of instructed muscle tension suggest that muscle activity and RT are related but in a more complex way.

As argued in the introduction, the observed additive effect of instructed muscle tension to those of S–R compatibility and signal degradation is a prerequisite for a motor interpretation of the effect of instructed muscle tension. These additive effects argue against the alternative interpretation that subjects slow down the reaction process as a whole because they feel that they are expected to do so. In that case a stronger effect of relaxation should occur in the more time-consuming incompatible and degraded conditions. The fact that MT was not systematically affected—as soon as the movement starts, relaxation ceases to have a consistent effect on performance—argues also against this view. Still another alternative explanation of the effect of instructed muscle tension could be that active relaxation transforms the task into a more demanding double task that has the effect of lengthening RT. But again this hypothesis predicts a stronger effect of relaxation as the other variables are more loading. In addition, a larger effect of relaxation should occur at the long-foreperiod condition—being the more demanding one—than at the short-foreperiod condition, whereas the results show the reverse (Experiments 1 and 2). As said, the results are consistent with a motor interpretation of the effect of instructed muscle tension. Of course this does not necessarily imply an exclusively peripheral locus. Also the operation of central-processing stages might be inhibited by relaxation, but it would be surprising if those stages were not at the motor side.

Relations With Foreperiod Duration and S–R Frequency. In both Experiments 1 and 2 an interaction between instructed muscle tension and foreperiod duration was found. The direction of this interaction suggests that motor preparation is less at the long foreperiod, because the difference between the tense and the relaxed condition is less at the long than at the short foreperiod. This result clearly supports a motor locus of the foreperiod effect. Corroborating evidence for this view comes from the relation between the size of the CNV and the duration of the foreperiod. Gaillard (this volume) has convincingly shown that the CNV reflects motor aspects of preparation. In addition, the results of Experiment 2 suggest that motor preparation has a pronounced direction. The interaction between instructed muscle tension and foreperiod duration reappears only in the case of the frequent S–R combination, whereas foreperiod duration as well as instructed muscle tension have only minor effects on RT in the case of infrequent S–R combinations.

This finding is obviously relevant to the inconsistent results on the relation between relative S–R frequency and foreperiod duration. As mentioned, an interaction as well as additive effects have been found by Bertelson and co-workers. In Fig. 3.2 both relations are observed, depending on the state of instructed muscle tension. The selective component of motor preparation seems absent when subjects are relaxed, which reconciles the inconsistent findings. Usually muscular activity during the foreperiod is an uncontrolled variable in choice reaction tasks. This is probably not harmful when the effects of central or sensory variables are studied, but it can cause serious troubles when variables affecting motor preparation are investigated.

Two Motor Stages?

Do the data of Fig. 3.2 imply that intensive and selective aspects of motor preparation are merely different sides of the same underlying process, where selectivity means no more than greater allocation of intensity? The considerable effect of relative frequency imbalance that is still found in the relaxed condition argues against this view. This remaining effect cannot be ascribed to the "choice" stage (Fig. 3.6), for the task in Experiment 2 was highly compatible. An attempt to locate the remaining effect can start from the fact

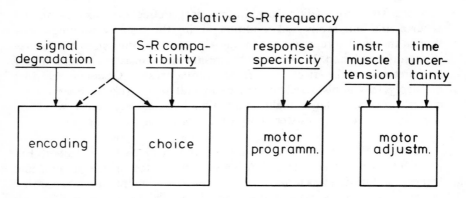

FIG. 3.6. A summary of the relations between the effects of the variables under investigation on RT. The dotted line connecting relative S-R frequency with encoding refers to the findings of Pachella and co-workers (Stanovich & Pachella, 1977).

that the first and second study did not use the same S-R display. The main difference was that in the first experiment the target buttons were fairly close together, whereas in the second experiment they were in widely different directions. The same can be said for the signals, but the instruction to fixate the warning light in Experiment 2 attempted to guarantee equal visibility of all signals. Thus the response movements all had a common direction in the first but not in the second study. This change was intentional, because pilot studies had shown virtually no effect of S-R frequency imbalance in the case of the common vector. This is reminiscent of the common phoneme condition discussed by Sanders (1970) and reviewed in the introduction, whereas the specific directions in the second study are analogous to the specific phoneme condition discussed in the same article. Assuming that this type of variable, labeled *response specificity,* may remove most of the remaining effect of relative S-R frequency, the picture in Fig. 3.6 might describe the results of the experiments.

Figure 3.6 assumes explicitly that response specificity on the one hand and foreperiod duration and instructed muscle tension on the other hand have additive contributions to RT, although this remains to be tested. The processing stage relating to response specificity and relative S-R frequency was called "motor adjustment" by Sanders (1977), but this term is probably a better label for the type of processes that are preset by intensive motor preparation. These may include straining the muscles but also more general processes, determining the distance to what Näätänen and Merisalo (1977) have called the motor-action limit. The remaining stage has been labeled "motor programming" and may well be the same as "response programming" as distinguished by Klapp (1977) to describe effects of variations in response complexity on RT. Klapp noticed that response programming can be abstract to some extent in the sense that it can develop without simultaneous commands to the muscles. If so, it would be plausible that the motor programming stage, as defined in Fig. 3.6, is not affected by instructed muscle tension. Although this reasoning has various loose ends, it seems to be open to experimental test.

Speed and Accuracy

With regard to errors, the average differences between the tense and relaxed conditions were small and not significant. In itself this does not exclude the possibility that the effect of instructed muscle tension reflects a shift in speed–accuracy tradeoff. Small and about equal average error percentages are not indicative, due to the logarithmic relation between speed and accuracy (Pachella, 1974; Pew, 1969). In an unpublished study, it was found indeed that a considerable part of the effect can be ascribed to a tradeoff shift. This is not surprising in view of the supposedly strategic nature of preparatory effects. Thus, Harm and Lappin (1973) have shown that the effect of relative S–R frequency is also largely determined by strategy shifts and the same has been suggested with regard to the effect of foreperiod duration (Posner & Klein, 1973). It should be noted, though, that this relation to speed–accuracy tradeoff does not basically affect the results of the present study. If interactions, and even main effects, can be completely removed by speed–accuracy corrections, then that does not mean that the phenomena—both in speed and accuracy—are not real! Obviously, however, the mode of operation of the underlying stages is specified as either more task or more strategy dependent (Ollman, 1977). The latter mode is probably predominant in preparatory activity.

REFERENCES

Bertelson, P., & Barzeele, J. Interaction of time uncertainty and relative signal frequency in determining choice reaction time. *Journal of Experimental Psychology,* 1965, *70,* 448–451.

Broadbent, D. E., & Gregory, M. On the interaction of S–R compatibility with other variables affecting reaction time. *British Journal of Psychology,* 1965, *56,* 61–67.

Brunia, C. H. M. Preparation: Some questions about the motor inhibition hypothesis. In E. H. Van Olst (Ed.), *The orientation response,* 1980.

Frowein, H. W., & Sanders, A. F. Effects of visual stimulus degradation, S–R compatibility and foreperiod duration on choice reaction time and movement time. *Bulletin of the Psychonomic Society,* 1978, *12,* 106–108.

Gottsdanker, R. The attaining and maintaining of preparation. In P. M. A. Rabbitt & S. Dornic (Eds.), *Attention and Performance V,* Academic Press, London, 1975.

Harm, O. J., & Lappin, J. S. Probability, compatibility, speed and accuracy. *Journal of Experimental Psychology*, 1973, *100*, 416–418.

Hawkins, H. L., MacKay, S. L., Holley, S. L., Friedlin, B. D., & Cohen, S. L. Locus of the relative frequency effect in choice reaction time. *Journal of Experimental Psychology*, 1973, *101*, 90–99.

Holender, D., & Bertelson, P. Selective preparation and time uncertainty. *Acta Psychologica*, 1975, *39*, 193–203.

Klapp, S. T. Response programming as assessed by reaction time does not establish commands for particular muscles. *Journal of Motor Behavior*, 1977, *9*, 301–312.

Klein, R. M., & Kerr, B. Visual signal detection and the locus of the foreperiod effects. *Memory & Cognition*, 1974, *2*, 431–435.

Laming, D. Choice reaction performance following an error. *Acta Psychologica*, 1979, *43*, 199–224.

Meyer, D. R. On the interaction of simultaneous responses. *Psychological Bulletin*, 1953, 50, 204–220.

Näätänen, R., & Merisalo, A. Expectancy and preparation in simple reaction time. In S. Dornic (Ed.), *Attention and performance VI*. Hillsdale, N.J.: Lawrence Erlbaum Associates, 1977.

Obrist, P. A. The cardiovascular-behavioral interaction as it appears today. *Psychophysiology*, 1976, *13*, 95–107.

Ollman, R. T. Choice reaction time and the problem of distinguishing task effects from strategy effects. In S. Dornic (Ed.), *Attention and performance VI*. Hillsdale, N.J.: Lawrence Erlbaum Associates, 1977, 99–113.

Pachella, R. G. The interpretation of reaction time in information processing. In B. Kautowitz (Ed.), *Tutorials in performance and cognition*. Hillsdale, N.J.: Lawrence Erlbaum Associates, 1974.

Pew, R. W. The speed–accuracy operating characteristic. In W. G. Koster (Ed.), *Attention and performance II*. *Acta Psychologica*, 1969, *30*, 16–26.

Posner, M. I., & Boies, S. J. Components of attention. *Psychological Review*, 1971, *78*, 391–408.

Posner, M. I., & Klein, R. M. On the functions of consciousness. In S. Kornblum (Ed.), *Attention and performance IV*. Academic Press, New York, 1973, 21–37.

Requin, J., Bonnet, M., & Semjen, A. Is there a specificity in the supraspinal control of motorstructures during preparation? In S. Dornic (Ed.) *Attention and performance VI*. Hillsdale, N.J.: Lawrence Erlbaum Associates, 1977, 139–174.

Sanders, A. F. Some variables affecting the relation between relative signal frequency and CRT. In A. F. Sanders (Ed.), *Attention and performance III*. *Acta Psychologica*, 1970, *33*, 45–55.

Sanders, A. F. Structural and functional aspects of the reaction process. In S. Dornic (Ed.), *Attention and performance VI*. Hillsdale, N.J.: Lawrence Erlbaum Associates, 1977, 3–25.

Sanders, A. F., & Andriessen, J. E. B. A suppressing effect of response selection on immediate arousal in a choice reaction task. *Acta Psychologica*, 1978, *42*, 181–186.

Stanovich, K. E., & Pachella, R. G. Encoding, stimulus-response compatibility and stages of processing. *Journal of Experimental Psychology: Human Perception and Performance*, 1977, *3*, 411–421.

Sternberg, S. The discovery of processing stages: Extensions of Donders' method. In W. G. Koster (Ed.), *Attention and performance II*. *Acta Psychologica* 1969, *30*, 276–315.

Theios, J. The components of response latency in simple human information processing tasks. In P. M. A. Rabbitt & S. Dornic (Eds.), *Attention and performance V*. London: Academic Press, 1975, 418–440.

Van Doorne, H., & Sanders, A. F. PSARP: A programmable stimulus and response processor. *Journal of Behavioral Methods and Instrumentation*, 1968, *1*, 29–32.

4 Cortical Correlates of Motor Preparation

Anthony W.K. Gaillard
Institute for Perception TNO
Soesterberg, The Netherlands

ABSTRACT

This study reviews the available evidence on two brain potentials that have been proposed as correlates of preparatory motor processes: the final component of the CNV (terminal CNV, late CNV, or E-wave) and the readiness potential, which precedes any voluntary movement. Both potentials are slow negative shifts that develop in the second or so before the execution of a motor response. In addition to their similarity in form they appear to have the same topographical distribution: Both potentials are most prominent at the vertex (C_z) over the precentral motor regions and show an asymmetry to the contralateral side of the responding hand. It is tentatively concluded that there is no reason for regarding the two negative shifts as reflections of different processes, whereas there are many arguments for the notion that they are generated by the same neurophysiological mechanism.

INTRODUCTION

Two brain potentials have been proposed as correlates of preparation for a motor response: The contingent negative variation (CNV) and the readiness potential (RP). The CNV is a slow negative shift, which is usually obtained in a so-called S_1–S_2 paradigm, where S_1 is a warning signal and S_2 an imperative signal (Walter, Cooper, Aldridge, McCallum, & Winter, 1964). The RP, also a slow negative shift, arises prior to voluntary movements (Kornhuber & Deecke, 1965). RPs are obtained by instructing the subject to make a series of movements (for example, finger presses) at a certain pace. The CNV and RP

75

differ in the type of task situation in which they are obtained and in the way they are averaged. The RP is derived from movement potentials, which are time-locked to the motor response, whereas the CNV is derived from averages time-locked to the S_1–S_2 paradigm.

The discovery of the CNV led to numerous experiments that attempted to specify its psychological significance. Although the CNV has been most pronounced in reaction-time (RT) tasks where S_2 requires a fast motor response, it has also been found in signal-detection tasks that involve only the perception of stimuli. Moreover, CNVs are found to precede complex or novel stimuli, even when there is no specified task at all. Thus, the CNV may be obtained in various task situations and is affected by many task variables.

From the reviews (Cohen, 1974; Hillyard, 1973; McAdam, 1974; Tecce, 1972) that attempt to relate the CNV to human behavior, it is evident that considerable disagreement prevails with regard to the functional meaning of this negative shift. Originally the CNV was called "expectancy wave," because it was thought that the expectancy of the subject for the arrival of S_2 was sufficient to produce the CNV. Other investigators preferred readiness to respond or motor preparation as the mechanism underlying the CNV, whereas it also has been associated with more broadly defined concepts, such as motivation, concentration, and attention. Most theoretical arguments boil down to the issue as to whether the CNV is related to the perception of S_2 or to the response to S_2. For example, Cohen (1974) maintains that the amplitude of the CNV is positively correlated to perceptual efficiency, whereas Hillyard (1973) regards the evidence as too meager for this conclusion. Indeed, a recent review (Gaillard, 1978) shows that only 3 out of 12 studies provide evidence for this hypothesis.

As long as the functional role of the CNV is unclear, its theoretical and applied value is limited, because possible effects cannot be interpreted in terms of psychological constructs. Of course, it is possible that the CNV is a general phenomenon that accompanies many types of behavior. Another possibility, however, is that the CNV consists of more than one slow potential shift. If these shifts differ in their functional meaning, they might confound each other, because they will be affected differentially by experimental manipulations.

Is the CNV a Unitary Phenomenon?

Recent studies that used interstimulus intervals (ISIs) of longer duration (≥ 3 sec) found at least two potentials that differ in their functional significance (e.g., Gaillard, 1976, 1977; Loveless & Sanford, 1974a,b; Rohrbaugh, Syndulko, & Lindsley 1976). As can be seen in the Fig. 4.1 and 4.2, the first potential has the form of an inverted U-curve, which reaches its peak within 1 sec after S_1, whereas the second potential gradually develops during the interstimulus interval (ISI). Because of its occurrence toward the end of the ISI and its

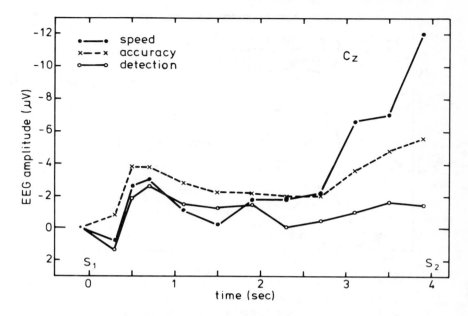

FIG. 4.1.   Slow brain potentials obtained from the vertex (C_z) and averaged across 10 subjects. The level of motor preparation was manipulated by instructions: Under *speed* instructions the subject is required to respond as quickly as possible, even at the cost of some errors; under *accuracy* instructions, the subject is also required to produce quick RTs, but the necessity to avoid errors is emphasized; under *detection* instruction the subject is instructed to delay his response by 1 sec. Under all instructions subjects had to make a visual discrimination at S_2, whereas S_1 was a 70-dB tone delivered via earphones (data derived from Gaillard & Perdok, 1980).

contingency to S_2 (or to the response to S_2), the second potential seems to resemble more closely the "classical CNV" obtained with short ISIs; therefore, it will be called *terminal CNV*. The term *CNV* will be used in its original meaning, to denote the negative shift preceding S_2 in studies with short ISIs, which generally did not discriminate between the two negative potentials described here. The first potential will be called *slow negative wave* (SNW) because of its similarity to the "slow wave" observed in selective listening tasks (e.g., Squires, Donchin, Herning, & McCarthy, 1977). The SNW appears to be dependent on the characteristics of S_1 in much the same way as the P_{300}. Therefore, both seem to belong to a family of slow potential shifts following S_1.

The SNW is regarded as a cortical component of the orientation reaction, because it is affected by the physical characteristics of S_1, such as modality, duration, and intensity. The SNW appears to be influenced also by the psychological properties of S_1. For example, enhanced amplitudes were

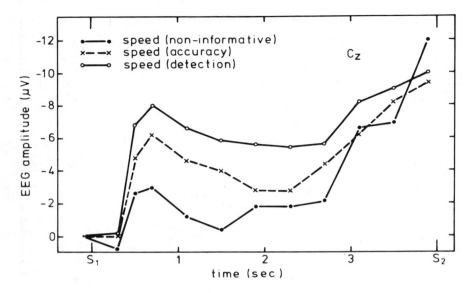

FIG. 4.2.   Slow brain potentials obtained from the vertex (C_z) and averaged across 10 subjects. The psychological significance of S_1 was manipulated by varying the information content of S_1: Either S_1 was a noninformative tone (i.e., only warned the subject that S_2 would arrive after 4 sec) or it indicated the instructions to be followed at S_2. This was done in two ways: In one condition speed and accuracy instructions and in the other speed and detection instructions were varied from trial to trial (see Fig. 4.1 for a description of the instructions). The instructions were indicated by the pitch of S_1, which had a frequency of either 500 or 2000 Hz. The figure shows the slow brain potentials under speed instructions, in the three experimental conditions just described (data derived from Gaillard & Perdok, 1980).

obtained when S_1 not only served as a time cue but also provided information about the task requirements at S_2 (see Gaillard, 1978, for review).

As shown in Fig. 4.2, the amplitude of the SNW is increased when S_1 indicates whether a speed or an accuracy instruction has to be followed—speed (accuracy), as compared to the situation where S_1 is noninformative. This effect is even larger when speed and detection instructions are varied within one block of trials—speed (detection). The larger effect is explained (see also Gaillard & Perdok, 1980) by the larger difference in task demands between speed and detection instructions (very quick RTs versus delayed response) than between speed and accuracy instructions (both RT tasks). It is to be noted that the amplitude of the terminal CNV is *not* affected by the manipulation of the information content of S_1 (see Fig. 4.2).

In contrast, the terminal CNV is dependent on the task demands required at S_2. Figure 4.1 shows that the amplitude of the negative shift preceding S_2 is twice as large under speed instructions than under accuracy instructions.

Under detection instruction, where the response to S_2 is delayed, the terminal CNV is virtually absent. In contrast the SNW is not affected by these instructions.

Recent studies suggest that the terminal CNV reflects the level of motor preparation: Larger amplitudes are expected when the subject prepares more intensively for the motor response to be given at S_2. For this view the following evidence can be given (Gaillard, 1978):

1. The terminal CNV is affected by task variables such as ISI duration, ISI variability, and relative signal frequency, all of which, on the basis of choice RT studies, have been assumed to affect the level of motor preparation (Sanders, this volume). For example, Loveless and Sanford (1974a) compared a regular ISI condition with an irregular ISI condition and found that the SNW was present in both conditions, whereas the terminal CNV was only observed in the regular ISI condition. In general, these results run parallel to the behavioral effect; RT is shorter in the regular condition and increases with increasing ISI duration.

2. The amplitude of the terminal CNV is not increased preceding difficult discriminations as compared to easy ones, either in RT tasks or in signal-detection tasks involving a delayed response. Also no enhanced amplitudes were found preceding hits or correct rejections as compared to errors (false alarms, misses).

3. In studies using longer ISIs ($\geq$ 3 sec) the terminal CNV was largely attenuated or even virtually absent in sensory tasks where no quick motor response was required.

4. Larger CNV amplitudes are obtained the larger the amount of muscular effort required for the response to S_2.

5. The amplitude of the terminal CNV is enhanced under speed instructions (see also Fig. 4.1). This result could also be taken as evidence for a motor-preparation hypothesis. If the CNV were positively related to perceptual sensitivity, larger amplitudes would be expected under accuracy instructions, where, of course, fewer errors are made.

6. The motor character of the terminal CNV is further supported by its similarlity to the RP. Both are negative shifts most prominent in the motor cortex, which gradually develop in the second before the execution of a motor response.

Terminal CNV and Readiness Potential

Studies using a 1-sec ISI have shown repeatedly that the amplitude of the CNV is attenuated when no response to S_2 is required (e.g., Donald, 1973; Järvilehto & Frühstorfer, 1970; Näätänen, Gaillard, & Mäntysalo, 1977; Peters, Knott, Miller, Van Veen, & Cohen, 1970; Syndulko & Lindsley, 1977). Irwin, Knott, McAdam, and Rebert (1966) have pointed out that the enhancement of the CNV amplitude by a subsequent motor response is of the same magnitude as the RP that precedes any voluntary movement. This again suggests that the CNV is not a unitary phenomenon but consists of more than one component. As argued previously, studies that have longer ISIs (≥ 3 sec) have indeed found two components, one of which (the terminal CNV) resembles the RP in form. Moreover, the terminal CNV seems to reflect the level of motor preparation and to be contingent on a motor response. Both notions suggest that the terminal CNV and the RP refer to the same neurophysiological mechanism, in other words, that they refer to the same phenomenon but are obtained in different task situations and by different averaging techniques. The major argument against this view has always been that the CNV is also present in sensory tasks where no quick response to S_2 is required. Since virtually no terminal CNV is found in task situations where the motor response is delayed or not required at all, the negative shift in sensory tasks (using a 1-sec ISI) can be attributed to the SNW.

It has also been argued that the CNV and the RP differ in their topographical distribution. It is generally found (e.g., Tecce, 1972) that the CNV obtained with a 1-sec ISI is located more anteriorly than the RP. This difference also can be attributed to the SNW, because this wave is frontally dominent, whereas the terminal CNV is most prominant over the motor cortex. In general, the anterior–posterior distribution, and also the form, of the CNV obtained with short ISIs will largely depend on the ratio between the two components (SNW and terminal CNV). The larger the SNW, the more ramp shaped the form of the CNV and the more anterior its midline distribution.

Another argument that has been used for the separation of the CNV and the RP is their lateral distribution. There is now a consensus that the RP is a few microvolts larger in the motor region contralateral to the responding limb (e.g., Deecke, Grözinger, & Kornhuber, 1976; Kutas & Donchin, 1977). For CNVs obtained with short ISIs, contradictory results have been found; some authors (Otto & Leifer, 1973; Syndulko & Lindsley, 1977) have reported differences in CNV amplitudes between hemispheres, but this asymmetry was not found by McCallum (1978).

In a recent study Rohrbaugh et al. (1976) compared the terminal CNV in a simple RT task (ISI of 4 sec) with the RP preceding voluntary finger movements. In general, the form and the topographical distribution of these two negative shifts were virtually the same: Largest amplitudes were found over the motor cortex (C_z), whereas amplitudes obtained from the hemisphere contralateral to the intended response were more negative than at the ipsilateral side.

In the experiment to be presented here this issue is further pursued. In addition to a simple RT task and voluntary movements, two intermediate conditions are included. In one experimental condition the subject had to respond 4 sec after S_1. In the other condition the subject was instructed to estimate the duration of the ISI and to indicate with a delayed response (1 sec after S_2) whether the interval had been of "normal" duration or had been (somewhat) longer.

It is expected that there will be no negativity in the latter condition because it is assumed that this detection task does not necessitate the involvement of motor systems before S_2. If the terminal CNV and the RP are the same phenomenon, the negativity preceding S_2 in the RT task and that preceding voluntary movements and delayed responses should have the same characteristics with regard to topography, form, and amplitude. To illustrate this, averages in the RT task and the detection task time-locked both to the S_1–S_2 paradigm and to the motor responses will be compared. If the negative shifts preceding the finger presses in all conditions are most prominent at the motor area and are larger in the hemisphere contralateral to the responding hand, this will localize these negative shifts and specify their functional role.

Another aspect of the present study was the comparison of cortical (EEG) and peripheral (EMG) measures of motor preparation. It is important to see whether the development of the slow cortical potential in the EEG has the same time course during the ISI as the muscular activity. Moreover, the recording of the EMG gives the opportunity to control whether the subjects followed the instruction (i.e., did not display motor activity before S_2 in the detection task or in the noninvolved arm in all four conditions).

METHODS

Subjects

The subjects were eight male students of the University of Utrecht who were paid for their participation. The data of four other subjects were discarded for having too many eye movements and/or DC drifts. Before the experiment the subjects completed a questionnaire about their hand preference. Only the subjects who preferred to use their right hand for most activities (writing, tooth brushing, etc.) were taken. For some activities (e.g., throwing a ball) bimanuality (i.e., no preference for either hand) was allowed.

Apparatus

The subjects were seated in a comfortable chair, which provided a neckrest and an armrest. S_1 and S_2 were both tones (70 dB), which were presented via earphones to either the left or right ear. The EEG was derived (time constant 10 sec) from the frontal (F_z), vertex (C_z), and parietal (P_z) regions and from the left (C_3) and right hemispheres (C_4). EOG signals were derived from the supra- and infra-orbital ridge. The EMG was recorded from the flexor muscles (in both the left and right forearms). Before averaging, the EMG was integrated using a 10-msec window. All physiological signals were recorded on magnetic tape, accompanied by a label that contained the experimental condition, the response knob, and the reaction time (RT) in milliseconds.

Procedure

The subject was required to give left- and right-hand presses in four experimental conditions. In one condition the subject was asked to give *voluntary movements:* The subject was trained to do this at intervals not shorter than 6 sec and not longer than 7 sec. The subject gave 48 finger presses for one hand, followed by 48 for the other. The order was balanced between subjects. In the *RT task* the subject was required to react as quickly as possible to S_2, which arrived 4 sec after S_1. In the *synchronization* task the subject had to respond as near to 4 sec after S_1 as possible. In this task S_2 was only present during the initial phase of the training sessions; thus S_2 was omitted in the experimental session. In the *detection* task the subject was instructed to estimate the time interval between S_1 and S_2 and to indicate with a delayed response (1 sec) on one of the buttons whether the interval had been of "normal" duration (4 sec) or had been longer. The arrival of S_2 was delayed on half of the trials by either 500 or 600 msec, depending on the subjects' performance during training. The delay was chosen such that 5–10% errors were made. In the latter three tasks S_1 indicated whether the subject had to respond with his left or with his right hand. If S_1 was presented to the left ear, a left-hand response was required and a right ear stimulus indicated a right-hand response. S_2 was always presented to the same ear as S_1.

The order of rotation of these four tasks was voluntary movements, RT task, detection task, and synchronization task. The task that was given first was varied between subjects (two subjects each started with the same task).

Data Analysis

The way in which the data were analyzed is described extensively in earlier reports (e.g., Gaillard, 1978); therefore only a short outline is given here. The physiological signals were analyzed in two ways: In the first analysis the EEG was time-locked to the S_1–S_2 paradigm, and in the second analysis it was time-locked to the closure of the response button.

In the first analysis, sampling (at a rate of 40 Hz) started 1 sec before S_1 and ended at the onset of S_2. For each trial the number of data points was reduced to 25 by taking the average of successive groups of 5 points. Due to memory limitations only 13 data points were retained for further analysis (see also Fig. 4.3). These data points were averaged across 40 trials, leaving 10 trials for the rejection of EOG artifacts. The average EEG activity in the period 200 msec before S_1 was taken as a baseline. The terminal CNV was measured as the average EEG activity in the 200 msec period before S_1.

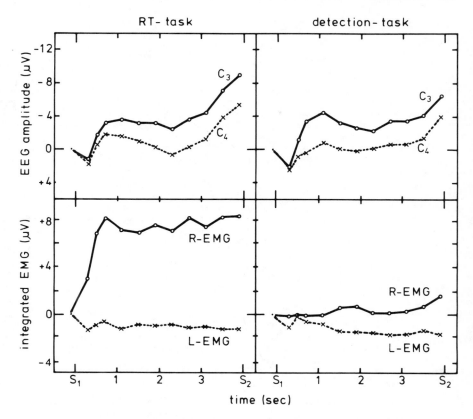

FIG. 4.3.   Slow brain potentials from left (C_3) and right (C_4) hemispheres and integrated EMG from left- (L-EMG) and right- (R-EMG) forearm muscles, separately for the RT task and the detection task.

The second analysis (sample interval 14 msec) started 3 sec before the response and ended 1 sec after it. As a measure for the negative shift preceding the response (Fig. 4.4) the EEG activity was taken in the period 284–144 msec before the response, referred to a baseline 3000–2860 msec before the response.

Two factor ANOVAs (experimental conditions × response side) were carried out on the amplitude of the terminal CNV and on the negative shift preceding the response. These ANOVAs were carried out for each of the five EEG channels, for the difference between left and right hemisphere (C_3–C_4), for the EOG channel, and for the left and right EMG. The ANOVAs on the terminal CNV involved only the RT and the detection conditions, because no stimulus-locked averages can be obtained with voluntary movements, and in the synchronization task rather low amplitudes were obtained. The latter may have been caused by the large variability in response latencies.

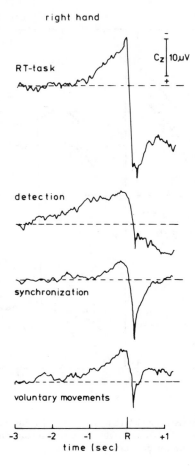

FIG. 4.4.   Vertex (C_z) potentials time-locked to right-hand finger presses for the RT task, detection task, synchronization task, and voluntary movements.

RESULTS

Figure 4.3 shows the changes during the ISI in slow potential for the left and right hemisphere (C_3 and C_4) and in muscular activity for left- and right-forearm muscles (L-EMG and R-EMG), separately for the RT and the detection task. In this figure (and in the following figures) only the data for the right-hand responses are presented. The data for the left-hand responses gave virtually the same results. Figure 4.3 shows that the terminal CNV was larger in the hemisphere contralateral to the responding hand. This effect was about the same in the RT and in the detection task (3.4 uV and 3.6 μV, across left- and right-hand responses). The EMG data run parallel to the EEG data:

Larger amplitudes were found in the RT task and in the involved arm, even with a delayed response in the detection task. It is to be noted that the time course of the EMG is quite different from the EEG. Instead of a gradually increasing curve, the EMG reaches a peak within 1 sec after S_1 and remains on a constant level thereafter.

The terminal CNV was affected by the type of task both at $C_z [F(^1/_7) = 6.8; p < 0.03]$ and at $P_z [F(^1/_7) = 7.4; p < 0.03]$; larger amplitudes were obtained in the RT task than in the detection task. At C_z this amplitude was about two times larger in the RT task (12.6 μV) than in the detection task (6.6 μV). The effect of the side of the response did not reach statistical significance for either C_3 or C_4, nor for the midline positions (F_z, C_z, P_z). However, a significant effect was found on the difference between C_3 and $C_4 [F (^1/_7) = 7.6; p < 0.03]$.

The EMG activity in the 200-msec period before S_2 was larger in the RT task than in the detection task, for both the left-arm $[F(^1/_7) = 16.6; p < 0.01]$ and right-arm EMG $[F(^1/_7) = 8.3; p < 0.01]$; the effects of response side were also significant for both the left arm $[F (^1/_7) = 21.1; p < 0.01]$ and the right arm $[F (^1/_7) = 18.5; p < 0.01]$.

Figure 4.4 presents the vertex potentials time-locked to the response. In general the negative shift preceding the response had the same form and amplitude in the four experimental conditions. Although this effect did not reach statistical significance, the negative shift was somewhat larger in the RT task and somewhat smaller in the synchronization task than in the other experimental conditions. In the detection task the shift started somewhat earlier. Response side had a significant effect on the amplitude of the negative shift preceding the response at the left hemisphere (C_3) $[F(^1/_7) = 5.9; p < 0.04]$ but not at the right hemisphere (C_4) $[F (^1/_7) < 1]$, whereas the difference between C_3 and C_4 was also significantly affected $[F (^1/_7) = 34.2; p < 0.01]$. Although the laterality effect was somewhat larger in the detection task and smaller in the RT task, experimental conditions did not have a significant effect on the difference between C_3 and $C_4 [F (^1/_7) < 1]$.

Figure 4.5 presents the EMG activity time-locked to the closure of the button switch. The EMG curves obtained from the noninvolved arm are not presented, because here virtually no activity was present. As with the movement potentials the EMG shows the same picture in the four experimental conditions. A large peak in the EMG precedes the response by 18 msec for voluntary movements and for the RT task and by 32 msec for the other two tasks. Although this peak was much larger in the RT task, the latency of the start of this peak was about the same for all conditions. Although modest in amplitude there is a gradual increase in EMG activity for 1 to 2 sec before the response. This gradual increase runs parallel to the slow negative shift preceding the response, as shown in Fig. 4.5. This gradual increase in EMG, largest in the RT and detection tasks, is also present in the averages time-locked to S_2 for both the RT task and the detection task (Fig. 4.3).

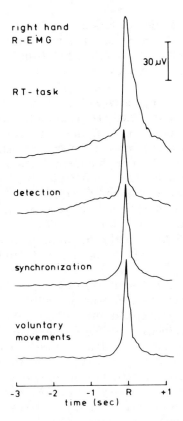

right hand
R-EMG

RT-task

30 µV

detection

synchronization

voluntary
movements

-3   -2   -1   R   +1
time (sec)

FIG. 4.5. The integrated EMG activity from the flexor muscles of the right forearm time-locked to right-hand finger presses in the RT task, detection task, synchronization task, and voluntary movements.

Experimental conditions did not have a significant effect on either of the EMG variables. Response side had an effect on both the left-arm EMG $[F\,({}^{1}\!/_{7}) = 8.7;\ p < 0.03]$ and on the right-arm EMG $[F\,({}^{1}\!/_{7}) = 9.6;\ p < 0.03]$.

DISCUSSION

The terminal CNV was twice as large in the RT task than in the detection task. This result corroborates earlier studies (Gaillard, 1977; Gaillard & Perdok, 1980; Lang, Öhman, & Simons, 1978; Loveless, 1975) in that it suggests that the terminal CNV is contingent on a fast motor response. However, it was expected that the terminal CNV would be virtually absent in the detection task, because it was assumed that before S_2 the involvement of motor systems would be minimal. That some negativity (6.6 µV) was still found might be caused by subjects having difficulty in inhibiting all motor activity until 1 sec after S_2. Even in the case of a delayed response, it is quite possible that at least some motor preparation takes place before S_2.

According to Syndulko and Lindsley (1977) the prominence of the vertex terminal CNV in motor tasks is so convincing that the occurrence of this slow potential in so-called sensory tasks, which do not involve specific, overt motor responses, suggests that the latter tasks also involve at least some "motor" elements. Sperry (1952) has suggested that, regardless of the manifest behavioral situation, the primary end product of the brain is motor output. Situations not involving specific, overt motor response may nevertheless produce generalized effector readiness, receptor orientation (fixation of eyes), and nonautomatic postural adjustments, in addition to specific motor concomitants of mental processes. Several other authors (see Festinger, Ono, Burnham, & Bamber 1967) have noted the strong relationship between stimulus input and efferent output. Sperry suggested (1952, p.301) that "insofar as an organism perceives a given object, it is prepared to respond with reference to it." In terms of the present experimental situation this may mean that although the requisite overt response is delayed, at least on a behavioral level, the subject may nevertheless encounter some difficulty in suppressing all motor preparation. The actual stimulus situation may be so compelling that he is unable wholly to suppress the motor processes for the motor response to be given later.

Some support for this notion is provided by the present EMG data: In the detection task the EMG activity before S_2 was larger in that forearm that had to give the delayed response. This result suggests that the subjects were so eager to respond that they tensed their muscles and prepared for the motor responses even before S_2. In an earlier experiment (Perdok & Gaillard, 1979), where unfortunately no EMG was recorded, the amplitude of the terminal CNV was larger preceding an easy discrimination than preceding a difficult one. In the light of the present data this result suggests that the more easy the discrimination and the more "obvious" the response, the more eager subjects are to indicate their observation by giving a response.

As argued more extensively elsewhere (Gaillard, 1978) the terminal CNV seems to be contingent on a motor response and its amplitude reflects the level of motor preparation. In fact, almost all experimental results reported in the literature can be explained in this way. In contrast, there is little support for theories that relate the (terminal) CNV to concepts such as attention, perception, decision, or expectancy.

The motor character of the CNV may be illustrated further by its similarity to the RP. In the present study the terminal CNV and the negative shifts preceding the response in the four experimental conditions had the same form and the same midline and lateral distributions. Both the terminal CNV and the RP consist of a gradually increasing negative shift, which starts 1 sec before the response. They are both most prominent over the motor region (C_z), and they both show an asymmetry contralateral to the responding hand. But the negative shift preceding the response was larger in the RT task than with voluntary movements. This may be explained as a larger involvement of motor systems in preparing the response in the RT task than in monotonously executing a series of finger presses. This larger involvement is also suggested by the EMG data time-locked to the response. The amplitude of the peak preceding the response and the gradual increase before this peak is larger in the RT task than preceding voluntary movements. Moreover, it has been shown that the RP is influenced by motivation (McAdam & Seales, 1969). In the latter study RP amplitudes preceding voluntary finger presses increased from 5 to 20 μV when subjects were told that they would receive 10 cents for each response given "at the right time." In fact, rewards for these "correct" responses were given in a random fashion. It could well be that the increased RP values reflect a higher level of motor preparation, caused by an enhanced interest in the task.

The present results corroborate earlier studies (Gaillard & Perdok, 1980; Rohrbaugh et al., 1976; Syndulko & Lindsley, 1977) with regard to form and topographical distributions of both the terminal CNV in RT tasks and the RP preceding responses in detection or synchronization tasks or preceding voluntary movements. In addition, Syndulko and Lindsley showed that the laterality effect only occurred in the motor cortex (i.e., it was *not* present in frontal, parietal, or occipital regions). The present laterality effect was much larger (3.4 μV) than in the Rohrbaugh et al. study. This difference is not easily explained in terms of task characteristics, because virtually the same task was used in both studies. However, one important difference from the Rohrbaugh et al. study is that in the present study the activity in the noninvolved response side was controlled by measuring the EMG. Moreover, during the training EMG was monitored and the subjects were informed when there was activity in the noninvolved arm. Thus, in the present study care was taken to limit motor preparation to the muscle groups involved in the response (see Syndulko & Lindsley, 1977).

At the moment there is no reason for regarding the vertex terminal CNV and the RP as reflections of different processes, whereas the notion that they are generated by the same neurophysiological mechanism is in line with the view that the terminal CNV reflects the level of motor preparation and is contingent on a motor response. Moreover, the RP is affected by task variables, such as muscle effort (e.g., Kutas & Donchin, 1977) and motivation (e.g., McAdam & Seales, 1969; McCallum 1979), which also influence the terminal CNV (Irwin et al., 1966; Low & McSherry, 1968; Rebert, McAdam, Knott & Irwin 1967; Waszak & Obrist, 1969).

It could be argued that RT tasks not only involve motor- but also perceptual- and decision-related processes. It is, however, unlikely that these are reflected in the negative shifts because the terminal CNV appears to be unrelated to these processes (see for review, Gaillard, 1978). Given the close relationship between terminal CNV and RP it is also unlikely that the negative shift preceding voluntary movements reflects other processes than motor preparation. Of course, it is quite possible that motivation, expectancy, attention, and time estimation affect the amplitude of the terminal CNV or the RP, insofar as they affect the level of motor preparation. If both potentials refer to the same neurophysiological generator but are obtained with different averaging techniques, the terminal CNV could be regarded as that part of the RP that precedes S_2. Of course, this is true only for single trials, because averaged potentials will diverge the larger the variability in RT. Because both the RP and the terminal CNV are slow phenomena, this effect will be negligible as long as the standard deviation of the RT is small (e.g., <50 msec). Thus, the amplitude of the terminal CNV can be predicted when the amplitudes and the waveform of the RP on the one hand and the latency and variability of the responses on the other hand are known. When the RP remains unchanged, the amplitude of the terminal CNV is determined by the RT. With shorter RTs the terminal amplitude increases, because a larger part of the RP precedes S_2.

As also noted by Rohrbaugh et al. (1976), this view enables the investigation of movement-related potentials within a much wider context. On the one hand, the study of the RP can be extended beyond the scope of repetitive stereotyped movements, and the influence of psychological variables can be investigated. On the other hand, a strict pairing of stimuli is no longer necessary, and new experimental paradigms can be used (for example, serial RT instead of warned RT tasks).

ACKNOWLEDGMENTS

The author wishes to thank C. Varey, J. Perdok, J. Th. Eernst, and A. J. Krul for their assistance during the experiment and for the analysis of the data.

REFERENCES

Cohen, J. Cerebral psychophysiology: The contingent negative variation. In R. F. Thompson & M. M. Patterson (Eds.), *Bioelectric recording techniques, Part B. Electroencephalography and human brain potentials.* New York: Academic Press, 1974.

Deecke, L., Grözinger, B., & Kornhuber, H. H. Voluntary finger movement in man: Cerebral potentials and theory. *Biological Cybernetics,* 1976, *23,* 99–119.

Donald, M. W. Discussion. Electroencephalograpy and clinical neurophysiology, Supplement 33, 1973, 241–242.

Festinger, L., Ono, H., Burnham, C. A., & Bamber, D. Efference and the conscious experience of perception. *Journal of Experimental Psychology,* Monograph, 74, 1967, *4,* Pt. 2.

Gaillard, A. W. K. Effects of warning-signal modality on the contingent negative variation (CNV). *Biological Psychology,* 1976, *4,* 139–154.

Gaillard, A. W. K. The late CNV wave: Preparation versus expectancy. *Psychophysiology,* 1977, *14,* 563–568.

Gaillard, A. W. K. *Slow brain potentials preceding task performance.* Doctoral dissertation. Soesterberg, Institute for Perception, 1978.

Gaillard, A. W. K., & Perdok, J. Slow brain potentials in the CNV-paradigm. *Acta Psychologica,* 1980, *44,* 147–163.

Hillyard, S. A. The CNV and human behavior. *Electroencephalograpy and Clinical Neurophysiology,* Supplement 33, 1973, 161–171.

Irwin, D. A., Knott, J. R., McAdam, D. W., & Rebert, C. S. Motivational determinants of the "contingent negative variation." *Electroencephalography and Clinical Neurophysiology,* 1966, *21,* 538–543.

Järvilehto, T., & Frühstorfer, H. Differentiation between slow cortical potentials associated with motor and mental acts in man. *Experimental Brain Research,* 1970, *11,* 309–317.

Kornhuber, H. H., & Deecke, L. Hirnpotential-änderungen bei Willkur-bewegungen und passiven Bewegungen des Menschen: Bereitschaftspotential und reafferent Potentiale. *Pleugers Archiv,* 1965, *284,* 1–17.

Kutas, M., & Donchin, E. Motor potentials, force of response and handedness. In J. E. Desmedt (Ed.), Attention, voluntary contraction and event-related cerebral potentials. Basel: Karger, 1977.

Lang, P. J., Öhman, A., & Simons, R. F. The psychophysiology of anticipation. In J. Requin (Ed.), *Attention and Performance VII.* Hillsdale, N.J.: Lawrence Erlbaum Associates 1978.

Loveless, N. E. The effect of warning interval on signal detection and event-related slow potentials of the brain. *Perception and Psychophysics,* 1975, *6,* 565–570.

Loveless, N. E., & Sanford, A. J. Effects of age on the contingent negative variation and preparatory set. *Journal of Gerontology,* 1974, *29,* 52–63. (a)

Loveless, N. E. & Sanford, A. J. Slow potential correlates of preparatory set. *Biological Psychology,* 1974, *1,* 303–314. (b)

Low, M. C., & McSherry, J. W. Further observations of psychological factors involved in CNV genesis. *Electroencephalography and Clinical Neurophysiology,* 1968, *25,* 203–207.

McAdam, D. W. The contingent negative variations. In R. F. Thompson & M. M. Patterson (Eds.), *Bioelectrical recording techniques, Part B. Electroencephalography and human brain potentials.* New York: Academic Press, 1974.

McAdam, D. W. & Seales, D. M. Bereitschaftspotential enhancement with increased level of motivation. *Electroencephalography and Clinical Neurophysiology,* 1969, *27,* 73–75.

McCallum, W. C. Relationships between Bereitschaftspotential and contingent negative variation. In D. A. Otto (Ed.), *Multidisciplinary Perspectives in Event-Related Brain Potential Research.* Washington, D.C.: U.S. Environmental Protection Agency, 1978.

Näätänen, R., Gaillard, A., & Mäntysalo, S. S_2 probability and CNV. *Activitatis Nervosa Superior (Praha),* 1977, *19,* 142–144.

Otto, D., & Leifer, L. J. The effect of modifying response and performance feedback parameters on the CNV in humans. *Electroencephalography and Clinical Neurophysiology,* Supplement 33, 1973, 29–37.

Perdok, J., & Gaillard, A. W. K. The terminal CNV and stimulus discriminability in motor and sensory tasks. *Biological Psychology,* 1979, *8,* 213–224.

Peters, J. F., Knott, J. R., Miller, L. H., van Veen, W. J., & Cohen, S. I. Response variables and magnitude of the contingent negative variation. *Electroencephalography and Clinical Neurophysiology,* 1970, *29,* 608–611.

Rebert, C. S., McAdam, D. W., Knott, J. R., & Irwin, D. A. Slow potential changes in human brain related to level of motivation. *Journal of Comparative and Physiological Psychology,* 1967, *63,* 20–23.

Rohrbaugh, J. W., Syndulko, K., & Lindsley, D. B. Brain wave components of the contingent negative variation in humans. *Science,* 1976, *191,* 1055–1057.

Sperry, R. W. Neurology and the mind-brain problem. *American Scientist,* 1952, *40,* 291–312.

Squires, K. C., Donchin, E., Herning, R. I., & McCarthy, G. On the influence of task relevance and stimulus probability on event-related potential components. *Electroencephalography and Clinical Neurophysiology,* 1977, *42,* 1–14.

Syndulko, K., & Lindsley, D. B. Motor and sensory determinants of cortical slow potential shifts in man. In J. E. Desmedt, (Ed.), *Attention, voluntary contraction and event-related cerebral potentials.* Basel: Karger, 1977.

Tecce, J. J. Contingent negative variation (CNV) and psychological processes in man. *Psychological bulletin,* 1972, *77,* 73–108.

Walter, W. G., Cooper, R., Aldridge, V. J., McCallum, W. C., & Winter, A. L. Contingent negative variation: an electrical sign of sensorimotor association and expectancy in the human brain. *Nature* (Lond.), 1964, *203,* 380–384.

Waszak, M., & Obrist, W. D. Relationship of slow potential changes to response speed and motivation in man. *Electroencephalography and Clinical Neurophysiology,* 1969, *27,* 113–120.

5

Time to Time in the Human Motor System

David A. Rosenbaum
Oren Patashnik
Bell Laboratories
Murray Hill, New Jersey
United States

ABSTRACT

To investigate how people control time intervals between successive movements, we have subjects attempt to produce specified time intervals between two finger presses and make the first finger press as quickly as possible after a reaction signal. Mean reaction times (RTs) are longer in these conditions than in a control condition where no second response is required (even when the second response is delayed by more than 1 sec), indicating advance programming of both responses. When produced intervals have to match required intervals precisely, mean RTs increase to an increasing degree the shorter the interval ($\geq$ 50 msec). This result suggests that there is a time-consuming "clock-setting" process that precedes the first response and whose duration depends on interval size. Under high-precision conditions, foreperiod duration and interval size have additive effects on mean RT, suggesting that clock-setting follows detection of the reaction signal rather than starting beforehand. The implications of these results for studies of motor programming and timing are discussed.

INTRODUCTION

How do people control time intervals between successive movements? This problem is confronted in walking, talking, typing, and many other motor activities. The ability to time movements precisely may be one of the main determinants of skilled performance.

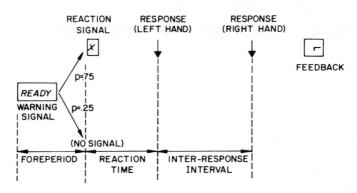

FIG. 5.1.   Overview of the experimental procedure. See text for details.

We have investigated the control of movement timing with a new experimental task (see Fig. 5.1). Our subjects are required to make two successive responses—key presses with the left and right index fingers—with specified time intervals between the two responses. On each trial we give feedback about the accuracy of the produced interresponse interval relative to the target interval. Besides producing correct intervals, the subjects are also required to make the first response as quickly as possible after the onset of a reaction signal. We have investigated how the reaction time (RT) to make the first response is affected by the length and precision of the produced interval.

The intervals we have required range from 0 to 1050 msec. Some of the intervals are too short for feedback from the first response to be used to control the second response (ballistic sequences) and some of the intervals are long enough for feedback to serve this purpose (nonballistic sequences). Given that the ballistic sequences must, by definition, be programmed in advance, the issue we have been primarily interested in is whether the nonballistic sequences are also preprogrammed.

To address this issue we have compared RTs for each of the intervals with RTs in a control condition where no second response is required (interval = ∞). Our working assumption is that both responses in a two-response sequence can be considered to be preprogrammed if the RT for the first response is longer than the RT for this same response performed in isolation. We expect RTs to be longer for the first of two responses than for isolated responses because it has been reported in several studies that RTs are longer for the first of two finger presses, made approximately simultaneously (and without precise timing requirements), than for single finger presses (Hammond & Barber, 1978; Kelso, Southard, & Goodman, 1979; Peterson, 1965;

Rabbitt, Vyas, & Fearnley, 1975; Ratz & Ritchie, 1961). By systematically varying required intervals here, we attempt to determine how large an interval must be in order for there to be no effect of the second response on the RT for the first response. If this critical interval is longer than the time required for feedback from the first response to be able to affect the second response,[1] we can conclude that there is preprogramming of both responses under nonballistic as well as ballistic conditions. Note that this method also allows us tentatively to identify the specific feedback loop that may be used for closed-loop timing. This would be the loop known from other studies—especially physiological studies—to have a time constant similar to the critical interval.

It should be noted that the question of whether preprogramming occurs for nonballistic as well as ballistic movement sequences is somewhat different from the more traditional question of whether feedback is necessary for skilled motor performance. In a number of studies addressed to the latter question it has been reported that skilled motor performance is indeed often possible when there are major disruptions of feedback—for example, after interruption of afferent pathways (for reviews, see Glencross, 1977; Keele, 1968; Kelso & Stelmach, 1976). Although these studies imply that motor programs play a role in movement control, they do not permit any firm conclusions about the functional importance of motor programs when feedback is not disrupted. Disrupting feedback may cause motor programs to be used more extensively than is normally the case. Because disrupting feedback may result in an abnormal mode of movement control,[2] we have preferred to use natural time limitations in feedback processing to investigate how programming is used.

The method of using RTs to investigate motor programming is not unprecedented (for reviews see Kerr, 1978; Klapp, 1978; Rosenbaum, in press; and Sternberg, Monsell, Knoll, & Wright, 1978), although very few RT studies have directly investigated programming of timing, and only one RT study that we are aware of has deliberately manipulated durations of required movements for purposes of influencing the availability of feedback. The latter study was conducted by one of us (Rosenbaum, 1976) and it used a procedure like the one to be reported here. Subjects were required to begin a sequence of two finger presses as quickly as possible after a reaction signal, and any one of six intervals between 10 and 220 msec could be required on a trial. The

---

[1]Physiological studies indicate that proprioceptive stimuli can produce cortical potentials in as little as 3 msec (see Adams, 1976, for review) and muscular effects in as much as 130 msec (see Spirduso, 1978, for review).

[2]We are also skeptical of claims, based on the finding that performance breaks down after feedback disruption, that feedback is essential for control of the gross features of voluntary movement. One effect of disrupting feedback may be to cause more attention to be paid to feedback than normal.

identity of the required interval was indicated by a warning signal (one of the letters A to F, corresponding to the six targets from 10 to 220 msec, respectively), which appeared 1.5 sec before the reaction signal. The main result was that mean RTs increased with mean produced intervals.

This study had at least two limitations. First, there was no control condition in which subjects made just one response in a trial. Second, there was no assurance that subjects had enough time between the warning signal and reaction signal to prepare even the first response; the time required for encoding of the warning signal may have increased with the length of the required interval or with the alphabetic position of the warning letter or both. (In view of data to be reported here, we are now led to believe that stimulus identification did in fact account for the positive relationship between intervals and RTs.)

To avoid ambiguities concerning the role of stimulus identification and response evocation in the present study, we have used a simple RT procedure in which only one interval is required in a block of trials and the same reaction signal (the letter X) is used for all intervals. In addition, to maximize practice for each required interval and to minimize possible range effects among intervals (Poulton, 1973) we have required only one interval in each session.

Our belief that the relationship between RTs and intervals may be affected by minimizing interval uncertainty is supported by several studies of Klapp (see Klapp, 1978, for review) in which subjects were required to produce short-duration finger presses and long-duration finger presses under simple and choice RT conditions. Klapp found that RTs increased with response duration in choice RT conditions but were unaffected by response duration in simple RT conditions. (Note that Klapp's choice RT result is open to the stimulus encoding criticism raised earlier in connection with Rosenbaum's results.) Simple RTs and response duration have also been found to be unrelated for more continuous movements, such as passing the hand over some distance to a target (see Kerr, 1978).

Unfortunately, the finding that simple RTs are unrelated to durations of such continuous movements does not allow for any strong conclusions about whether such movements are preprogrammed. Although one can argue, as Klapp has, that the absence of a duration effect reflects preprogramming, one can also argue that there is preprogramming of only the initial phases of the movements and reliance on feedback for later phases (for discussions of feedback-based timing, see Adams, 1977; Bizzi, 1974; Greer & Harvey, 1978, Kelso, 1978; and Schmidt, 1971).

How can one distinguish between these two interpretations? One method that may prove useful is to vary the precision with which movement durations must be controlled. If the RT to begin a movement is affected by that movement's required temporal precision, then it seems reasonable to conclude that at least some programming of the entire movement occurs in advance.[3] To our knowledge, the issue of required temporal precision in motor control has not been experimentally investigated. Because this issue seems critical for understanding the timing of "discrete" movements (of the kind used here) as well as continuous movements, we have chosen to explore the timing-precision issue with our interval production task.

We have done this, in Experiment 1, by either requiring low interval variances or allowing high interval variances when subjects are otherwise encouraged to produce the same mean intervals (0, 50, 150, 300, 500, 750, or 1050 msec). An advantage of using this manipulation is that if RTs are found to depend on the relative precision of produced intervals, we will have a relatively strong basis for concluding that response *timing* is preprogrammed. (If RTs were found to depend on interval means but required interval precision were not experimentally varied, it would be possible to invoke a *response competition* explanation, in which case it would not be necessary to assume that timing control *per se* influences latencies.) As will be seen later, mean RTs do in fact turn out to depend on the relative precision of intervals, suggesting that some kind of clock-setting process occurs during the RT.

In the second experiment reported here we ask whether this hypothesized clock-setting process only occurs after the reaction signal. An alternative is that the process normally occurs in anticipation of the reaction signal, although there are occasional failures of anticipation that cause the process to extend into the RT. We present evidence against the anticipation hypothesis.

In the General Discussion section we consider some of the implications of this study for other studies of motor programming and timing.

EXPERIMENT 1

Method

On each trial (see Fig. 5.1) a warning signal (*READY*) was displayed on a cathode-ray tube screen for .5 sec. A half second later, on 75% of the trials, a reaction signal (*X*) appeared where the letter *A* had appeared and remained on the screen until the last required response was made. On the remaining 25% of the trials no reaction signal was presented; these "catch" trials were included to discourage anticipation. A half second after the last required response, feedback was given for 2.5 sec about the RT and produced interval. Feedback about the RT took the form of a horizontal line that extended from the center of the screen toward the right over a distance proportional to the

---

[3]This inference assumes that the initial elements of the movement are unaffected by the precision requirement—one case of the *element invariance* assumption of Sternberg *et al.* (1978). The alternative is that the initial elements are performed differently—and consequently with different RTs—so that resultant feedback can be used more effectively to time the second response.

RT, for RTs greater than 130 msec and less than 642 msec; for RTs greater than or equal to 642 msec, the horizontal line reached the right edge of the screen. Feedback about the produced interval took the form of a vertical line that extended up from the center of the screen if the produced interval was too long or down if the produced interval was too short. Different feedback scales were used depending on whether subjects were required to have low interval variances (*stringent* condition) or were allowed to have high interval variances (*relaxed* condition). In the *stringent* condition the length of the vertical line was proportional to the percentage deviation of the produced interval from the required interval, so that the line reached the top or bottom of the screen for percentage deviations greater than or equal to 100%; when the required interval was 0 msec, the length of the vertical line was proportional to the length of the produced interval, so that the line either reached the top of the screen when the left finger led the right by more than 20 msec or reached the bottom of the screen when the right finger led the left by more than 20 msec. In the *relaxed* condition the feedback scale was reduced by a factor of 25 so that generally subjects could only see whether their produced intervals were too long or too short.

In all experimental conditions, subjects were instructed to make the vertical line point up and down about equally often. This made it possible for subjects to produce intervals with approximately correct median values (and also approximately correct means if they produced symmetrical interval distributions) but different variances in the *stringent* and *relaxed* conditions. Subjects were also instructed to minimize the lengths of the vertical and horizontal lines, and scores and cash bonuses were given to motivate quick and accurate responding. Subjects were also instructed to respond only with the left finger before the right, except when the required interval was 0 msec, and to keep the first key depressed until the second key was depressed.

Responses were made on two standard telegraph keys and the subjects in this computer-controlled experiment were tested individually in a sound-proof booth. The subjects were three right-handed women between the ages of 28 and 38 who had extensive practice in earlier versions of the experiment.

Each subject participated in fifteen 1-hour sessions consisting of 11 blocks of 60 trials each, with the first block for practice. In each session only one interval was tested at only one level of required accuracy. The sessions were ordered so that on each day any given target was given to only one subject; no subject was tested on the same or adjacent intervals in adjacent sessions; and each target was first tested under *relaxed* and *stringent* conditions about equally often.

Results

Errors of responding on catch trials or responding first with the right finger when nonzero intervals were required occurred on less than 2% of the trials in

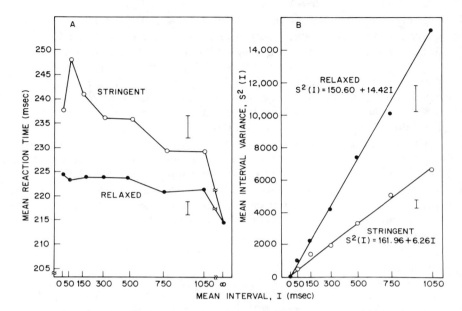

FIG. 5.2.   Results of Experiment 1, averaged over the three subjects: Speeded production of one response in isolation (∞) or of one response followed by another with a target interresponse interval of from 0 to 1050 msec, with *relaxed* or *stringent* interval accuracy requirements; about 1300 observations per point. (A) Mean RTs and estimates of standard error (±SE) for the two accuracy conditions. (B) Mean interval variances, fitted linear functions, and estimates of ±SE. Estimates of ±SE based on mean squares from fits of mean functions to individual subject data.

each of the 15 conditions of the experiment. The remaining discussion is concerned with results from errorless trials only.

Figure 5.2 illustrates the main results. The vertical alignment of filled and empty points indicates that the subjects produced similar mean intervals in the *stringent* and *relaxed* conditions. As is seen in Panel B, interval variances increased approximately linearly with interval means, both in the *stringent* and *relaxed* conditions. For the three subjects the slopes of the fitted linear functions were 5.74, 6.37, and 6.60 in the *stringent* condition and 15.69, 12.04, and 15.47 in the *relaxed* condition. Linear regression accounted for 99.7% and 99.9% of the variance among mean variances (averaged over subjects) in the *stringent* and *relaxed* conditions, respectively. In both conditions fitted quadratic functions did not account for significantly more variance among mean variances than did the best-fitting linear functions. The difference between intercepts for the two best-fitting linear functions, tested relative to the errors of estimate for the intercepts, was not statistically significant.

Panel A of Fig. 5.2 shows that mean RTs were shorter for the infinite interresponse interval (where only one response was required) than for every finite interval; this was true for every subject. For the conditions in which two responses were required, mean RTs were longer under *stringent* conditions than under *relaxed* conditions, $F(1, 28) = 10.43$, $p < .01$. There was a significant interaction between target and accuracy condition, $F(6, 28) = 2.75$, $p < .05$, such that mean RTs decreased with targets less in the *relaxed* condition than in the *stringent* condition.

In the *stringent* condition the decrease in RTs for the 0-msec target was not attributable to short latencies for responses in which the right finger led the left; these latencies were in fact about 3 msec *longer* than latencies for left-first responses. Subjects said that they controlled interresponse intervals differently in the 0-msec condition and other experimental conditions, in part by keeping their wrists and fingers stiff in the 0-msec condition but loose in the other conditions.

Discussion

One dramatic result of Experiment 1 is that the RT to make an isolated response was shorter than the RT to make one response followed even more than 1 sec later by another response. This result suggests that there was some preprogramming of both responses even when there was almost certainly enough time to use feedback from the first response to time the second. Our data suggest, then, that the availability of feedback does not eliminate the need—or at least the tendency—for preprogramming.

Another dramatic result is that interval variances increased linearly with interval means. This relationship can be explained by a *stochastic wait* process (Wing & Kristofferson, 1973a, b) in which interval variance increases with the number of "ticks" of an internal clock for which times between ticks fluctuate randomly about a mean and successive intertick times are stochastically independent. The difference between slopes for the *stringent* and *relaxed* conditions can then be explained by a difference in the mean and/or variance of intertick times.

These considerations help us interpret the RT data. If we regard the stochastic wait process as the running of an internal alarm clock, we can hypothesize that the alarm clock is set during the RT. In Fig. 5.3 we present one embodiment of such a model. According to the model, after the desired number, n, of clock ticks has been specified (i.e., after the clock has been set), the motor initiation of response 1 begins and the clock is allowed to start ticking. After the nth tick has occurred (i.e., after the alarm has gone off), the motor initiation of response 2 begins. We assume in the model that the variance associated with processing of the visual reaction signal and motor initiation of the two responses is constant. The model says that more

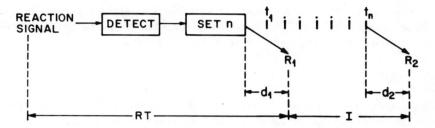

FIG. 5.3. An *alarm clock* model for the qualitative aspects of performance in Experiment 1. See text for details.

time is required to set the clock more precisely and that shorter intervals require more precise setting, although the specific mechanism responsible for these effects is as yet unclear.[4]

EXPERIMENT 2

The next experiment was concerned with the question of whether the hypothesized clock-setting process normally awaits the reaction signal or normally occurs in anticipation of the reaction signal. If there were occasional anticipation errors, the clock-setting process could occasionally extend into the RT. In addition, if the magnitude or frequency of such errors depended on the required precision of intervals to be produced, one could obtain RT effects like those found in Experiment 1.

To determine whether the clock-setting process awaits the reaction signal, we took advantage of the fact that as foreperiods increase above about 500 msec, people become less able to prepare for reaction signals; that is, their RTs tend to increase (Alegria & Bertelson, 1970; Bevan, Hardesty, & Avant, 1965; Botwinick & Brinley, 1962; Karlin, 1959; Klemmer, 1956). In Experiment 2 we varied the foreperiod (in blocked fashion), using values of 500, 1250, and 2000 msec, and we obtained RTs for the same target intervals as in Experiment 1 (using stringent accuracy requirements only). Following Sternberg's (1969) additive factor logic, we predicted that if the clock-setting

---

[4]After preparing the text for this chapter, we were able to develop a more specific model of the clock-setting process (see Rosenbaum & Patashnik, in press). In this model, we assume that after the clock is set to a target position for production of an interresponse interval in one trial, the clock setting drifts randomly to a new position from which it must be reset during the RT of the next trial. The time needed to reset the clock is inversely related to the range of allowable settings, and this range decreases as required interval precision increases. This model accounts for the RT and interval variance data from Experiment 1.

process awaits the reaction signal, target intervals and foreperiods should have additive effects on RTs. In addition, the accuracy of produced intervals should be unaffected by the length of the foreperiod.

Method

Each subject was tested on one target interval per session with all three foreperiods used in each session. Each foreperiod was used in four consecutive blocks of 60 trials each. The order of the foreperiods was balanced so that the six possible foreperiod orders were distributed approximately equally across target intervals, subjects, and sessions. At the start of each $1\frac{1}{4}$-hour session, 60 practice trials were given, using the foreperiod to be used in the first four experimental blocks. Between foreperiod conditions a rest period was provided. At the start of the second and third foreperiod conditions, 30 practice trials were given with the foreperiod that was about to be used. There were three right-handed female subjects, one of whom had participated in Experiment 1. In all other respects the design, procedure, and apparatus were the same as in Experiment 1.

Results

As in the previous experiment, errors of responding on catch trials and responding with the right finger before the left when nonzero intervals were required occurred on less than 2% of the trials in each condition. The following discussion of results is concerned with errorless trials only.

Panel B of Figure 5.4 shows that interval variances increased approximately linearly with interval means, as in Experiment 1, and that foreperiod durations had no systematic effect on interval means or variances. Slopes and intercepts of fitted linear functions for the 500-, 1250-, and 2000-msec foreperiod conditions were 5.56 and 78.93, 6.08 and 84.81, and 5.57 and 85.32, respectively. Linear regression accounted for 98.1%, 99.1%, and 99.4% of the variance among mean variances for the 500-, 1250-, and 2000-msec foreperiod conditions, respectively. The fitted linear function for mean variances pooled over foreperiods, which is shown in Fig. 5.4, accounted for 99.2% of the variance of those means. A quadratic function fitted to the pooled variance data did not account for significantly more variance than did the fitted linear function.

Panel A of Fig. 5.4 shows that mean RTs increased with foreperiods, $F(2, 4) = 10.93$, $p < .01$, and depended on target intervals, $F(7, 14) = 4.20$, $p < .01$. However, the interaction between target interval and foreperiod was not statistically significant, $F(14, 28) = 1.27$, $p > .10$, and accounted for less than 1% of the variance of mean RTs.

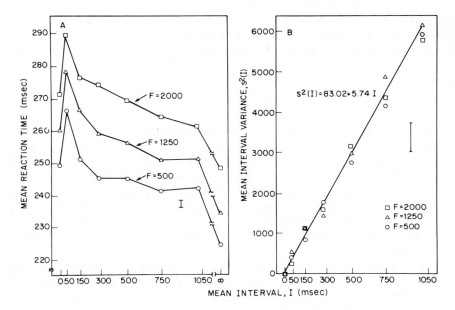

FIG. 5.4.   Results of Experiment 2, averaged over the three subjects: Speeded production task, as in Experiment 1, with fixed foreperiods (*F*) of 500, 1250, and 2000 msec; about 530 observations per point. (A) Mean RTs and estimate of ±SE. (B) Mean interval variances, linear function fitted to mean interval variances pooled over foreperiods, and estimate of ±SE. Estimates of ±SE based on *targets × foreperiods × subjects* interaction.

Discussion

The results of Experiment 2 are consistent with the hypothesis that the time-consuming process of setting a clock for a forthcoming interresponse interval (or preparing the interval in some other way) awaits the reaction signal. As far as we can tell, there is no straightforward way to explain the relationship between RTs and intervals in terms of occasional failures to anticipate the reaction signal.

It is worth noting that a qualitatively similar conclusion was reached by Sternberg, Wright, Knoll, and Monsell (1980) in a study of rapid speech production. Their subjects attempted to minimize the time after a reaction signal to say an entire list of previously specified words. Sternberg *et al.* found that mean latencies increased linearly with the number of words to be said. The intercept of the latency function was higher with random foreperiods than with fixed foreperiods, but the slope was about the same. The latter result led Sternberg *et al.* to conclude that the process responsible for the linear increase in latency began after the reaction signal was presented. Thus, their data, like ours, indicate that some aspects of the preparation of a response sequence must be postponed until immediately before execution of the sequence.

GENERAL DISCUSSION

Our data suggest that people may control interresponse intervals by using an internal alarm clock that is set just before response sequences are executed. One of the major theoretical implications of this conclusion is that the availability of proprioceptive feedback does not eliminate the need (or tendency) for motor preprogramming. (It should be noted, however, that we have not demonstrated that proprioceptive feedback plays no role in the control of interresponse intervals; we have merely demonstrated that proprioceptive feedback by itself is not used to control delays between responses.)

If it is true that part of the preparation for a movement sequence entails setting a clock that controls the timing of the sequence, many questions immediately come to mind. What are the detailed characteristics of the clock-setting process? (We consider some possibilities in another paper—Rosenbaum & Patashnik, in press.) Why is the clock-setting process postponed until just before movement execution? Is a similar clock-setting process used for continuous movements? What happens when sequences involving more than two discrete responses must be rhythmically controlled? And how does programming of timing information interact with programming of other kinds of movement information? (See Klapp, 1977, for some relevant work.) We hope to address these and related questions in future studies.

One strong conclusion that the present study allows takes the form of a methodological recommendation: In future RT studies of motor programming, investigators should consider varying the required precision of the movement variables they ask subjects to control. Here, when subjects were merely supposed to control the means of their interresponse intervals (in the *relaxed* condition of Experiment 1), there was a tiny effect of intervals on RTs. Increasing the required precision of the intervals yielded a robust RT effect that has helped us gain insight into the mechanisms of motor programming and timing.

ACKNOWLEDGMENTS

We thank O. Fujimura, C. S. Harris, J. C. Johnston, R. L. Knoll, J. F. Kroll, T. K. Landauer, R. S. Nickerson, R. T. Ollman, S. Sternberg, and B. L. Wattenbarger for helpful comments and L. Christofferson and G. Salyer for assistance with data collection.

REFERENCES

Adams, J. A. Issues for a closed-loop theory of motor learning. In G. E. Stelmach (Ed.), *Motor control: Issues and trends.* New York: Academic Press, 1976.

Adams, J. A. Feedback theory of how joint receptors regulate the timing and positioning of a limb. *Psychological Review,* 1977, *84,* 504–523.

Alegria, J., & Bertelson, P. Time uncertainty, number of alternatives and particular signal–response pair as determinants of choice reaction time. In A. F. Sanders (Ed.), *Attention and performance III. Acta Psychologica,* 1970, *33,* 36–44.

Bevan, W., Hardesty, D. L., & Avant, L. L. Response latency with constant and variable interval schedules. *Perceptual and Motor Skills,* 1965, *20,* 969–972.

Bizzi, E. The coordination of eye–head movements. *Scientific American,*1974, *231*(4), 100–106.

Botwinick, J., & Brinley, J. F. An analysis of set in relation to reaction time. *Journal of Experimental Psychology,* 1962, *63,* 568–574.

Glencross, D. J. Control of skilled movements. *Psychological Bulletin,* 1977, *84,* 14–29.

Greer, K., & Harvey, N. Timing and positioning of limb movements: Comments on Adams' theory. *Psychological Review,* 1978, *85,* 482–484.

Hammond, N., & Barber, P. Evidence for abstract response codes: Ear–hand correspondence effects in a three-choice reaction-time task. *Quarterly Journal of Experimental Psychology,* 1978, *30,* 71–82.

Karlin, L. Reaction time as a function of foreperiod duration and variability. *Journal of Experimental Psychology,* 1959, *58,* 185–191.

Keele, S. W. Movement control in skilled motor performance. *Psychological Bulletin,* 1968, *70,* 387–403.

Kelso, J. A. S. Joint receptors do not provide a satisfactory basis for motor timing and positioning. *Psychological Review,* 1978, *85,* 474–481.

Kelso, J. A. S., Southard, D. L., & Goodman, D. On the coordination of two-handed movements. *Science,* 1979, *203,* 1029–1031.

Kelso, J. A. S., & Stelmach, G. E. Central and peripheral mechanisms in motor control. In G. E. Stelmach (Ed.), *Motor control: Issues and trends.* New York: Academic Press, 1976.

Kerr, B. Task factors that influence selection and preparation for voluntary movements. In G. E. Stelmach (Ed.), *Information processing in motor control and learning.* New York: Academic Press, 1978.

Klapp, S. T. Response programming, as assessed by reaction time, does not establish commands for particular muscles. *Journal of Motor Behavior,* 1977, *9,* 301–312.

Klapp, S. T. Reaction time analysis of programmed control. In R. Hutton (Ed.), *Exercise and sport sciences reviews* (Vol. V). Santa Barbara, Calif.: Journal Publishing Affiliates, 1978.

Klemmer, E. T. Time uncertainty in simple reaction time. *Journal of Experimental Psychology,* 1956, *51,* 179–184.

Peterson, J. R. Response–response compatibility effects in a two-hand pointing task. *Human Factors,* 1965, *7,* 231–236.

Poulton, E. C. Unwanted range effects from using within-subject experimental designs. *Psychological Bulletin,* 1973, *80,* 113–121.

Rabbitt, P. M. A., Vyas, S. M., & Fearnley, S. Programming sequences of complex responses. In P. M. A. Rabbitt & S. Dornic (Eds.), *Attention and performance V.* London: Academic Press, 1975.

Ratz, H. C., & Ritchie, D. Operator performance on a chord keyboard. *Journal of Applied Psychology,* 1961, *45,* 303–308.

Rosenbaum, D. A. *Mental time and real time in the production of manual responses.* Paper presented at the Seventeenth Annual Meeting of the Psychonomic Society, St. Louis, 1976.

Rosenbaum, D. A. Human movement initiation: Specification of arm, direction, and extent. *Journal of Experimental Psychology: General,* in press.

Rosenbaum, D. A., & Patashnik, O. A mental clock setting process revealed by reaction times. In G. E. Stelmach (Ed.), *Tutorials in motor behavior*. Amsterdam: North-Holland Publishing Co., in press.

Schmidt, R. A. Proprioception and the timing of motor responses. *Psychological Bulletin*, 1971, *76*, 385–393.

Spirduso, W. W. Hemispheric lateralization and orientation in compensatory and voluntary movement. In G. E. Stelmach (Ed.), *Information processing in motor control and learning*. New York: Academic Press, 1978.

Sternberg, S. The discovery of processing stages: Extensions of Donders' method. In W. G. Koster (Ed.), *Attention and performance II. Acta Psychologica*, 1969, *30*, 276–315.

Sternberg, S., Monsell, S., Knoll, R. L., & Wright, C. E. The latency and duration of rapid movement sequences: Comparisons of speech and typewriting. In G. E. Stelmach (Ed.), *Information processing in motor control and learning*. New York: Academic Press, 1978.

Sternberg, S., Wright, C. E., Knoll, R. L., & Monsell, S. Motor programs in rapid speech: Additional evidence. In R. A. Cole (Ed.), *The perception and production of fluent speech*. Hillsdale, N.J.: Lawrence Erlbaum Associates, 1980.

Wing, A. M., & Kristofferson, A. B. The timing of interresponse intervals. *Perception & Psychophysics*, 1973, *13*, 455–460. (a)

Wing, A. M., & Kristofferson, A. B. Response delays and the timing of discrete motor responses. *Perception & Psychophysics*, 1973, *14*, 5–12. (b)

6 Response Planning and the Organization of Speed Movements

D. J. Glencross
Discipline of Psychology
The Flinders University of South Australia
Bedford Park, South Australia

ABSTRACT

A series of experiments is reported, concerned with the advance planning of movements, that were themselves systematically varied in the complexity of their serial organization. Response complexity is defined in terms of the response units that are mapped onto an invariant motor schema. Response units are specified in three forms: (1) the number of muscle synergies; (2) the number of phases of muscle activity; (3) the number of sequencing instructions. Probe RT procedures are used with speed movements that varied systematically in terms of these three factors. Probes are presented both before and during the primary movement. The results show that probe RT is lengthened for probes presented during the latency phase of the movement, as well as during the early part of some of the movements. The lengthening of the probe RT is closely related to the number of sequencing instructions. It is proposed that two forms of advance planning have been observed: one in which the whole response is planned in advance of execution and another in which the planning continues into the early stages of the execution of the movement. The latter form of planning is associated with the more complex movements.

INTRODUCTION

What details of a response can be planned in advance of its execution? The answer to this question is a primary objective of motor control theory; for it relates to the central issues of the organization of sequences of action that are "too fast" to be controlled by long-loop feedback mechanisms and the serial organization of complex patterns of movement that characterize the skilled performer (Glencross, 1977; Lashley, 1951). This chapter addresses the issue of response planning in a series of experiments in which the complexity of the serial organization of the response was systematically varied in a speed movement.

Response Planning

Reaction time (RT) has been used as an index of the planning of the response, on the general assumption that preparation for a complex movement would take longer than that for a simple movement, particularly if this preparation is completed prior to the actual start of the movement phase. However, the results from an extended series of experiments, in which duration, extent, direction, and sequencing of the movement were varied, have been conflicting and contradictory (Glencross, 1972, 1973; Henry, 1960, 1961; Klapp & Wyatt, 1976; Klapp, Wyatt, & Lingo, 1974). It is suggested that this pattern of equivocal findings is primarily a consequence of the unsuitability of RT as an index of the variety of planning possibilities and also the result of the inadequate theoretical framework defining response complexity. First, it is proposed that RT measures may not be appropriate in the investigation of response planning, particularly when the planning may take a variety of forms. For example, the response could be planned completely in advance of the stimulus and just triggered into action. Again, the planning may occur partly before the stimulus or may continue after the stimulus, or even during the early phase of execution. In all of these instances RT will not be a valid expression of the duration of the advance planning of the response.

An alternative to the RT technique that may permit a more direct investigation of the range of planning possibilities is the probe RT procedure (Posner & Keele, 1969). The potential value of this procedure is that it will permit inferences about processes occurring not only during the preparatory phase of the response but also during the actual execution. For example, Posner and Keele (1969), in a wrist-rotation task to a target, found that probe RT was lengthened most at the initiation and end of the movement (in the region of the target). Further, the probe was lengthened more for the small-target condition, but only for probes presented during the latter stages of the movement. In a similar study Ells (1973) demonstrated that the lengthening of the probe was related to the number of possible alternative actions, when the probe occurred before the actual movement. However, probe RT during the movement was related to the specified precision of the movement. In the present study it is proposed to use this probe procedure to investigate more specifically the planning of responses that varied systematically in the complexity of their serial organization.

Response Complexity

It is apparent that the motor system can produce an extensive variety of movements and that different movements (and hence muscles) can subserve identical goals. Thus one might speculate that at one level of the motor control system is a general representation or schema of a class of movements, independent of the units of action (Bernstein, 1967; Turvey, 1977). The idiosyncratic features of a particular response are then specified by the response units and parametric details that are mapped onto the general framework (schema), presumably during the preparatory phase of the response. Although this description has wide acceptance (Connolly, 1970; Fitch & Turvey, 1978), the actual representation of the response units, the parametric specifications, the interaction of these properties and the time course of their preparation are not clearly understood. An attempt was made in the present study to increase response complexity by manipulating the organization of a number of response units onto an invariant motor scheme (a lateral arm sweep movement). Tentatively, a response unit was described in three possible forms:

1. The number of agonistic and antagonistic muscle synergies involved in the movement.
2. The number of phases of activity of the agonistic and antagonistic muscle synergies.
3. The number of sequencing instructions required to pattern the specified movement.[1]

These forms are clarified with respect to the movements used in the present experiments (see Table 6.1).

Sweep S. The basic task was a lateral arm sweep in which the arm was moved rapidly from the midline, horizontally a distance of some 35 cm. There were no target constraints. In making the movement the shoulder joint was extended and abducted and the elbow joint extended. It is assumed that in this movement there is only *one* functional synergy, the extensors of the shoulder and elbow; there is *one* phase of muscle activity; and there is *one* sequencing instruction, the "sweep" instruction.

---

[1]The number of sequencing instructions may be closely related to the number of halts or pauses in the movement sequence and, as such, may be inextricably associated with the timing of the segments of the action.

TABLE 6.1
Task Analyses in Terms of Muscle Synergies, Phase of Muscle Activity and
Sequencing Instructions

Task	Movement Pattern	Muscle Synergies	Phases of Activity	Number of Instructions
Sweep S		(1) Extension	(1)	(1) Sweep
Reversal R		(2) Extension Flexion	(2)	(3) Sweep Reverse Sweep
1-tap T		(2) Extension Flexion	(3)	(3) Sweep Tap Sweep
2-tap 2T		(2) Extension Flexion	(5)	(4) Sweep Tap Tap Sweep
2-tap 2TR Reversal		(2) Extension Flexion	(5)	(4) Sweep Tap Tap Sweep

Reverse R.   The lateral arm sweep was modified so that after traveling 35 cm the movement had to be reversed and the hand returned to the start. In this case there are *two* functional synergies, the extensors and the flexors that reverse the action; there are *two* phases of muscle activity; and there are *three* sequencing instructions: sweep, reverse, sweep.

Single-Tap T.   The lateral arm sweep was further modified so that after 20 cm the hand had to tap a large target and then continue. Thus, there are *two* functional synergies, *three* phases of muscle activity, and *three* sequencing instructions: sweep, tap, sweep.

Double-Tap 2T. If the lateral arm sweep is further modified so that midway through the movement the hand has to tap two adjacent large targets and then continue, there will be *two* functional synergies, *five* phases of muscle activity, and *four* sequencing instructions: sweep, tap, tap, sweep.

Double-Tap Reversal 2TR. If the hand is required to tap first the further target block and then reverse to the closer target block and then to reverse and continue the sweep, there are *two* functional synergies, *five* phases of muscle activity, and *four* sequencing instructions: sweep, tap, tap, sweep.

Speed movements of relatively short duration (< 500 msec) were used to ensure that the planning of the response would occur, in part at least, before the initiation of the movement. Further, it is assumed that by making the accuracy constraints minimal, the use of feedback for control purposes would be avoided. Finally, if the movements were made in a simple reaction-time situation, any confounding effects due to perceptual and response selection would be controlled. Probe RT procedures were used, and probes were inserted during the preparatory phase of the movement as well as during the execution of the movement.

EXPERIMENT 1

Method

Subjects. Six right-handed subjects aged between 20 and 36 years participated in the experiment.

Apparatus and Task. In this experiment the first three tasks outlined in Table 6.1 were used, namely the lateral arm sweep (S), the single-tapping action (T), and the reversing action (R).

The subject sat at a table on which was centrally mounted a box containing two response keys 10 cm apart; 9 cm above and slightly behind the right response key was a neon pea lamp that served as the stimulus for the arm sweep response; 15 cm to the right of the right response key was a photoelectric switch and a further 20 cm to the right in the same horizontal plane was a second photoelectric switch. The vertical distance between the light cells in the switches was 18 cm. In between these switches were two adjacent target blocks each 8 × 23 cm mounted at the same height as the response keys. The arm movement started from the right response key that was depressed by the right index finger on the commencement of each trial. At the completion of each movement the subject was required to hold the arm in place until the signal for the next trial was presented.

The probe task was an auditory tone of 1000 Hz and approximately 25 dB delivered to the subject over headphones. The subject was required to release the left response key on the occurrence of the probe tone. The probes occured randomly at intervals of 100, 250, 350, 450, or 650 msec after the onset of the visual stimulus used to initiate the movement response. The control was a condition in which the probe occurred after the movement had been completed (at 1000 msec after the visual stimulus). A probe was presented on each trial except for a few catch trials.

A second auditory signal of 3000 Hz was used to indicate the beginning of a new trial and also served to initiate the foreperiod, which varied randomly between 1 and 4 sec.

Signal presentation and data collection was controlled by a PDP 11/10 computer. The measures recorded were reaction for the movement response (stimulus RT), reaction time to the probe (probe RT), intermediate movement time (MT) (to the first photoelectric switch), and total movement time (MT) (to the second photoelectric switch).

Procedure.   The procedure was essentially a simple reaction-time situation. The subject was informed of which movement response was required for the particular block of trials. Following completion of the first block of trials the procedure was repeated with the second movement response and then again with the third. All subjects performed each movement condition in a counterbalanced order in accordance with a 3 × 3 Latin square (S, T, R; T, R, S; R, S, T).

Prior to the beginning of each block of trials extensive practice was given. When it was apparent that both the stimulus RTs and probe RTs showed some consistency, then 90 randomly presented test trials were conducted (15 trials per probe). Knowledge of results was given after the practice trials but not after the test trials. A new trial was initiated every 6 sec.

Subjects were instructed to make the movement response as fast as possible; they were also advised to respond to the auditory probe as quickly as possible but to consider the movement task of primary importance.

Results and Discussion

The results are based upon median probe RT, median stimulus RT, mean intermediate MT, and mean total MT. The data were screened for extreme scores using a rejection criterion of $p \leq .043$ after Snedecor and Cochran (1967).

Probe RT.   The main results of interest is the lengthening of probe RT, relative to the control probe RT, when the probe occurs before and during the movement, for each of the three tasks. For the purposes of analysis, probes

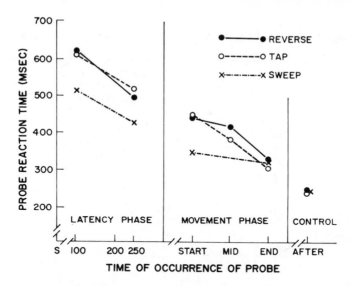

FIG. 6.1.   Probe reaction times during sweep (S), tap (T), and reversal (R) movements in Experiment 1.

that occurred at the same temporal phase, before (latency phase) and during the movement (start, mid, end phases), were compared. The results are shown in Fig. 6.1.

There was a highly significant main effect of time-of-probe occurrence, $F(4, 24) = 39.94$, $p < .01$, but not for movement complexity, $F(2, 6) = 2.43$, $p > .05$. However, there was a significant probe occurrence × movement complexity interaction, $F(8, 24) = 4.80$, $p < .01$. Post hoc tests of simple effects were based on Lindquist's (1953) critical difference procedure. First, comparing the effects of the time of occurrence of the probe before and during the movement, with the control probe, when the probe occurred before the movement (during the latency phase), probe RT was significantly lengthened on the three movement conditions compared with the control probe RT ($p < .01$). Probes that occurred during the actual tapping and reversing movements at the "start" and "mid" phases were significantly lengthened but not those presented at the end of the movement. The probes during the sweeping movement were not lengthened significantly.

Second, comparing the probe RTs for each movement, the probe RTs during the tapping and reversing movements were not significantly different, at any phase. However, these probe RTs were significantly longer than those for probes presented during the sweeping movement at the latency phase and the start of the movement ($p < .01$) and to a lesser extent at the mid phase ($p < .05$) but not at the end of the movement.

TABLE 6.2

Means, Medians and S.D. for Stimulus Reaction Time and Movement Time in
Experiment 1

| | Task | Time of Probe Occurrence | | |
		Latency Phase[a]	Movement Phase[a]	Control
Median	Sweep M	333	330	339
Stimulus	S.D.	29	29	20
Reaction	Tap M	320	317	332
	S.D.	31	31	43
Time	Reverse M	341	334	340
(msec)	S.D.	29	30	24
Mean	Sweep M	149	149	155
Total	S.D.	28	28	30
Movement	Tap M	334	335	333
	S.D.	66	61	64
Time	Reverse M	147[b]	148	143
(msec)	S.D.	37	39	28
Mean	Sweep M	86	86	89
Intermediate	S.D.	24	21	20
Movement	Tap M	111	111	112
	S.D.	27	25	28
Time	Reverse M	78	80	82
(msec)	S.D.	20	18	19

[a]Time of probe occurrence collapsed.
[b]Time measured for outward movement only.

Stimulus RT. The RTs for the start of each movement were just significantly different, $F(2, 6) = 7.05$, $p < .05$ (see Table 6.2). The latency of the
tapping movement was shorter than the latency for the sweep or reverse
movements, which were not significantly different. There was a significant
effect of time-of-probe occurrence, $F(5, 15) = 7.09$, $p < .01$, but this was
largely due to the longer latencies for the control trials compared with the test
(probed) trials.

Movement Time. There was a significant main effect of movement complexity on both total movement time, $F(2, 6) = 70.31$, $p < .01$, and intermediate movement time, $F(2, 6) = 40.16$, $p < .01$, the tapping response being the
slowest. There were no other main effects or interactions (see Table 6.2).

It is apparent that the presentation of the probe does not disrupt the
primary movement task, as both total and intermediate movement times for
the control and test trials are not significantly different. Even though the
stimulus RTs are lengthened on the control trials compared to the test trials,

this suggests some enhancing effect rather than a disruption to the task. Thus, because the probe has little or no effect on the primary tasks, then the changes in probe RTs can be related to the processing demands of the movements. The observed probe RTs suggest that the planning of the reversing and tapping movements is more complex and demanding than that of the sweeping movement. The differences seem to be more a consequence of the "number of instructions" than just the phases of activity. This issue is followed up in Experiment 2 where the complexity of the response was further increased.

EXPERIMENT 2

In the second experiment a single-tapping action was compared with a double-tapping action. It was hypothesised that if complexity was related to the number of sequencing instructions or phases of activity, then the probe RTs would be further delayed during the latency phase of the double-tapping action compared with the single-tapping action.

Method

Subjects.   There were 15 right-handed subjects from an introductory psychology course, with an age range from 18.5 to 29 years.

Apparatus and Task.   There were three conditions as described in Table 6.1: (1) the single-tapping action as used in Experiment 1; (2) a double-tapping action in which the subject was to make two taps, one on each of the target blocks that were separated by a cardboard barrier 5 cm high; (3) a new control condition was introduced in which when the stimulus occurred, no movement was made but the subject still responded to the probes when they occurred. In each of these conditions the probes were presented randomly at 100, 300, 450, 500 msec after the first stimulus. A control probe also occurred at 1000 msec. Probes occurred on approximately 80% of the trials. All other details were the same as for Experiment 1, although the first photoelectric switch was now placed between the two target blocks to give a better estimate of movement time to the first target.

The procedure and design were as reported for Experiment 1. In addition, however, each movement task alone and the probe alone were included as controls.

Results and Discussion

Probe RT.   For the median probe RTs (see Fig. 6.2) there were significant main effects-of-movement complexity, $F(1, 4) = 13.32, p < .02$, and of time-of-probe occurrence, $F(4, 16) = 125.01, p < .01$. There was also a significant

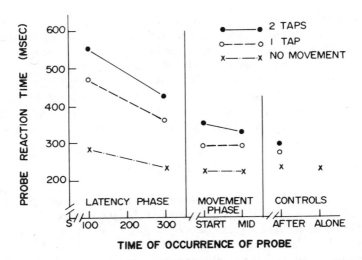

FIG. 6.2.   Probe reaction times during one-tap (1T), two-tap (2T), and "no" movements in Experiment 2.

movement complexity × probe occurrence interaction, $F(4, 16) = 7.90, p <$ .01. The tests of the simple effects showed that probe RT was significantly lengthened on the double-tapping task compared with the single-tapping condition, particularly when the probes occurred during the latency phase ($p < .01$), and also at the start of the actual movement ($p < .05$) but not in the region of the targets. The probe delays for both tasks were longer when the probe occurred during the latency phase of the movement than when it occurred during the movement phase.

Stimulus RT.   The latencies of the two-movement tasks were significantly different, $F(1, 4) = 14.74, p < .02$, with the latency of the single-tap condition being longer than that for the two-tap condition, although this difference was not apparent in control-alone trials (see Table 6.3). There was a significant effect of time-of-probe occurrence, $F(4, 20) = 12.21, p < .01$, and a small-movement complexity × probe occurrence interaction, $F(5, 20) = 2.80, p <$ .05. However, there were no differences in stimulus RT when probed trials were compared with the trials on which no probe occurred (1 tap, 321 V 339 msec; 2 tap, 305 V 308 msec).

Movement Time.   As would be expected there was a higly significant difference in total-movement time between the two tapping conditions, $F(1, 4) = 250.37, p < .01$, the double-tapping action taking almost twice as long as the single tap (see Table 6.3). There was a similar difference for intermediate-movement time, $F(1, 4) = 84.80, p < .01$. It is clear that one of the effects of

TABLE 6.3
Means, Medians, and S.D. for Stimulus Reaction Time and Movement Time in
Experiment 2

		Time of Probe Occurrence			
				Controls	
	Task	Latency Phase[a]	Movement Phase[a]	After	Alone
Median	1-tap M	316	325	334	292
Stimulus	S.D.	31	36	38	27
Reaction	2-tap M	297	312	309	293
Time	S.D.	26	35	31	29
(msec)					
Mean	1-tap M	224	235	236	211
Total	S.D.	53	56	60	50
Movement	2-tap M	408	423	429	403
Time	S.D.	55	59	56	53
(msec)					
Mean	1-tap M	115	119	124	107
Intermediate	S.D.	28	28	34	25
Movement	2-tap M	221	228	224	207
Time	S.D.	28	29	33	25
(msec)					

[a]Time-of-probe occurrence collapsed.

making a second tap is to slow down the first phase of the movement, in approaching, striking, and leaving the first target.

The introduction of the "no-movement" control condition in this experiment provides strong support for the conclusion that the observed differences in probe RT on the two-movement tasks must be associated with response factors. Further, the results support those from the first experiment that the differential lengthening of probe RT is related to the increased complexity in the movement task, particularly when the probes occurred during the latency phase.

EXPERIMENT 3

In Experiment 3, two-tapping actions were compared in which the phases of muscle activity were quite different but in which the number of sequencing instructions were the same. It was hypothesized that if complexity was related to the number of instructions rather than the phases of activity, the probe RTs would be similar on both tasks.

Method

Subjects.   Six right-handed subjects with an age range from 21 to 31 years were used.

Apparatus and Task.   There were three conditions (see Table 6.1): (1) the double-tapping action described in Experiment 2; (2) a reverse double-tapping action in which the subject first moved to the more distant target block and then back to the nearer target block and then on through the second photo-electric switch; (3) the no-movement control condition as used in Experiment 2. Probes occurred randomly at 100, 300, 450, and 550 msec after the first stimulus. The control probe occurred at 1500 msec and the probe-alone controls were the same as for Experiment 2. The procedure and all other details were the same as for Experiment 2.

Results and Discussion

Probe RT.   There were significant main effects of movement complexity, $F(2, 10) = 25.67$, $p < .01$, and time-of-probe occurrence, $F(4, 20) = 20.92$, $p < .01$. The movement complexity × probe occurrence interaction was not significant. The probe RTs for the two-tapping conditions were not significantly different at any of the probe positions. However, the probe RTs for the no-movement control condition were significantly shorter than those for the two-tapping movements ($p < .01$) (see Fig. 6.3).

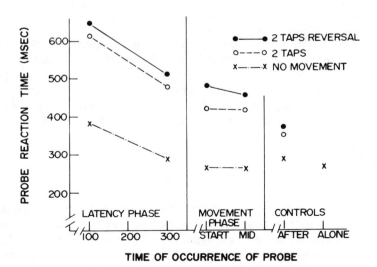

FIG. 6.3.   Probe reaction times during two-tap (2T), two-tap reversal (2TR), and "no" movements in Experiment 3.

Stimulus RT. The difference in stimulus RT between the two-tapping tasks was not significant, $F(1, 5) = 0.11$, $p > .05$, (2T = 350 msec, 2TR = 345 msec). There were no other significant main effects or interactions.

Movement Time. There was no main effect of movement complexity on total MT, $F(1, 5) = 5.11$, $p > .05$, (2T = 446 msec, 2TR = 455 msec), but this effect was significant for intermediate MT, $F(1, 5) = 43.58$, $p < .01$, which is a consequence of the first tap occurring on the second target for the reversal condition (2T = 277 msec, 2TR = 148 msec).

The results of Experiment 3 corroborate the finding from Experiment 1, that it is the number of instructions rather than the phases of activity that is important in defining response complexity. This finding seems to hold for the two double-tapping actions studied, as well as for the single-tap and reversal actions reported in Experiment 1.

In the experiments so far there has been a consistent finding that RTs to probes presented during the early phase of the tapping movements were significantly lengthened. This is an interesting finding, for it was proposed that if a movement was planned completely in advance and then run off ballistically, then probes presented during the actual movement (execution) phase would not be lengthened. This seemed to occur for the sweep movement in Experiment 1 but not for any other movements studied. Several explanations may account for this finding; for example, the planning may still be ongoing even though the movement has started, or attention may be directed to feedback from the movement. In order to investigate these two explanations, two further experiments were conducted in which related visual feedback was eliminated during the movement task.

EXPERIMENTS 4 AND 5

In these two experiments the single-tapping action and double-tapping action were performed under normal conditions and when vision was excluded. These two experiments are described together.

Method

Subjects. Nine right-handed subjects were used in both experiments with an age range from 18 to 36 years.

Apparatus and Task. In each experiment three movement conditions were used: (1) the lateral arm sweep as used previously; (2) the single-tapping action (in Experiment 4), the double-tapping action (in Experiment 5); and (3) these same tapping actions with vision excluded. The only change in the apparatus was that for the tapping-blind conditions a cardboard shield was placed between the subject and the apparatus in such a way that the visual stimulus was still in view, but the right response key, the right hand and arm, the photoelectric switches and the tapping target blocks were not visible. The probes occurred randomly at 50, 100, 200, 350, and 500 msec after the first stimulus. A control probe occurred at 1000 msec. The other controls and procedure were essentially the same as those of Experiment 2.

Results and Discussion

Probe RT. The results of both experiments were very similar, and in particular that the probe RTs on each of the tapping conditions (normal versus blind) were not significantly different at any of the times of occurrence during the latency phase of each movement (see Fig. 6.4 and 6.5).

In Experiment 4 there was a significant main effect of time-of-probe occurrence, $F(5, 30) = 46.15, p < .01$, but not for movement complexity, $F(2, 12) = 2.91, p > .05$. There was a small-movement complexity × probe occurrence interaction, $F(10, 60) = 2.10, p < .05$. The only significant difference in probe RT on the two single-tapping conditions was in the region of the target, where there was a slight lengthening of probe RT for the blind-tapping condition $(p < .05)$.

In Experiment 5 there was a significant main effect of time-of-probe occurrence, $F(5, 30) = 44.92, p < .01$, and movement complexity, $F(2, 12) = 12.93, p < .01$. There was also a significant-movement complexity × probe

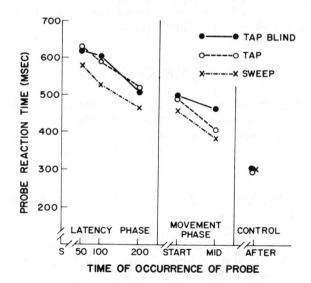

FIG. 6.4. Probe reaction times during sweep (S), one-tap (T), and one-tap blind (TB) movements in Experiment 4.

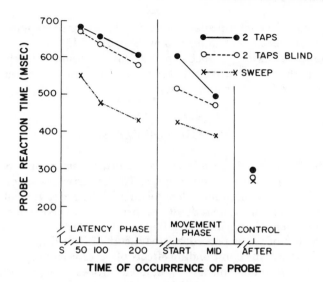

FIG. 6.5.   Probe reaction times during sweep (S), two-tap (2T), and two-tap blind (2TB) movements in Experiment 5.

occurrence interaction, $F(10, 60) = 4.48$, $p < .01$. The probe RTs on both double-tapping conditions were similar for all corresponding times of probe occurrence, except at the start of the movement where the probe RT for the blind condition was significantly longer ($p < .05$) than that for the visual condition.

Stimulus RT.   In both experiments the movement complexity effect was not significant ($p > .05$). However, there was a significant main effect of time-of-probe occurrence for Experiment 4, $F(5, 30) = 6.57$, $p < .01$, and for Experiment 5, $F(5, 30) = 3.53$, $p < .01$).

Movement Time.   As would be expected the total movement time for tapping movements was slower than the sweeping movement, and in Experiments 4 and 5 the blind-tapping conditions were 40 and 47 msec, respectively, slower than the corresponding "visual" condition. In Experiment 4 the main effect-of-movement complexity was $F(2, 12) = 51.34$, $p < .01$, and for Experiment 5, $F(2. 12) = 99.93$, $p < .01$. For intermediate-movement time there was no significant effect-of-movement complexity in Experiment 4, $F(2, 12) = 3.51$, $p > .05$, and a small effect in Experiment 5, $F(2, 12) = 4.49$, $p < .05$. There were no other significant main effects or interactions.

The results of these two experiments, taken together show that probe RT is largely unaffected by the exclusion of vision in the tapping movements.

Further because the intermediate movement times for the tapping conditions in each experiment were similar and in the order of 150–175 msec, it is likely that the tapping phase is planned in part at least in advance. It is thus apparent that the lengthening of probe RT is not associated with attention directed to visual feedback for control purposes.

GENERAL DISCUSSION

The probe RT procedure was used in the present series of experiments to investigate response planning processes. The underlying assumption of this approach is that the differential lengthening of the probe RT will reflect the processing (attention) demands of the primary movement tasks (Posner, 1978). A number of important methodological considerations are incorporated with the use of probe procedures (McLeod, 1977, 1978). In particular, in the present study, the confounding effects of perceptual and response selection processes were controlled or eliminated. Probes were presented temporally rather than spatially in order to reduce anticipation and expectancy effects. Further the primary movement task and secondary probe task involved two highly compatible (although different) manual responses, which although competing for the same common process were unlikely to conflict through structural interference. Finally, although probe RT reflects the interval between the probe stimulus and response and although it is not always evident when the processing actually occurs, however it is the difference in probe RTs on tasks of differing complexity that provides the basis for interpreting the differential processing demands of two primary movement tasks.

Probes During the Latency Phase

In all the present experiments, RTs to probes presented during the latency phase of the movement task were lengthened significantly relative to RTs to probes presented after the movement or alone or when no movement was required to the first stimulus. Thus, apparently the differences in probe RT between the movement conditions are the result of factors associated with response processes. In as much as the situation was a simple reaction-time setup, these response processes must be concerned with response preparation or planning and not the selection between alternative responses. Further, even though there is a clear psychological refractory period effect to probes presented during the latency phase of the movements, the process demands are indicated by the difference in probe RT between movement tasks rather than the absolute value.

The most significant differences in probe RT were obtained when the arm sweep was compared with the tapping and reversing responses (Experiment 1) and the single-tap was compared with the double-tap response (Experiment 2). The differences between tapping and reversing responses (Experiment 1) and the double-tap and double-tap reversal responses (Experiment 3) were not significant. Relating these differences to the analysis of task dimensions in Table 1, the lengthening of probe RT is most closely related to the number of sequencing instructions and not the phases of muscle activity. Although "sequencing instruction" has been defined quite arbitrarily, it is an attempt to specify in a function-descriptive sense the units of action (rather than the units of movement). This distinction is somewhat similar in principle to that of Sternberg, Monsell, Knoll, and Wright (1978), who found that in vocal responses the "stress groups" were more closely related to latency than the number of syllables. It seems that what is important is the number of sequencing instructions rather than the actual "content" of the instruction. Thus in Experiment 1, the instruction to "reverse" and the instruction "to tap" produced equivalent lengthening in probe RT, as did the double-tap and double-tap reversal instructions in Experiment 3, However, in each case the sequence of movement and detailed pattern of the muscles' activity were quite different.

Probes During the Movement Phase

It was proposed that if a response was planned completely in advance of its execution, then RT would not be lengthened for a probe presented during the movement phase. However, there was clear evidence in all the experiments of the significant lengthening of RTs to probes presented at the start of some movements and also in some cases in the midphase (target region) of the movement.

Why should probe RT be lengthened at the start of the movement? Welford (1977) has suggested that part of the lengthening of RT in psychological refractory period experiments is associated with a feedback monitoring signal that "clears" the decision mechanism. However, this explanation cannot account for the present finding that the lengthening in RT to probes presented at the start of the movement is related to the complexity of the response. For the same reason it is unlikely that the differential lengthening of probe RT is a result of structural interference. Not only are the initial actions of the primary movement and probe response highly compatible, but also the probe stimulus always occurred after the primary movement had commenced.

On the other hand, if the planning of the complex response is still ongoing, whereas the simpler response has been completed or will be completed sooner than that of the complex response, then the lengthening of the probe will be sensitive to response complexity, as indeed the data suggest; that is, the central processor (whatever its form) is still committed to planning the response, even though the actual execution of that response has commenced.

During execution, when the probes occurred in the region of the target, there was some evidence that the RTs were lengthened for the reversal movement compared with the sweep movement in Experiment 1. There were also small differences in probe RT for the tapping movements in Experiments 2 and 3, but these were not significant. Are these differences associated with attention directed to visual feedback for control purposes? The results of the two blind-tapping experiments, in which the probe delays in the target regions were approximately equivalent under blind and visual conditions, would seem to rule such an explanation. Of course kinaesthetic information was still available and the removal of visual feedback that usually dominates other feedback sources in most situations (Klein & Posner, 1974) may force the subject to attend to the more novel and diffuse kinaesthetic feedback. But, because of the speed of movement, such information will be out of phase for current control purposes. However, it is still possible that subjects may attend to the target areas to update and amend the response on subsequent trials.

A further general finding relates to stimulus RT. These RTs for the primary tasks did not consistently reflect the complexity of the response as Henry (1960) had proposed. The latencies reported for the range-of-movements studies in the present experiments were generally not significantly different. Klapp and Wyatt (1976) and Klapp et al., (1974) have argued that relatively simple responses can be "preprogrammed in preparation" for the stimulus in a simple reaction-time situation; that is, simple RT is independent of response complexity. However, it was proposed earlier in the chapter that where the planning of the response may take a variety of forms, then RT was not a valid measure of the planning process. This seems to be the case in the present experiments, where the planning of relatively complex movements seemed to continue even after execution of the action had commenced. Indeed in this case one may well expect to find "reduced" latencies for complex responses. Such a time-sharing strategy may shorten the duration of the whole task and thus increase the overall efficiency of performance.

Finally, the potentiality of the probe procedure to investigate some of the issues of motor control raised in this paper should be evident from the present series of experiments. Indeed if the position of McLeod (1977, 1978) is elaborated, then the use of a number of different probes may permit a task analysis and profile description in terms of its component processes, for example, at various stages of skill acquisition, in the comparison of skilled and unskilled operators and in the direct comparison of tasks themselves.

ACKNOWLEDGMENTS

I am grateful to Alan Welford and Michael Posner who both made valuable comments on aspects of this work.

I would like to acknowledge the assistance given by John Gould, Judith Nilsson, and Paul Tildesley in the conduct of the experiments and data analyses.

This project was supported by a grant from the Australian Research Grants Commission.

REFERENCES

Bernstein, N. *The coordination and regulation of movement.* Oxford, England: Pergamon Press, 1967.

Connolly, K. J. Skill development problems and plans. In K. J. Connolly (Ed.), *Mechanisms of motor skill development.* London: Academic Press, 1970.

Ells, J. A. Analysis of temporal and attentional aspects of movement. *Journal of Experimental Psychology,* 1973, *99,* 10–21.

Fitch, H. L., & Turvey, M. T. On the control of activity: Some remarks from an ecological point of view. In D. M. Landers & R. W. Christina (Eds.), *Psychology of motor behavior and sport.* Champaign, Ill.: Human Kinetic Pub., 1978.

Glencross, D. J. Latency and response complexity. *Journal of Motor Behavior,* 1972, *4,* 448–458.

Glencross, D. J. Response complexity and the latency of different movement patterns. *Journal of Motor Behavior,* 1973, *5,* 95–104.

Glencross, D. J. Control of skilled movements. *Psychological Bulletin,* 1977, *84,* 14–29.

Henry, F. M. Increased response latency for complicated movements and a "memory drum" theory of neuromotor reaction. *Research Quarterly,* 1960, *30,* 448–459.

Henry, F. M. Stimulus complexity, movement complexity, age, and sex in relation to reaction latency and speed in limb movements. *Research Quarterly,* 1961, *32,* 356–366.

Klapp, S. T., & Wyatt, E. P. Motor programming within a sequence of responses. *Journal of Motor Behavior,* 1976, *8,* 19–26.

Klapp, S. T., Wyatt, E. P., & Lingo, W. Response programming in simple and choice reaction times. *Journal of Motor Behavior,* 1974, *6,* 263–271.

Klein, R. M., & Posner, M. I. Attention to visual and kinaesthetic components of skill. *Brain Research,* 1974, *71,* 401–411.

Lashley, K. S. The problem of serial order in behavior. In L. A. Jeffress (Ed.), *Cerebral mechanisms in behavior,* New York: Wiley, 1951.

Lindquist, E. G. *Design and analyses of experiments in psychology and education.* Boston: Houghton Mifflin, 1953.

McLeod, P. A dual task response modality effect: Support for multiprocessor models of attention. *Quarterly Journal of Experimental Psychology,* 1977, *29,* 651–667.

McLeod, P. Does probe RT measure central processing demand? *Quarterly Journal of Experimental Psychology,* 1978, *30,* 83–89.

Posner, M. I. *Chronometric explorations of mind.* Hillsdale, N.J.: Lawrence Erlbaum Associates, 1978.

Posner, M. I., & Keele, S. W. Attention demands of movement. *Proceedings of XVIIth Congress of Applied Psychology, Amsterdam, Zeitlinger,* 1969.

Snedecor, G. M., & Cochran, W. G. *Statistical methods.* Ames, Iowa: University Press, 1967.

Sternberg, S., Monsell, S., Knoll, R. L., & Wright, C. E. The latency and duration of rapid movement sequences: Comparisons of speech and typewriting. In G. Stelmach (Ed.), *Information processing in motor control & learning.* New York: Academic Press, 1978.

Turvey, M. T. Preliminaries to a theory of action with reference to vision. In R. Shaw & J. Bransford (Eds.), *Perceiving, acting and knowing: Toward an ecological psychology.* Hillsdale, N.J.: Lawrence Erlbaum Associates, 1977.

Welford, A. T. Serial reaction times, continuity of task, single-channel effects and age. In S. Dornic (Ed.), *Attention and performance VI.* Hillsdale, N.J.: Lawrence Erlbaum Associates, 1977.

II STIMULUS CLASSIFICATION AND IDENTIFICATION

7

Models of Identification

J. E. Keith Smith
University of Michigan
Ann Arbor, Michigan
United States

ABSTRACT

A number of models of the identification experiment (Luce, 1968) are presented and compared. The Thurstonian successive intervals model is the only one depending explicitly on the notion of distance, but it has difficulty in dealing with more than one dimension of variation. The remainder of the models describe the data in terms of response bias and pairwise similarity, leaving the notion of distance aside.

Aside from the Thurstonian models, the remainder are all closely related to "sophisticated guessing" as defined by Broadbent (1967). One of these, proposed by Nakatani (1970), is promising but leads to considerable difficulties in parameter estimation and has a somewhat troublesome process interpretation. A new model presented here, called *symmetric sophisticated guessing* (SGM) has a reasonable process interpretation, but in its most general form it has too many parameters to be estimated. However, it does impose testable conditions on the data, and several specializations including Townsend's stimulus activation model (1971) are discussed.

The major point of this chapter is that all SGM are special cases of the Luce biased choice model (1968). The biased choice model is a log–linear model, and recent advances in the statistical theory of such models permit extensive exploratory analyses of identification data using maximum likelihood techniques.

Several examples of such analyses are included to illustrate the range of possibilities.

INTRODUCTION

A ubiquitous paradigm in experimental psychology is that of the identification experiment (Luce, 1963). Briefly, the subject is asked which of a finite set of possible stimuli has been presented on a particular trial. The choice is made difficult by degrading or deforming the stimulus, by making the presentation time brief, by making the subject react rapidly, or by making the subject remember the correct identification over a long period of time before being called upon to recall it. The correct response may depend only on the class to which the particular stimulus belongs, and the class definition may be exceedingly difficult to remember or learn.

In most cases the purpose of the experiment is to produce errors and to relate the number of errors or the kinds of errors to particular experimental conditions. In sensory psychophysics, the principal reason for using this method has been to reduce or control certain nonsensory variation in the measurement of detection probability. For that reason the existence of certain kinds of error is likely to be deplored, and subjects are trained not to make them. If, for example, in a four-alternative forced choice experiment, the subject is prone to say "3" when the stimulus is in the second interval but not so much when it is in the first or fourth, this suggests that the subject has more information about the stimulus than his correct percent score will indicate and that analysis ignoring this information will be incomplete.

In alphabet confusion studies, on the other hand, the overall number of errors is relatively uninteresting. The point of the study is to determine, for theoretical or practical reasons, which unique confusions are relatively common. The designer of an air defense console cannot afford to let operators confuse the symbol E for enemy with the symbol F for friendly.

In a memory study (Clark & Stafford, 1969) the experimenters were concerned with precisely which errors were common and how the pattern of errors was related to the three dimensions along which the stimuli varied. Holyoak and Glass (1978) had subjects remember which of a set of adjective quantifiers had been used in sentences heard earlier. They were interested in which of two theories best described the confusions generated in their experiment.

In our laboratory we have been concerned with the effects of stimulus probability and stimulus degradation in deadline reaction time and tachistoscopic tasks (Pachella, Smith, & Stanovich, 1978). By stimulus degradation I mean to include not only degradation of the visual stimulus itself but also short deadlines and short exposure durations. Our stimuli are alphabetic characters or sets of alphabetic characters (words, paralogs, etc.). As in the memory studies and other alphabet studies, and unlike the signal detection tasks, in our studies there is no direct physical characterization of the stimuli, so the use of number of errors itself as a dependent variable is not particularly valuable. Rather it is most valuable as a conditioning variable. It is important, when comparing kinds of confusions across experimental conditions or across subjects, to control the total proportion of errors. We have been quite successful in maintaining total errors at a relatively constant level ($\pm 5\%$) by adjusting exposure time or response deadline time appropriately for individual subjects, so much so that the number of total errors is used as a blocking or independent variable.

Although this chapter is concerned entirely with confusion matrices, it should be said that I do not imply that other aspects of the data obtained in these experiments are unimportant. Indeed they are likely to be crucial in distinguishing among the models discussed. Certainly the time the subject takes to make his response, the confidence with which he makes his identification, the effects of previous stimuli and previous responses on his behavior in the current trial, and his latent preferences among nonselected responses are potentially important data, and some of these are likely to be essential to a complete understanding of the underlying processes involved in identifying and recognizing stimuli.

My purpose here is to discuss several existing models of identification experiments and elucidate similarities and differences among them. Emphasis is given to paradigms using three or more stimuli, not because they are necessarily more important but because the patterns of confusion are richer and more interesting.

Conceptual Bases of the Identification Process

As far as I know, all models of the identification process concern two sources of variation affecting the data, which can be conveniently labeled as *response bias* and *similarity*. Response bias refers to the tendency of subjects to use some of the permissible responses more frequently than others. The label suggests that its originator felt this tendency was maladaptive, if not perverse. Later it is shown that for at least one of the models, even when stimuli are presented equally often, it may be quite adaptive to have severely different biases in order to maximize the number of correct responses. It is also demonstrated that different models, even when they agree precisely on the predicted data, may differ substantially in the numbers they use to describe response bias. This discussion and the literature seem implicitly to suggest that response bias is to some extent under the congitive control of the subject, but that is an open question at the moment.

The notion of stimulus similarity, however it is captured in a model, seems to be even more of an enigma. Some models interpret similarity as a distance in some conceptual space: The smaller the distance, the greater the similarity. Others, such as Nakatani's (1970) model and the version of sophisticated guessing, to be discussed here, are less ambitious, assuming only that the similarity of Stimuli A and B is directly related to the probability that the subject will remain undecided between A and B as responses even after the stimulus has been presented. Luce's biased choice model (1963), the principal topic here, is even more noncommittal, merely assigning a parameter to each pair, a parameter that is large when confusions between them are common. All of these interpretations use the term *similarity* as a symmetric concept, but even this interpretation has been called into question (Tversky, 1977). My own predilection is to retain the symmetry property in my use of the term, recognizing that everyday semantics may differ. Although the linguistic habits of subjects clearly lead them to use the term asymmetrically, I expect the analyst in most cases will be aided by separating such usage into its symmetric and antisymmetric parts and retaining the scientific term *similarity* for the symmetric part.

On the representation of similarity as distance, I remark that even the models just mentioned that do not do so do not deny the possibility. Rather their object is to arrive at a precise specification of data, leaving for later the empirical question of whether a distance function can be defined, at a reasonable cost in precision. It seems more valuable to discover a distance function than to impose one.

As a final point I must warn you about sharing my own failing of assuming that similarity is a kind of "given," a relational property of two stimuli independent of situation. This is clearly not so, if for no other reason than that similarity is a function of selective attention. Although I know of no experiment precise enough to justify my opinion, I feel certain that making a particular error expensive not only will reduce the response bias toward that error but also will change the measured similarity involved, whatever model is used.

MATHEMATICAL MODELS

Three general classes of model are discussed. These are the Thurstonian model, a special case of which is analyzed using the *method of successive intervals* (Torgerson, 1958). It captures the notion of similarity through a distance measure and the notion of response bias through unequal separations of category boundaries.

The second class of model is the *sophisticated guessing model* (SGM), originally described by Broadbent (1967). One SGM model is that proposed by Nakatani (1970), and another, briefly discussed earlier (Pachella et al., 1978) is fully developed here. Two special cases of the latter model are also discussed. These models characterize similarity by using the probability that a particular set of responses remains appropriate to the subject even after stimulus presentation. These particular sets are called *confusion sets,* and two stimuli are similar if the confusion sets containing both their appropriate responses have high probability. Response bias is introduced directly as the conditional probability of a particular response given that it is a member of the confusion set. These models are characterized by a partition of the identification process into two stages: an information input stage, yielding hopefully a small confusion set, followed by a response selection stage, in which a response is chosen from the confusion set.

The third class of model discussed is the *biased choice model* (BCM), proposed by Luce (1963). It holds that the probability of any particular response to a stimulus is proportional to the product of a similarity index between the stimulus presented and that stimulus appropriate to the particular response and a bias index appropriate to the response. Because the similarity index is assumed symmetric, any asymmetry in the data is attributed to differential response bias.

Most of the discussion is centered on SGM and BCM, the relations between them and appropriate statistical techniques.

Thurstonian Models

The only Thurstonian model that has been fully developed is appropriate for the case in which stimuli can be considered to be ordered along one dimension and this ordering is known, at least to the experimenter. It is assumed that when a stimulus is presented, a representation (called a *discriminal process*) is perceived by the subject and that for each stimulus the discriminal process has a distribution along the dimension characterized by a density function $f[(x - \mu_s / \sigma_s]$. Two stimuli are "similar" to the extent that

$$\frac{\mu_s - \mu_{s'}}{\sqrt{\sigma_s^2 + \sigma_{s'}^2}} \text{ is small.}$$

In order to make a response it is assumed that the subject has developed a collection of cut points, t_g or "category boundaries" dividing the dimension into M regions where M is the size of the simulus set, and the response S occurs when the discriminal process falls in the appropriate interval. If the interval assigned to S is short, the subject would be said to have a bias against saying S.

Excellent computer programs are available (Dorfman & Alf, 1968; Schonemann & Tucker, 1967) for deriving maximum likelihood estimates of μ, σ, and t, the category boundaries, if the density function f is assumed to be either normal or logistic. A program is described in Bock and Jones (1968) which calculates the asymptotically equivalent weighted least-squares solution for normal densities and which can be easily modified to use other density functions as well. Not only estimates but their standard errors are available.

It is conceptually straightforward to extend this model to higher dimensions of stimulus differences. The discriminal dispersion can be replaced by a vector, as can μ_s and σ_s, and the category boundaries by (say) bounding hyperplanes yielding again M regions for M responses. The problem is really the converse of the classical multiple discriminant function problem. Essentially we are given the subjects' classifications and misclassifications and asked to describe their discriminant functions. Unfortunately the problem is unsolved. This is the model preferred by Professor Broadbent (1967, p. 7). For another approach to this problem, using auxiliary data, see Getty, Swets, and Swets (this volume).

I should point out, before moving on to other models, that the *successive intervals* method was devised to solve quite another problem, essentially that of rating-scale psychophysics and similar choice paradigms. Those are not identification experiments and thus there is no identification function relating stimuli and responses and no "correct" and "incorrect" answers. It happens that the same estimation procedure is appropriate for both paradigms.

Sophisticated Guessing Models

To quote Broadbent (1967),

> A more complex model is one in which, even when a stimulus word has not been correctly perceived, the information which has arrived at the senses nevertheless rules out some English words as being impossible, and leaves a restricted set of alternatives as still consistent with what has been heard. If now S chooses at random out of this restricted set, but with a bias towards the more probable words, he will, just as in the simple model, score some correct answers on common words by chance [p. 2].

This brief paragraph comes very near a complete specification of a mathematical model. The important features of it from a mathematical point of view are, first, that it clearly places the response appropriate to the presented stimulus in the confusion set and, second, that it clearly specifies the response selection process. What it lacks is any specification of the relative frequencies of the various confusion sets. Nakatani's early model does this in one way; the class proposed here does it in another way. *Some* further specification is needed. As it stands, with M stimuli there are $2^M - 1$ possible confusion sets for any particular stimulus with the additional possibility that any multi-response set could have different probabilities of occurring depending on which stimulus had generated it, making a total of $M \cdot 2^M - 1$ parameters. Because the data consist of only $M(M - 1)$ independent observations, there is little hope of much detailed analysis. The Nakatani model takes one tack on this problem; I take another.

Nakatani's Model (1970)

Suppose that for each pair of stimuli, i and j, there is a probability P_{ij} that when one of them is presented, both appropriate responses will be in the confusion set. So stated, $P_{ij} = P_{ji}$. Then the probability of any particular confusion set when Stimulus i is presented is given by the formula

$$P_i(C) = \prod_{j=1}^{M} P_{ij}^{\delta_j} Q_{ij}^{1-\delta_j} \qquad \text{where } Q_{ij} = 1 - P_{ij}, \tag{1}$$

where $\delta_j = 1$ if $R_j \in C$; O otherwise. If we denote the class of confusion sets containing Response i as C_i and the class of sets containing both Response i and j as C_{ij} and the bias toward Response j as b_j, then the data matrix P_{ij} (conditional probability of response) given stimulus i is given by

$$P_{ij} = b_j \sum_{c=C_i} \frac{P_i(c)}{\sum_{r \in c} b_r} \qquad i \neq j \tag{2}$$

and

$$P_{ii} = 1 - \sum_{j \neq i} P_{ij}.$$

This system has $M - 1$ bias parameters, $M(M-1)/$ P_{ij}'s and thus leaves $(M - 1)(M - 2)/2$ degrees of freedom for testing goodness of fit. Nakatani used a heuristic algorithim for estimating parameters and attained quite impressive appearing fits to several classic data sets.

Aside from the difficulty of estimating parameters this model has an interesting feature. Although the pairwise confusion probabilities are symmetric, the observed confusion set probabilities $P_i(C)$ depend on the stimulus. In a five-element experiment, for example, the confusion set [1, 2, 3] would occur with different probabilities depending on the correct stimulus. Thus

$$P_1(C) = P_{12}P_{13}Q_{14}Q_{15}$$

while

$$P_2(C) = P_{12}P_{23}Q_{24}Q_{25}$$

Thus the set C might occur rather frequently when Stimulus 1 is presented and rather rarely when Stimulus 2 is presented. Under those conditions one might expect the sapient observer who had reached this point of indecision to hazard a guess of "1" much more frequently than $b_1/(b_1 + b_2 + b_3)$. This problem occurs unless $P_{ij} = k$ for all i, j.

Since I have been able to obtain equal or better fits to Nakatani's examples with the models yet to be discussed, I pass on to those models with the lingering wish that the estimation problem could be solved and crucial experiments devised to make the choice more testable.

Symmetric Sophisticated Guessing Model[1]

In order to avoid ascribing to the subject the less than adaptive mode of behavior just mentioned, my form of SGM assumes that $P_i(C)$ and $P_j(C)$ are identical if $C \epsilon C_{ij}$. This has two disadvantages. First, although there is a great reduction of parameters to be estimated, it is nowhere near sufficient. There remain $2^M - 1$ confusion sets, and although these are constrained by the boundary conditions,

$$\sum_{C \epsilon C_i} P(C) = 1$$

this leaves $2^M - M - 1$ parameters as well as $M - 1$ biases to be estimated, again from only $M(M - 1)$ observations. Second, no easily interpretable similarity indices remain.

A second feature of this model I consider to be a somewhat unexpected advantage: Although there are in general many more parameters than can be estimated, it may nevertheless not fit! To see this, consider the extensive form of the data matrix

$$P_{ij} = b_j \sum_{c = C_i} \frac{P(C)}{\sum_{r \epsilon c} b_r} \qquad i \neq j \tag{3}$$

$$P_{ii} = 1 - \sum_{j \neq i} P_{ij}.$$

Note that p_{ij} is written as the product of two terms, b_j and the remainder that is a symmetric function of i and j; call it $\theta_{ij} = \theta_{ji}$. This implies that

$$P_{ij}P_{jk}P_{ki} = P_{ji}P_{ik}P_{kj} \qquad \text{for all } i, j, \text{ and } k. \tag{4}$$

---

[1]Throughout the remainder of this chapter SGM refers to the symmetric sophisticated guessing model described here. Other sophisticated guessing models, besides this one and the Nakatani model, may yet be defined, not having either of the symmetry features characteristic of these models.

This condition is closely related to Tversky's feature additivity (1977, p. 332). This important quality, which comes up again later, need not agree with the data; if it does not, within reasonable statistical variation, the model must be rejected, even with its multitude of parameters.

Another somewhat weaker testable condition can be seen by writing the diagonal probability in more extensive form.

$$P_{jj} = P(j) + b_j \sum_{c=C_j} \frac{P(c)}{\sum_{r=c} b_r} \tag{5}$$

Because $C_{ij} \subseteq C_j$, it must be the case that $p_{ij} \leq p_{jj}$ for all i, j (i.e., the probability of correctly identifying Stimulus j is necessarily larger than the probability of misidentifying Stimulus i as Stimulus j). Although this seems a reasonable thing to expect of well-controlled data, it is not necessarily always observed.

Both these properties become important in exploring the relation between this model and the biased choice model.

Special Cases of SGM

As is usually helpful when dealing with overparametrized models, we now consider special cases obtained by making simplifying assumptions.

1. The Linear Guessing Model. If the stimuli vary along one dimension as in the Thurstonian discussion, a plausible reduction in the number of nonzero confusion set parameters is possible. If, for example, stimuli are ordered 1, 2, 3, 4, 5, one might expect any confusion set containing 2 and 4 to contain 3 as well. If one assumes that only stimulus sets contained in an interval have nonzero probability as confusion sets, the number of parameters to be estimated is greatly reduced. Indeed, taking into account the marginal constraints just mentioned, there remain only $M(M-1)/2$ independent confusion set probabilities to be estimated. An example of such a confusion matrix is presented in Table 7.1. In these fictitious data, confusion sets of size 2 have probability 0.10, sets of size 3 have probability 0.25, and the total confusion set has probability 0.10. Response biases were set at (0.4, 0.3, 0.2, 0.1). For example, the linear guessing model specifies that the Response 3 to Stimulus 1 is possible when either the confusion set (1, 2, 3) or the confusion set (1, 2, 3, 4) occur. If the confusion set (1, 2, 3) occurs, Response 3 is emitted with probability $2/9 [.2/(.4 + .3 + .2)]$. The confusion set (1, 2, 3, 4), "total confusion," leads to Response 3 with probability $.2 [.2/(.4 + .3 + .2 + .1)]$. In sum this particular error has probability $2/9 (.25) + 2/10 (.10) = 0.076$. Response 3 to Stimulus 2 happens much more often, because it can

TABLE 7.1
Fictitious Confusion Matrix

		Response			
		1	*2*	*3*	*4*
	1	.758	.156	.076	.010
Stimulus	2	.204	.545	.199	.052
	3	.151	.298	.466	.085
	4	.040	.155	.170	.635

result from the two additional confusion sets (2, 3) and (2, 3, 4). These contribute, respectively, 0.040 and 0.083 to this error probability.

This is not an unusual confusion matrix, especially for ordered responses. Probabilities decrease from the diagonal in an orderly way. The end responses are more frequently correct, mainly because they are elements of fewer confusion sets. We return to this matrix in later sections.

2. The Simple Guessing Model.   This model is not identifiably different from the *approximation* Broadbent developed for his criterion placement model (1967, pp. 6–10). This point is discussed in the following.

This model was also discussed in the Broadbent (1967) paper. As a special case of SGM it arises when one assumes that either the subject identifies the stimulus correctly (i.e., has a confusion set with one element) or he has no information (i.e., has a confusion set of size M and guesses according to his biases). This leads to what has been called a *quasiindependent* data matrix, in that all nondiagonal cells can be written as the product of a row factor and a column factor. Analysis of such tables has been discussed elsewhere (Smith, 1973; Bishop, Fienberg, & Holland, 1975). It is a special case of the Nakatani model as well, corresponding to $P_{ij} = k$ for all i and j.

In itself it is not particularly interesting in that it implies a rather homogeneous set of stimuli. It is appropriate for the N-alternative forced choice psychophysical experiment, with a somewhat different interpretation than that just given. If one assumes that each time interval gives rise to an independent decision index and that the subject's response is determined by the largest of these, then when an error is made, the conditional probability of any particular one of the N-1 error responses is independent of the stimulus used. There may be bias either because the N-1 error processes have different means or for some nonsensory reason.

Its greatest value, however, is as a base line for other more incisive models. It is a special case of all models to be discussed here. To the extent that it provides an adequate description of the data, there is no reason to infer anything about the similarity structure of the data. When complex programs such as multidimensional scaling are used, they should be preceded by a simple check of this hypothesis.

3. Stimulus Activation (Townsend, 1971). Townsend proposes a special case of SGM in which he assumes that all confusion sets have either one or two elements. This model has precisely the same number of parameters as the Nakatani model or the linear guessing model. It is particularly useful when error rates are relatively low.

As pointed out elsewhere (Pachella et al., 1978), the stimulus activation model has an increasingly difficult time as the experimental task is made more difficult. Intuitively if the subject is never choosing between more than two stimuli, his *average* error rate can never increase beyond 0.5. For a particular stimulus of course he may very seldom be correct, but the only explanation within this model is response bias. If response bias is low for one stimulus, it must be high for some others; and that high bias will at least compensate by yielding more correct responses to those stimuli. This is easily proved. This unnatural upper bound, however many stimuli or however difficult the task, greatly limits the utility of this model to situations in which the probability of multielement confusion sets is a priori low.

The concentration of this model on two-element confusion sets suggests a similarity of this model with that of Nakatani. The suggestion is incorrect. Nakatani includes confusion sets of all sizes, but their probabilities are *based* on two-element confusions. His model is not limited in the same way the stimulus activation model is.

4. The Informed Guessing Model. In our laboratory we have found the stimulus activation model appealing because of its process description and have cast about for a modification allowing higher error rates. The informed guessing model (Pachella et al., 1978) is the result. To Townsend's pairwise confusions we have added one confusion set that contains all responses. The IGM is thus a mixture of simple guessing and stimulus activation. Because the stimulus activation model uniquely specifies all table probabilities, this additional parameter, which one might call the probability of a pure guess, returns us in a small way to the indeterminancy of the general sophisticated guessing model; that is, there is a range of parameter value sets, each of which makes the same data prediction, so that there is no intrinsic way to choose among them. This range corresponds to a range on g, the pure guess probability, and if the range on g is small, inferences may not be seriously affected. Stimulus activation can be considered to be a special case of informed guessing when $g = 0$. When the average percentage correct is less than 50, the range of g does not include 0.

As the value of g used increases, the estimates of pairwise confusion decrease, so we typically use the upper bound to obtain conservative confusion estimates. One could also imagine using different estimates of g so as to match comparable data sets on other parameters. It should be pointed out again that which value of g is used has no effect whatever on the fit of the model to data; each is equally good or bad.

Returning to Table 7.1, it can be seen that stimulus activation cannot fit. To show this I present the mathematical form of *informed guessing*. The parameters are: b_j, response biases; ξ_i, the probability of the confusion set (c); ξ_{ij}, the probability of the confusion set (ij); and g, the probability of a pure guess.

$$p_{ii} = \xi_i + b_i \sum_{j \neq i} \frac{\xi_{ij}}{b_i + b_j} + b_i g$$

$$\text{(6)}$$

$$p_{ij} = b_j \left(\frac{\xi_{ij}}{b_i + b_j} + g \right)$$

With $g = 0$ it is clear that $\xi_{ij} = p_{ij} + p_{ji}$ for $i \neq j$. For Stimulus 2 in the table, we obtain estimates

$$\xi_{12} = .360 = .156 + .204$$
$$\xi_{23} = .497$$
$$\xi_{24} = .207.$$

Summing we see that when Stimulus 2 is presented, the probability of a two-element confusion set is 1.064, leaving less than nothing for ξ_2.

The Informed Guessing Model takes this sum to be

$$\xi_{12} + \xi_{23} + \xi_{24} + (b_1 + 3b_2 + b_3 + b_4)g,$$

or

$$\xi_{12} + \xi_{23} + \xi_{24} + (1 + 2b_2)g.$$

Because $\xi_{12} + \xi_{23} + \xi_{24} + g$ must be less than or equal to 1,

$$2b_2 g \geq 0.064 \quad \text{or} \quad g \geq 0.107;$$

that is, $g = 0$ is not possible as we have already seen. At the other end of the scale, Equation 6 asserts that the smallest cell frequency must be at least $b_j g$. Checking through the matrix we find that cells $(1, 4)$ and $(4, 1)$ both imply that $g \leq 0.100$. In these data there is no permissable value of g, and we must conclude that there is at least one three-element confusion set with nonzero probability.

Even having one more parameter than we can estimate is not sufficient to force a fit. Generally speaking this has not occurred often in our work. Pragmatically the value of the informed guessing model for us has been that it provides a reasonable unified summary of tables in which a number of low-frequency cells exist, allowing us to ascribe all of them to a guessing response rather than to assign each to a different pairwise confusion.

5. *Summary.* The sophisticated guessing model has been shown to have a number of interesting and useful specializations. Even though the general model is over specified, it *is* rejectable because of the two special conditions data generated by it must satisfy. This testability as well as its straightforward process interpretation maintains its value. A model with too many parameters need not necessarily fit.

Technically the kind of indeterminacy noted here is called nonidentifiability. Because this concept plays a large part in the rest of the chapter, I define it now. A model is a function with unknown parameters describing a set of data. When the parameters are specified numerically, the result is a model instance. Two models are said to be nonidentifiable with respect to a set of data, if for any instance of one model there exists an instance of the other model that makes the same prediction for those data. One model (say A) can be said to be nonidentifiable *within* another model (say B) with respect to a data set if for every instance of Model A there exists an instance of Model B such that the two instances make the same prediction for those data. Two models are nonidentifiable if each is nonidentifiable within the other. This is not to say that the models are "mathematically identical," or equivalent, except with respect to the specific data involved. The controversy around the 1967 Broadbent paper involved confusion over this point. Broadbent's criterion bias model and the simple guessing model were shown to be nonidentifiable with respect to a confusion matrix, not "mathematically identical." Two extremely different models with very different structure and justification may nevertheless be nonidentifiable with respect to a particular paradigm. To put the point in classical terms what one needs is a "crucial experiment." Only if a crucial experiment were inconceivable would one be justified in calling the models equivalent, mathematically or otherwise.

The Biased Choice Model (Luce, 1963)

A major point of this work is that the model "sophisticated guessing" is nonidentifiable within the model "biased choice." Any sophisticated guessing model of the sort defined here, including all the special cases, makes predictions that can be matched, cell by cell, by a biased choice model, if the data form is a confusion matrix resulting from an identification experiment.

Whatever index of goodness of fit is used, there will be a biased choice model that fits at least as well as the best sophisticated guessing model.

In order to explore the relation between these two models, I first describe the biased choice model and some of its special cases and extensions in detail and in the next section some joint implications are explored.

The biased choice model consists of a set of bias parameters summing to one and a set of $M(M - 1)/2$ similarity parameters, one for each pair of stimuli. It is assumed that the conditional probability of Response j when Stimulus i has been presented is proportional to the product of the bias β_j toward Response j and the similarity (η_{ij}) of stimuli i and j, this similarity being symmetric. Mathematically,

$$p_{ij} = \frac{\beta_j \eta_{ij}}{\alpha_i}, \tag{7}$$

where

$$\alpha_i = \sum_j \beta_j \eta_{ij}, \qquad \sum \beta_j = 1, \qquad \eta_{ij} = \eta_{ji}, \quad \text{and} \quad \eta_{ii} = 1.$$

Using the notation introduced earlier, in which the sophisticated guessing equation is $p_{ij} = b_j \, \theta_{ij}$, we see that defining

$$\eta_{ij} = \frac{\theta_{ij}}{\sqrt{\theta_{ii}\theta_{jj}}} \qquad \beta_j = \frac{b_j\sqrt{\theta_{jj}}}{\sum_l b_i\sqrt{\theta_{ii}}} \tag{8}$$

yields the biased choice model directly. The inverse conversion

$$\theta_{ij} = \eta_{ij} \; \left(\frac{\beta_j}{\alpha_i} + \frac{\beta_i}{\alpha_j}\right) \qquad b_j = \frac{\beta_j \alpha_j}{\sum_i \beta_i \alpha_i} \tag{9}$$

is formally correct, but it can lead to inadmissible values for confusion set probabilities in the sophisticated guessing model.

Luce originally made the eminently sensible suggestions that $\eta_{ij} \leq 1$ and $\eta_{ij}\eta_{jk} \leq \eta_{ik}$ for all i, j, k. This was partially in order to allow him to define – ln η_{ij} as a distance function and also it seemed reasonable not to allow two different stimuli to be more similar than a stimulus is to itself. The work reported here does not impose these restrictions: the first because we have seldom, if ever, seen data that violated it and the second because it seems somewhat arbitrary, precisely as arbitrary as the choice of a distance function. If eventually distance functions *are* to be used, some similar restriction will be needed, as it will be necessary, when Stimulus *i* is very close to Stimulus *j* and Stimulus *j* very close to Stimulus *k*, that Stimulus *i* not be too far from Stimulus *k*. It seems reasonable not to introduce this restriction, however, when stimuli differ on separable dimensions and the notion of distance may be less appropriate.

An extremely valuable property of the biased choice model is that it is a log–linear model; that is, the model asserts that the logarithms of cell probabilities are linear functions of the logarithms of the parameters. If one further assumes that the data for each stimulus are drawn from a multinomial distribution, it is quite simple using existing techniques (Bishop et al., 1975) to obtain maximum likelihood estimates of the parameters. Indeed almost all the modern techniques of statistical analysis are available, providing a proved methodology for the kind of "data snooping" so valuable in the exploration of complex data.

In Table 7.2 I present a set of data published by Wayne Wickelgren (1965). Subjects were presented with lists of subsets of the CV and VC digrams made up of *f, n, a,* and *o*. As the lists were presented, subjects copied them and shortly afterward were asked to recall them serially. The data presented represent the digrams recalled that had been correctly copied. The data have been summed over subjects, so the analysis I present (as well as Wickelgren's) makes a rather strong assumption of subject homogeneity and independence. The biased choice model has been fitted with the resulting chi-square 15.00

TABLE 7.2
Wickelgren Data (BCM estimates)

		Response (%)								
		fa	af	fo	of	na	an	no	on	N
Data	fa	.756	.045	.060	.037	.033	.027	.022	.020	849
(Pred.)		(.756)	(.046)	(.066)	(.032)	(.028)	(.032)	(.021)	(.020)	
	af	.076	.698	.025	.097	.032	.038	.016	.017	812
		(.076)	(.698)	(.021)	(.103)	(.027)	(.039)	(.018)	(.017)	
	fo	.095	.014	.690	.083	.017	.018	.039	.044	902
		(.090)	(.017)	(.690)	(.082)	(.015)	(.021)	(.042)	(.044)	
	of	.021	.056	.046	.777	.009	.024	.036	.030	755
		(.026)	(.049)	(.048)	(.777)	(.014)	(.021)	(.032)	(.033)	
	na	.056	.029	.022	.043	.679	.075	.055	.040	782
		(.062)	(.035)	(.024)	(.039)	(.679)	(.071)	(.052)	(.038)	
	an	.051	.033	.024	.034	.040	.740	.023	.056	792
		(.045)	(.032)	(.021)	(.037)	(.045)	(.740)	(.027)	(.054)	
	no	.033	.020	.055	.061	.035	.037	.687	.072	705
		(.034)	(.018)	(.051)	(.065)	(.039)	(.032)	(.687)	(.074)	
	on	.023	.012	.039	.050	.019	.045	.054	.758	753
		(.023)	(.012)	(.039)	(.048)	(.020)	(.046)	(.053)	(.758)	

Chi-Square = 15.00, d.f. = 21.

with 21 degrees of freedom (d.f.). This is astonishingly small, given the 6350 responses it represents, perhaps because the technical assumption of subject independence was not met. In any case, as a summary of the data the biased choice model seems completely sufficient. In no cell is there an error of more than six observations. The stimulus activation model fits the data precisely as well, because of the relatively low error rate and its nonidentifiability within the biased choice model.

In Table 7.3 are data published by Clark and Stafford (1969). Here subjects were presented sentences and were asked to remember the verb. Verbs differed in tense and whether or not they were progressive or perfect forms, yielding eight possible verbs. Again the fit is impressive, perhaps too much so. Here the maximum error is less than seven observations. The stimulus activation model cannot fit because of the low average percentage correct (0.344).

These data sets were introduced here not only to impress the reader with the promise of the biased choice model but to illustrate some of the specializations of it that are useful. In both sets, as frequently is the case, there is an a priori structure on the stimuli that the general model has not taken into account. There are many ways to utilize this structure and I discuss only a few.

In Wickelgren's original analysis he arrived at a number of interesting conclusions but avoided testing others because of the response bias in the data. A particularly simple model might be that errors are due to (1) missing

TABLE 7.3
Clark–Stafford Data (1969)

		Response (%)							
		A	B	C	D	E	F	G	H	N
	A	.217	.136	.118	.204	.093	.087	.050	.096	323
(BCM Predicts)		(.217)	(.136)	(.108)	(.214)	(.087)	(.090)	(.048)	(.099)	
	B	.132	.253	.102	.227	.053	.089	.049	.095	304
		(.132)	(.253)	(.103)	(.221)	(.057)	(.096)	(.043)	(.095)	
	C	.037	.046	.287	.277	.067	.079	.079	.128	328
		(.046)	(.045)	(.287)	(.272)	(.076)	(.074)	(.074)	(.127)	
	D	.067	.053	.160	.347	.077	.063	.073	.160	300
		(.056)	(.059)	(.166)	(.347)	(.065)	(.062)	(.087)	(.157)	
	E	.024	.024	.069	.075	.240	.243	.060	.266	334
		(.030)	(.020)	(.060)	(.085)	(.240)	(.224)	(.065)	(.277)	
	F	.030	.036	.045	.068	.172	.320	.059	.270	337
		(.026)	(.029)	(.050)	(.069)	(.190)	(.320)	(.056)	(.259)	
	G	.015	.009	.053	.123	.067	.061	.424	.249	342
		(.016)	(.015)	(.057)	(.110)	(.063)	(.064)	(.424)	(.251)	
	H	.015	.012	.036	.071	.110	.098	.095	.563	336
		(.012)	(.012)	(.037)	(.074)	(.100)	(.110)	(.093)	(.563)	

Chi-Square = 11.35, d.f. = 21.

TABLE 7.4
Feature Analysis of Wickelgren Error Data

Model	d.f.	Chi-Square	Average Absolute Error
BCM	21	15.00	2.34
Independent features	38	87.13	5.50
No bias	45	179.66	7.84
No order effect	39	141.85	6.55
No vowel effect	39	205.89	9.14
No consonant effect	39	251.65	10.09

the consonant; (2) missing the vowel; or (3) missing the order and that these features are missed independently. If one assumes that the similarity of two digrams is reduced by a factor for each of the features on which they differ, one obtains a model that is a special case of the Luce model and is still log–linear in form. In Table 7.4, the results of testing this independent feature model are presented and we see that this model is clearly rejected, the increase in chi-square of 72.13 being compensated by only 17 degrees of freedom. Nevertheless the average absolute error only increases to 5.5 observations.

Wickelgren's assumption of response bias is quite strongly confirmed, the biases being in favor of syllables that are words (*of* and *on* most strongly). It is quite clear that the consonant most strongly affects the similarity, followed by the vowel and finally the order. Looking at deviations from the independent feature model it appears that its major failing is that the order and consonant features interact in such a way that errors involving both order and consonant differences are more common than the independent feature model predicts. What has been gained is the ability to check rather complex relations within a simple unified framework.

A graduate student, Susan Duffy, has done a definitive analysis of the Clark and Stafford data[2]. She was able to obtain an almost equally good fit with many fewer parameters. Among her results were two that were particularly interesting. The first is that a rather more parsimonious fit was obtainable by assuming that confusions were primarily based on the word length of the verb rather than its grammatical form. This is somewhat tentative due to the high correlation between word length and grammatical form, but it does suggest the a posteriori obvious control for word length in such experiments. The other was that by giving up the symmetry of η, but staying within log–linear models, she could achieve a better fit.

---

[2]Class Project, April, 1977. Susan Duffy, University of Michigan.

Using the same sort of analysis carried out earlier on the Wickelgren data, it was clear that errors on any one of the dimensions were correlated positively with errors on the others. An error in tense was most likely if an error in progressiveness or perfection (?) or both was also made. This might have been due to a certain proportion of clear correct recalls and that hypothesis could also be checked within this framework.

The response bias parameters can also be looked at more carefully. In the Clark–Stafford data there appeared to be a bias toward *past* relative to *present*, toward *nonprogressive* relative to *progressive*, and toward *imperfect* rather than *perfect*. This was tested and it was found that although these three independent feature biases explained most of the seven degree of freedom response bias vector, the remaining portion was still significant. The past–present bias did seem independent of the others, however.

To summarize these analyses, note that first a BCM model is fitted to the total confusion matrix. This model ignores the a priori structure of the stimulus set. If that model provides a reasonable description of the data, special cases of the model utilizing the prior structure can be entertained, checking for separable contributions of the various features built into the stimulus set, either to the similarities or to the response biases. In both the Wickelgren data and the Clark and Stafford data the independent feature hypotheses provide a good description of the data, but they are measurably poorer than the general model. The attempt to fit an independent feature hypothesis is worthwhile for two reasons, however. First if it had worked, a 35-parameter model would be replaced by a 6-parameter model; and second, even when the attempt failed, the way in which it failed was of interest in itself.

Garner and Haun Data (1978)

Another illustrative data set is that provided by Garner and Haun (1978). This analysis is merely illustrative, because the data reported in detail have been averaged over subjects and noise conditions, throwing most of the statistical assumptions into grave doubt. The biased choice model parameters and goodness-of-fit statistics are presented in Table 7.5. If statistical assumptions were justified, these chi-square values range from significance levels of 0.01 for G & H Table 7 to 0.20 for G & H Table 5. More descriptive might be the average absolute cell deviation for error cells that is 5.4 out of the average error cell entry of 101.2.

The data represent the results of a 2 × 2 experiment, with the first factor being whether the stimulus letters form a "feature set" (I, L, Γ, ⊏) or a "dimension set" (*p, b, g, d*) and the second being whether identification was hampered by process limitation (i.e., the adding of noise features) or by state limitation (i.e., reduction in display time). The first two subtables contain

TABLE 7.5
Garner and Haun Parameters (1978)

G & H Table 1		Eta			Beta	Chi-Square (3 d.f.)
p	1	.050	.101	.054	0.276	6.87
b		1	.051	.115	0.241	
d			1	.066	0.243	
g				1	0.240	
G & H Table 3		Eta			Beta	Chi-Square (3 d.f.)
I	1	.086	.084	.020	0.200	7.19
L		1	.024	.089	0.243	
Γ			1	.096	0.245	
⊏				1	0.313	
G & H Table 5		Eta			Beta	Chi-Square (3 d.f.)
p	1	.196	.129	.109	0.246	3.36
b		1	.082	.100	0.230	
d			1	.198	0.190	
g				1	0.333	
G & H Table 7		Eta			Beta	Chi-Square (3 d.f.)
I	1	.185	.164	.068	0.359	9.76
L		1	.059	.134	0.305	
Γ			1	.160	0.206	
⊏				1	0.131	

parameters for the process limited condition; the second two, the stage limited condition.

The major result of this analysis is that every statement made by the authors concerning the characteristics of the average data is unequivocally supported by the analysis reported here. I point out some specifics shortly.

My only disagreement with the authors is with their statement that "distances" between letters are not always symmetric. It is not really clear what the authors mean by "distance," but if distance is measured by similarity in the BCM sense, that conclusion is not required by these data. The interpretation proposed by the authors that state limitation of feature sets leads to loss of features seems eminently sensible, but the effect using BCM is to modify strongly the response bias observed. In subtable 3, the data reflect a rather strong bias in favor of C, and against I; whereas in subtable 7 that bias has been completely reversed. In addition, a bias for L and against T has been introduced, as noted by Garner and Haun but unexplained by them. This change is clearly one of the largest in the data set and it seems unreasonable to pass it off so easily.

Inspection of subtables 3 and 7 also reveals a large change in similarities. This hypothesis can be checked with log–linear analysis, essentially by fitting the same similarity matrix to both sets of data, resulting in an increase in chi-square of 196.5 with 6 degrees of freedom. This number should provide some additional feeling of the goodness of fit represented by the values reported in Table 7.4. How much of this change is attributable to the greater difficulty of the state limited task? Subtable 3 has an overall error rate of 17% whereas subtable 7 has an overall rate of 30%. One may check this question by fitting a model in which the similarities of subtable 7 are a constant multiple of those in subtable 3. The single degree of freedom attributable to this parameter ($\hat{\lambda}$ = 1.93) has a chi-square of 172.8, accounting for 88% of the difference in similarities, leaving a slight significant remainder but one less than twice as large as that due to lack of fit of the full model.

Summarizing, state limitation leads to a drastic modification of response bias. If feature loss were operating independently on the two features, we would estimate bias in subtable 7 as (.375, .289, .190, .146), not very different from that observed. Even this difference is highly significant, however (chi-square = 17.2, 1 d.f.), such that feature losses are negatively related, as would seem natural in a tachistoscopic task; that is, missing the upper limb is less likely when the lower limb has been missed.

The bias errors in the process limited feature set are consistent with occasional assimilation of noise features. In the state limited condition, the data are consistent with the notion that about 14% of the times a lower limb was presented it was missed, whereas the upper limb was missed roughly 40% of the time and that S's adjusted their biases in line with the "perceived" frequencies of the letters. This notion as a process description is of course highly speculative and certainly not justified by the data analysis presented here. It is presented merely as an example of the detailed analysis possible within the BCM framework.

Generalizations of BCM

The previous analyses were carried out using special cases of the biased choice model. Experimental considerations suggested more specialized values of the general bias and similarity parameters. In much of the work in our laboratory, generalizations of biased choice have been valuable. In an early experiment, subjects identified the letters B, C, D, and E under progressively more stringent response deadlines. We were interested in the effect of speed stress on parameter values. Four different models were proposed. Defining p_{ijk}, the probability of Response j to Stimulus i under speed stress condition k, the models are

$$p_{ijk} = \frac{\beta_j \eta_{ij}}{\alpha_i} \tag{10a}$$

$$p_{ijk} = \frac{\beta_j \eta_{ijk}}{\alpha_{ik}} \tag{10b}$$

$$p_{ijk} = \frac{\beta_{jk} \eta_{ij}}{\alpha_{ik}} \tag{10c}$$

and

$$p_{ijk} = \frac{\beta_{jk} \eta_{ijk}}{\alpha_{ik}} \tag{10d}$$

The first of these asserts the total independence of response frequencies from speed stress. The second asserts that similarities but not biases are affected. The third asserts that biases but not similarities are changed by speed stress, whereas the fourth estimates different parameters of both kinds for different conditions. The models form a lattice

in which each model is a special case of those below it on a path. The differences in chi-square between Models A and B or between Models C and D are atributable to differences in similarity structure due to the experimental variable. The C–D difference allows for an experimental effect on biases as well, whereas the A–B difference assumes no effect on bias. In the experiment described, both of these were highly significant, but the A–C and B–D differences attributable to response bias effects were small.

In another experiment (see Table 7.6) deadlines were held constant, but stimulus frequencies were manipulated. The data of Table 7.6, Condition 1, were obtained from Subject CD when the four stimuli were presented equally often, whereas the data in Table 7.6, Condition 2, were obtained with stimulus frequencies of (0.40, 0.25, 0.25, 0.10). The model fit here is somewhat better than typical. The expected values shown are those for Model D. Chi-square values for Models, A, B, and C are given in Table 7.7. The major differences are those between A and C and between B and D, showing that stimulus

TABLE 7.6
Pachella–Smith Data
Subject C.F.   *Speed Stress*

		B	C	D	E	N
		— Condition 1		Response (%)		
		B	C	D	E	N
	B	.838	.038	.110	.015	400
(Pred)		(.838)	(.037)	(.106)	(.020)	
	C	.052	.800	.038	.110	399
		(.053)	(.800)	(.044)	(.103)	
	D	.140	.050	.800	.010	398
		(.142)	(.041)	(.800)	(.015)	
	E	.048	.142	.025	.078	400
		(.042)	(.149)	(.023)	(.785)	
		Condition 2				
	B	.814	.053	.127	.006	640
		(.814)	(.049)	(.125)	(.012)	
	C	.065	.855	.042	.038	400
		(.072)	(.855)	(.044)	(.030)	
	D	.210	.052	.732	.005	400
		(.213)	(.051)	(.732)	(.004)	
	E	.112	.131	.013	.744	160
		(.089)	(.151)	(.015)	(.744)	

Chi-Square = 7.366; d.f. = 6.

TABLE 7.7
Submodels

		A	Chi-Square = 44.075	d.f. = 15
Chi-Square = 24.250	B	C	Chi-Square = 27.319	d.f. = 12
d.f. = 9		D	Chi-Square = 7.366	d.f. = 6

frequency affects response bias. Although numerically similar, the bias differences correspond to only 3, rather than 6 degrees of freedom.

Despite these data, the caution expressed earlier about interpreting bias and similarity as, respectively, pure response tendency and perceptual similarity bear repeating. If the stimuli are somewhat more complex and if the frequency of E were even more severely reduced, one could expect a shift of attention away from those features unique to E with a consequent apparent increase in the similarity of E to the other stimuli. Increasing the speed stress surely increases the measured similarity among the stimuli. If these similarities are differentially changed, the subject may be led to change his response biases, because by so doing he would improve his recognition score. This is discussed briefly in the following but, even ignoring this subtle effect, response bias may change merely to take advantage of differences in response speed. In this experiment stimuli were carefully chosen, as were responses, resulting in a relatively clean separation of bias and similarity effects.

Optimum Response Bias

In another paper[3] I have discussed the implications of the biased choice model for how a subject with control of his response biases should apportion them. Although stimulus frequency and differential payoffs have the same sort of effect here as is ascribed to them in signal detection theory, the change to more than two stimuli introduces a new complication. Even when all stimuli occur equally often and when the payoff is the same for each correct response, the biased choice observer may be well advised not to use responses equally often. Consider the similarity matrix of Table 7.8, and assume equal payoff for being correct on each stimulus and equal frequency of presentation. The subject who chooses a bias vector of ($\frac{1}{3}$, $\frac{1}{3}$, $\frac{1}{3}$) will be correct 45.15% of the time, whereas the subject who chooses (0, $\frac{1}{2}$, $\frac{1}{2}$) (i.e., never responds l) will be correct 51.28% of the time, corresponding to a 13% improvement. If Stimuli A and B are very similar, and A is much more similar to C than B is similar to C, the tendency to say *A* should be reduced. This is not the place to explore this phenomenon in detail and it has been discovered so recently that it is yet to be studied systematically in an experiment, but it may help explain what have seemed to be anomalously large individual differences in response bias.

TABLE 7.8
Similarity Matrix (η)

		Stimulus		
		A	B	C
	A	1	.9	.6
Stimulus	B	.9	1	.3
	C	.6	.3	1

In addition to the special questions addressed here, tests and confidence intervals can be applied to answer questions concerning ratios of particular similarity indices and biases, the equality of subsets of parameters, interesting relations among parameters (e.g., is η_{ik} equal to $\eta_{ij} \eta_{jk}$), and the contribution of particular stimuli or stimulus pairs to the lack of fit of the model.

This concludes the section on the biased choice model in and of itself. We have found it to provide a powerful analytic tool for discovering the effects of many experimental variables on the identification of stimuli. The next section

---

[3] *On optimum bias in the biased choice model.* Unpublished manuscript, July, 1978.

explores some of the relations between the biased choice model and sophisticated guessing.

Sophisticated Guessing and Biased Choice

I have pointed out earlier that sophisticated guessing is not identifiable within the biased choice model. For every realization of a sophisticated guessing model, there exists a realization of a biased choice model yielding precisely the same predictions for each cell of the confusion matrix. One might say that therefore sophisticated guessing is a special case of biased choice. Although this is true, it is not sufficiently precise. This use of the term *special case* is quite different from its use when we were discussing the effect of stimulus frequency on response bias. There the parameter space of Model B was a subspace of the parameter space of Model D; specifically it is of lower dimension than that of Model D. Roughly speaking, if one picked "at random" a realization of Model D, there would be virtually no chance that it would satisfy Model B. Even more colloquially, if one kicked a football, the chance of its landing precisely on the 50-yard line would be extremely small. In contrast the sophisticated guessing model has a parameter space the image of which is measureable in the parameter space of the biased choice model. Picking a "random" biased choice realization and finding it to satisfy sophisticated guessing would be like having the football land between the 20-yard line and the goal line. Perhaps a small probability, but measureable. The theorems that allow us to subtract chi-squares in the previous examples do not work for testing sophisticated guessing within biased choice, for with some finite probability the difference would be zero, contrary to the chi-square distribution.

It would be ideal to be able to characterize those biased choice models that *do* correspond to some sophisticated guessing model. This can be done for the stimulus activation model in a rather uninteresting way, to wit: All biased choice models for which

$$\sum_{i \neq j} \frac{\beta_j \eta_{ij}}{\alpha_i} + 1 - \frac{\beta_j}{\alpha_j} > 0 \qquad \text{for all } j.$$

It is somewhat more interesting to characterize the simple guessing model within biased choice. That model satisfies the condition

$$\eta_{ij} = f_i f_j \qquad i \neq j \text{ for some } f;$$

that is, the similarities can each be factored into a product of a number depending only on i and another depending only on j.

But no such characterization has been discovered for the general sophisticated guessing model. The nonidentifiability of sophisticated guessing within biased choice comes from the fact that sophisticated guessing satisfies the "circular order" property; that is,

$$p_{ij} \cdot p_{jk} \cdot p_{ki} = p_{ji} \cdot p_{ik} \cdot p_{kj} \quad \text{for all } i, j, \text{ and } k,$$

and that any model satisfying this property is a biased choice model. Several necessary and interesting restrictions on biased choice models that match sophisticated guessing models follow from the other feature we noted earlier, namely that $p_{ij} \leq p_{jj}$ for all i and j. Translating this restriction into biased choice parameters, this means that

$$\frac{\beta_j \eta_{ij}}{\alpha_l} \leq \frac{\beta_j}{\alpha_j}, \qquad \frac{\beta_i \eta_{ij}}{\alpha_j} \leq \frac{\beta_i}{\alpha_i}, \tag{11}$$

which together imply that $\eta_{ij} \leq 1$, just as Luce had earlier required. Even further, suppose that for some $i, j, \eta_{ij} = 1$. Returning to SGM, we see that this implies that all confusion sets containing Response i also contain Response j and vice versa, and this means that if

$$\eta_{ij} = 1$$

then

$$\eta_{ik} = \eta_{jk} \quad \text{for all } k.$$

that is, two stimuli that are maximally similar to one another must be equally similar to all other stimuli. Finally, from Equation 11 we have

$$\eta_{ij}\alpha_j \leq \alpha_i,$$

and expanding α_i and α_j we find

$$\eta_{ij} \sum_k \beta_k \eta_{jk} \leq \sum_k \beta_k \eta_{ik}$$

$$\sum \beta_k(\eta_{ik} - \eta_{ij}\eta_{jk}) \geq 0.$$

This means that if a similarity matrix along with a bias vector is the image of an SGM model *for all possible choices* of a bias vector, then the similarity parameters must satisfy the equation

$$\eta_{ik} \geq \eta_{ij}\eta_{jk} \qquad \text{for all } k.$$

This is the condition Luce imposed to make $-\ln \eta$ a distance measure. Here it arises as a necessary condition for the similarity matrix to correspond to a sophisticated guessing model. Unfortunately it is merely necessary. It is quite possible to write down a similarity matrix satisfying all these conditions and a bias vector that together still are the image of no SGM model.

The reasonableness of these necessary conditions as well as the simplicity of the process underlying the sophisticated guessing model motivate continued study of its properties and attempts to circumvent the multiple parameter problem. The problem in general is hopeless. In a 26-letter alphabetic confusion problem there could be as many as 64 million parameters to estimate. With three or four or even five stimuli, reasonable possibilities exist. One is the informed guessing model that we have used with four stimuli, but as the number of stimuli becomes large, the likelihood of having only stimulus activation plus pure guessing decreases.

Another approach would be to change the experiment. One might for example introduce second choices. If one assumed such a modification did not change the conditions of the experiment too much, this would allow estimation at least of three-element confusion set probabilities. It would provide a direct test of the stimulus activation model, because that model implies that either the first or the second choice will be correct. In the case of three stimuli it could even test the sophisticated guessing model directly, because whatever the stimulus, the probability of the three-element confusion set could be estimated experimentally independently on the basis of trials in which neither choice is correct. One would have to assume that second choices were based on the same biases as first choices.

Still a third possibility would be to precue or postcue subjects on each trial as to subsets of the stimuli containing the correct response. One would be concerned about the attention shifts due to precueing and the disruption of response selection by postcueing.

A mathematical approach using linear programming techniques is possible. The maximum likelihood estimates obtained from the biased choice model provide a set of linear equations that the confusion set probabilities must satisfy. In addition, the sum of the probabilities of confusion sets containing any of the responses must be one. Finally inequalities are introduced by the restriction that confusion set probabilities are nonnegative. The final element of this procedure is the objective function to be maximized. One might search for the solution that maximized the probability of one-element confusion sets or minimized that probability or both. These solutions would provide a range of parameter values to consider. This technique would also detect systematically those data matrices that could not be fitted by a sophisticated guessing model or rather those matrices whose maximum likelihood estimates were different under SGM from those under biased choice.

A sometimes annoying relation between the two models is that they both present response bias vectors, but these vectors do not in general agree. In an earlier paper[4] I presented a worst case example and repeat that example here in Table 7.9. The simple guessing model just discussed can also be described by the equation.

$$p_{ij} = p_i + \Pi_j(1 - p_i) \qquad i = j$$
$$= \Pi_j(1 - p_i) \qquad i \neq j.$$

In this equation p_i is the probability of identifying Stimulus i when it is presented and Π_j is the probability of Response j when no stimulus is identified. The Π vector is a response bias vector. The three data sets in Table 7.9 all satisfy the simple guessing model, and because this model is a special case of both, they also satisfy biased choice and sophisticated guessing, so there is no statistical goodness of fit involved. The data have been constructed so that for each set one of the three models yields a flat response bias vector, usually interpreted as "no bias," but for each set the other models sometimes describe considerable bias.

I hope this final section will help others as it has helped me to avoid confusing the name of a concept with its meaning.

TABLE 7.9 (a)
Constructed Data (No Bias, PRB)

		Response					
		1	2	3	4	5	Total
	1	840	40	40	40	40	1000
	2	60	760	60	60	60	1000
Stimulus	3	120	120	520	120	120	1000
	4	140	140	140	440	140	1000
	5	180	180	180	180	280	1000

Response Biases

		Response				
		1	2	3	4	5
	GM	0.200	0.200	0.200	0.200	0.200
Model	SGM	0.399	0.266	0.133	0.113	0.089
	BCM	0.346	0.269	0.157	0.134	0.094

---

[4]Paper presented at Psychonomics Convention, St. Louis, Mo., 1972.

TABLE 7.9 (b)
Constructed Data (No Bias, BCM Model)

		Response					
		1	2	3	4	5	Total
	1	369	263	193	123	52	1000
	2	285	400	165	105	45	1000
Stimulus	3	236	187	453	87	37	1000
	4	181	143	105	543	28	1000
	5	103	81	59	38	719	1000

Response Biases

		Response				
		1	2	3	4	5
	GM	0.346	0.273	0.200	0.127	0.054
Model	SGM	0.255	0.235	0.208	0.173	0.129
	BCM	0.200	0.200	0.200	0.200	0.200

TABLE 7.9 (c)
Constructed Data (No Sophisticated Guessing Bias)

		Response					
		1	2	3	4	5	Total
	1	435	235	173	110	47	1000
	2	235	505	136	87	37	1000
Stimulus	3	173	136	600	64	27	1000
	4	110	87	64	722	17	1000
	5	47	37	27	17	872	1000

Response Biases

		Response				
		1	2	3	4	5
	GM	0.346	0.272	0.200	0.128	0.054
Model	SGM	0.200	0.200	0.200	0.200	0.200
	BCM	0.168	0.181	0.197	0.216	0.238

Note: Negative correlation between GM and BCM.

CONCLUSION

I have attempted to describe and discuss here a number of models useful in understanding data obtained from multialternative identification experiments. Two alternative experiments have been discussed at length in the literature.

I have concentrated on models that stay rather close to the original data, the confusion matrix or matrices, avoiding models, particularly multidimensional scaling models, that build in even more theoretical structure. My own bias is that such models are potentially so important that they should be based upon a solid understanding of the basic similarities and biases they are meant to explain.

The Luce biased choice model has received a great deal of attention here for two reasons: (1) It seems to capture the structure of many data sets; and (2) as a log–linear model it lends itself to extremely powerful analytic methods for exploratory data analysis. The close connection between it and the sophisticated guessing model not only opens up methods for exploring sophisticated guessing but lends meaning to biased choice as, if nothing else, a compact way of representing sophisticated guessing.

ACKNOWLEDGMENT

This work was carried out under a grant from the National Science Foundation (BNS-76-82815) to Professor Robert G. Pachella and the author.

REFERENCES

Bishop, Y. M. M., Fienberg, S. E., & Holland, P. *Discrete multivariate analysis: Theory and practice.* Cambridge, Mass.: MIT Press, 1975.

Bock, R. D., & Jones, L. V. *The measurement and prediction of judgement and choice.* San Francisco: Holden-Day, 1968.

Broadbent, D. E. Word-frequency effect and response bias. *Psychological Review*, 1967, *74*, 1–15.

Clark, H. H., & Stafford, R. A. Memory for semantic features in the verb. *Journal of Experimental Psychology*, 1969, *80*, 326–334.

Dorfman, D. D., & Alf, E., Jr. Maximum likelihood estimation of parameters of signal detection theory—A direct solution. *Psychometrika*, 1968, *33*, 117–124.

Garner, W. R., & Haun, F. Letter identification as a function of type of perceptual limitation and type of attribute. *Journal of Experimental Psychology: Human Perception and Performance*, 1978, *4*, 199–209.

Holyoak, K. J., & Glass, A. L. Recognition confusions among quantifiers. *Journal of Verbal Learning and Verbal Behavior*, 1978, *17*, 249–264.

Luce, R. D. Detection and recognition. In R. D. Luce, R. R. Bush, & E. Galanter (Eds.), *Handbook of mathematical psychology* (Vol. I). New York: Wiley, 1963.

Nakatani, L. H. *A confusion-choice stimulus recognition model applied to word recognition.* Ph.D. Dissertation, University of California, Los Angeles, 1970.

Pachella, R. G., Smith, J. E. K., & Stanovich, K. E. Qualitative error analysis and speeded classification. In N. John Castellan, Jr., & Frank Restle (Eds.), *Cognitive theory* (Vol. 3). Hillsdale, N.J.: Lawrence Erlbaum Associates, 1978.

Schonemann, P. H., & Tucker, L.R. A maximum likelihood solution for the method of successive intervals allowing for unequal dispersions. *Psychometrika,* 1967, *32,* 403–417.

Smith, J. E. K. On tests of quasi-independence in psychological research. *Psychological Bulletin,* 1973, *80,* 329–333.

Torgerson, W. S. *Theory and methods of scaling.* New York: Wiley, 1958.

Townsend, J. T. Theoretical analysis of an alphabetic confusion matrix. *Perception & Psychophysics,* 1971, *9,* 40–50.

Tversky, A. Features of similarity. *Psychological Review,* 1977, *84,* 327–352.

Wickelgren, W. A. Similarity and intrusions in short-term memory for consonant-vowel digrams. *Quarterly Journal of Experimental Psychology,* 1965, *9,* 241–246.

8 Effect of Prior Context on Two-Choice Absolute Judgments Without Feedback

John Long
*Medical Research Council Applied Psychology Unit**
Cambridge, England

ABSTRACT

Three experiments explored the effect on judgment of prior context (signal–response events on the preceding trial) in two-choice discrimination without immediate feedback. Auditory frequency was the independent variable in Experiment 1 and visual intensity in Experiment 2. The results of the two experiments showed that following errors, as opposed to correct responses, there was: (1) a significant reduction in discriminability (d'), which interacted with modality (frequency larger than intensity); and (2) a significant change in measured bias (β), away from the previous signal and toward the previous response, which was independent of modality. The two effects were significantly correlated only for frequency. A single theoretical account is thus inadequate for the changes in bias and the impairment of intensity judgment. Experiment 3 evaluated organismic state versus modality process contributions to the discriminability reduction and general versus specific accounts of the bias change, by interleaving auditory-frequency and visual-intensity signals on alternate trials. Presenting prior context in a different modality: (1) produced a small but reliable impairment of judgment following errors, which was independent of modality; and (2) eliminated the effect on bias. However, analysis of the same data conditional on two trials back (i.e., in the same modality) showed a reduction of discriminability that interacted with modality and a change in bias (as in Experiments 1 and 2). These results indicate that the reduction in discriminability following errors was multiply determined: for visual intensity (1) by an organismic state variable, such as attention or arousal; (2) by sequential variance; and in addition for

---

*Now at Ergonomics Unit, University College London, London, England

auditory frequency (3) by a modality process variable involved in the judgment itself. Concerning bias, the findings argue against models based on generalized response bias and in favor of those that assume that bias is specific to the way in which judgments are made. Two of these models—*memory trace* and *memory state*—are used to interpret the frequency-specific component of reduced discriminability following errors.

INTRODUCTION

There are basically two kinds of psychophysical question (Luce, 1972). One concerns the recoding of the physical stimulus into an internal representation (e.g., Green & Luce, 1973). The other concerns the processing of the representation as required by the experimental task (e.g., Helson, 1964; Poulton, 1968). A question of the second kind is the effect that prior context exerts on judgments of simple signals. Of interest here are one-dimensional signals, such as auditory frequency and visual intensity, having two possible values and for which no immediate feedback is provided. Two general sorts of prior-context effect are considered: biasing and changes in accuracy.

Early work concerning bias shows a substantial effect of prior context, defined as events occurring on the previous trial. In general, subjects tend to be more accurate in their judgments following a stimulus alternation than after a repetition, and they tend to repeat the last response (Parducci, 1964; Parducci & Sandusky, 1965). Subsequent work indicates that these tendencies represent changes only in measured bias and not in detectability (as distinguished within the framework of decision theory analysis—Green & Swets, 1974). Following correct trials, measured bias favors the previous response, the previous signal, or both (the values are the same). Following incorrect trials, measured bias favors the previous response and contrasts with the previous signal (the values are different). The accuracy of alternations and the repetition of responses occur because the change in measured bias is small following the two possible types of correct response and large following the two types of incorrect response (Kinchla, 1966; Sandusky, 1971; Tanner, Haller, & Atkinson, 1967). Although different theoretical accounts have been proposed for these findings, they all suppose prior context to affect only measured bias.

No such agreement exists, however, concerning the possible effect of prior context on the other parameter of decision theory analysis, detectability, or (more appropriately in the case of absolute judgments) discriminability. If greater accuracy following signal alternations results from differential changes in measured bias following correct and incorrect responses, then none of the research cited earlier indicates a true change in discriminability. Other studies, however, do suggest such an effect. Most involved auditory detection tasks in which performance tended to be worse following an incorrect response than following a correct one (Pastore & Sorkin, 1971; Shipley, 1961;

Swets, Shipley, McKey, & Green, 1959). A similar effect is suggested by studies involving two-choice recognition. In loudness judgments John (1973) reported a tendency for an error on the previous trial to be repeated. In judgments of auditory frequency, MacDonald (1974) found a significant dependency between errors on successive trials, as well as between responses. Further, one of the data sets from the studies reporting only changes in bias also suggests a tendency for discriminability to be worse following errors (Sandusky, 1971, Fig. 2).

In summary, there is clear evidence that prior context affects measured bias. The evidence for an effect on discriminability is suggestive only and appears confined to the auditory domain, particularly frequency.

Given that prior context may affect discriminability as well as measured bias, the question arises of the relation between the two effects. If they are related, then it should be possible to explain the effect on discriminability by means of the models proposed to account for the effect on bias (Sandusky, 1971; Tanner et al., 1967). If the two are unrelated, then additional assumptions are required, either in terms of processes unrelated to bias or in terms of nonsensory variables involving the state of the organism. The relation between the effects was tested here using auditory-frequency judgments in the first experiment and visual-intensity judgments in the second.

The experiments had an additional aim. There are theoretical reasons for assuming that context exerts some effect on discriminability, given the difference in magnitude of the change in measured bias following correct and incorrect responses, if performance is analyzed only as a function of error rather than of error type on the previous trial. If judgment moves back and forth between two decision criteria or response biases, the average ROC point will lie on a straight line connecting them. Since the straight line falls below the curvilinear ROC curve, measured discriminability is reduced (Green & Swets, 1966, p. 411; Lee, 1971, p. 230). The reduction following errors would be greater than following correct responses due to the larger shift in measured bias. The effect, termed *criterion averaging,* has been reported elsewhere to contribute to poorer performance under conditions of divided attention. Changes in measured bias on one dimension have been shown to result from the "present" context provided by the signal–response events associated with the simultaneous presentation of a second dimension (Long, 1975; 1976; 1977). The present experiments thus also evaluated the contribution of criterion averaging to changes in discriminability.

EXPERIMENTS 1 AND 2

The two experiments are reported and analyzed together for ease of exposition.

Method

In Experiment 1, two independent Wien-network oscillators generated signals at different frequencies, which were presented binaurally through Astrolite headphones. The two possible signals were 1000 and 991 Hz pure tones of 1-sec duration, presented at a sound pressure level 25dB above the ambient noise level (45 dB). A signal occurred every 6 sec. Signals were presented in blocks of 100 trials, four blocks per session. Two initial daily sessions were used for training. Subsequently, a 1-hour session was run each day for 6 days, making 2400 trials per subject. Knowledge of results concerning the previous day's performance was provided at the beginning of each session. Signal values were presented with equal frequency and equal transition probability, and subjects were informed of the fact. Subjects rated responses on a six-point scale for confidence (*very sure, fairly sure, unsure* for each response type). The subjects were 11 young male volunteers from the Royal Navy, tested in groups of 6 and 5.

In Experiment 2, the visual intensity signals were presented at a line-of-sight viewing distance of 1.8 m by means of a 5 × 60 mm frosted glass-covered aperture in a viewing box. The two visual intensities were dim, 31.4 lx; bright 36.6 lx. The method was otherwise the same as that of Experiment 1 including the identical presentation sequence of large and small signal values and the wearing of headphones. A further 11 young male volunteers from the Royal Navy were tested in groups of 6 and 5.

Results

Performance was analyzed as a function of the four possible previous-trial outcomes (two types of correct and two types of incorrect response). The four sets of rating data from each experiment were summarized in the form of ROC curves, each curve consisting of five data points, representing the five category boundaries of the six-point rating scale (see Fig. 8.1). The decision theory parameters for the ROC curves of individual subjects were estimated using a maximum-likelihood procedure described by Grey and Morgan (1972). Mean values appear in Fig. 8.1. Discriminability was measured by the index d', based on the geometric mean of the standard deviations of the signal distributions. Bias was measured by the index β. Central $\log_e \beta$ values are reported and evaluated statistically (referred to as $\ln \beta_c$). The β_c values are associated with the third datum point of each ROC curve, that is, at the category boundary between one type of response and the other (e.g., for auditory frequency between 'LOW' and 'HIGH'). The slope of the normalized ROC curve was computed as the ratio of the larger signal value to the smaller. Changes in performance over the initial three sessions, measured by the percentage of correct responses was +5% for frequency, −3% for intensity,

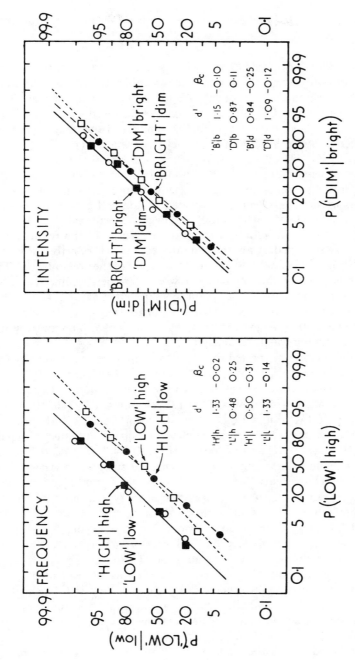

FIG. 8.1. Experiment 1: Auditory frequency recognition; Experiment 2: visual intensity recognition: Rating data summarized in the form of normalized ROC curves and plotted as a function of the context provided by the previous trial (lowercase words = signals; uppercase words = responses). d' and central ln β values are averaged over subjects.

163

and over the last three 0% and +2%, respectively. Significance levels for terms and interactions from analyses of variance was $p < .05$.

Discriminability.   Analysis of variance using d' values from the two experiments assessed three factors: one between subjects (modality) and two within (signal, response). The signal × response interaction was significant [$F(1, 20) = 23.12, p < .001$], as was the signal × response × modality interaction [$F(1, 20) = 6.06, p < .025$]. Further analysis of the interaction indicated an effect only in the case of frequency [frequency: $F(1, 20) = 26.45, p < .001$; intensity: $F(1, 20) = 2.76, p > .05$). Analysis of the intensity data alone indicated a significant signal × response interaction [$F(1, 10) = 27.14, p < .001$]. Thus, discriminability was worse following an error than following a correct response. The effect is illustrated in Fig. 8.1 by the downward displacement of the ROC curves along the negative diagonal.

To compute the contribution of criterion averaging to the reduction in discriminability provided by an undifferentiated analysis of errors, the data were reanalyzed conditional only on the correctness of the previous trial. The contribution is given by the difference between these new estimates and the mean value for correct and error response values cited earlier. The contribution was .02 unit of d' or 2.4% of the reduction for frequency. In the case of intensity, the size of the effect was increased by .03 unit of d'. The contribution of criterion averaging was thus negligible.

Figure 8.1 shows an unexpected change in the slope of the normalized ROC curves following errors, as illustrated by different ROC curves following errors and identical ROC curves following correct responses (frequency: 'LOW'/low = 1.04, 'HIGH'/low = 1.22, 'LOW'/high = .84, 'HIGH'/high = 1.04; intensity: 'DIM'/dim = 1.05, 'BRIGHT'/dim = 1.06, 'DIM'/bright = .93, 'BRIGHT'/bright = 1.03). Analysis showed a significant effect of signal [$F(1, 20) = 10.01, p < .01$] and of response [$F(1, 20) = 4.72, p < .05$] but no interaction with modality. The contribution of sequential variance to the reduction of discriminability given by the analysis of differentiated errors was estimated by recalculating d' following each error type in units of the less variable distribution (for example, low following 'HIGH'/low and high following 'LOW'/high). The amount was .09 unit of d' or 10.7% of the reduction for auditory frequency and .03 unit of d' or 11.1% for visual intensity. The contribution was thus important. This outcome is interpreted as a selective increase following errors, in the variance of one of the underlying distributions on which judgments are assumed to be based. The increase effectively reduced discriminability on trials following errors compared to those following correct responses. The phenomenon is termed *sequential variance* following Treisman (1977). The reduction occurs regardless of which distribution is used to scale the measure or whether as here some combination is used (Simpson & Fitter, 1973).

Bias.   Analysis of ln β_c values showed a significant effect of signal [$F(1, 20) = 31.03, p < .001$]; of response [$F(1, 20) = 7.46, p < .025$]; and of signal- × response interaction [$F(1, 20) = 5.24, p < .05$]. There was no interaction of any of these terms with modality. Measured bias, thus, changed significantly following errors. Responses were assimilated to the previous response value and were contrasted with the previous signal value. The effect is illustrated in Fig. 8.1 by the distance between the central datum points (and indeed the noncentral points) along the ROC curves, which is greater following errors than following correct responses.

Relationship Between Discriminability and Bias.   The relationship between the two effects was assessed by correlating the reduction in d' following errors (compared with correct responses) with the shift in ln β_c values toward the previous response and hence away from the previous signal following errors (compared with correct responses). A significant positive relationship was shown for frequency but not for intensity (Spearman Rank correlation coefficient: frequency $r_s = .75, p < .01$; intensity $r_s = .14, p > .05$).

Discussion

Prior context affects both discriminability and bias. For auditory frequency and visual intensity, judgments were less accurate as well as biased following errors. The relationship between the effects is complex. Changes in measured bias are always accompanied by some change in discriminability. Bias changes, however, may occur in the absence of a large reduction in discriminability, as in the case of intensity. When a large reduction does occur, it is positively correlated with the change in bias, as in the case of frequency.

The complexity of the relationship, however, did not result from criterion averaging. Criterion averaging contributes only to a reduction in discriminability based on an analysis of undifferentiated errors; and the contribution was negligible. Note that the contribution will vary with the magnitude of the changes in bias, which were small in the present experiments compared to those reported elsewhere. Differences among studies in this regard might be due to practice effects (Parducci & Sandusky, 1965), differences in frequency of repetition of signal values across conditions in the same experiment, changes in a priori probability (Kinchla, 1966; Tanner et al., 1967), or changes in transitional probability (Sandusky, 1971).

Nor did the complexity of the relationship result entirely from sequential variance. The contribution of sequential variance accounted for about 10% of the reduction and was the same for both frequency and intensity. This is a new component of the reduction, which has not been previously reported and for which there is no obvious explanation. A possible account is to combine the notion of (1) a selective attention band that samples primarily at one region in sensory space, for example at the location of the previous signal, hence deriving a larger sample for repeated signals and so reducing their variance compared with alternating ones (Green & Luce, 1974) with (2) a selective use of response criteria that increases the variance with repeated use, perhaps because the requirement to hold them in perceptual memory adds noise (Kinchla & Smyzer, 1967; see also Treisman, 1977 for an alternative view). The two types of selection, involving both a relative decrease and an increase in variance, affect the same underlying distribution following correct responses but different distributions following errors. Hence, the suggestion is consistent with a change in the slope of ROC curves following errors.

Thus, the complex relationship between the effects resulted from neither criterion averaging nor sequential variance. Since the magnitude of the reduction in discriminability was larger for auditory frequency and unrelated to the change in bias for visual intensity, the factor responsible for the impairment of intensity judgments following errors cannot be explained within the framework of the models proposed to account for the effect of prior context on measured bias, without additional assumptions.

EXPERIMENT 3

The previous experiments indicated that the impairment of intensity judgments following errors was unrelated to the judgmental processes involved in the changes of measured bias. The simplest explanation of the deficit not associated with sequential variance is to suppose organismic "state" or "non-sensory" variables responsible (Garner & Morton, 1969). "Attention" and "arousal" are assumed to fluctuate over time, but slowly enough so as not to change abruptly between two successive judgments (Collier, 1954; Isgur & Trehub, 1971; Kahneman, 1973, chap. 3). Hence poor performance on one trial is followed by poor performance on the next, because both involve the same lowered state of the organism's efficiency. By this account, the impairment of frequency judgments consists of at least two components, in addition to sequential variance—one small, in common with visual intensity, and unrelated to the changes in bias; the other large, related to changes in bias occurring only for frequency. This account is termed the *organismic "state" hypothesis*.

An alternative view is also consistent with the results of the previous experiments. It supposes that the intensity impairment may or may not be shared by frequency. In either case, the deficit depends on part of the judgmental process not involved in the bias effect. This view is termed the *modality "process" hypothesis*.

The contrast between the two hypotheses lies in the function ascribed to the dimension used to present the signals. For the modality process view, no effect of prior context on discriminability would be expected unless the same dimension occurred on the preceding trial. The process is assumed to be specific to the dimension. For the organismic state view, the effect is independent of the dimension and the modality of presentation on the previous trial. The effect is exerted by an organismic state and, therefore, is common to both.

Suppose auditory and visual signals are interleaved on alternate trials, for example a high tone following a dim light and so on. The modality process view predicts no impairment of judgment following errors in a different modality (shown schematically in Fig. 8.2 a and c) whereas the organismic state view predicts an impairment of the same order of magnitude as in the intensity experiment (illustrated in Fig. 8.2 b and d).

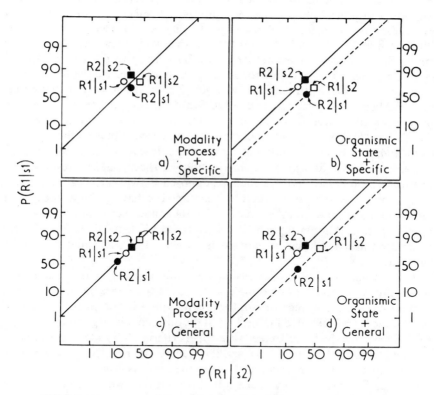

FIG. 8.2.   A summary of the predictions considered in the text concerning the effect of prior context: (1) on discriminability by the organismic state (b, d) versus modality process (a, c) hypotheses and (2) on measured bias by the general (c, d) versus specific (a, b) hypotheses. Signals are labeled s1, s2; responses R1, R2. Performance is plotted as a function of the context provided by the previous trial. In the interests of clarity, a single datum point only is associated with each type of prior context. The point corresponds to the central cutoff of the normalized ROC curves shown in Fig. 8.1, 8.5, and 8.6.

Interleaving frequency and intensity signals on alternate trials does not change the structure of the stimulus sequences. For example, the sequence of signals "low, high, high, low" in the first experiment became "dim, bright, bright, dim" in the second and "low, bright, high, dim" in the present experiment. This has some interesting implications for models of signal recognition proposed to account for the change in measured bias following errors. The models can be divided into two classes—those involving general biases and those that assume a relationship between the sensory information (or its effect) on one trial and the next.

Models of generalized response bias assume two response tendencies—to alternate the preceding response, perhaps in order to maintain the known a priori probabilities of the signals over the short term, and to repeat the preceding response, perhaps because processes associated with it have been more recently used and are therefore facilitated. This class of model is illustrated in Fig. 8.3, which shows that if the two tendencies are of similar strength, they offset one another following correct responses. Following errors, however, the tendency to repeat dominates, because the tendency to alternate decreases with confidence, which is itself monotonic with correctness and hence is low for errors. In other words, the subjects tend to alternate only when they have reason to believe the previous response was correct. Generalized bias is independent of the dimension used to present the signals—both high and bright counting as large values, low and dim as small ones. Thus, at the level at which the implications of the signal-and-response sequence are processed, equivalence is supposed between values on the two dimensions. The sequence structure is assumed to have a single underlying semantic representation in terms of which the tendencies to alternate and to repeat operate. Alternating modalities, thus, should leave the effect of prior context on measured bias unchanged as shown in Fig. 8.2c and d. This is the "general" view of bias.

The second class of model assumes specific aspects of the judgmental process to be involved. For example, subjects may compare the percept of the current signal with the memory for the previous one (Tanner et al., 1967). This type of model is illustrated in Fig. 8.4a. If the difference is large and positive—the evidence for the signal exceeds the upper criterion (C2)—then the subjects respond 'HIGH' (for frequency), and if it is large and negative—the evidence falls below the lower criterion (C1)—then the subjects respond 'LOW.' If the difference is small—the evidence falls between the two criteria—then the current signal is identified as the same as the previous one and the last response is repeated. The memory trace for errors is less extreme on average than for correct responses, and this increases the number of "different" judgments made to signals opposite in value to those of the previous trial. Because the cutoffs producing "same" responses remain unchanged, measured bias is larger following errors.

Model of Generalized Response Bias

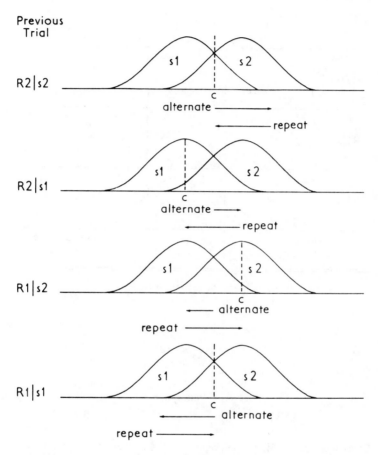

FIG. 8.3. Illustration of a generalized response bias model, showing the underlying distributions on the present trial following four typical signal–response values on the previous trial (signals, s1, s2; responses, R1, R2). The underlying distributions are assumed fixed. The final criterion cutoff (dotted line marked C) is set by two response tendencies: to alternate and to repeat (details are provided in the text). For illustrative purposes only, the tendency to alternate is shown as (1) acting before the tendency to repeat and (2) beginning at the crossover point of the two distributions.

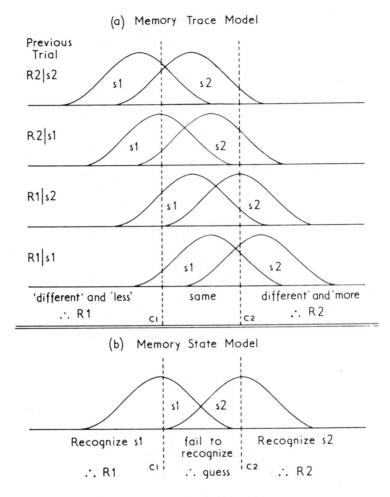

(a) Memory Trace Model

Previous Trial

R2|s2

R2|s1

R1|s2

R1|s1

'different' and 'less'   same   'different' and 'more'

∴ R1   C1   C2   ∴ R2

(b) Memory State Model

Recognize s1   fail to recognize   Recognize s2

∴ R1   C1   ∴ guess   C2   ∴ R2

Guessing Rules: if n−1 recognized, then alternate response.
if n−1 not recognized, then alternate or repeat response.

FIG. 8.4.   Illustration of (a) *memory-trace model,* assuming fixed decision criteria (shown by dotted lines marked C1, C2), and underlying distributions varying as a function of the size of the trace on the previous trial (signals, s1, s2; responses, R1, R2). Four typical signal–response values on the previous trial are shown; (b) *memory-state model,* assuming fixed decision criteria (C1, C2) and fixed underlying distributions, with guessing rules dependent on the recognition outcome of the previous trial. The text provides further details on both models.

An alternative model is illustrated in Fig. 8.4b. This model assumes subjects' judgments to be absolute at extreme signal values—above C2 or below C1 (Sandusky, 1971). These judgments result from "true" recognitions and hence are correct. Intermediate values falling between C1 and C2 are not recognized and are therefore guessed. The guessing response depends on the "sensory state" remaining from the preceding trial. If the signal was recognized, the subjects alternate their responses. If the signal was not recognized, the subjects alternate or repeat their responses according to personal bias. Larger changes in bias following errors of the kind reported here occur if subjects display a repetition bias on the second of successive nonrecognition trials. Alternating modalities in both of these cases should eliminate the effect of prior context on measured bias, as illustrated in Fig. 8.2a and b, because both the previous sensory trace and sensory state are inappropriate. This is the "specific" view of bias.

The organismic state versus modality process predictions concerning the discriminability and the general versus specific predictions concerning bias (illustrated in Fig. 8.2) were tested in the third experiment.

Method

The method was identical with that of the first two experiments except that auditory and visual signals were alternated. They also were made somewhat easier to discriminate in an attempt to equate performance with the earlier experiments: frequency, high—1000 Hz, low—989 Hz; intensity, bright—36.6 lx, dim—29.1 lx. A further group of 11 young male volunteers from the Royal Navy were tested.

Results

The rating data summarized in the form of ROC curves are shown in Fig. 8.5

Discriminability.   Analysis of variance with signal, response, and modality as within-subject factors showed only a significant signal × response interaction [$F(1, 10) = 7.40, p < .025$]. Impaired judgments followed errors in a different modality, seen in Fig. 8.5 by the downward displacement along the negative diagonal of the ROC curves.

Bias.   Analysis of variance showed no effect of prior context on measured bias, seen in Fig. 8.5 by the proximity of the central datum points along the ROC curves. All relevant F ratios were < 1.

Relationship Between Discriminability and Bias.   For neither frequency nor intensity was there a significant relationship between the two effects

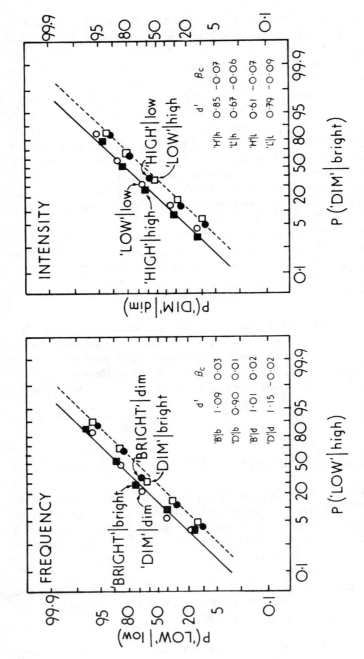

FIG. 8.5. Experiment 3. Auditory-frequency and visual-intensity recognition: Rating data summarized in the form of normalized ROC curves and plotted as a function of the context provided by the previous trial (signal presented to a different modality) (lowercase words = signals; uppercase words = responses). d' and central ln β values are averaged over subjects.

(Spearman Rank correlation coefficient: frequency $r_s = .-17$; intensity $r_s = .11, p > .05$).

Presenting prior context in a different modality eliminated the frequency-specific impairment reported in the first experiment and the change in measured bias noted in both earlier experiments. The elimination of these effects raised the question of their robustness. In order to establish whether they had withstood an intervening judgment of a signal presented to a different modality, a within-modality analysis of the data was also undertaken. The data were reanalyzed, conditional on two trials back, when the signal was in the same modality.

The pattern of outcomes (Fig. 8.6) was similar to that found in the first two experiments (Fig. 8.1). Discriminability showed a significant signal × response interaction [$F(1, 10) = 16.05$, $p < .01$], which itself interacted with modality [$F(1, 10) = 6.86, p < .05$]. Further analysis of the interaction showed impaired performance following errors for frequency but not for intensity [frequency: $F(1, 10) = 22.83, p < .001$; intensity: $F(1, 10) = 2.67, p > .05$]. Bias showed a significant effect of signal [$F(1, 10) = 16.96, p < .01$]. There were no interactions with modality. The correlation between the two effects was significant for frequency but not for intensity (Spearman Rank correlation coefficient: frequency $r_s = .63, p < .05$; intensity $r_s = .36, p > .05$).

Discussion

Prior context does not have to be in the same dimension and modality to produce a small but reliable reduction in discriminability following errors. Prior context does have to be in the same dimension and modality however to affect measured bias. Together the results support the organismic state hypothesis and the specific view of bias (compare central datum points in Fig. 8.5 and Fig. 8.2b—change in d', no change in β_c).

A number of possible confounding factors affecting these results can be discounted. First, in as much as the impairment occurred for both dimensions, it is unlikely that the intensity effect was simply due to subjects failing to look up at the visual signal following an auditory one. The long signal duration (1 sec) also argues against this possibility. Second, the impairment was not due to interference from a previous erroneous trial (in tasks requiring fine discrimination, errors take longer than correct responses—Pickett, 1967), because subjects in these experiments were highly practiced and the response interval (4 sec) was much longer than typical error reaction times. Further, manipulation of interval duration has not been found to affect changes in discriminability (MacDonald, 1974). Third, the impairment was not an artefact of the reduction in data. A reanalysis of the data from Experiments 1 and 2 as performed in Experiment 3 (alternate trials) showed only a slight decrease in the size of the effect. Concerning measured bias, the absence of a change

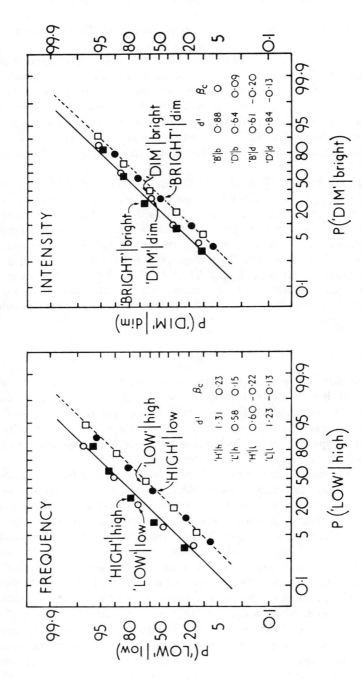

FIG. 8.6. Experiment 3. Auditory-frequency and visual-intensity recognition: Rating data summarized in the form of normalized ROC curves and plotted as a function of the context provided by two trials back (signal presented to the same modality) (lowercase words = signals; uppercase words = responses). d' and central ln β values are averaged over subjects.

174

was not due to subjects having strong biases that differed in direction. The differences following correct and incorrect responses were small even when calculated independently of their direction. The organismic state and specific bias hypotheses are thus retained.

GENERAL DISCUSSION

The third experiment indirectly demonstrated the contribution of organismic state or nonsensory variables to the reduction in discriminability following errors. This contribution added to that of sequential variance would seem to account for all the impairment shown by intensity in the second experiment. This conclusion is consistent with the absence of any relationship between discriminability and bias effects for intensity. The small but reliable effect of organismic state variables means that error dependencies cannot automatically be interpreted in process terms, unless the appropriate control conditions have been tested (MacDonald, 1974).

Given the interaction of the discriminability effect with modality in the first two experiments and in the data conditionalized on two trials back in the third, a further component of impairment must be assumed. This component appears to be related to the judgmental processes involved in the bias effect, because the two effects were significantly correlated. The question thus arises as to why it occurs with auditory frequency and not with visual intensity.

The frequency-specific nature of the impairment might be explained in three different ways. First, the specificity may depend on the modality to which the signal is presented. Persistence effects in vision may be less long lasting than in audition (Darwin, Turvey, & Crowder, 1972; Penney, 1975; Vanthoor & Eijkman, 1973). The impairment may thus originate in the processing of the auditory trace from the previous trial. This notion is inconsistent however with the absence of a discriminability effect in auditory judgments of loudness (Kinchla, 1966; Tanner et al., 1967; McNicol, this volume). Second, the specificity may be related to classes of judgments that differ systematically, for example, qualitative or metathetic (frequency) versus quantitative or prothetic (intensity) (Stevens & Galanter, 1957). But this notion is inconsistent with the absence of an effect using visual spatial location (qualitative—Sandusky, 1971). Unlike the modality explanation, it is consistent with the absence of an effect using auditory amplitude (Kinchla, 1966; Tanner et al., 1967). Further tests between these two approaches could be designed using sound duration for which only the modality explanation predicts an effect or color and orientation for which only the class of judgment explanation predicts an effect. Neither approach predicts an effect for visual area, line length, or dot numerosity. Third, the specificity may be related to frequency itself, perhaps because people's familiarity with pitch is not usually in the form of pure tones and hence differences in direction are more difficult to identify. Alternatively, the cyclic nature of the musical scale of pitch may lead to confusion in direction. How these approaches relate to the models most able to account for the change in measured bias following errors is considered later.

The results of the three experiments argue against models of generalized bias, because the effect on bias only occurred when the same dimension was used to present the prior context. The conclusion is similar to one reached elsewhere concerning the biasing effect on one dimension of the present context provided by the signal–response events associated with the simultaneous presentation of a second dimension (Long, 1977). Varying the association between simultaneous signal values from .2 to 1.0 without the subjects' knowledge, while maintaining the a priori probabilities for each dimension, left overall bias unchanged on the two dimensions. The finding argues in favor of a mechanism which assumes that biasing at some level of processing depends on the mutually contingent interaction of discrete events on the two dimensions and against one which assumes biasing to depend on memory and expectations of the relative frequency of conjoint events. Matching the relative frequency of signal events is a basic assumption of the model of generalized response bias tested here. The two conclusions are thus similar.

The results are also inconsistent with two-factor models of the effect of prior context on bias, which include generalized bias as one of the factors. The conclusion seriously weakens this class of model, because a single factor does not result in a greater effect on bias following errors as opposed to correct responses. Suppose subjects alternate their responses, or in line with the common experience that a medium tone sounds lower following a high tone than following a low one they adjust their criteria in the direction of the sensory information received on the previous trial, thus favoring a 'HIGH' response following a low signal (Broadbent, 1971, chap. 6; John, 1973; Thomas, 1975). Then adjustment by a constant amount predicts a similar change in bias following errors and correct responses, and adjustment proportional to the sensory value predicts a smaller change following errors, because small values lead to error.

There remains the question of how the specific models of bias noted earlier cope with the frequency-specific component of the reduction in discriminability following errors that was shown to be related to bias (Fig. 8.4). The memory-trace model can account for the effect, if it is assumed that the mental computation of the difference between a current signal and the trace of the previous one and the computation of the direction of the difference are two separable operations. If the direction of frequency is difficult to code (for modality, class of judgment or for reasons specific to auditory frequency—see earlier), then confusion may occur when a significant difference does not involve a change of response. This would be most likely after an error, because the effect of the trace is less extreme and the chance of having a "different" decision requiring the same response would be greater (see Fig. 8.4 center panels). This account predicts that cuing direction should eliminate the effect. The memory-state model can account for the effect if it is assumed that the labeling of the true recognition states become reversed. It is unclear from the model, however, why the reversals should follow errors.

CONCLUSIONS

1. Prior context affected discriminability as well as bias.
2. The reduction in discriminability following errors was multiply determined—by an organismic state or nonsensory variable, by sequential variance for visual intensity, and in addition by a modality process variable for auditory frequency.
3. Changes in measured bias following errors did not result from generalized bias.
4. A positive relation between discriminability and bias occurred in the case of the modality process variable but not in the case of the organismic state variable.
5. A memory-trace and a memory-state model of signal recognition are able to account for these results.

ACKNOWLEDGMENTS

I would like to thank Mr. Keith Taylor for developing and running the analysis programs for this research and Dr. Ian Nimmo-Smith and Dr. Dan Weber for helpful discussions. Thanks are also due to the Royal Navy, who made available the subjects.

REFERENCES

Broadbent, D. E. *Decision and stress.* London: Academic Press, 1971.
Collier, G. Intertrial association at the visual threshold as a function of intertrial interval. *Jounal of Experimental Psychology,* 1954, *48,* 330–334.
Darwin, C. J., Turvey, M. T., & Crowder, R. G. An auditory analogue of the Sperling partial report procedure: Evidence for brief auditory storage. *Cognitive Psychology,* 1972, *3,* 255–267.
Garner, W. R., & Morton, J. Perceptual independence: Definitions, models and experimental paradigms. *Psychological Bulletin,* 1969, *72,* 233–259.
Green, D. M., & Luce, R. D. Speed-accuracy trade-off in auditory detection. In S. Kornblum (Ed.), *Attention and performance IV.* New York and London: Academic Press, 1973.
Green, D. M., & Luce, R. D. Variability of magnitude estimates: A timing theory analysis. *Perception and Psychophysics,* 1974, *15,* 291–300.
Green, D. M., & Swets, J. A. *Signal detection theory and psychophysics.* New York: Wiley, 1966; reprinted New York: Krieger, 1974.
Grey, D. R., & Morgan, B. J. T. Some aspects of ROC curve fitting: Normal and logistic models. *Journal of Mathematical Psychology,* 1972, *9,* 128–139.

Helson, H. *Adaptation-level theory*. New York: Harper and Row, 1964.

Isgur, J., & Trehub, A. Detection efficiency and evoked brain activity. *EEG and Clinical Neurophysiology*, 1971, *31*, 96–98.

John, I. D. Sequential effects in absolute judgements of loudness without feedback. In S. Kornblum (Ed.), *Attention and performance IV*. New York and London: Academic Press, 1973.

Kahneman, D. *Attention and effort*. Englewood Cliffs, N.J.: Prentice-Hall, 1973.

Kinchla, R. A. A comparison of sequential effects in detection and recognition. *Experimental Psychology Series*, Psychology Department, New York University, Technical Reports, *1*, 1966.

Kinchla, R. A., & Smyzer, F. A diffusion model of perceptual memory. *Perception and Psychophysics*, 1967, *2*, 219–229.

Lee, W. *Decision theory and human behavior*. New York: Wiley, 1971.

Long, J. B. Reduced efficiency and capacity limitations in multidimension signal recognition. *Quarterly Journal of Experimental Psychology*, 1975, *27*, 599–614.

Long, J. B. Dividing attention between non-verbal signals: All-or-none or shared processing? *Quarterly Journal of Experimental Psychology*, 1976, *28*, 47–69.

Long, J. B. Contextual assimilation and its effect on the division of attention between non-verbal signals. *Quarterly Journal of Experimental Psychology*, 1977, *29*, 397–414.

Luce, R. D. What sort of measurement is psychophysical measurement? *American Psychologist*, 1972, *27*(2), 96–106.

MacDonald, R. R. Intertrial dependence in detection and recognition tasks. *Acta Psychologica*, 1974, *38*, 357–365.

Parducci, A. Sequential effects in judgement. *Psychological Bulletin*, 1964, *61*, 163–167.

Parducci, A., & Sandusky, A. Distribution and sequence effects in judgement. *Journal of Experimental Psychology*, 1965, *69*, 450–459.

Pastore, R. E., & Sorkin, R. D. Adaptive auditory signal processing. *Psychonomic Science*, 1971, *23*, 259–260.

Penney, C. G. Modality effects in short-term verbal memory. *Psychological Bulletin*, 1975, *82*, 68–84.

Pickett, R. M. Response latency in a pattern perception situation. In A. F. Sanders (Ed.), *Attention and performance I*. Amsterdam: North-Holland Pub. Co., 1967.

Poulton, E. C. The new psychophysics: Six models for magnitude estimation. *Psychological Bulletin*, 1968, *69*, 1–19.

Sandusky, A. Signal recognition models compared for random and Markov presentation sequences. *Perception and Psychophysics*, 1971, *10*, 339–347.

Shipley, E. F. Dependence of successive judgements in detection tasks: Correctness of the response. *Journal of the Acoustical Society of America*, 1961, *33*, 1142–1143.

Simpson, A. J., & Fitter, M. J. What is the best index of detectability? *Psychological Bulletin*, 1973, *80*, 481–488.

Stevens, S. S., & Galanter, E. H. Ratio scales and category scales for a dozen perceptual continua. *Journal of Experimental Psychology*, 1957, *54*, 377–411.

Swets, J. A., Shipley, E. F., McKey, M. J., & Green, D. M. Multiple observations of signals in noise. *Journal of the Acoustical Society of America*, 1959, *31*, 514–521.

Tanner, T. A., Haller, R. W., & Atkinson, R. C. Signal recognition as influenced by presentation schedules. *Perception and Psychophysics*, 1967, *2*, 349–358.

Thomas, E. A. C. Criterion adjustment and probability matching. *Perception and Psychophysics*, 1975, *18*, 158–162.

Treisman, M. On the stability of d_s. *Psychological Bulletin*, 1977, *84*, 235–243.

Vanthoor, F. L. J., & Eijkman, E. G. J. Time course of the iconic memory signal. *Acta Psychologica*, 1973, *37*, 79–85.

9 Multiple Regression Analyses of Sequential Effects in Loudness Judgments

D. McNicol
School of Psychology
University of New South Wales
New South Wales, Australia

ABSTRACT

Sequential effects in loudness judgments were studied in a four-stimulus absolute judgment task, a two-stimulus × two-response identification task, and a two-stimulus task with confidence ratings. Multiple regression analyses of the data showed that the current stimulus, previous stimulus, and previous response influenced the choice of the current response, which was contrasted with the previous stimulus and assimilated to the previous response in all three tasks. It was proposed that subjects judge the difference between the current and previous stimuli rather than the current stimulus itself and shift their response criteria so as to reduce biases created in the sensory evidence by the shifting value of the trial $n - 1$ comparison stimulus. Reaction-time data showing that responses were slower on trials when the current stimulus was a repetition of the previous one also supported the hypothesis that judgments involve sampling from the distribution of differences between the trial $n - 1$ and trial n stimuli to choose a response.

Ward and Lockhead (1971) showed that the size and sign of the error in an absolute judgment task was related to the values of stimuli and responses from earlier trials in the series. There seemed to be two key findings about sequential effects in this type of task that needed explanation. First was the apparent assimilation of R_n, the response on the current trial, to R_{n-1}, the response (or S_{n-1}, the stimulus) from the immediately preceding trial; second was the apparent contrast between R_n and responses (or stimuli) from trials before the immediately preceding one. Although the size of the contrast effect decreased as preceding trials became more remote, it could be detected in trials at least five back from the current one. Explanations of these phenomena have generally assumed that subjects acquire information about the frequency with which members of the stimulus set occur and the range of values they cover, either from trial-by-trial feedback, or from memory of the stimulus values presented on earlier trials. This information is used in conjunction with certain response strategies to select a response to the current stimulus. This chapter considers only cases where feedback was not given and subjects could only gain information from the stimulus series or from their own responses. Ward and Lockhead (1971) proposed that in this situation the current stimulus indicates a range of possible response values, and the one chosen is that which is closest to the response on the previous trial. Additionally, longer-term sequential effects may also arise from attempts to use all areas of the response scale equally frequently within 5 to 10 trials. Other explanations of sequential effects in absolute judgments have been based on the range–frequency principle (Parducci, 1973) or on the role of end anchors and of error perseveration (John, 1973).

By contrast, explanations of sequential effects in the two-stimulus identification task without feedback have assumed that only events on the immediately preceding trial directly influence the response made on the current trial. Models for this task have usually been based on the signal detection theory concepts of distributions of sensory evidence corresponding to S_n and S_{n-1}, the current and previous stimuli, and of a criterion that partitions the sensory continuum into two response regions. Data have normally been presented in the form of conditional probabilities, $P(R_j|S_iS_kR_l)$s, of responses, R_js, occurring on trial n to stimuli, S_is, given the stimuli, S_ks, and responses, R_ls, on trial $n - 1$. Typically it has been found that R_j is more likely to occur on the current trial if it also occurred on the preceding trial but is less likely to occur on the current trial if S_j occurred on the preceding trial (Parducci & Sandusky, 1965; Sandusky, 1971; Tanner Haller, & Atkinson, 1967; Tanner, Rauk, & Atkinson, 1970). To explain these response assimilation and stimulus contrast effects, Tanner et al. (1970) suggested that subjects judge the difference between S_n and their memory of S_{n-1}, giving response R_1 if the difference is large and negative, R_2 if it is large and positive, and repeating R_{n-1} if it is small. Other models based on a psychophysical learning theory (Schoeffler, 1965) or a four-state Markov process (Sandusky, 1971) have also been suggested. All the models noted are applicable to cases where feedback is not given, but others have been developed that predict sequential effects when subjects are informed about the correctness of their responses (Dorfman & Biderman, 1971; Kac, 1962; Larkin, 1971; Lee, 1966).

Apparent dissimilarities between the results from the two-stimulus and many-stimulus tasks has led to the belief that different explanations are needed for sequential effects in the two cases (Parducci, 1973), but these dissimilarities may reflect differences in methods of data analysis rather than in the way subjects make judgments. John (1973) used Ward and Lockhead's (1971) procedure to analyze data for 2-, 3-, and 10-stimulus identification tasks and reported assimilation to the previous trial's stimulus in each case. Jesteadt, Luce, and Green (1977) and Green, Luce, and Duncan (1977) have analyzed sequential effects in magnitude estimation and production tasks by a multiple regression procedure, concluding that sequential effects extend back only to the immediately preceding trial and that the current response is assimilated to the previous response and is contrasted with the previous stimulus. Their original regression equation was of the form:

$$f(R_n) = B_1 f(S_n) + B_2 f(S_{n-1}) + B_3 f(R_{n-1}) + A \tag{1}$$

where the B_is are raw score regression coefficients and A is the additive constant. The terms $f(S_n), f(R_n), f(S_{n-1})$, and $f(R_{n-1})$ are appropriate functions of the current and previous stimuli and responses. In Jesteadt et al. (1977) and Green et al. (1977), logarithmic functions were used, as they seemed appropriate to tasks where subjects were instructed either to make judgments so that the ratio of successive response values reflected the ratio of successive stimulus values or to adjust the stimulus level on successive trials to equal the ratio of successive numbers. However, other transformations may be appropriate to tasks not emphasizing ratio judgments. For example, if a signal-detection model of the type suggested by Tanner et al. (1970) is applied to the two-stimulus identification task, the expression for $P(R_j|S_iS_kR_l)$ in z-score form is:

$$z(R_j|S_iS_kR_l) = B_1 \mu_i + B_2 \mu_k + B_3 c_l + A \tag{2}$$

where μ_i and μ_k are the means of the distributions of sensory effect for the current and previous stimuli and c_l is the position of the response criterion on trial $n - 1$. As subjects are presumed to base their judgments on the distribution of differences between S_n and S_{n-1}, B_2 should be negative; and as there is a bias toward repeating the trial $n - 1$ response, B_3 should be positive. The similarity between these formulations of the two-stimulus identification task and the many-stimulus × many-response task is obvious; it offers a framework for comparing judgment processes in the two cases and for testing some of the models advanced to explain sequential effects. The Ward and Lockhead (1971) and Parducci (1973) models of the many-stimulus task and Schoeffler's (1965) model of the two-stimulus task propose assimilation to the previous response but do not postulate involvement of the previous stimulus. Thus B_3 should be positive, and B_2 should be near zero. Adaptation level theory proposes that the present judgment is influenced by previous stimulation (Helson, 1964) and predicts that B_2 should be negative, whereas B_3 should be near zero. Models that assume that the previous stimulus acts as a standard for comparative judgment, while the previous response has a biasing effect on the current response, such as John's (1973) model for the many-stimulus task or Tanner *et al.*'s (1970) and Sandusky's (1971) models for the two-stimulus task, predict that B_2 will be negative and that B_3 will be positive.

The present study used the regression model in three stimulus-identification situations: four-stimulus absolute judgments, the two-stimulus × two-response task, and the two-stimulus task with the response scale extended to include confidence judgments. If a single model can account for judgment processes in these situations, then a common pattern should occur in the values of the regression coefficients for sequential effects in the three cases.

EXPERIMENT 1: ABSOLUTE JUDGMENTS

Jesteadt *et al.* (1977) performed regression analyses by using log R_n as the dependent variable and by successively including the log values of the five immediately preceding stimuli or the five immediately preceding responses as independent variables. Only the current stimulus and the stimulus and response of the immediately preceding trial contributed significantly to predicting R_n. The regression analysis was therefore restricted to events on the current and immediately preceding trial, and the equation solved was that given by Eq. (1) using logarithmic functions of stimulus and response variables. The procedure used in this experiment was slightly different. Stimulus sequences were constructed where the probability of any stimulus being repeated on successive trials was varied, thus making S_{n-1} predictable from S_n. In these sequences the overall probabilities of stimuli were equal, and only the repetition probability of a stimulus on successive trials was constrained. If the stimuli are considered to lie on an ordinal scale, where the numbers 1 to m represent them from smallest to largest, then the mean ordinal value $\bar{S}_{n-1}$, of the previous stimulus can be obtained from the ordinal value, S_n, of the current stimulus and from m and $P(rep)$, the number of stimuli in the set and the repetition probability, respectively. Thus:

$$\bar{S}_{n-1} = P(rep)S_n + [1 - P(rep)] \cdot \left[\frac{m(m + 1) - 2S_n}{2(m - 1)}\right] \tag{3}$$

The regression equation can then be formed by substituting S_n, R_n, $\bar{S}_{n-1}$, and R_{n-1} for $f(S_n)$, $f(R_n)$, $f(S_{n-1})$, and $f(R_{n-1})$, in Eq. (1).

Two remarks should be made about this procedure. First, it may seem inappropriate to use ordinally scaled variables in a regression analysis, but most models can be distinguished according to whether the regression coefficients are positive or negative, or significantly different from zero, and these tests can be made on ordinally scaled variables (Cohen & Cohen, 1975). Second, varying repetition probability ensures that S_n is highly correlated with S_{n-1} for any subject, thus making it difficult to assess their independent effects on that person's performance. However, by choosing high repetition probabilities for some subjects and low repetition probabilities for others the correlation between S_n and S_{n-1} can be made to be low between subjects, making it possible to estimate group regression coefficients without encountering problems of multicolinearity between these independent variables.

Method

Forty members of an introductory psychology course at the University of New South Wales made absolute judgments of the loudness of four 600-Hz tones that differed from one another in steps of 1 dB, with the softest tone set to give a sound pressure level of about 75 dB, re .0002 microbar. Subjects listened to the tones through Pioneer SE300 headphones and made their judgments by pressing one of four keys labeled 1 to 4 from left to right, where key 1 corresponded to the softest, and key 4, to the loudest tones in the set. The keys were spaced about 4 cm apart, and throughout the experiment the subjects rested the middle and index fingers of the left hand on keys 1 and 2 and the index and middle fingers of the right hand on keys 3 and 4. They were told that their reaction times were to be measured and were asked to respond as quickly and accurately as possible. They were also informed that there was a 5-sec deadline for responding, but this was never exceeded during the experiment.

A trial began with a .5-sec warning light, and 1 sec later a stimulus tone was presented for .25 sec. After the response there was a delay of 4.25 sec before the next trial. A total of 200 experimental trials were run during the session, with each of the four decibel levels occurring 50 times in a quasirandom order. As the experiment was computer controlled, it was possible to run several subjects simultaneously, but each received a different stimulus sequence. The requirement that all four stimuli were to occur an equal number of times in the sequences of 200 trials precluded their generation by varying transition probabilities in a Markov process as in Sandusky (1971). The sequences were, in fact, permutations containing exactly 50 events (each of four different types) but constrained so that if event i occurred on trial n, the probability of it occurring again on trial $n + 1$ was $P(rep)$; whereas the probability of any of the other three events occurring was $\frac{1}{3}[1 - P(rep)]$. The procedure used to generate a sequence ensured that these transition probabilities were stationary over the entire sequence and that events occurred in a quasirandom order. For half the subjects, a high repetition probability was used [Mean $P(rep)$ = 59, Range = .55–.64]; for the others, it was low [Mean $P(rep)$ = .13, Range = .09–.19]. Subjects were told nothing of this variable, however, only being informed that all stimuli would occur equally often during the experiment.

Before the experimental session, subjects were acquainted with the range of stimuli to be used and were given experience with the response keys. Just prior to the experimental trials, 20 practice trials were attempted under the conditions that pertained during the experiment. Responses and reaction times for each subject's experimental series were sorted by the computer program into 4×4 matrices containing the mean response, $\bar{R}_n$, and the mean latency, $\bar{L}_n$, on trial n, for each of the 16 $(S_n \times R_{n-1})$ combinations.

Results

A hierarchical multiple regression analysis (Cohen & Cohen, 1975, section 3.6.2) was carried out on the 640 mean response values obtained from the 40 subjects under the 16 experimental conditions. The independent variables, in order of entry to the analysis, were S_n, $\bar{S}_{n-1}$, R_{n-1}, and $P(rep)$. The results of the analysis in Table 9.1 show that the current and previous stimuli and the previous response all contributed significantly to determining the current response and, between them, accounted for about 24% of its variance. Repetition probability made no significant contribution to the current response. The

TABLE 9.1

Hierarchical Multiple Regression Analysis of Mean Response Values, and Mean Reaction Times on Trial n in the Four-Stimulus Absolute Judgment Task

Independent Variable	Raw Score Regression Coefficient, B_i	Normalized Regression Coefficient, β_i	Significance of Coefficient, F_i	Cumulative R^2
Mean Response Value for Trial n				
S_n	.13	.27	24.48^{ab}	.042
$\bar{S}_{n-1}$	−.31	−.22	31.32^{ab}	.100
R_{n-1}	.16	.32	83.12^{ab}	.239
$P(rep)$	−.10	−.04	N.S.	.241
Constant	2.62			
Mean Latency for Trial n (*Coefficient values in msec*)				
R_n	25.4	.02	N.S.^{c}	.000
S_n	−13.8	−.02	N.S.^{c}	.000
$\bar{S}_{n-1}$	24.7	.01	N.S.^{c}	.000
R_{n-1}	−30.8	−.04	N.S.^{c}	.002
$P(rep)$	89.9	.25	54.42^{ac}	.096
Constant	489.5			

[a] $P < .05$
[b] d.f. = (1,581)
[c] d.f. = (1,580)

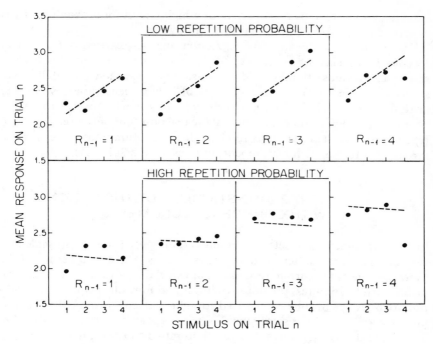

FIG. 9.1.   Mean response on trial n in the absolute judgment task, plotted as a function of the current stimulus, S_n, and previous response, R_{n-1}, for subjects receiving sequences with high or low probabilities of stimulus repetition on trials $n - 1$ and n. Regression lines have been fitted with the coefficients for S_n and R_{n-1} for each group.

signs of the regression coefficients indicated contrast of the current response to S_{n-1} and assimilation to R_{n-1}. The variable that had the strongest effect on $\bar{R}_n$ was R_{n-1}, then S_n, and finally S_{n-1}.

As the finding that R_{n-1} contributed more to $\bar{R}_n$ than S_n was unexpected, the response data were examined further by separating the results of the 20 subjects with low repetition probabilities from those with high repetition probabilities and conducting separate regression analyses with the variates S_n and R_{n-1}. (S_{n-1} could not be included because it was almost perfectly correlated with S_n within each group.) The normalized regression coefficients for S_n and R_{n-1} for the low repetition group were .37 and .17, respectively, and they accounted for 18% of the variance in $\bar{R}_n$. For the high repetition group, the normalized coefficients for S_n and R_{n-1} were −.02 and .49, respectively, accounting for 26% of $\bar{R}_n$'s variance. The effects are illustrated in Fig. 9.1, which gives plots of $\bar{R}_n$ against S_n and R_{n-1} for the two groups that are fitted by the regression lines. It can be seen that with a low repetition probability the current response is mainly determined by the current stimulus and, to a lesser extent, by the previous response. With a high repetition probability, $\bar{R}_n$ is governed largely by R_{n-1} and hardly at all by S_n.

The results of a hierarchical regression analysis, carried out on mean reaction times, classified according to the values of the current stimulus and response, previous stimulus and response, and repetition probability, are shown in Table 9.1. The order of entry of independent variables into the analysis was $\bar{R}_n$, S_n, $\bar{S}_{n-1}$, R_{n-1}, and $P(rep)$. Only repetition probability accounted for a significant proportion of the reaction-time variance. The mean reaction time of the 20 subjects receiving low repetition rates was 651 msec; for the 20 subjects with high repetition rates, it was 987 msec.

EXPERIMENT 2: TWO-STIMULUS IDENTIFICATION WITH CONFIDENCE JUDGMENTS

In this experiment, subjects rated their certainty on a four-point scale that they had heard the softer or louder of two tones. The design permitted the average value of the current response to be calculated, given any combination of the current stimulus, previous stimulus, and previous response. In addition, two groups of subjects received stimulus sequences with either high or low probabilities of the same stimulus being repeated on trials $n - 1$ and n. This enabled investigation of two questions raised by Experiment 1. First, do subjects with high stimulus repetition probabilities make less use of S_n and more use of R_{n-1} in choosng R_n than do those with low repetition probabilities? Or was the apparently lower weight given to S_n by high repetition subjects in Experiment 1 merely a consequence of the strategy to base judgments on the difference between S_n and S_{n-1}, which will normally be large, and informative about S_n's value, when the repetition probability is low but will normally be small and less informative about S_n, when the repetition rate is high? Second, were the faster reaction times of the low repetition condition in Experiment 1 due to the facilitation of a response alternation strategy by the structure of the stimulus sequence? Or were they due to the fact that the normally large differences between S_n and S_{n-1} in the low repetition condition speeded comparisons between the current and previous stimuli, whereas the normally small differences between S_n and S_{n-1} in the high repetition condition slowed them down?

Method

Forty members of an introductory psychology course at the University of New South Wales judged the loudness of two 600-Hz tones, differing from one another by 1 dB. The softer tone was set to give a sound pressure level of about 75 dB re .0002 microbar. The equipment and procedure used were the same as in Experiment 1, except that subjects were told that the four response keys corresponded to steps on a rating scale, where key 1 (the leftmost) indicated moderate certainty that the softer tone had been presented, key 4 (the rightmost) indicated moderate certainty that the louder tone had been presented, and keys 2 and 3 (the center keys) were to indicate uncertain soft and loud responses, respectively.

Practice and experimental trials were conducted as in Experiment 1, with a total of 250 experimental trials being given during the session, half being the softer and half being the louder tone, in a quasirandom order that differed for each subject. For half the subjects, the mean probability of the same stimulus being repeated on trials $n - 1$ and n was .70 (range .66–.73), whereas for the others it was .28 (range .22–.35). As in Experiment 1, subjects were told nothing about this manipulation, only being informed that all stimuli would occur equally often during the experiment. Responses and reaction times for each subject's experimental series were sorted by the computer program into 4×4 matrices containing the mean response and mean latency for trial n for each of the 16 $S_n \times S_{n-1} \times R_{n-1}$ combinations.

Results

As in Experiment 1, mean response values on trial n for the high and low repetition probability groups under the various $S_n \times S_{n-1} \times R_{n-1}$ combinations were subjected to a multiple regression analysis to estimate the degree to which the current response was determined by S_n, S_{n-1}, R_{n-1}, $P(rep)$, and the interaction between $P(rep)$ and S_n. This interaction is of interest because it can be used to test the hypothesis that subjects give different weights to the current stimulus when judging it under different stimulus repetition conditions. As the independent variables were combined factorially, the regression analysis was equivalent to a $2 \times 2 \times 2 \times 4$ analysis of variance on the factors groups × current stimulus × previous stimulus × linear trend on the previous confidence rating. Thus the regression coefficients were estimated via an analysis of variance as described by Cohen and Cohen (1975, section 5.5). There was no significant difference between the mean response values of the high and low repetition probability groups. A summary of the within-subjects analysis is given in Table 9.2 and shows that the value of the current response was contrasted with that of the previous stimulus and assimilated to that of the previous response, with S_{n-1} having a greater weight than R_{n-1} in determining $\bar{R}_n$. The interaction between repetition probability and S_n was insignificant, giving no support to the hypothesis that a high repetition probability decreases the weight of S_n in determining R_n. In fact the mean response data were adequately fitted by the regression lines found from the coefficients for S_n, S_{n-1}, and R_{n-1}, as shown in Fig. 9.2 The variables accounted for about 80% of the variance in $\bar{R}_n$.

TABLE 9.2

Multiple Regression Analysis of Mean Response Values on Trial *n* in the Two-Stimulus Confidence Judgment Task

Independent Variable	Raw Score Regression Coefficient, B_i	Normalized Regression Coefficient, β_i	Significance of Coefficient, F_i, d.f. = (1, 38)	Proportion of Variance
S_n	1.37	.83	479.55^a	.68
S_{n-1}	−.44	−.27	30.87^a	.07
R_{n-1}	.16	.21	19.27^a	.04
$S_n \times P(rep)$	−.05	−.01	N.S.	.00
Constant	.74			

$^aP < .05$

Mean reaction times for the two groups were submitted to a 2 × 2 × 2 × 2 × 2 analysis of variance with factors groups × current stimulus × previous stimulus × previous response × confidence level. These last two factors were defined by coding rating categories 1 and 2 as response 1, categories 3 and 4 as response 2, categories 1 and 4 as high confidence, and categories, 2 and 3 as low confidence. The high confidence mean of 542 msec was significantly smaller than the low confidence mean of 1268 msec: $F(1, 38) = 10.30, p < .05$,

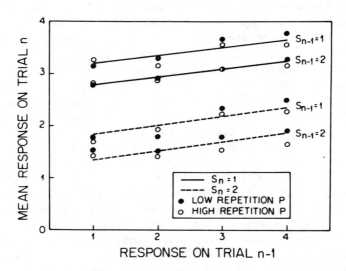

FIG. 9.2.   Mean response on trial *n* in the two-stimulus task with confidence ratings, plotted as a function of the current stimulus, S_n, previous stimulus, S_{n-1}, and previous response, R_{n-1}, for subjects receiving sequences with high or low stimulus repetition probabilities on trials *n* − 1 and *n*. Regression lines have been fitted using the coefficients for S_n, S_{n-1}, and R_{n-1} from Table 9.2.

MSE = 4652.6. Also the high repetition group mean of 594 msec was smaller than the low repetition group mean of 820 msec: $F(1, 38) = 4.12$, $p < .05$, MSE = 1979.5. Thus responding appeared to be facilitated by stimulus sequences with high repetition rates, which made it more likely that the same response would be made on successive trials, when the experimental design controlled for the fact that high repetition sequences also required more comparative judgments where $S_n = S_{n-1}$, and which were likely to slow down reaction time. However, an examination of reaction times classified according to whether the same or a different response had been made on trials $n - 1$ and n showed that a repeated response was not always faster than an alternated one. For subjects in the high repetition condition, mean reaction time was 569 msec when $R_n = R_{n-1}$ and 645 msec when $R_n \neq R_{n-1}$; in the low stimulus repetition condition, mean reaction time was 760 msec when $R_n = R_{n-1}$ and 678 msec when $R_n \neq R_{n-1}$. This interaction between the repetition probability condition and whether the trial n and $n - 1$ responses were an alternation or a repetition was significant: $F(1, 38) = 5.71$, $p < .05$, MSE = 2203.8. Thus response repetitions were faster than alternations when the stimulus reptition rate was high, but alternations were faster when the stimulus repetition rate was low.

EXPERIMENTS 3 AND 4:
TWO-STIMULUS × TWO-RESPONSE
IDENTIFICATION TASK

Two versions of this task were conducted. Experiment 3 was a conventional two-stimulus × two-response task without feedback, where the response on the preceding trial was followed by an empty intertrial interval of 5.5 sec. Experiment 4's intertrial interval was also 5.5 sec long but contained an interpolated series of four tones that were presented after the trial $n - 1$ response was made. The first three of these tones were 1 dB louder, 1 dB softer, or the same intensity as the stimulus tone used on trial $n - 1$. The last tone of the interpolated series always had the same intensity as that used on trial $n - 1$. The purpose of this task was to see if the current judgment was only affected by the stimulus event immediately preceding the current trial or if it also depended on earlier events. One difficulty created by using earlier stimuli in the series to explore for sequential effects prior to trial $n - 1$ in an absolute judgment task is that these stimuli are both remote in time from S_n and followed by their own response events. On the other hand, in Green et al.'s (1977) magnitude production task, the trial $n - 1$ stimulus was found to influence judgments of the trial n stimulus, despite the fact that it was both more separated in time from the trial n stimulus than in their magnitude estimation task and that the magnitude production response resulted in a wide range of tones being interpolated between S_{n-1} and S_n. Why the effect of S_{n-1} should be apparently immune to interpolated events in magnitude production, but susceptible to them in estimation is a puzzle, but it was hoped that the use of the interpolated tones in an estimation task would provide a more sensitive test of the cumulative effects of prior stimulation on judgments of the current stimulus.

Method

Twenty-five members of an introductory psychology course at the University of New South Wales participated in Experiment 3, and 32 participated in Experiment 4. In both tasks subjects were asked to judge whether a 600-Hz stimulus tone was the louder or softer of two possible tones. The tones differed by 1 dB, and the softer tone had a sound pressure level of about 75 dB re .0002 microbar. Responses were made on a two-key response board, with either the right or left key being assigned to response 1 or 2 in a random manner. The keys were spaced 4 cm apart, and subjects rested their thumbs or index fingers on top of the keys throughout the task. Reaction times were recorded in Experiment 3, and subjects in that task were asked to respond as quickly and as accurately as possible. Each subject in Experiment 3 attended six experimental sessions, spread over a period of 2 weeks and, during each session, received 100 presentations each of the softer and louder tone. All experimental sessions were preceded by at least 20 practice trials. A trial consisted of a .5-sec visual warning signal, followed by a delay of .5 sec, a .5-sec stimulus presentation, and then the response. Following the response there was an empty interval of 5.5 sec before the next trial.

Subjects in Experiment 4 attended three experimental sessions, spread over a period of 1 week. In each, there were 100 presentations of the softer and of the louder tone. All experimental sessions were preceded by at least 20 practice trials. The trial structure was the same as that of Experiment 3, except that the 5.5-sec intertrial interval began with an empty period of .5 sec and then four interpolated tones were heard, each lasting for .5 sec and with a .25 -sec delay after each of them. An empty interval of 2 sec followed the interpolated task, and then another trial began. A different version of the interpolated series was used in each of the three experimental sessions, the order of administration being randomized over subjects. In the low version, the first three tones of the interpolated series were set at 1 dB below the intensity of the stimulus presented on the preceding trial; in the medium version, the three tones were the same intensity as the trial $n - 1$ stimulus; in the high version, the three tones were 1 dB above the intensity of S_{n-1}. The fourth interpolated tone always had the same intensity as S_{n-1}. Half the subjects were assigned to the instructed group where they were told that the final tone of the interpolated series would always be a repetition of the stimulus they had judged on the previous trial. The other subjects were assigned to the uninstructed group and were told nothing about the interpolated tones except that they were not to respond to them.

Results

Response data from both experiments were used to find $P(R_1|S_iS_kR_l)$, the probability of making response 1 on the current trial, conditional on the current stimulus being i, the previous stimulus, k, and the previous response, l, for each of the eight possible combinations of S_i, S_k, and R_l. The probabilities were then transformed to z-scores, which were then used to estimate the regression coefficients of Eq. (2) via an analysis of variance as described in Experiment 2. Experiment 3 corresponded to a $2 \times 2 \times 2$ factorial design with factors, current stimulus × previous stimulus × previous response. Experiment 4 was a $2 \times 2 \times 2 \times 2 \times 3$ design, the first three factors being the same as in Experiment 3 and the other two being instruction group and type of interpolated series. Neither of these factors had significant effects on the trial n response, so that, as in Experiment 3, only S_n, S_{n-1}, and R_{n-1} were used as variables in the regression equations for Experiment 4. The results of these regression analyses are shown in Table 9.3. In both experiments there was contrast of the current response with S_{n-1} and assimilation to R_{n-1}, with the previous stimulus accounting for more of the variance in the current judg-

TABLE 9.3
Multiple Regression Analyses of $z(R_1|S_iS_kR_l)$s in the Two-Stimulus × Two-Response Tasks of Experiments 3 and 4

Independent Variable	Raw Score Regression Coefficient, B_i	Normalized Regression Coefficient, β_i	Significance of Coefficient, F_i	Proportion of Variance
Experiment 3				
S_n	1.17	.87	276.15[a]	.77
S_{n-1}	−.34	−.25	96.64[a]	.06
R_{n-1}	.14	.10	4.52[a]	.01
Constant	−1.45			
Experiment 4				
S_n	1.60	.70	209.83[b]	.50
S_{n-1}	−.74	−.33	115.77[b]	.11
R_{n-1}	.34	.15	14.90[b]	.02
Constant	−1.86			

[a]d.f. = (1,24), $P < .05$
[b]d.f. = (1,30), $P < .05$

ment than the previous response. It also appears that S_{n-1} exerted more influence on the current response in Experiment 4, where it was repeated just prior to the presentation of S_n, than in Experiment 3, where it occurred some 6 sec prior to S_n, with R_{n-1} being interpolated between it and S_n. The obtained values of $z(R_1|S_iS_kR_l)$ for the two experiments are shown in Fig. 9.3 fitted to Eq. (2) by the regression coefficients in Table 9.3. These variables accounted for 84% of the variance of the $z(R_1|S_iS_kR_l)$s in Experiment 3 and for 64% of their variance in Experiment 4. Coefficients for S_{n-1} were larger in Experiment 4 than in Experiment 3: $t(55) = 5.79$, $p < .05$.

Mean correct and error reaction times were found for the 16 combinations of S_n, R_n, S_{n-1}, and R_{n-1} in Experiment 3 and are shown in table 9.4. An analysis of variance showed that correct responses were faster than errors [$F(1, 24) = 22.47$, $p < .05$, MSE = 560.28] and that for correct responses the reaction times were faster when a stimulus repetition occurred on trials $n - 1$ and n [$F(1, 24) = 29.32$, $p < .05$, MSE = 15.665] and when a response alternation occurred on trials $n - 1$ and n [$F(1, 24) = 10.86$, $p < .05$, MSE = 28.830]. These effects were not significant in the error data, however.

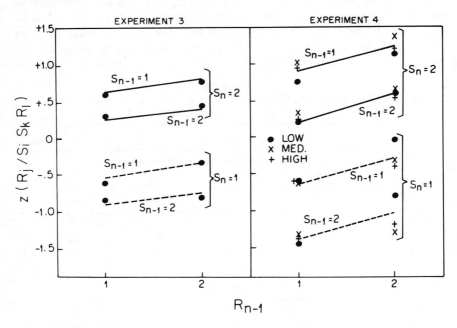

FIG. 9.3.   Mean $z(R_1 | S_iS_kR_l)$ values for Experiments 3 and 4, plotted as a function of the current stimulus, S_n, previous stimulus, S_{n-1}, and previous response, R_{n-1}. Regression lines have been fitted using the coefficients for S_n, S_{n-1}, and R_{n-1} from Table 9.3. Points for the low, medium, and high interpolated tasks of Experiment 4 are shown separately.

TABLE 9.4

Mean Reaction Time (msec) for Correct and Error Responses on Trial n
Classified by the Current Stimulus, S_n, the Previous Stimulus, S_{n-1}, and the
Previous Response, R_{n-1}

S_n	S_{n-1}	R_{n-1}	Correct Reaction Time	Error Reaction Time
1	1	1	421	455
1	1	2	426	504
1	2	1	406	470
1	2	2	384	507
2	1	1	386	485
2	1	2	418	538
2	2	1	404	479
2	2	2	427	470

DISCUSSION

The response data from the four experiments show a consistent pattern of contrast with the previous stimulus and assimilation to the previous response. Together, these two variables accounted for an average of 13% of the variance of the current response in the four experiments, whereas the addition of the current stimulus increased the average variance accounted for to 57%. There was no evidence that other variables examined in these studies, such as repetition probability in Experiments 1 and 2 or unjudged interpolated tones more remote than the one just prior to S_n in Experiment 4, gave improved predictions of R_n. Thus the results of the regression analyses generally agreed with those of Jesteadt *et al.* (1977) for magnitude estimation and provide further evidence against models that attribute sequential effects in judgments entirely to previous stimuli or to previous responses.

An adequate account of how a series of stimuli is judged must begin with the fact that the sensory evidence frequently reflects the difference between weighted values of the current stimulus and the one immediately preceding it. It may not even be necessary that this previous stimulus be judged explicitly, as the effects of S_{n-1} were even greater in Experiment 4 where it was repeated as the last member of the unjudged interpolated sequence than in Experiment 3 where R_{n-1} occurred between S_{n-1} and S_n. Thus although the process may be interpreted as a deliberate comparison of S_n and S_{n-1}, as if subjects treat judgments of single stimuli as implicit paired comparisons, it may simply be that the current stimulus impinges on a sensory system whose adaptation level has been shifted by the previous stimulus. If the subject did nothing more than choose a response that was a monotonic function of the signed difference between S_n and S_{n-1}, there would always be contrast with the trial $n - 1$

stimulus, just as there is to an explicit but unjudged anchor stimulus presented just prior to S_n (McNicol & Pennington, 1973). However, as S_{n-1} was judged, the subject had some information, albeit unreliable, that would allow him to correct his response for variations in the size of the comparison stimulus, S_{n-1}. In terms of the signal detection model of Eq. (2), the subject may attempt to avoid response biases by adopting a low criterion for response 1 if he believes that the mean of the difference distribution between S_n and S_{n-1} will be low, as will tend to be the case if he judged a large stimulus was presented on trial $n - 1$; or by adopting a high criterion for response 1 if he belives that the mean of the difference distribution will be high, as will tend to be the case when a small stimulus was judged to have occurred on trial $n - 1$. (This assumes, of course, that there is a moderate correlation between the physical and judged values of the stimuli.) The bias correction procedure will produce the assimilation effect to R_{n-1} shown in these experiments, and in those of Jesteadt *et al.* (1977), and will account for the tendency to repeat responses from the previous trial noted in a number of experiments (Parducci & Sandusky, 1970; Verplanck, Collier, & Cotton, 1952; Ward & Lockhead, 1971). It should be noted that the bias correction procedure is equivalent to Tanner *et al.* 's (1970) decision rule to give response 1 when the $S_n - S_{n-1}$ difference is large and negative, to give response 2 when it is large and positive, and to repeat R_{n-1} when it is small. However, their decision rule is not easily applicable to tasks involving more than two levels of the stimulus variable and would need to be modified to incorporate confidence judgments.

Some additional facts suggest that this account of sequential effects is too simple. First, Jesteadt *et al.* (1977) found that the correlation between successive magnitude estimates decreased as the decibel difference between successive stimuli increased. This suggests that the second term of Eq. (1) should be modified to reflect the difference between S_n and S_{n-1} rather than just the value of S_{n-1} itself. If $f(S_n) - f(S_{n-1})$ is substituted for S_{n-1} in Eq. (1), some rearrangement gives:

$$f(R_n) = (B_1 + B_2)f(S_n) - B_2 f(S_{n-1}) + B_3 f(R_{n-1}) \qquad (4)$$

If there is contrast between the current response and the $S_n - S_{n-1}$ difference, then Eq. (4) implies that the absolute value of the coefficient for $f(S_{n-1})$ should be bigger than that for $f(S_n)$. However, this would only be a weak test of the model proposed by Eq. (4), as B_1 would normally be expected to exceed B_2. Jesteadt *et al.* 's (1977) procedure of examining individual S_n and S_{n-1} pairings has provided more convincing evidence for such a model.

A second complication for a model that proposes that the judged value of a stimulus depends only on events from the preceding trial is that the distribution of stimuli over the range being judged may make some of them particularly salient. Such anchor stimuli have been shown to influence judgments of other members of the series (Weber, Green, & Luce, 1977).

The reaction-time data give some additional support for a decision process based on the difference between S_n and S_{n-1}. These show two effects, the first of which appears to be one of response facilitation similar to that reported by Bertelson (1961) and Kornblum (1967); that is, response alternations may be faster than repetitions, or vice versa, depending on the transition probabilities between trial $n - 1$ and n stimuli. This effect was noted in Experiment 2, and a similar response alternation effect occurred in Experiment 3. Of more interest, however, were the slower reaction times in Experiment 3 on trials when $S_n = S_{n-1}$ than when $S_n \neq S_{n-1}$, as these could reflect the time needed to compare the trial n and $n - 1$ stimuli in order to determine whether the difference was positive or negative. A number of models for decision times (e.g., Audley & Pike, 1965; Vickers, 1970; Vickers, Caudrey, & Willson, 1971) have proposed that a response is chosen by cumulating samples from the distribution of differences between two stimuli in two counters corresponding to responses 1 and 2, according to whether each sample lies below or above the response criterion, and terminating sampling when one or the other counter reaches a critical level. It is characteristic of these models that when the differences between the stimuli are small, decision times will be longer than when they are large and that, except under extreme bias of the criterion, error reaction times will be longer than correct reaction times (Pike & Ryder, 1973). The expected difference between correct and error times occurred in Experiment 3, and the slower times on trials where $S_n = S_{n-1}$ than when $S_n \neq S_{n-1}$ are consistent with the idea that the current response is based on a series of samples of differences between the current and previous stimuli.

ACKNOWLEDGMENTS

I am grateful to Connie Humphries who assisted in gathering the data for these experiments, to John Long of the MRC Applied Psychology Unit in Cambridge, England who commented on an earlier draft of this paper, and to the Department of Psychology, University of Toronto, for allowing me the use of its facilities while the paper was being written.

REFERENCES

Audley, R. J., & Pike, A. R. Some alternative stochastic models of choice. *British Journal of Mathematical and Statistical Psychology,* 1965, *18,* 207–225.

Bertelson, P. Sequential redundancy and speed in a serial two-choice responding task. *Quarterly Journal of Experimental Psychology,* 1961, *12,* 90–102.

Cohen, J., & Cohen, P. *Applied multiple regression/correlation analysis for the behavioral sciences.* Hillsdale, N.J.: Lawrence Erlbaum Associates, 1975.

Dorfman, D. D., & Biderman, M. A learning model for a continuum of sensory states. *Journal of Mathematical Psychology,* 1971, *8,* 264–284.

Green, D. M., Luce, R. D., & Duncan, J. E. Variability and sequential effects in magnitude production and estimation of auditory intensity. *Perception and Psychophysics*, 1977, *22*, 450–456.

Helson, H. *Adaptation-level theory.* New York: Harper, 1964.

Jesteadt, W., Luce, R. D., & Green, D. M. Sequential effects in judgments of loudness. *Journal of Experimental Psychology: Human Perception and Performance*, 1977, *3*, 92–104.

John, I. D. Sequential effects in absolute judgments of loudness without feedback. In S. Kornblum (Ed.), *Attention and performance IV.* New York: Academic Press, 1973.

Kac, M. A note on learning signal detection. *IRE Transactions on Information Theory*, 1962, *IT-8*, 126–128.

Kornblum, S. Choice reaction time for repetitions and nonrepetitions: A re-examination of the information hypothesis. *Acta Psychologica*, 1967, *27*, 178–187.

Larkin, W. Response mechanisms in signal detection experiments. *Journal of Experimental Psychology*, 1971, *91*, 140–153.

Lee, W. Conditioning parameter model for reinforcement generalization in probabilistic discrimination learning. *Journal of Mathematical Psychology*, 1966, *3*, 184–196.

McNicol, D., & Pennington, C. W. Sensory and decision processes in anchor effects and aftereffects. *Journal of Experimental Psychology*, 1973, *100*, 232–238.

Parducci, A. A range-frequency approach to sequential effects in category ratings. In S. Kornblum (Ed.), *Attention and performance IV.* New York: Academic Press, 1973.

Parducci, A., & Sandusky, A. Distribution and sequence effects in judgment. *Journal of Experimental Psychology*, 1965, *69*, 450–459.

Parducci, A., & Sandusky, A. Limits on the applicability of signal detection theories. *Perception and Psychophysics*, 1970, *7*, 63–64.

Pike, R., & Ryder, P. Response latencies in the yes/no decision task: An assessment of two basic models. *Perception and Psychophysics*, 1973, *13*, 224–232.

Sandusky, A. Signal recognition models compared for random and Markov sequences. *Perception and Psychophysics*, 1971, *10*, 339–346.

Schoeffler, M. S. Theory for psychophysical learning. *Journal of the Acoustical Society of America*, 1965, *37*, 1124–1133.

Tanner, T. A., Haller, R. W., & Atkinson, R. C. Signal recognition as influenced by presentation schedules. *Perception and Psychophysics*, 1967, *2*, 349–358.

Tanner, T. A., Rauk, J. A., & Atkinson, R. C. Signal recognition as influenced by information feedback. *Journal of Mathematical Psychology*, 1970, *7*, 259–274.

Verplanck, W. S., Collier, G. H., & Cotton, J. W. Nonindependence of successive responses in measurements of the visual threshold. *Journal of Experimental Psychology*, 1952, *44*, 273–282.

Vickers, D. Evidence for an accumulator model of psychophysical discrimination. *Ergonomics*, 1970, *13*, 37–58.

Vickers, D., Caudrey, D., & Willson, R. Discriminating between the frequency of occurence of two alternative events. *Acta Psychologica*, 1971, *35*, 151–172.

Ward, L. M., & Lockhead, G. R. Response system processes in absolute judgment. *Perception and Psychophysics*, 1971, *9*, 73–78.

Weber, D. L., Green, D. M., & Luce, R. D. Effects of practice and distribution of auditory signals on absolute identification. *Perception and Psychophysics*, 1977, *22*, 223–231.

10 Selectivity in Character Classification

Wolfgang Prinz
Abteilung Psychologie
Universität Bielefeld
West Germany

ABSTRACT

When similar stimuli are mapped onto different responses in speeded classification tasks $(A \rightarrow R^+; a \rightarrow R^-)$, response performance is usually impaired as compared to appropriate control conditions with dissimilar stimuli $(B \rightarrow R^+; c \rightarrow R^-)$. A framework for the analysis of the effect is presented. The impairment is assumed to reflect an increase in response competition that arises from the similarity of the stimuli. The increase can be avoided if the subject bases his response decisions on internal representations which do not contain those attributes which are shared by the competing alternatives. The selective reduction of the attributes can pertain either to the internal representations which are automatically activated by the stimulus information (set of stimulus-induced attributes) or to the representations of the response criteria which are constructed on the basis of the information in the instructions (sets of response-defining attributes). It is argued that these two modes of selective reduction can be separated from each other under bias conditions. Illustrative data suggest the conclusion that the structure of the attribute lists (selectivity) depends on stimulus bias whereas their dynamical state (readiness) is controlled by response bias.

A FRAMEWORK FOR ASKING QUESTIONS

Theories of performance in choice reaction-time tasks usually assume that the period between the presentation of the stimulus and the initiation of the response is filled by a sequence of stages. Several investigators have postulated a distinction between stimulus categorization and response selection (Rabbitt, 1971; Welford, 1968). More elaborate conceptualizations of the whole sequence have also considered the peripheral processes of stimulus encoding and response programming (Smith, 1968).

The present study, which pertains to the mechanisms of selective information reduction, starts from the following tentative account of the stage sequence.

1. The operation of *stimulus encoding* forms an internal representation (output) from the external stimulus information (input). The internal representation of the stimulus can be conceived as a set of physical features that are automatically extracted from the stimulus.

2. On the basis of the stimulus representation (input) the operation of *stimulus categorization* locates an appropriate memory address and retrieves its content (output). The content of the address can be conceived as a set of attributes, with attributes defined as pieces of stored knowledge.

3. The operation of *response selection* implies a choice of one out of several response alternatives. The decision is based on two kinds of input information: information pertaining to the stimulus and information pertaining to the response criteria. The first input is supplied from the set of stimulus-induced attributes that was activated in stage 2 (SI set). The response criteria can be conceived as sets of response-defining attributes (RD sets), with one set for each alternative. Each RD-set specifies the attributes that are necessary for the selection of the corresponding response. One of the RD sets is selected (output), depending on its overlap with the SI set.

4. On the basis of the particular RD sets selected (input), the operation of *response programming* triggers and controls the execution of the response (output).

According to this view, the coordination of stimuli and responses is mediated by a comparison between two kinds of attribute sets. The first of them is evoked by the actual stimulation. The second one is evoked by the instructions regarding the S-R mapping rules of the task. Both of these sets do not only contain attributes that are related to the physical properties of the objects. It is assumed that the attributes can also be related to nonphysical object characteristics such as names, category memberships, and associative connotations. This has been demonstrated convincingly by Posner and his co-workers for stimulus-induced attributes (Posner, 1969, 1973; Posner & Boies, 1971). It is reasonable to assume that it also applies to response-defining attributes.

The basic structure of the response selection operation is illustrated in Fig. 10.1a for a task with two stimuli (S_1, S_2) mapped onto two responses (R_1, R_2). When S_1 is presented, a corresponding attribute set is generated (upper left circle). When it is compared with the response-defining sets for R_1 and R_2 (lower circles), a match is observed for the set that specifies the conditions for R_1 because it comprises the same attributes that are contained in the SI set for S_1. When S_2 is presented a match is observed for R_2. The first illustration represents the fictitious case of zero overlap between the competing attribute sets. The second one (Fig. 10.1b) faces the more realistic situation of some degree of similarity between the two stimuli. Though the attribute set induced by one of the stimuli (say, S_1) leads to a complete match with the corresponding response criterion (R_1: thick vertical arrow between S_1 and R_1), there will

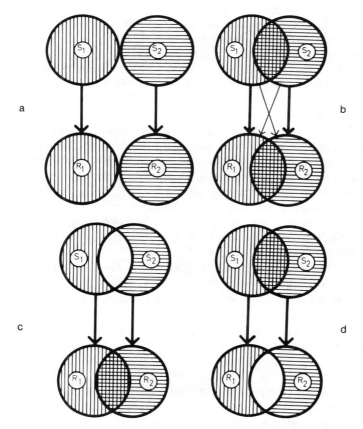

FIG. 10.1.   Hypothetical relations between stimulus-induced and response-defining attribute sets (upper versus lower circles) in a binary classification task under conditions of low and of high similarity (*a* versus *b, c, d*) and different assumptions regarding the selection of attributes. (b) No selection. (c) Selection of stimulus-induced attributes. (d) Selection of response-defining attributes. See text for further explanation.

also be a partial match with the criterion set for the competing response (R_2: thin oblique arrow between S_1 and R_2) that results from the partial overlap between the response-defining sets. Suppose, for example, that a red square is mapped on R_1 and a red circle on R_2. In this case the color of the alternative stimuli is a possible source of response competition that would be absent in a nonoverlap control condition with a red square and a green circle.

This increase in response competition can be reduced or even avoided by an appropriate selective reduction of the attribute sets involved. The reduction can pertain either to the stimulus-induced attributes (Fig. 10.1c) or to the response-defining attributes (Fig. 10.1d). In the first case the stimuli are represented by reduced attribute sets. The selective reduction pertains to those attributes that are shared by both alternatives. Though the RD sets still overlap, response conflict is not increased because the reduced SI sets will never lead to a partial match with the RD sets of the competing response. In the second case the response criteria are represented by reduced sets. Again the reduction pertains to those attributes that are shared by both alternatives. An increase of response conflict is avoided because the critical attributes that are contained in each of the two SI sets are not included in the RD sets.

The illustrations in Fig. 10.1c, d represent two different conceptualizations of the mechanism of selective response control. They virtually restate two rivaling views in a longstanding discussion that inquires about the locus of selection in information reduction tasks. A similar distinction was first drawn by Külpe (1904) who asked whether the selective abstraction of attributes occurs at the level of sensation (Empfindung) or (ap)perception (Auffassung). More recent investigators have postulated that selective response control can be exerted at both perceptual and response level, depending on task conditions (Broadbent, 1971; Haber, 1966).

If the present approach is adopted, the distinction between SI set selection and RD set selection is not regarded as a distinction between two different loci or levels of selection. Instead, it refers to two kinds of attribute sets that are generated in the same attribute space. It should therefore be understood as a distinction between two objects of selection rather than of two loci of the selective process.

A METHOD FOR FINDING ANSWERS

As can be derived from Figure 10.1c, d, the selective reduction of SI sets and of RD sets leads to the same result. The two modes of selection can therefore not be separated from each other in such simple tasks. This should perhaps be possible, however, under conditions where the competing alternatives differ in bias. Figure 10.2 illustrates a task structure where a positive bias in favor of one of the alternatives (S^+/R^+) is introduced at the cost of a negative bias of

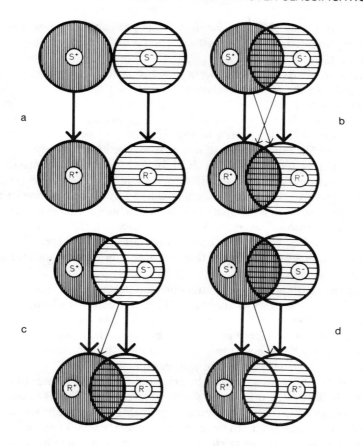

FIG. 10.2.   Hypothetical relations between stimulus-induced and response-defining attribute sets under conditions of bias toward S^+/R^+ (dense vertical hatching). (a)–(d) See Fig. 10.1. In (c) and (d) selectivity is assumed to be correlated with bias. See text for further explanation.

the other one (S^-/R^-). The bias is assumed to affect the dynamical state of the attributes involved. It increases the readiness of the attributes of the positive alternative relative to those of the negative one. This is coded in the figures by a difference in the density of hatching between the corresponding parts of the attribute space $(S^+/R^+$ versus $S^-/R^-)$.

Under bias conditions an increase of response conflict must again be expected for the high-similarity task (Fig. 10.2b) as compared to the low-similarity control task (Fig. 10.2a)—provided that no attribute selection occurs. The increase must be different for the two alternatives, however. When S^+ is presented, the correct response is dynamically strong and the wrong response is weak (R^+ versus R^-): Response competition will be low. When S^- is presented, the reverse is true (R^- versus R^+) and response competition will be high.

If some kind of attribute selection occurs, the pattern of response competition depends on the assumed relationship between bias and selectivity. If selectivity is unrelated to bias, the increase in response competition can be avoided for both alternatives by deleting the overlapping attributes from either attribute set as illustrated in Fig. 10.1c, d. However, if selectivity is correlated with bias, the increase of response competition can only be partially avoided. This is illustrated in Fig. 2c, d. In both cases it is assumed that the selective reduction is asymmetric with respect to the two alternatives (i.e., that it is only applied to the positive alternative and not to the negative one). In Fig. 10.2c the asymmetry pertains to the SI sets. This will decrease the (weak) response competition evoked by S^+ without affecting the (strong) conflict evoked by S^-. In Fig. 10.2d the asymmetry pertains to the RD sets. This leads to the somewhat paradoxical result that response conflict is avoided for S^- but not for S^+.

Thus, if the assumption of a positive correlation between bias and selectivity is valid, the two basic views about the object of selection can be differentiated from each other by means of asymmetries in response conflict.

How can the degree of response conflict be assessed? In principle, it should be reflected in both response times and error rates. Response time should be delayed to the degree where two responses compete with each other. On the other hand, response time can also be delayed to the degree where one of the two hypothetical attribute sets is selectively reduced. This is because the selective elaboration of an attribute set reduces the amount of evidence (number of attributes) that can be used to compare the sets. Therefore, when a delay of response times due to similarity is observed, it can imply either that selective elaboration did occur (and the number of attributes was reduced) or that it did not occur (and response conflict was increased).

This ambiguity does not apply to the interpretation of error rates. Increasing the overlap between the competing attribute lists will cause some errors of confusion in addition to the basic error rate in the nonoverlap control task. This cannot be expected in case of selective reduction. The error rates must therefore be considered as more valid indicators of selectivity than the response times.

Though the nature of the very relationship between these crude speed and error statistics and the operations underlying the response decision is left unspecified, some preliminary tests of the usefulness of the present approach can be made. In the following section, its application is illustrated by an appropriate reanalysis of data from two previous experiments.

PRELIMINARY APPLICATIONS

Selection of Stimulus-Induced Attributes

The first illustration is taken from a binary classification task where subjects had to map four letter stimuli on two responses (Prinz, 1978). Positive and negative set sizes were equal ($s = 2$), and each set contained an uppercase and a lowercase (UC/LC) letter. Similarity was varied in terms of nonphysical stimulus characteristics. In one condition the positive and negative sets contained items that had the same name (*Ab/Ba*; condition *SN*); in the other condition the two sets contained completely different items (*Ab/Cd*; condition *DN*). There was a slight frequency unbalance ($S^+:S^- = 7:5$) that introduced some bias toward the positive set. This response bias was further supported by the instructions that enumerated the positive items but left the negatives unspecified. The instructions also introduced some (stimulus) bias toward the uppercase member of the positive set: The uppercase letter was always in the first (left-hand) position on the cardobard, which showed the two positive items for a given task. Note that similarity was varied in the experiment, whereas the conditions affecting stimulus and response bias were kept constant.

The relevant error data are summarized in Table 10.1. The effect of response bias is reflected in the error rates for S^+ and S^-. The error rate for S^- exceeds that for S^+ under both conditions, and similarity increases the error rate for S^- but not for S^+. As outlined previously, this pattern of results must be expected under the assumption that the difference in the error rates indicates a difference in the dynamical properties of the corresponding attribute sets. The effect of stimulus bias is reflected in the error rates for UC and LC. There is no systematical difference in *DN*, but there is a reliable effect in

TABLE 10.1
Error Rates for Uppercase and Lowercase Items (UC/LC) in the Positive and Negative Set (S^+/S^-) Under Conditions *SN* and *DN*[a]

Percent	SN			Percent	DN		
	S^+	S^-			S^+	S^-	
UC	7.3	13.4	10.4	UC	8.4	14.5	11.5
LC	11.8	20.1	16.0	LC	10.8	10.8	10.8
	9.6	16.8	13.2		9.6	12.6	11.1

Note: Data from 16 subjects and 4 sessions = 64 experimental sessions with about 800 stimulus presentations each.
[a]Data from Prinz (1978).

SN. This seems to imply that stimulus bias does not affect the dynamical state of the assumed attribute sets, but only their structural properties. As the error rate is lower for the biased as compared to the unbiased stimuli (UC versus LC), the selective reduction must pertain to the SI sets.

Figure 10.3a illustrates how the effects of stimulus bias and response bias are combined in the *SN* condition. Each *SN* task can be partitioned into two subtasks. In the first subtask S^+ is an uppercase item and S^- is its lowercase

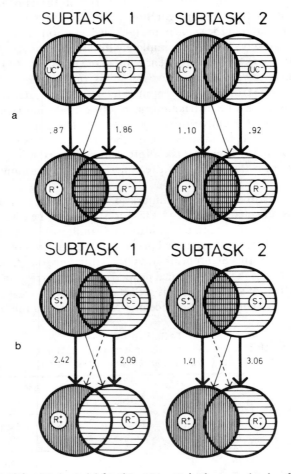

FIG. 10.3. (a) A model for the error rates in the two subtasks of the first illustration. Subtask 1: S^+ is uppercase and S^- is lowercase (UC$^+$/LC$^-$; Subtask 2: vice versa. (b) Same for the second illustration. Subtask 1: positive correlation between stimulus and response bias (S_+^+/S_-^-); Subtask 2: negative correlation (S_-^+/S_+^-). The entries are ratios of error rates (SN/DN). See text for further details.

version; in the second subtask the reverse relation holds (A/a and b/B in the previous example). In the first subtask UC^+/LC^-) stimulus bias and response bias are positively correlated. Due to the assumed selective reduction of the SI set, conflict is completely avoided for UC^+. It is not avoided for LC^- where the degree of conflict must be quite high because the competing RD set (R^+) is dynamically strong. In the second subtask (LC^+/UC^-) stimulus bias and response bias are negatively correlated. In this case the assumed selective reduction pertains to the stimulus-induced attributes of UC^-, and conflict is avoided for this stimulus. Some conflict should arise for LC^+, but it must be much weaker as compared to that for LC^- in the first subtask, because the competing RD set (R^-) is dynamically weak.

From the data in Table 10.1 a ratio of the error rates in the two conditions (SN/DN) can be obtained for each stimulus. This figure gives an indication of the error rate in SN as related to DN. These ratios are also given in Fig. 10.3a. The results fit quite well with what must be expected from the combined effects of the assumed dynamical and structural properties of the attribute sets.

Selection of Response-Defining Attributes

The second illustration is taken from an experiment where same-name and different-name stimuli were combined in the same task (Prinz, 1976, Exp. I). In the SN task of the first illustration the subject could reduce the attribute sets for many (all?) stimuli simultaneously if he ignored their names and based his response decisions solely on their physical attributes. Such switching off of the name level would be less efficient when SN and DN stimuli are mixed in the same task. If selection occurs at all with this task structure, it should be specific to each particular stimulus.

The task was to map 18 letter stimuli onto three responses. The stimulus items were divided into three categories: S^+, S_b^-, and S_c^-. The subject was instructed to respond to S^+ and S_b^- items but not to S_c^- items. Each category contained three lowercase and three uppercase letters. Similarity was again varied by manipulating the name relation. There were four SN items in the S^+ category. Two of them (one for each case) had the same names as two corresponding items in the S_b^- category. Two others corresponded to two S_c^- items. The two remaining positions in the S^+ category and the four remaining positions in each of the S^- categories were filled by DN items.

In this task the instructions were explicit with respect to all categories. The information about the required $S-R$ mapping was provided by cardboards that remained visible during the experiment. The cardboard that defined the S^+ category was always placed in the center, as illustrated by the following example:

S_b^-	S^+	S_c^-
kse	qra	duc
LYQ	EGD	APV

For one group of subjects the capital letters were stencilled above the small letters and for the other group the positions were reversed (stimulus bias conditions emphasizing uppercase and lowercase items, respectively). Some response bias towards the S^+ category was provided by its central position in the instructions. It was further strengthened by a slight frequency bias (S^+ : S_b^- : S_c^- = 6 : 5 : 5).

The error data from the two emphasis instruction groups are combined in Table. 10.2. The results for S_+ and S_- refer to UC and LC items under uppercase emphasis instructions and to LC and UC under lowercase emphasis. Response bias is again observed in the error rates for S^+ and S^- for both DN and SN stimuli, and again similarity increases the error rate for S^- much more than for S^+. So far the present data replicate the previous results and confirm the conclusions drawn from them. For stimulus bias a different picture emerges, however. First, some effect of the emphasis instructions shows up in the DN stimuli. This seems to imply that the attribute sets of emphasized and unemphasized stimuli are dynamically different in the DN condition—much in the same way as those of S^+ and S^- items. Second, there is an effect of emphasis in the SN stimuli that goes in the reverse direction. As pointed out previously, this paradoxical result can only be explained under the assumption of a selective reduction of the response-defining attribute sets.

Figure 10.3b summarizes the inferences drawn from these results. In the first subtask (S_+^+/S_-^-), stimulus and response bias are positively correlated. If the RD set for the emphasized stimulus (R_+^+) is selectively reduced, conflict should, in principle, be avoided for S_-^- but not for S_+^+. In the second subtask

TABLE 10.2

Error Rates for Emphasized and Unemphasized Items (S_+/S_-) in Stimulus Categories S^+ and S^- for SN and DN Stimuli[a]

Percent	SN			Percent	DN		
	S^+	S^-			S^+	S^-	
S_+	10.9	18.1	14.5	S_+	4.5	5.9	5.2
S_-	9.6	15.2	12.4	S_-	6.8	7.3	7.0
	10.2	16.6	13.4		5.6	6.6	6.1

Note: Data from 6 subjects and 9 sessions = 54 experimental sessions with 600 stimulus presentations each. Error rates are averaged from b-errors (R_b^- instead of R^+ and vice versa) and c-errors (R_c^- instead of R^+ and vice versa).

[a]Data from Prinz (1976).

where the correlation is negative, conflict should arise for S_+^- but not for S_-^+. In its strictest form the model postulates that response conflict is completely avoided for the nonemphasized items (S_-^- and S_+^+). In a more realistic version it assumes that the selective reduction is not perfect on each trial. This results in some minor degree of response conflict even for these stimuli (as indicated by the dotted arrows in Fig. 10.3b). The differences in the error ratios between the two emphasized stimuli (2.42 versus 3.06) and the two nonemphasized stimuli (2.09 versus 1.41) can be derived from the dynamical properties of the competing attribute lists.

The results of the two illustrations differ in the inferred object of attribute selection. Why should this selection pertain to the SI sets in the first task and to the RD sets in the present one? As the present task is mixed from *SN* and *DN* stimuli, the reduction of attributes is only required for some stimuli. Under this condition the selection of stimulus-induced attributes might be inappropriate if it is based on switching off the name code for all or many stimuli simultaneously. It is therefore replaced by the selection of response-defining attributes for each particular stimulus. One might speculate that such differential processing of each stimulus is easier in the RD sets than in the SI sets because the subject has more direct control over the contents of the RD sets (which he constructs from the information in the instructions) as compared to the SI sets (which are automatically generated from the stimulus information).

Notwithstanding this difference the results from the two illustrations join in the more general conclusion that the structure of the attribute lists (selectivity) depends on stimulus bias whereas their dynamical state (readiness) is controlled by response bias.

CONCLUSIONS

1. The findings from these experiments are clearly limited to the type of stimulus materials used. The stimuli were specific in three respects. (a) Similarity was varied by using same versus different names (i.e., at a nonphysical level of coding). Different results are perhaps obtained if similarity is varied on other dimensions. (b) Letter stimuli are extremely familiar and the associations between the physical and the name attributes are highly overlearned. With such stimuli the selective elaboration of an attribute set can only take the form of a reduction of attributes (i.e., of the deletion of attributes that are usually included in the set). (c) Physical and name attributes should probably be considered as nonintegral attributes that can, in principle, be separated from each other in spite of the strength of their association. Different results are perhaps obtained with less separable stimulus dimensions (Garner, 1970; Prinz & Scheerer-Neumann, 1974; Treisman, Sykes, & Gelade, 1977).

2. The validity of the conclusions drawn from these results is heavily dependent on the validity of the basic assumption that the increase in error rates under conditions of high similarity is due to an increase of perceptual confusions and not to an increase of motor errors (Rabbitt & Vyas, 1970). Though the response times for the wrong responses were not studied in detail, it was occasionally observed that wrong responses were considerably faster than correct ones in the low-similarity conditions but only slightly faster in the high-similarity conditions. Equivalent results were obtained by Rabbitt & Vyas in an experiment where the physical similarity of the stimuli was varied (1970, p. 71). These findings seem to imply that the additional errors that arise from similarity are slower than those that contribute to the basic error rate in the control task. This suggests that the additional errors do not result from premature responses (motor errors) but from perceptual confusions instead (i.e., that they are based on some degree of stimulus processing. More research is needed to corroborate this assumption.

3. A final comment is needed on the notion of selective elaboration. Though it was only used in the restricted sense of a selective reduction or deletion of attributes, it should perhaps be understood in the broader sense of a selective reorganization of an attribute set. If an attribute set is regarded not only as a set of attributes that can vary in size but as an organized structure of attributes, the problem of selection is more adequately stated as that of restructuring the set (e.g., of reorganizing its hierarchical arrangement) than that of reducing it. As Külpe noted (1904), a theory of abstraction must deal not only with negative abstraction (ignoring irrelevant information) but also with positive abstraction (stressing relevant information). An attribute can be irrelevant for a response decision because it is deleted from the attribute set (negative abstraction) or because other attributes are dominant (positive abstraction). The notion of selective elaboration should comprise both of these meanings.

ACKNOWLEDGMENTS

The experiments reported in this chapter were supported from Sachbeihilfe PR 118/1-2 by the Deutsche Forschungsgemeinschaft. The manuscript was prepared under Akademie-Stipendium I/34218 by the Stiftung Volkswagenwerk to the author.

REFERENCES

Broadbent, D. E. *Decision and stress.* London and New York: Academic Press, 1971.
Garner, W. R. The stimulus in information processing. *American Psychologist* 1970, *25*, 350–358.
Haber, R. N. Nature of the effect of set on perception. *Psychological Review,* 1966, *73*, 335–351.

Külpe, O. Versuche über Abstraktion. *Bericht über den 1. Kongress für Psychologie* (Gieben, 1904), pp. 56–68. Leipzig: J. A. Barth, 1904.

Posner, M. I. Abstraction and the process of recognition. In G. Bower & J. T. Spence (Eds.), *Advances in learning and motivation* (Vol. 3). New York: Academic Press, 1969.

Posner, M. I. Coordination of internal codes. In W. G. Chase (Ed.), *Visual information processing*. New York: Academic Press, 1973.

Posner, M. I., & Boies, S. J. Components of attention. *Psychological Review,* 1971, *78,* 391–408.

Prinz, W. Bereitschaft und Selektivität von Reaktionscodes. *Archiv für Psychologie,* 1976, *128,* 45–65.

Prinz, W. Selektivität von Reiz- und Gedächtnisrepräsentationen. *Archiv für Psychologie,* 1978, *130,* 107–119.

Prinz, W., & Scheerer-Neumann, G. Component processes in multiattribute stimulus classification. *Psychological Research,* 1974, *37,* 25–50.

Rabbitt, P. M. A. Times for the analysis of stimuli and for the selection of responses. *British Medical Bulletin,* 1971, *27,* 259–265.

Rabbitt, P. M. A., & Vyas, S. M. An elementary preliminary taxonomy of some errors in laboratory choice reaction time tasks. In A. F. Sanders (Ed.), *Attention and Performance III.* Amsterdam: North-Holland Pub. Co., 1970.

Smith, E. E. Choice reaction time: An analysis of the major theoretical positions. *Psychological Bulletin,* 1968, *69,* 77–110.

Treisman, A. M., Sykes, M., & Gelade, G. Selective attention and stimulus integration. In S. Dornic (Ed.), *Attention and performance VI.* Hillsdale, N.J.: Lawrence Erlbaum Associates, 1977.

Welford, A. T. *Fundamentals of skill.* London: Methuen, 1968.

III MEASUREMENT OF ATTENTION AND EFFORT

11 The Measurement of Attention

R. A. Kinchla
Princeton University
Princeton, New Jersey
United States

ABSTRACT

Rather than treating *attention* as a single entity, it seems more useful to assume that a variety of cognitive mechanisms mediate selectivity in human information processing. Any theoretical characterization of such a mechanism would seem to qualify as a theory of attention. Furthermore, if the mechanism can be mathematically modeled, estimates of its parameters based on experimental data constitute quantitative measures of attention. This chapter presents a number of illustrative examples of such measures. It also examines the type of negative trading relation various models predict between the processing of one source of information and another. These relations, termed *attention operating characteristics*, seem to provide a basic characterization of selectivity in human information processing.

INTRODUCTION

This chapter is not intended to be a comprehensive review of recent work on attention. Rather it is an attempt to consider what is meant by the term *attention* and how one measures it. Of course these are issues that have bedeviled experimental psychologists for some time. Although the term *attention* is often used as if its definition were self-evident, it has remained a remarkably elusive concept. Edward Bradford Titchener wrote in 1908 that:

The discovery of attention didn't result in any immediate triumph of experimental method. It was something like the discovery of a hornet's nest: The first touch

> brought out a whole swarm of insistant problems.... The discovery of a reliable measure of attention would appear to be one of the most important problems that await solution by the experimental psychology of the future.

Unfortunately the hornets Titchener referred to are still on the wing. There still is not any widely accepted definition of, or method of measuring, *attention*. Rather, I argue, the only consistent feature of attentional research is an interest in the selective aspects of information processing. By *selective,* I mean the degree to which one may choose to process specific sources of information and ignore others. The phrase *sources of information* is used rather than *stimuli,* because in some instances it seems useful to think of memory as a source of information, the processing (accessing, recovery) of which may or may not be compatible with the processing of stimulation from external sources.

The major theme of this chapter is that attention should *not* be thought of as a single entity. It seems more useful to assume that a variety of cognitive mechanisms mediate selectivity in information processing. A theoretical characterization of any such mechanism would seem to qualify as a *theory of attention.* Furthermore, if the theoretical mechanism can be mathematically modeled, estimates of its parameters based on experimental data constitute quantitative measures of attention. Note that this view does not equate *attention* and *consciousness.* The idea that we are conscious of things to which we attend is intuitively appealing and has a long history in psychology. Unfortunately there is virtually no experimental evidence bearing directly on this issue. The position that I take is that some selective cognitive mechanisms (e.g., rehearsal, visualization, mental rotation, memory search) may involve *conscious* real-time operations that have important subjective properties. Nevertheless it is primarily the selectivity of the information processing that defines the mechanism as *attentional.*

There seem to be three major lines of work bearing on the issue of selectivity in information processing. The first, which is the major focus of this chapter, is the study of *information tradeoffs:* The study of situations in which increased processing of information from one source is inevitably associated with reduced processing of information from another source. For example, increased comprehension of one conversation at a cocktail party normally means reduced comprehension of conversations occurring at the same time; or, increasing the number of letters correctly reported from one row of a briefly presented letter matrix usually reduces accuracy in reporting the letters in other rows. A second line of work bearing on selective information processing could be termed the study of *perceptual intrusions:* the study of situations in which certain sources of information seem difficult to ignore. For example, the so-called Stroop effect (Stroop, 1935) whereby subjects have difficulty ignoring printed color names when their task is simply to report the color of ink in which those names are printed. It is as if certain highly practiced perceptual processes become so automatic they are difficult to suppress; such perceptual automaticity is discussed by Laberge and Samuels (1977) and Shiffrin and Schneider (1977). Finally, a third line of work is the study of *attention switching:* situations which seem to involve a shift from processing information from one source to processing that from another. For example, when listening to two people speaking simultaneously, comprehension of one seems to preclude, or at least hinder, comprehension of the other. The study of how attending to one voice reduces comprehension of the other is a study of information tradeoff; however, the study of the manner in which one shifts (e.g., the time required) from attending to one voice to the other is a study of attention switching. Sperling and Reeves consider the problem of visual attention switching later in this volume. The three lines of work are interrelated, and all contribute to our understanding of selectivity in information processing; however, the study of information tradeoffs has been the most characteristic and extensive form of attentional research. It is the primary focus of this chapter and most of the chapters in this volume.

STUDYING INFORMATION TRADEOFFS

Many information-processing tasks involve multiple sources of information. For example, a subject may be asked to listen to two people speaking at once (two sources) or to identify the letters appearing in N different locations in a tachistoscopically presented letter matrix (N sources). Yet how the number of *sources* is determined depends to some extent on the type of analysis one wishes to make. Thus a single voice might be thought of as a pattern of stimulation from several *sources* corresponding to different sound frequency bands. A single letter might be thought of as a pattern of stimulation from various *sources* corresponding to specific components of the letter (e.g., the separate points of light that often comprise computer-generated characters in CRT displays. In fact, if one were asked to listen to two voices and simultaneously monitor briefly presented letter matrices, it might be useful for analytic purposes to treat the task as involving only two sources of information; one acoustic and the other visual.

Although it is possible to consider information tradeoffs in situations involving more than two sources of information, it is easier when a subject can be represented as processing only two sources. Performance of such *dual tasks* can then be characterized by the efficiency with which each source is processed. An information tradoff is simply evidence of a gain in the speed or accuracy of processing one source, accompanied by a loss in speed or accuracy of processing the other. Figure 11.1 presents some graphic examples of how the information a subject processes from each of two sources may be

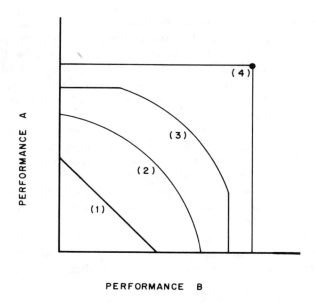

FIG. 11.1.   Illustrative types of information tradeoffs.

related. Each of the functions labeled 1 through 4 indicates a range of performances defined by pairs of processing levels. Function 4 implies that the subject can achieve the maximum level of processing source A and source B at the same time (the intersection of the horizontal and vertical components). Function 3 indicates the subject can only achieve the maximum processing level of one source by processing less than the maximum level from the other, although this tradeoff occurs only at relatively high levels of processing. Functions 1 and 2 indicate two forms of continuous tradeoff between processing of the two sources; any increase in processing one source involves reduced processing of the other.

Dual-task paradigms were a common feature of early work on attention (see Moray, 1969). For example, in the classic cocktail party problem, the two sources of information were two voices speaking simultaneously, and the subject's ability to process each voice was assessed by some measure of comprehension. Figure 11.2 indicates how interest generally focused on only three points of the trading relation. When subjects were asked to *listen to* (or *shadow*) one voice only, they exhibited the highest level of comprehension for that voice (a_3 or b_3). They also showed some limited comprehension of the other voice (a_1 or b_1). Much of the theoretical work on this problem focused on the type of information likely to be comprehended in the *nonattended* voice (e.g., one's own name, or material closely related to the information in the attended voice). It was also clear that comprehension of both voices was

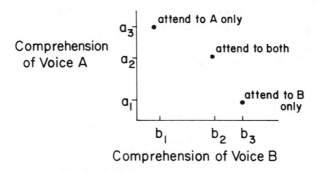

FIG. 11.2. Hypothetical data from a "cocktail party" experiment indicating an information tradeoff.

less than optimal when the subject was asked to listen to both simultaneously (a_2 or b_2). There was, however, little interest in assessing the exact form of trading relation between comprehension levels for each voice. This was due partly to the lack of any consistent metric for measuring comprehension and also to the lack of any theoretical basis for predicting the forms of trading functions. Comprehension of speech was too complicated a task to model effectively. Recently there have been attempts to assess the exact form of the trading relation in simpler dual-task situations that are susceptible to theoretical analysis. However, before considering the variety of theories that can be used to generate specific theoretical trading relations, it seems useful to consider some simple empirical examples of such relations.

At Attention and Performance III (Kinchla, 1969) I presented a paper entitled "An Attention Operating Characteristic in Vision."[1] It dealt with performance of a simple visual dual task: monitoring two, laterally separated ~2.5°) points of light for the occurrence of "signals", brief blinks (3-msec off periods) of either or both lights. Figure 11.3a shows the trading relation

[1]The reference, Kinchla (1969), is a technical report summarizing a more extensive paper given at the Attention and Performance III meeting in Soesterberg, The Netherlands, in 1969. Because this author was in the midst of changing academic positions at that time, the more extensive paper was not written up in time to be included in the subsequently published proceedings. However, the work is cited in Moray's (1969) book on attention (p. 27) and described in some detail in Swets and Kristofferson's (1970) chapter on attention in the *1970 Annual Review of Psychology*. Sperling and Melchner (1979) were apparently unaware of this earlier work when they presented their paper at Attention and Performance VII in 1976. Although they employed a more sophisticated visual recognition task, their concept of an AOC and the type of mathematical model they employ are equivalent to the one proposed earlier by this author: Subjects attend primarily to one of two regions of the display on each trial, being more accurate if the target is in the attended region, and a negative linear AOC is generated by varying the tendency to attend to a particular region.

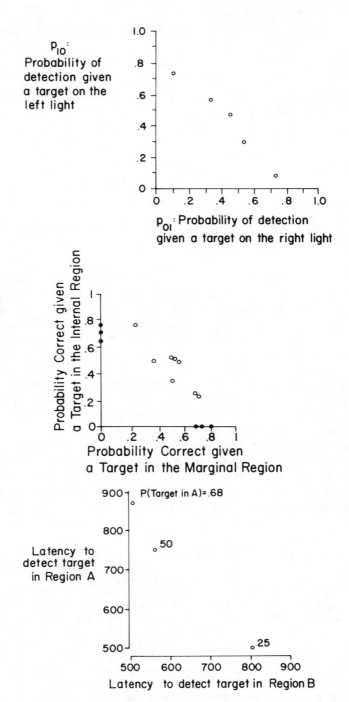

FIG. 11.3. Empirical attention operating characteristic (AOC) functions: (a) Data from Kinchla's (1978) visual detection experiment. (b) Data from Sperling and Melchner's (1978) letter recognition experiment. (c) Data from Shaw's (1978) visual reaction-time experiment.

between accuracy in detecting a signal on the left and right lights. The five data points, from top left to bottom right respectively, were generated by instructing the subject to *attend only to the left light, mostly to the left light, equally to both, mostly to the right light,* or *only to the right light.* I termed this empirical trading relation the *attention operating characteristic* (AOC), because it characterized the range of performances (pairs of accuracy levels) a subject could exhibit on this dual task. Instructions to *attend* more or less to specific lights seemed to move the performance along this AOC function, just as instructions to be more or less *conservative* in reporting a signal move a subject's performance (pairs of *hit* and *false-alarm* rates) along a receiver operating characteristic (ROC) function in a conventional signal detection task.

At a subsequent Attention and Performance meeting (VII in 1976), Sperling and Melchner (1978) presented a similar AOC analysis of a visual recognition task. They asked subjects to monitor briefly presented letter arrays for the presence of target letters. Each rectangular array consisted of larger letters occurring in the periphery or margin of the display and smaller letters in the internal region of the display (around a central fixation point). Figure 11.3b illustrates the trading relation they found between recognition accuracy for targets occurring in marginal and internal regions of the array. They obtained this tradeoff by varying the "importance" of recognizing central versus peripheral targets (e.g., "it is twice as important to recognize targets occurring in the center as in the periphery").

Shaw (1978) presented data from a letter recognition task that can be plotted in the form of a latency AOC function. Her visual displays consisted of two strings of letters, symmetrically positioned on either side of a fixation point. The subject's task was to indicate which of two target letters occurred in each display by pressing one of two buttons as rapidly as possible after the display was turned on. The trading relation shown in Fig. 11.3c was generated by varying the a priori probability that a particular string of letters would contain the target. There is clearly a negative relation between the probability of a particular string containing the target and time to make the recognition response.

A final example of an empirical trading relation is provided by what Posner refers to as "cost–benefit analysis." Figure 11.4a presents the results of a study (Posner, Nissen, & Ogden, 1978) in which subjects responded as rapidly as possible to the onset of a light. The light could occur in one of four positions on each trial: .5° to the left or right of a fixation point, termed the *near positions,* or 6.9° to the left or right of the same fixation point, termed the *far positions.* Just prior to each trial the subject was presented with one of three equally likely cues. The probability that the light would come on in one of the far positions rather than one of the near positions was conditional on the cue; specifically, .8, .5, or .2, depending on the cue. Figure 11.4a gives Posner's original graph of the results in which he shows the subject's median reaction

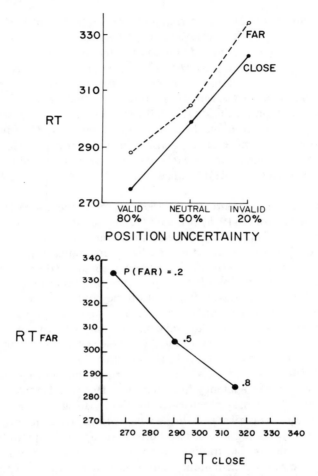

FIG. 11.4.   Data from Posner et al.'s (1978) visual reaction-time experiment:
(a) Illustrating Posner's "cost-benefit" analysis. (b) Replotted as an AOC
function.

time to lights occurring in the more probable location (*valid cue*), in one of the
less probable positions (*invalid cue*), or in either position given the neutral
cue. Posner argues that the difference in median reaction time for valid versus
neutral cues is a measure of the *benefit* a subject accrues by using the cue
information. The difference between reaction time for invalid versus neutral
cues is a measure of the *cost*. Figure 11.4b is a replotting of Posner's data
showing how the cue appears to move the subject's performance along a
latency AOC function.

A common-explanation for the type of empirical trading relations that have
just been considered is that subjects are limited-capacity information-proces-

sing systems and the demands of the dual task exceed this capacity. Thus the subject is forced to share (allocate) limited processing resources (attention, capacity, etc.) between the tasks. Increased allocation to one task improves performance on it but reduces the resources available for the other task, thereby producing the tradeoff. It seems clear that this form of "explanation" is little more than the acknowledgment of a trading relation between perform-ance levels on each task (i.e., if there were no limit to a subject's capacity, both tasks could be performed simultaneously as well as either alone). Any deeper meaning to the concept of capacity would seem to require some specification of the theoretical mechanisms mediating the tradeoff.

Norman and Bobrow (1975) made some very general and useful points regarding joint performance levels in dual-task situations, although they refer to such trading relations as *performance operating characteristic* (POC) functions rather than AOC functions. They place particular emphasis on a distinction between regions of a POC (AOC) in which there is a trading relation, indicating a *resource limitation,* and regions in which there is none, indicating a *data limitation.* For example, function 3 in Fig. 11.1 has two linear regions where a reduction in the performance level on one task is *not* accompanied by an increased level on the other. According to Norman and Bobrow this implies that the additional *resources* made available by the reduced demands of one task cannot improve performance on the other. They attribute this invariant upper bound on performance to the quality of infor-mation available for processing on that task, a *data limitation.* In contrast the curvilinear region of the same POC (AOC) function defines a performance tradeoff between the two tasks consistent with performances limited by shared resources, a *resource limitation.* This type of distinction will be made more explicit in terms of specific theoretical mechanisms discussed later in this chapter. First, however, it seems important to consider an implicit assumption of the Norman and Bobrow analysis, the idea that both tasks share a single limited resource. An alternative assumption is that there are many different processing resources or mechanisms (e.g., iconic and echoic memory systems, verbal rehearsal systems, and memory scanning and search processes). The extent to which dual tasks compete for particular resources would depend on the specific tasks.

Reduction in the performance level for one task might involve reduced utilization of a particular resource that was irrelevant to the second task. Thus the absence of an improvement on the second task would not prove it was *data limited.* It could be competing for a different limited resource whose use was unaffected by the lowered performance level on the first task.

The manner in which two tasks may utilize *multiple resources* is considered in a recent article by Navon and Gopher (in press).[2] They employ microeco-

---

[2]Navon and Gopher also discuss these ideas in their article in this volume.

nomic concepts in an analysis of POC (AOC) functions, treating dual-task problems as similar to those a company might encounter in the production of two products. Just as the production of each product may draw on a variety of shared resources (staff, machinery, supplies, etc.), each perceptual task may draw on a variety of shared processing resources. Their analysis stresses the way in which various competing demands on common resources determine the form of a POC (AOC) function. Although they do not consider the specific nature of these resources, their approach is consistent with the one advanced here, that is, many different "processes" or "mechanisms" are employed in human information processing. If two perceptual tasks compete for the use of a common perceptual mechanism (resource), an information tradeoff may be required. This is illustrated in terms of specific theoretical processes in the next section.

An important aspect of Navon and Gopher's analysis is their consideration of the effect of practice on the form of a POC (AOC) function. It is clear that extensive practice alters the form of information tradeoff in most dual-task situations. In general, practiced subjects seem able to achieve higher levels of performance on both tasks simultaneously. In fact, under certain circumstances the tradeoff in performance levels may disappear completely (the POC may look like function 4 in Fig. 11.1). Navon and Gopher consider a variety of ways in which practice could produce such effects: Each task may utilize resources more efficiently; alternative ways of performing a task may be employed that reduce the competition for limited resources, or resources utilized in the allocation or distribution of resources become available as the process of allocation becomes more efficient or practiced. These considerations seem particularly relevant to the issue of *automaticity* in perception that was mentioned earlier.

SOME ILLUSTRATIVE THEORETICAL PROCESSES

The theoretical processes we shall consider are not presented as representing the most recent or sophisticated theoretical views. They were selected primarily to illustrate simply, and yet specifically, how a variety of theoretical mechanisms can determine the form of an AOC function. The first is a model I presented at Attention and Performance III to account for the empirical AOC functions presented in Fig. 11.3a.

An All-Or-None Attentional Model

As indicated earlier (see footnote 1) the data presented in Fig. 11.3a were obtained in a visual dual-detection task in which an observer was asked to monitor two laterally displaced ($\sim 2.5°$) lights for the occurrence of brief "blink" signals (3-msec off periods of the lights). He was told to respond *yes* if he detected a signal on either or both lights. There were four possible stimulus patterns: S_{ij}, which occurred with equal (.25) probability on each of a series of trials: S_{11}, S_{10}, S_{01}, and S_{00}, where the subscripts indicate the stimulus event on the left and right light, respectively, a value of 1 indicating a signal and a 0, no signal. For example, S_{10} denotes a signal on the left light and none on the right.

The central assumption of the all-or-none model is that the observer adopts one of *two alternative attentional strategies* on each trial: He attends to the left light, denoted A_L, with probability α or to the right light, denoted A_R, with probability $1 - \alpha$. Each presentation of a stimulus pattern (S_{ij}) evokes two *subjective impressions*, one of the stimulus event on the left light, denoted X_L, and the other the event on the right light, denoted X_R. These impressions are represented as Gaussian random variables whose expected values and variances are a joint function of the specific stimulus pattern (S_{ij}) and the observer's attentional strategy (A_L or A_R). Presenting a signal on a light increases the expected value of the evoked impression, whereas attending to a light reduces its variance (noise level). The subject responds *yes* if the impression from either light exceeds his *decision criterion* for that light. The criteria for the left and right lights will be denoted by β_L and β_R, respectively. This sort of *independent decisions* model is considered in some detail in the paper by M. Shaw presented in this volume.

For our present purposes only one characteristic of the all-or-none model need be considered. It can be expressed most easily in terms of two attention-conditional probabilities denoted p_{ijL} and p_{ijR} where

$$p_{ijL} = P(\text{Yes}|S_{ij}A_L) \tag{1}$$

and

$$p_{ijR} = P(\text{Yes}|S_{ij}A_R). \tag{2}$$

The probability of a *yes* response given S_{ij} is simply a weighted average of these two probabilities, reflecting the mixture of A_L and A_R trials: specifically,

$$P(\text{Yes}|S_{ij}) = \alpha p_{ijL} + (1 - \alpha)p_{ijR} \tag{3}$$

In the general form of the model the subject may obtain some stimulus information from the nonattended light. Furthermore the same factors that induce a dchange in α may alter the subject's decision criteria. However, the simple linear relation between p_{10} and p_{01} apparent in Fig. 11.3 suggests certain simplifying assumptions. If the variability (noise level) of the impression obtained from the nonattended light is very high, the observer may adopt an extremely high decision criterion for that impression that has a negligible chance of being exceeded. Thus the probability of a *yes* response would correspond to the probability that the impression from the attended light exceeded its decision criterion:

$$p_{ijL} = P(X_L > \beta_L) \tag{4}$$

and

$$p_{ijR} = P(X_R > \beta_R). \tag{5}$$

If instructions to vary attentional strategy only influence the value of α and do not affect the decision criteria, then Equation 3 defines a linear trading relation (AOC) of the sort shown in Fig. 11.5. This is the type of relation suggested. The fact that estimates ($\hat{P}$) of p_{10R}, p_{01L}, and p_{00} were essentially equal supported the idea that the response depends solely on the impression from the attended light.

Thus one interpretation of the empirical AOC functions in Fig. 11.3a is that the subjects attended to only one light on each trial, basing their response solely on the impression obtained from that light, and that the instructions to attend more or less to specific lights influenced the attentional allocation parameter α. When α equals 1, response tendencies to signals on each light are given by p_{01L} and p_{10L}, and when α equals 0, by p_{01R} and p_{10R}.

Sperling and Melchner (1978) interpreted the AOC function obtained in their letter-recognition task in a very similar manner, although they refer to

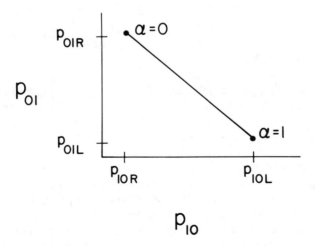

FIG. 11.5.   Theoretical AOC functions derived from Kinchla's (1969) model.

their model as a "switching model." In order to compare their analysis with the preceding one, it will be useful to introduce some simple notation.

Their stimulus displays were rectangular arrays of letters consisting of an *internal* array and a surrounding *marginal* array. A target letter occurred either in the internal region, a T_I display, or in the marginal region, a T_M display. They assumed that the observer adopted one of two alternative *attentional strategies* on each trial: attending to the internal letters, and A_I strategy, with probability α, or to the marginal letters, and A_M strategy, with probability $1 - \alpha$. The probability of correctly identifying the target letter depended on the four possible combinations of target location (T_I or T_M) and attentional strategy (A_I or A_M). Thus there are four corresponding conditional probabilities of a correct identification that can be denoted by p_{II}, p_{IM}, p_{MI}, and p_{MM}, where the first subscript indicates the location of the target and the second the attentional strategy. This allows one to write expressions for the probability of a correct identification of an internal target, denoted $p(C|T_I)$, and of a marginal target, denoted $p(C|T_M)$:

$$P(C|T_I) = \alpha p_{II} + (1 - \alpha)p_{IM} \tag{6}$$

and

$$P(C|T_M) = \alpha p_{MI} + (1 - \alpha)p_{MM}. \tag{7}$$

This implies a linear trading relation (AOC) between these two probabilities similar to that shown in Fig. 11.5. Specifically, suppose values of $P(C|T_M)$ were represented on the ordinate and $P(C|T_I)$ on the abcissa. As α varies from 0 to 1, a linear AOC is swept out from the point p_{IM}, p_{MM} to the point, p_{II}, p_{MI}. Sperling and Melchner induced their subjects to adopt values of α between 0 and 1 by varying the probability that a particular region would contain the target. They induced them to attend always to the internal region ($\alpha = 1$) by always presenting targets there or to attend always to the margins ($\alpha = 0$) by always presenting targets there. Note that in these cases they could only estimate $P(C|T_I)$ equal to p_{IM} or $P(C|T_M)$, equal to p_{MI}, respectively. These correspond to the solid points in Figure 11.3b, which allowed them to fix the end points of a linear functions fitted to the open points. Those points were obtained in conditions in which both T_I and T_M displays were presented. Note in Fig. 11.3b that the values of p_{IM} and p_{MI} are close to chance guessing (.5) indicating that the observer obtained virtually no target information from the unattended regions of the display.

A Weighted Integration Model

The preceding models characterize an observer as responding on the basis of information from only one of the two stimulus sources on each trial (the left or the right light in the Kinchla study and the internal or the marginal display regions in the Sperling and Melchner study). An alternative assumption is that the response is based on an integration or combination of information from two sources. (M. Shaw considers this issue in detail in this volume.) Collyer and I proposed a model of this sort to characterize the detection of target letters in multiletter arrays (Kinchla & Collyer, 1974). The subject was seen as reporting a target letter only if a weighted average of "impressions," $X_i(i = 1, 2, \ldots N)$, obtained from the N letters exceeded some response criterion β; specifically,

$$P(\text{Yes}) = P(\Sigma\ \omega_i X_i > \beta) \tag{8}$$

where each X_i is a Gaussian random variable whose expected value is larger if the target is in that location and each ω is a nonnegative number with $\Sigma\ \omega_i = 1$. Note that the degree to which a particular letter influences the response is determined by the product of the impression it evokes (X_i) and the weight (ω_i) assigned to that impression. The subject will appear less sensitive to letters in locations assigned low weights, just as if they were not "seen" as well. Furthermore, because the weights sum to unity, any increase in the subject's apparent sensitivity to one location must be accompanied by an apparent reduction in sensitivity elsewhere. The exact form of this trading relation can be derived for a two-letter ($N = 2$) display specifying an AOC function. In this case the observer obtains only two impressions, X_1 and X_2, on each trial. Because ω_1 must equal $1 - \omega_2$, the response rule can be written more simply as

$$P(\text{Yes}) = P(Y > \beta) \tag{9}$$

where Y, termed the *integrated impression*, is defined as

$$Y = \omega X_1 + (1 - \omega)X_2. \tag{10}$$

The four possible combinations of target or no target in each location can be represented as S_{ij} stimulus patterns: S_{11}, S_{10}, S_{01}, and S_{00}, where the subscripts i and j indicate the stimulus in the first and second locations, respectively: a 1 indicating a target and a 0, no target. Suppose each of the four S_{ij} patterns were presented with equal (.25) probability over a series of trials. A subject's performance can be summarized by the probability of a yes response given each of the four S_{ij}. These will be denoted by p_{ij} that is,

$$p_{ij} = P(\text{Yes}|S_{ij}: \tag{11}$$

It can be shown (Kinchla & Collyer, 1974) that the letter stimuli in each location have an additive influence on a particular transformation of these response measures: Specifically, let each p_{ij} be transformed to a measure Z_{ij} such that

$$\Phi(Z_{ij}) = p_{ij} \tag{12}$$

where Φ is simply the standard cumulative normal function (i.e., Z_{ij} is simply a Z-transformation of p_{ij}). The additivity of the two effects is illustrated graphically in Fig. 11.6a. Note that the *influence measures* I_1 and I_2 are simply the additive effects of varying the stimulus event (target versus no target) in locations 1 and 2, respectively. When all the weight is assigned to X_1 ($w = 1$), the effect of location 1 (I_1) corresponds to a conventional d' signal detectability measure (d'_1), and there is no effect of the stimulus in location 2 ($I_2 = 0$); conversely, when $\omega = 0$, I_2 equals a similar measure d'_2 and $I_1 = 0$. Thus the measures I_1 and I_2 reflect the relative influence of the stimuli in each location and are independent of the response criterion β. Varying ω generates the curvilinear form of AOC function shown in Fig. 11.6b.

An empirical AOC function of this sort was obtained in a study by this author (Kinchla, 1977) on the role of structural redundancy in visual detec-

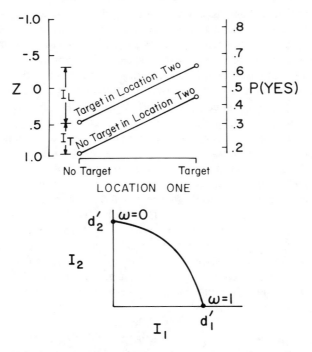

FIG. 11.6. Kinchla's (1977) weighted integration model: (a) Inference measures I_1 and I_2. (b) AOC relating I_1 to I_2 as weight ω is varied from 0 to 1.

tion. Subjects in a tachistoscopic visual detection task had to decide whether a particular, barely perceptible, detail was imbedded in either of two larger, and more readily perceptible, forms. They seemed to integrate information from the two large forms in a weighted manner, placing more weight on the impression from that form that had the highest a priori probability of containing the target detail. Varying such a priori probabilities seemed to induce shifts in weighting (ω) consistent with the AOC function in Fig. 11.6b. Thus the subjects exhibited a trading relation between their apparent "sensitivity" to the details in each form, *as if* they were attending more to one form or the other.

Serial Coding Models

Many influential models of the perceptual process characterize the initial internal representation of a stimulus as held in a *sensory register* (e.g., iconic or echoic memory). These representations are assumed to be fairly rich but unprocessed. They also decay rapidly and are susceptible to the masking effects of subsequent stimulation. Some early theories saw attention as something like a switch (Broadbent, 1958) or filter (Treisman, 1969) that determined what information was extracted or coded from the sensory registers. A number of models represent such coding processes as serial in nature, so that there is a sort of race between the decay and/or masking of information in the sensory register and the serial coding process. For example, Sperling in his seminal work on tachistoscopic letter recognition proposed that letters were serially identified from a visual sensory register at the rate of about one every 10 msec. He reached this conclusion by progressively delaying a postletter mask that seemed to halt further coding of the letters. Although Sperling has subsequently revised this early theoretical view, it is a simple example of a potential selective mechanism. If only so many letters could be coded or identified, the subject might selectively choose which letters to process.

Rumelhart (1970) quantitatively characterized just this sort of selective mechanism in terms of a serial *feature-extraction* process. In his model the observer successively extracted (coded) "features" (rather than letters) from a sensory register. The delay between successive feature extractions was Poisson distributed, with the mean number of features extracted per unit of time a parameter λ. The probability that the next feature identified was from a particular part of the visual display, (i.e., a particular letter) was under the subject's control and constituted a kind of allocation of attention. Specifically, if the visual display consisted of N letters, the subject was seen as assigning N probabilities $\theta_1, \theta_2, \ldots, \theta_N$ to these N letter locations, where θ_i denotes the probability that the next feature identified comes from the ith letter. If a postletter masking stimulus halted this serial feature identification process, the number of features successfully identified from each location would be positively related to the θ_i assigned to that location. Note that λ, the mean number of features identified per unit of time, is an example of a specific *capacity limitation,* whereas the list of θ_i values corresponds to a particular pattern of *attentional allocation.* Thus estimates of these theoretical parameters based on experimental data would constitute quantitative measures of *attention.* One obvious question is whether estimates of the *capacity* parameter λ remain invariant given apparent shifts in attentional allocation (θ_i values). Unfortunately, because of the range of questions Rumelhart chose to consider, he offers no clear answer to this question.

Although one could derive a specific AOC function for two-letter displays from Rumelhart's model, an even simpler example of an AOC based on a conception of serial coding is a model proposed by Estes and Taylor (1964). They proposed that a subject could successfully identify an average of K letters from a briefly viewed (e.g., 50 msec) letter matrix. Each letter matrix contained $N - 1$ randomly arranged nontarget letters plus a single target letter, either F or D with equal probability. Thus the probability of correctly identifying the target letter, denoted $P(C)$, was simply

$$P(C) = \frac{K}{N} + \left(1 - \frac{K}{N}\right)(.5) \tag{13}$$

[i.e., the probability that the K letters identified included the target letter, plus one minus that probability times the probability of a correct guess (.5)]. Now suppose the letter matrix consisted of two rows of R letters, and the target letter could either be presented in the top row, a T_1 display, or the bottom row, a T_2 display. Furthermore, suppose an observer could selectively allocate his processing so as to identify k_1 letters from the top row and k_2 from the bottom row, where k_1 plus k_2 must equal K. The probability of a correct identification given a T_i display, denoted $P(C|T_i)$, can then be written as

$$P(C|T_i) = \frac{k_i}{R} + \left(1 - \frac{k_i}{R}\right)(.5) \tag{14}$$

This also implies a linear AOC function of the sort shown earlier in Fig. 11.5. Here however it is a tradeoff between accuracy in reporting targets presented in one row or the other. Specifically, suppose values of $P(C|T_1)$ were represented on the ordinate and $P(C|T_2)$ on the abcissa. As k_1 varies from K to 0, a linear AOC is swept out from the point $P(C)$, .5 to the point .5, $P(C)$, where $P(C)$ is defined by Equation 13. Again, estimates of K would constitute a measure of a capacity limitation, whereas estimates of k_1 and k_2 would constitute measures of attentional allocation.

Models of Selective Memory Processes

A number of perceptual theories involve selective mechanisms operating on stimulus information that has already evoked (activated, primed) associated information in memory. For example, an early paper by Deutsch and Deutsch (1963) emphasized such a view of attention.

A simple illustration of such processes is afforded by Sperling's initial interpretation (Sperling, 1960) of how subjects reported the letters they had seen in a briefly presented letter matrix. They seemed to "see" many more letters than they could subsequently report, *as if* the limit on their report was imposed by the capacity of a short-term memory process that retained the names of the identified letters until they could be written down. Sperling suggested this was a sort of "verbal rehearsal" process that had an upper capacity of four or five names. Thus, even if the subject successfully "coded" or identified many more letters, he would be unable to remember more than four or five.

Consider how a limited capacity verbal rehearsal process might combine with a serial coding process to determine the form of an AOC function. Suppose, for example, the letter matrix contained two rows of 8 letters each. Even if one could successfully code all 16 letters, one's ability to report the letters could be limited by the capacity of the subsequent verbal rehearsal process. Suppose this capacity were 6 letters. If one could selectively maintain the names of *any* 6 letters in the display, one could choose to remember r_1 letters from the top row and r_2 from the bottom row, so long as r_1 plus r_2 equaled 6. This would imply a linear AOC function relating number of letters reported from each row shown by the solid function in Fig. 11.7. However, suppose a mask were presented after the letter display degrading the letters so

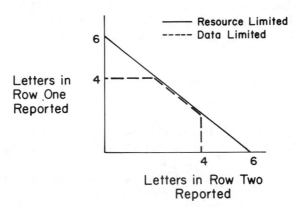

FIG. 11.7.   Theoretical AOC functions based on Sperling's original (1960) conception of serial coding and rehearsal stages illustrating "resource-limited" (solid function) and "data-limited" (broken function) processes.

that each letter had only a .5 probability of being legible. This would mean that an average of 4 letters would be legible in each row. No matter how much rehearsal capacity was allocated to maintaining letters from a particular row, no more than 4 letters could be accurately reported. Thus the AOC would have the form indicated by the broken line in Fig. 11.7b. Note that this provides a specific example of Norman and Bobrow's distinction between data-limited regions of an AOC function (the horizontal and vertical components of the broken curve) and resource-limited regions (the diagonal component of the same function). As indicated earlier such distinctions seem reasonable in terms of specific models of the perceptual process. However, the possibility of complicated competition for multiple resources makes it difficult to interpret such functions in the absence of an explicit theory.

Recently a number of more sophisticated models have been proposed in which selectivity is mediated by the order in which information is processed in memory (Hoffman, 1978; Shiffrin & Geisler, 1973; Shiffrin & Schneider, 1977.) A model proposed by Falmagne and Theios (1969, 316–323) provides a simple example of how such processes may lead to attentional or selective information processing, as well as specific AOC functions. According to their model, stimulus prototypes held in memory are sequentially compared to a test stimulus, until a match occurs producing recognition. In the simplest case there are only two memory prototypes, M_1 and M_2, and the test stimulus S_1 or S_2, matches one of them. Note that the order of comparison should influence the recognition latency for each stimulus (e.g., if S_1 is presented, then recognition latency should be lower if the subject is prepared to compare in the order M_1M_2 than in the order M_2M_1. More generally, if the subject is prepared to compare in the order M_iM_j, his latency to recognize an S_k stimulus can be denoted by $L_k(M_iM_j)$, where

$$L_1(M_1M_2) < L_1(M_2M_1) \tag{15}$$

and

$$L_2(M_2M_1) < L_2(M_1M_2) \tag{16}$$

It can be shown that this also implies a linear trading relation of the sort shown earlier in Fig. 11.5. However here it is a linear tradeoff between the latency to recognize S_1 and S_2 stimuli. Specifically, as one varies the probability of comparisons in the order M_1M_2, the latency to respond to S_1 stimuli goes from $L_2(M_1M_2)$ to $L_1(M_2M_1)$, whereas latency to S_2 stimuli goes from $L_1(M_1M_2)$ to $L_2(M_2M_1)$. Falmange and Theios proposed that "preparatory set" represented in this process was a form of "attentional allocation." In fact, the idea that "set" is a form of attention can be traced back at least as far as William James (1890). Thus it seems reasonable to treat the linear trading

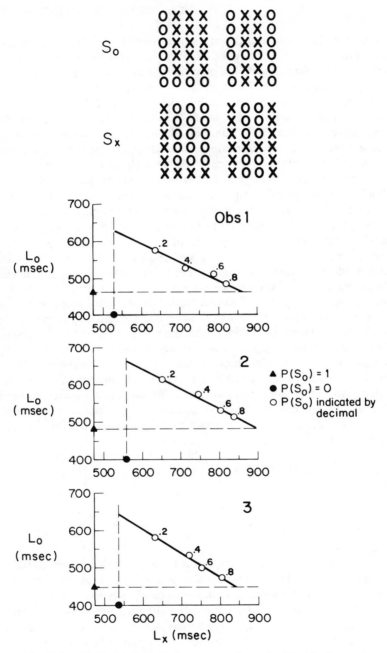

FIG. 11.8. (a) Illustrative stimulus patterns from the Kinchla (in press) "figure ground" experiment, which can be seen as a large L or H with X's defining the "figure" (S_x) or O's defining the figure (S_o). (b) Empirical and theoretical organizational operating characteristic (OOC) function from Kinchla's (in press) figure-ground experiment.

relation defined by Falmagne and Theios as a type of AOC function. Estimates of the parameters of this process would, therefore, represent quantitative measures of an attentional (selective) aspect of information processing.

I have recently developed a very similar model to characterize certain aspects of "figure-ground organization" in vision (Kinchla, in press). Figure 11.8 presents four illustrative stimulus patterns. Note that the top two patterns can be seen to define the large letters L and H as *figures* made up of small X's against a background of small O's. The bottom two patterns can also be seen as defining the large letters L and H, but with the opposite "figure-ground" organization (the small O's define the figure and the X's the background). Any alphabetic character can be defined in this manner, defining the figure either with the small X's an S_x pattern, or small O's, an S_o pattern. These can be presented to an observer in the following trial-by-trial *recognition task*. Each trial begins with the specification of a randomly selected three-letter *target set,* followed a few moments later by the presentation of a *test pattern* similar to those shown in Fig. 11.8. With probability $P(S_o)$ this is an S_o pattern, and with probability $1-P(S_o)$, an S_x pattern. Whether the display is an S_o or S_x pattern, the large letter defined by this pattern will be a member of the target set on a randomly selected 75% of the trials. When it is, the subject is to respond by pressing a pushbutton; otherwise no response is to be made.

The central assumption of the model is that the subject initially perceives (organizes) the pattern in one of two ways: with the small X's defining the figure, an F_x organization, or with the O's defining the figure, an F_o organization. If this initial *figure-ground organization (F_x or F_o)* is appropriate for the type of stimulus pattern (S_x or S_o), the subject should recognize the large letter faster than if it is inappropriate. Thus increasing the probability of an initial F_o organization should reduce the latency of a response to an S_o pattern, denoted L_o, and increase the latency to an S_x pattern, denoted L_x. These assumptions lead to a predicted trading relation of the same form as that shown in Fig. 11.7c. Only here it is the probability of an initial F_o organization rather than the probability of an M_1M_2 comparison sequence, which moves performance along the theoretical function. Although the choice of initial organization should be partially determined by physical features of the specific stimulus pattern (intrinsic determinants), it should also be related to the subject's expectancy regarding the type of pattern (S_o or S_x) most likely to be presented. Figure 11.8 presents data from three observers indicating how the probability of an S_o pattern within a testing session, $P(S_o) = 1 - P(S_x)$, determined mean response latencies to S_o and S_x patterns (L_o and L_x). The results are quite consistent with the linear trading relation predicted by the model.

Psychologists have traditionally treated *figure-ground organization* as an *attentional* process, so it seems reasonable to consider the trading relations shown in Fig. 11.8 as AOC functions. Again, estimates of theoretical parameters, such as the probability of an initial F_o organization, would seem to be legitimate measures of one type of attention. Furthermore, the difference in latency given a correct or incorrect initial organization may represent the time required to switch organizations, a measure of attention switching.

Shaw's Search Model

The last model to be considered was developed by Shaw (1978) drawing on earlier theories of optimal search (Koopman, 1957). It is of special interest because it provides a quantitative measure of processing capacity with few assumptions concerning the specific mechanisms involved.

The model can be explained most easily in terms of the following *visual recognition task*. On each of a series of trials an observer is asked to monitor simultaneously N different locations for the occurrence of a target character. On each trial one of three equally likely target characters is presented in a single randomly selected location. Let $L_1, L_2, \ldots, L_N$ denote the N locations, and let $P(T_i)$ denote the probability of a target occurring in location L_i. The observer's task is to report which of the three targets occurred on each trial.

Shaw proposed that the total processing resources an observer may utilize to perform the task is fixed and that these resources must be allocated or shared among the N locations; specifically, let a quantity Φ denote the *total processing resources* and ϕ_i, the resources allocated to position L_i. This means that

$$\Phi = \Sigma \phi_i \tag{17}$$

Shaw also assumed that the probability of identifying a target occurring in location L_i, denoted $P(C|T_i)$, can be written as follows:

$$P(C|T_i) = 1 - (1 - \alpha)e^{-\phi_i} \tag{18}$$

where α is the probability of a correct guess given no identification (i.e., α equals .33 in this instance, because there are three equally likely targets). Note that Equation 18 implies that the probability of correctly identifying the target character progressively increases as more resources are allocated to location L_i, with accuracy reaching an upper bound of $1 - (1 - \alpha)e^{-\phi_i}$ when all resources are allocated to that location.

An estimate of the resources allocated to location L_i, denoted $\hat{\phi}_i$, can be obtained by rewriting Equation 18 as

$$\hat{\phi}_i = \ln (1 - \alpha) - \ln [1 - P(C|T_i)] \tag{19}$$

and substituting the observed proportion of correct recognitions given a target in location L_i, denoted $\hat{P}(C|T_i)$, for $P(C|T_i)$. Furthermore, as estimate of the total processing resources Φ, denoted $\hat{\Phi}$, is given by

$$\Phi = \Sigma \; \hat{\phi}_i$$
$$= \Sigma \; \{\ln (1 - \alpha) - \ln [1 - \hat{P}(C|T_i)]\} \tag{20}$$

By varying the probabilities of targets in specific locations, $P(T_i)$ values, Shaw (Shaw & Shaw, 1977) induced large shifts in an observer's apparent allocation of resources (i.e., targets were much more likely to be correctly recognized in locations where they were most probable). Yet the estimated value of Φ remained essentially invariant. Thus Shaw has some claim to having derived an invariant measure of visual processing capacity.

An accuracy AOC function can be derived from Shaw's model for the case in which there are only two locations ($N = 2$). It's general form is illustrated in Fig. 11.9a. Each point on the curvilinear trading relation corresponds to a specific pair of values for $P(C|T_1)$ and $P(C|T_2)$, given a particular pattern of allocation, ϕ_1 and ϕ_2. The end points of the function correspond to pure guessing for targets in the location allocated *no resources* and a probability correct of $1 - (1 - \alpha)e^{-\Phi}$ for the location allocated *all the resources*.

Shaw (1978) has recently generalized her original model to deal with reaction-time data. The central idea is that information is processed from a visual display at a constant overall rate V, which is the sum of the rates of processing at each location. For example, if an observer processes information from N locations in a visual display, then

$$V = \Sigma_i \, v_i \tag{21}$$

where V is the overall rate of processing and v_i is the rate of processing from each location L_i, $i = 1, 2, \ldots, N$. Although the value of each v_i can change from moment to moment as an observer reallocates processing resources (attention), the overall rate of processing V should remain invariant. Empirical evidence supporting this invariance assumption was obtained by Shaw (1978). One of two equally probable targets (the letters P and T) was presented in one of N locations on each of a series of trials. The subject was to respond as rapidly as possible on each trial, pressing one button or another, depending on the target presented on that trial. The experimental variables were the number of locations to be monitored ($N = 3, 4, 5,$ or 6) and the a priori probabilities of the target occurring in particular locations. Both had substantial effects on the pattern of reaction times. Times were faster when N was small or the target occurred in an a priori probable location. Although this implies shifts in the rate at which information was processed from each location, estimates of the overall rate V were essentially invariant across all conditions.

A latency AOC can be derived from Shaw's (1978) model for a two-location ($N = 2$) reaction-time task in which one of two equally likely targets occurs in one of two locations on each trial. Figure 11.9b presents the relation between the mean reaction time to targets in location L_1, denoted T_1, and in location

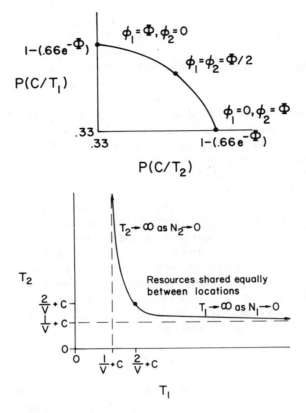

FIG. 11.9. AOC functions derived from Shaw's (1978) search model: (a) Accuracy AOC. (b) Latency AOC.

L_2, denoted T_2. Note that the parameters of the AOC are the overall processing rate V, the individual processing rates v_1 and v_2, and a constant C that can be interpreted as a constant motor component of reaction time added to the time to identify a target. As an observer allocates more processing capacity to location L_i (increases v_i), the latency for targets in that position approaches an asymptote equal to $(1/V) + C$. Sharing resources equally between locations yields latencies of $(2/V) + C$ in each location. Based on the Shaw (1978) study the value of V would be about .02 msec and C, about 150 to 200 msec.

CONCLUSION

We have considered a number of theoretical models that characterize selective aspects of human information processing. These have been used to illustrate how estimates of certain theoretical parameters can be interpreted as quantitative measures of attention. They also show how the range of information-processing options (from which one makes a selection) can be represented by attention operating characteristics. Further analysis of such functions, both empirical and theoretical, would seem to be central to the study of attentional or selective aspects of human information processing.

REFERENCES

Broadbent, D. E. *Perception and communication.* New York: Pergamon Press, 1958.

Deutsch, J. A., & Deutsch, D. Attention: Some theoretical considerations. *Psychological Review,* 1963, *70,* 80–90.

Estes, W. K., & Taylor, H. A. A detection method and probabalistic models for assessing information processing from brief visual displays. *Proceedings of the National Academy of Sciences of the United States of America,* 1964, *52,* 446–454.

Falmagne, J. C., & Theios, J. On attention and memory in reaction time experiments. In W. G. Koster, (Ed.), *Acta Psychologica 30 Attention and Performance II,* North Holland Pub. Co., Amsterdam, 1969.

Hoffman, J. E. Search through a sequentially presented visual display. *Perception and Psychophysics,* 1978, *23,* 1–11.

James, W. *The principles of psychology.* New York: Holt, 1890 (New York: Dover, 1950).

Kinchla, R. *An attention operating characteristic in vision. Technical Report No. 29,* Department of Psychology, McMaster University, Hamilton, Ont., 1969.

Kinchla, R. A. The role of structural redundancy in the detection of visual targets. *Perception & Psychophysics,* 1977, *22,* 19–30.

Kinchla, R. A. "Figure-ground" processing in vision: An organizational operating characteristic. *Perception & Psychophysics,* in press.

Kinchla, R. A., & Collyer, C. E. Detecting a target letter in briefly presented arrays: A confidence rating analysis in terms of a weighted additive effects model. *Perception & Psychophysics,* 1974, *16,* 117–122.

Koopman, B. O. The theory of search: Pt. III: The optimal distribution of searching effort. *Operations Research,* 1957, *5,* 613–626.

Laberge, D., & Samuels, S. J. *Basic processes in reading: Perception and comprehension.* Hillsdale, N.J.: Lawrence Erlbaum Associates, 1977.

Moray, N. *Attention: Selective processes in vision and hearing.* New York: Academic Press, 1969.

Navon, D., & Gopher, D. On the economy of the human processing system, *Psychological Review,* 1979, *86–3.* 214–255.

Norman, D. A., & Bobrow, D. G. On data-limited and resource-limited processes. *Cognitive Psychology,* 1975, *7,* 44–64.

Posner, M. I., Nissen, M. J., & Ogden, W. C. Attended and unattended processing modes: The role of set for spatial location. In H. L. Pick & I. J. Saltzman (Eds.), *Modes of perceiving and processing information.* Hillsdale, N.J.: Lawrence Erlbaum Associates, 1978.

Rumelhart, D. E. A multicomponent theory of the perception of briefly exposed visual displays. *Journal of Mathematical Psychology,* 1970, *7,* 191–218.

Shaw, M. A. A capacity allocation model for reaction time. *Journal of Experimental Psychology: Human Perception and Performance,* 1978, *4,* 586–598.

Shaw, M. L., & Shaw, P. Optimal allocation of cognitive resources to spatial locations. *Journal of Experimental Psychology: Human Perception and Performance,* 1977, *3,*(No. 2), 201–211.

Shiffrin, R., & Geisler, M. Visual recognition in a theory of information processing. In R. L. Solso (Ed.), *Contemporary issues in cognitive psychology: The Loyola Symposium.* Washington, D.C.: V. H. Winston, 1973.

Shiffrin, R. M., & Schneider, W. Controlled and automatic human information processing: II Perceptual learning, automatic attending, and a general theory. *Psychological Review,* 1977, *84*(2), 127–190.

Sperling, G. The information available in brief visual presentations. *Psychological Monographs,* 1960, *74.*

Sperling, G., & Melchner, M. J. The attention operating characteristic: Examples from visual search. *Science,* 1978, *202,* 315–318.

Sperling, G., & Melchner, M. J. Visual search, visual attention, and the attention operating characteristic. In J. Requin (Ed.), *Attention and performance VII.* New York: Academic Press, 1979.

Stroop, J. R. Studies of interference in serial verbal reactions. *Journal of Experimental Psychology,* 1935, *18,* 643–652.

Swets, J. A., & Kristofferson, A. B. Attention. In P. H. Mussen & M. R. Rosenzweig (Eds.), *Annual Review of Psychology.* Palo Alto, Calif.: Annual Reviews, Inc., 1970.

Titchener, E. B. *Lectures on the elementary psychology of feeling and attention.* New York: McMillan, 1908-Chapter 5.

Treisman, A. M. Strategies and models of selective attention. *Psychological Review,* 1969, *76,* 282–299.

12 The Structure of Attentional Resources

Christopher D. Wickens
Department of Psychology
University of Illinois at Urbana-Champaign

ABSTRACT

Structural and capacity theories of dual-task performance are contrasted and a hybrid conception of structure-specific capacity is proposed in which processing resources reservoirs are defined by processing structures. A review of the literature identifies candidates for structural resource reservoirs, defined by input and output modalities, stages of processing, and hemispheres of processing. An experiment is reported in which encoding and response modalities of a digit-processing task are varied, as it is time-shared with a tracking task, whose difficulty is manipulated. The results are interpreted in terms of the concepts of capacity, structure, and resource pools.

STRUCTURE, CAPACITY, AND STRUCTURE-SPECIFIC RESOURCES

When two tasks are performed concurrently in a dual-task paradigm, the concept of attention is an inferred construct used to describe the *cost* in performance of the tasks associated with their concurrence. Research and theory have generated two theoretical conceptions to account for attentional phenomena in dual tasks:

Structural theories infer attention to be related to the competition of tasks for specific information-processing mechanisms (structures) neccesary for performance (e.g., Keele, 1973; Kerr, 1973; Welford, 1967). Such theories often assume processing structures to be dedicated and treat this competition as a discrete state, all-or-none process: Tasks either compete for the common mechanisms or not, and processes either demand attention or not.

239

Capacity theories, in contrast, conceptualize attention as a processing resource that can be allocated in continuous modulated quantities as required by task demands. The allocation of this resource is assumed to be under some level of cognitive control (Kahneman, 1973; Moray, 1967; Navon & Gopher, 1979, this volume; Norman & Bobrow, 1975).

In distinguishing between the two conceptions, Roediger, Knight, and Kantowitz (1977) have argued that capacity interference is related to variations in the task performance produced by manipulations of concurrent task difficulty, whereas structural interference is more often associated with the difference between single- and dual-task performance. Capacity and structural theories are not of course mutually exclusive: Both seem to have a considerable amount to contribute in accounting for time-sharing phenomena, and both appear capable of being integrated into a common conceptual framework (e.g., Kahneman, 1973; Kantowitz & Knight, 1976; Navon & Gopher, 1979).

A basic assumption underlying the original formulation of capacity theories is that capacity (which is henceforth referred to as *resource*) resides within a single undifferentiated reservoir and can be allocated in graded quantity to tasks as required (Knowles, 1963; Moray, 1967). As the demands of one task increase rendering fewer resources available for other tasks, performance on the latter will thereby deteriorate to a degree proportional to the increased demand of the manipulated task. Evidence in the literature abounds to suggest that this conception, although a useful metaphor, cannot be applied literally.

In numerous cases inference effects appear to be related to task structure: One loading task interferes more with a primary task than does another, even though the second task may be equivalent in its information-processing requirements to the first: The two tasks differ only in the processing structures required for their performance (e.g., modality of input or output). Such instances will be termed *examples of structural alteration effects* (e.g., Baddeley, Grant, Wight, & Thomson, 1975; Kinsbourne & Hicks, 1978; McLeod, 1977, 1978; Treisman & Davies, 1973).

In several studies increases in the difficulty or demand for resources of one task (the manipulated task) leaves performance on the other (the measured task) unaffected. This phenomenon, which will be termed *difficulty insensitivity,* can be accounted for by three possible explanations:

1. Performance on the manipulated task may not remain constant. If it does deteriorate, the subject can be inferred to be maintaining a constant resource supply to the manipulated task despite the increase in demand. In these circumstances, a corresponding constant resource supply would be available to the measured task, performance of which should therefore not change.

2. Performance on the measured task is *limited by the quality of data* and not by resources expended, so that further withdrawal of resources will not yield further deterioration of its performance (Norman & Bobrow, 1975).

3. Both these explanations are still compatible with the conception of undifferentiated capacity, but the patterns of data in a number of time-sharing studies suggest a third explanation that tasks draw for their performance upon a number of structure-specific reservoirs of processing resources (Kantowitz & Knight, 1976; Kinsbourne & Hicks, 1978; Navon & Gopher, 1979, this volume; Sanders, 1979; Wickens & Kessel, 1979, in press). A time-shared task pair in which the manipulated demand of one task draws from a pool also used by the shared task will manifest a performance-difficulty tradeoff. However, if the pool affected by the manipulation is not required or only minimally required by the second task, difficulty insensitivity will be the consequence.

The view put forward here argues that structures can share or divide their processing resources between concurrent activities (e.g., Long, 1976a). This sharing is, however, subject to the constraint that resources within a structure are limited; shared resources will thereby diminish performance on a task to a degree determined by the relative contribution of those resources to the overall performance of the task. As a consequence, task performance might be diminished equivalently in one of two ways: by a relatively small demand (of a concurrent task) for the resources of a structure heavily involved in measured task performance or by a large demand for resources of a structure that only minimally contributes to measured task performance. An example of the first might be the deterioration in signal detection resulting from performance of an easy concurrent perceptual task; of the second, the detection decrement that results from a heavily demanding response-related task. The two might also be differentiated in terms of their effects on different aspects of performance: Encoding resources would influence d', whereas response-related resources would influence β (beta).

An alternative to the concept of structure-specific resources proposed here is the modification of undifferentiated capacity theory proposed by Kahneman (1973) in light of the ample data-relating task interference to structural effects. These two theoretical conceptions must be contrasted to identify the distinguishable and testable differences between them. Kahneman proposes that in addition to capacity interference—that related to the limited supply of resources—task inference can also be determined by the competition for processing structures. A distinction is thus drawn between *structures,* as mechanisms that cannot be voluntarily modulated in their availability between tasks, and the central *resources* whose utilization and deployment between tasks can be governed by a cognitive allocation strategy dictated by task demands and priorities (Fisher, 1975; Roediger et al., 1977; Navon & Gopher, 1979, this volume).

It is proposed that dedicated processing structures and processing resources (either undifferentiated, or residing within structures) may be operationally distinguished by results from two experimental paradigms.

1. Priority manipulation: If two tasks share a common resource pool, a continuous tradeoff may be observed as the priorities between tasks are shifted inducing a change in allocation of common resources between tasks. This tradeoff is graphically expressed in the form of the performance-operating characteristic or POC (Norman & Bobrow, 1975; Sperling & Melchner, 1978). If a dedicated structure is involved, the tradeoff will not be manifest and a discontinuous POC will result (Navon & Gopher, 1979, this volume).

2. Difficulty manipulation: If difficulty manipulations affect a resource reservoir shared by two tasks, a continuous difficulty-performance tradeoff will result as the subject reallocates resources to deal with demand changes. If these manipulations affect dedicated structures, the extent of tradeoff will be minimized or of a discrete, all-or-none nature. Thus the major conceptual difference between the view suggested by Kahneman and that proposed here concerns the existence of only a single entity with resource-like properties, instead of a number of entities.

The assertion that resources reside in part or entirely within separate processing structures represents only an initial step in the much more challenging venture of establishing the identity of the specific structural resources in a way that achieves at least some degree of parsimony. Parsimony is essential since the entire concept of structure-specific resources can rapidly lose its predictive and explanatory value as the number of proposed reservoirs begins to approach the number of different tasks and task elements.

Three plausible candidates for the structural composition of resource reservoirs that are suggested by research results from a variety of dual-task paradigms are related to *stages of processing, cerebral hemisphere of operation,* and *modalities of processing* (both encoding and response).

Stage of Processing.   The concept of processing stages has obtained considerable acceptance through the application of additive and subtractive factors methodology to reaction-time data (e.g., Pachella, 1974; Sternberg, 1969), although the assumption of complete seriality of processing by different stages is probably not entirely valid (McClelland, 1978). Whereas the conceptual separation of processing stages does not of itself imply that stages draw processing resources from independent reservoirs, other evidence employing dual-task methodology suggests that they do. For example, studies of verbal transcription (Shaffer, 1971, 1973) indicate that processes of encoding, central processing or translation, and responding can proceed concurrently and with minimal mutual interference, as if all were relying upon resources from nonoverlapping reservoirs. In addition, a number of experiments provide evidence that (1) tasks making perceptual encoding demands can be efficiently time-shared with tasks whose demands are primarily response related (e.g., Trumbo, Noble, & Swink, 1967; Wickens, 1976; Wickens & Kessel, in press) but not with each other (Long, 1976b; Treisman & Davies, 1973); and (2) manipulation of demands on one stage of processing generates only minimal interference effects with tasks that appear to rely heavily upon a different stage (e.g., Isreal, Chesney, Wickens, & Donchin, 1980; Kantowitz & Knight, 1976; Roediger et al., 1977; Wickens, Isreal, & Donchin, 1977; Wickens & Kessel, 1979). This second line of evidence often draws upon the procedures adopted by Briggs, Shulman and their colleagues in which additive factors logic in a reaction-time task is coupled with a dual-task paradigm (Briggs, Peters, & Fisher, 1972; Damos & Wickens, 1977; Logan, 1978; Shulman & Briggs, 1971). Because the manipulations of reaction-time task demands are assumed to affect specific processing stages, the magnitude of their interaction with dual-task loading can provide an index of the degree of resource commonality between the manipulated reaction-time variable (inferred stage of processing) and the concurrently performed task.

Hemisphere of Processing. The recent experimental and theoretical research of Kinsbourne and Hicks (1978) has argued for the concept of functional cerebral space. This view posits that the two cerebral hemispheres act partially as separate resource reservoirs by virtue of their greater functional and spatial separation. Indeed much of their research supports the view that tasks presumed to involve a common hemisphere for their processing (e.g., verbal tasks, and tasks requiring right-handed manipulation) will generate a greater level of mutual interference than tasks depending on separate hemispheres. The results of time-sharing studies involving memory are also consistent with hemispheric reservoirs, assuming that the processes of verbal and spatial working memory (Baddeley & Lieberman, this volume) are associated with the left and right hemispheres, respectively.

Modalities of Processing. Perhaps the clearest demonstration that structures can behave as separate resource pools is provided by those studies in which auditory versus visual encoding and manual versus vocal responses have been contrasted in the dual-task paradigm. Harris, Owens, and North (1978) and McLeod (1977, 1978) for example have observed large changes in interference patterns as structural alterations are made between vocal and manual responses. Evidence for corresponding structural alteration effects between auditory and visual encoding has also been provided by a number of time-sharing investigations (e.g., Glucksberg, 1963; Treisman & Davies, 1973; Wewerwinke, 1976).

On the other hand, Lindsay, Taylor, and Forbes (1968) observed no difference in the interference patern of simultaneous detection as different versus common modalities were employed. Also, Trumbo and Milone (1971) failed to identify a reliable difference in the extent to which manual versus local responding in a serial anticipation task interfered with concurrent step-tracking performance. Although such results initially appear to be at odds with the concept of structure-specific resources, they are troublesome only if resources are viewed as absolutely nontransferrable between structures. Instead it may be assumed that if demands on one pool are sufficiently heavy, resources from another pool may be transferred and applied to the demanding task, albeit with considerably reduced efficiency (Navon & Gopher, 1979). In a time-sharing investigation of verbal and spatial detection and memory, Hellige and Cox (1976) argue for a related concept of "hemispheric overflow:" If the demands on one hemisphere (for spatial or verbal processing) become sufficiently intense, then the opposite hemisphere can assume some of the processing, and the pools are thereby no longer functionally separate.

According to such a view, the advantage of structural separation between time-shared tasks will be reduced as tasks become exceedingly demanding (Kinsbourne & Hicks, 1978). As demands become greater, the activity at the center concerned will spread, increasing the likelihood of disruption of activity in adjacent but functionally separate centers. Stated in different terms, the variation in dual-task performance induced by demand manipulations on one task will be related to the extent of difficulty manipulation but will be attenuated in proportion to some measure of functional distance between the structures primarily employed in performing the measured task and those affected by the manipulated task.

SUMMARY OF DUAL-TASK LITERATURE AND IMPLICATIONS FOR PROCESSING STRUCTURES

Table 12.1 and Figs. 12.1 and 12.2 set out the results of dual-task experiments in which either or both of the following manipulations have been employed:

1. The modality of encoding (auditory vs. visual), memory (verbal versus spatial), or response (speech versus manual) of an interfering task has been altered, whereas the processing demands (difficulty) of that task have been held relatively constant so that structural alteration effects can be assessed.
2. The demands of one task are manipulated as its structure is held constant so that instances of difficulty insensitivity can be identified. Table 12.1 presents examples of structural alteration effects and provides evidence that structure-specific reservoirs may be defined equally well by encoding, memory, and response modalities.

Figure 12.1 represents studies that have paired tracking with other infor-mation-processing tasks. In all the tracking investigations located, three

TABLE 12.1
Structural Alteration Effects (Each entry corresponds to a study identified by a number in the references.)

Stage in Which Modality Is Altered	Encoding: Visual vs. Auditory		Memory: Spatial vs. Verbal		Response: Vocal vs. Manual	
Structural Alteration Effect:	Present	Absent	Present	Absent	Present	Absent
Paired task						
Detection	52D[a]	51D	45M	9M		
	59D	39R				
	64M					
Memory/Reasoning	8S	15R	17D		58P	32R
	45D					35P[b]
Reaction time/	1M		1M	35P[b]	27T[c]	
Shadowing	13D				37R	
	28M					
	45.5T					
	47S					
Tracking	14R	53S	3M		7R[c]	
	(23, 24)R	54S	4M		15R	
					24R	
					36D	
					54R	

Nature of Manipulated Task
D = detection, discrimination   P = response production
M = memory   S = shadowing
R = reaction time   T = tracking
[a]Detection was of both spatial and verbal material.
[b]Effect is absent above age 9.
[c]Response structure altered is hand of control (and thereby controlling cerebral hemisphere).

categories of manipulated difficulty dimensions could be identified: the band-width of the disturbance or input function to be tracked, the number of dimensions or axes to be tracked, and the complexity of the controlled element dynamics (normally 0, 1, or 2 time integrations). The origin of the arrows from tracking therefore indicates the nature of these manipulations. The categories associated with the nontracking tasks identify either the tasks themselves (e.g., memory, detection) or, when such is possible, the clearly defined locus of processing within which the manipulated task had its effect. Thus an arrow originating from auditory encoding might for example indi-cate either the manipulation of difficulty in auditory detection or the manipu-lation of encoding demand in an auditory reaction-time task.

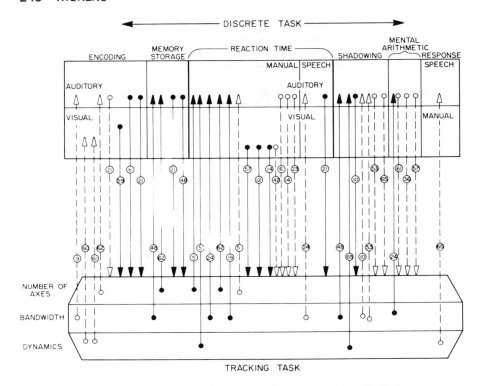

FIG. 12.1. Difficulty-performance tradeoffs between tracking and other in-formation-processing tasks. Each line or arrow corresponds to a study, identi-fied by its number in the references. The circled end of the arrow lies in the task whose difficulty was manipulated (the manipulated task), and the arrowhead indicates the paired task. Solid lines and filled arrows or circles indicate that a significant effect of the difficulty manipulation on performance of the paired task was obtained. Dashed lines (and open symbols) indicate difficuly insen-sitivity.

A number of conclusions are suggested by the data presented in Fig. 12.1:

1. Tasks that show difficulty insensitivity with tracking appear to be primary those that involve verbal or cognitive activity such as shadowing and mental arithmetic.

2. Memory processes and tracking apparently depend on some common resources for their performance because the performance-difficulty tradeoff is invariably present.

3. There is no strong evidence of modality-related pools. Because all tracking tasks were visual–manual, this evidence might have been provided by more cases of difficulty insensitivity when an auditory- or speech-discrete

task was time-shared. However, there is no apparent difference in the proportion of tasks showing difficulty insensitivity between the two modalities.

4. There is some tendency to asymmetry of effect: For example, whereas tracking demand manipulation fails to affect encoding performance, the converse is not true. Again, whereas three out of five tracking manipulations affect shadowing or mental arithmetic tasks, manipulation of shadowing or arithmetic difficulty fails to affect tracking in five out of six cases. Such asymmetry cannot be predicted by undifferentiated resource models. It is however quite compatible with the notion of structure-specific resources in which interference is a joint function of the manipulated structure *and* the relative contribution of that structure to performance of the measured task. If that contribution is small, difficulty insensitivity can be expected.

5. Difficulty manipulations of tracking fail to influence encoding performance, lending some support to the conception of tracking as a "response-loading" task (Navon & Gopher, this volume). However, the three manipulations of tracking demand (number of axes, bandwidth, and dynamics) fail to distinguish or separate themselves in terms of their effects on stages of processing, thereby behaving as if either each variable influences all stages of processing or resources were undifferentiated across stages.

Figure 12.2 presents data when reaction-time tasks have been time-shared with other tasks. The figure suggests the following conclusions with regard to difficulty insensitivity and reaction time.

1. As in Fig. 12.1, memory demands appear to draw heavily upon resources employed in reaction time, particularly those related to encoding. There is no evidence that the performance-difficulty tradeoff is affected by the nature (verbal versus spatial) of the memory processes.

2. In contrast to the results of Fig. 12.1, it is apparent in Fig. 12.2 that the demand manipulations of reaction time do influence the performance of mental arithmetic.

3. When tracking is paired with reaction time, manipulations of demand at response-selection stages do provide some support for modality-specific resources. Such manipulations, when the RT stimulus is visual, appear to have a greater influence on tracking performance (2, 12, 38) than those when the stimulus is auditory (6, 14, 24, 46).

4. When paired with nontracking tasks, reaction time shows little evidence for modality-specific resources. In pairings of encoding with monitoring (20, 33), response selection with reaction time (22), and memory with response selection (26), instances are provided in which cross-modal paired tasks show a reliable difficulty-performance tradeoff. It was argued previously, however, that failure to show difficulty insensitivity when separate modalities are used does not of necessity imply a single common resource pool. It only suggests the absence of a complete independence of resources.

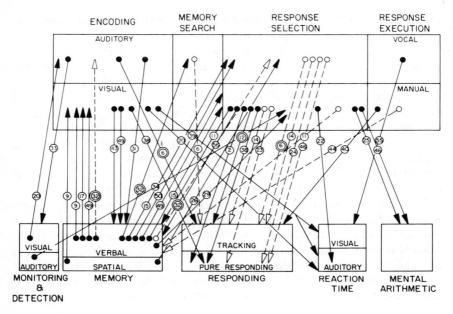

○ Stage determined by additives factors logic.

FIG. 12.2. Difficulty-performance tradeoffs between reaction time and other information-processing tasks. Processing stages rather than tasks appear across the upper portion of the figure. For arrows originating in the reaction-time stage representation, the origin represents the stage of processing affected by the difficulty manipulation. If the manipulation was one of speeding the response process, as by decreasing the interstimulus interval in a forced-paced serial reaction-time task, then the origin is in response selection. For arrows originating in the tasks identified across the bottom of the figure, the locus of termination indicates the locus of effect in processing stages, revealed by additive factors methodology. If this locus was not identified by the study and only total response latency was measured, then arrows terminate at response selection.

The combined implications of Table 12.1 and Fig. 12.1 and 12.2 are complex. There is evidence for separate structural resource pools but because few studies have manipulated encoding demand of a task paired with a response task, or apparently manipulated the responding demand of tasks paired with encoding tasks (Fig. 12.2), it is difficult to draw any conclusions concerning the presence or absence of stage-related resource pools. The table and both figures suggest that short-term memory processes draw upon a general resource pool that is available to and used by all concurrent tasks, whatever their modality and processing stage. With regard to the distinction just drawn between resource pools and structures, the status of processing modalities appears uncertain. The modality-related structural alteration effects observed in Table 12.1 are compatible with either conception, whereas neither Fig. 12.1 nor 12.2 provides substantial evidence that the likelihood of observing difficulty-performance tradeoffs is altered as modalities are shifted, an alteration that if obtained would favor the resource pools conception.

EXPERIMENT

The objective of the experiment reported here was to establish the extent to which input (auditory versus visual) and output (speech versus manual) modalities were defined by separate resource reservoirs. In formulating the experimental design, the following logic was applied. The difficulty of one task is varied across all processing stages and if modalities define pools, then the magnitude of the difficulty-performance tradeoff should vary as a function of the number of processing stages in which modalities are shared between the two tasks (0, 1, or 2). If instead modalities are better represented as processing structures, different tradeoffs will not be observed, but the absolute *decrement* in performance will be related to the number of shared modalities. Finally an undifferentiated resource conception predicts no difference in interference effects as long as processing demands remain constant. Tracking was chosen as the manipulated task with the bandwidth of the tracking disturbance function employed as the demand variable manipulated. This variable is assumed to influence all stages of processing. A running memory mental arithmetic task was performed concurrently. In this task, stimuli could be presented auditorily or visually, and responses could be vocal or manual.

Method

Subtraction (Digit) Task. The subject was presented with a random series of digits (1–9) either visually on a CRT display or auditorily over headphones. Following the occurrence of each digit after the first, the subject was required to compute the difference between that digit and its predecessor, and to indicate this either with a left-handed key press (manual response condition) or vocally (speech response condition). A new digit was presented immediately following a correct response. The series was constrained so that the differences were never greater than 4. The auditory digit stimuli were generated by a Model VS-6 VOTRAX voice synthesizer system, and the subject's speech responses were analyzed for latency and correctness on line by a Scope Electronics Model 1632 VDETS voice recognition system.

Tracking. In the tracking task, the subject manipulated a control stick in a left–right direction, with the right hand, in order to keep the displayed error cursor centered on a target in the middle of the CRT display. The target was immediately above (1.5° visual angle) the digit display on visual digit trials. Tracking dynamics were those of a pure first-order (velocity) system and the input was generated by summing three nonharmonically related sinusoids of adjustable frequency and amplitude. Three levels of tracking difficulty defined by the amplitude and value of the constitutent frequencies were generated. An index of tracking difficulty (ITD) was assigned to each input function according to the formula $ITD = \Sigma_{i=1}^{3} freq_i \times \log amp_i$. This is a quantitative index that accounts for both the increasing difficulty observed with the logarithm of control amplitude as characterized in Fitts's law of movement time (Fitts, 1954) and the exponential rise in difficulty or effort that Micko (1969) observed as responses are decreased in time. The ITDs generated for the three inputs are spaced at equal intervals with values of 4.5 (.068, .111, .154 Hz), 9.5 (.063, .154, .642 Hz), and 14.5 (.063, .310, .670 Hz). Experimental control over the tracking and the digit task was by a NOVA 800 computer.

Subjects

Subjects were 10 officer candidates enrolled in the Naval Flight Training Program at Naval Air Station, Pensacola, Florida. All were voluntary participants in the experiment and were right-handed.

Procedure

Trials for each task, whether single or dual, lasted for 2 min and were preceded by a 1-sec warning indicator on the display. After the initial 30 sec, each dual-task trial was interrupted and the subject viewed a feedback display representing his performance on both the paired tasks so far. This was to aid the subject in allocating his resources equally between tasks for the remaining 90 sec. This information was presented both graphically and verbally.

Design

All subjects participated in three sessions on consecutive days. Half were randomly assigned to the keyboard response group and half to the vocal. On the first day subjects received one trial with each of the five single-task conditions (three levels of tracking difficulty followed by the auditory and visual digit-task input with the appropriate response modalities), in order to gain familiarity with the tasks. Subjects were then told the nature and purpose of the dual-task feedback display they were to see, and the importance of equal allocation of attention between tasks was emphasized. They then performed each of the six dual-task combinations once.

During the second and third sessions, subjects received one calibration trial on each single-task condition, in order that the feedback display could be adjusted to the performance of each individual. Following this, they received a total (across both days) of two trials with each single-task condition and three with each dual-task condition. Trials were presented in a quasirandom order, partially counterbalanced across subjects. Tracking RMS error, the latency of correct digit responses, and the proportion of incorrect responses were calculated and stored for later data analysis.

RESULTS

For each subject, the decrement in task performance was computed by subtracting the dual-task tracking RMS error and digit latency and proportion of errors on each trial from their single-task control scores. Each of these differences was then converted to a normal deviate score by dividing by the within-trial standard deviation. A combined digit-task performance decrement was computed as the average of the latency and error normalized decrements.

The decrements for the 12 dual-task conditions, averaged over subjects and trials, are plotted in the performance operating characteristic (POC) space in Fig. 12.3a (Navon & Gopher, 1979). In this figure tracking decrements are cross-plotting against digit-task decrements with the positive diagonal indicating loci of equal decrement. Better performance (smaller decrements) lie in the upper right of the space. The figure indicates generally greater decrements associated with manual as opposed to speech response and with visual as opposed to auditory encoding. There is no consistent evidence of increasing decrement with increasing difficulty. With the exception of the easy manual conditions, most points lie near the equal decrement and, therefore, equal allocation axis.

Statistical evaluation of the results required that a single number capture the combined dual-task decrement. Because across the three sets of trials priorities varied somewhat from one task to the other, only a single trial of each condition was selected for each subject to represent this decrement, that being the trial on Day 3 that fell closest to the equal allocation axis.[1] The dual-task decrement of this trial was then computed as the average of the decrements in the digit and tracking tasks. The mean of these scores across subjects is shown in Fig. 12.3b and reflects the trends described in Fig. 12.3a. A four-way ANOVA performed on these trials indicated reliable effects of response modality ($F_{1,7}$ = 5.79, $p < .05$) and encoding modality ($F_{1,7}$ = 7.92, $p < .05$). The main effect of difficulty was not statistically reliable ($p > .10$) nor were any of the interactions.

---

[1]It is assumed that these points represented the best estimate of the subjects' dual-task efficiency when equal priority instructions were followed. If points are averaged that fall off the equal allocation axis, assumptions are required concerning the nature of the underlying POC (Navon & Gopher, 1979).

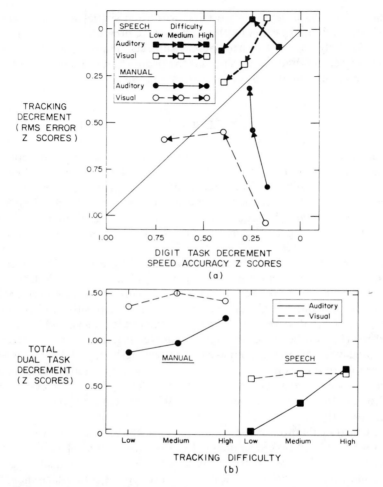

FIG. 12.3.   Dual-task decrements of tracking and digit processing. (a) Performance operating characteristic (POC) space representation. (b) Combined task decrement.

DISCUSSION

Figure 12.3 indicates that structural alteration effects were obtained with regard to both encoding and response modality. Both were in the expected direction indicating a lesser cost associated with time-sharing when separate rather than common modalities were employed between tasks. These results are not surprising and confirm conclusions of previous studies with regard to encoding modality (e.g., Treisman & Davies, 1973) and response modality (e.g., McLeod, 1977, 1978). Unlike the absoute performance decrements, the magnitude of difficulty-performance tradeoffs was not found to vary with the number of shared processing modalities, as would be predicted by modality-defined resource pools. In fact, although all modalities manifest difficulty insensitivity, the one condition in Fig. 12.3 that approached a difficulty-performance tradeoff was that involving auditory input and speech response, that is, the digit task that shared the fewest modalities with tracking.

These results suggest one of two alternative explanations. It is possible that the hydraulic analogy of capacity is not appropriate when applied to modality-defined structures; modalities of encoding and response behaved more as dedicated processors, with a fixed cost associated with time-sharing that does not vary with demand. Such a conception is quite compatible with a structural view of task interference but is seemingly at odds with arguments that resources can be shared in continuous, graded fashion between and within encoding modalities (e.g., Long, 1976a; Sperling & Melchner, 1978).

An alternative explanation is that the hypothetical processing structure most affected as bandwidth is manipulated is one that is neither heavily used in digit processing nor associated closely with encoding and responding. Consequently, no tradeoff or interaction of these modes with difficulty was observed. For the present, the identity of this hypothetical processing structure must remain tentative, as Fig. 1 provides little clarification on this point. The fact that the structure is seemingly unrelated to mode of encoding or response (no reliable interactions with bandwidth were obtained) suggests central processing as a plausible candidate. This result however appears inconsistent with Isreal, Chesney, Wickens, and Donchin's (1980) conclusion that bandwidth manipulation is "response loading." The observation that the difficulty-performance tradeoff was greatest in the auditory–speech condition suggests that the left hemisphere might have been the locus of resource competition (Kinsbourne & Hicks, 1978). This hemisphere was required for speech production in all subjects and because manual control was right-handed, it served as the control center for all tracking performance. Furthermore, it has been argued that this hemisphere is used in the temporal sequencing of responses (Krashen, 1977). As a consequence, further demands would be placed on the left hemisphere as the sequencing became more complex with higher bandwidth.

It must be emphasized that this interpretation is highly speculative. The question of which processing structures behave as dedicated processors and which follow the hydraulic metaphor of resource pools and how these combine to predict task interference patterns remains an intriguing area for further investigation.

ACKNOWLEDGMENTS

This research was supported in part by the Navy Aerospace Medical Research Laboratory, Pensacola, Florida, and the experiment reported was conducted at this facility. Lieutenant Steven Harris, USNMSC, was a collaborator in all phases of the experiment and the author wishes to acknowledge his invaluable contributions.

The theoretical position presented in this paper was formulated in large part on the basis of research sponsored by the Air Force Office of Scientific Research Life Sciences Directorate (Grant No. AFOSR 77-3380). Dr. Alfred Fregly was the technical monitor. Dr. Colin Kessel was a collaborator in much of this research and his contributions to the chapter are greatly acknowledged. In addition the author wishes to acknowledge the contributions of Jack Isreal to the ideas presented here and of Becky Williams for her assistance in data collection and analysis.

REFERENCES

1. Allport, D. A., Antonis, B., & Reynolds, P. On the division of attention: A disproof of the single channel hypothesis. *Quarterly Journal of Experimental Psychology*, 1972, *24*, 225–235.
2. Baddeley, A. The capacity for generating information by randomization. *Quarterly Journal of Experimental Psychology*, 1966, *18*, 119–129.
3. Baddeley, A., Grant, S., Wight, E., & Thomson, N. Imagery and visual working memory. In P. M. Rabbitt & S. Dornick (Eds.), *Attention and performance V*. London: Academic Press, 1975.
4. Baddeley, A., & Lieberman, K. Spatial working memory and imagery mnemonics. In R. Nickerson (Ed.) *Attention and performance VIII*. Hillsdale, N.J.: Lawrence Erlbaum Associates (this volume).
5. Baty, D. Human transinformation rates in one to four axis tracking. *7th Annual Conference on Manual Control*, NASA S.P. No. A281, 1971.
6. Briggs, G., Peters, G., & Fisher, R. P. On the locus of the divided attention effects. *Perception and Psychophysics*, 1972, *11*, 315–320.
7. Briggs, G. G. A comparison of attentional and control shift models of the performance of concurrent tasks. *Acta Psychologica*, 1975, *39*, 183–191.
8. Brooks, L. An extension of the conflict between reading and visualization. *Quarterly Journal of Experimental Psychology*, 1970, *22*, 91–96.
9. Chow, S. L., & Murdock, B. B. Concurrent memory load and rate of readout from iconic memory. *Journal of Experimental Psychology: Perception and Performance*, 1976, *2*, 179–190.
10. Cliff, R. C. Attention sharing in the performance of a dynamic dual task. *IEEE Transactions on Systems Man and Cybernetics*, 1973, *SMC-3*, 241–248.
11. Crowder, R. G. Short-term memory for words with a perceptual-motor interpolated activity. *Journal of Verbal Learning and Verbal Behavior*, 1967, *6*, 753–761.
12. Danos, D. L., & Wickens, C. D. Dual task performance and Hick's law. *Journal of Motor Behavior*, 1977, *9*, 209–215.
Fisher, S. The microstructure of dual task interaction 1. The patterning of main task responses within secondary task intervals. *Perception*, 1975, *4*, 267–290.
Fitts, P. The information capacity of discrete motor responses. *Journal of Experimental Psychology*, 1964, *67*, 103–112.

13. Geffen, G., Bradshaw, S. L., & Nettleton, N. C. Attention and hemispheric differences in reaction time during simultaneous audio-visual tasks. *Quarterly Journal of Experimental Psychology*, 1973, *25*, 404–412.
14. Glucksberg, S. Rotary pursuit tracking with divided attention. *Journal of Engineering Psychology*, 1963, *2*, 119–125.
15. Griffeth, D., & Johnston, W. An informational processing analysis of visual imagery. *Journal of Experimental Psychology*, 1973, *100*, 141–146.
16. Harris, S., Owens, J., & North, R. A system for the assessment of human performance in concurrent verbal and manual control tasks. *Behavior Research Methods and Instrumentation*, 1978, *10*, 329–333.
17. Hellige, J., & Cox, P. Effects of concurrent verbal memory on recognition of stimuli from the left and right visual fields. *Journal of Experimental Psychology: Human Perception and Performance*, 1976, *2*, 210–221.
18. Henderson, A. I. A note on the interference between verbal output and a cognitive task. *Acta Psychologica*, 1975, *39*, 495–497.
19. Isreal, J., Chesney, G., Wickens, C., & Donchin, E. P-300 and tracking difficulty: evidence for multiple resources in dual task performance. *Psychophysiology*, 1980, *17*, 259–273.
20. Isreal, J., Wickens, C., Chesney, G., & Donchin, E. The event related brain potential as selective index of display monitoring load. *Human Factors* (in press).
21. Johnston, W., Greenberg, S., Fisher, R., & Martin, D. Divided attention: A vehicle for monitoring memory processes. *Journal of Experimental Psychology*, 1970, *83*, 164–171.
Kahneman, D. *Attention and effort*. Englewood Cliffs, N.J.: Prentice-Hall, 1973.
22. Kalsbeek, J., & Sykes, R. Objective measurement of mental load. *Acta Psychologica*, 1967, *27*, 253–261.
23. Kantowitz, B. H., & Knight, J. Testing tapping and time-sharing. *Journal of Experimental Psychology*, 1974, *103*, 331–336.
24. Kantowitz, B. H., & Knight, J. Testing tapping and time-sharing II: Use of auditory secondary task. *Acta Psychologica*, 1976, *40*, 343–362.
25. Keele, S. W. Compatibility and time-sharing in serial reaction time. *Journal of Experimental Psychology*, 1967, *75*, 529–539.
Keele, S. W. Attention and human performance. Pacific Pallisades, Calif.: Goodyear, 1973.
26. Kelley, R. T., & Martin, D. Dual task analysis of memory for random shapes. *Journal of Experimental Psychology*, 1974, *103*, 224–229.
Kerr, B. Processing demands during mental operations. *Memory & Cognition*, 1973, *1*, 401–412.
27. Kinsbourne, M., & Hicks, R. Functional cerebral space. In J. Requin (Ed.), *Attention and performance VII*, Hillsdale, N.J.: Lawrence Erlbaum Associates, 1978.
Knowles, W. B. Operator loading tasks, *Human Factors*, 1963, *5*, 151–161.
Krashen, S. D. The left hemisphere. In M. C. Wittrock (Ed.), *The human brain*. Englewood Cliffs, N.J.: Prentice-Hall, 1977.
28. Kroll, N. Short term memory and the nature of interference from concurrent shadowing. *Quarterly Journal of Experimental Psychology*, 1972, *24*, 414–419.
29. Lansman, M. *An attentional approach to individual differences in immediate memory*. ONR Final Report, University of Washington, June 1978.
30. Lindsay, P. H., Taylor, M. M., & Forbes, S. M. Attention and multidimensional discrimination. *Perception & Psychophysics*, 1968, *4*, 113–117.
31. Lindsay, P., & Norman, D. Short term retention during a simultaneous detection task. *Perception & Psychophysics*, 1969, *5*, 201–205.
32. Logan, J. Attention in character classification tasks: Evidence for automaticity of component stages. *Journal of Experimental Psychology*, 1978, *107*, 32–63.
Long, J. Division of attention between non-verbal signals: All-or-none or shared processing. *Quarterly Journal of Experimental Psychology*, 1976, 28, 47–69. (a)

33. Long, J. Effect of task difficulty on the division of attention between non-verbal signals: Independence or interaction. *Quarterly Journal of Experimental Psychology,* 1976, *28,* 179–192. (b)

34. Martin, M. Reading while listening: A linear model of selective attention. *Journal of Verbal Learning and Verbal Behavior,* 1977, *16,* 453–463.

McClelland, J. On the time relations of mental processes: A framework for analyzing processes in cascade. Center for Human Information Processing. CHIP Report No. 77. University of California, San Diego, October 1978.

35. McFarland, K., & Ashton, R. A developmental study of the influence of cognitive activity on an ongoing manual task. *Acta Psychologica,* 1975, *39,* 447–456.

36. McLeod, P. A dual task response modality effect: Support for multiprocessor models of attention. *Quarterly Journal of Experimental Psychology,* 1977, *29,* 651–667.

37. McLeod, P. Does probe RT measure central processing demand? *Quarterly Journal of Experimental Psychology,* 1978, *30,* 83–89.

38. Michon, J. A. Tapping regularity as a measure of perceptual motor load. *Ergonomics,* 1966, *9,* 401–412.

Micko, H. C. A psychological scale for RT measurement. *Acta Psychologica,* 1969, *30,* 324–338.

39. Millar, K. Stimulus capacity requirements of stimulus encoding. *Acta Psychologica,* 1975, *39,* 393–410.

Moray, N. Where is capacity limited? A theory and a model. *Acta Psychologica,* 1967, *27,* 84–92.

40. Navon, D., & Gopher, D. On the economy of the human processing system. *Psychological Review,* 1979, *86.*

Navon, D., & Gopher, D. Interpretation of task difficulty in terms of resources: Efficiency, load, demand and cost composition. In R. Nickerson (Ed.), *Attention and performance VIII.* Hillsdale N.J.: Lawrence Erlbaum Associates (this volume).

41. Naylor, J., Briggs, G., & Reed, W. Task coherence, training time and retention interval effects on skill retention. *Journal of Applied Psychology,* 1968, *52,* 386–393.

Norman, D. A., & Bobrow, D. J. On data limited and resource limited processes. *Cognitive Psychology,* 1975, *7,* 44–64.

42. North, R. A. Task functional demands as factors in dual task performance. *Proceedings 21st Annual Meeting of the Human Factors Society,* San Francisco, 1977.

North, R. A., & Gopher, D. Measures of attention as predictors of flight performance. *Human Factors,* 1976, *18,* 1–9.

Pachella, R. The use of reaction time measures in information processing. In B. Kantowitz (Ed.), *Human information processing,* Potomac, Md.: Lawrence Erlbaum Associates, 1974.

43. Poulton, C. C. Measuring the order of difficulty of visual-motor tasks. *Ergonomics,* 1958, *2,* 234–239.

44. Roediger, H. L., Knight, J. L., & Kantowitz, B. H. Inferring decay in short term memory: The issue of capacity. *Memory & Cognition,* 1977, *5,* 167–176.

Sanders, A. In N. Moray (Ed.), *Mental workload: Its theory and measurement.* New York: Plenum Press, 1979.

45.5. Schori, T. R. A comparison of visual, auditory and cutaneous tracking displays when divided attention is required to a cross-adaptive loading task. *Ergonomics,* 1973, *16,* 153–158.

46. Schouten, J. F., Kalsbeek, J. W., & Leopold, F. F. On the evaluation of perceptual and mental load. *Ergonomics,* 1962, *5,* 251–260.

45. Segal, S., & Fusella, V. Influences of imaged pictures and sounds on detection of visual and auditory signals. *Journal of Experimental Psychology,* 1970, *83,* 458–463.

Shaffer, L. H. Attention in transcription skill. *Quarterly Journal of Experimental Psychology,* 1971, *23,* 107–112.

Shaffer, L. H. Latency mechanisms in transcription. In S. Kornblum (Ed.), *Attention and performance IV.* New York: Academic press, 1973.

47. Shaffer, L. H. Multiple attention in continuous tasks. In P. M. Rabbitt & S. Dornic (Eds.), *Attention and performance V.* London: Academic Press, 1975.

48. Shulman, H. G. & Briggs, G. *Studies of performance in complex aircrew tasks.* Ohio State University Research Foundation. Air Force Project 2718, Final Report, 1971.
49. Shulman, H. G., & Greenberg, S. N. Perceptual deficit due to division of attention between perception and memory. *Journal of Experimental Psychology,* 1971, *88,* 171–176.

Sperling, G., & Melchner, M. Visual search and the attention operating characteristic. In J. Requin (Ed.), *Attention and performance VII.* Hillsdale, N.J.: Lawrence Erlbaum Associates, 1978.

50. Stanners, R. F., Meunier, G. F., & Headley, D. B. Reaction time as an index of rehearsal in short term memory. *Journal of Experimental Psychology,* 1969, *82,* 566–570.

Sternberg, S. The discovery of processing stages: An extension of Donders' method. *Acta Psychologica,* 1969, *30,* 276–315.

51. Taylor, B., Lindsay, P., & Forbes, S. Quantification of shared capacity processing in auditory and visual modalities. *Acta Psychologica,* 1967, *27,* 223–229.
52. Treisman, A., & Davies, A. Divided attention between eye and ear. In S. Kornblum (Ed.), *Attention and performance IV.* New York: Academic Press, 1973.
53. Trumbo, D., Noble, M., & Swink, J. Secondary task interference in the performance of tracking tasks. *Journal of Experimental Psychology,* 1967, *73,* 232–240.
54. Trumbo, D., & Milone, F. Pirmary task performance as a function of encoding retention and recall in a secondary task. *Journal of Experimental Psychology,* 1971, *91,* 273–279.
55. Van Galen, G., & TenHoopen, G. Speech control and single channelness. *Acta Psychologica,* 1976, *40,* 245–255.
56. Wagenear, W. *Sequential Response Bias.* Institute for Perception, TNO Soesterberg: The Netherlands, 1972.
57. Watson, B. L. *The effect of secondary tasks on pilot describing functions in a compensatory tracking task.* University of Toronto Institute for Aerospace Studies Technical Note No. 178, June 1972.
58. Weber, R., & Blagowski, J. Metered memory search and concurrent chanting, *Journal of Experimental Psychology,* 1971, *89,* 162–168.

Welford, A. T. Single channel operation in the brain. *Acta Psychologica,* 1967, *27,* 15–24.

Welford, A. T. Mental workload as a function of demand, capacity, strategy and skill. *Ergonomics,* 1978, *21,* 151–167.

59. Wewerwinke, P. *Human monitoring and control behavior.* Netherlands National Aerospace Laboratory Technical Report, NLR TR 77010 U, 1976.

Wickens, C. D. The effects of divided attention on information processing in tracking. *Journal of Experimental Psychology: Human Perception and Performance,* 1976, *1,* 1–13.

60. Wickens, C., & Kessel, C. The effect of participatory mode and task workload on the detection of dynamic system failures. *IEEE Transactions on Systems Man and Cybernetics,* 1979, *13,* 21–31.
61. Wickens, C. D., & Kessel, C. *The processing resource demands of failure detection in dynamic systems. Journal of Experimental Psychology: Human Perception and Performance* (in press).
62. Wickens, C., Isreal, J., & Donchin, E. The use of the event related cortical potential as an index of task workload. *Proceedings 19th Annual Meeting of the Human Factors Society,* San Francisco, Calif., October 1977.
63. Williams, H., Beaver, W., Spence, M., & Rundell, O. Digital and kinesthetic memory with interpolated information processing. *Journal of Experimental Psychology,* 1969, *80,* 530–536.
64. Wright, P., Holloway, C., & Aldrich, A. R. Attending to visual or auditory verbal information while performing other concurrent tasks. *Quarterly Journal of Experimental Psychology,* 1974, *26,* 454–463.
65. Zeitlin, L. R., & Finkleman, J. Subsidiary task techniques of digit generation and digit recall as measures of operator loading. *Human Factors,* 1975, *17,* (2), 218–220.

13 Does Oculomotor Readiness Mediate Cognitive Control of Visual Attention?

Raymond Klein
Dalhousie University
Halifax, Nova Scotia
Canada

ABSTRACT

Cognitive control of visual attention (i.e., the allocation of processing resources to locations in visual space in the absence of eye movements) has been amply demonstrated in recent years. The role of the eye movement system in producing these internal shifts of attention has been disputed. In this chapter, I review the evidence on cognitive control of visual attention and propose an explicit oculomotor readiness mechanism that is consistent with that evidence and several other findings as well. This proposal predicts that (1) a readiness to move the eyes to a particular location will facilitate detection of stimuli appearing at that location; and (2) cognitive control of visual attention is produced by preparing to move the eyes to the to-be-attended location. These predictions were tested in two dual-task experiments and both were clearly disconfirmed. It is concluded that cognitive control of visual attention is independent of the eye movement system, even though attentional shifts may be reflexively linked to overt shifts in eye position.

INTRODUCTION

Where are you looking? This simple question and your response are basically ambiguous. "Looking" may refer to the locus of gaze (i.e., the portion of the visual field falling upon the sensitive fovea) or to the locus of visual attention (i.e., active information pickup). On the basis of their own introspection judgments, early psychologists claimed that these two locations are not necessarily the same. Helmholtz (1925), for instance, claimed that "the observer may be steadily gazing at the fixation mark, and yet at the same time he can concentrate his attention upon any part of the field he likes"; Wundt (1912) drew a similar conclusion. In more recent years, the independence of gaze and visual attention has been reinforced in work by Kaufman and Richards (1969). Using a technique known as *Haidinger's brush* to monitor eye position while the subject examined a visually presented figure, they concluded that "the fovea is not always oriented toward the point to which attention is directed."

In the past decade or so a variety of experimental paradigms have been brought to bear on this issue (Engel, 1971; Eriksen & Hoffman, 1973; Jonides, 1976; Posner, Nissen, & Ogden, 1975, 1978; Shaw & Shaw, 1977; Van Voorhis & Hillyard, 1977). These studies not only provide objective evidence for the independence viewpoint that had been based upon subjective introspection but also valuable information characterizing the attentional process itself.

I concentrate here on the paradigm that is employed in the present study: the priming, expectancy, or cost-benefit paradigm. In this paradigm, the subject is encouraged (via payoffs, probability, instructions, or some combination of these) to allocate attention (processing resources) to one of several possible stimuli (Posner & Snyder, 1975), sensory modalities (Klein, 1977), or memory locations (Neely, 1977). Performance on expected and unexpected dimensions is compared to that in a neutral condition, in which no attentional shift is generated. This allows determination of the costs and benefits of attentional allocation.

In a typical priming experiment on the allocation of attention in space, the subject is looking at a fixation stimulus, and a foveal warning cue is presented. This cue may be neutral (e.g., a plus sign), conveying no information about the location of an impending detection stimulus, or it may be priming (e.g., an arrow), informing the subject of the likely location of a detection stimulus. On most of the priming trials the arrow is valid, and the target appears on the expected side. It is invalid on the remaining trials. The subject's task is to make a simple manual response as soon as a stimulus at either location is detected. Subjects are instructed not to move their eyes, and trials with eye position shifts are excluded from the analysis. Typically, the valid condition is faster (benefits), and the invalid condition is slower (costs), when compared to the neutral condition.[1]

---

[1]Much of the work on the allocation of visual attention using this paradigm is due to Posner and colleagues. I shall try to cite the appropriate unpublished papers in the text; published reviews can be found in Posner (1978) and Posner et al. (1978).

Some Characteristics of the Orienting Mechanism

Posner et al., (1975) and Posner and Davidson (1976) have shown that the costs and benefits are the same whether the detection stimuli are in the fovea (.5° left or right of fixation) or in the periphery (6.9° and 25°). Posner infers from this that orienting does not depend on the saccadic eye movement system, because if it did, peripheral targets that would normally elicit eye movements might be expected to show greater costs and benefits. This inference is questionable, because subjects can make .5° saccades. Nevertheless, the results do demonstrate that for simple detection the fovea does not have special access to attention. If it did, one would expect little or no costs for unexpected foveal stimuli. Posner, Snyder, and Davidson (1977) have also demonstrated that it is difficult or impossible to divide visual attention between nonadjacent locations that were defined by the presence of intervening "nonattended" target positions. Finally, there is evidence (Remington, Shulman, & McLean, 1978) suggesting that the orienting process is a continuous one in which attention moves through intermediate points as it is shifted from one location to another.

The experiments just mentioned measured the speed of a simple manual response to a luminance increment. When comparing these results to those of other studies, it is worth keeping this in mind, because detection is one of the simplest tasks we can set for a subject. For example, whereas Posner and colleagues (Posner et al. 1975, 1978) have demonstrated that the retina is equipotential with respect to detection of a large luminance change, they also suggest that the fovea may play a special role if fine discriminations are required.

Jonides (1976) measured the time course of the costs and benefits in a speeded letter identification task with four possible target locations. His time-course data are incomplete because the largest prime-stimulus interval he used was 200 msec.[2] Nevertheless, he reports some interesting findings. One experiment compared foveal cues with peripheral ones, presented just eccentric to the target locations. The benefits with the two cues were about the same, but the costs were much greater with the peripheral cues. In another experiment, peripheral cues produced large costs even if they were uninformative concerning target location. These results suggest that peripheral stimuli reflexively attract attention.

---

[2]Jonides did not monitor eye movements and for this reason used no prime-stimulus interval longer than 200 msec so that subjects would have insufficient time to fixate the primed location while the stimulus was still on. It should be kept in mind that eye movements may have been executed in this experiment, and they may have been more likely in the peripheral cue condition (see p. 273).

The generality of the orienting mechanism is fortified by studies using dependent measures other than reaction time. Several investigators have found improved accuracy for stimuli appearing at attended locations (Engel, 1971; Shaw & Shaw, 1977; Sperling & Melchner, 1978). Converging evidence is also available from studies of evoked potentials in man (Eason, Harter, & White, 1969; Van Voorhis & Hillyard, 1977) and single-cell responses of parietal cortex neurons in monkey (Bushnell, Robinson, & Goldberg, 1978). Van Voorhis and Hillyard, for example, recorded evoked potentials to target and nontarget flashes of light 20° to the left and right of fixation under focused (e.g., attend left), divided, and passive instructions. They found enhanced responses for stimuli appearing at the attended locus, with enhancement beginning as early as 155 msec following stimulus onset. Similarly, Bushnell et al. (1978) found enhanced responses of parietal cortex neurons to receptive field stimuli that required the monkey's attention.

An Oculomotor Readiness Theory of Visual Attention

In my view, the data reviewed so far strongly suggest that the allocation of attention to a position in space involves either improved processing along the pathway from that location or improved access to attention for stimuli from that location. I would like to turn our attention to *how* these shifts might be mediated. On the basis of the powerful effects of peripheral cues, Jonides (1976) suggests "... to the extent that peripheral information is also quite effective in capturing eye fixations, perhaps shifts of attention, or movements of the mind's eye are intimately related (in an as yet unspecified way) to movements of the body's eye." Posner, on the other hand, has concluded that "the ability to move attention around in the visual field is not parasitic upon the saccadic eye movement system [Posner & Davidson, 1976]."

In order to distinguish between these opposing viewpoints, two experiments were designed to test a specific oculomotor mechanism for producing shifts of attention in vision. Movements of the mind's eye might depend on the saccadic eye movement system in the following specific manner: *When attention to a particular location is desired, the observer prepares to make an eye movement to that location; the oculomotor readiness, via as yet unknown feedforward pathways, has the effect of enhancing processing in or from sensory pathways dealing with information from the target location.* Evidence supporting this proposal comes from several sources.

First, there is a plausible neural substrate in the close correspondence between the system producing saccadic eye movements and the visual mosaic. For instance, cells in the superior colliculus which respond before the eye moves to a particular location and which, when stimulated, produce eye movements to that location also respond to visual stimuli presented at that location (Schiller & Koerner, 1971; Schiller & Stryker, 1972). This arrangement seems to be designed to select visual targets for fixation (Wurtz & Mohler, 1974). Perhaps these pathways or closely related ones can be used to select visual loci for purposes other than eye movements. Recently, Mohler and Wurtz (1976) have shown that some cells in the intermediate layers of the superior colliculus begin to increase their response rate if the monkey is preparing to make an eye movement. Feedforward from these neurons to corresponding sensory areas might provide a neural mechanism for the oculomotor readiness hypothesis proposed here. The enhancement in parietal cortex reported by Bushnell et al. (1978) might be produced by such a feedforward mechanism.

Second, Jonides'(1976) data on the reflexive allocation of attention toward peripheral targets are consistent with the proposal. In this situation, however, the "readiness" is imposed by the stimulus, whereas, in the aforementioned studies, it is cognitively generated by the subject.

Third, several investigators have demonstrated that perception of stimuli is enhanced if the stimuli are to be the target for an eye movement (Bryden, 1961; Crovitz & Daves, 1962; Rayner, McConkie, & Ehrlich, 1978, Experiment 3). In the Crovitz and Daves experiment, for example, a horizontal array of digits was briefly presented and subjects were instructed to move their eyes to one side of the string or the other, at their dirscretion. Even though the stimulus was turned off by the time the eye movement had been initiated, it was found that the digits on the side to which movement was made were more accurately reported than those on the other side. This finding is not definitive with respect to the proposed oculomotor readiness mechanism, because the features of the visual stimulus that attract the eye movement system may independently also attract attention.[3] Nevertheless, Crovitz and Daves (1962) did anticipate the present proposal when they suggested that "the neural activity responsible for an eye movement may itself play an important role in perceptual integration whether or not an eye movement occurs."

Lastly, there is an anomalous finding in the literature on stimulus–response compatibility that would be explained by the oculomotor readiness proposal. Posner and Davidson (1976) and Klein (1978) have shown that incompatible eye movements (those directed away from a stimulus) take 50 msec longer to initiate than compatible movements even when the direction of movement is known in advance of the stimulus. This finding is anomalous because for most other stimulus–response mappings (e.g., hand–eye or hand–ear) compatibility effects are absent or reduced in simple reaction time (see Posner, 1978, Fig. 7.5). The authors of both studies explain the anomaly in terms of the difficulty

---

[3]This objection does not apply to the Rayner et al. (1978) study, because their subjects were instructed to move to the left or right target for a whole block of trials. See, however, p. 273.

of overriding the very direct input–output connections of the saccadic eye movement system. The present proposal predicts this effect for different reasons. In simple RT paradigms, the subject is told in advance of the trial (or block of trials) what response to make when any stimulus is detected. In the Klein (1978) and Posner and Davidson (1976) experiments just mentioned, the subject would prepare to make a leftward (or rightward) movement prior to the left or right stimulus appearing. If subjects voluntarily move attention around by preparing to make eye movements, then, in this type of experiment, attention will be directed toward the location that is to be foveated, and, thus, benefits will be obtained on compatible trials and costs will be obtained on incompatible trials. If this analysis is correct, then it may not be a coincidence that the compatibility effect (moving left to left vs right stimuli) is about 40–50 msec; this is the typical size of the cost–benefit effect in studies of the allocation of visual attention without eye movements.

Two forms of dependence between attention and eye movements are entailed in the oculomotor readiness mechanism just outlined. One is that a readiness to move the eyes to a certain locus produces an attentional bias toward that locus. The other is that attention to a location in space involves a readiness to move one's eye to that locus. Each of these predictions will be tested in dual-task paradigms combining manual responses to a brief luminance increment with saccadic responses to the appearance of an asterisk.

EXPERIMENT 1

According to the oculomotor hypothesis, if the subject is ready to move his eyes to a particular location, then stimuli appearing at that location should be detected more rapidly than if the readiness is directed elsewhere. On the other hand, if attention in space is independent of the eye movement system, then detection latency should be unaffected by oculomotor readiness. A dual-task paradigm was used to discriminate between these two predictions. In the saccadic response task, the subject was instructed to make a saccadic eye movement from the central fixation point to one of two peripheral target dots when an asterisk appeared at either of the target locations. The direction of movement was constant for a block of trials and, thus, did not depend on the location of the asterisk. It was assumed that in such a simple reaction-time procedure the subject would prepare the saccadic eye movement in advance of the imperative stimulus. On occasional trials, a different stimulus, one of the peripheral targets briefly brightening, occurred. In response to either target brightening the subject's task was to make a simple manual response. The question of interest was whether performance on this detection task would be affected by the direction of the prepared eye movement. The two types of stimuli occurred equally often at each target location; therefore, no cognitive shift of attention was expected. However, the oculomotor readiness hypothesis predicts that detection of the luminance increment should be faster when the target that brightens is the one to which the subject is ready to move his eyes.

METHOD

Subjects

Ten Dalhousie undergraduates were paid $3 per hour for their participation. Subjects were informed of the approximate probabilities of the possible events in each type of block. They were instructed to respond as quickly and as accurately as possible and were discouraged from making anticipatory responses. Subjects were tested in three sessions.

Apparatus

The subject sat with his head in a chin rest, facing a Tektronix 604 display monitor in a dimly illuminated room. The distance from the chin rest to the screen was 36 cm. A biometrics eye movement monitor was used to monitor horizontal position of the subject's right eye. The device was mounted in eyeglass frames and worn with supporting straps. A response bar was placed on the table in front of the subject. A PDP11/10 computer controlled the sequence of events in the experiment.

Task and Procedure

Each block of trials began and ended with an eye position calibration procedure. After the initial calibration, the word READY appeared on the screen. When the subject was ready, he pressed the response bar to initiate the block of trials. Each trial began with the display of three horizontally arranged dots in the middle of the screen. The dots were evenly spaced, the distance between the left and right dots being 8° of visual angle. The subjects were instructed to depress and hold down the response bar when they had foveated the central dot. One-half second after this response a warning cue (+) was displayed superimposed over the central dot, and sampling of eye position every 2 msec was initiated. After 1 sec, one of three possible types of event occurred: (1) the left or right dot brightened for 100 msec;[4] (2) an asterisk was displayed

---

[4]Brightening was accomplished by refreshing the point three times every 10 msec instead of once.

superimposed over the left or right dot until the end of the trial; or (3) there was no change in the fixation field (catch trial). The subject's task was to release the bar if a dot brightened (manual task) or to make a lateral saccadic eye movement in a prespecified direction if an asterisk appeared (saccadic task). Subjects made no response on catch trials. Eye movement sampling continued for 1 sec, after which the screen went blank.

In order to reject trials with obvious eye movement artifacts the experimenter monitored the subject's eye position and performance in another room. After the experimenter coded the trial, feedback was presented to the subject on the oscilloscope. This feedback could be reaction time (for the saccadic task), the work CORRECT (for the manual task), and/or a series of error messages. If the subject shifted his eye position by more than ½° in the 1-sec warning interval, the message EYE SHIFT ERROR was displayed.[5] In this case, no other feedback was provided. If the subject made a manual response on a catch or saccadic trial, the message HAND ERROR was displayed. Similarly, if the subject made an eye movement on a manual or catch trial, the message EYE ERROR was displayed. Finally, if the subject made a manual response before the warning interval had elapsed, the message TOO FAST was displayed; and if the subject did not make a response at all when one was required the message TOO SLOW was displayed.

In each session, each subject was tested in three types of blocks, which differed with respect to the frequency of occurrence of the three types of events (see Table 13.1). The saccadic block consisted entirely of saccadic (asterisk) and catch trials, whereas the manual block consisted entirely of manual (brightening) and catch trials. The dual-task blocked contained all three types of trial, but a majority of the trials required saccadic responses. In each session subjects were tested on one manual, two saccadic, and two dual-task blocks. Prior to each saccadic and dual block, subjects were told which peripheral dot was to be the target for their eye movement in that block. Note that half the saccadic responses were compatible with the location of the asterisk, that half were incompatible because the direction of movement was constant for an entire block, and asterisks appeared equally often at the two locations.

Results and Discussion

Response latencies for the various conditions are shown in Fig. 13.1. The eye movement latencies from the saccadic and dual-task blocks reveal a consistent compatibility effect. Interactions between location of stimulus and direc-

---

[5] In most of the following analyses reported, eye movement shifts greater than ¾° during the warning interval have been excluded from the analysis. The percentage of trials excluded for this reason over all subjects and conditions was 8% for Experiment 1 and 5% for Experiment 2. Analysis of the results with these trials included does not change any of the conclusions. Overt shifts in eye position do not seem to be contaminating the results.

TABLE 13.1
Composition of the Three Types of Blocks in Experiment 1 (The
number of trials is shown in parentheses)

Response	Stimulus	Location	Type of Block (%)		
			Manual (50)	Saccadic (50)	Dual (100)
Manual	Luminance	Left	40	—	10
	increment	Right	40	—	10
Saccadic	Asterisk	Left	—	40	30
		Right	—	40	30
None	Nothing (catch)	—	20	20	20

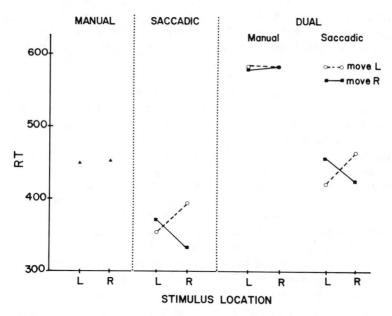

FIG. 13.1.   Reaction times from manual-, saccadic-, and dual-task blocks as a
function of stimulus location and direction of oculomotor readiness (circles-
= moving left; squares = moving right) (Experiment 1).

tion of eye movement are significant for the saccadic block ($F_{1,9}$ = 13.94,
$p < .01$) and for the dual block ($F_{1,9}$ = 22.97, $p < .001$). Collapsed across
direction of movement, subjects are 37 (dual) and 38 (saccadic) msec faster
when the target appears where they are ready to look, a result that is in
reasonable agreement with previous work. The oculomotor readiness hypothesis predicts a similar effect for the manual task in the dual block. It can

be seen by inspecting Fig. 13.1 that manual latencies in the dual-task block were totally unaffected by the relationship between the location of the luminance increment and direction of oculomotor readiness. Mean manual latencies were 581 msec when the dot brightening was the one to which the subject was ready to look and 579 msec when it was the other one. It was worth noting that there was also no difference in the proportion of detection failures (omissions) in these two conditions (.126 and .128, respectively).

These results demonstrate that shifts of visual attention do not necessarily occur when subjects get ready to move their eyes to a target location.

EXPERIMENT 2

The oculometer readiness hypothesis claims that the allocation of attention in visual space is accomplished by preparation of a saccadic eye movement to the to-be-attended locus. This claim was tested in the second experiment by inducing attentional shifts for detection of a luminance increment (manual response) and occasionally requiring the subjects to make saccadic eye movements (in response to an asterisk) to the attended or unattended location. The attentional shifts were induced by the use of priming cues that either informed the subject of the likely location of the luminance increment (arrows pointing left or right) or provided no information (a plus sign) (see p. 260 and following). If the attentional shift is accomplished by preparation of a saccade to the attended location, then saccades to the attended locus should be initiated faster than those to the unattended locus.

In order to test the oculomotor readiness proposal adequately, two eye movement conditions are necessary. To see why this is so, imagine that the subject is attending to the right location for the luminance increment and an asterisk appears at the left or right position. The oculomotor readiness proposal predicts that the subject will be faster to move his eyes *to* the asterisk (compatible condition) when it appears at the right location. This is so because the subject is already prepared to move in that direction. If, however, the perception of the asterisk is affected by the subject's attentional bias, one need not resort to oculomotor readiness to account for the effect. The problem with compatible eye movements is that the costs and benefits that presumably occur in the perception of the stimulus are confounded with those proposed to occur due to oculomotor readiness. By comparing compatible and incompatible eye movement conditions (subjects instructed to move toward or away from the asterisk), it is possible to separate these two effects. To illustrate, suppose that the subject is attending the right target and an asterisk is presented in the *incompatible* condition. If the asterisk appears at the right location, the subject may detect it more rapidly because of his attentional set, but he will be required to move against the hypothesized prepared movement. Conversely, if the asterisk appears at the left location, detection may be delayed, but the eye movement should benefit from advance preparation. Thus, if the oculomotor readiness hypothesis is correct, prime condition (neutral, valid, or invalid) should interact with compatibility of eye movements; the exact form of this interaction cannot be predicted, because the sensory and motor costs cannot be independently assessed. Nevertheless, the expected pattern of results would be costs and benefits (see p. 260 for an explanation) for compatible eye movements and a reduction or reversal to the effect with incompatible movements. Alternatively, if the eye movement system does not mediate movements of the mind's eye, then compatibility and prime condition should produce additive effects.

METHOD

Because, in general, the method for Experiment 2 is similar to that of Experiment 1, only the differences will be noted here. Eight students were randomly assigned to two groups (compatible and incompatible) and were tested in seven sessions. One group of subjects was instructed to move toward the asterisk when it appeared (compatible), and the other group was instructed to move away from the asterisk to the other target location (incompatible). Both groups made the simple manual response (releasing the bar) when a target dot brightened.

There were three types of blocks that differed with respect to the frequency of occurrence of the various events (see Table 13.2). The manual-task block consisted entirely of manual and catch trials. The saccadic-task block consisted entirely of saccadic and catch trials, and the dual-task block contained all three types of trial but the majority of trials required manual responses. In the

TABLE 13.2
Composition of the Three Types of Blocks in Experiment 2 (The number of trials is shown in parentheses.)

			Type of Block (%)					
			Manual			Saccadic	Dual		
			+ (24)	← (24)	→ (24)	+ (55)	+ (44)	← (44)	→ (44)
Manual	Luminance	Left	42	67	17	—	36	64	9
	Increment	Right	42	17	67	—	36	9	64
Saccadic	Asterisk	Left	—	—	—	45	9	9	9
		Right	—	—	—	45	9	9	9
None	Nothing (catch)	—	16	16	16	10	9	9	9

manual- and dual-task blocks three types of warning cues (primes) were used to induce attentional allocation. A plus sign was the neutral cue, providing the subject with no information on the likely location of the luminance increment. The other warning cues, arrows pointing either to the left or right, signaled the probable location of the luminance increment. The prime condition is neutral when the prime is a plus sign, valid when the location of either stimulus matches the prime, and invalid when it mismatches. Note that the saccadic stimuli (asterisks) were always equally likely to appear at either location, and therefore subjects should have no reason to prepare specific eye movements, except if such preparation is required to mediate attentional shifts. Reaction-time feedback was provided for the manual task, and the messages CORRECT and INCORRECT were appropriately displayed for the saccadic task.

On Day 1, subjects were tested only on the manual-task blocks, to familiarize them with the procedure in general and to give them practice using the warning cues. On Days 2–7, subjects were tested on each of the three blocks in the following order: manual, saccadic, dual.

RESULTS AND DISCUSSION

Response latencies for the various conditions are shown in Fig. 13.2. Before one can assess the oculomotor readiness hypothesis, it is necessary to demonstrate that an attentional set is, in fact, produced by the priming stimuli. An analysis of variance performed on the reaction-time data from the manual-task blocks revealed a highly significant effect of prime condition ($F_{2,12}$ = 78.90, $p < .001$) and a significant interaction between prime condition and stimulus location ($F_{2,12}$ = 10.22, $p < .01$). There was a tendency for the incompatible group to show a smaller effect of prime condition, but this interaction was only marginally significant ($F_{2,12}$ = 3.53, $p < .10$). Nevertheless, the cost-benefit effect (invalid–valid) was significant for each group, and its average magnitude was 41 msec. An analysis of the cost–benefit effect for the eight manual-task blocks (two on Day 1, one on each other day) revealed no change in the size of the effect over sessions ($F_{7,42}$ = .49). Omissions in the manual task were infrequent, and an analysis of variance revealed no significant or marginal effects. The proportion of omissions for the valid, neutral, and invalid conditions were .011, .022, and .030, respectively. Thus, in the manual-task blocks, subjects were using the prime stimuli to allocate attention for detection of the luminance increment.

It is still possible that attentional shifts are not made in the dual-task blocks because the combination of the two tasks is too difficult. An analysis of variance performed on the manual-task data from these blocks revealed a significant effect of prime condition ($F_{2,12}$ = 13.86, $p < .001$), a significant interaction between prime condition and location of stimulus ($F_{2,12}$ = 7.30,

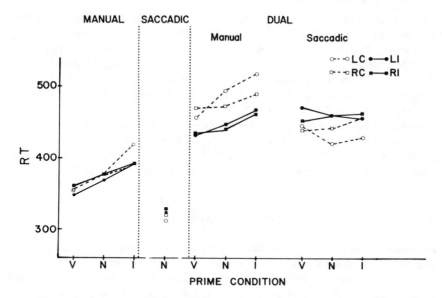

FIG. 13.2. Reaction times from manual-, saccadic-, and dual-task blocks as a function of prime condition (V = valid; N = neutral; I = invalid), group (open symbols = compatible; closed symbols = incompatible), and location of stimulus (circles = left; squares = right) (Experiment 2).

$p < .01$), and a significant three-way interaction between prime condition, location, and group (compatibility) ($F_{2,12} = 7.98$, $p < .01$). Once again the cost–benefit effect was significant for each group, and its average magnitude was 32 msec. An analysis of variance of the omissions revealed no significant effects. The proportion of omissions for valid, neutral, and invalid conditions were .044, .056, and .042, respectively.

Despite the significant effect of prime on performance of the manual task in the dual-task blocks, inspection of the individual data revealed one subject in the incompatible group whose valid and invalid manual response latencies were identical. Because evaluation of the oculomotor readiness hypothesis in the dual-task blocks necessitates an attentional shift for the manual-task stimuli, the eye movement data from this subject were not included in the following analysis. Furthermore, all the data shown in Fig. 13.2 excludes this subject, so that comparisons across conditions involve the same subjects.[6] An analysis of variance performed on the saccadic response times from the dual-task blocks revealed no significant effects or interactions. Most impor-

---

[6]All ANOVAS in this experiment have been performed on the original eight subjects and on the seven who showed a cost–benefit effect in the dual-task blocks. Both sets of analyses lead to the same conclusions.

tantly, there was no effect of prime ($F_{2,10}$ = .48, ns) and no prime by group (compatibility) interaction ($F_{2,10}$ = .42, ns).[7] As pointed out previously, any interaction between prime condition and compatibility would support the idea that the eye movement system plays some role in producing attentional shifts. Inspection of the data in Fig. 13.2 reveals almost perfect additivity between prime and compatibility, suggesting that oculomotor motor readiness does not accompany shifts of visual attention.

It should be noted that the expected costs and benefits were not obtained with compatible eye movements. Two possible explanations for this finding are treated in the following general discussion (see also Footnote 9), because there is no definitive evidence for either one in the present data.[8]

GENERAL DISCUSSION

An oculomotor readiness mechanism for cognitive control of visual attention was proposed and shown to be consistent with several findings in the literature. Nevertheless, as outlined here, this proposal makes two straightforward predictions both of which were clearly disconfirmed.[9] First, readiness to move one's eye does not seem to induce an attentional shift toward the targeted location. Second, attentional shifts to a location in space are not accompanied by oculomotor readiness.

The independence between the eye movement system and detection performance with manual responses observed in both experiments confirms Posner's view (Posner, 1978; Posner & Davidson, 1976) that the allocation of attention in space is not "parasitic" upon the saccadic eye movement system. The data presented here suggest that central adjustments other than oculomotor readiness must be assumed to explain how subjects allocate attention in vision.

---

[7]With so few subjects per group, one should be cautious in interpreting nonsignificant interactions involving groups. Nevertheless, because the sample data do not reveal even a hint of the interaction predicted by the oculomotor readiness proposal, it seems unlikely that the lack of significance is due to insufficient power.

[8]Because type of stimulus (brightening versus asterisk) is confounded with type of response (manual versus saccadic), it might be suggested that the failure to obtain an effect of prime upon eye movement latency is due to the stimulus differences. That the failure is not due to the stimuli used to elicit eye movements (asterisks) was demonstrated in a pilot experiment in which a signficant effect of prime (36 msec) was obtained with manual responses to the detection of asterisks [$F_{(1,12)}$ = 9.22, $p < .01$].

[9]It might be claimed that the dual-task blocks in both experiments were too difficult for the subjects and that, therefore, performance on the secondary tasks (those which were low in probability) could not provide an adequate assessment of the prediction of the oculomotor readiness proposal. Because improbable secondary tasks have provided sensitive measures of the attentional allocation in many complex task situations (see Kerr, 1973, for a review), we feel our data strongly challenge the oculomotor readiness proposal.

It should be pointed out that I am not claiming that eye movements are not related to attention. There is no question that shifts of visual attention are often, if not usually, accomplished through shifts in eye position. This is necessary because many activities require the sensitive fovea and its associated neural machinery. The claim is that when shifts of attention are accomplished without eye movements, readiness to move the eyes plays no role in these shifts.

This distinction may help to explain why the present data seem to conflict with the findings described earlier in support of the oculomotor readiness hypothesis. In Jonides' (1976) study, for example, readiness to move the eyes was induced by stimulus onset rather than generated cognitively in advance of the stimulus. As mentioned earlier (p. 263), the onset of a stimulus may attract both the eye movement system and attentional mechanisms without any causal relationship between the two systems being implicated. In the Bryden (1961), Crovitz and Daves (1962), and Rayner et al. (1978, Experiment 3) studies, eye movements (whether or not they are planned in advance) were actually executed (see also Footnote 2). It is possible that the actual execution of an eye movement is preceded by an attentional shift (see Nissen, Posner, & Snyder, 1978), even if a readiness to move in the absence of execution is not (Experiment 1). In the studies just mentioned, this shift might operate on the iconic representation of the stimulus after it is turned off. Thus, the linkage between the eye movement system and attention may be a reflexive one, not under cognitive control. Looking necessitates an attentional shift, whereas cognitive preparation to look does not.

Although the disconfirmation of the oculomotor readiness hypothesis seems to be clear-cut, one finding of Experiment 2 is problematic. Costs and benefits for compatible eye movements were expected but not obtained. It was expected that a directional prime would induce subjects to attend to the primed *location* and that any stimulus appearing there would benefit from this bias, whereas any stimulus appearing at the nonattended locus would be delayed. In fact, eye movements in both the compatible and incompatible conditions were insensitive to the locus of attention. There are at least two explanations for this unexpected finding.

One explanation rests upon the distinction between two visual systems: one mediating conscious processing of shape and form, the other mediating localization (Schneider, 1969; Trevarthen, 1968). Weiskrantz (1977) has reviewed experimental work with animals and human clinical evidence supporting this distinction. For example, patients with a cortical scotoma may be unaware of stimuli presented to the affected area of the visual field. Nevertheless, they can localize these stimuli with hand or eye movements at better than chance accuracy. In terms of the present paradigm, the visual pathways leading to saccadic eye movements and other localization responses are separable from those mediating conscious detection. Although early visual processing may be common to both systems, it is possible that attention

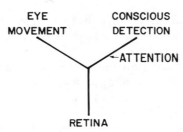

FIG. 13.3.   Schematic view of two visual systems, one mediating conscious processing of shape, form, etc., and the other mediating eye movements and localization in space. Internal attentional mechanisms may operate only upon the former system.

operates upon the conscious detection pathways after separation of the two systems (see Fig. 13.3).

The present experiments have presupposed that the cognitive allocation of attention in vision is to a location in the visual field, and Posner (1978; Posner et al., 1978) has implicitly made this assumption as well. A second explanation of the failure to obtain costs and benefits for eye movement stimuli appearing at the attended and unattended loci is based upon rejection of this assumption. The subject's attention may be allocated not to a position in visual space but to the set of known properties of the expected (primed) stimulus. Brightening of one of the peripheral dots should be expected following a priming stimulus (because its probability is .64). Asterisks are equally likely to appear at either location; therefore, the subject may be equally prepared (or because of their low probability, unprepared) for the two possible eye movement stimuli. This view would be consistent with an explanation of costs and benefits in terms of the subject's use of conditional probabilities to optimally allocate his processing resources (Shaw & Shaw, 1977).

Further experimentation is necessary before we shall be able to choose between these explanations for the failure of the eye movement system to be sensitive to shifts of visual attention.

ACKNOWLEDGMENTS

This research was supported by the National Research Council of Canada. I would like to thank John Barresi for commenting upon earlier versions of this manuscript, John Calcott for collecting pilot data as part of his honors thesis, and Ed Hansen for invaluable assistance in preparation of the final version.

REFERENCES

Bryden, M. P. The role of post-exposural eye movements in tachistoscopic perception. *Canadian Journal of Psychology,* 1961, *15,* 220–225.

Bushnell, M. C., Robinson, D. L., & Goldberg, M. E. Dissociation of movement and attention: Neuronal correlates in posterior parietal cortex. *Neurosciences Abstracts,* 1978, *4,* 621.

Crovitz, H. F., & Daves, W. Tendencies to eye movement and perceptual accuracy. *Journal of Experimental Psychology,* 1962, *63,* 495–498.

Eason, R., Harter, M., & White, C. Effects of attention and arousal on visually evoked cortical potentials and reaction time in man. *Physiology and Behavior,* 1969, *4,* 283–289.

Engel, F. L. Visual conspicuity, directed attention and retinal locus. *Vision Research,* 1971, *11,* 563–575.

Eriksen, C. W., & Hoffman, J. E. The extent of processing of noise elements during selective encoding from visual displays. *Perception & Psychophysics,* 1973, *14,* 155–160.

Helmholtz, H. von. *Hondbuch der Physiologischen optik.* English translation, Southall J. P. C., *3,* 1925.

Jonides, J. *Voluntary vs reflexive control of the mind's eye movement.* Presented at Psychonomic Society, St. Louis, November 1976.

Kaufman, L., & Richards, W. Spontaneous fixation tendencies for visual forms. *Perception & Psychophysics,* 1969, *5,* 85–88.

Kerr, B. Processing demands during mental operations. *Memory & Cognition,* 1973, *1,* 401–412.

Klein, R. M. Attention and visual dominance: A chronometric analysis. *Journal of Experimental Psychology: Human Perception and Performance,* 1977, *3,* 365–378.

Klein, R. M. Chronometric analysis of saccadic eye movements: Reflexive and cognitive control. In D. Landers and R. Christina (Eds.), *Psychology of Motor Behavior and Sport, 1977.* Champaign, Ill.: Human Kinetics Pub., 1978.

Mohler, C. W., & Wurtz, R. H. Organization of monkey superior colliculus: Intermediate layer cells discharging before eye movements. *Journal of Neurophysiology,* 1976, *39,* 722–742.

Neely, J. H. Semantic priming and retrieval from lexical memory: Roles of inhibitionless spreading activation and limited-capacity attention. *Journal of Experimental Psychology: General,* 1977, *106,* 226–254.

Nissen, M. J., Posner, M. I., & Snyder, C. R. *Relationship between attention shifts and saccadic eye movements.* Paper presented at Psychonomics Society, San Antonio, Texas, November 1978.

Posner, M. I. Chronometric explorations of mind. Hillsdale, N.J.: Lawrence Erlbaum Associates, 1978.

Posner, M. I., & Davidson, B. J. *Automatic and attended components of orienting.* Paper presented at the International Congress of Physical Activity Sciences, Quebec City, July 1976.

Posner, M. I., Nissen, M. J., & Ogden, W. *Attending to a position in space.* Paper presented at Psychonomics Society, Denver, November 1975.

Posner, M. I., Nissen, M. J., & Ogden, W. C. Attended and unattended processing modes: The role of set for spatial location. In H. L. Pick & I. J. Saltzman (Eds.), *Modes of perceiving and processing information.* Hillsdale, N.J.: Lawrence Erlbaum Associates, 1978.

Posner, M. I., & Snyder, C. R. R. Attention and cognitive control. In R. L. Solso (Ed.), *Information processing and cognition: The Loyola Symposium.* Hillsdale, N.J.: Lawrence Erlbaum Associates, 1975.

Posner, M. I., Snyder, C. R., & Davidson, B. J. *Attention and the detection of signals.* Paper presented at Psychonomics Society, Washington, D.C., October 1977.

Rayner, K., McConkie, G. W., & Ehrlich, S. Eye movements and integrating information across fixations. *Journal of Experimental Psychology: Human Perception and Performance,* 1978, *4,* 529–544.

Remington, R., Shulman, G., & McLean, J. *Moving attention through space: Evidence for the continuous nature of attentional movement.* Paper presented at Western Psychological Association, 1978.

Schiller, P. H., & Koerner, E. Discharge characteristics of single units in superior colliculus of the alert rhesus monkey. *Journal of Neurophysiology,* 1971, *34,* 920–936.

Schiller, P. H., & Stryker, M. Single unit recording and stimulation in superior colliculus of alert rhesus monkey. *Journal of Neurophysiology,* 1972, *35,* 915–924.

Schneider, G. E. Two visual systems. *Science,* 1969, *163,* 895-902.

Shaw, M. L., & Shaw, P. Optimal allocation of cognitive resources to spatial location. *Journal of Experimental Psychology: Human Perception and Performance,* 1977, *3,* 201-211.

Sperling, G., & Melchner, M. J. Visual search, visual attention and the attention operating characteristic. In J. Requin (Ed.), *Attention and performance VII.* Hillsdale, N.J.: Lawrence Erlbaum Associates, 1978.

Trevarthen, C. B. Two mechanisms of vision in primates. *Psychologische Forshung,* 1968, *31,* 299-337.

Van Voorhis, S., & Hillyard, S. A. Visual evoked potentials and selective attention to points in space. *Perception & Psychophysics,* 1977, *22,* 54-62.

Weiskrantz, L. Trying to bridge some neurophysiological gaps between monkey and man. *British Journal Psychology,* 1977, *68,* 431-445.

Wundt, W. *Introduction to psychology.* (R. Pinter, trans.). London: George Allen, 1912.

Wurtz, R. H., & Mohler, C. W. Selection of visual targets for the initiation of saccadic eye movements. *Brain Research,* 1974, *71,* 209-214.

14 Identifying Attentional and Decision-Making Components in Information Processing

Marilyn L. Shaw
Douglass College
Rutgers—The State University
New Brunswick, New Jersey
United States

ABSTRACT

The present chapter offers a systematic method for the analysis of selective information processing within the framework of the independent-decisions model. First, simple, parameter-free consequences derived from the model provide a way of using detection data to distinguish among three different attentional strategies. Second, it is shown how localization data can be used to answer the question: Does attention affect the quality or clearness of the internal stimulus representation?

INTRODUCTION

Many theories of information processing postulate two internal stages. First the stimulus (which may be visual or auditory) is transformed into some internal representation (iconic or echoic storage). Second, a decision is made regarding which response to make. From the viewpoint of such theories an important issue is whether the quality or clearness of any one part of the representation depends, in part, on the amount of attention allotted to it.

One of the most popular variables in studies of visual attention is the number of signal locations (set size). Interest in this variable arises from the assumption that increasing the number of signal locations means less attention can be paid to each. In fact, error rate and response time typically do increase with increases in the number of signal locations. This set–size effect cannot, however, be attributed simply to attentional factors. Increasing the number of signal locations also increases the complexity of the decision-making process. Thus, attentional determinants of the stimulus representation are confounded with the characteristics of the decision-making process. In fact, an analysis of the statistical considerations involved in decision making may provide a complete account of the effect of number of signal locations on performance; it may not be necessary to postulate an effect of attention on the quality of the stimulus representation. This point has been made by a number of authors, including Eriksen and Spencer (1969), Gardner (1973), Kinchla (1969b), and Shiffrin and Gardner (1972).

The present chapter is concerned with the separation of attentional factors from decision-making processes. The analysis will focus on a simple experimental paradigm: a trial-by-trial detection task, in which the subject monitors two or more locations for the presence of a target stimulus and makes a binary response on each trial. In particular, first I examine the situation in which the subject's response choices are *yes,* a target occurred, or *no,* a target did not occur.

The problem of separating attentional and decision-making processes is complicated by the fact that the relevant decision-making considerations depend on which response-selection rule is assumed (Shaw, 1979). The present discussion operates within the framework of an *independent-decisions* model. This type of model has a long history in psychology (e.g., Gardner, 1973; Graham, in press; Green & Swets, 1966; Starr, Metz, Lusted, & Goodenough, 1975).

The Independent-Decisions Model.   In the independent-decisions model described by Green and Swets (1966), the subject makes a decision on the basis of statistically independent observations or sources of information (e.g., several signal locations or several observations of the same location). For each observation a separate, binary decision (positive or negative) is made. The response is based on all the observations; it is *yes* if any one of the separate decisions is positive and *no* if all are negative. Thus, the overall probability of a *yes* response is

$$P = 1 - \prod_{k=1}^{n} (1 - P_k), \tag{1}$$

where P_k is the probability of a positive decision on the kth observation.

EXPERIMENTAL PARADIGM

We shall consider the application of the independent-decisions model to a hypothetical visual-detection experiment. In this paradigm, the stimulus consists of two or more signals, each of which may appear in two or more signal locations. One or more of the possible signals are designated as targets. This subset is termed the *target* set; its complement is the *distractor* set. The subject's response options consist of a simple binary choice. The first part of this discussion will concentrate on the yes–no case, in which the subject judges whether or not a target was present on a given trial. Later, a second response option will also be considered: which of several possible target locations contained a target.

Consider an experiment in which there are two signal locations, denoted L_a and L_b. There is one item in the target set; there may be one or several items in the distractor set. Because two types of signal (target or distractor) may occur in each location, for every trial there are four possible stimulus patterns. These will be denoted by S_{ij}. The first subscript, i, indicates the signal in location L_a, $i = 1$ indicating a target and $i = 0$, a distractor. Similarly, the second subscript, j, indicates the signal in location L_b. Thus, for example, S_{10} denotes a target in position L_a and a distractor in position L_b. Notice that it is possible for a target to appear in both locations at once (S_{11}).

The Dependent Measure. The basic dependent variable is the conditional response probability P_{ij}, which is defined here as the probability of a *no* response given stimulus pattern S_{ij}. Thus, P_{10} refers to the probability of a *no* response when there is a target in location L_a and a distractor in L_b. The probability of a *no* response is used—rather than its complement, the probability of a *yes* response—because the expression of predictions is thereby greatly simplified.

The probability P_{ij} should be understood to be conditional, not only upon a given stimulus pattern but also upon a given set of attentional instructions, a priori stimulus probabilities, and criterial instructions.

Attentional instructions are of two kinds, specifying undivided or divided attention. In the undivided condition, subjects may be instructed to respond *yes* only when a target is detected in location L_a or, alternatively, to respond only to a target in L_b. The divided attention condition directs the subject to respond *yes* when a target is detected in either L_a or L_b, or in both. The subjects may be directed to divide their attention equally or unequally between the two locations. The division of attention can also be influenced by the a priori stimulus–probability distribution.

The a priori stimulus-probability distribution may or may not be symmetrical. When it is symmetrical, targets appear at L_a or L_b with equal likelihood, and it is expected that subjects will pay equal attention to the two locations unless otherwise directed. When it is not symmetrical, subjects will generally attend more to the location with the higher target probability. The probability that a given stimulus pattern will occur is determined by the separate target probabilities at the two locations: For example, the probability of S_{10} is the product of the probability of a target at L_a and the probability of a distractor at L_b.

Clearly, the target probabilities will influence the subjects' response tendencies, as well as their division of attention. For example, as the probability of a target decreases, it is expected that the subjects will become more inclined to say *no*—that is, more conservative. Such response tendencies are also directly influenced by the criterial instructions.

Criterial instructions involve telling the subject to (1) "respond *yes* even when you are only slightly sure you saw the target"; or (2) "respond *yes* only when you are very sure you saw the target." These are termed, respectively, *liberal instructions* and *conservative instructions*.

THE FORMAL MODEL

It is assumed that each presentation of a stimulus pattern evokes some internal or sensory response within the subject. This internal state will be specified by two random variables, one for each target location. Their means and variances depend on the signal event in that location: For each variable there is one set of parameters corresponding to a target, another set for a distractor. The four probability distributions are assumed to have finite means and variances. Otherwise, no assumptions are made about these distributions—they may be Gaussian or non-Gaussian. The random variables are denoted by the terms X_{ai} and X_{bj}, with the first subscript indicating the location (L_a or L_b) and the second subscript, the objective signal event in that location (1 = a target, 0 = a distractor).

The subject is seen as making two independent decisions based on the values of the random variables X_{ai} and X_{bj} and the values of two corresponding decision criteria β_a and β_b. Specifically, the decision regarding location L_a will be positive if $X_{ai} \geq \beta_a$ and negative if $X_{ai} < \beta_a$. Similarly the decision regarding location L_b will be positive if $X_{bj} \geq \beta_b$ and negative if $X_{bj} < \beta_b$. The subject is represented as making an overt *yes* response if the decision about either location is positive and a *no* response otherwise.

If we wish to separate decision-making and attentional effects on performance, it is necessary to specify more precisely what is meant by attention. The issue is not whether there *is* such a thing as attention—obviously there is—but whether it influences the quality and clearness of the stimulus representation. Introspection suggests that the less attention we pay to a part of the visual or auditory world, the less sensitive we are to that part. This notion can be represented within the framework of the independent-decisions model by the assumption that the mean and/or variance of the internal random variables X_{ai} and X_{bj} are, in part, functions of how much attention is paid to the stimulus components they represent. For example, the variances ("noise levels") of X_{ai} and X_{bj} may be assumed to increase monotonically with decreases in the amount of attention paid: the less attention, the more noise.

Alternatively, attention may not affect the clarity of the stimulus representation but only the parameters of the decision process, such as the decision criteria. Then attentional instructions will have no effect on the parameters of the internal random variables.

In order to decide between these two possibilities it will be useful first to distinguish among several alternative versions of the independent-decisions model. This will be done by generating parameter-free predictions from the different models—predictions that do not require estimation of the models' parameters. Because their accuracy does not rest on the accuracy of estimated model parameters, these predictions hold whether or not attention influences the means or variances of the internal random variables.

Two Kinds of Attention Allocation

This section examines several ways in which attention may influence the decision-making process. Two major variations of the independent-decisions model will be considered.

The Sharing Model.   The first will be termed the *sharing model.* It can be interpreted in one of two ways: Attention may be given to both locations simultaneously, or attention may be switched rapidly back and forth between the two locations within a single trial. For the present purposes, these two alternatives are considered to be equivalent.

A principle feature of this model is that the allocation of attention does not change from trial to trial. Thus, the conditional probability of a *no* response given stimulus S_{ij}, written P_{ij}, remains constant—it is simply the product of the probabilities that each of the two random variables does not exceed its corresponding criterion:

$$P_{ij} = P(X_{ai} < \beta_a)P(X_{bj} < \beta_b). \tag{2}$$

Bear in mind that the equations in this section are neutral regarding the issue of whether or not attention affects the parameters of the random variables X_{ai} and X_{bj}. Attention may affect only the decision criteria β_a and β_b or only the parameters of the random variables or it may affect both.

The Mixture Model.   The second kind of attention-allocation model is termed the *mixture model,* because processing is characterized as a mixture of two discrete allocation rules. (This has been called an "all or none" process by Kinchla, 1969a, and "attention switching" by Sperling & Melchner, 1978.) On each trial the observer allocates attention primarily to one location or primarily to the other, in a probabilistic fashion. Thus, on a given trial the observer is in one or the other of two different states, which differ in that each has its own set of criteria. (Again, the parameters of the random variables X_{ai} and X_{bj} may be the same or different in the two states.) Overall performance will be a weighted mixture of what would occur if each of the attentional states were used exclusively.

Two types of mixture model will be considered. In the first, information on a given trial is obtained either from one location or from the other. This will be called the *type 1 mixture model,* because information comes from only *one* location. The *type 2 mixture model,* on the other hand, allows for some impression from the unattended location: Information is obtained from *two* locations (as it is with the sharing model).

Let the probability that attention is directed primarily to L_a be α and the probability that attention is directed primarily to L_b be $1 - \alpha$. Then for the type 1 mixture model, the conditional probability of a *no* response is simply

$$P_{ij} = \alpha P(X_{ai} < \beta_a) + (1 - \alpha)P(X_{bj} < \beta_b). \tag{3}$$

With this model, a *no* response is as likely to occur when there is a target in both locations as when there is a target only in the attended location.

For the type 2 mixture model, the conditional probability of a *no* response becomes

$$P_{ij} = \alpha P(X_{ai} < \beta_a)P(X_{bj} < \beta'_b) + (1 - \alpha)P(X_{ai} < \beta'_a)P(X_{bj} < \beta_b), \tag{4}$$

where β_k is the criterion when attention is directed primarily to location L_k and β'_k is the criterion when attention is *not* directed primarily to L_k. The attentional state in which criteria β_a and β'_b are used occurs with probability α, and the state in which β'_a and β_b are used occurs with probability $1 - \alpha$.

There are several different ways to characterize the difference between the type 1 and type 2 mixture models. The failure to make use of information from the unattended location, in the type 1 model, may be attributed to one of the following causes:

1. The parameters of the internal random variable corresponding to the unattended location may be such that the information coming from that location is practically worthless. If the signal and noise distributions overlap almost completely, then the criterion for that location (β') may be set so high that it is virtually never exceeded.

2. The parameters of the random variable may be unaffected by the allotment of attention, but the criterion for the unattended location may nevertheless be set high enough that it is unlikely ever to be exceeded.

3. The internal random variable and the criterion may both be unaffected by attention, but the information about whether the criterion has been exceeded may simply not be used in the later stages of the decision-making

process. The message may be lost or ignored and play no role in determining the overt response.

Predictions

Table 14.1 summarizes the three types of independent-decisions model, as well as the parameter-free predictions that will now be derived from these models.

Consider first the attention-sharing model. From Equation 2 it follows that

$$P_{01} = P(X_{a0} < \beta_a)P(X_{b1} < \beta_b)$$

and

$$P_{11} = P(X_{a1} < \beta_a)P(X_{b1} < \beta_b).$$

Then

$$\frac{P_{01}}{P_{11}} = \frac{P(X_{a0} < \beta_a)P(X_{b1} < \beta_b)}{P(X_{a1} < \beta_a)P(X_{b1} < \beta_b)} = \frac{P(X_{a0} < \beta_a)}{P(X_{a1} < \beta_a)}.$$

Similarly,

$$\frac{P_{00}}{P_{10}} = \frac{P(X_{a0} < \beta_a)P(X_{b0} < \beta_b)}{P(X_{a1} < \beta_a)P(X_{b0} < \beta_b)} = \frac{P(X_{a0} < \beta_a)}{P(X_{a1} < \beta_a)}.$$

Assuming that none of the above probabilities are equal to zero, the sharing model predicts equality between the two ratios:

$$\frac{P_{01}}{P_{11}} = \frac{P_{00}}{P_{10}}. \tag{5}$$

The mixture models, on the other hand, do not predict the equality of Equation 5. Whether or not the unattended location is assumed to have an effect, the mixture models predict response probabilities by a sum rather than a product, so the cancellations just shown do not occur.

Returning to the sharing model, the second parameter-free prediction concerns the two sums of conditional response probabilities, $P_{01} + P_{10}$ and $P_{00} + P_{11}$. From Equation 2 it follows that:

$$
\begin{aligned}
(P_{01} + P_{10}) - (P_{00} + P_{11}) = & \\
P(X_{a0} < \beta_a)P(X_{b1} < \beta_b) &+ P(X_{a1} < \beta_a)P(X_{b0} < \beta_b) \\
- P(X_{a0} < \beta_a)P(X_{b0} < \beta_b) &- P(X_{a1} < \beta_a)P(X_{b1} < \beta_b) \\
= [P(X_{a0} < \beta_a) - P(X_{a1} < \beta_a)] &\times [P(X_{b1} < \beta_b) - P(X_{b0} < \beta_b)].\tag{6}
\end{aligned}
$$

TABLE 14.1
Contrasting Predictions for Probability of a *No* Response, Assuming Independent Decisions

Model	Description	Equation	Predictions	
Sharing model	a single allocation rule	$P_{ij} = P(X_{ai} < \beta_a)P(X_{bj} < \beta_b)$	$\dfrac{P_{01}}{P_{11}} = \dfrac{P_{00}}{P_{10}}$	$P_{01} + P_{10} < P_{00} + P_{11}$
Mixture model, type 1	No information from unattended location	$P_{ij} = \alpha P(X_{ai} < \beta_a) + (1 - \alpha)P(X_{bj} < \beta_b)$	$\dfrac{P_{01}}{P_{11}} \neq \dfrac{P_{00}}{P_{10}}$	$P_{01} + P_{10} = P_{00} + P_{11}$
Mixture model, type 2	Some information from unattended location	$P_{ij} = \alpha P(X_{ai} < \beta_a)P(X_{bj} < \beta'_b)$ $+ (1 - \alpha)P(X_{ai} < \beta'_a)P(X_{bj} < \beta_b)$	$\dfrac{P_{01}}{P_{11}} \neq \dfrac{P_{00}}{P_{10}}$	$P_{01} + P_{10} < P_{00} + P_{11}$

Note: Two locations are assumed, with attention divided equally between them.

But the probability that a variable will fall below the criterion obviously must be greater in the case of a distractor than in the case of a target, so

$$P(X_{a0} < \beta_a) > P(X_{a1} < \beta_a) \tag{7}$$

and

$$P(X_{b0} < \beta_b) > P(X_{b1} < \beta_b). \tag{8}$$

Thus, of the two multiplicands in Equation 6, the first is positive and the second is negative, so the expression in Equation 6 is negative and

$$(P_{01} + P_{10}) - (P_{00} + P_{11}) < 0.$$

Therefore

$$P_{01} + P_{10} < P_{00} + P_{11}. \tag{9}$$

The same inequality shown in Equation 9 is predicted for the type 2 mixture model, which uses the assumption that there is some information gained from the unattended location. For this kind of model, the probability of a *no* response is given by Equation 4, from which it follows that:

$$(P_{01} + P_{10}) - (P_{00} + P_{11}) =$$
$$\alpha\{[P(X_{a1} < \beta_a) - P(X_{a0} < \beta_a)] \times [P(X_{b0} < \beta'_b) - P(X_{b1} < \beta'_b)]\}$$
$$+ (1 - \alpha)\{[P(X_{a1} < \beta'_a) - P(X_{a0} < \beta'_a)] \times [P(X_{b0} < \beta_b) -$$
$$P(X_{b1} < \beta_b)]\}.$$

From the inequalities in Equations 7 and 8, the first two multiplicands are, respectively, negative and positive; the second two are also negative and positive. Thus both of the summed terms are negative, and as in Equation 9

$$P_{01} + P_{10} < P_{00} + P_{11}. \tag{10}$$

The above inequality does not hold for the mixture model that uses the assumption of *no* information gained from the unattended location. On the contrary, the type 1 mixture model predicts that the two sums will be equal. From Equation 3 it follows that

$$P_{01} + P_{10} = \alpha P(X_{a0} < \beta_a) + (1 - \alpha)P(X_{b1} < \beta_b)$$
$$+ \alpha P(X_{a1} < \beta_a) + (1 - \alpha)P(X_{b0} < \beta_b) \tag{11}$$

and

$$P_{00} + P_{11} = \alpha P(X_{a0} < \beta_a) + (1 - \alpha)P(X_{b0} < \beta_b)$$
$$+ \alpha P(X_{a1} < \beta_a) + (1 - \alpha)P(X_{b1} < \beta_b) \tag{12}$$

Inspection of Equations 11 and 12 shows that both $P_{01} + P_{10}$ and $P_{00} + P_{11}$ are equal to:

$$\alpha[P(X_{a0} < \beta_a) + P(X_{a1} < \beta_a)] + (1 - \alpha)[P(X_{b0} < \beta_b) + P(X_{b1} < \beta_b)].$$

Therefore

$$P_{01} + P_{10} = P_{00} + P_{11}. \tag{13}$$

It is important to remember that the preceding parameter-free predictions depend on neither the parameters of the internal random variables nor the subjects' decision criteria. It should also be noted that these statistics distinguish among the models only when attention is divided. When attention is directed exclusively to one location, the models make the same predictions. For example, when attention is given solely to location L_a the prediction for P_{00} is the same as for P_{01}; namely,

$$P_{ij} = P(X_{a0} < \beta_a).$$

For both P_{10} and P_{11} the prediction is

$$P_{ij} = P(X_{a1} < \beta_a).$$

Thus

$$\frac{P_{00}}{P_{10}} = \frac{P_{01}}{P_{11}} \tag{14}$$

and

$$P_{01} + P_{10} = P_{00} + P_{11}. \tag{15}$$

These predictions for the case when attention is not divided provide an additional test of the models.

Quantitative Predictions.   Table 14.2 illustrates how these statistics allow one to distinguish between the models. Quantitative predictions are generated here for the sharing model and for the type 1 mixture model, in which no information is gained from the unattended location. Exact predictions are not possible for the type 2 mixture model, because inequalities are predicted both

TABLE 14.2

Quantitative Predictions for the Probability of a *No Response*

Model	Hypothetical Data					Predictions			
	Accuracy	P_{00}	P_{11}	P_{01}	P_{10}	P_{01}/P_{11}	P_{00}/P_{10}	$P_{01}+P_{10}$	$P_{00}+P_{11}$
Sharing model	High	.90	.20	.42	.42	2.12	2.12	.84	1.11
	Low	.90	.42	.61	.61	1.46	1.46	1.23	1.32
Mixture model, type 1	High	.90	.20	.55	.55	2.75	1.64	1.11	1.11
	Low	.90	.42	.66	.66	1.57	1.36	1.32	1.32

for the ratios P_{01}/P_{11} and P_{00}/P_{10} and for the sums $P_{01} + P_{10}$ and $P_{00} + P_{11}$. Thus if experimental results indicate that the ratios are not equal and also that $P_{01} + P_{10}$ is less then $P_{00} + P_{11}$, these data will lend support to the type 2 mixture model, in which some information is obtained from the unattended location.

The predictions shown in Table 14.2 are computed under two conditions: (1) high accuracy, where P_{00} = .90 and P_{11} = .20; and (2) low accuracy, where P_{00} = .90 and P_{11} = .42. Given the response probabilities for the two-target and two-distractor stimulus patterns, one can easily compute the response probabilities for the one-target patterns, P_{01} and P_{10}. (For these examples it will be assumed that the attentional instructions are for equal attention and that the a priori probability of S_{01} equals that of S_{10}, so we expect P_{01} to equal P_{10}.

In the case of the sharing model, from Equation 5 we know that

$$P_{01}P_{10} = P_{00}P_{11}. \tag{16}$$

Because P_{01} = P_{10}, both are equal to $\sqrt{P_{00}P_{11}}$, or .42 in the high-accuracy condition and .61 in the low-accuracy condition.

For the type 1 mixture model, from Equation 13 it follows that P_{01} and P_{10} are computed from $(P_{11} + P_{00})/2$. This equals .55 with high accuracy and .66 with low.

From the values for P_{00}, P_{11}, and P_{01} (or P_{10}), the other predictions in Table 14.2 are readily derived. Notice that the predicted ratios for P_{01}/P_{11} and P_{00}/P_{10} are equal in the case of the sharing model, whereas with the mixture model P_{01}/P_{11} is larger. This is true for both levels of accuracy; however, the effect is greater at the higher accuracy level. The models' predictions for the two sums, $P_{01} + P_{10}$ and $P_{00} + P_{11}$, also differ more at higher accuracies. These sums are equal in the case of the sharing model, whereas the mixture model predicts that $P_{00} + P_{11}$ will exceed $P_{01} + P_{10}$. Clearly, any experiment designed to test these models must involve sufficiently high levels of accuracy, or these statistics will not discriminate among them.

A final cautionary note concerns the matter of individual differences. It is quite possible for Subject A to behave according to the sharing model, Subject B according to the type 1 mixture model, and Subject C according to the type 2 mixture model. Averaging data would, of course, obscure this fact. Moreover, it is also possible that a given subject may operate in different ways at different times, depending on the type or complexity of the task.

The Set–Size Effect

At this point we return to the question of why the error rate goes up with set size, which in this context refers to the number of possible signal locations. When there are more locations to be monitored, less attention is presumably available for each location. Thus, if attention does affect the quality of the stimulus representation, four locations will appear less clear than two—or, in terms of the model, the parameters of the internal random variables will be influenced by the number of signal locations. This would result in a greater decline in accuracy, as set size increases, than would be expected from decisional factors alone.

Before attacking this problem directly, it was necessary to distinguish among the three models of attention allocation, which are variations of the independent-decisions model. This was important because the interpretation of the second stage of the analysis depends on the outcome of the preceding investigation.

Location Judgments. The paradigm of the hypothetical experiment will now be expanded. There will be two display conditions: one with two target locations and one with four. The target can appear in only one location on a given trial. The subject will now be asked not only to decide whether a target appeared but to give its location as well. The percentage of correct location judgments becomes the dependent measure of interest.

The independent-decisions model is extended to location judgments by the following postulate: that the signal location chosen is the one evoking the strongest impression of the presence of the target (the largest value of X_{ki}). Assume for a moment that increasing the number of attended locations from two to four does *not* change the parameters (mean and/or variance) of the internal random variable corresponding to a given display location. Given the probability distribution of such an internal random variable, it is possible to compute the expected change in the probability of a correct location judgment as the number of locations increases from two to four.

I have explored the expected change in probability correct under a number of different assumptions about the shape of the underlying probability distributions. The predictions for two of these assumed distributions, the Gaussian and the exponential, are shown in Fig. 14.1. In this figure the predicted probability of a correct location judgment in the four-location condition (P_4) is plotted against the probability of a correct two-location judgment (P_2). Each of the four solid lines in Fig. 14.1 was generated by a different set of assumptions. The curve labeled *Gaussian* is based on the assumptions of normally distributed random variables, equal variance for the target and distractor distributions, and no effect of set size on the parameters of these distributions. The *exponential* curve is based upon the same assumptions except for the postulated shape of the distributions.

As a predicted function moves to the right and downward in Fig. 14.1, increasingly greater drops in accuracy are predicted for the four-location task. The exponential model predicts the least decline in accuracy as the number of target locations goes from two to four; the Gaussian model predicts a slightly greater decline. For both of these models, there is no change

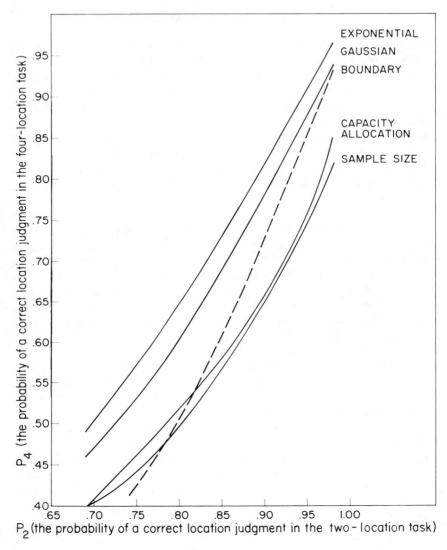

FIG. 14.1. Predictions of several models for correct location judgment in the four-location task (P_4) plotted against the probability of a correct location judgment in the two-location task (P_2).

in the parameters of the random variables when set size increases. Thus, a model based on either Gaussian or exponential that *does* call for a change in the parameters with set size would produce a greater drop in four-location accuracy than predicted by the Gaussian and exponential models shown in Fig. 14.1.

A set of points for the pairs of probabilities (P_2, P_4) can be generated empirically by varying, for example, display energy. Given such a set of data points, when is it possible to say that these points cannot be generated by a model that assumes no effect of set size on the parameters of the internal random variables; that is, when can we reject the null hypothesis of no effect of attention on the quality or clearness of the internal representation?

If the analysis of the two-location yes–no data indicates that the subject used either the sharing model or the type 2 mixture model, an answer is readily available. It consists of the boundary curve shown in Fig. 14.1. Any empirical function lying significantly below and to the right of that boundary must derive from a model in which set size *does* affect the parameters of the random variables.

The boundary function is based on the following arguments. The signal location chosen is assumed to be the one evoking the strongest impression of the target's presence, in other words, the largest value of X_{ki}. Thus, location k is chosen out of N locations if the value of X_{ki} is greater than the values of all the other $N - 1$ random variables. Suppose that each X_{k0} (distractor variable) is distributed as $F_d(x)$ with density function $f_d(x)$ and that X_{k1} (the target variable) is distributed as $F_t(x)$ with density function $f_t(x)$. Suppose also that as N (the number of random variables) increases, the functions F_d and F_t retain the same mean and variance. Then the probability P_N that the target random variable is larger than any of the $N - 1$ distractor variables is

$$P_N = \int_{-\infty}^{\infty} f_t(x) F_d^{N-1}(x)\, dx. \tag{17}$$

Using Holder's inequality (Royden, 1963) it is easily shown (see Appendix) that

$$\int_{-\infty}^{\infty} f_t(x) F_d^{N-1}(x)\, dx \geq \left[\int_{-\infty}^{\infty} f_t(x) F_d(x)\, dx \right]^{N-1}. \tag{18}$$

This inequality simply says that P_N is always larger than or equal to the result of raising P_2 (probability correct for two locations) to the power $N - 1$:

$$P_N \geq P_2^{N-1}. \tag{19}$$

Thus, P_2^{N-1} forms the lower boundary for P_N, given that the parameters of the random variables do not change. The boundary curve for P_4 shown in Fig. 14.1 is P_2^{4-1}, or P_2^3.

The two curves in Fig. 14.1 that lie mostly below and to the right of the boundary are based on the capacity-allocation model and the sample-size model. Both of these models use the assumption that attention *does* influence the parameters of the random variables. The capacity-allocation model

(Shaw, 1978; Shaw & Shaw, 1977) is discussed by Professor Kinchla in this volume, so it is not necessary to elucidate it here. Notice, however, that the curve for this model crosses the boundary curve where P_2 equals .82. What this means is that an experiment using the predictions shown in Fig. 14.1 should aim for a P_2 greater than .82. It would be best if the task were in the .85 to .95 range. This, of course, can be achieved through control of display energy.

The curve labeled *sample size* is based on a model that is similar to the sample-size model proposed by Luce and Green (Green & Luce, 1974; Luce, 1977). With this model each internal random variable X_{ki} is a sample mean based on N_k observations of that location, where the total number of observations over all locations remains constant. Thus, the variance of each X_{ki} depends directly upon N_k:

$$\sigma_k^2 = \frac{\sigma^2}{N_k} \tag{20}$$

where σ^2 is the variance of a single observation of one random variable.

For the reader's convenience, the numerical values used to construct Fig. 14.1 are given in Table 14.3.

TABLE 14.3
Probabilities of Correct Location Judgments for Two (P_2) and Four (P_4) Locations, as Predicted by Several Models

P_2	Exponential	Gaussian	Boundary (P_2^3)	Capacity Allocation	Sample Size
.69	.49	.46	.33	.40	.39
.71	.52	.49	.36	.43	.41
.74	.57	.52	.41	.45	.43
.76	.59	.55	.44	.48	.46
.78	.62	.58	.47	.50	.48
.80	.66	.61	.51	.52	.50
.82	.69	.64	.55	.55	.53
.84	.72	.67	.59	.58	.55
.85	.73	.70	.61	.59	.57
.87	.77	.73	.65	.62	.59
.88	.78	.75	.68	.63	.61
.90	.82	.78	.73	.66	.64
.91	.84	.80	.75	.68	.65
.92	.85	.82	.78	.70	.67
.93	.87	.84	.80	.72	.70
.94	.89	.86	.83	.74	.73
.95	.91	.88	.86	.76	.75
.96	.93	.90	.88	.78	.78
.97	.95	.92	.91	.81	.80
.98	.96	.95	.94	.85	.82

The Type 1 Mixture Model. It was pointed out previously that the arguments used to construct Fig. 14.1 hold only if information is gained from more than one location on a given trial. What if the analysis of attention-allocation strategy implicates the type 1 mixture model? In this case attention appears to have a dramatic effect, because the information from the un-attended location plays no role in the decision-making process.

Suppose that a subject using this strategy is given the task of choosing the target location. Because there is information from only the attended location, the subject must decide whether the information from that location is suffi-ciently favorable to suggest that a target was present. If it is, then that location is chosen; if it is not, another location is chosen at random. How will a subject fare with such a strategy?

There is an answer to this question (Shaw, in preparation) in the case of the capacity allocation model. Given a fixed amount of resources (processing capacity or attention) to be distributed among N locations, the strategy that maximizes the number of correct location judgments is as follows: Ignore one location and allocate the resource among $N - 1$ of the locations; should it appear that the target is not in one of the $N - 1$ locations, then guess the ignored location. For the capacity allocation model, it is not possible to find a strategy that will maximize both location and detection judgments. When there are only two locations, the mixture strategy can achieve a higher level of correct location judgments than the sharing strategy. Suppose that when four locations are searched only one location is attended, with failure to detect the target resulting in a guess among the three ignored locations. Then, overall percent correct location judgments will be lower than for the sharing strategy. Now suppose four locations are searched and attention is shared among three of the four locations with the ignored location being guessed if detection search fails. This strategy involves both the sharing and mixture strategies and will achieve a higher level of percent correct location judgments than a strategy in which attention is shared among all locations and response selec-tion is based on the maximum rule. Furthermore, the optimal strategy will give values of P_2 and P_4 that may fall above the boundary curve. These results would give the impression that set size does not influence the parameters of the internal random variables, despite the fact that performance is based upon a model that does involve an effect on the parameters. For this reason, it is extremely important to determine whether or not subjects share attention between locations. (A more detailed discussion of this topic is presented in Shaw, in preparation.)

To summarize, given evidence for the sharing model of decision making, location data lying below and to the right of the boundary curve of Fig. 14.1 provide evidence that attention does influence the quality of the internal representation. The converse, however, is not true. Empirical functions that lie above and to the left of the boundary curve do not prove that attention has no effect on the parameters of the random variables. With some models of attention allocation the underlying distribution of the random variables may be such that $P_N \geq P_2^{N-1}$. If this is the case, it will be necessary to determine the underlying distributions directly, in order to test whether set size influences the parameters of the internal random variables.

Finally, it might seem that a quick answer to the questions explored in this chapter could have been provided by the measure d' based on detection data. Although d' is a measure of "sensitivity" and would thus be affected by any change in the parameters of the random variables, an answer to the set–size question does not emerge from simply plotting an ROC curve for different set sizes. There are two reasons for this.

First, the usual d' is based on the assumption of normally distributed random variables with equal variances. Although this assumption is worthy of consideration, other assumptions are also possible and have been considered here.

Second, plotting an ROC for different set sizes requires that the criteria for the different locations be equal. If they are not equal, the resulting ROC curves cannot be expressed in a two-dimensional graph: The points lie on a surface. This makes it impossible to discriminate between the effects of criterial changes and an effect of set size on the parameters of the internal random variables.

The previous explanation applies only to the independent-decisions model, which was the assumption underlying this entire chapter. Under a different assumption—for example, the integration model (Green & Swets, 1966)—it is possible to make use of ROC curves.

Conclusions

The present chapter has illustrated how the independent-decisions model can be used to generate testable predictions regarding the effect of dividing attention on the quality of the stimulus representation. Two kinds of data are required for a complete analysis: detection and localization. Detection data are used to distinguish among three different strategies of attention allocation. Two of these strategies allow the subject to utilize information, within a given trial, from more than one location at once. Should the detection data favor one of these strategies, localization data can then be used to answer the question: Does attending to more locations at once decrease the quality (i.e., increase the noise level) of the internal representation?

ACKNOWLEDGMENTS

I would like to thank Arnold Glass, Tom Wallsten, Mark Altom, and an anonymous reviewer for their comments on an earlier draft of this paper. Special thanks are due Ron Kinchla and Judith R. Harris for their extensive editorial assistance. I would like to thank Duncan Luce for pointing out that Equation 18 is easily proved using Holder's inequality. To Roy C. Milton, I am indebted for preparing extensions of tables published in his book *Rank Order Probabilities: Two Sample Normal Shift Alternatives* (1970). These were used in making the predictions of the Gaussian and sample-size models.

REFERENCES

Eriksen, C. W., & Spencer, T. Rate of information processing in visual perception: Some results and methodological considerations. *Journal of Experimental Psychology Monograph*, 1969, *79*(2, Pt. 2).

Gardner, G. T. Evidence for independent parallel channels in tachistocopic perception. *Cognitive Psychology*, 1973, *4*, 130–155.

Graham, N. Spatial-frequency analysis in human vision: Detecting edges without edge detectors. In C. S. Harris (Ed.), *Visual coding and adaptability*. Hillsdale, N.J.: Lawrence Erlbaum Associates, in press.

Green, D. M., & Luce, R. D. Variability of magnitude estimates: A timing theory analysis. *Perception & Psychophysics*, 1974, *15*, 291–300.

Green, D. M., & Swets, J. A. *Signal Detection Theory and Psychophysics*. Wiley, New York: 1966.

Kinchla, R. A. *An Attention operating characteristic in vision*. Paper presented at the International Conference on Attention and Performance, Institute for Perception RVO-TNO, Solsterberg, Netherlands, 1969. (a)

Kinchla, R. A. Temporal and channel uncertainty in detection: A multiple observation analysis. *Perception & Psychophysics*, 1969, *5*, 129–136. (b)

Luce, R. D. Thurstone's discriminal processes fifty years later. *Psychometrika*, 1977, *42*, No. 4, 461–489.

Milton, R. C. *Rank Order Probabilities: Two Sample Normal Shift Alternatives*. New York: Wiley, 1970.

Royden, H. L. *Real Analysis*. New York: Macmillan, 1963.

Shaw, M. L. A capacity allocation model for reaction time. *Journal of Experimental Psychology: Human Perception and Performance*, 1978, *4*, 586–598.

Shaw, M. L. *Selective mechanisms in visual search*. Paper presented at the Joint US–USSR Seminar on Normative and Descriptive Models of Decision Making, Tbilisi, USSR, March 1979.

Shaw, M. L. On the difference between detecting and locating targets in visual search. *Psychological Review*, in press.

Shaw, M. L., & Shaw, P. Optimal allocation of cognitive resources to spatial locations. *Journal of Experimental Psychology: Human Perception and Performance*, 1977, *3*, No.2, 201–211.

Shiffin, R. M., & Gardner, G. T. Visual processing capacity and attentional control. *Journal of Experimental Psychology*, 1972, *93*, 72–83.

Sperling, G., & Melchner, M. J. The attention operation characteristic: Examples from visual search. *Science*, 1978, *202*, 315–318.

Starr, S. J., Metz, C. E., Lusted, L. B., & Goodenough, D. J. Visual detection and localization of radiographic images. *Radiology*, 1975, *116*, 533–538.

APPENDIX

Theorem. Let f_t and f_d be two probability density functions, then

$$\int_{-\infty}^{\infty} f_t \, F_d^{\,N} \, dx \geq \left[\int_{-\infty}^{\infty} f_t \, F_d \, dx \right]^N.$$

Holder's Inequality. Suppose $p, q > 0$, $p + q = pq$, and f and g are functions such that

$$\int |f|^p \, dx \quad \text{and} \quad \int |g|^q \, dx$$

exist. Then,

$$\left| \int fg \, dx \right| \leq \left(\int |f|^p \, dx \right)^{1/p} \left(\int |g|^q \, dx \right)^{1/q}.$$

Because f_t and f_d are densities, we can drop the absolute value signs. Let $q = N$, $p = N/(N - 1)$, $f = f^{N-1/N}$, and $g = f_t^{1/N} F_d$. Then,

$$\int f_t F_d \, dx = \int f_t^{N-1/N} f_t^{1/N} F_d \, dx$$

$$\leq \left[\int (f_t^{N-1/N})^{N/N-1} \, dx \right]^{N-1/N} \left[\int (f_t^{1/N} F_d)^N \, dx \right]^{1/N}$$

$$= 1 \times \left[\int f_t F_d^{\,N} \, dx \right]^{1/N}.$$

Therefore,

$$\left[\int f_t F_d \, dx \right]^N \leq \int f_t F_d^{\,N} \, dx.$$

15

Task Difficulty, Resources, and Dual-Task Performance

David Navon
University of Haifa

Daniel Gopher
Technion-Israel Institute of Technology
Haifa, Israel

ABSTRACT

The effect of task difficulty on dual-task performance is conceptualized within two alternative theoretical frameworks: One posits that performance depends on the use of resources from a common pool; the other views the processing system as comprised of a number of mechanisms, each having its own capacity that may be considered as a separate resource. It is shown that under the central capacity model difficulty should most often interact with resource investment in such a way that effects of resource investment on quality or speed of performance are more pronounced the easier the task is. The implication of this result to performance in dual-task situations is discussed. If multiple resources are assumed, then a difficulty manipulation may differentially affect the use of each of those resources. If in a dual-task situation a manipulation of the difficulty of one task affects the use of a mechanism that is not required by the other task, processing of the latter may remain intact in some circumstances. To obtain a complete picture of how difficulty affects dual-task performance, it is proposed to manipulate task priorities as well as difficulty parameters and to present their joint effect by families of *performance operating characteristics*. An application of this approach to the study of pursuit tracking is briefly described and interpreted in terms of the multiple resources approach.

It is often found that performance of a task is affected not only by its own difficulty but also by the existence or by the difficulty of another task with which it is time-shared. This has been taken to indicate that both tasks apply demands to the same capacity (or resources, effort, attention, etc. See Broadbent, 1971; Kahneman, 1973; Kerr, 1973; Moray, 1967; Norman & Bobrow, 1975). The notion of capacity is widely used, but there is little agreement about what it is or how to go about testing it. In particular, one would be at a loss to extract from the literature a clear prediction from capacity models about the effect of task difficulty on concurrent task performance or about the joint effect of difficulty levels of both tasks. A recent reminder of this fact is the exchange between Kantowitz & Knight (1976, 1978) and Lane (1977). In this chapter, we address these problems from a point of view that is based on some ideas borrowed from microeconomics, an approach that we describe and discuss in detail elsewhere (Navon & Gopher, 1979).

It seems that much of the confusion about predictions can be traced to obscurity of terminology. The term *task difficulty* is considered by different researchers to denote quite different things. It is not a priori clear that all manipulations that are regarded as difficulty manipulations would have similar effects on performance in a dual-task situation. We therefore start by proposing a conceptual framework. Within it we distinguish among various senses of task difficulty and then examine their effects on dual-task performance.

PERFORMANCE AND RESOURCES

Resources and Processing Output

Let us postulate that the human processing system possesses a limited amount of *resources*, such as processing facilities, that it uses to produce *processing output*, such as information transmission. That processing output is required for performance but should not be equated with it. To illustrate this distinction, the amount of feature extraction (processing output) that is done in the course of letter recognition is not the only determinant of recognition accuracy (performance); another obvious component is the number of features that *have* to be extracted (assuming no contextual cues). In general, most tasks can be regarded as assignments posed to the processing system: The objective of a task specifies some criterial amount of processing output that is to be attained by the operation of the relevant processing mechanisms. Quality of performance is typically defined in reference to that criterion. Let us stay now within the level of operation of the mechanisms and return later to the issue of how measures of performance depend on the relation between the actual and required outputs of the mechanisms.

The *mental input* the system invests to produce processing output is the duration of usage of its allocated resource units (e.g., seconds of occupying channels of a certain processing device). Processing output is positively related to the amount of mental input used to produce it (see, e.g., the output–input functions in Fig. 15.1A). Hence, the amount of *invested resources* (vis., mental input per unit time) determines *output rate* (viz., proces-

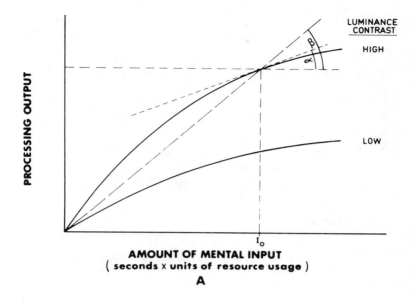

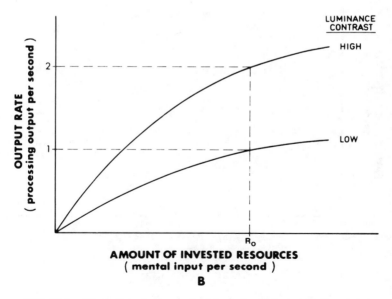

FIG. 15.1. Illustrations for two output–input functions (panel A) and their corresponding rate-resource functions (panel B), and for four accuracy-resource functions (panel C) and two latency-resource functions (panel D) derived from one of the rate-resource functions.

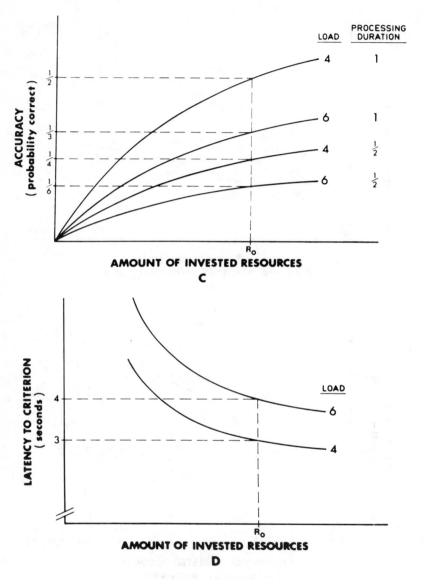

FIG. 15.1. (continued)

sing output per unit time). For example, how many locations of long-term memory are visited *in a second* of memory search depends on the amount of resources that are committed to that search during that second. Thus, output–input functions as in Fig. 15.1A can be translated to rate–resource functions as in Fig. 15.1B. This work-rate (or energy–power) distinction is called for, because it is the availability of processing facilities *per unit time* that is limited, whereas in many tasks the outcomes of processing can be aggregated *over* time (see Kahneman, 1973, p. 25).[1]

Senses of Difficulty

Output depends not only on how much is invested but also on what the investment can produce. The contribution of a unit of input to the total output (or of a unit of resources to output rate) may be termed *processing efficiency*.[2] Some factors that are regarded as difficulty variables, such as luminance-contrast or signal-to-noise ratio, may affect processing efficiency. The two curves in Fig. 15.1A B correspond to two different efficiencies due to variation of luminance contrast. This could arise, for example, if the rate of feature extraction was positively correlated with luminance contrast. In sum, an efficiency manipulation is one that affects the productivity of the basic mechanisms involved in generating the output needed to accomplish the task in question. However, one can conceive of other ways in which the difficulty of a task can be manipulated: The amount of required output may be increased and/or the time to attain it may be curtailed.

The criterial amount of output required to satisfy the objective of a task may be called task *load,* because it determines how much mental input should be invested to meet the criterion. Different variants of a task may differ with respect to the load they impose on the processing system to meet the same objective. For example, the size of the memory set in a search task affects the amount of processing required per decision; the redundancy of a stimulus ensemble affects the average number of features that are sufficient for identifying a single stimulus.

In many tasks the *processing duration* is limited, either because response rate is externally paced (e.g., tapping) or because stimuli are available for processing for a brief period (e.g., externally paced visual search). Variants of a task may differ in the period they allow for processing a stimulus or for preparing a response (e.g., externally paced visual search tasks with different stimulus onset asynchronies).

A special case is the class of continuous tasks such as tracking or externally paced reading. Those may be construed as a sequence of assignments each of which is to be met fast enough to keep up with the change of stimuli. Each of the assignments has a load and a processing duration; hence the requirement

---

[1]A similar distinction had independently been made by Shaw (1978). She refers by *capacity* to what we call *mental input* and by *capacity rate* to what we call *resources* and assumes that the latter is a fixed parameter. Our choice of terms was influenced by our commitment to the convention that whatever is limited is called capacity (or resources).

[2]If the output–input relation is not linear, then a distinction should be made between *marginal efficiency,* which is the output gain resulting from the last unit of input (e.g., α in Fig. 15.1A is the marginal efficiency at input I_0), and *average efficiency,* which is the average contribution of all units invested (e.g., β in Fig. 15.1A is the average efficiency at I_0).

such a task poses to the system is the ratio of average load to average processing duration, a ratio that may be termed *criterial rate*.

Thus, difficulty manipulations fall mainly in four classes according to what variable they affect: efficiency, load, processing duration, or criterial rate.

Measures of Performance

To see how difficulty manipulations of the various types affect performance, let us digress to a redefinition of performance measures in terms of resources. Performance is measured in terms of accuracy, latency, or rate.

Accuracy of performance must be directly related to the ratio

actual output/load

(i.e., to the ratio of actual to criterial output).[3] Accuracy measures are typically relevant in situations in which processing duration is limited. When that duration is too short to reach the criterion at the rate determined by invested resources, one of two things may happen, depending on the nature of the task: Either the assignment will be partly completed (e.g., inaccurate movement in tracking) or the insufficient output will lead to correct responses with a certain probability. It is easy to see that this ratio can also be expressed as

processing duration × (output rate/load)

(i.e., the proportion of criterial output produced in a unit time multiplied by the length of the processing period).[4]

In tasks in which the performer is free to continue processing until the criterial output is met, the relevant aspect of performance is the *latency to criterion,* which can be defined as

c + load/output rate

where c is some constant period representing the contribution of factors that are unrelated to processing done with the resources in question.

Finally, in tasks that may be conceptualized as a sequence of similar assignments, the attainment of which is paced by the subject (e.g., subject-paced typing), the convenient measure of performance is

output rate/load per assignment.

To distinguish this rate from output rate, let it be called *performance rate.*

---

[3] For continuous tasks, accuracy can be defined as a function of actual output rate/criterial rate.

[4] Of course, ratios that are greater than 1 are equivalent with regard to their effect on accuracy.

Types of Performance-Resource Functions

Now, how are the various measures of performance affected by the various manipulations of difficulty? We derive three types of performance-resource functions (Norman & Bobrow, 1975) from rate-resource functions (as in Fig. 15.1B).

The function relating accuracy to amount of invested resources can be derived from the underlying rate-resource function by dividing each rate by the load and multiplying it by processing duration. As an illustration, consider the four functions in Fig. 15.1C that depict the accuracy of four variants of a task whose processing efficiency is presented in Fig. 15.1B. For example, suppose the task is to identify one of a certain type of stimuli at a high luminance contrast. If the rate of feature extraction with R_0 resources is 2 units per second, then if 4 units are required for an absolutely certain identification, probability of correct responses with R_0 resources will be $\frac{1}{2}$ at a 1-sec exposure duration and a $\frac{1}{4}$ at $\frac{1}{2}$-sec duration.[5]

The function relating latency to amount of invested resources can be derived from the underlying rate-resource function if we know the values of c and task load. For example, the two functions in Fig. 15.1D describe the latency-resource relationships for two variants of the task in Fig. 15.1B given a high luminance contrast. When c is 1 sec and R_0 resources are invested, then if the load is 4 units, 3 sec will be required to reach the criterion; if the load is 6 units, 4 sec will be required. If the performer aims at a level of accuracy that is less than perfect, hence at a level of output that is different from the criterial one, latency-resource functions can still be derived in a similar fashion (where load is replaced by that other level of output).

The function relating rate of performance in continuous subject-paced tasks to amount of invested resources can be derived from the underlying rate-resource function by dividing each rate by the load. For example, if the ordinate of Fig. 15.1C is taken to represent the rate of identification of stimuli presented at a high contrast, then the two upper curves corrspond to loads of 4 and 6 output units per identificiation.

Thus, there are three major types of function that relate performance to amount of invested resources: accuracy-resource functions, latency-resource functions, and performance-rate–resource functions. All of them are affected by characteristics of the task in the following way: All of them are affected by processing efficiency, because all are derived from the underlying function relating output rate to resources. All are affected by task load, because it appears in the definitions of all three measures of performance. Only accuracy-resource functions are affected by processing duration.

---

[5]This assumes, of course, no guessing and that accuracy exactly equals the ratio of actual to criterial output.

Demand

The inverse of a performance-resource function may be called a *demand* function, because it specifies the demand for resources associated with every specific level of performance of a given task. Thus, aiming for *a certain level of performance* of a task determines its demand for resources.

PREDICTIONS FOR DUAL-TASK PERFORMANCE

It follows from this discussion that the effect of any difficulty manipulation on performance will probably interact with the amount of resources: The output is the aggregate of the contributions of all units of resources invested. If an efficiency manipulation affects the marginal efficiency of *all* units of resources of some extent, then the effect cumulates so that the functions diverge (see Fig. 15.1B). Because all measures of performance are functions of the ratio of output rate to load, and output rate is a monotonic function of resources, it follows that manipulation of load must interact or even multiply with the amount of resources invested. So does manipulation of processing duration.

Thus, it is quite safe to expect that effects of difficulty and available capacity will interact, in that effects of resource investment on rate or accuracy will be more pronounced the easier the task is (and the reverse will hold for effects on latency[6]). Note, however, that if the functions approach a ceiling dictated by the nature of the performance measure (what Norman & Bobrow, 1975, call a "data-limit"), that interaction may disappear or even be reversed in some regions of the performance functions (see Lane, 1977). If the limit is imposed by the difficulty manipulation itself, a different picture emerges, and we later touch on this issue.

How can the amount of invested resources in a task be experimentally controlled? A common approach is to pair the task with another concurrent one. To lay the ground for the discussion of performance in a dual-task situation, we briefly digress and touch on some concepts presented in detail in Navon and Gopher (1979).

Resource Allocation

In a dual-task situation, given the structure of the tasks and the capacity of the performer, some levels of *joint* performance are feasible and some others are

---

[6]To be precise, this reversal will take place when the following condition is met: Let A and B denote output rates under the difficult variant with a small or large investment of resources respectively; let C and D denote the corresponding output rates under the easy variant. Then the condition is $D-C/B-A < D{\times}C/B{\times}A$. This condition is necessarily met when the two rate-resource functions are related by a constant multiplication, for example when difficulty is manipulated through changing the load. But even if the functions interact in some other way, this condition will probably be very often satisfied.

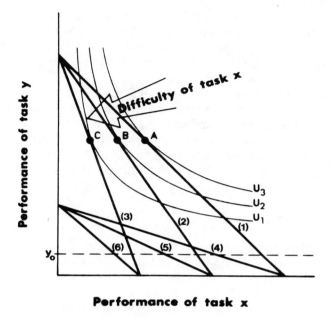

FIG. 15.2.   Bold curves 1, 2, and 3 are POCs for three variants of task x paired with an easy variant of task y. Curves 4, 5, and 6 are POCs for the same three variants of task x paired with a difficult variant of y. The thin curves are indifference curves. A, B, and C are points of optimal resource allocation for easy, medium, and difficult task x, respectively.

not. The set of performance combinations that can be produced when the performer operates at his full capacity, can be represented as a curve of the type called by Norman and Bobrow (1975) a *performance operating characteristic* (or POC in short; see bold curves in Fig. 15.2), or by Sperling and Melchner (1978) an *attention operating characteristic*. The POC comprises a set of alternative combinations only one of which is realized in a particular situation. So, if the performer can control the selection among the alternative combinations, he or she will probably consider their utility. Preferences can be represented by means of *indifference curves* each of which is a locus of all combinations among which the person is indifferent (see thin curves in Fig. 15.2). The optimal combination of performance levels is at the point of the POC that is tangent to the "northeasternmost" indifference curve (e.g., point A in Fig. 15.2). At that point the slopes of the POC and the indifference curve are equal, which means that no extra utility can be gained by trading either more x for less y or vice versa.

Because task difficulty is assumed to affect the slope of the performance-resource function, it will also change the slope of the POC, provided that the difficulty of the concurrent task is held constant. Thus, the effect of difficulty on dual-task situations can be described by means of a *family of POCs*. When task x is made more difficult, the POC has a smaller x intercept (see transition from curve 1 to curve 3 through curve 2 in Fig. 15.2). When task y is made more difficult, the y intercept is smaller (see, e.g., transition from curve 1 to curve 4). Making both tasks more difficult should depress both intercepts (see, e.g., transition from curve 1 to curve 6).

How does one obtain an empirical POC? If we assume that the subject controls his own processing devices, then the experimenter should fix parameters for both tasks and try to influence resource allocation by inducing the subject to change the relative emphasis on the tasks by means of payoffs or instructions (Norman & Bobrow, 1976). A family of POCs can be obtained by varying the difficulty of one task and plotting a POC for every level of difficulty.

Back to the Predictions

Figure 15.2 illustrates two predictions from models of central capacity.

One, difficulty of a task should interact with its relative emphasis, as reflected by the increase in horizontal separations of the curves 1, 2, and 3 toward the bottom.

Two, the difficulties of the two concurrent tasks should interact in their effect on the performance of one of the tasks holding the other one constant, as can be seen from the larger horizontal separations of curves 1, 2, and 3 at y_0, as compared with those of curves 4, 5, and 6.

This is how difficulty affects the *set* of feasible alternatives for joint performance. We now discuss how it affects the actual combination selected given a certain pattern of task preferences. Does difficulty affect the demand for resources? It does, of course, affect the demand per unit performance, so that to maintain all aspects of performance at the same level the performer has to respond to increased difficulty by a larger resource investment. However, it rarely happens that all aspects of performance remain intact when difficulty is increased. Thus, difficulty may be reflected in deterioration with *no* concomitant change in resource allocation. Only if both speed and accuracy are to be maintained at some desired level, will the performer have to recruit more resources to compensate for increased difficulty. So absence of difficulty effects on concurrent performance (e.g., Briggs, Peters, & Fisher, 1972; Kantowitz & Knight, 1976) is not very surprising, if it is found that the difficulty affects the performance of the task itself. Furthermore, it is often the most expected result: Task difficulty is usually more likely to affect the performance of the same task rather than the performance of the concurrent one. This prediction becomes clear when one inspects the illustration in Fig. 15.2: Increasing the difficulty of task x under the task preferences represented by the indifference curves shifts optimal joint performance from point A to point B and then to point C. Of course, a precise prediction is not possible without knowledge of the exact shape of the indifference curves and the POC.

In sum, families of POCs serve to separate effects of difficulty from effects of allocation policy; they are obtained by joint manipulation of task priorities and difficulty manipulations; and they enable testing various predictions from capacity models.

TASK DIFFICULTY AND MULTIPLE RESOURCES

Up to this point resources have been construed as a sort of general undifferentiated entity; tasks have been assumed to interfere to the extent that they depend on resources from that general pool. Elsewhere (Navon & Gopher, 1979) we advanced, discussed, and reviewed some evidence for the idea that there may be various types of resources as there are various factors that may be input to production. The human processing system may be viewed as composed of a number of processing mechanisms each having *its own* capacity. Each specific capacity constrains the output rate of a specific mechanism, and it can be shared by several processes; thus it constitutes a distributable resource.

If several specific resources exist, the performance depends on the amounts of each of them. First, suppose that to perform a certain task resources are used in *fixed proportions* [e.g., exactly 2 units of STM capacity with 1 unit of VIS (visual information storage) capacity]; any increase in one of them without a concomitant increase in the other would not improve performance at all.

To be exact, a task is characterized by a required mixture of outputs (or output rates, in case synchronization of activity is essential) of the various resources. The proportions as well as actual amounts of the various resources needed to realize that output mixture depends on their efficiencies. Let the combination of specific resources used to obtain a unit of performance be called a *cost composition*. The intention to maintain a certain level of performance determines the combination of *total* amounts of specific resources demanded by the task, which may be called a *demand composition*. It follows from these definitions that the cost composition is determined both by the nature of the task and by the eficiencies of the various resources. Manipulating a difficulty variable may, theoretically, affect equally the efficiencies of all relevant resources, so that the cost composition will vary in terms of amounts but not in terms of proportions. In this case we may say that the manipulation affects performance quantitatively. However, we suspect that most often a certain manipulation of difficulty has a differential effect on different processing facilities, so that it changes the *relative* weights of the various resources in the cost composition. That may be regarded as a qualitative modification in the nature of the task.

Different tasks may have different compositions of specific resources. A task may even use resources of a type that are not used at all by another task (let that be called a *disjoint* resource). Tasks interfere with each other to the extent that their cost compositions are similar so that they have to compete for some common types of resource (see Navon & Gopher, 1979, for a detailed analysis).

Let us now consider the implications of the notion of multiple resources for difficulty effects in dual-task situations. Suppose the performance of task y is observed to be related to the manipulation of a certain parameter. It may mean that that manipulation affects the cost of the task in terms of some relevant types of resources. If that task is conjoined with another one x that does *not* use those types of resources, the manipulation will have no effect on the performance of the latter task. Note that this can happen in two cases: one, when the tasks do not overlap at all in their use of resources; two, when they do overlap but the difficulty manipulation of task y has a differential effect on the components of the cost composition, so that it taps only resources from the set which is relevant only for task y.

The effect of the difficulty manipulation in the first case is illustrated in Fig. 15.3A: there is no performance tradeoff at all, so manipulating the difficulty of a task affects just the maximal level of performance of that task. In the second case, however, there is some tradeoff, but because the manipulation has no bearing on the cost composition of common resources, it affects neither the performance of the competing task nor the amount of tradeoff. A simple example may best illustrate this point. Suppose the system possesses 20 units of R^1 and 20 units of R^2. Further, suppose that the demand for resources for a unit increase of both tasks is constant over all levels of performance: Task x demands 1 unit of R^1; task y demands 1 unit of R^1 *and* 1 unit of R^2. The corresponding POC is curve 1 in Fig. 15.3B. Now suppose that a parameter of task y is manipulated so as to increase its demand for R^2 to 2 units. This sets a new limit to the performance of y, which is 10, but because to achieve that level the performer needs no more than 10 units of R^1, the rest can be directed to task x. The resulting POC is curve 2 in Fig. 15.3B.[7]

Now let us examine what happens when we relax the requirement that resources must be employed in fixed proportions. Suppose there is more than one way to do a task. There may be one optimal composition of resources, but deviations are tolerated and performance usually benefits to some extent

---

[7]The family of POCs in Fig. 15.3B could arise even if there was just one pool of resources. One could conjecture that some task parameters do not affect efficiency of resources but rather the limit of their effectiveness, namely the ceiling of performance (or "data limit"; see Norman & Bobrow, 1975). For example, masking may disrupt some features so that they cannot be recovered at all. However, in that case performance cannot be improved by enabling a longer processing duration, whereas in the case illustrated in Fig. 15.3B performance should be sensitive to processing duration.

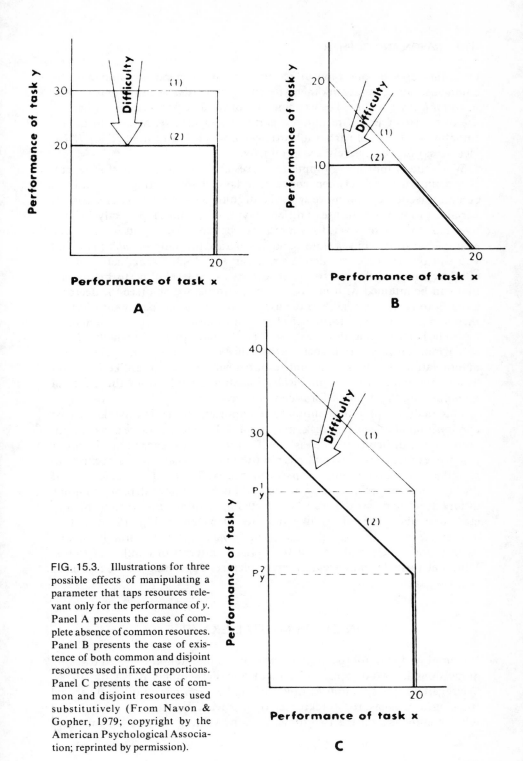

FIG. 15.3. Illustrations for three possible effects of manipulating a parameter that taps resources relevant only for the performance of y. Panel A presents the case of complete absence of common resources. Panel B presents the case of existence of both common and disjoint resources used in fixed proportions. Panel C presents the case of common and disjoint resources used substitutively (From Navon & Gopher, 1979; copyright by the American Psychological Association; reprinted by permission).

309

from increases of one type of resource, even when not accompanied by commensurate increases of other types; in other words, resources may be used in *variable proportions*. The extreme case of variable proportions is when the use of the two types of resource is perfectly substitutive. More typical presumably is the case of partial substitution in which substituting R^1 for R^2 (or vice versa) is progressively less productive.

When the proportions of input resources are not fixed, the performer can reduce interference between concurrent tasks by operating less with the common resources and more with the disjoint ones. In the extreme case of variable proportions the use of different types of resource is perfectly disjunctive, namely *any* of several resources can be employed by itself. Take the example illustrated in Fig. 15.3B and just change the italicized *and* to *or*, and you will obtain the effect demonstrated in Fig. 15.3C: A reduction in the efficiency of the disjoint resource R^2 decreases the level of performance of y that can be attained with no cost to the performance of x (see the decrease from P_y^1 to P_y^2 in Fig. 15.3C). If the use of resources is just partly substitutive, then to maintain the performance of y at the same level a larger amount of R^1 has to be invested in it; thus task x suffers. It is hard to predict whether it will suffer more or less with higher performance of y. If it suffers more, then a manipulation that taps a disjoint resource will produce a fanlike family of bowed-out POCs that is practically indistinguishable from the effect of manipulating the demand for a common resource.

This analysis calls our attention to an important point: The overlap in cost composition of concurrent tasks may be partial. Hence, a failure of a manipulation of the difficulty of one task to affect the performance of the other one just proves that resource overlap is not total but not that it does not exist. On the other hand, even when joint performance exhibits a considerable tradeoff due to shifts in resource allocation, the tasks may still depend on some different mechanisms that can be detected by manipulating various parameters and observing effects like the ones depicted in Fig. 15.3B and C. Therefore, researchers should manipulate several difficulty variables as well as task preferences and present their effects in terms of families of POCs. Different variables may yield different pictures depending on the resources that they tap.

AN EXPERIMENTAL EXAMPLE

We employed this approach in a study of the interaction between tracking dimensions in two-dimensional pursuit tracking (Gopher & Navon, 1978). We regarded this situation as time-sharing between horizontal and vertical tracking and measured tracking error in each dimension. We controlled relative emphasis on the two dimensions by varying the ratio of tolerance levels for error in each and manipulated the difficulty of each dimension independently by varying some parameter of tracking in that dimension. In the first experiment the manipulated variable was the cutoff *frequency* for the low-pass filter applied to the output of a random-noise generator to yield the changes of target directions. In the second experiment difficulty was manipulated by changing the target *velocity* (which was also higher on the average than the velocity in the other experiments). In the third experiment we varied the ratio of acceleration to velocity in the *control dynamics* of the hand controller (this ratio was also higher on the average than in the other two experiments). Some of the results are presented in Fig. 15.4 as families of POCs.

In the first experiment (see Fig. 15.4A) task emphasis had a large effect on performance, which was nevertheless negatively accelerated as indicated by the strong curvature of the POCs: subjects did respond to a lower requirement in one dimension by increasing tracking error, but that yielded very little improvement in the other dimension. The difficulty effects were much smaller: The frequency of the target vertical movement affected vertical accuracy linearly but horizontal accuracy curvilinearly, and it did not interact with the task emphasis variable nor with the frequency of horizontal movement.

The results of the second and the third experiments (see Fig. 15.4B and C, respectively) are characterized by a smaller effect of task emphasis and a larger effect of the difficulty manipulations. The limited performance tradeoff exhibited in the first experiment recurs in the second one. The velocity manipulations had linear effects just on the manipulated axes and did not interact either between themselves or with task emphasis. The latter result also indicates that the concavity of the POCs would not vanish by different scaling. In contrast, the fanlike family of almost linear POCs in Fig. 15.4C reveals that in the third experiment performance tradeoff was considerable and that the manipulation of the control dynamics interacted with task emphasis.[8]

The results can be accommodated within a post hoc account based on the notion of multiple resources. Suppose that, despite the apparent similarity between vertical and horizontal tracking, their cost compositions are fairly dissimilar. Suppose further that the two tasks require the same kind of motor-related resource but different kinds of perceptual or "computational" resources. Now, in the first two experiments the load on the motor system, which was the common resource was relatively small; hence the tasks hardly interfered with each other. However, because of the higher average ratio of

---

[8]To give an idea of the goodness of fit of the curves to the data, the actual performance combinations in the second experiment are presented in Fig. 15.4D averaged across subjects and levels of difficulty for each of the levels of task emphasis, along with the POC curve fitted to them. The fit is slightly better in the first experiment and slightly worse in the third one.

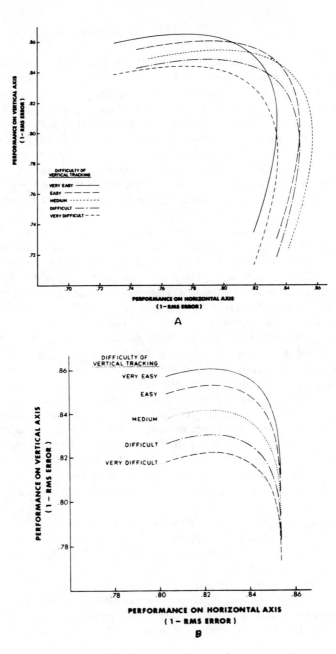

FIG. 15.4.   A family of POCs representing tracking accuracy (1 root mean square error) on each of the axes in dual-axis tracking as a function of task emphases. Each POC corresponds to a different level of difficulty of vertical tracking and is obtained by jointly solving two second-order multiple regression equations for predicting performance on the two axes from the task emphases variable. The different panels correspond to different difficulty

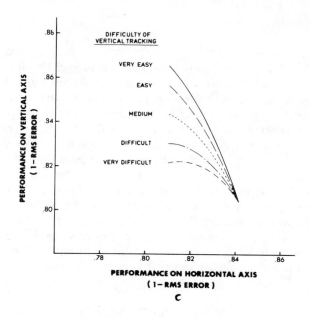

C

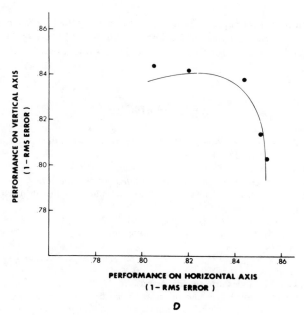

D

manipualtions: frequency of target movement in panel A (scaled down due to space limitation), target velocity in panel B, and control dynamics in panel C. Panel D presents average performance combinations in each level of task emphasis in the second experiment with the POC fitted to them. Actual averages cannot be plotted on the family diagram, because the design was a fractional one (Response Surface Methodology, see Myers, 1971).

acceleration to velocity in the third experiment, both tasks required more motor capacity, so they had more for which to compete. The different effects of the difficulty manipulations may be interpreted once we realize that the only parameter that seems to affect the motor system is the control dynamics manipulation in the third experiment. Manipulations that tap a common resource are expected to yield a fanlike family of POCs (see Fig. 15.2), whereas those that tap disjoint resources may yield a family like the one illustrated in Fig. 15.3C (which is basically what was found in the second experiment).

However, if these two tasks are not similar enough to call for exactly the same resources, one might wonder whether the number of different resources identified empirically will not turn out to be too large to make the notion of multiple resources useful. Thus, the analysis of this experimental example illustrates, in addition to the potential utility of interpretations in terms of multiple resources, the difficulties that may arise as well.

ACKNOWLEDGMENTS

The preparation of this chapter was supported in part by the Life Sciences Program, Air Force Office of Scientific Research, under Grant No. AFOSR 78-3131. We thank our referees and the editor for their comments and suggestions for improvement in presentation.

REFERENCES

Brigges, G. E., Peters, G. L., & Fisher, R. P. On the locus of divided attention effects. *Perception & Psychophysics,* 1972, *11,* 315–320.

Broadbent, D. E. *Decision and stress.* London: Academic Press, 1971.

Gopher, D., & Navon, D. *How is performance limited: Testing the notion of central capacity.* The Technion-Israel Institute of Technology, Haifa, Israel: Faculty of Industrial and Management Engineering. TR AFOSR-78-2, 1978.

Kahneman, D. *Attention and effort.* Englewood Cliffs, N.J.: Prentice-Hall, 1973.

Kantowitz, B. H., & Knight, J. L., Jr. Testing tapping time-sharing, II: Auditory secondary task. *Acta Psychologica,* 1976, *40,* 343–362.

Kantowitz, B. H., & Knight, J. L., Jr. When is an easy task difficult and vice versa? *Acta Psychologica,* 1978, *42,* 163–170.

Kerr, B. Processing demands during mental operations. *Memory & Cognition,* 1973, *1,* 401–412.

Lane, D. M. Attention allocation and the relationship between primary and secondary task difficulty. A reply to Kantowitz and Knight. *Acta Psychologica,* 1977, *41,* 493–495.

Myers, R. H. Response surface methodology. Boston: Allyn & Bacon, 1971.

Moray, N. Where is capacity limited? A survey and a model. *Acta Psychologica,* 1967, *27,* 84–92.

Navon, D., & Gopher, D. On the economy of the human processing system. *Psychological Review,* 1979, *86,* 214–255.

Norman, D. A., & Bobrow, D. J. On data-limited and resource-limited processes, *Cognitive Psychology,* 1975, *7,* 44–64.

Norman, D. A., & Bobrow, D. J. On the analysis of performance operating characteristics. *Psychological Review,* 1976, *83,* 508–510.

Shaw, M. L. A capacity allocation model for reaction time. *Journal of Experimental Psychology: Human Perception and Performance,* 1978, *4,* 586–598.

Sperling, G., & Melchner, M. J. The attention operating characteristics: Examples from visual search. *Science,* 1978, *202,* 315–318.

IV VISUAL INFORMATION PROCESSING

16

Recent Themes in Visual Information Processing: A Selected Overview

Lynn A. Cooper
Cornell University
Ithaca, New York
United States

ABSTRACT

In this chapter two themes in the recent literature in visual information processing are discussed and illustrated with a selected set of experiments. The first theme is a renewed interest in structural and organizational aspects of visual information. The second theme is the idea that qualitatively different modes of visual information processing can operate on perceptual input. It is argued that these themes represent general concerns in that they cut across a variety of experimental paradigms and seemingly distinct theoretical issues. Furthermore, research reflecting these themes points to the inadequacies of simple models of visual information processing based primarily on the independent extraction of local visual features.

I begin this chapter with a general disclaimer and an outline of what I shall discuss. The field of visual information processing—which I have been asked to review—is a broad and heterogeneous one that encompasses in some sense many of the major areas represented in other chapters of this volume. If we think of visual information processing as the study of the mechanisms that transform visual input into an internal representation of the visual world, then clearly issues in attention, memory, and even problem solving are relevant. In terms of levels of analysis, research in visual information processing ranges from investigation of sensory processes to the study of higher-level cognitive activities. In terms of content, issues in visual information processing include the recognition of objects, the processing of visually presented text, the perception of motion, and the mechanisms and representations underlying mental imagery, to name but a very few.

Because of the diversity of concerns in visual information processing, it would be extremely difficult to attempt a comprehensive review of the recent literature in this field. Nor would it be particularly useful for purposes of this volume to select one or two more delimited subareas (such as word perception or iconic memory) and review the recent studies in those areas. Instead, I have chosen to identify two *themes* emerging in the recent literature in visual information processing and to discuss selectively experimental and theoretical work that reflects these themes. I believe that these themes cut across different content areas and levels of analysis and, thus, illustrate some general concerns in recent work on visual information processing.

The plan of the chapter is as follows. First, I present a simplified outline of a traditional model for visual information processing. Then, I briefly discuss some of the central questions that are natural to this model. Finally, for the bulk of the chapter, I suggest some issues (the recent themes) that are not captured well by the traditional model. The first of these is a growing concern with structural and organizational characteristics of the visual information coming into the system and with the processing consequences of such structure and organization. The second is the idea that visual processing may proceed in qualitatively different ways depending on the level of visual analysis required, the particulars of the task, the strategies of the individual subject, and the stage of development being studied.

A Simple Model of Visual Information Processing

Figure 16.1 illustrates schematically a simple and very general view of visual information processing. According to this view, visual input enters the system and is subjected to a variety of processing operations. The outcome of all this processing is the construction of an internal representation of the visual input that may or may not contain all the information in the input itself. The internal representation can then be used to guide response processes. Central to models like the one in Fig. 16.1 is the idea that the nature of the visual information or its "coded form" is actively transformed by the different processing operations. (See Fig. 16.1 for a partial list of typical processes and codes studied in visual information processing.) Note too that processing need not act in solely a "bottom-up" or "data-driven" fashion (Lindsay & Norman, 1977). "Top-down" or "conceptually driven" operations, such as the generation of expectations or the use of contextual information, can influence the selection and processing of the visual input.

Given a framework like the one outlined in Fig. 16.1, several sorts of questions tend naturally to emerge, and these questions have been and continue to be the focus of much research in visual information processing. One sort of question concerns a quantitative specification of processing

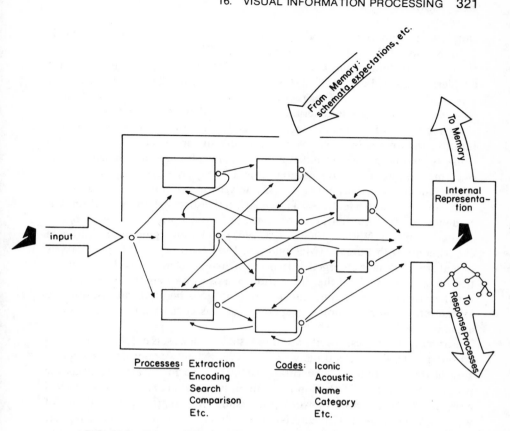

FIG. 16.1. Schematic illustration of a model for visual information processing. Boxes denote internal processes, and open circles denote the output of the processes. Typical processes and codes studied in visual information processing are listed at the bottom of the figure.

operations. For example, does processing of visual input occur in parallel or serially (Townsend, 1974)? What are the durations of different processing operations (Sternberg, 1969)? Do certain processes operate independently, or do they interact (Sternberg)?

Another sort of question that has loomed large in visual information-processing research concerns changes in the coded form of the visual input over time. Is visual information, in some cases, recoded in an acoustic–verbal form (Conrad, 1964)? Can the change in the form of visual input over time be characterized as toward greater abstraction (Posner, Boies, Eichelman, & Taylor, 1969)? Is the representation of visual information in some cases "analog" as studies of mental manipulations suggest (Cooper & Shepard, 1978; Kosslyn & Pomerantz, 1977; Shepard, 1975)? Or is it more appropriate to view visual memory representations as abstract and propositional in nature (Anderson, 1978; Palmer, 1975)? (Note that the somewhat fanciful "internal representation" portion of the model in Fig. 16.1 allows for either possibility.)

A matter on which the general outline of visual information processing, as shown in Fig. 16.1, is silent concerns a specification of the nature of the visual input to the processing system. In many current versions of visual information-processing models, visual stimuli are conceptualized as concatenations of elementary attributes or features. One of the early stages of processing in many models invariably involves the analysis or extraction of features and relationships among features. This is attractive because there is abundant evidence for feature analyzers or detectors from both neurophysiological studies (Hubel & Wiesel, 1962, 1965, 1968) and converging psychophysical experiments with humans (McCollough, 1965; Stromeyer, 1969). The types of features that have emerged as important are very elementary, local properties of patterns such as the orientation or position of single line segments. Furthermore, by arranging feature detectors in a hierarchical fashion, the extraction of more complex properties such as corners and angles can be accomplished.

For many purposes, specification of visual input as sets of features extracted independently works quite well. However, when we consider the processing of displays that are structurally rich, the case for local features as the proper specification of the input or the unit of visual analysis becomes less compelling. In the area of word processing, the superior perceptibility of words—as compared with unrelated letter strings, various sorts of regular nonword strings, and perhaps single letters—have led some investigators to propose that units larger than the individual features of letters are the important ones in perceiving printed words (Gibson, 1969; Spoehr & Smith, 1975). Further demonstrations of contextual or overall structural effects in visual processing suggest that an analysis of global properties of a display can precede and then guide the extraction of lower-level features. For example, Biederman's (1972; Biederman, Glass, & Stacey, 1973; Biederman, Rabinowitz, Glass, & Stacey, 1974) experiments on scene perception show that the structural coherence of a picture influences the detection and identification of individual objects in the picture.

The purpose of these examples is simply to set the stage for discussion of the two themes that are the focus of this paper—viz., that visual processing depends on the structure of the information being processed and that different types of processes may interact in interpreting a complex visual display. I turn now to a more detailed consideration of recent work on the effects of structure and organization in visual information processing.

STRUCTURAL AND ORGANIZATIONAL FACTORS
IN VISUAL INFORMATION PROCESSING

The idea that analysis of independent features of patterns is inadequate to explain visual processing is hardly a novel one. The well-known Gestalt laws of organization—such as good continuation, proximity, closedness—certainly question the independent-features notion by showing that properties of configurations of elements, not necessarily the properties of the elements themselves, determine perceptual experience (Koffka, 1963; Wertheimer, 1958). But, the Gestalt principles of perceptual grouping, however compelling experientially, have remained little more than demonstrations of possible organizational effects (see Hochberg, 1974, for further discussion); that is, more effort has been directed toward this phenomenal level than toward specifying quantitatively the contributions of the various organizational principles or toward clearly examining the perceptual conditions under which these principles operate. [A notable exception to this generalization is the work of Hochberg, Attneave, and their associates (Attneave, 1954; Hochberg, 1968; Hochberg & Brooks, 1960; Hochberg & McAlister, 1953.] Viewed in the context of an information-processing approach to perception, the Gestalt demonstrations of organizational effects have been unsatisfying in that they have failed to show the nature of processing consequences of variables of pattern structure. [A notable exception to this generalization is the extensive work of Garner (1974) and his colleagues. Not only has Garner provided a quantitative measure of variables like "pattern goodness," he has also shown that goodness affects performance on a variety of tasks including discrimination, recognition, and reproduction.]

When discussing the effects of organizational variables on visual information processing, a difficult problem rapidly arises. This problem concerns the locus of the organizational effects. When performance is influenced by some structural property of the visual display being processed, are we to attribute this affect to the structure of the display alone, to the nature of the processing operations that act on the visual information, or to some interaction between visual structure and processing? Clearly an explanation based on processing alone is inadequate, because structural effects arise in the presence of certain configurations of information and not in the presence of others. An explanation based exclusively on the nature of the visual information also seems wanting, for structural effects will presumably emerge as a consequence of certain processing demands but not as a consequence of others (Bartram, 1978). If we accept the remaining position—that structural effects result from an interaction between the organization of visual information and the nature of the processing mechanisms that operate on the visual information—then the task for theory and research on visual structure becomes a difficult one.

Not only must potent stimulus variables that can produce structural effects be isolated, but also a clear account of the processing operations that mediate the structural effects must be provided.

Renewed attention to effects of organization and structure is one recent theme in research on visual information processing. This research can be seen as an effort to specify the nature of the *input* in Fig. 16.1—the effective information coming into the processing system—at a level beyond that of sets of independent, local visual features. Another part of this effort is to propose processing mechanisms that make use of structured visual information. In the two sections that follow, I review some recent experiments showing the effects of various structural and organizational variables in a variety of visual information-processing situations. I consider separately the effects of visual structure in *low-level* processing tasks such as detection and discrimination and in *higher-level* tasks including recognition, reproduction, mental manipulation, and direct judgments of visual organization. Throughout, discussion will focus on both the isolation of effective stimulus variables and proposals concerning mechanisms that might mediate structural effects. It will be evident that much more progress has been made on the former issue than on the latter.

Configural and Contextual Effects in Detection, Identification, and Discrimination

In the past several years, a number of investigators have reported striking effects on configural factors in simple visual-processing situations. All of these demonstrations share the property that configural or contextual effects are found *even when information about a single feature of a visual display (e.g., the orientation of a line segment) is all that is logically required to perform the task.* Perhaps the best known of these demonstrations is the "object-superiority effect," reported by Weisstein and Harris (1974). In this experiment, the subject's task was to identify which of four line segments appeared in a visual display that sometimes contained contextual information in addition to the target line. The important finding was that target lines were identified more accurately when they were embedded in contexts that appeared coherent and three dimensional than when they were embedded in patterns that appeared less coherent and two dimensional. Figure 16.2 shows examples of the displays used in this and related experiments.

Subsequent research (Williams & Weisstein, 1978) has extended this finding even further by showing that identification of single lines in coherent, object-like contexts can be superior to identification of the lines when presented alone. Clearly, these experiments challenge the idea that features are extracted independently of the larger configurations in which they appear. They offer less in the way of an account of the mechanisms responsible for the

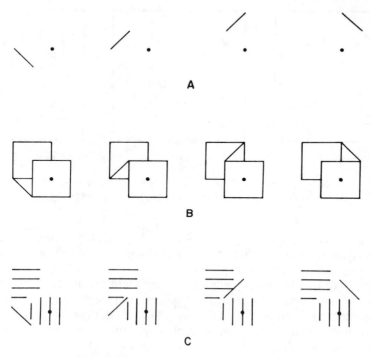

FIG. 16.2. Examples of displays used in studies of the "object superiority effect." (Adapted from Weisstein & Harris, 1974.)

contextual effect, except to suggest that higher-order structural components of objects might be analyzed *directly* rather than via an analysis of their constituent line segments. This latter idea is further supported by a series of experiments by McClelland (1978) showing that structural characteristics of masking stimuli can selectively influence detection of line segments in object-like and single-line displays. In particular, object-like masks lead to better identification of lines alone than lines in object contexts like those used by Weisstein and Harris (1974). Conversely, masks containing incoherent arrangements of line segments impair detectability of single lines as compared to lines presented in object contexts. (See McClelland, 1978, for alternative interpretations of these data.)

Another very clever set of experiments on configural effects has been done by Pomerantz and his collaborators (Pomerantz, 1978; Pomerantz & Garner, 1973; Pomerantz, Sager, & Stoever, 1977; Pomerantz & Sager, 1976; Pomerantz & Schwaitzberg, 1975). The basic form of one of these demonstrations is shown by the visual displays in Fig. 16.3. In the case of all three displays, the task is to determine as rapidly as possible which quadrant of the display is

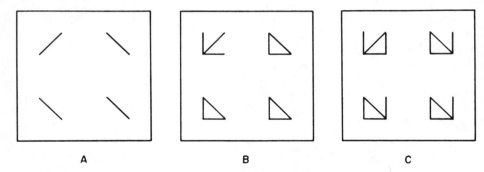

FIG. 16.3.   Examples of displays used by Pomerantz and his collaborators to study configural effects in perception. (Adapted from Pomerantz, Sager, & Stoever, 1977.)

different from the others. And, in all three displays, the disparate quadrant differs from the others only by virtue of the slope of a single line segment (the same segment in all three displays).

Detecting the differing quadrant is most rapid for display B, next most rapid for display A, and slowest for display C (but see Pomerantz et al., 1977, Experiment 5). Presumably, in the case of display B the contextual information interacts with the target line segment to produce "emergent features" that can be processed directly rather than via an analysis of local parts of a visual array. But not all contexts interact with targets to produce easily discriminable emergent features as the inferiority of display C demonstrates. Indeed, one of the important contributions of Pomerantz's research program has been to identify just what sorts of stimulus variables produce perceptual organizations that help or hinder performance in a variety of tasks. The mechanism that he proposes to explain instances of configural superiority is the direct access of global, higher-order visual features to detection processes beyond the level of analysis of single line segments (see Pomerantz, 1978).

As a final example of configural effects in visual processing, consider the recent experiments by Banks and Prinzmetal (1976; Prinzmetal & Banks, 1977). Subjects had to detect the presence of alternative target characters in a briefly presented visual array containing a target and noise elements sharing features with the target. Banks and Prinzmetal manipulated the organization of the arrays according to Gestalt principles of perceptual grouping (figural "goodness" and good continuation). In some cases the array was structured such that the target letter was perceived as grouped with the noise elements (e.g., it was part of a good pattern or a continuing line, as in Fig. 16.4A). In other cases the noise items were grouped together and the target was perceived as separate (as in Fig. 16.4B). The results of these experiments are quite clear. Detection speed and accuracy were poorer when the target item was

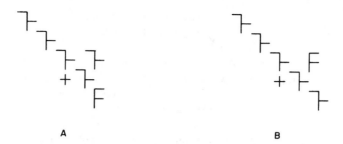

FIG. 16.4.   Examples of displays used in the detection experiments of Banks and Prinzmetal. (Adapted from Prinzmetal & Banks, 1977.)

organized with the noise elements than when the target was grouped by itself or as part of a less coherent structure.

Banks and Prinzmetal conclude that their results challenge accounts of visual detection based on simple interactions among local feature detectors (Estes, 1972), and they offer some ideas concerning how visual organization might affect processing in the detection situation. Specifically, a perceptual "parser" might act on the visual input, segregating it into units or groups on the basis of Gestalt principles. Only subsequent to this initial organization would more analytic processing of the elements in each group occur. In the example in Fig. 16.4, the principle of good continuation would result in a grouping of the array into two units—one containing a string of elements and the other containing an isolated element. Further analysis of the elements in each unit would lead to poor performance on one display (Fig. 16.4A) owing, perhaps, to inhibition among the features shared by the target and the noise items with which the target has been grouped. For the other display (Fig. 16.4B), target detection should be quite good, because the target is grouped by itself and thus can be analyzed efficiently without inhibition from other elements. Configural effects arise, then, from the operation of an initial parsing process that cannot work effectively on unstructured visual arrays.

Structural Effects in Recognition, Recall, Perceptual Judgment, and Mental Manipulation

A rather different sort of evidence concerning the role of structure in visual processing has come from experiments involving memory, perceptual comparisons, mental manipulations, and other sorts of *cognitively based* judgments. In general, these studies demonstrate powerful effects of the organization of pattern parts, as well as overall configural effects. For example, Reed (1974; Reed & Johnsen, 1975) has shown that some subparts of patterns are easier to recognize as parts of the pattern than are others. This finding in itself argues strongly against the idea that patterns are coded in terms of independent sets of visual features, and it suggests that higher-order pattern units are stored and used in recognition.

An extensive investigation of the role of part structure in memory and perception of simple visual patterns has recently been reported by Palmer (1977, 1978). Examples of the sorts of patterns used in these studies are shown in Fig. 16.5. Palmer's basic idea is that patterns such as these are represented internally in the form of a hierarchical network. At each level of the hierarchy, structural units of the pattern are represented in terms of both their global properties and their component parts. At the highest level in the hierarchy, the structural unit would be the pattern itself (with global properties like overall symmetry), and at the lowest level the units would be the individual line segments of which the pattern is composed. Intermediate levels would represent higher-order pattern units that are groupings of lower-level pattern elements. These higher-order units can be accessed directly on the basis of their global properties without an analysis of their component elements.

One crucial feature of Palmer's representation is its *selective organization;* that is, only some groupings of elements in a pattern will be represented as intermediate-level structural units. To predict which pattern components will be organized as structural units, Palmer has developed a quantitative measure of the relationships among segments in a pattern based on Gestalt grouping principles such as proximity, connectedness, and similarity in orientation. The notion is that *good* subparts of patterns, as defined by Palmer's measure, will have a high probability of being grouped as a structural unit, and *bad* subparts will have a low probability of being represented as a structural unit

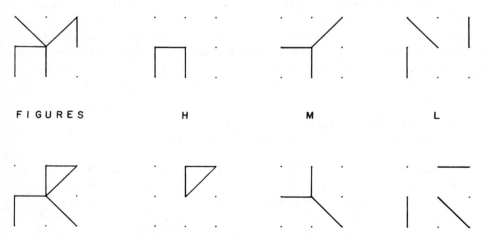

FIGURES   H   M   L

FIG. 16.5. Figures with high, medium, and low goodness parts used in Palmer's experiments. (Adapted from Palmer, 1977.)

of the pattern. (See Fig. 16.5 for examples of pattern subparts varying in goodness.)

Palmer (1977) presents considerable converging evidence that is consistent with his hierarchical representation of visual patterns. His goodness-of-subpart measure predicts the way people divide six-line-segment patterns like those in Fig. 16.5 into three-segment parts, and it also accounts for direct ratings of the *goodness* of such parts in whole patterns. Part goodness or coherence is related to the time needed to *synthesize mentally* two separate three-segment parts into a complete pattern for *same–different* matching against a subsequently presented pattern. Finally, when subjects must determine whether a three-segment unit is part of a simultaneously presented six-segment pattern, part verification time increases with increasing *badness* of the part as a unit of the pattern.

Palmer provides a process model to account for these part verification reaction-time data. Quite briefly, the model holds that matching of a part to a network representation of a figure proceeds from the highest level of the hierarchy down. Since *good* parts of a figure have a high probability of being encoded as single higher-level structural units in the representation of the pattern, they will be directly matched early in the comparison operation. *Bad* parts, however, are not likely to be represented as structural units; so, verification of their presence in the pattern requires matching at a lower level in the hierarchical representation of the pattern—possibly at the level of individual line segments. Although this model is not sufficiently well specified to be tested rigorously, it is commendable that Palmer offers ideas about both the representation of structure in patterns and possible mechanisms that process that structure. At the very least, Palmer's data provide another form of evidence that individual features of visual patterns (in the case of his stimuli, single line segments) are not processed independently (see, also, Palmer, 1978).

Cunningham (1979) has used tasks and stimuli similar to those of Palmer to study the organization of information in visual patterns; however, his approach is considerably different. Rather than defining a measure of pattern structure beforehand (such as Palmer's goodness measure), Cunningham uses data from ratings of the goodness of parts in patterns and from timed part verification to derive structural representations of individual visual patterns. The representations that he extracts from the data are weighted trees. (See Cunningham, 1978, for a description of the method for deriving the tree representations.) He has found impressive agreement among the structural representations of single visual patterns across a variety of tasks, including the sequence of drawing strokes that subjects make in reproducing a simple visual pattern. Cunningham's method can be used to study the structure in more complex visual patterns and in more varied processing situations. His approach has the advantage of being able to specify the representation of structure in individual visual patterns. With such a specification available, it might be possible to develop and test richer process models (e.g., models of how information is retrieved from the representation of a visual pattern).

Experiments designed to assess the recall of visual information from memory (often via reproduction of a visual pattern) have also uncovered effects of pattern structure. For example, Bower and Glass (1976) had subjects reproduce simple line drawings from memory. Cues consisting of parts of the pattern were provided before each recall, and a cue could be a good, mediocre, or bad part of the pattern. (Part goodness was defined by intuition and Gestalt principles of common direction and proximity.) *Good* cues led to much better recall than poorer cues. Again, the inference is that the good cues correspond to single structural units in the memory representations of the patterns.

Structural properties of entire patterns, not only subunits of patterns, have been shown to affect recall or reproduction. One pattern variable that has received much attention is the size of the equivalence set of a pattern (Garner, 1966, 1974). Good or structured patterns are redundant, coming from small subsets defined by the operations of rotation and reflection. The size of a pattern's equivalence class is inversely related to the ease of encoding, recognizing, or reproducing the pattern (Checkosky & Whitlock, 1973; Garner, 1974; Schnore & Partington, 1967). An interesting extension of this work has recently been reported by Bell and Handel (1976). These investigators have shown that good patterns are more resistant to masking than are poor patterns. Superior performance on reproducing good patterns holds up over variations in the goodness of the masking stimulus, and, interestingly, good patterns appear to be less effective maskers than poor patterns.

In other types of recall experiments, performance also depends on the visual organization of the stimulus materials. For example, Bartram (1978) had subjects reproduce random arrays of 10 disks following tachistoscopic presentation. When order of recall was not specified, subjects reproduced the arrays by generating successive "chunks" of about three or four spatially adjacent disks. This result is interesting, because, in the absence of any compelling structure in the random arrays, subjects used the only available organization—spatial adjacency of disks—as a basis for encoding and recalling the patterns.

Another psychological task in which structural properties of patterns very obviously are potent variables is direct perceptual judgment. We all have intuitions concerning which visual patterns are good and what sort of part constitutes a coherent structural unit of a pattern. Indeed, just such intuitions about pattern structure provided a basis for formulating the Gestalt laws of organization. And, ratings of pattern or subpart goodness are often used to validate more objecitve, quantitative measures of structure. Perhaps of more interest (or, at least, greater subtlety) is the use of one variable of pattern structure to predict judgments concerning another aspect of the pattern or its relationship to other patterns. For example, Palmer (1978) had used similarity ratings of pairs of visual patterns to make inferences about the nature of higher-order structural units in patterns. In another recent experiment by Hemenway and Palmer (1978), organizational principles were used to bias both ratings of the three dimensionality of projection drawings of objects and the time required to perceive the drawings as three dimensional. Organization was manipulated by coloring various sections of the objects according to principles designed to emphasize two- or three-dimensional interpretations.

Still another example of the role of structure in judgments about properties of patterns concerns rated complexity. Earlier studies have pointed to the effects of symmetry and number of sides as determinants of perceived complexity (Arnoult, 1960; Attneave, 1957). In a very extensive investigation, Chipman (1977) has explored the role of these and other variables in judgments of complexity of visual patterns. Her results indicate a functional separation between quantitative variables, such as number of sides in a pattern, and structural variables, such as forms of symmetry and repetition, in complexity ratings. Number of *turns* in her patterns set an upper bound on perceived complexity, and the effects of structural variables were assessed by how great a reduction in complexity they produced from the upper value set by the quantitative variables. A variety of structural properties (10 were investigated in all) affected perceived complexity, and Chipman provides a quantitative account of the contribution of each property to the perceptual judgments.

As a final example of a visual information-processing situation in which effects of structural variables have been sought, consider tasks requiring mental manipulations of internal representations of patterns. Palmer's (1977) mental synthesis experiment is one such task, and he found that the time taken to synthesize two pattern parts into an integrated whole was greatly affected by the goodness of the parts as structural units of the pattern. Thompson and Klatzky (1978) have also reported that mental synthesis is quicker and more complete when the pattern eventually synthesized is a closed form than when it is an assemblage of partially disconnected line segments. Akin and Chase (1978) have examined the effects of structural variables such as symmetry, compactness, planarity, and linearity on the time taken to report how many blocks are present in drawings of three-dimensional objects formed by concatenating up to 10 cubical blocks. Their idea was that structural variables should affect the ease with which sets of blocks could be perceptually grouped and then added. Somewhat surprisingly, only the variable of compactness had a consistent and substantial effect on quantification latencies, though each of the other three structural variables did account for small portions of the variance in the latencies.

Summary

In the preceeding two sections, I provide a review of some experiments demonstrating the influence of stimulus organization and structure on visual information processing. The tasks surveyed range from detecting some property of a single line segment to reproducing a whole visual pattern from memory. Even so, the review is far from complete in terms of both range of tasks and diversity of structural variables. Notably absent are discussions of structural variables like dimensional integrality and separability (Garner, 1974; Monahan & Lockhead, 1977) and less well-defined factors like familiarity, to mention but a few. Also, I have tried to confine my survey to studies done in the past several years, thus ignoring earlier and important work. Even from this brief review, two things emerge clearly. First, the tacit assumption of models, like the one in Fig. 16.1, that inputs to the visual-processing system need be specified only at the level of independent features is certainly wrong. And, the role of structure in visual information processing is currently a topic of vigorous investigation in many laboratories.

I suggested at the beginning of the discussion of organization and structure that both an identification of stimulus variables and proposals for mechanisms that mediate structural effects were needed. As the studies reviewed attest, we are well on the way to understanding the kinds of stimulus factors that produce organizational effects. I think, too, that these experiments go beyond the observations of the Gestalt psychologists by showing the range of performances that are helped or hindered by visual structure. What, though, of theories of how processes operate on structured visual information? In answering this question, much less progress has been made. (In fact, many of the references cited close with a statement to the effect that it is not yet clear just what the mechanisms are that underlie perceptual grouping or the perception of visual structure.) However, some interesting and promising suggestions have been made. These include Pomerantz's notion of the direct detection of emergent configural features, Banks and Prinzmetal's idea of a structural perceptual parsing followed by more fine-grained analysis of visual input, and Palmer's approach to modeling the internal representation of visual figures. Hopefully, in the next few years more progress will be made on elucidating the processing mechanisms by which structural effects operate, just as progress in demonstrating the range of those effects has been made in the past few years.

QUALITATIVE DIFFERENCES IN MODES OF VISUAL INFORMATION PROCESSING

In this section, I consider another theme in some of the recent literature in the field of visual information processing. As with the earlier theme, this one is not captured well nor represented explicitly in the simple model of visual information processing shown in Fig. 16.1. The idea is that qualitatively different kinds of processing can operate on visual input depending on factors such as the kind of visual analysis required, strategies employed by the individual perceiver, and the level of development of the perceiver. Recently, a number of investigators have suggested sets of such *modal* differences in perception and information processing. (See Pick & Saltzman, 1978, for an entire volume devoted to this issue.) Types of modal differences that have been proposed include the difference between *automatic* and *attended* or *controlled* processing (Posner, Nissen & Ogden, 1978; Shiffrin & Schneider, 1977; Schneider & Shiffrin, 1977), the distinction between categorical and noncategorical perception (Studdert-Kennedy, Liberman, Harris, & Cooper, 1970), and the difference between processing visual information with respect to subjective versus objectve reference systems (Attneave & Benson, 1969; Rieser & Pick, 1976), to name but a few.

The distinction that I focus on is between *holistic* and *analytic* modes of processing visual information. These dichotomous labels have been used to characterize processing differences in a variety of situations—from differences in the operations underlying *same* and *different* responses in visual comparison tasks (Bamber, 1969) to differences in the way the two cerebral hemispheres of the brain operate on visual information (Cohen, 1973; Egeth & Epstein, 1972). Because the domains in which these descriptive terms have been applied is so diverse, it is unlikely that any unitary form of holistic or analytic processing underlies all the performance differences characterized in these ways. However, the very use of the dichotomous terms suggests qualitative differences in information processing that may be specific to particular types of tasks. Following, I discuss just three cases to which the holistic-analytic distinction seems to apply. Again, the suggestion is not that a single type of holistic or analytic processing is appropriate in all three cases. However, similarities among the processing differences in the three cases will be pointed out when they exist.

Sequencing of Types of Visual Analysis

A currently popular view of the processes involved in perceiving and interpreting complex visual input is one that holds that an early holistic, global, or preattentive type of processing is followed by more analytic processing of detailed local information (Broadbent, 1977; Neisser, 1967). This is similar to Banks and Prinzmetal's idea of a perceptual parser that identifies regions of a visual array on the basis of overall configural properties and then analyzes local features of the segregated regions. The purpose of the first analysis of the input as a whole is to make a preliminary identification of potentially useful and informative parts of the input to which later analysis can be efficiently directed and from which additional information can be extracted (cf., Neisser's, 1976, concept of the perceptual cycle). Presumably, a single global stage of processing is not necessarily followed by an analytic stage whose cessation terminates interpretation of visual input. Rather, global and local types of processing are continually interacting in perceiving complex visual displays.

There have been many experimental demonstrations of this idea of an initial holistic mode of processing followed by a more analytic mode, and I mention only two recent sets of studies. One is a series of experiments by Navon (1977) designed to put global information against local information in an interference situation. The stimuli in some of Navon's experiments were visual displays of a large letter (either *H* or *S*) composed of small letters that were the same in identity as the large letter or different. In one experiment, the stimulus letters were presented tachistoscopically, and subjects had to determine whether an *h* or an *s* had been presented. In one condition, the judgments were made with respect to the global identity of the letter; in the other condition, the identity of the local elements was to be indicated. Overall, *global-directed* response times were faster than *local-directed* times. Of particular interest is the finding that the identity of local elements had no effect (either beneficial or harmful) on response times when subjects were to base their decisions on the global identity of the letter. However, when decisions were based on the local identity of component letters, conflicting global information led to a substantial increase in response time. These results indicate that global processing must be undertaken even when only local information is relevant to the task but not vice versa. (However, see Kinchla & Wolf, 1979, for an alternative interpretation of this and related experiments.)

Another and somewhat different sort of evidence for a holistic level of visual processing followed by an analytic one comes from an experiment on recognition memory for line drawings of scenes done by Parker (1978). Subjects studied target pictures that were line drawings of scenes containing six objects. They were then shown a recognition series in which the distractors were systematic transformations of the targets. The transformations included deletion of an object or a change in an object. The changes could be in the object's size, the substitution of one object by an object with a different identity, or the substitution of an object with an object of the same identity but different physical characteristics. On each recognition trial, both the time time to respond *same* or *different* and the subject's pattern and duration of eye fixations were recorded.

Of particular relevance is the finding that on *different* trials on which the distractor had one object deleted, reaction times were quite rapid, and subjects often failed to fixate the position corresponding to the missing object. This suggests that an initial global analysis of the test picture was sufficient to determine that the overall configuration—the relative portions of figure and ground—had changed. On other types of *different* trials, subjects often broke away from their typical order of scanning objects in the picture (that was found on *same* trials) and jumped ahead to the differing object before initiating a response. This suggests that an initial holistic processing of the picture provided enough information to form a hypothesis about the changed region and to direct fixation to that location for further, more detailed analysis. In summary, then, both the studies of Navon and Parker and other considerations (see Lockhead, 1972) indicate the existence of two qualitatively different types of visual processing—holistic or global parsing of regions of a visual array, followed by and interacting with an analysis of local information from one (or more) of the segregated regions.

Differences in Strategies
for Visual Memory Comparison

The holistic–analytic distinction may also apply to individual differences in strategies for processing visual information. The case that I consider in detail is a series of experiments on *same–different* visual comparison done in my laboratory (Cooper, 1976, 1979a, b; Cooper & Podgorny, 1976). In these experiments, subjects were shown an initial or standard visual shape and had to determine whether a sequentially presented second shape was identical to or different from the first shape. Fig. 16.6 shows the standards and test shapes from a typical experiment. *Different* test shapes were random perturbations of the standard shapes, and they varied in their similarity to the standards, ranging from highly similar to very dissimilar.

At the level of the group data, reaction time for responding *different* decreased monotonically with increasing dissimilarity between the standard and the test shapes, and *same* responses were of intermediate speed. At the level of single subject data, though, the picture changes considerably. Some subjects (generally, the majority) show the same pattern as the group data but in a more accentuated form. For other subjects, there is no effect of the similarity between the standard and the test shape on *different* reaction times, and *same* responses are faster than all *different* responses. This latter group of subjects has response times that are considerably faster than subjects in the first group. It is also important that these differences in patterns of reaction times occur in the absence of any differences in the pattern or magnitude of errors for the two types of subjects. For both subject groups, error rates decrease monotonically with increasing dissimilarity between the standard and the test shape. So, in the case of the subjects affected by similarity, reaction times and error rates are positively correlated; in the case of the other subjects, there is no correlation between times and errors. Figure 16.7 shows reaction time and error data for the two subject types from a typical experiment.

Because the difference between these two types of subjects involves an entire pattern of performance—including sensitivity to similarity, overall response speed, relative speed of the *same* response, and the relationship

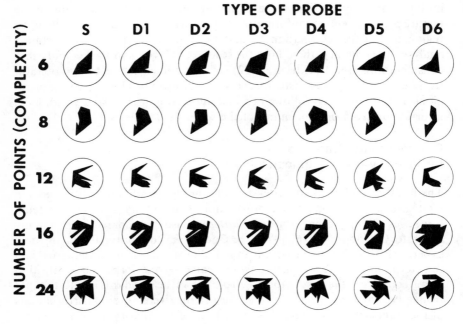

FIG. 16.6.   Standard shapes and distractors varying in their similarity used in *same–different* visual comparison experiments. (From Cooper & Podgorny, 1976.)

between reaction time and error rate—I have interpreted it as reflecting qualitatively different strategies for comparing a visual memory representation with an external visual test shape. If the two strategies are conceptualized in the following way, the principal patterns in the data can be accounted for. The subjects unaffected by similarity could be comparing a visual memory representation with a test shape in a holistic, perhaps parallel, fashion, attempting to find a match between the two visual representations. If a match is found, the *same* response is executed; if no match is achieved, the *different* response is made essentially by default without further analysis.

The subjects affected by similarity could be using a more analytic comparison process specialized for detecting differences between the visual features of the memory representation of the standard and the test shape. If a *different* response is executed as soon as this process finds a feature that distinguishes the memory representation from the test shape, then the greater the dissimilarity between the two visual representations, the earlier a difference will be detected and the faster will be the response. A second process (perhaps like the single holistic comparison process of the other subject type) could operate simultaneously with the difference detection process and lead to the execution of the *same* response. (See Bamber, 1969, for a description of this *dual-*

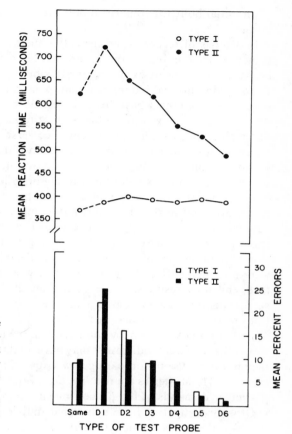

FIG. 16.7. Mean reaction time and mean percent error in a *same–different* visual comparison task reported by Cooper (1979b). Reaction times and errors are plotted separately for the holistic (Type I, open circles and bars) and analytic (Type II, filled circles and bars) processors.

process model of same–different comparison and Cooper, 1976, 1979a, b, for a more detailed account of the nature of these comparison strategies and how they account for the obtained performance differences.)

Note that the holistic–analytic distinction is used in a somewhat different way to charcterize the differences in individual subjects' comparison strategies than it was in the earlier section on types of visual analysis used to interpret a complex visual display. Unlike that earlier case, in the present case the *quality* of visual information extracted by the two types of processes does not differ, because the two types of subjects have virtually equivalent error rates. Like the earlier case, though, the holistic process postulated for some subjects in the present experiments proceeds more rapidly than the analytic process postulated for other subjects. Note, too, that the holistic comparison operation is all that is logically needed to perform the same–different discrimination. Thus, the more analytic comparison operation used by some of the subjects may be an optional, additional process used to check the outcome

of an initial holistic comparison of the test shape with the memory representation.

In a series of recent experiments (Cooper, 1979b), I have tried to gain a
firmer understanding of the nature of the comparison processes used by
individual subjects by exploring the flexibility of the strategies in the face of
various stimulus and judgmental manipulations. To summarize these experiments very briefly, I have been successful in creating processing demands
that will cause a given individual subject to switch from holistic to analytic
processing and, to a limited extent, vice versa. When the comparison task
requires an explicit report of information differentiating a memory representation from a test shape, as well as an overall same–different comparison,
some holistic subjects will switch to an analytic strategy. And, when multidimensional stimuli composed of separable dimensions (size, shape, and
color) are used in the visual memory comparison task, all subjects exhibit
data consistent with analytic processing. The only task thus far in which all
subjects give evidence of holistic processing involved same–different comparison of photographs of female faces. For all subjects, *different* reaction times
were minimally affected by similarity between a face in memory and a test
face, and *same* responses were faster than all *different* responses. What this
suggests is that the photographs of faces were treated as holistic configurations rather than being analyzed into constitutent features that could serve as
a basis for analytic memory comparisons. In summary, this line of research
shows that different individuals may have qualitatively distinct strategies that
they normally use in comparing new visual input with visual information in
memory. The strategies are flexible, however, and can be manipulated by the
particular demands of the processing situation.

Other investigators have uncovered individual differences that might be
thought of as holistic–analytic-processing distinctions. For example, Hock
and his collaborators (Hock, 1973; Hock, Gordon, & Gold, 1975; Hock,
Gordon, & Marcus, 1974) have found quantitative differences among subjects in same–different visual comparison experiments. The *same* responses of
some subjects are relatively more affected by stimulus variables like symmetry, rotation, and uppercase–lowercase difference than are the responses of
other subjects. Hock labels the more affected subjects *structural* processors
and the less affected subjects *analytic* processors. Although some kind of
processing dichotomy certainly exists in Hock's experiments, it does not
appear to be related to the differences just presented (Cooper, 1979c).

Developmental Trends in Modes
of Processing Visual Information

A third area in which the analytic–holistic distinction may be useful is the
development of ways of processing visual information. Many theorists have
argued that perceptual development proceeds from a holistic or undifferen-

tiated mode to a more analytic or differentiated one (Bruner, Olver, & Greenfield, 1966; Gibson, 1969). Recently, Smith and Kemler (1977; Kemler and Smith, 1978) have done an interesting set of experiments testing and further articulating this hypothesis. The basic notion behind their experiments is that stimuli composed of dimensional combinations that are perceived separably (Garner, 1974) by adults might be perceived integrally or more holistically by young children. They found that young children classified visual stimuli varying in size and brightness on the basis of overall similarity relations (implicating integral perception), whereas older children classified the same stimuli on the basis of their dimensional composition (Smith & Kemler, 1977).

The developmental picture is not quite so simple as a progression from perceptual integrality to increasing separability, however. In subsequent experiments, Kemler and Smith (1978) have shown that even young children can access the dimensional structure of stimuli and use this structure as a basis for responding. But, they tend not to use dimensional relations unless the task is very difficult to perform on the basis of similarity relations. These studies thus suggest that the use of holistic versus analytic modes of processing is determined by a host of factors including the structure of the stimuli, the nature of the task, and the developmental status of the perceiver.

Evidence of a quite different sort pointing to a developmental discontinuity in visual information processing has been provided by Carey and Diamond's (1977; Diamond & Carey, 1977) investigation of the perception of faces. Carey and Diamond argue that processing of faces by young children is done on the basis of "piecemeal" information—or analysis of individual features of a face. Older children and adults, however, make use of overall configural information in recognizing faces. Their evidence for this claim is twofold. First, young children are more likely than older children to accept as the same two different faces that share some extraneous feature, such as an article of clothing like a hat. Second, young children's recognition performance on upright and inverted faces is about equal, whereas older chlidren show a marked superiority in recognizing upright over inverted faces. Presumably, holistic processing of configural information is possible only when faces are shown in the canonical, upright orientation. So, the fact that young children do no better on upright than on inverted faces indicates that they cannot make use of configural information in recognizing faces.

At first blush, these findings seem to contradict Kemler and Smith's contention that visual information processing generally proceeds from holistic to analytic with development. However, Carey and Diamond's claim of a developmental trend from analytic to holistic processing may apply only to the peculiar case of human faces. They found that recognition of houses—another visual stimulus with a canonical orientation—was no better when the stimulus was presented upright than when it was presented inverted, for older children. Younger children, though, had worse recognition for inverted than for upright houses. So, the developmental trend in visual processing for materials other than faces may be toward greater efficiency in the analysis of component features.

Summary

In this section, I have selected one *modal* distinction between types of visual information processing—loosely termed *holistic* and *analytic*—and have shown that the distinction may be useful in understanding quite varied problems. The three cases to which I have tried to apply the distinction include levels of visual analysis, individual differences in processing strategies, and developmental changes in modes of processing visual information. No doubt there are other problems to which this processing distinction could be applied (e.g., differences in the way the hemispheres process visual information), as well as a host of other qualitative processing differences, some of which were mentioned at the beginning of this section. The general approach of isolating modal processing differences is, I think, a promising one. It emphasizes the diversity of processing strategies available and the flexibility in the use of processing skills in different situations. This approach represents renewed attention in the field of visual information processing toward investigation of large-scale sources of processing differences—including developmental changes and individual differences—rather than exclusive concentration on the processes by which a typical subject performs a particular task.

CONCLUDING REMARKS

I close this chapter much as I began it, emphasizing what I have and have not tried to accomplish. I have not provided a review of the field of visual information processing. Because of the variety of problems, levels of analysis, and experimental techniques studied and used by workers in this area, visual information processing is not a coherent field of study. Rather, I have pointed to two themes or recent concerns in work on visual information processing. The first of these themes is a renewed interest in the role of visual structure and organization in information processing, and the second is the idea of qualitative or modal differences in types of visual analysis.

Within each theme, I have presented a selected review of recent relevant literature. One purpose of these reviews has been to show that a variety of research using different experimental paradigms and addressing seemingly distinct problems coherently reflects the two central themes. In the case of the theme of organization and visual information processing, evidence was reviewed from experiments ranging from detection situations to judgments of aspects of perceptual structure. In the case of the theme of modes of visual information processing, problems of individual differences and developmental trends were shown to be relevant. Nonetheless, the work reviewed was drawn almost exclusively from the "traditional" information-processing literature. For example, the significant and continuing contributions of Gibson and his co-workers (Gibson, 1950, 1966, 1979) to an understanding of the nature and structure of visual information have not been mentioned, for such a discussion—though certainly relevant—is beyond the designated scope of this chapter.

Another purpose of these reviews has been to point out inadequacies in general conceptualizations of visual information processing similar to that schematized in Fig. 16.1. The outline in Fig. 16.1 presents a large number of processing operations interacting in complex ways. Yet, clearly, the model is oversimplified in the two respects discussed in this chapter. First, the nature of the information that serves as input to the processing system is not specified except, perhaps, at the level of visual features. Second, the model does not capture the flexibility implied by differences in strategies or processing modes that might characterize individual subjects, stages of development, or levels of visual analysis. Recent attention to issues of visual organization and processing flexibility may indicate a growing awareness that simple feature analysis followed by a series of processing operations does not provide an adequate account of the complexities of visual information processing. Hopefully, continuing research effort will help to unravel some of these complexities.

ACKNOWLEDGMENTS

Preparation of this chapter was supported by National Science Foundation Grant BNS 76-22079 to the author.

REFERENCES

Akin, O., & Chase, W. Quantification of three-dimensional structures. *Journal of Experimental Psychology: Human Perception and Performance,* 1978, *4,* 397–410.

Anderson, J. R. Arguments concerning representations for mental imagery. *Psychological Review,* 1978, *85,* 249–277.

Arnoult, M. D. Prediction of perceptual responses from structural characteristics of the stimulus. *Perceptual and Motor Skills,* 1960, *11,* 261–268.

Attneave, F. Some informational aspects of visual perception. *Psychological Review,* 1954, *61,* 183–193.

Attneave, F. Physical determinants of the judged complexity of shapes. *Journal of Experimental Psychology,* 1957, *53,* 221–227.

Attneave, F., & Benson, B. Spatial coding of tactual stimulation. *Journal of Experimental Psychology,* 1969, *81,* 216–222.

Bamber, D. Reaction times and error rates for "same"–"different" judgments of multidimensional stimuli. *Perception & Psychophysics*, 1969, *6*, 169–174.

Banks, W. P., & Prinzmetal, W. Configurational effects in visual information processing. *Perception & Psychophysics*, 1976, *19*, 361–367.

Bartram, D. J. Post-iconic visual storage: Chunking in the reproduction of briefly dislayed visual patterns. *Cognitive Psychology*, 1978, *10*, 324–355.

Bell, H. H., & Handel, S. The role of pattern goodness in the reproduction of backward masked patterns. *Journal of Experimental Psychology: Human Perception and Performance*, 1976, *2*, 139–150.

Biederman, I. Perceiving real-world scenes. *Science*, 1972, *177*, 77–79.

Biederman, I., Glass, A. L., & Stacey, E. W., Jr. Searching for objects in real-world scenes. *Journal of Experimental Psychology*, 1973, *97*, 22–27.

Biederman, I., Rabinowitz, J. C., Glass, A. L., & Stacey, E. W., Jr. On the information extracted from a glance at a scene. *Journal of Experimental Psychology*, 1974, *103*, 597–600.

Bower, G. H., & Glass, A. L. Structural units and the redintegrative power of picture fragments. *Journal of Experimental Psychology: Human Learning and Memory*, 1976, *2*, 456–466.

Broadbent, D. E. The hidden preattentive processes. *American Psychologist*, 1977, *32*, 109–118.

Bruner, J. S., Olver, R. R., & Greenfield, P. M. *Studies in cognitive growth*. New York: Wiley, 1966.

Carey, S., & Diamond, R. From piecemeal to configurational representation of faces. *Science*, 1977, *195*, 312–314.

Checkosky, S. F., & Whitlock, D. The effects of pattern goodness on recognition time in a memory search task. *Journal of Experimental Psychology*, 1973, *100*, 341–348.

Chipman, S. F. Complexity and structure in visual patterns. *Journal of Experimental Psychology: General*, 1977, *106*, 269–301.

Cohen, G. Hemispheric differences in serial versus parallel processing. *Journal of Experimental Psychology*, 1973, *97*, 349–356.

Conrad, R. Acoustic confusions in immediate memory. *British Journal of Psychology*, 1964, *55*, 75–84.

Cooper, L. A. Individual differences in visual comparison processes. *Perception & Psychophysics*, 1976, *19*, 433–444.

Cooper, L. A. Spatial information processing: Strategies for research. In R. E. Snow, P. A. Federico, & W. E. Montague (Eds.), *Aptitude, learning, and instruction: Cognitive process analyses.* Hillsdale, N.J.: Lawrence Erlbaum Associates, 1980 (a)

Cooper, L. A. *Individual differences in visual processing I: Comparison strategies and processing flexibility.* Paper in preparation, 1980. (b)

Cooper, L. A. *Individual differences in visual processing II: Exploring relationships among sets of processing dichotomies.* Paper in preparation, 1980. (c)

Cooper, L. A., & Podgorny, P. Mental transformations and visual comparison processes: Effects of complexity and similarity. *Journal of Experimental Psychology: Human Perception and Performance*, 1976, *2*, 503–514.

Cooper, L. A., & Shepard, R. N. Transformations on representations of objects in space. In E. C. Carterette & M. Friedman (Eds.), *Handbook of perception, (Vol. VIII), Perceptual coding.* New York: Academic Press, 1978.

Cunningham, J. P. Free trees and bidirectional trees as representations of psychological distance. *Journal of Mathematical Psychology*, 1978, *17*, 165–188.

Cunningham, J. P. *Trees as memory representations for simple visual patterns.* Unpublished manuscript, 1979.

Diamond, R., & Carey, S. Developmental changes in the representation of faces. *Journal of Experimental Child Psychology*, 1977, *23*, 1–22.

Egeth, H., & Epstein, J. Differential specialization of the cerebral hemispheres for the perception of sameness and difference. *Perception & Psychophysics*, 1972, *12*, 218–220.

Estes, W. K. Interactions of signal and background variables in visual processing. *Perception & Psychophysics*, 1972, *12*, 278–286.

Garner, W. R. To perceive is to know. *American Psychologist*, 1966, *21*, 11–19.

Garner, W. R. *The processing of information and structure*. Potomac, Md: Lawrence Erlbaum Associates, 1974.

Gibson, E. J. *Principles of perceptual learning and development*. Englewood Cliffs, N.J.: Prentice-Hall, Inc., 1969.

Gibson, J. J. *The perception of the visual world*. Boston: Houghton Mifflin, 1950.

Gibson, J. J. *The senses considered as perceptual systems*. Boston: Houghton Mifflin, 1966.

Gibson, J. J. *An ecological approach to visual perception*. Boston: Houghton Mifflin, 1979.

Hemenway, K., & Palmer, S. E. Organizational factors in perceived dimensionality. *Journal of Experimental Psychology: Human Perception and Performance*, 1978, *4*, 388–396.

Hochberg, J. In the mind's eye. In R. N. Haber (Ed.), *Contemporary theory and research in visual perception*. New York: Holt, Rinehart and Winston, 1968.

Hochberg, J. Organization and the gestalt tradition. In E. C. Carterette & M. Friedman (Eds.), *Handbook of perception* (Vol. 1). New York: Academic Press, 1974.

Hochberg, J., & Brooks, V. The psychophysics of form: Reversible perspective drawings of spatial objects. *American Journal of Psychology*, 1960, *73*, 337–354.

Hochberg, J., & McAlister, E. A quantitative approach to figural "goodness." *Journal of Experimental Psychology* 1953, *46*, 361–364.

Hock, H. S. The effects of stimulus structure and familiarity on same–different comparison. *Perception & Psychophysics*, 1973, *14*, 413–420.

Hock, H. S., Gordon, G. P., & Gold, L. Individual differences in the verbal coding of familiar visual stimuli. *Memory & Cognition*, 1975, *3*, 257–262.

Hock, H. S., Gordon, G. P., & Marcus, N. Individual differences in the detection of embedded figures. *Perception & Psychophysics*, 1974, *15*, 47–52.

Hubel, D. H., & Wiesel, T. N. Receptive fields, binocular interaction and functional architecture in the cat's visual cortex. *Journal of Physiology*, 1962, *160*, 106–154.

Hubel, D. H., & Wiesel, T. N. Receptive fields and functional architecture in two nonstriate visual areas (18 and 19) of the cat. *Journal of Neurophysiology*, 1965, *28*, 229–289.

Hubel, D. H., & Wiesel, T. N. Receptive fields and functional architecture of monkey striate cortex. *Journal of Physiology*, 1968, *195*, 215–243.

Kemler, D. G., & Smith, L. B. Is there a developmental trend from integrality to separability in perception? *Journal of Experimental Child Psychology*, 1978, *14*, 653–673.

Kinchla, R. A., & Wolf, J. The order of visual processing: "Top-down," "bottom-up," or "middle-out"? *Perception & Psychophysics*, 1979, *25*, 225–231.

Koffka, K. *Principles of gestalt psychology*. New York: Harcourt, Brace and World, 1963.

Kosslyn, S. M., & Pomerantz, J. R. Imagery, propositions, and the form of internal representations. *Cognitive Psychology*, 1977, *9*, 52–76.

Lindsay, P. H., & Norman, D. A. *Human information processing*. New York: Academic Press, 1977.

Lockhead, G. R. Processing dimensional stimuli. *Psychological Review*, 1972, *79*, 410–419.

McClelland, J. L. Perception and masking of wholes and parts. *Journal of Experimental Psychology: Human Perception and Performance*, 1978, *4*, 210–223.

McCollough, C. Color adaptation of edge-detectors in the human visual system. *Science*, 1965, *149*, 115–116.

Monahan, J. S., & Lockhead, F. R. Identification of integral stimuli. *Journal of Experimental Psychology: General*, 1977, *106*, 94–110.

Navon, D. Forest before trees: The precedence of global features in perception. *Cognitive Psychology*, 1977, *9*, 353–383.

Neisser, U. *Cognitive psychology*. New York: Appleton-Century Crofts, 1967.

Neisser, U. *Cognition and reality*. San Francisco: Freeman, 1976.

Palmer, S. E. Visual perception and world knowledge: Notes on a model of sensory-cognitive interaction. In D. A. Norman & D. E. Rumelhart (Eds.), *Explorations in cognition.* San Francisco: Freeman, 1975.

Palmer, S. E. Hierarchical structure in perceptual representation. *Cognitive Psychology,* 1977, *9,* 441–474.

Palmer, S. E. Structural aspects of visual similarity. *Memory & Cognition,* 1978, *6,* 91–97.

Parker, R. E. Picture processing during recognition. *Journal of Experimental Psychology: Human Perception and Performance,* 1978, *4,* 284–293.

Pick, H. L., & Saltzman, E. *Modes of perceiving and processing information.* Hillsdale, N.J.: Lawrence Erlbaum Associates, 1978.

Pomerantz, J. R. Are complex visual features derived from simple ones? In E. Leeuwenberg & H. Buffart (Eds.), *Formal theories of visual perception.* Sussex, England: Wiley Ltd., 1978.

Pomerantz, J. R., & Garner, W. R. Stimulus configuration in selective attention tasks. *Perception & Psychophysics,* 1973, *14,* 565–569.

Pomerantz, J. R., & Sager, L. C. Line-slope vs. line-arrangement discrimination: A comment on Ambler and Finklea's paper. *Perception & Psychophysics,* 1976, *20,* 220.

Pomerantz, J. R., Sager, L. C., & Stoever, R. J. Perception of wholes and of their component parts: Some configural superiority effects. *Journal of Experimental Psychology: Human Perception and Performance,* 1977, *3,* 422–435.

Pomerantz, J. R., & Schwaitzberg, S. D. Grouping by proximity: Selective attention measures. *Perception & Psychophysics,* 1975, *18,* 355–361.

Posner, M. I., Boies, S. J., Eichelman, W. H., & Taylor, R. L. Retention of visual and name codes of single letters. *Journal of Experimental Psychology Monograph,* 1969, *79* (1, Pt. 2).

Posner, M. I., Nissen, M. J., & Ogden, W. C. Attended and unattended processing modes: The role of set for spatial location. In H. L. Pick, Jr., & E. Saltzman (Eds.), *Modes of perceiving and processing information.* Hillsdale, N.J.: Lawrence Erlbaum Associates, 1978.

Prinzmetal, W., & Banks, W. P. Good continuation affects visual detection. *Perception & Psychophysics,* 1977, *21,* 389–395.

Reed, S. K. Structural descriptions and the limitations of visual images. *Memory & Cognition,* 1974, *2,* 329–336.

Reed, S. K., & Johnsen, J. A. Detection of parts in patterns and images. *Memory & Cognition,* 1975, 569–575.

Rieser, J. J., & Pick, H. L., Jr. Reference systems and the perception of tactual and haptic orientation. *Perception & Psychophysics,* 1976, *19,* 117–121.

Schneider, W., & Shiffrin, R. M. Controlled and automatic human information processing: I. Detection, search, and attention. *Psychological Review,* 1977, *84,* 1–66.

Schnore, M. M., & Partington, J. T. Immediate memory for visual patterns: Symmetry and amount of information. *Psychonomic Science,* 1967, *8,* 421–422.

Shepard, R. N. Form, formation, and transformations of internal representations. In R. Solso (Ed.), *Information processing and cognition: The Loyola Symposium.* Hillsdale, N.J. Lawrence Erlbaum Associates, 1975.

Shiffrin, R. M., & Schneider, W. Controlled and automatic human information processing: II. Perceptual learning, automatic attending, and a general theory. *Psychological Review,* 1977, *84,* 127–190.

Smith, L. B., & Kemler, D. G. Developmental trends in free classification: Evidence for a new conceptualization of perceptual development. *Journal of Experimental Child Psychology,* 1977, *24,* 279–298.

Spoehr, K. T., & Smith, E. E. The role of orthographic and phonotactic rules in perceiving letter patterns. *Journal of Experimental Psychology: Human Perception and Performance,* 1975, *1,* 21–34.

Sternberg, S. The discovery of processing stages: Extensions of Donders' method. In W. G. Koster (Ed.), *Attention and performance II. Acta Psychologica,* 1969, *30,* 276–315.

Stromeyer, C. F. Further studies of the McCollough effect. *Perception & Psychophysics*, 1969, *6*, 105–110.

Studdert-Kennedy, M., Liberman, A. M., Harris, K. S., & Cooper, F. S. The motor theory of perception: A reply to Lane's critical review. *Psychological Review*, 1970, *77*, 234–249.

Thompson, A. L., & Klatzky, R. L. Studies of visual synthesis: Integration of fragments into forms. *Journal of Experimental Psychology: Human Perception and Performance*, 1978, *4*, 244–263.

Townsend, J. T. Issues and models concerning the processing of a finite number of inputs. In B. H. Kantowitz (Ed.), *Human information processing: Tutorials in performance and cognition*. Hillsdale, N.J.: Lawrence Erlbaum Associates, 1974.

Weisstein, N., & Harris, C. S. Visual detection of line segments: An object superiority effect. *Science*, 1974, *186*, 752–755.

Wertheimer, M. Principles of perceptual organization. In D. D. Beardslee & M. Wertheimer (Eds.), *Readings in perception*, Princeton, N.J.: Van Nostrand, 1958.

Williams, A., & Weisstein, N. Line segments are perceived better in a coherent context than alone: An object-line effect in visual perception. *Memory & Cognition*, 1978, *6*, 85–90.

17
Measuring the Reaction Time of A Shift of Visual Attention*

George Sperling
New York University, New York and
Bell Laboratories, Murray Hill, New Jersey

Adam Reeves†
New York University, New York
United States

ABSTRACT

The reaction time for shifting attention from a target letter at the left of fixation to a stream of numerals at the right of fixation is measured by noting the earliest-occurring numeral an observer can report. In addition to this attention reaction time (ART), the observer produces a conventional motor reaction time (MRT) by indicating target detection with a finger movement. ARTs and MRTs have comparable distributions over trials, but ARTs vary more with the difficulty of targets than do MRTs to the same targets. The results are accounted for by a two-stage three-component model of reaction times consisting of a shared *detection* component (in which detection for attention responses requires 50% longer processing than detection for motor responses) followed by independent attention and motor response-generating components. A *metal snapshot* model is proposed to account for the functioning of the attention response-component.

†Now at Institut für Arbeitsphysiologie, Universität Dortmund, West Germany. The experimental work was carried out at New York University, and the article was prepared while the second author was a postdoctoral fellow at Bell Laboratories, Murray Hill, N.J.

*A summary of the material in this article was first presented at the Psychonomic Society, 17th Annual Meeting, St. Louis, Mo., 11 Nov. 1976. For reprints, write to G. Sperling, Room 2D-518, Bell Laboratories, Murray Hill, N.J. 07974.

INTRODUCTION

As any party goer or student can testify, it is possible to look fixedly at one thing while paying attention to another. Psychologists, too, have long believed that one's visual attention can be shifted from one object to another with no discernable outward sign such as a change in eye position (Helmholtz, 1924, p. 455; James, 1890, p. 437; Wundt, 1924, p. 20). The experimental procedure described here is an objective method for measuring such a covert shift in visual attention.

PROCEDURE

Outline. A subject is instructed to maintain steady eye fixation on a fixation dot shown on a cathode-ray oscilloscope. To the left of the fixation dot a steady stream of letters appears; to the right is a steady stream of numerals. The letters appear one after the other, in the same location, at a rate of 4.6 letters per second. The subject's task is to detect a target in the letter stream and then, without moving his eyes from the dot, to report the earliest possible numeral from the numeral stream—preferably the numeral that occurred simultaneously with the target.

In our experiments, the target was any one of the three symbols: the letters U or C or an outline square. It was presented at a randomly determined location in the letter stream between the ninth and the twentieth letters. The numerals appeared, in various conditions, at rates of 4.6, 6.9, 9.1, or 13.4 per second. The stimulus conditions are designed so that subjects report they have to give "full attention" to the letter stream in order to detect the targets reliably, and they have to "shift attention" to report the numeral. In fact, subjects seldom succeeded in reporting the simultaneous numeral, and they actually reported a numeral that occurred later. The time delay between the target letter on the left and the reported numeral on the right defines an attention reaction time (ART): The earlier in the sequence is the reported numeral, the quicker is the inferred ART. From a series of trials, we can obtain an entire distribution of ARTs.

Stimuli. The stimuli were composed of vectors generated by a Digital Equipment Corp. PDP/15 computer on an oscilloscope with a fast P4 phosphor. Stimuli were viewed binocularly at a distance of 0.69 m. The height of the letters and numbers was 1.75 cm (1.45 deg) and they were separated (center to center) by 2.25 cm (1.87 deg). Characters were refreshed three times during a display period of 3.6 msec. The screen was blank between characters. The total luminous energy per character varied from 1.92×10^{-6} cd-sec for I to $3.33 \ 10^{-6}$ cd-sec for W. Background luminance of the display was 0.10 cd/m^2

for subject AR, and the room illumination was approximately 0.9 m-cd. For the other two subjects, these figures were, respectively, 0.35 cd/ m² and 0.5 m-cd. See Sperling (1971) for calibration methods.

Eye Position.   Objective measurements of eye position showed that subjects did indeed maintain fixation as instructed. (1) One subject's eye movements were measured by an electro-oculogram method whose sensitivity was determined to be amply sufficient to detect a movement from the fixation dot to either of the character streams. In several sessions that yielded typical data, such eye movements did not occur. (2) A saccadic eye movement made during viewing of the displays frequently causes the apearance of multiple images of the display. In the early practice sessions, subjects quickly learned to suppress eye movements to avoid these multiple images.

Motor Reaction Time, Critical Interval.   On each trial, in addition to reporting the numeral, the subject also had to make a more traditional response to each appearance of the target: He had to lift his finger from a key as soon as he detected the target. The set of motor reaction times (MRTs) for the finger response serves as a standard of comparison for the covert attention response in which we were primarily interested. The motor reaction time includes the time of many component processes (e.g., detection of the target, response selection, muscle contraction, and finally, sufficient movement of the finger to activate the response key). As we shall show later, the components of an attention reaction time include some processes shared in common with the motor reaction and others that are particular to the numeral selection task. By analogy to the MRT, the ART refers not merely to a single component but to all the component processes that intervene between the occurrence of a target and the response (finger movement or numeral selection) being measured.

As in traditional reaction-time experiments, the subject was instructed to make the motor response (lifting his finger from the key) as quickly as possible (i.e., as early as possible in an interval immediately following the onset of the target stimulus, called the *critical interval*). The reaction-key response terminated the display after 1 sec. In reaction-time experiments, when a subject responds too soon or too late, he is admonished to be more careful; those responses are assumed to be false and are discarded. Based on preliminary experiments, we defined the critical interval as 170 to 1700 msec after the target onset. When a response occurred outside the critical interval, the subject was so informed, and the trial was omitted from the data analysis. Overall, this occurred on 1.6% of the trials. As subjects became more experienced, it became obvious that the critical interval was overly generous—it could have been shortened to less than 1 sec without substantially altering the fraction of rejected data.

Attention Reaction Times, Critical Sets.   In measuring the attention reaction times, the *critical interval* is replaced by a *critical set* of numerals in the
numeral stream. Usually, the critical set was defined as the seven consecutive
numerals that begin with the first numeral occurring subsequent to the target.
However, the position of the critical set was adjusted somewhat with conditions to ensure that it did not limit the subject's performance. For example,
with very slow numeral rates, when the subject could occasionally report the
numeral simultaneous with the target, the critical set included the numerals in
the zero position (simultaneous) and in the −1 position.

On every trial, the seven numerals of the critical set, plus the two preceding
and the one following, always comprised a sequence of 10 all-different
numerals. The subject was instructed to detect the target letter and then to
report the earliest-seen numeral in the critical set of numerals. He typed his
response on a keyboard in front of him and immediately received feedback in
the form of a display of the critical set. If a numeral had been typed in that was
not in the critical set, the word *WRONG* was displayed. Overall, this occurred
3% of the time.

RESULTS

MRTs and ARTs

Typical Results.   The procedure and some typical data are summarized in
Fig. 17.1. The columns on the left side show a sample of a typical stimulus
sequence. The fixation point was always present. A new letter appeared every
218 msec in the letter stream, and (in this example) a new numeral, every 109
msec in the numeral stream. The target here was the letter C. The numeral that
appeared at the same time as the target—in this case a 6—is defined as being in
position 0; the critical set consists of the numerals in positions 1 through 7.

Sample responses are shown in the middle columns of Fig. 17.1. For the
attention-shift response, the subject typed in the numeral 9 (the third numeral
in the critical set). The motor response occurred with an RT of about 400
msec.

The graphs on the right side of Fig. 17.1 show actual data of one subject for
this condition. The graph of attention reaction time (ART) shows the proportion of times the subject responded with numerals in each position of the
critical set. The numeral in the +3 position was the most frequently made
response. The mean ART occurred 457 msec after the target; the standard
deviation was 79 msec. The graph of motor reaction time (MRT) shows the
distribution of latencies for the finger-lifting response. The mean of this
distribution was 436 msec; the standard deviation, 73 msec. In this example,
the mean ART is slower than the mean MRT; however, ARTs can be either
faster or slower than the MRTs, depending on the conditions and the subjects.

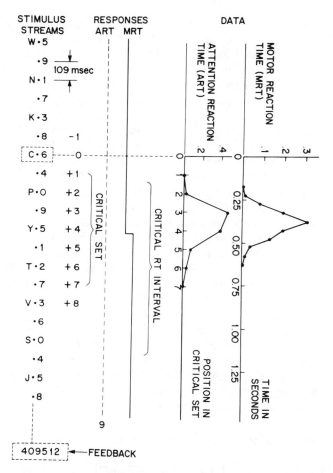

FIG. 17.1. Procedures and typical results of the ART and MRT measurements. Stimulus streams are shown at left. The subject sees only the letters, the fixation dots, and the numerals. Each row represents a single display, briefly flashed and superimposed on the preceding display. The target letter is a C. The critical set of numerals and the critical reaction-time periods are indicated. MRT indicates the finger (motor) reaction-time key, and ART indicates the attention-shift reaction "9". Feedback indicates the answer display (first six numerals of critical set) shown to the subject after his ART response. The results show the actual observed MRT distribution and the observed ART distribution (proportion of times a numeral corresponding to each position is named) for 414 trials in this particular condition: letter stream rate 4.6 per second, target C, numeral rate 9.1 per second, recall of one letter, subject AR.

Statistical Problems in the Treatment of ART Responses

The MRT distribution is a complete probability distribution and all moments can be estimated directly from the data by conventional statistics. The ART distribution is not complete because a nonnegligible number of ARTs occur outside the critical set, typically 1–5%. To estimate the ART moments, we find the Gaussian density function over the whole numeral sequence that best fits the ART distribution (in a least-squares sense) within the critical set and that predicts the observed number of reports outside the critical set. We use the moments of this Gaussian as estimates of the ART moments. The estimation method is most sensitive to the central part of the distribution and relatively insensitive to the tails, where our data are incomplete. Although we offer no proof that this unusual Gaussian fitting procedure has desirable properties in general, it is easy to demonstrate its good properties in a case very similar to the ART distributions, namely, the MRT distributions. By applying the Gaussian fitting procedure to the MRT distributions for which true sample means are available, we can compare the Gaussian estimates of the means with the true sample means. The Gaussian procedure gives estimates of the MRT means that differ absolutely from the true sample means by less than 1 msec (.5%) on the average—very good agreement, indeed. The fit of the Gaussian distribution was tested with the Kolgomorov–Smirnov D statistic and was rejected ($p < .05$) for only 8 of the 59 observed ART distributions.

Another complication is that the lateral position (but not the shape) of the ART distribution depends somewhat on the assumptions made. It is assumed here that, after an attention shift occurs, the subject reports the most recently presented numeral. For example, if numerals occur every 109 msec, and if the subject shifts attention from the target to the numerals in less than 109 msec, then he would report the numeral that occurred simultaneously with the target. For more details, see Reeves (1977).

Subjects' Knowledge of Position; Order Information

We wondered why three highly motivated, well-practiced subjects—each extensively trained before the start of the experiments and then serving in 17 experimental sessions for a total of almost 5000 trials with full feedback— were not able to name earlier-occurring numerals. Why could they not, for example, pay partial attention to the numeral stream, remember the order of the numerals, and give a response based on reconstruction from this memory? In an attempt to answer this question, two different procedures were used.

Position Judgments. In the first procedure, subjects were asked to estimate the position within the critical set of the numeral they reported (i.e., to say whether it occurred *early, middle,* or *late* in the critical set). We found that, with slow numeral rates, the subjects quickly learned to judge whether the first numeral they could report occurred early or late in the numeral stream. But at the fastest numeral rates, subjects were unable to estimate reliably the position of their response numeral, even after much practice. For one subject, the ART distribution for responses designated as *early* coincided exactly with the distribution for responses designated as *late*. Evidently, at the fastest rates, the subjects have little or no order information available to them—they do not know the actual temporal order of the numerals.

Recall-4 Procedure.   This conclusion was further supported by the results of our second procedure, "Recall-4." Subjects were instructed to report not only the earliest numeral they could in the critical set but also the next three numerals. Although complete analysis of these Recall-4 data is more complex than of the single response data (Recall-1), the results of the analysis (Reeves, 1977) are unambiguous: at the slower numeral rates the subjects succeeded quite well at the task. At the fastest numeral rates, their responses showed no evidence of order information.[1]

Covariation of MRT, ART

Target Difficulty.   The motor reaction time (MRT) depends on which target occurs. Mean MRT is slowest for U and quickest for the square. These MRTs are consistent with the ease of detection of these targets against the letter background. To create the easiest possible detection task, in another experiment, the background letters were eliminated and the target was simply an arrow pointing at the numeral stream. This arrow condition gave the fastest MRTs. The order of mean *attention* reaction times (ARTs) to the four kinds of targets corresponded within measurement error to the order of the MRTs. These data, illustrated in Fig. 17.2, show that targets that slow the ART also slow the MRT, though to a lesser extent.

Numeral Rate.   Insofar as both MRTs and ARTs depend only on target processing, numeral rate should have no effect on them. In fact, numeral rate has a small effect on MRTs (MRTs are slow at slow numeral rates) and a large effect in the opposite direction on ARTs. However, an analysis of variance shows that there is no significant interaction between the main effects (upon MRT or ART) of target difficulty and of numeral rate: These factors work independently (i.e., the curves of Fig. 17.2 are approximately parallel). The effect of numeral rate upon the ART is analogous to the effect upon the MRT

---

[1]When Ss listen to repeated sequences of *unfamiliar* sound, they are absolutely unable to report correctly the order of these sounds even when the duration of individual sounds is long enough to permit the easy discrimination of the order in sequences composed of familiar speech sounds (Warren, Obusek, Farmer, & Warren, 1969). Warren (1974) proposes that discrimination of order at high item rates requires the prior learning of overall patterns. At high visual presentation rates, the difficulty our subjects experienced in discriminating order is analogous to the difficulty Warren's subjects experienced with unfamiliar sounds. By analogy this would suggest that our subjects did not learn the overall patterns produced by consecutive visual numbers.

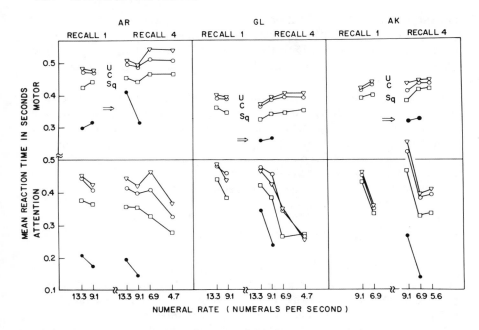

FIG. 17.2.   Mean ART (left) and mean MRT (right) as a function of numeral rate (reciprocal of the time T from one of one numeral to the next). Target type is the parameter. Targets U ($\triangle$), C ($\bigcirc$), and Square ($\square$) were run in a mixed list; the arrow condition was run separately. Data of three subjects are shown in both conditions, Recall-1 and Recall-4 (see text). The ARTs in the Recall-4 data are for the first numeral (of four) reported, and all ART means are computed by the method described in the text.

of changing the finger being used or the mechanical characteristics of the reaction key. Absolute RTs change but differences are preserved. Thus, fast and slow numeral rates give identical estimates of the *differences* in ARTs and in MRTs for the various targets.

Factor independence means, for example, that if ARTs are 40 msec longer for the U target than for the $\square$ target, this same 40 msec difference will be found whether the ART is measured at fast or at slow numeral rates. Factor independence of target difficulty and of numeral rate upon the variance of MRT and ART also was tested and found to hold (see Reeves, 1977). Thus, the choice of numeral rate for an ART experiment is a matter of convenience. All conclusions about the relative speeds of processing different targets would be the same at all the numeral rates tested.

Foreperiod Effect.   The foreperiod refers to the position of the target letter within the letter stream. *When* a target occurs (i.e., early or late) has a significant influence upon reaction time, presumably because late-occurring targets are more predictable (Nickerson, 1965, 1967; Nickerson & Burnham,1969; Snodgrass, 1969). Averaging ARTs and MRTs over all subjects and conditions, we find that RTs to targets in the last quartile (target positions 18, 19, 20) are 33 msec faster than RTs to stimuli in the earliest quartile (target positions 9, 10, 11); this decrease in reaction times is linear over quartiles. Averaging over subjects and conditions, the foreperiod effect is the same for ARTs and MRTs. Analysis of variance shows the foreperiod effect does not interact with the effect of target identity on ART or MRT (i.e., the two effects are additive). That foreperiod and target difficulty have a similar effect on ART and on MRT can be regarded as a further substantiation of the ART method. These two variables produce their expected effects on both MRT and ART.

Other Results

Numeral Identity. There is a small but statistically significant tendency for subjects to report the numeral 1 less often than the other numerals which, within measurement error, are reported equally often. There is no significant tendency for any numeral (including 1) to be reported earlier or later than any other. As far as we have been able to determine, ARTs are independent of which particular numerals happen to occupy the critical positions.

Subjects' Guessing Strategies. In other experiments, not reported here, in which the numeral stream was augmented to contain 16 characters (rather than just 10 numerals), characters from certain positions *never* appeared in the response. Because a random selection of characters would have produced characters from every position, the systematic absence of certain positions indicates there was no purely random guessing. Additionally, the data of the present experiments were subjected to various analyses by a procedure that corrects for sophisticated guessing strategies (Sperling & Melchner, 1976). The "corrected" and uncorrected data do not differ in any respects that are important for the issues under consideration.

THEORY

Two-Stage, Three-Component Model for MRT and ART

All the previous results and many others are encapsulated in a two-stage three-component model consisting of a detection–recognition component d that contributes both to the MRT and the ART; a motor component m that contributes only to the MRT; and an attention component a that contributes only to the ART. The model is distribution-free; each component contributes to a mean μ and a variance σ^2 to the observed reaction-time distribution.

MRTs. Let i represent a particular target and j, a numeral rate. The predicted means $\overline{MRT}(i, j)$ and variances $VAR[MRT(i, j)]$ of the MRT distributions are:

$$\overline{MRT}(i, j) = \mu_d(i) + \mu_m \tag{1}$$

$$VAR[MRT(i, j)] = \sigma_d^2(i) + \sigma_m^2. \tag{2}$$

ARTs. To a first approximation, MRTs are independent of the various numeral rates, so we omit rate parameters in predicting them. ARTs, however, do depend strongly on the numeral rate and this must be incorporated in the prediction. Moreover, to account for the somewhat greater effect of target on ART than on MRT, the model assumes that processing of stimuli by the detection–recognition component takes longer for initating the attention response than for initiating the motor response, by a factor of $1 + h$, where $h > 0$. For concreteness, the detection–recognition process can be represented by a random walk, information-accumulation process (Laming, 1968; Link & Heath, 1975; Stone, 1960) with a lower threshold for initiating the motor response process than for initiating the attention response process. The predicted means $\overline{ART}(i, j)$ and variances $VAR[ART(i, j)]$ of the ART distributions are:

$$\overline{ART}(i, j) = (1 + h)\,\mu_d(i) + \mu_a(j) \tag{3}$$

$$VAR[ART(i, j)] = (1 + h)\sigma_d^2(i) + \sigma_a^2(j). \tag{4}$$

In a given condition of target i and numeral rate j, the predicted covariance between MRT and ART, COV (MRT, ART$|i, j$), is simply

$$COV(MRT, ART|i, j) = \sigma_d^2 \tag{5}$$

Parameter Estimation. In any one condition (i, j), there are seven model parameters $[(h, \mu_d(i), \sigma_d(i), \mu_a(j), \sigma_a(i), \mu_m, \sigma_m]$ and only five observables. However, 18 conditions were conducted in a balanced design for each of subjects AR and GL and 15 conditions for AK. The 18 conditions yield 90 observable quantities and require only 17 model parameters so that parameter estimation is feasible in principle.

Predictions of means and of variances are separable in the model. The additive effects of target difficulty and of numeral rate on the predicted mean $\overline{ART}$s and $\overline{MRT}$s is essentially an embodiment of the finding of no significant interaction from an analysis of variance. It is not suprising, therefore, that predictions of the means are reasonably good, accounting for .69 to .88 of the variance to the observed means.

The model correctly predicts the linear regression [with slope $(1 + h)^{-1}$] of the $\overline{MRT}$s upon the $\overline{ART}$s between conditions (i.e., the way mean MRTs and mean ARTs vary together with different targets). This aspect of the predictions is incoporated in the parameter h; the average value of h for the three subjects was 0.51. This means that on the average there is a 51% greater effect of increasing target difficulty on ARTs than on MRTs. In the model, an *h* greater than zero means that a target initiates an attention response process only some time after it has already initiated a motor response process (i.e., the ART undergoes more processing in the detection component than the MRT).

Predictions. There are three important predictions from the variances in the model:

1. *The correlation, within conditions, between individual ARTs and MRTs elicited by the same stimulus.* This correlation is predicted to be positive (because it is proportional to the fraction of total response variance that is shared between ARTs and MRTs) and small (because the sharing is restricted to the first part of the joint detection stage). In the data, all these ART–MRT correlations were small and positive, as predicted.

2. *The slope of the MRT variances upon the ART variances.* At each numeral rate, for the various targets, the slope of the MRT variances upon the ART variances is predicted to be the same as the corresponding slope of the means $(1 + h)^{-1}$. This prediction assumes the variation in additional processing that the ART undergoes in the joint detection component is uncorrelated with the shared processing. [The slope would be predicted to be $(1 + h)^{-2}$ if the ARTs' additional detection processing were perfectly correlated with the shared processing. This would occur if the trial-to-trial variation in detection latency were due to stimulus variations, such as target context, rather than to internal fluctuations within the information-accumulation process.]

3. *Absolute estimation of variances.* The model enables absolute estimation individually of σ_d, σ_m, and σ_a. In contrast to previous MRT models, there is no arbitrary constant that can be exchanged between these quantities without producing an observable change in MRT (or ART) variances.

Unfortunately, none of these three predictions could be critically tested because meaningful estimation of model parameters from variances requires much greater precision of sample variances (relative to their own variability) than we had.

Mental Snapshot Model for ARTs

By considering a broader set of data that includes, in addition to the observables in Equations 1 and 2, the subjects' introspections and a comprehensive analysis of report order, we have arrived at a "mental snapshot" model of the attention component. The model represents activity in a higher-level visual short-term memory (VSTM) that simultaneously maintains representations of several successively presented stimuli (Scarborough, 1972; Sperling & Kaufman, 1978). We shall not dwell here on how these processes actually might be carried out in the brain but rather on the formal analogy to taking and examining a photograph.

The memory model assumes there is a representation of each of the numerals in a *visual processor*. Every time a particular numeral is viewed by the subject, a corrsponding representation in this visual processor is activated. The representation remains active at least until the next numeral is displayed to the subject, when the new representation becomes active. As soon as a target is detected in the letter stream, the activity pattern in the processor begins to be registered in the visual short-term memory. Registration of activity is not instantaneous, however, but occurs during an interval of about .25 sec (during which several numerals become active.) Ultimately, numerals are reported in an order that corresponds to their total, cumulated activity during the registration interval.

The visual processor is analogous to a panel of numbers on which a number lights up whenever it is being presented. The VSTM system corresponds to a camera pointed at the panel. Target detection is analogous to triggering the camera to take a picture of the panel. The registration process corresponds to the camera shutter opening gradually and closing gradually, with a minimum exposure time of about .25 sec. Thus, several numerals may appear on the same piece of film, each exposed by different amounts depending on how wide open the shutter was during the time the numeral was illuminated. The photographic image on the film represents the contents of VSTM. The process by which a sequence of numerals is retrieved from VSTM corresponds to the following reporting strategy vis a vis the photograph: The most visible (most exposed) numeral is reported first. When more than one numeral is asked for, the second most visible is reported next, and so on. It follows that numerals that were partially exposed (i.e., numerals that were presented as the shutter was opening or when it was closing) will be reported in haphazard order after the numerals that were presented while the camera shutter was wide open.

Two Factors Determine Order of Report. Temporal order information in VSTM is hypothesized to consist of a radically different kind of information: a marker associated with each numeral indicating its time of occurrence in the snapshot independently of its strength. Useful markers are assumed to require more time for their formation than is available at the highest rates of numeral presentation, but markers become quite effective at low rates. Thus, there is a single factor (exposure strength) that determines order of report at high presentation rates, but there are two factors (strength and relative time of occurrence) that combine to determine the response sequence at low numeral rates. This two-factor model leads to a precise mathematical representation that provides accurate descriptions of the sequences of response numerals that subjects produced in the various Recall-4 conditions (Reeves & Sperling, 1977).

The model clarifies the answer to the problem of reconstructive memory. Where marker-type order information is lacking, as at high numeral rates, there is no possibility of effective reconstruction from memory; "working backward" in memory to retrieve earlier items could be attempted, but it would primarily increase the variance and not reliably alter the mean reported position. Therefore, at high rates, the ART distribution directly estimates the moment of maximal attention to the numerals (i.e., the moment of fastest registration—the moment at which the shutter is fully open).

Where there is marker-type order information, as at slow numeral rates, the subject can use the markers to partially reconstruct the actual order of the numerals in the critical set; the response numerals then come from the early phase of the attentional response. At low numeral rates there is the possibility of complication if there is partial attention to the numeral stream even during target search. In the mental snapshot model, partial attention corresponds to the shutter being left slightly open and the film being advanced from time to time. When events occur very slowly in the numeral stream, the order traces are better, the film needs to be advanced less often, and therefore it is easier to reconstruct the sequence backward from the time attention is shifted. Thus, in the case of a simple detection task (an "arrow" target when the background characters are blanks) and a slow numeral rate (4.6 per second), we find good order memory and evidence of continuous partial attention to the numerals. For example, subjects occasionally report the numeral from the –1 position. But these factors are easily manipulable. By choosing a detection task sufficiently difficult to require full attention to the letter stream and by choosing a sufficiently high rate of numeral presentation to minimize pointer-type order information, we obtain an ideal situation for measuring attention shifts, a situation corresponding to the "shortest exposure" of a mental snapshot.

To return again to the main results, we now interpret the decrease in mean ART with decreasing numeral rate as due to reconstructive memory at the slow rates. Because there is no interaction of numeral rate and target difficulty in the data or in the two-stage model, the choice of numeral rate for an ART experiment is a matter of convenience. As noted previously, any conclusion about the relative speeds of processing different targets would be the same at all the numeral rates tested.

Perceived Temporal Order

Finally, the present analysis has direct applicability to the classical psychological problem of how simultaneity judgments are made (Boring, 1950). We propose that simultaneity judgments (e.g., of a light and a click) are based on attention shifts from one modality or stimulus channel to another[2] and, in the

---

[2]For a model that proposes attention shifts without memory from one modality to another, see Kristofferson (1967).

case of sophisticated subjects, also on reconstructive memory. The lability of simultaneity judgments is explained as being a property of the memory-reconstruction algorithms that are available to subjects in typical test situations. The extraordinary dependence of simultaneity judgments on mental "set" is due to the choice of which channel is the trigger for the attention shift.

REFERENCES

Boring, E. G. *A history of experimental psychology*. New York: Appleton-Century, 1950.

Helmholtz, H. von. *Handbuch der Physiologischen Optik*. English translation J. P. C. Southall (Ed.) (Vol. III) (Optical Society of America, 1924). Reprinted: New York: Dover, 1962.

James, W. *The principles of psychology* (Vol. 1). New York: Holt, 1890.

Kristofferson, A. B. Attention and psychophysical time. In A. F. Sanders (Ed.), *Attention and performance, Acta Psychologica*, 1967, *27*, 93–100.

Laming, D. R. *Information theory of choice reaction time*. New York: Wiley, 1968.

Link, S. W., & Heath, R. A. A sequential theory of psychological discrimination. *Psychometrika*, 1975, *40*(1), 77–105.

Nickerson, R. Response times for "same"–"different" judgments. *Perceptual and Motor Skills*, 1965, *20*, 15–18.

Nickerson, R. Expectancy, waiting time and the psychological refractory period. In A. F. Sanders (Ed.), *Attention and performance, Acta Psychologica*, 1967, *27*, 23–34.

Nickerson, R., & Burnham, D. Response times wtih nonaging foreperiods. *Journal of Experimental Psychology*, 1969, *79*, 452–457.

Reeves, A. *The detection and recall of rapidly displayed letters and digits*. Unpublished doctoral dissertation, City University of New York, 1977.

Reeves, A., & Sperling, G. *Attentional theory for order information in short-term visual memory*. Paper presented at the Tenth Annual Mathematical Psychology Meeting, Los Angeles, Calif., August 1977.

Scarborough, D. L. Memory for brief visual displays of symbols. *Cognitive Psychology*, 1972, *3*(3), 408–429.

Snodgrass, J. Foreperiod effects in simple reaction time: Anticipation or expectancy? *Journal Experimental Psychology Monograph*, 1969, *79*, (3, Pt. 2), 1–19.

Sperling, G. The information available in visual presentations. *Psychological Monographs*, 1960, *74*(11, Whole No. 498).

Sperling, G. The description and luminous calibration of cathode ray oscilloscope visual displays. *Behavior Research Methods & Instrumentation*, 1971, *3*(3), 148–151.

Sperling, G., & Kaufman, J. *Three kinds of visual short-term memory*. Paper given at Attention and Performance VIII, Educational Testing Service, Princeton, N.J., August 22, 1978.

Sperling, G., & Melchner, M. Estimating item and order information. *Journal of Mathematical Psychology*, 1976, *13*(2), 192–213.

Stone, M. Models for choice reaction time. *Psychometrika*, 1960, *25*(3), 251–260.

Warren, R. M. Auditory temporal discrimination by trained listeners. *Cognitive Psychology*, 1974, *6*, 237–256.

Warren, R. M., Obusek, C. J., Farmer, R. M., & Warren, R. P. Auditory sequence: Confusion of patterns other than speech or music. *Science*, 1969, *164*, 586–587.

Wundt, W. *An introduction to psychology*. (2nd German ed., R. Pinter, trans. London: Allen & Unwin, 1924. Edinburgh: Ballentyre Press, 1912).

18

The Observer's Use of Perceptual Dimensions in Signal Identification

David J. Getty,
Joel B. Swets,
John A. Swets
Bolt Beranek and Newman Inc.
Cambridge, Massachusetts
United States

ABSTRACT

We examine a model of the process of stimulus identification, which assumes that complex visual or auditory stimuli are represented as vectors in a multidimensional perceptual space and which postulates a simple probabilistic decision process based on the geometric structure of the perceptual space. We present evidence from several conditions of an identification task that human observers engage in a continuing, dynamic process in which dimension salience weights are tuned to optimize identification performance. In addition, we verify the reliability of the INDSCAL multidimensional scaling procedure in deriving the geometric structure of the observers' perceptual space for the set of visual spectrograms used in our identification tasks. We also present evidence supporting an assumption of dimensional decomposability made in the decision process. Finally, we observe that the model is successful in accounting for approximately 90% of the variance in individual confusion matrices, averaged over 18 observers × conditions.

INTRODUCTION

The process of identifying a complex visual or auditory stimulus from a set of similar stimuli requires both a psychological representation for each candidate stimulus and an appropriate decision process to govern the choice among them. In recent work (Getty, Swets, Swets, & Green, 1979), we describe an approach to understanding complex stimulus identification that involves two parts: (1) the derivation of a multidimensional perceptual space for a set of complex stimuli from the application of a multidimensional scaling (MDS) procedure to judgments of stimulus similarity; and (2) the use of a probabilistic decision model to predict the identification confusion matrix based on the geometric structure of the MDS-derived perceptual space. Using this approach with a set of eight visual spectrograms of real underwater sounds, we were quite successful in predicting the confusion matrices for individual observers, accounting for an overall average of 94% of the observed variance across several conditions of both complete- and partial-identification tasks. In another study that proposed a related type of probabilistic decision model—and again using a MDS procedure to determine the perceptual space—Howard, Ballas, and Burgy (1978) were able to account for between 61 and 96% of the variance in individual confusion matrices obtained for a set of 16 complex acoustic patterns.

In our previous study, we found that observers appeared to weight differentially information derived from the several perceptual dimensions in such a way as to maximize the average probability of a correct identification. Similarly, Howard et al. (1978) reported that their model estimates of dimension "emphasis" supported the hypothesis that relative emphasis was allocated to dimensions by listeners so as to maximize the average probability correct.

In this chapter, we pursue the implication of the findings that observers are flexible in their use of perceptual dimensions. Specifically, we suggest that observers are engaged in a continuing, dynamic process of adaptive tuning of dimension weights so as to optimize a particular, task-dependent criterion of performance. In the usual identification task, this criterion is either explicitly stated or implicitly understood to be maximizing the probability of a correct identification. Clearly, however, changes in the task could invoke other criteria, such as maximizing the probability of correctly identifying some subset of the stimuli or maximizing the probability of correctly classifying the stimuli into a particular set of categories. Different criteria would dictate different optimal patterns of relative dimension weights.

The optimal pattern of dimension weights is obviously stimulus-dependent as well as task-dependent. For example, given the optimal pattern of relative dimension weights for a particular set of stimuli, if we now decrease the range of stimulus variation on one of the perceptual dimensions toward zero, we may expect the optimal weight on that dimension, relative to the others, to decrease likewise toward zero. In the identification experiment that follows, we made use of this manipulation in several different conditions to produce different expected patterns of dimension weights. Our objectives in these conditions were to determine whether tuning of dimension weights occurs and, if so, whether the optimization criterion seems to be maximization of the probability of correct identification.

We had several other objectives in this experiment as well. First, we wished to test the reliability of the perceptual space derived from INDSCAL (Carroll, 1972; Carroll & Chang, 1970; Carroll & Wish, 1974), which is the MDS procedure we applied to judgments of stimulus similarity. Second, we wished to test a decomposability assumption of the decision model. Finally, we wished to obtain multiple tests of the model's adequacy in predicting individual confusion matrices under a variety of conditions, using a set of stimuli that were sufficiently similar to yield a high rate of confusion errors. Each of these goals is elaborated at appropriate points in the discussion.

THE IDENTIFICATION MODEL

We describe here, briefly, the decision model that predicts the distribution of response probabilities for each stimulus, given the relative loci of the stimuli in the observer's multidimensional perceptual space. (For a fuller discussion of the model, see Getty et al., 1979).

We assume that the distance between stimulus S_i and stimulus S_j in the perceptual space is given by a weighted Euclidean metric:

$$D_{i,j} = \left[\sum_k w_k(\psi_{i,k} - \psi_{j,k})^2 \right]^{1/2} \tag{1}$$

where w_k is a salience weight measuring the relative importance of dimension $k(w_k \geq 0$ and $\sum w_k = 1)$ and $\psi_{i,k}$ is the coordinate value of stimulus S_i on dimension k. The salience weights are model parameters; the stimulus coordinates are obtained from the MDS procedure applied to judgments of stimulus similarity.

We define a set of confusion weights $C_{i,j}$ such that the confusability of stimulus S_i with stimulus S_j is given by

$$C_{i,j} = \exp{(-aD_{i,j})} \tag{2}$$

where a is an observer sensitivity parameter, greater than zero. This exponential relationship has received support both in our earlier experiments and in Shepard's related work on stimulus generalization (1957; 1958a, b).

Finally, the conditional probability of giving the response assigned to stimulus S_j, namely, R_j, when stimulus S_i was presented is given by Luce's biased-choice model (1963):

$$\Pr(R_j | S_i) = \frac{b_j C_{i,j}}{\sum_k b_k C_{i,k}} \tag{3}$$

where b_j is a response bias weight describing the relative bias toward making response R_j ($b_j \geq 0$ and $\Sigma\ b_j = 1$), and k is an index over the set of stimuli.

METHOD

Stimuli

Our stimuli were synthesized visual spectrograms of complex, two-formant sounds. The stimuli were displayed as frequency (horizontal axis) versus time (vertical axis) versus energy (darkness—the greater the energy, the darker the trace). They varied along three physical dimensions: (1) location of the center of the first formant; (2) location of the center of the second formant; and (3) the frequency of sinusoidal amplitude modulation (AM) in the temporal direction (corresponding to a low-frequency periodicity in the sound).

A basic set of 27 stimuli was defined by all combinations of three equally spaced values on each of the three dimensions. The values for the location of the first formant were 20, 25, and 30 elements from the left edge of the stimulus image. (The stimulus was 126 elements wide by 128 elements high.) The three values for the location of the second formant were 90, 95, and 100 elements from the left edge. The three frequencies of amplitude modulation were 15, 17, and 19 cycles per stimulus. The 27 stimuli were "randomly" partitioned into three sets of 9 stimuli, subject to two constraints: (1) no two stimuli within a set shared more than one coordinate value in common; (2) for each set, each of the three values on each of the three dimensions occurred with exactly three of the stimuli. The purpose of these constraints was to obtain a uniform distribution of stimuli throughout the space within each set. The resulting three sets, labeled A, B, and C, are given in Table 18.1.

The stimulus image was constructed by subtracting profiles of the two formants from a background of random, Gaussian-distributed noise. The noise consisted of a 126×128 ($w \times h$) matrix of elements, each element having an independent gray value sampled anew on each trial from a Gaussian distribution with a mean of 128 gray units and a standard deviation of 25 gray units. The first and second formants were given Gaussian-shaped horizontal profiles with a peak amplitude of 40 gray units and standard deviations of 10 and 18 display pixels, respectively. The amplitude modulation was imposed on the resulting image in the vertical direction with a modulation depth of 50%. Finally, each element was expanded to fill a 2×2 pixel area, resulting in an image 252×256 pixels on the display monitor. The experimental apparatus is described elsewhere (Getty et al., 1979).

These high-contrast stimuli were used in the similarity-judgment task. In order to increase confusability of the stimulus set for the identification task and to increase their realism, the stimuli were modified in two ways. First, we

TABLE 18.1

Physical Values Defining Each Stimulus on the Three Primary Dimensions
(AM, F1, F2) and the Two Derived Dimensions (Width, Location)

Stimulus Number	AM	F1	F2	Width[a]	Location[b]
Stimulus Set A					
1	17	30	100	70	65.0
2	17	25	90	65	57.5
3	19	25	100	75	62.5
4	15	25	95	70	60.0
5	15	20	100	80	60.0
6	17	20	95	75	57.5
7	19	20	90	70	55.0
8	15	30	90	60	60.0
9	19	30	95	65	62.5
Stimulus Set B					
1	15	20	95	75	57.5
2	15	25	90	65	57.5
3	15	30	100	70	65.0
4	17	20	90	70	55.0
5	17	25	100	75	62.5
6	17	30	95	65	62.5
7	19	20	100	80	60.0
8	19	25	95	70	60.0
9	19	30	90	60	60.0
Stimulus Set C					
1	15	20	90	70	55.0
2	15	30	95	65	62.5
3	19	20	95	75	57.5
4	17	30	90	60	60.0
5	15	25	100	75	62.5
6	17	25	95	70	60.0
7	19	30	100	70	65.0
8	17	20	100	80	60.0
9	19	25	90	65	57.5

[a]Width = $F2 - F1$.
[b]Location = $(F1 + F2)/2$.

introduced temporal variability or "wobble" into the displayed value of the
stimulus on each of the three dimensions. Thus, scanning down each of the
examples shown in Fig. 18.1, you will see (independent) wobble in the
location of each of the two formants and in the period of the amplitude
modulation. For each dimension, the temporal pattern of deviation from the
value specified for the stimulus was generated by summing together four

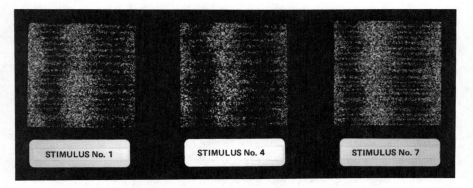

FIG. 18.1.   Examples of high-contrast stimuli with wobble present on all three physical dimensions. All three values used on each of the three dimensions are shown across the three stimuli; these values are given for stimuli 1, 4, and 7 (stimulus set A) in Table 18.1.

sinusoids with frequencies 1, 2, 3, and 4 cycles per stimulus, each beginning at a different random phase that was sampled anew on each trial. By summing only integral frequencies, we guaranteed that the total deviation about the specified dimension value, integrated down the length of a stimulus image, was always zero. As the second modification to increase confusability we reduced the signal-to-noise ratio considerably by decreasing the peak amplitude of the first and second formants from 40 gray units to 8 and 10, respectively. As a result, the formants were barely perceptible within the stimulus.

Observers

Two groups of three observers, referred to as Groups A and B, participated in the experiment. Four of the six observers were recruited from an observer pool and paid for their assistance; the other two were members of BBN's technical staff, including one of the experimenters (JBS).

Procedure

Similarity Judgment Task.   The observers were instructed to rate similarity of pairs of stimuli on a seven-point scale, with the scale end points 1 and 7 indicating very dissimilar and very similar stimuli, respectively. Each of the 36 possible pairs for a particular set of nine high-contrast, wobbleless stimuli was presented side by side on the display monitor for 15 sec, followed by an observer-paced response interval. Four blocks of 36 trials were presented, using a different random order for each block, with the left–right position of stimuli within a given pair counterbalanced over blocks.

All six observers participated in two different conditions of the similarity-judgment task. The two conditions were run successively between the first and second conditions of the identification task.

Identification Task.   Each trial began by blanking of the display monitor screen, followed approximately 2.5 sec later by a low-contrast, wobbly display of a stimulus image, chosen randomly from the set of nine being used. Each observer then made a self-paced identification response (from the numbers 1 to 9 on the keyboard), making reference to a folder of labeled, high-contrast, wobbleless Polaroid photographs of the nine stimuli. After all observers had responded, the number of the presented signal was displayed on each observer's terminal. The stimulus number and stimulus image remained on display for approximately 2 sec after which the next trial began. Trials were grouped into 50-trial blocks, with 3 blocks presented each day for 7 days for each of three conditions of the task for each group. The nature of each condition for each group is discussed later as each arises.

DERIVATION OF THE PERCEPTUAL SPACE

The primary purpose of the first similarity-judgment condition was to derive a multidimensional representation of the observers' perceptual space in terms of both the identity of the psychological dimensions comprising the space and the relative loci of the stimuli within the multidimensional space. Stimulus set A (as defined in Table 18.1) was used in this condition—the same set of nine stimuli used for all observers in the immediately preceding identification condition. It was hoped that by running the similarity-judgment task immediately after a condition of the identification task and by using the same stimulus set in both cases that the same perceptual dimensions salient to the observers in the identification task would remain salient in the similarity-judgment task. Our concern stemmed from a previous study (Getty et al., 1979) in which one dimension (low-frequency periodicity or amplitude modulation) that was apparently utilized by observers when identifying the stimuli was not used when they rated similarity of the stimuli. In anticipation of our present results, that problem did not arise here.

The objectives of the second similarity-judgment condition were to provide a test of the reliability of the INDSCAL procedure and to test the decomposability property of INDSCAL. Decomposability is the assumption that the distance between any two points in the derived multidimensional space can be decomposed into independent contributions from each of the derived dimensions (Tversky & Krantz, 1970). Stimulus set B, the stimuli used in this condition and defined in Table 18.1, shared with Stimulus set A the same three values on each of the three physical dimensions, although in different, unique combinations. Given that these new stimuli lay in the same region of the physical space, we would expect to derive the same perceptual dimensions from INDSCAL in the second condition as in the first condition and to find the same psychophysical mapping of each physical dimension into its corresponding psychological dimension. This latter expectation requires, in part, that decomposability be satisfied.

Results

We calculated the average similarity rating for each of the 36 stimulus pairs, separately for each observer and each condition. The average for each pair was based on judgments from the second, third, and fourth blocks of trials; the first block of trials was regarded as practice and excluded from analysis. The average ratings for each observer were then submitted to MDS analysis, separately for the two conditions, using the metric version of INDSCAL.

Condition 1. The rating data for stimulus set A were fitted well by a three-dimensional solution that accounted for 89% of the variance in the data. The first psychological dimension is clearly identified with the physical AM dimension. The psychophysical relationship, shown in the top, left panel of Fig. 18.2, appears to be highly linear, at least over the physical range utilized.

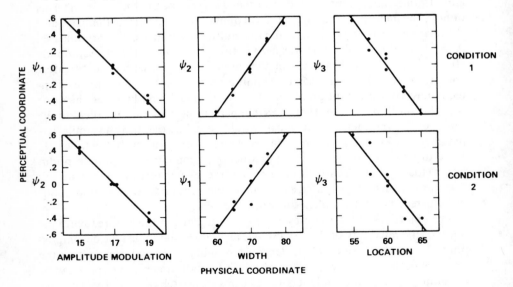

FIG. 18.2.   The observed psychophysical relations between the three physical dimensions (AM, width, and location) and the corresponding INDSCAL-derived perceptual dimensions (ψ_1, ψ_2, and ψ_3), for each of the two similarity-judgment conditions. In each case, the best-fitting straight line is shown.

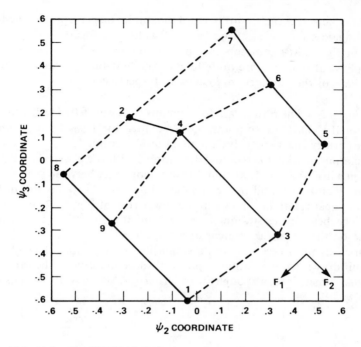

FIG. 18.3. The INDSCAL-derived coordinates of each of the nine stimuli in stimulus set A on perceptual dimension 3 plotted against coordinates of the stimuli on perceptual dimension 2. Stimuli sharing the same $F1$ ($F2$) value are connected by solid (dashed) lines.

The best-fitting straight line accounts for 99% of the observed variability in the psychological dimension.

Suprisingly, the identities of the other two psychological dimensions are not the locations of the first and second formants, those being the other two physical dimensions manipulated in the construction of the stimuli. Rather, they appear to be identified with a related pair of physical dimensions obtained by a 45° rotation of the $F1$ and $F2$ axes. This geometric relationship can be seen in Fig. 18.3, which shows the stimuli plotted in the ψ_2, ψ_3 plane. Stimuli sharing the same vlaue of $F1$ are connected by solid lines; those sharing the same value of $F2$ are connected by dashed lines. A possible basis for the obtained psychological dimensions becomes apparent if one regards each stimulus as being composed of a central vertical column bounded on either side by $F1$ and $F2$ (see Fig. 18.1). Then the physical dimension corresponding to ψ_2 is the width of the column—the distance between $F1$ and $F2$—and the physical dimension corresponding to ψ_3 is the location of the column, that is, the location of the midpoint between $F1$ and $F2$, given by $(F1 + F2)/2$.

Plotting the perceptual coordinates of the stimuli on perceptual dimensions 2 and 3 against the physical measures of width and location, respectively, shown in the right-hand, top two panels of Fig. 18.2, we see that both psychophysical relations are quite linear. The best-fitting lines account for 97 and 96% of the variance in ψ_2 and ψ_3, respectively.

Condition 2. The rating data for stimulus set B were fitted well by a three-dimensional INDSCAL solution that accounted for 86% of the variance in the data, nearly the same value obtained in Condition 1.

Correlating the three perceptual dimensions with the physical dimensions determined in Condition 1, we found a correspondence between ψ_1 and width, between ψ_2 and AM, and between ψ_3 and location. As in Condition 1, the psychophysical relations, shown in the lower row of Fig. 18.2, are all quite linear. The best-fitting straight lines account for 89, 99, and 87% of the variance on the ψ_1, ψ_2, ψ_3 dimensions, respectively.

We are thus able to account for the similarity rating of two independent sets of stimuli drawn from a common physical space in terms of the same three perceptual dimensions, although the ordering of AM and width dimensions is

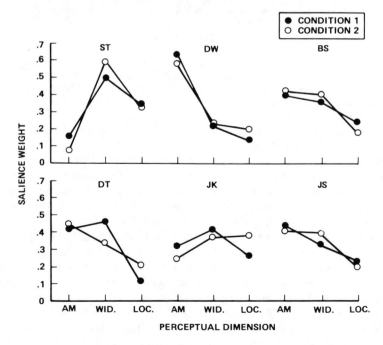

FIG. 18.4.   Relative dimension salience weights from INDSCAL for each of the three perceptual dimensions derived from INDSCAL in the two conditions of the similarity-judgment task, for each of the six observers.

reversed in the INDSCAL solution of the second condition. Moreover, both sets of data support the conclusion that the perceptual dimensions are *linearly* related to their respective physical dimensions.

Salience Weights. In addition to the coordinates for each stimulus in the multidimensional space, INDSCAL also produces a vector of salience weights for each observer reflecting the relative importance of each dimension for that observer. The derived salience weights for each observer in both conditions of the task are shown in Fig. 18.4. The results indicate that there are substantial individual differences in the pattern of salience weights across observers but that there is considerable stability in the pattern of weights for a given individual across the two conditions.

PREDICTION OF IDENTIFICATION CONFUSION MATRICES

The first condition of the identification task was the same for both groups of observers and made use of the nine patterns comprising stimulus set A. It provided a first test of the model's accuracy in predicting confusion matrices and served as a reference for the other conditions.

Prior to starting this condition, all observers received six sessions of practice (150 trials per session) identifying high-contrast, wobbleless stimuli and 1 day of practice identifying low-contrast, wobbly stimuli. Identification data were then collected for 7 days; the resulting confusion matrix for each observer contained 1050 trials.

Model Analysis

Parameter Estimation. Model parameters were estimated separately for each observer in a two-stage process. First, an iterative parameter-estimation procedure was used to determine the set of response bias weights, b_j, that minimized the summed squared deviation between obtained and predicted confusion matrices (as given by Equation 3). The response bias weights were then fixed at their estimated values and a second estimation procedure carried out using the full structure of the model (Equations 1, 2, and 3) and the normalized three-dimensional loci of the stimuli obtained from the INDSCAL analysis of the similarity-judgment task. Estimates were obtained for the three salience weights, w_1, w_2, and w_3, and the sensitivity parameter, a.[1]

---

[1]We estimated the dimension salience weights instead of using the INDSCAL-derived weights for each observer, because the requirements of the identification task may well result in salience weights different than those of the similarity-judgment task.

Prediction of Individual Confusion Matrices.   The model predicts the individual confusion matrices very well, accounting for an average of 92% of the variance across the six observers. Moreover, we did not find any obvious violations of model assumptions in the remaining variance not accounted for. The goodness-of-fit and the estimated model parameter values are shown in Table 18.2 (Condition 1) for each observer. The relative importance of the three dimensions appears to vary to some extent across observers; however, there is a general tendency for width and location to be weighted about equally and both to be weighted more heavily than AM.

The predicted and obtained response distributions for each stimulus are shown in Fig. 18.5 for three of the six observers, chosen to represent the worst (DT), median (ST), and best (DW) fits of the model to the data. The overall probability of a correct identification was 0.50, averaged over stimuli and observers. Thus, about half of the approximately 100 responses contributing to each distribution were confusion errors. In Fig. 18.5, it can be seen that the model generally predicts with considerable accuracy both the probability of a correct identification—the highest peak in most distributions—and the patterns of confusion errors. Even in cases where the prediction of the exact magnitude of a major confusion response is not accurate—for example, response 3 to stimulus 1 for observer ST—the model has at least successfully predicted the response to be a major confuser.

One can also see in Fig. 18.5 that although the patterns of confusion errors for a particular stimulus are often similar across observers, there are some differences—occasionally large. The model accounts for these individual differences based on a different pattern of dimension salience weights for each observer.

A TEST OF DIMENSIONAL DECOMPOSABILITY

The decision model assumes that the measure of interstimulus distance is decomposable into independent contributions from each of the perceptual dimensions (Equation 1). Our objective in a second condition of the identification task was to test the decomposability assumption using the perceptual space derived from one set of nine stimuli (stimulus set A in Table 18.1) to predict the confusions for an independent set of nine stimuli (stimulus set C). These new stimuli share with the old set the same three values on each of the three dimensions but in new, independent combinations. If each dimension contributes independently to interstimulus distance, then we should do as well at predicting the confusion matrix for stimulus set C as for stimulus set A, when both predictions are based on the perceptual space derived from stimulus set A.

TABLE 18.2
Proportion of Variance Accounted for by the Model and Estimated Parameter Values
for Each Observer

OB	r^2	w_1 (Amp. Mod.)	w_2 (Width)	w_3 (Loc.)	a
		CONDITION 1			
Group A					
BS	.95	.07	.46	.47	5.9
ST	.91	.00	.45	.55	4.5
DW	.98	.43	.34	.24	6.1
AVG	.95	.17	.42	.42	5.5
Group B					
JK	.86	.23	.38	.38	4.3
JS	.97	.22	.45	.34	5.4
DT	.83	.12	.47	.41	3.6
AVG	.90	.19	.43	.38	4.4
COND. AVG.	.92	.18	.43	.40	5.0
		CONDITION 2			
Group A					
BS	.96	.09	.31	.61	5.8
ST	.92	.00	.44	.56	5.1
DW	.99	.36	.34	.31	7.3
AVG	.96	.15	.36	.49	6.1
Group B					
JK	.81	.43	.08	.48	3.3
JS	.83	.33	.11	.56	4.2
DT	.64	.10	.52	.38	3.1
AVG	.76	.29	.24	.47	3.5
		CONDITION 3			
Group A					
BS	.97	.00	.50	.50	6.0
ST	.94	.00	.49	.51	4.8
DW	.96	.50	.34	.16	6.8
AVG	.95	.17	.44	.39	5.9
Group B					
JK	.89	.17	.42	.42	4.2
JS	.96	.20	.38	.42	5.6
DT	.91	.34	.33	.34	4.0
AVG	.92	.24	.38	.39	4.6

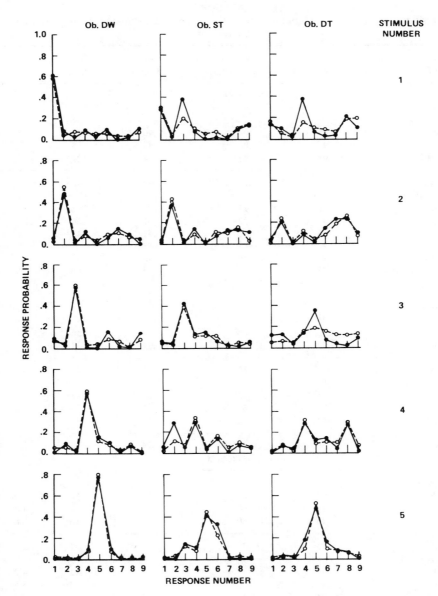

FIG. 18.5.   Distribution of response probability for each of the nine stimuli in Condition 1, for three of the six observers. Obtained distributions are given by filled circles; predicted distributions are given by open circles.

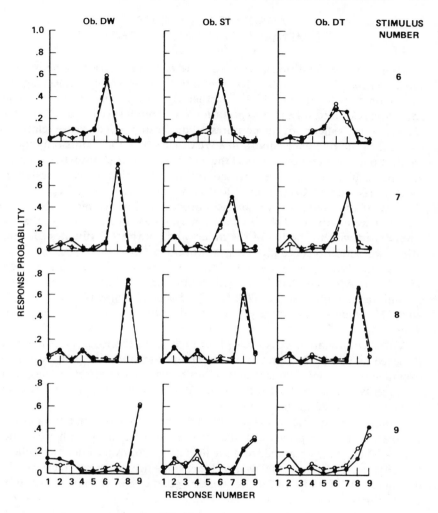

FIG. 18.5. (continued)

The results are shown in Table 18.2 under Condition 2, Group A. The model accounted for an average of 96% of the variance in the observed confusion matrices, a figure almost identical to the 95% of the variance accounted for in the first condition for these same observers. Moreover, the percentages of variance accounted for in the two conditions agree within 1% for each of the three observers individually. This result offers strong support for the model's assumption of dimensional decomposability.

ADAPTIVE TUNING OF
DIMENSION SALIENCE WEIGHTS

In each of three conditions, we made one of three physical dimensions—width, $F1$ location, and AM—less useful to the observer by "squeezing" the values on the dimension closer together than they were in the reference condition (Condition 1). Our expectation—and model prediction—is that, in each case, the salience of the compressed dimension will decrease relative to its value in the reference condition.[2] We discuss here the results only for the condition in which we compressed the width dimension (Group B, Condition 2). The results for the other two conditions, in which we compressed $F1$ location (Group B, Condition 3) and AM values (Group A, Condition 3), showed effects similar in type but less pronounced in magnitude due to the fact that we compressed the $F1$ location and AM dimensions less than we compressed width. The fits of the model and parameter estimates for those other two conditions are included, however, in Table 18.2.

The stimuli in the compressed width condition were identical to those in stimulus set A, except that the five values of width represented among the nine stimuli were compressed from 60, 65, 70, 75, and 80 elements to 68, 69, 70, 71, and 72 elements, respectively—a fivefold reduction in the range on this dimension.

A confusion matrix was obtained for each of the three observers in Group B, based on 900 trials from the last six of seven sessions; the first session was excluded as practice. Compressing width had a marked effect on the overall probability of a correct identification, reducing it from .45 for this group in Condition 1 to .29 in this condition.

In order to fit the model to the observed confusion matrices, estimates were required of the perceptual locations corresponding to the new physical width values. These were obtained from the linear psychophysical function relating the physical and perceptual width dimensions derived from the similarity-judgment task (see Fig. 18.2). The resulting goodness-of-fit values and parameter estimates are given in Table 18.2 (Condition 2, Group B) for each observer. For two of the observers (JK and JS), the salience weight for width dropped markedly, as expected, from .38 and .45 in Condition 1 to .08 and .11 in Condition 2, respectively. For the third observer (DT), however, the width salience weight increased slightly from .47 to .52, contrary to our expectation based on adaptive tuning.

---

[2]Another plausible intuition suggests that as the discriminability on a dimension is decreased by compression, the observer should compensate by devoting *more* attention to that dimension. The model does not support this prediction because the total amount of attention to be distributed over dimensions is fixed (at unity in the model). Thus, an increase in the salience of a dimension of reduced utility would be achieved only *at the expense* of a decrease in the salience of some other dimension of relatively enhanced utility.

A further analysis aids our understanding of these results considerably. In order to determine the temporal course of tuning, we reanalyzed the Group B data of both Conditions 1 and 2 in successive 300-trial blocks (thirds of a condition) and fitted the model separately to each of these successive blocks. The estimated salience weights for the final 300-trial block of Condition 1 and each successive block of Condition 2 are shown for each observer by the solid lines in the left-hand panels of Fig. 18.6. In addition, for a particular set of stimuli—and given the obtained estimates of an observer's response biases and sensitivity—it is possible to determine from the model the pattern of salience weights that would maximize the observer's probability of a correct identification. We determined these optimal weights, shown in Fig. 18.6 by the dashed lines, for each successive block, for each observer.

Comparing observed and optimal salience weight patterns we see that observers JK and JS demonstrate relatively optimal weight patterns in the final blocks both of Conditions 1 and 2. The optimal weight pattern for Condition 2 is quite different than that for Condition 1. Both observers JK and JS redistribute their salience weights to match the new optimal patterns by the second block of 300-trials. The tuning process is sufficiently gradual, however, so that the observed pattern for both observers for the first 300-trial block of Condition 2 is intermediate between that present at the end of Condition 1 and that arrived at by the middle of Condition 2.

In contrast, a comparison of the obtained and optimal salience weight patterns for observer DT shows little evidence of tuning. Over successive thirds, the observed weight pattern changes considerably, but in ways that appear to bear little relationship to the optimal weight pattern. A possible explanation of this result becomes clear when we compare the probability of a correct identification, $Pr(C)$, obtained when the optimal weight pattern is used with that obtained when the observed, nonoptimal weight pattern is used. These optimal and observed correct identification probabilities are shown for each successive 300-trial block in the right-hand panels of Fig. 18.6. Not surprisingly, the observed $Pr(C)$ is no more than a few percent below the optimal value in all cases for observers JK and JS, both of whom adopted nearly optimal weight patterns. What is surprising, however, is that the observed $Pr(C)$ for observer DT is, on the average, no more than 6% below the optimal value. For our stimuli, the optimization surface determined by the three salience weights is very flat, so that relatively large departures in the weights from the optimal pattern result in only a modest decrement in identification accuracy. According to this reasoning, we may interpret the performance of observers JK and JS as indicating a high sensitivity to small deviations from optimal $Pr(C)$, whereas the performance of observer DT indicates a lesser sensitivity. We speculate that if stimuli were chosen in such a way that the optimization surface were steep, we would find evidence of tuning in the performance of all observers, including that of observer DT.

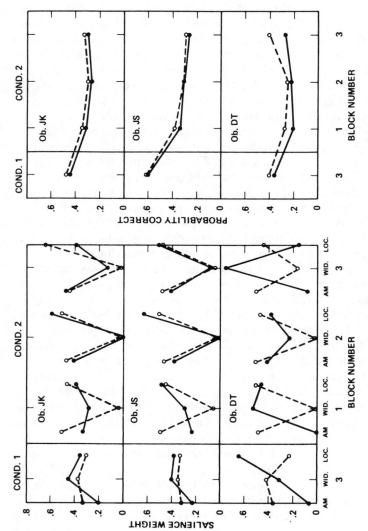

FIG. 18.6. Left panels: The observed (filled circles) and predicted (open circles) relative salience weights for each of the three perceptual dimensions for the final 300-trial block of Condition 1 and successive blocks of Condition 2, for each observer in Group B. Right panels: The observed (filled circles) and predicted (open circles) probability of a correct identification for successive blocks of trials in Conditions 1 and 2 for each observer in Group B.

CONCLUSIONS

Our results demonstrate the existence of an adaptive process of tuning of dimension salience weights in the identification process. For the identification task, the data are consistent with the hypothesis that observers tune to maximize the average probability of correct identification. Starting from a very nonoptimal weight distribution, we observed that the tuning process may take place over tens or hundreds of trials. These results support the view that the human observer is indeed flexible in his or her use of perceptual dimensions in pattern identification or classification, adjusting the weighting of dimensions to the characteristics of the set of stimuli at hand and the particular requirements of the identification or classification task.

The results of the two conditions of the similarity-judgment task affirm the reliability of the INDSCAL MDS procedure in that we derived the same three perceptual dimensions and linear psychophysical functions on all three dimensions, in both conditions.

We also obtained support for the model's assumption of dimension decomposability. Having obtained estimates of the perceptual loci for one particular set of stimuli, we were then able to predict the confusion matrix equally well for several different combinations of the same set of values on the three dimensions.

Finally, we note the overall success of the model in predicting the confusion matrices over the three conditions of the identification task for each of the two groups of observers. Averaged over the 18 comparisons of predicted and observed confusion matrices (Table 18.2), the model accounted for 91% of the observed variance.

ACKNOWLEDGMENT

This research was supported by a contract with the Engineering Psychology Programs, Office of Naval Research.

REFERENCES

Carroll, J. D. Individual differences and multidimensional scaling. In R. N. Shepard, A. K. Romney, & S. Nerlove (Eds.), *Multidimensional scaling: Theory and applications in the behavioral sciences.* New York: Seminar Press, 1972.

Carroll, J. D., & Chang, J. J. Analysis of individual differences in multidimensional scaling via an *N*-way generalization of "Eckart–Young" decomposition. *Psychometrika,* 1970, *35,* 288–319.

Carroll, J. D., & Wish, M. Models and methods for three-way multidimensional scaling. In D. H. Krantz, R. C. Atkinson, R. D. Luce, & P. Suppes (Eds.), *Contemporary developments in mathematical psychology,* (Vol. II). San Francisco: Freeman, 1974.

Getty, D. J., Swets, J. A., Swets, J. B., & Green, D. M. On the prediction of confusion matrices from similarity judgments. *Perception & Psychophysics,* 1979, *26,* 1–19.

Howard, J. H., Jr., Ballas, J. A., & Burgy, D. C. *Feature extraction and decision processes in the classification of amplitude modulated noise patterns.* (Technical Report ONR-78-4) Washington, D.C.: The Catholic University of America, July, 1978.

Luce, R. D. Detection and recognition. In R. D. Luce, R. R. Bush, & E. Galanter (Eds.), *Handbook of mathematical psychology.* New York: Wiley, 1963.

Shepard, R. N. Stimulus and response generalization: A stochastic model relating generalization to distance in psychological space. *Psychometrika,* 1957, *22,* 325–345.

Shepard, R. N. Stimulus and response generalization: Deduction of the generalization gradient from a trace model. *Psychological Review,* 1958, *65,* 242–256. (a)

Shepard, R. N. Stimulus and response generalization: Tests of a model relating generalization to distance in psychological space. *Journal of Experimental Psychology,* 1958, *55,* 509–523. (b)

Tversky, A., & Krantz, D. H. The dimensional representation and the metric structure of similarity data. *Journal of Mathematical Psychology,* 1970, *7,* 572–596.

19 Retrieval of Information from a Mental Map

Pekka K. Lehtiö
Department of Psychology
University of Helsinki

Laila Poikonen
Kirsti Tuunainen
University of Turku
Finland

ABSTRACT

In four experiments described in this chapter, the subjects had to solve simple tasks using information they have stored about the city in which they live. When they had to decide if a place is to the left or to the right of a reference line, the subjects used more time if the distance between the reference and the place in question was longer than when it was shorter. A similar negative correlation between the distance between two streets and the time required to answer if they cross each other was obtained. On the other hand when subjects had to judge if four streets were parallel or not, RT increased with the distance between these streets. A mechanism based on sequential utilization of a hierarchical data base might explain these results as well as other memory comparison results.

INTRODUCTION

In a previous experiment, subjects were asked first to memorize a picture rich in detail and afterward to decide if certain details had appeared in the memorized picture (Lehtiö & Kauri, 1973). The task presumed that the subjects based their decisions successively on different parts of the original picture. It was shown that the recognition time for a series of part pictures is dependent on the *distance* between adjacent part pictures in the original display. It was therefore proposed that the retrieval operation is analogous to scanning a visual display.

Kosslyn and his co-workers (Kosslyn, 1973; Kosslyn, Reiser, & Ball, 1978) have reported similar results. In their experiments the Ss first learned simple drawings. They then attended selectively to one portion of the visual image; after receiving an instruction to focus their attention on a new part of the image, they shifted their attention to the target area. The time to verify a visual feature of the target area, measured from the time at which they received the instruction, increased as a function of the distance between the initial focus and the target.

Kosslyn et al. (1978) have also contrasted two possible explanations for these results. According to the first explanation the internal representation is analogous to the actual picture in the sense that the spatial relations between corresponding portions of the picture are preserved in the spatial relations between corresponding portions of the image; the subject, while shifting his attention, passes the intermediate areas of the image. The second explanation attributes the distance effect to the time needed to process a kind of list structure representing intervening items between successive targets. In support of the first alternative, Kosslyn et al. (1978) have shown that (1) more time was required to scan greater distances, even when the same number of items fell between the focus and the target locations; and (2) subjectively larger images required more time to be scanned than did subjectively smaller ones.

The idea that images are mentally scanned may be regarded as an example of the paradigm of second-order isomorphism put forward by Shepard and Chipman (1970) [see also Shepard (1978) for a review]. According to this view the brain processes that underlie a mental image must necessarily contain information that could in principle permit the reconstruction of a picture with a high degree of isomorphism to the external object image, and the subjects use very similar mental processes when they perceive an external object and when they attain information from its memorized image (Shepard, 1978). Within this framework the scanning of an image should be considered an internalized counterpart to the processes of sampling information during successive fixations.

The results establishing a positive correlation between the time required to scan a visual mental image and the distance to be scanned (measured on the memorized picture) were obtained in experimental situations in which the visual images arose as a result of a short learning period during which the S examines a picture. Four experiments in which we tried to question the effect of physical coordinates on retrieving environmental information from memory are reported in this chapter. This information is assimilated during a longer time period, and its overall organization is learned in everyday activity.

The environmental information gives rise to vivid mental images, a fact that the reader may easily verify by walking "mentally" from home to a nearby shopping center, for instance.

In the first two experiments the S had to imagine himself standing on a certain street corner in his hometown and facing a given direction. He then had to decide for each of a number of places displayed to him whether they were situated to the right or to the left of his imagined line of sight.

In the third experiment the S had to decide if two streets crossed each other or not. In the last experiment, four streets were presented simultaneously and the S had to judge if they all were parallel or not.

EXPERIMENTS 1 AND 2

Method

Each subject was seated in front of a rear projection screen. A map of the city area of Turku was then shown, and the experimenter first pointed at the marketplace of Turku and then at one of its corners. The S was instructed to imagine himself standing at that corner and his imagined line of sight was shown on a map. He was then told that a set of slides, each representing a place in the city, would be displayed and that he would have to decide for each place whether it was located to the left or to the right of his imagined line of sight. He was asked to press the left or the right reaction key as soon as possible to indicate his decision.

Different stimulus materials and subjects were used in Experiments 1 and 2, but the reaction times were recorded under identical conditions. An electromechanical shutter exposed the stimulus slide and simultaneously a digital timer was started. For each slide the experimenter recorded the reaction time and the key pressed.

In Experiment 1 the stimulus material consisted of a set of 82 color slides displaying a place in the downtown area of Turku. Twenty slides were used during a training period and 62 during the experiment. One-half of the slides implied LEFT and one-half, RIGHT responses, and the order of displays was randomized.

For Experiment 2 two different stimulus sets were constructed. The first set consisted of 30 names of buildings or monuments and the second set, 30 names of street corners. The stimulus slides in Experiments 1 and 2 covered the same area of the city. Both sets were presented sequentially, each set preceded by two training slides.

The subjects were afterward asked to judge the stimulus slides according to their familiarity. They were instructed to make these judgments so that they would reflect how familiar these places were for inhabitants of Turku in general and to try to disregard their individual idiosyncracies. The ratings were made on a five-point scale, 1 standing for a very well-known place and 5 for a very poorly known place.

In the first experiment, 32 girls from a local high school served as Ss. Their age varied from 16 to 18 years. All of them were permanent residents in the city of Turku.

In the second experiment, 21 students from the University of Turku served as voluntary subjects. They were all permanent residents in Turku.

Results

The error rates were 15% for pictures, 7% for buildings, and 5% for street corners. Only correct reaction times were submitted to further analysis. A linear regression model with two independent variables was first fitted to each set of data. The mean RT was always the dependent variable and the first independent variables (X_1) was the distance from the line of sight to the target place along the shortest possible route; the second independent variable (X_2) was the mean of the familiarity ratings of that place. The contribution of distance was significant in the case of pictures ($t = 2.629$, $df = 59$, $p < 0.02$) and street corners ($t = 3.337$, $df = 27$, $p < 0.01$) and approached significance in the case of buildings ($t = 1.721$, $df = 27$, $p < 0.10$). The contribution of familiarity was significant in the case of pictures ($t = 4.880$, $df = 59$, $p > 0.01$) and buildings ($t = 5.093$, $df = 27$, $p < 0.01$) and nearly significant in the case of street corners ($t = 1.780$, $df = 27$, $p < 0.10$).

A more careful inspection of the data showed, however, that there was an interaction between the familiarity rating and the effect of physical distance on reaction time. The data were therefore grouped to form three subsets according to familiarity. The group limits were set so that they divided the results of Experiment 1 into three groups of almost equal size, and these same limits were applied to all observations in this paper. The mean RTs and the correlations between RT and the distance are listed in Table 19.1. It can be seen that RT decreases as a function of familiarity as might be expected. Inspection of correlation coefficients shows that the negative correlation between distance and RT increases as familiarity decreases.

The negative correlation between distance and RT contradicts the previous image-scanning results, but the result is similar to memory-comparison effects first reported by Moyer (1973). The results were analyzed in terms of angles between the imagined line of sight and the target place, but no systematic trends were found.

These experiments have been later replicated by the first author. The control experiment was carried out in the city of Helsinki. Six different reference lines were used and the test stimuli consisted of names of places and buildings. The trials were blocked so that in each block only one reference line

TABLE 19.1

Mean Reaction Times and Correlations Between RT and Distance for Different
Set and Different Familiarity Ratings.

Stimulus Set	Familiarity Rating (1: high, 5: Low)	Mean RT (sec)	Correlation Between RT and Distance
Pictures	0.00–1.25	4.355	0.00
	1.26–1.75	4.725	−0.32
	1.76–5.00	5.290	−0.41
Places	0.00–1.25	1.956	−0.03
	1.26–1.75	2.585	−0.55
	1.76–5.00	3.207	−0.85[a]
Street corners	0.00–1.25	—	
	1.26–1.75	3.216	−0.31
	1.76–5.00	3.732	−0.65[a]

[a]$p < 0.01$

was given. All stimulus slides were successively run with all the seven subjects. *Before* the experiment the subjects estimated the familiarity of all the names, and only those slides having familiarity within ± 1 standard error from the average were used. The distance–RT correlation computed over all the reference lines and all the stimuli was −.883.

EXPERIMENT 3

The results of Experiments 1 and 2 can be understood, if we assume that (1) subjects have different representations of the city in their memory; (2) these representations vary in scale and area covered; and (3) a low resolution representation is activated first. Thus subjects would first locate each place on an approximate mental map, and if places are far from each other, they could resolve their relationship on the basis of this information only. If on the other hand the places are near each other, they would need a more accurate representation and its recall would require more time.

Experiment 3 was intended to test this hypothesis. We tried to design a task in which subjects could use inaccurate location information to bypass a detailed analysis. Subjects had to decide if two streets crossed each other or not. It was supposed that if two streets were far from each other, they could be classified as belonging to different parts of the city and a further analysis was not needed. When the distance between streets shortens, they more and more often belong to a common category in a low resolution representation, and more information is needed to decide if they cross. This in turn requires more time.

Method

Fifty pairs of streets in the city area of Turku were selected. Thirty-four of these streets crossed each other, and 16 did not cross. A slide was produced of each pair by photographing a text written according to the formula "the corner of street A and street B." The same street name could appear on several slides.

Each subject was first asked to estimate the degree of familiarity of the streets (not the corners) used as in Experiments 1 and 2. The aim of the rating task was to activate the material in the subjects' memories and it preceded the measurement of latencies. The interaction between the effect of distance on reaction time and familiarity had not yet been found when this experiment was performed, and the rating task was intended to attenuate the effect of familiarity variation.

The reaction-time task was then demonstrated to the subject, and the measurement proceeded as in Experiments 1 and 2. The key labeled YES was pressed if the streets crossed and a key labeled NO was pressed if the streets did not cross.

After the measurement of latencies, the subject had to indicate for each street the location that he first came to think of when he tried to imagine that street. The answers were tape-recorded.

The subjects were 20 students from the University of Turku who had lived in Turku all their lives. They all volunteered in Experiments 3 and 4.

Results

For each stimulus slide the familiarity score was computed by averaging the ratings obtained for each street on the slide.

The distance scores were based on the places the subjects reported when asked to mention the first place that appeared in their minds when they heard a particular street name. The places were plotted on a map and if one place was mentioned by the majority of the subjects, this was used for measuring the distances. Otherwise the reference points were found by computing the mean distance of different points mentioned from one end of the street. The distance score of the slide was the physical distance between these reference points.

This method for determining the distance scores was motivated by an intention to use this slide set in different experiments without the time-consuming interview phase. We accepted the method when we found that all answers were well clustered.

In order to obtain distance scores, only reaction latencies to slides representing nonexistent corners were included in further analysis. For these responses the error rate was 5.8%. Only correct responses were analyzed.

TABLE 19.2
Mean Reaction Time and Correlations Between RT and
Distance for Different Familiarity Ratings in Experiment 3

Familiarity Rating (1: high, 5: Low)	Mean RT (sec)	Correlation Between RT and Distance
0.00–1.25	2.915	–0.42
1.26–1.75	2.843	–0.68[a]

[a]$p < 0.001$

Analysis of mean latencies for each stimulus slide showed a statistically significant relationship between the distance score and the mean latency ($t = 4.50$, $df = 14$, $p < 0.001$). The relationship between the familiarity rating and the RT was not significant.

The data points were grouped according to familiarity rating to see if they showed the same trend as the results of Experiments 1 and 2. These results are displayed in Table 19.2. There is again a significant negative correlation between the distance and RT, and this correlation increases as the familiarity decreases.

EXPERIMENT 4

The three experiments reported previously show a negative correlation between physical distance and decision latency in a task demanding the subject to locate places or streets on his mental map and to report their relative locations. It is possible that this results follows from the fact that higher-level categories may be used as the basis for reactions. In Experiment 4 we tried to design a task that would require more detailed information of the mental map.

Method

The only difference between Experiments 3 and 4 was that in the latter each stimulus slide consisted of four street names in rows one below the other. The subjects were instructed to start from the first name and to proceed downward as rapidly as possible until they found a street that was not parallel to the others. The key labeled YES was pressed if a nonparallel street was found; otherwise the NO key was pressed. Of the 37 stimulus slides constructed for this experiment, 21 included a nonparallel street, whereas on 16 slides all the streets were parallel. The ratings collected before Experiment 3 were used in this experiment, too.

Results

The distance score for each slide was computed by adding the distances between the reference points of each pair of successive streets on the slide taking the nonparallel street as the last one. If all streets were parallel, the sum of distances between all the streets was used.

The familiarity score was again computed as the mean of the ratings for different streets, and the nonparallel street was the last one included into the average. It was thus assumed that subjects processed the streets sequentially and terminated the process if they found a crossing street.

The error rate was 15%. Only correct RTs were analyzed. The correlation between distance scores and RT was computed separately for the slides in which the nonparallel street was the second, the third, or the fourth street. These correlation coefficients were then pooled for one estimate of the correlation. There was a positive correlation of +.66 ($p < 0.01$) between distance score and reaction time when the slide included a nonparallel street but no correlation when all the four streets were parallel.

The data were again grouped on the basis of familiarity ratings. The results of this analysis are displayed in Table 19.3. In the case of positive slides the correlations were computed from the residuals obtained when the linear equation relating the position of the nonparallel street and the RT was first fitted to the data. This way the results do not reflect the effect of list position. For the negative slides the correlation was computed from raw scores. High familiarity again attenuates the correlation. The lack of correlation in the case in which all the streets were parallel may follow from the fact that all the slides in this group belonged to the second familiarity group.

TABLE 19.3
Mean Reaction Time and Correlations Between RT and
Distance for Different Familiarity Ratings in Experiment 4

Familiarity Rating (1: high, 5: Low)	Mean RT (sec)	Correlation Between RT and Distance
Positive slides (All streets not parallel)		
0.00–1.25	—	—
1.26–1.75	4.113	0.28
1.76–5.00	5.083	0.59[a]
Negative slides (All streets parallel)		
0.00–1.25	—	
1.26–1.75	4.730	−0.06
1.76–5.00	—	

[a] $p < 0.05$

DISCUSSION

In all the experiments reported here the actual physical distances did affect the decision latencies. The results of the first three experiments do not, however, lend support to the idea of mental scanning in its simplest sense; that is, the time needed to locate a place to the right or to the left from a known reference does not increase as the distance between these places increases. On the contrary the Ss are able to make decisions more rapidly when the distance is longer. Similar results are obtained when the subjects are required to decide if two streets cross each other or not.

In contrast, when the Ss have to decide if two or more streets are parallel, the decision latencies increase as the distance between the streets increases.

The results of the first three experiments display the so-called "symbolic distance effect." This effect was first found when Ss were required to make memory comparisons of animal size (Moyer, 1973). The time was inversely related to the subjects' estimate of the differences in the sizes of the animals compared. Another example of the symbolic distance effect is obtained when the Ss have to decide which of two letters occurs later in the alphabet or whether a letter pair is in correct alphabetic order (for a recent analysis of alphabetic-order judgments, see Hamilton & Sanford, 1978). RT is again inversely related to the ordinal distance.

In the study of symbolic distance effects a line of theorizing adopted by many writers emphasizes the similarity between perceptual and memory processes (Kerst & Howard, 1978; Moyer & Bayer, 1976; Paivio, 1975). They explain the symbolic distance effect by referring to the fact that perceptual judgments of stimuli that are actually present are made more rapidly as the difference between the sizes of the objects compared increases. It is also thought that the symbolic distance effect provides support to the idea that analogue representations are used by the human information-processing system, since such representations are appropriately processed by mechanisms usually recruited during perception.

The symbolic distance effect in our experiments is based on situations that are not actually size-comparison tasks. After discovering these symbolic distance effects, we did an experiment to measure symbolic distance effects more carefully (Lehtiö & Tervonen, 1976). We used six different distances in the city of Helsinki as standards (each in turn) and measured the decision latencies when the subjects had to compare a given distance with a standard. For each standard, two well-known places in the city of Helsinki were described to subjects who were asked to use the straight-line distance between those places as a standard. Similarly each test slide consisted of two names of places and their straight-line distance was compared to that of the standard. For each standard a block of 40 test slides was presented. Figure 19.1 shows

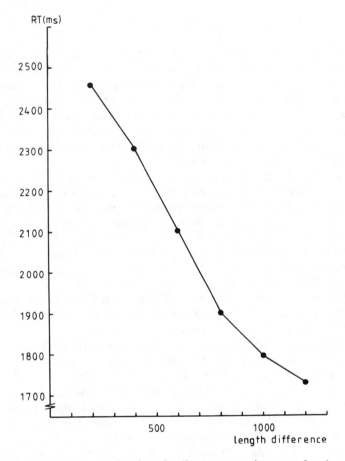

FIG. 19.1. Mean reaction times for distance comparisons as a function of
length differences. The length difference ranges were 100...299, 300...499,
500...699, 700...899, 900...1099, and 1100...1299 m. Each group mean is
based on approximately 180 RT measurements.

the relation between RT and the difference between the compared distance
and the distance of the standard averaged over all standards. The graph in
Fig. 19.1 displays a very pronounced symbolic distance effect.

It is proposed that the results of the previous experiments may be understood in terms of hierarchical memory organization. People usually acquire
information about a city piecewise: They learn that around a certain landmark certain places are located; they also learn how to move from one area or
landmark to another using public transportation or driving along main
streets. This information is then used during the planning of daily activities.

We think that it is important to assume that the image of the city we have is also modified by this planning activity. It is supposed that the way we acquire information from the environment, as well as the way we use it, induces hierarchical structure to the memory representation. This means that people have multiple representations of a city. These representations allow different degrees of resolution in making decisions about features of the city. When memory is activated, people first obtain access to a low resolution representation that enables them to solve problems within its resolution limits. Subjects also spontaneously report that they first have a fuzzy image of a part of the town memorized, including perhaps the most important building in that area. Depending on the task, subjects may have to recall more and more details and this is effected by activated lower levels of the representation.

When our subjects are classifying places to the left or to the right of a reference line or categorizing streets as crossing and noncrossing ones, they are able to solve these tasks using a higher level of the hierarchical representation of the city when the places are further away from each other. On these higher levels, fewer relations need be processed. While comparing distances the Ss again take advantage of the levels of the hierarchy: They are able to extract enough metric information to solve the comparison problems on a higher level of hierarchy when the difference between the distances is large but not when it is small.

Finally when Ss have to answer if two streets are parallel, they have to use a detailed representation and to construct a path from one street to the other using relational information and this activity takes longer when the distance is longer.

It has been demonstrated by many authors (for a recent review, see Friedman, 1978) that memory comparisons display the symbolic distance effect even when comparisons are based on a nonperceptual dimension. It is not unrealistic to speculate that both perceptual and memory comparisons are based on mechanisms having access to representations of different resolution and that this information is utilized sequentially.

REFERENCES

Friedman, A. Memorial comparisons without the "mind's eye." *Journal of Verbal Learning and Verbal Behavior,* 1978, *17,* 427–444.

Hamilton, J. M. E., & Sanford, A. J. The symbolic distance effect for alphabetic order judgments: A subjective report and reaction time analysis. *Quarterly Journal of Experimental Psychology,* 1978, *30,* 33–43.

Kerst, S. M., & Howard, J. H., Jr. Memory psychophysics for visual area and length. *Memory & Cognition,* 1978, *6,* 327–335.

Kosslyn, S. M. Scanning visual images: Some structural implications. *Perception & Psychophysics,* 1973, *14,* 90–94.

Kosslyn, S. M., Reiser, B. J., & Ball, T. M. Visual images preserve metric spatial information: Evidence from studies of image scanning. *Journal of Experimental Psychology: Human Perception and Performance*, 1978, *4*, 47–60.

Lehtiö, P. K., & Kauri, T. An experiment in memory scanning. In S. Kornblum (Ed.), *Attention and Performance IV*, New York: Academic Press, 1973.

Lehtiö, P. K., & Tervonen, T. An unpublished experiment, 1976.

Moyer, R. S. Comparing objects in memory: Evidence suggesting an internal psychophysics. *Perception & Psychophysics*, 1973, *13*, 180–184.

Moyer, R. S., & Bayer, R. H. Mental comparisons and the symbolic distance effect. *Cognitive Psychoogy*, 1976, *8*, 228–246.

Paivio, A. Perceptual comparisons through the mind's eye. *Memory & Cognition*, 1975, *3*, 635–647.

Shepard, R. N. The mental image. *American Psychologist*, 1978, *33*, 125–137.

Shepard, R. N., & Chipman, S. Second-order isomorphism of internal representations: Shapes of states. *Cognitive Psychology*, 1970, *1*, 1–17.

V LANGUAGE COMPREHENSION

20 Comprehension and Memory in Rapid Sequential Reading

Mary C. Potter
Massachusetts Institute of Technology

Judith F. Kroll
Institute for Cognitive Studies
Rutgers University

Carol Harris
Massachusetts Institute of Technology
United States

ABSTRACT

In RSVP (rapid serial visual presentation—Forster, 1970), text is presented one word at a time, each word appearing at fixation. Single RSVP *sentences* can be read and accurately recalled when presented at a rate as high as 12 words a second, twice as fast as people normally read. Although RSVP *paragraphs* seem to be understood when presented at that rate, they are remembered poorly. Four models of comprehension give different explanations of that deficit. The models were investigated by presenting paragraphs that were difficult to structure unless the topic was known. A sentence that mentioned the critical topic was presented at the beginning, in the middle, or at the end of the paragraph, or was omitted; the effect on recall of the preceding and following text was measured. At each of three rates of presentation (4, 8, and 12 words a second plus a two-word pause between sentences), readers were able to comprehend RSVP text at both local and global or schematic levels, contrary to models in which local processing takes place before global integration or vice versa. The results support a model in which higher-level schemas interact with ongoing sentence processing. Memory impairment at higher rates may reflect disruption of a process of consolidation because RSVP readers evidently understood much more than they could remember immediately thereafter. Listening to spoken text at 3.3 words a second was similar to RSVP reading at that rate. Readers of conventional text remembered more of what they did read than either listeners or RSVP readers, but they could not read as fast as the higher RSVP rates even when pressed.

INTRODUCTION

What factors limit the rate at which people read? A skilled adult reads nontechnical material at about 300 words a minute, or 5 words a second. Advocates of speed reading have claimed that a more efficient pattern of eye fixations (among other things) can lead to much faster reading than that. But others (e.g., Gibson & Levin, 1975) argue that reading rate is limited by the speed of comprehension. If the first view is correct, people might be able to read faster (without impairment of comprehension) if eye movements were bypassed. One way to accomplish this is to present the words of a sentence one at a time at the point of fixation; eye movements are unnecessary and so the rate of reading is controlled by the experimenter. Forster (1970) called this method *RSVP* (rapid serial visual presentation). Research to be reviewed showed that single RSVP sentences can be perceived adequately when presented at about twice the normal reading rate. The purpose of the experiments reported here was to examine the ability to understand and remember RSVP paragraphs.

RSVP SENTENCES

As a background to the present experiments, it is important to consider how well readers can process RSVP sentences presented in isolation. A body of work by Forster (1970) and his colleagues (cf. Forster, 1974, for a review) demonstrated that RSVP sentences of six to eight words are not recalled perfectly when presented at 16 words per second (wps); some 30% of the words are omitted. Nonetheless, viewers appeared to process such a sequence as a sentence, because syntactic complexity, plausibility, and word order (correct versus scrambled) all affected the accuracy of recall. Forster (1974) concluded that readers identify more of the words than they can remember; words may be forgotten if the sentence structure into which they fit is difficult to compute during presentation.[1]

---

[1]Mitchell (1979) has recently questioned Forster's interpretation; in Mitchell's experiment, report of the first four words of a seven-word RSVP sentence was reduced when the last three words were nonsensical rather than reasonable. Mitchell argues that such a backward-acting effect demonstrates that sentence processing did not take place word by word during presentation but was probably carried out after presentation, using a short-term visual representation. The criticism is not compelling, because Mitchell used a rate of 20 wps (higher than Forster's) and because the nonsensical words could have caused subjects to forget the initial part of the sentence, even if it had been processed.

Even though Forster and his colleagues argued that more of a sentence was seen than was retained, they acknowledged that visual masking may have prevented the adequate registration of many words. Therefore, Potter, Kroll, Yachzel, & Cohen (1978) used a slower rate of 12 wps at which visual masking was minimal. They presented RSVP sentences of 8 to 14 words and required subjects to judge the plausibility of each sentence before writing it down. Plausibility hinged on the last word of a sentence; for example, *Judy needed the stool to reach the lightbulb* was made implausible by replacing *lightbulb* with *moon*. Plausibility judgments were made accurately (11% errors) and rather rapidly (the mean RT was 1293 msec, from the onset of the last word of the sentence). In recall, 87% of the words were correct. Unlike some previous experiments in which different strategies were adopted by subjects reading for recall and reading for comprehension (Aaronson, 1976), in this experiment groups of subjects who just judged sentence plausibility or just recalled the sentence differed little from subjects who did both tasks.

REBUS Sentences. To investigate the extent to which readers were processing RSVP sentences during presentation, Potter et al. replaced nouns in some of the sentences with pictures of objects (they termed these *REBUS sentences*). For example, in the sentence given earlier, replaced *stool*.

Earlier work (Potter & Faulconer, 1975) had shown that pictured objects are understood at least as fast as written names of the same objects, but the pictures take some 200–300 msec longer to name aloud than the words. If RSVP readers simply retain an ordered string of words in short-term memory and process sentence meaning later, a picture should disrupt processing because of the delay in retrieving its verbal code—the code necessary to retain a rapid ordered sequence (Paivio & Csapo, 1971). Although it did turn out that plausibility decisions were 100 msec slower for REBUS sentences than for all-word sentences, there was no difference in decision accuracy and virtually no difference (86% versus 87%) in recall accuracy. Order errors in recall, which might have been expected to be frequent for the REBUS sentences, occurred for only 1.5% of the words and pictures, compared with 0.8% in all-word sentences. The ease with which subjects could read REBUS sentences suggested that RSVP sentences are understood word by word or phrase by phrase as they are presented.

Scrambled Sentences. Given the difficulty of detecting the order of even a short sequence of random items presented at rates of 6 per second and higher (Aaronson, Markowitz, & Shapiro, 1971; Scarborough & Sternberg, 1967), it was conceivable that subjects were unable to register the input order of the words (and the picture). Instead, they might have constructed a plausible order after presentation—contrary to the tentative conclusion that understanding occurs during presentation. Forster (1970) had already rejected that counterargument, because recall of scrambled sentences was less accurate than recall of normally ordered sentences. Potter et al. (1978) replicated Forster's result, using the materials already described and again presenting the sentences as 12 wps. It was immediately apparent that readers could not judge sentence plausibility until they had engaged in a lengthy process of reconstruction, so subjects were not required to make a plausibility judgment. Recall of the sentences—whether requested in the order of presentation or in the order of the reconstructed original sentence—was markedly lower for the scrambled sentences. Only 61% of the words were recalled, compared with 90% when the same sentences were presented in normal order. (Scrambled REBUS sentences fared no worse than scrambled all-word sentences.) Order errors were numerous; 26% of the words recalled were out of order, compared with 1% in the normally ordered sentences.

These results showed unambiguously that the order of presentation was perceived and used in RSVP reading at 12 wps, thus confirming that sentence processing took place during presentation. Not only were words incorporated into a representation of the sentence as they appeared but so were the REBUS pictures. As already indicated, a lexical entry for a picture cannot be retrieved until at least 200 msec after that of a written word, but conceptual meaning is available for a picture as fast as for a word. Evidently the developing representation of an RSVP sentence was conceptual, not exclusively linguistic, so the picture could be incorporated easily.

Telegraphic Sentences.   Another hypothesis considered by Potter et al. was that observers were not really reading RSVP sentences normally but were seeing content words and guessing the short, hard-to-see function words. When predictable function words were omitted and the resulting "telegrams" were presented in RSVP, however, numerous errors were made in guessing the missing words; there were also somewhat more errors in recall of the words actually presented. With blank frames replacing the missing words, comprehension and recall were still impaired. So, as in normal language processing, both sentence order and "redundant" function words play significant roles in RSVP reading.

Conventional Reading Versus RSVP.   Finally, to make a direct assessment of the similarities and differences between conventional reading and RSVP reading, Potter et al. (1978) presented single sentences in a conventional simultaneous form for the same total time as the RSVP sentences. Subjects were unable to read the whole sentence in the time available and therefore made more recall errors than with RSVP. When an extra 300-msec viewing time was added (an increase of about 30%), recall equaled that for RSVP, but RT to make a plausibility decision was still about 400 msec longer; thus, a conventional sentence required about 700 msec longer than an RSVP sentence to read and understand.

Single RSVP Sentences: Conclusions and Implications

It is plain from these studies and others not reviewed here (Frauenfelder, Dommergues, Mehler, & Segui, 1979; Fischler & Bloom, 1978; Pfafflin, 1974) that all or most of a sentence can be understood and recalled, at a presentation rate of 12 words a second. Further, there is evidence that such sentences are processed and understood during presentation. In answer to our initial question about the limits on the rate of reading, the results seem to support the view that people could read twice as fast as they do if they were not held back by inefficient eye fixations. Reading at 12 words a second is a somewhat breathless experience, however, and some viewers doubted that they could read a paragraph at that rate. Perfetti and Lesgold (1977) give a description of slow readers that might apply to RSVP reading: "In comprehension there are recurrent input and output events for short-term memory. The slow coder [or the normal reader of RSVP text] will . . . fall behind in the cycle of comprehension events, revert to less efficient patterning of the various comprehension process components, and finally fail to comprehend some of the discourse [p. 17]." To see whether RSVP reading could be sustained over several sentences, the following experiments examined understanding and retention of RSVP paragraphs.

RSVP PARAGRAPHS

An initial experiment (Potter & Kroll, 1977) was carried out to see whether RSVP reading would simply break down when a paragraph was presented. The paragraphs were followed by questions about the content. For example, one paragraph included the sentence *Weapons and pots of food were buried with them to protect them in their new life;* subjects were asked, *With what were dead Egyptians buried?* Responses were scored on a scale from 0 (no answer or entirely wrong answer) to 1 (verbatim answer); a partially correct answer was scored .50; a paraphrase, .75. When the sentences were presented at the rate of 12 words a second with a 167-msec pause between sentences (the equivalent of two words), the mean score was .52, demonstrating that readers had picked up a substantial amount of information from the paragraphs. By comparison, when other subjects read the paragraphs in conventional form at their own pace, taking more than three times as long, scores averaged .65.

Two other reading conditions were examined in that experiment. In one, the RSVP sentences were followed by a 1-sec pause instead of a 167-msec pause. Scores rose to .59, approaching the accuracy of the much slower self-paced readers. In the final condition the paragraphs were presented conventionally but subjects were given the same brief time to read as the first RSVP group. The scores averaged .47, slightly below the RSVP group's .52. Accuracy was particularly low for questions about material at the end of the paragraph; it was clear that conventional readers could not finish the paragraph in the time available.

Models of Comprehension

The experiment just described showed that RSVP paragraphs presented at 12 words a second could be understood and remembered at least in part. Increasing the total processing time by lengthening the pause between sentences did improve performance, however; evidently one or more aspects of processing could not be completed when time was limited. Theories of language comprehension and retention make different predictions about what component of processing should fail first, as presentation speeds up. Consider the following four models of comprehension.

First, the *cyclic model:* Readers may simply fall behind in a fixed processing cycle, as in Perfetti and Lesgold's description of poor readers. Readers would still be processing the first sentence when the next appeared, so they would pick up only part of the second sentence, and so on; that is, the language-processing apparatus would jam, and readers would process only fragments of the subsequent text. Although recall in the experiment just described did not exhibit the pattern of disintegration that the cyclic model would predict, the retention test may have been insufficiently sensitive.

A second model of text comprehension contrasts processing of individual sentences with integration of sentence information into the higher-order structure of the text—its main topic or theme. The *sentence-first model* proposes that each sentence is initially processed in a context-free manner and then integrated into the higher-order structure. A reason for entertaining this two-stage hypothesis is that the syntax and perhaps the semantics of a sentence is designed for autonomous processing. Mitchell and Green (1978) report that relevant prior context caused readers to pause longer at the end of a sentence but did not alter reading time within a sentence. They take this result as support for the sentence-first model: Integration with context occurs *after* initial sentence comprehension. The sentence-first model would predict that when less time is available for processing, the second stage (integration with higher-order structure) would not be completed.

A third view of text comprehension, the *schema-first model,* is one that speed-reading advocates have suggested: As reading is speeded, individual sentences are not fully processed, but higher-level structures are nonetheless built up. The idea is not unreasonable. Conceptual processing based on spreading activation from individual word concepts has been proposed as a supplement to syntactic parsing (Anderson, Kline, & Lewis, 1977), and in Quillian's (1969) model such spreading activation is the first step in processing. Higher-level structures might be built directly on the crude conceptual representation, even if processing time was too short for complete parsing and interpretation of individual sentences.

The fourth view of text comprehension, the *interactive model*, proposes that the processing of each sentence is influenced by the higher-order structure already developed, so that the sentence is incorporated directly into the growing text structure *as* it is processed, not afterward. For example, retrieval of the referent of a pronoun may occur as soon as the pronoun appears rather than after the sentence has been processed (Carpenter & Just, 1977).

EXPERIMENT 1:
ROLE OF A TOPIC SENTENCE IN
COMPREHENSION OF RSVP PARAGRAPHS

The purpose of Experiment 1 was to distinguish among the four models of comprehension. We describe the experiment briefly, before giving the predictions of each model. RSVP paragraphs were presented at three within-sentence rates, 4, 8, or 12 wps—the slowest rate being close to that of normal speech and reading. (There was a pause equivalent to two words after each sentence, so the overall rates averaged 3.3, 6.7, and 10 wps.) Immediately after viewing a paragraph, subjects wrote down what they remembered. To assess readers' ability to incorporate higher-order structure, we used paragraphs that appeared to be ambiguous and poorly integrated unless the topic of the discourse was known (a method adopted by Bransford & Johnson, 1972; Dooling & Lachman, 1971; and others). A sentence that mentioned the topic was placed at the beginning, middle, or end of the paragraph or was omitted altogether, thus controlling the availability of a schema that would presumably assist comprehension.

The following paragraph is an example:

> It seemed like hours since I had called. Finally it arrived, richly colored but a little thin. I wondered if it was too hot to touch. The smell was so strong that I couldn't help but try. I pulled at one section, but it was difficult to remove, so I tried another. Elastic fibers developed, attaching it to the rest. I exerted more force. As I pulled, however, droplets of hot oil splashed off one side, burning my hand. I dropped it. Perhaps I could last a couple more minutes. I was impatient, but it was very hot.[2]

In this version, the topic sentence "I was hungry, but the pizza was very hot" was modified to delete information about the topic.

---

[2]We thank Helene Intraub for writing this paragraph about pizza; the reader may wish to attempt verbatim recall without rereading the paragraph.

In previous studies using this paradigm, the topic was presented explicitly as the title or theme of the paragraph. Bransford and Johnson (1972) found that recall of the paragraph was improved when the title was given in advance, whereas giving the title only after the paragraph was little better than not giving it at all. Similar results were obtained by Dooling and Mullet (1973). Both sets of authors concluded that advance knowledge of the topic led to more effective encoding of the paragraph, not simply to better retrieval or reconstruction.[3]

Predictions of the Four Models. Paragraphs like the previous one should be recalled more accurately and completely when the topic sentence appears at the beginning, provided that readers understand the topic sentence and have time to make use of the schematic knowledge elicited by the topic as they read the paragraph. All four models agree on that basic assumption, so all predict that when text is presented at a normal reading rate, the topic sentence will lead to an improvement in recall of text that follows it.

The models make different predictions when text is presented more rapidly than normal, although all predict a deficit in recall. The *cyclic* model predicts that recall will decline markedly after the first sentence or two, as readers fall behind. The topic sentence will help only if it appears at the beginning, because it will simply be missed when it appears later in the paragraph. The *sentence-first model* predicts that when processing time is reduced, there will be time only to process each sentence independently, not to carry out the second step of integrating it with an overall schema. Therefore the usefulness of the topic sentence will *diminish* as rate increases. The *schema-first model* predicts the opposite: Because a higher-level schema can be built on a crude initial analysis of a sentence, an integrating topic will be *increasingly* helpful as rate increases. The availability of a higher-order structure may partially compensate for failure to complete the processing of individual sentences. A corollary of this prediction is that paraphrase should replace verbatim recall as rate increases.

Finally, the *interactive model* predicts that because sentence processing and higher-order processing are carried out together, a reduction in reading time will have similar effects on both aspects of processing; that is, knowledge of a paragraph's topic will be helpful at all rates of reading. Unlike the cyclic model, the interactive model does not predict that comprehension will decline markedly after the first few sentences. No one aspect of processing fails under time pressure; rather, the whole process becomes less accurate.

---

[3]When recall is delayed for a day or more, the topic-after condition is superior to the no-topic condition; that is, reconstructive processes become increasingly important over time, as Bartlett (1932) observed. Because our interest is in initial encoding rather than reconstruction, immediate recall is the relevant measure.

Method

The materials were four paragraphs of 87 to 128 words; one was the pizza paragraph given previously and the other three (given in the Appendix) were adapted from paragraphs of Dooling and Lachman (1971) and Bransford and Johnson (1972). There were also two practice paragraphs. The topic of the paragraph was mentioned in a sentence that was part of the paragraph, written so that it could appear naturally as the first sentence, the last sentence, or a sentence near the middle of the paragraph. When the topic was omitted, a substitute sentence similar to the topic sentence was placed at the end of the paragraph, to keep the overall length approximately constant in all four conditions.

Each subject saw one of the four paragraphs in each of four conditions: The topic sentence was the first, middle, or last sentence or was omitted. The four conditions were counterbalanced over the four paragraphs, so that there were four versions of the materials. The four versions were filmed one word per frame on 16-mm black-and-white film, developed so that the words were white on black. Two blank frames were inserted between sentences. A warning row of asterisks preceded the beginning of each paragraph by nine frames.

Three groups of 16 subjects read the paragraphs at the rate of 4, 8, or 12 wps (when the two extra frames between sentences are included, the overall rates averaged 3.3, 6.7, and 10 wps—33, 17, or 11 sec per paragraph). The slowest rate was similar to a brisk rate of reading aloud. The two practice paragraphs were presented at the same rate as the test paragraphs.

The subject's task was to read the paragraph and then write it down as completely and accurately as possible. Subjects were encouraged to attempt a verbatim recall but were instructed to include anything they remembered even if they knew it was not verbatim. They were also told that they would do better if they just attempted to understand the paragraph rather than trying to "memorize" it during presentation. Subjects were not told about the topic sentences. Because the topic was only mentioned casually as part of the paragraph, the design of the experiment was not obvious, and no subject reported having figured out that giving or not giving the topic was the main variable.

Scoring

Report of the Topic.   If the topic (e.g., *pizza*) was directly mentioned at any point in recall (whether or not the rest of the topic sentence was recalled), the topic was scored as understood (or guessed, in the no-topic condition).

Verbatim and Paraphrase Recall.   Recall of each half of the paragraph was scored separately, excluding the topic sentence. A count of the number of words correct is difficult to obtain for paragraph recall because of the large number of repeated words in a paragraph, including many function words that are likely to be used by a subject even if he or she is simply guessing. Moreover, verbatim word counts fail to give credit for paraphrased but otherwise correct recall or gist recall that condenses and summarizes the ideas in a paragraph. For that reason we used a scoring system that permitted us to look at both verbatim recall and paraphrase. The paragraphs were broken down into idea units such that most function words were included with a content word. The following are examples; slashes separate the units. *A newspaper/is better than/a magazine. A rock/will serve as/an anchor. Finally/it arrived,/richly/colored/but a little/thin.* There were 1.7 words per idea unit, overall. As will be evident from these examples, the division into minimal idea units was pragmatic, guided by common sense (Hasher & Griffin, 1978). If a subject wrote down all the words in the idea unit in correct order, verbatim credit for that idea unit was given. If a synonym or paraphrase that adequately conveyed the idea was reported or if the content words but not the function words were accurate or if word order was altered, credit for a paraphrase was given. For example, *can be used for* was considered as a paraphrase of *will serve as,* and *the anchor* for *an anchor.*

Logical Errors.   Whenever idea units were reported in a combination that contradicted the sense of the paragraph [e.g., by reversing two ideas, as in *A magazine is better than a newspaper*—see previous example] a logical error was scored. Similarly, any intrusions that were incompatible with the message of the paragraph were considered logical errors.

Thematic Intrusions and Paraphrases.   Recall of each half of the paragraph (again excluding the topic sentence) was examined for evidence—in the form of an intrusion or paraphrase—that the topic had been understood. For example, several subjects wrote *Soon they will all be dirty again* instead of *Soon they will all be used again.* The substitution of *dirty* was taken as an indication that the topic—doing the laundry—had been understood. The score was binary: Such evidence was scored as present or absent in a given half. Exactly the same criteria were applied whether or not the subject had known the topic when reading that part of the text, so this measure also gave an indication of the extent of guessing or reconstruction.

Results and Discussion

Report of the topic.   The left panel of Fig. 20.1 shows the percentage of paragraph recalls in which the topic (e.g., *pizza* or *kite*) was directly mentioned. Note first that the topic was rarely guessed in the no-topic condition. When the topic sentence was included, however, the topic was highly likely to

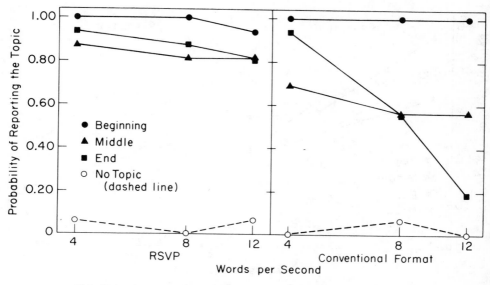

FIG. 20.1.   Probability of reporting the topic, as a function of the position of the topic sentence in the paragraph, for Experiment 1 (RSVP) and Experiment 2 (conventional reading).

be perceived and recalled, especially when presented in the first sentence. Moreover, pickup of the topic was almost as likely at a presentation rate of 12 wps as it was at 4 wps, showing that most of the sentences were comprehended at even the fastest presentation rate. This result conflicts with the cyclic model, which predicts a failure (at high rates) to process the topic sentence when it appears in the middle of the paragraph.

Recall of Paragraph Halves.   The percentages of idea units recalled in each condition (combining verbatim and paraphrase) are shown in Fig. 20.2. Recall of the topic sentence itself is *not* included in these scores. The results are broken down by paragraph half in order to assess the effect of presenting the topic in the middle of the paragraph. (Because the two halves were not matched for difficulty, absolute comparisons between halves are unwarranted, but interactions with rate or topic position may be examined.) Clearly, having the topic beforehand improved recall. In the first half, having the topic at the beginning increased recall by 23%, compared with the other three conditions combined. In the second half, the effect of the topic was even more marked. When it had appeared at the beginning, there was a 66% improvement, compared with the conditions in which it appeared at the end or not at all; when the topic appeared in the middle (i.e., just before the second half), recall was improved by 38%. Moreover, reading the topic sentence *after* the

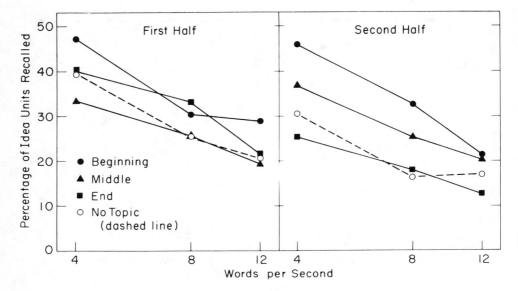

FIG. 20.2.   Experiment 1 (RSVP): Percentage of idea units recalled in each half of the paragraph, as a function of the position of the topic sentence in the paragraph.

text had no positive effect on recall: There was no systematic difference between giving the topic at the end and not at all, and having the topic in the middle only helped the material that followed. Thus reconstruction or guessing played no visible role in the improvement brought about by reading the topic sentence.

In the analysis of variance with topic position and paragraph half as within-subjects variables (and rate as a between-subjects variable) the main effect of topic, $F(3, 135) = 6.05$, and the interaction of topic and half, $F(3, 135) = 4.84$, were significant at the .01 level. The main effect of decreasing the *time* to process the paragraph is also clear. Overall, as less time was available for processing, recall decreased from 37% of the idea units at 4 wps to 26% at 8 wps to 20% at 12 wps, $F(2, 45) = 14.75$, $p < .01$.[4]

The main theoretical question is whether the topic was differentially effective at different rates of presentation. There was no marked change in the contribution of the topic as rate increased. Rate did not interact significantly

---

[4]Measured as the percentage recalled per second of presentation (including pauses), the 12-wps rate was the most efficient. The mean number of idea units recalled per second of presentation, across all topic conditions, was .74, 1.02, and 1.20 for rates of 4, 8, and 12 wps, respectively. Keesey (1973) presented successive *lines* of text at various rates and found that the most efficient rate with that technique was 8 wps.

with either topic position or half; all F's were less than 1.0. Overall (considering both halves of the paragraph), recall increased by 31% in the 4-wps group when the topic was known at the time of reading, by 32% in the 8-wps group, and by 40% in the 12-wps group.[5] Again, the obvious ability of readers to see and use topic sentence at all rates of presentation, even when it appeared in the middle of the paragraph, contradicts the cyclic model; nor did recall of the second half of the paragraph suffer more than the first half, as rate increased.[6] Neither the sentence-first nor the schema-first model is supported by these results, because the predicted interaction between rate of presentation and topic availability did not materialize. Only the interactive model is consistent with this outcome.

Paraphrase Versus Verbatim Recall. The schema-first model predicts that paraphrase will replace verbatim recall as rate increases, because a higher-level schema will be constructed without complete processing of each sentence. The ratio of paraphrase recall to total recall was .41 at 4 wps, .47 at 8 wps, and .51 at 12 wps, which offers a modicum of support for the model. In other respects, including the effect of knowing the topic, the results for verbatim and paraphrase recall were remarkably similar.

Logical Errors. In addition to a reduction in recall, failure to understand could result in mistaken interpretations that we termed "logical errors." Errors of this kind increased significantly as rate of presentation increased. Of the idea units recalled, 3, 8, and 13% were logical errors in the 4-, 8-, and 12-wps conditions, respectively. Logical errors were less than half as likely when the topic was known at the time of reading, however. There was no consistent interaction of topic and rate of presentation, again indicating that the topic helped comprehension at even the highest rate of presentation.

Thematic Intrusions. Each subject's recall of each paragraph half was scored as including or not including a paraphrase or intrusion that indicated understanding of the topic. In the 4-wps condition, the percentage of paragraph halves with a thematic intrusion in recall rose from 5% when the theme

---

[5]Although the percentage of improvement due to the topic increased slightly with faster rates of presentation, the absolute change in amount recalled became slightly smaller (see Fig. 20.2): An absolute increase of 10.6, 7.2, and 7.1% in the percentage of ideas recalled for the 4, 8, and 12 wps, respectively.

[6]Presenting the topic in the middle of a paragraph, however, did not help recall of the second half of the paragraph as much as presenting it at the beginning. Is that evidence for processing failure? A different explanation is that subjects had already set up an ad hoc schema for the information in the first half and were unable to switch instantly to the new schema indicated by the topical information (Kieras, 1978). Consistent with that hypothesis, recall of the *first* half of the paragraph was poorest when the topic appeared in the middle (Fig. 20.2a).

had not appeared yet to 44% when it had; in the 8-wps condition, the corresponding percentages were 5 and 33%; in the 12-wps condition, 8 and 14%. Statistical analyses showed that the main effect of the topic and the interaction between rate of presentation and the topic were significant. When the topic was presented after a given half of the paragraph, topic intrusions were no more frequent than when the topic was omitted altogether. Clearly most of the intrusions reflected initial encoding, not just reconstruction during recall. (Incidentally, intrusions in recall that did not paraphrase material in the paragraph were infrequent, about 12% of total recall.) In contrast to the results for correct recall, then, the pattern of theme-relevant paraphrases and intrusions is consistent with the sentence-first model: There was less evidence for schema-related intrusions at higher rates of presentation.

Conclusions from Experiment 1

As the earlier experiment with RSVP paragraphs had also suggested (Potter & Kroll, 1977), the cyclic model underestimates a reader's capacity to keep up with RSVP paragraphs presented at 12 wps. The sentence-first model received support from the pattern of theme-related intrusions, which were less frequent at higher rates of presentation. But the opposite model, the schema-first model, received support from the increase in paraphrase relative to verbatim recall as rate increased. None of these three models, though, gives an explanation of the principal result: Knowledge of the topic had a consistently positive effect at all rates of presentation.

That leaves the interactive model, which proposes that available context is directly used during the processing of each successive sentence. This model has been supported in studies of text processing at normal rates of presentation (Marslen-Wilson & Welsh, 1978), but it is somewhat surprising to discover that context can be used at a reading rate of 12 wps. The interactive model, however, does not give a specific explanation for the overall drop in recall as rate of presentation increases (Fig. 20.2). The other three models specified particular loci of the breakdown in text processing when rate is increased, but all three were rejected. One possibility not yet considered is that the breakdown is in a later stage of processing than comprehension, a stage of consolidation. Consideration of this and other explanations is postponed until the final discussion.

EXPERIMENT 2:
FAST CONVENTIONAL READING

The conclusions reached from Experiment 1 were based on the assumption that RSVP reading engages normal language processing mechanisms, although it pushes them beyond a rate that most people can adopt in conventional reading. A possible objection to RSVP is that it causes viewers to adopt a mode of processing that is not like normal reading but might be more like skimming or skipping over material. A parallel criticism has been made of speed reading—that it amounts to skimming rather than rapid but complete reading (Gibson & Levin, 1975). The purpose of Experiment 2 was to compare conventional reading with RSVP reading, when subjects are given the same total time to read.

We considered two possible outcomes. First, readers might be able to read and understand conventional text as rapidly, when pressed, as RSVP readers. If so, that would place RSVP reading in the same category as normal skimming. Second, readers of normal text might not be able to finish the paragraphs at the faster rates without skipping. This outcome would support the assumption that RSVP permits a higher rate of reading than is otherwise possible, although still ensuring that almost all words are perceived. In either case, the costs and benefits of RSVP and conventional reading could be compared.

Method

The paragraphs of Experiment 1 were typed in a conventional format and subjects were given the same total times to read them (silently) as the RSVP subjects, that is, about 33, 17, or 11 sec per paragraph. In all other respects the design, procedure, and scoring were identical to Experiment 1. As before, a different group of 16 subjects read the paragraphs at each rate.

Results and Discussion

One of the main characteristics of skimming is that some words, phrases, or sentences are not seen. Work of Rayner (1978) and others has shown that only the two or three words at or near the point of fixation can yield semantic information, so a skimmer is obliged to guess or omit any words that do not fall within such a fixation window. RSVP readers were very likely to see and recall the topic of the pragraph, which was conveyed by a key word or two in the topic sentence (pizza, kite, Christopher Columbus, laundry). Would conventional readers do as well? The right panel of Fig. 20.1 gives the results. The topic was never missed at the beginning, often missed in the middle, and when time was shortest, it was almost always missed at the end. (As in RSVP, the topic was rarely guessed when it had been omitted.) The difference between RSVP readers and conventional readers is summed up in these results. RSVP permitted at least superficial comprehension of all sentences, whereas conventional readers frequently skipped material or were unable to finish the paragraph.

Recall of Paragraph Halves.   Figure 20.3 shows the percentage of idea units recalled in each condition and can be compared with Fig. 20.2. In the

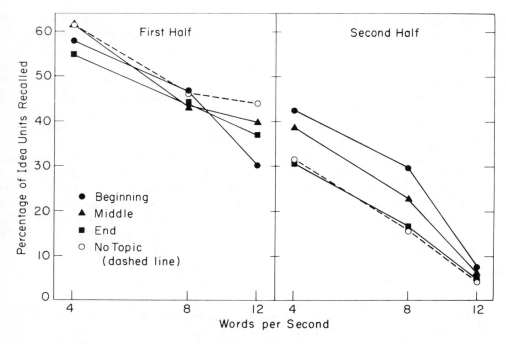

FIG. 20.3.   Experiment 2 (conventional reading): Percentage of idea units recalled in each half of the paragraph, as a function of the position of the topic sentence in the paragraph.

first half of the paragraph, conventional reading led to better recall than RSVP; in the second half, however, RSVP was better than conventional reading (these results and others reported here were statistically significant at the .05 level or better; details are omitted for brevity). The effect of having or not having the topic sentence at the beginning was different in the two experiments. In conventional reading, presence of the topic sentence had *no* effect on amount recalled from the first half of the paragraph but did affect recall of the second half.

 Why was only the second half aided? The result is unlikely to be a sampling error, for the same pattern was obtained at all three rates, with different groups of subjects. Our tentative explanation is the following. A reader of conventional text controls his or her rate of reading indirectly, by setting a comprehension criterion (or perhaps a comprehension-plus-memory criterion: See the final discussion). A given level of comprehension was reached more rapidly when a topic sentence was available, so subjects could read faster and therefore completed more of the second half of the paragraph before the time was up. Hence the topic only affected the amount read and recalled from the second half. This account assumes that the topic was used (when available) in comprehending the first half. In support of this assumption, there was a marked increase in topic-relevant paraphrases and intrusions in the first half of the paragraph when the topic was presented at the beginning, just as in Experiment 1.

Overall, the proportion of recalled idea units that were reported verbatim, rather than paraphrased, was higher in conventional reading (66%) than in RSVP (54%), particularly at the higher rates of presentation. Consistent with that result, the proportion of logical errors was higher in RSVP, at the two higher rates. Whereas in conventional reading there were between 3 and 4% logical errors at all three rates, in RSVP there were 3, 8, and 13% such errors, for increasing rates. (Particularly in RSVP, logical errors were more frequent when the topic had not yet appeared in the paragraph.)

Conclusions From Experiment 2

The ability of RSVP readers to pick up the topic, even at 12 wps, is the single most persuasive testimony for comprehension of most of the text during presentation. To select and remember that critical word, subjects had not only to see and understand it but also to appreciate its relevance to the rest of the paragraph. Although readers of conventional text digested rather completely the sentences they *did* read, under marked time pressure they failed to complete the paragraph or skipped sections of text. Unlike RSVP readers, therefore, they often missed the critical topic.

EXPERIMENT 3: SPOKEN PARAGRAPHS

In comparing Experiments 1 and 2, some differences were noted between recall of paragraphs read in RSVP and read conventionally. Conventional readers had the option of varying their rate of intake, but RSVP readers did not. Listening to speech is like RSVP in this respect, for listeners cannot ordinarily control a speaker's rate. The purpose of Experiment 3 was to see whether listening to a paragraph is more like RSVP reading than conventional reading is. Such an outcome would further support the assumption that RSVP reading elicits normal language processing. Previous work comparing memory for spoken and written discourse suggests that they are similar (Kintsch, Kosminsky, Streby, McKoon, & Keenan, 1975; Sticht, 1972), so no marked departure from the results of Experiments 1 and 2 was expected.

Only one rate of speech was used, corresponding to the slowest condition in Experiments 1 and 2. (It would be possible to compress speech artificially to achieve higher rates, but Miron and Brown, 1971, found that compressed speech declines markedly in intelligibility at rates above 6 wps.) This rate was not the most efficient for RSVP (see Footnote 4), so the absolute level of recall in listening, RSVP reading, and conventional reading was of less interest than the patterns of recall.

Method

The materials and procedure were identical to those of Experiments 1 and 2 except that only one group of 16 subjects was tested (because only one rate was used), and the paragraphs were recorded and played aloud to the subjects. They were read in normal intonation at a fairly brisk rate, 303 msec per word (in slow RSVP the rate within a sentence was 250 msec per word but including blanks between sentences it was 300 msec per word). Thus in Experiment 3 the overall time to process the paragraph was the same as in the slowest condition in Experiments 1 and 2.

Results and Discussion

The topic was invariably recalled, whatever its location in the paragraph, but rarely guessed—a pattern similar to that of conventional reading at the slow rate and RSVP at all rates. In all three modes of presentation, subjects recognized the significance of the topic sentence and recalled the topic. Recall of the two halves of the paragraph (omitting the topic sentence) is shown in Fig. 20.4, together with the results of the equivalent groups from Experiments 1 and 2. [The condition(s) in which the topic had already appeared are combined, as are the conditions in which the topic appeared afterward or not at all.] In an analysis comparing recall in the three modes of presentation, the main effect of presentation mode was not significant but the interaction between mode and half was (details are again omitted for brevity). In the first half of the paragraph, conventional reading led to significantly better recall than the other two modes, but in the second half there were no differences among the three modes. Recall was distributed more evenly over the whole paragraph in the spoken and RSVP conditions than in conventional reading.

In most other respects, performance in the three modes was similar. The overall effect of the placement of the topic sentence on recall was similar and highly significant in the three modes. (Inspection of Fig. 20.4 shows, however, that in the first half of the paragraph conventional readers did not benefit from having the topic in advance.) Of the total number of idea units recalled, the proportion paraphrased rather than recalled verbatim was .42 in RSVP, .38 in listening, and .33 in conventional reading. In Experiment 3, as in Experiments 1 and 2, logical errors decreased when the topic was known, whereas the probability of topic-relevant intrusions increased markedly. There was no evidence for reconstructive recall when the topic sentence was presented at the end of the paragraph.

In sum, recalling a briskly spoken text was much like recalling an RSVP text presented for the same total time, about 3.3 wps overall. Both differed

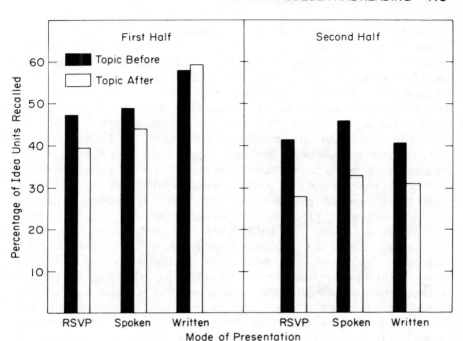

FIG. 20.4. Percentage of idea units recalled after presentation at an overall rate of about 3.3 wps (equivalent to 4 wps within RSVP sentences) in Experiment 1 (RSVP), Experiment 2 (conventional text), and Experiment 3 (spoken text), in each half of the paragraph.

from recall of a conventional written paragraph seen for the same rather generous reading time; readers of conventional paragraphs processed the first half of the paragraph more completely than did subjects in either of the other conditions. The result supports the assumption that RSVP reading, at least at this relatively slow rate, is much like listening. Although speech provides many cues such as stress pattern and within-sentence pauses that are absent in written prose, it is possible that written words are recognized more easily than spoken words. But the similarity in recall for all three modes suggests that the major determinant of memory is processing that occurs at a level beyond modality-specific language mechanisms.

GENERAL DISCUSSION

What *can* a reader manage to do, when reading at 12 words a second? Evidently he or she can parse and comprehend sentences, at least superficially. This comprehension includes retrieval of a good deal of specific knowledge about mentioned entities such as pizzas and kites, and use of that knowledge in interpreting subsequent sentences. To review briefly, the evidence for this claim is that even when readers were able to recall relatively little of the text, they were highly likely to note and remember a critical piece of information, the topic, wherever in the paragraph it appeared—even though it was not explicitly labeled as the topic. Further, material that followed the topic sentence was more completely and accurately recalled, and there was an increase in topic-consistent paraphrases and intrusions. None of those effects was observed when the topic sentence appeared after the part of the paragraph in question, so the whole impact of the topic was on comprehension at the time of reading rather than reconstruction at the time of recall.

Previous experiments with single sentences (Potter et al., 1978) also supported the conclusion that a great deal of processing is accomplished during presentation of an RSVP sentence at 12 wps. A pictured object, for example, was readily incorporated into REBUS sentences, implying that a conceptual level of representation was attained directly. Moreover, scrambled RSVP sentences and sentences in which inessential function words were omitted (as in a telegram) were markedly more difficult to read than full, ordered sentences, again suggesting that the words of an RSVP sentence are fitted into the sentence structure as they appear, not organized after the sentence has been presented. These and other observations indicate that semantic and syntactic processing take place word by word and phrase by phrase, following as closely on the heels of presentation as the sentence permits (cf. Fodor & Frazier, 1978, and Marslen-Wilson & Welsh, 1978 for related views of speech processing).

Nonetheless, reading at 12 wps (more than twice as fast as our subjects normally read) is not equivalent to reading more slowly: Fast readers cannot recall as much of the material. At 4 wps, subjects recalled 37% of the idea units in a paragraph; at 8 wps, 26%; at 12 wps, only 20%. The theoretical question addressed by Experiment 1 was where in processing that loss occurs.

Four models of comprehension were considered.[7] The cyclic model assumes that a fixed cycle of processing must be completed in phase with the uptake of new information from the printed page; as readers fall behind in the cycle, reading comprehension is disrupted. That model may correctly de-

---

[7]There is another hypothesis about comprehension that should be mentioned briefly: The setting up of any form of higher-order organization may take capacity. Britton, Holdredge, Curry, and Westbrook (1979) recently reported an experiment in which readers of versions of several of the paragraphs used here responded more *slowly* to click probes when the topic had been named in advance. The authors suggest that additional capacity is required to process the cohesive relations made available by the topic. One might then expect that the topic would be less and less useful as rate of presentation increases—contrary to the present results. But tradeoff between increased capacity demands and better memory for cohesive material makes an exact prediction difficult.

scribe what ultimately happens at rates of presentation higher than 12 wps. But it cannot easily account for the reduction in recall as rate increased from 4 to 12 wps, because the evidence just reviewed shows that subjects were able to comprehend the text even at 12 wps. A different explanation is offered by the sentence-first and schema-first models. They both propose that processing takes place serially, and so later stages of processing are maximally disrupted by speeding up the presentation (under conditions that are not data-limited in Norman & Bobrow's sense, 1975). The two models make opposite predictions about the order in which two stages—sentence processing and schematic integration—occur. Neither model was supported consistently by the results.

The fourth model considered was the interactive model, which proposes that context and higher-level schemas interact with the ongoing processing of a sentence. This model correctly predicted that availability of a higher-level schema (provided by the topic sentence) would be equally helpful at all rates of processing. But the interactive model does not explain why much less is recalled from very rapidly presented paragraphs, even though readers appear to comprehend most of the material while it is being presented.

If the rate-limiting process in remembering RSVP text is neither sentence-by-sentence comprehension nor higher-level structuring of the information, what is it? Possibly a rapid sequence of material disrupts a still later stage of processing—a stage in which new information is consolidated. An RSVP reader may momentarily understand what he or she is reading but forget it because of retroactive interference while the memory is still vulnerable. A hypothesis of this kind has been proposed to explain the understanding and immediate forgetting of words in a list (Massaro, 1970) and pictured scenes (Potter, 1976); experiments of Marcel (this volume) on perception of words without subsequent awareness represent a similar phenomenon. The disrupted process might be consolidation of what has already been understood, or perhaps there is a failure to establish more detailed connections among ideas in the paragraph. Although the main topic of a paragraph could be understood and used in subsequent processing even at 12 wps, other inferences and interpretations that a slower reader makes may not have been completed.

In conclusion, the present experiments show that when eye movements are not required, readers are able to comprehend text presented as rapidly as 12 wps, more than twice as fast as people normally read. That result is superficially consistent with the hypothesis that eye movements, not comprehension, limit our rate of reading. But a more significant determinant of reading rate appears to be the time required to stabilize material in memory, because fast RSVP text was poorly remembered even though it was understood at the time of reading. Comprehension can outpace eye movements, but at a cost to memory.

ACKNOWLEDGMENTS

This work was supported by grant BNS77-2 5543 from the National Science Foundation and by Contract MDA 903-76-0441 from ARPA. We thank Virginia Valian and David Rosenbaum for their comments on the manuscript and Bruce Renken and Beverly Colby for assistance.

REFERENCES

Aaronson, D. Performance theories for sentence coding: Some qualitative observations. *Journal of Experimental Psychology: Human Perception and Performance,* 1976, *2,* 42–55.

Aaronson, D., Markowitz, N., & Shapiro, H. Perception and immediate recall of normal and "compressed" auditory sequences. *Perception and Psychophysics,* 1971, *9,* 338–344.

Anderson, J., Kline, P., & Lewis, C. A production system model of language processing. In M. A. Just & P. A. Carpenter (Eds.), *Cognitive processes in comprehension.* Hillsdale, N.J.: Lawrence Erlbaum Associates, 1977.

Bartlett, F. C. *Remembering: A study in experimental and social psychology.* Cambridge, England: Cambridge University Press, 1932.

Bransford, J. D., & Johnson, M. K. Contextual prerequisites for understanding: Some investigations of comprehension and recall. *Journal of Verbal Learning and Verbal Behavior,* 1972, *11,* 717–726.

Britton, B. K., Holdredge, T. S., Curry, C., & Westbrook, R. D. Use of cognitive capacity in reading identical texts with different amounts of discourse level meaning. *Journal of Experimental Psychology: Human Learning and Memory,* 1979, *5,* 262–270.

Carpenter, P. A., & Just, M. A. Reading comprehension as eyes see it. In M. A. Just & P. A. Carpenter (Eds.), *Cognitive processes in comprehension.* Hillsdale, N.J.: Lawrence Erlbaum Associates, 1977.

Dooling, D. J., & Lachman, R. Effects of comprehension on retention of prose. *Journal of Experimental Psychology,* 1971, *88,* 216–222.

Dooling, D. J., & Mullet, R. L. Locus of thematic effects in retention of prose. *Journal of Experimental Psychology,* 1973, *97,* 404–406.

Fischler, I., & Bloom, P. A. *Effects of rapidly presented contexts on word retrieval in reading.* Paper presented at the meeting of the Southeastern Psychological Association, Atlanta, Ga., March 1978.

Fodor, J. D., & Frazier, L. The sausage machine: A new two stage parsing model. *Cognition,* 1978, *6,* 291–325.

Forster, K. I. Visual perception of rapidly presented word sequences of varying complexity. *Perception and Psychophysics,* 1970, *8,* 215–221.

Forster, K. I. The role of semantic hypotheses in sentence processing. In *Current problems in psycholinguistics,* CNRS International Colloquium, Paris: CNRS, 1974.

Frauenfelder, U., Dommergues, J. Y., Mehler, J., & Segui, J. L'integration perceptive des phrases. *Bulletin de Psychologie,* 1979, *32,* 893–902.

Gibson, E. J., & Levin, H. *The psychology of reading.* Cambridge: MIT Press, 1975.

Hasher, L., & Griffin, M. Reconstructive and reproductive processes in memory. *Journal of Experimental Psychology: Human Learning and Memory,* 1978, *4,* 318–330.

Keesey, J. C. Memory for logical structure and verbal units in prose material at increased rates of presentation. *Psychological Reports,* 1973, *33,* 419–428.

Kieras, D. E. *How readers identify topics in technical prose.* Paper presented at the Psychonomic Society Meetings, San Antonio, Tex., November 1978.

Kintsch, W., Kozminsky, E., Streby, W., McKoon, G., & Keenan, J. Comprehension and recall of text as a function of content variables. *Journal of Verbal Learning and Verbal Behavior,* 1975, *14,* 196–214.

Marslen-Wilson, W. D., & Welsh, A. Processing interactions and lexical access during word recognition in continuous speech. *Cognitive Psychology,* 1978, *10,* 29–63.

Massaro, D. Perceptual processes and forgetting in memory tasks. *Psychological Review,* 1970, *77,* 557–567.

Miron, M., & Brown, E. The comprehension of rate incremented aural coding. *Journal of Psycholinguistic Research,* 1971, *1,* 65–76.

Mitchell, D. C. The locus of the experimental effects in the rapid serial visual presentation (RSVP) task. *Perception and Psychophysics,* 1979, *25,* 143–149.

Mitchell, D. C., & Green, D. W. The effects of context and content on immediate processing in reading. *Quarterly Journal of Exerimental Psychology,* 1978, *30,* 609–636.

Norman, D. A., & Bobrow, D. G. On data-limited and resource-limited processes. *Cognitive Psychology,* 1975, *7,* 44–64.

Paivio, A., & Csapo, K. Short-term sequential memory for pictures and words. *Psychonomic Science,* 1971, *24,* 50–51.

Perfetti, C. A., & Lesgold, A. M. Discourse comprehension and sources of individual differences. In M. A. Just & P. A. Carpenter (Eds.), *Cognitive processes in comprehension.* Hillsdale, N.J.: Lawrence Erlbaum Associates, 1977.

Pfafflin, S. M. The total time hypothesis, recall strategies, and memory for rapidly presented word strings. *Memory and Cognition,* 1974, *2,* 236–240.

Potter, M. C. Short-term conceptual memory for pictures. *Journal of Experimental Psychology: Human Learning and Memory,* 1976, *2,* 509–522.

Potter, M. C., & Faulconer, B. A. Time to understand pictures and words. *Nature,* 1975, *253,* 437–438.

Potter, M. C., & Kroll, J. F. *RSVP paragraphs.* Technical Report No. 4, ARPA Contract MDA 903-76-C-0441, July 1977.

Potter, M. C., Kroll, J. F., Yachzel, B., & Cohen, J. *Pictures in sentences: Conceptual and lexical representation in language comprehension.* Technical Report No. 8, ARPA Contract MDA 903-76-C-0441, July 1978.

Quillian, M. R. The teachable language comprehender. *Communications of the ACM,* 1969, *12,* 459–476.

Rayner, K. Eye movements in reading and information processing. *Psychological Bulletin,* 1978, *85,* 618–660.

Scarborough, D. L., & Sternberg, S. *Processing items and their order in sequential visual displays.* Paper presented at the meeting of the Eastern Psychological Association, Boston, Mass., April 1967.

Sticht, T. G. Learning by listening. In J. B. Carroll & R. O. Freedle (Eds.), *Language comprehension and the acquisition of knowledge.* Washington, D.C.: Winston, 1972.

APPENDIX: PARAGRAPHS USED
IN EXPERIMENTS 1–3

The topic sentence (and its neutral version) is shown as the last sentence. An asterisk indicates the location of the topic sentence, when it appeared in the middle of the paragraph. In the fourth paragraph (on pizza—see text), the middle location followed the word *try.*

1. A newspaper is better than a magazine. A seashore is a better place than the street. At first it is better to run than to walk. You may have to try several times. It takes some skill but it's easy to learn. Even young children can enjoy it. Once successful, problems are minimal.* Birds seldom get too close. Rain, however, soaks in very fast. Too many people doing the same thing can also cause problems. One needs lots of room. If there are no complications, it can be very peaceful. A rock will serve as an anchor. If things break loose, however, you will not get a second chance. There are just these few simple things to remember when [making and flying your own kite/doing this activity].

2. With pawned jewels financing him, our hero bravely defied the scornful laughter of people who tried to prevent his scheme. "Your eyes deceive," he had said. "An egg, not a table, corectly typifies this unexplored region."* Now with three sturdy sisters he sought proof, forging along sometimes through calm vastness, yet more often over turbulent peaks and valleys. Days became weeks, as many doubters spread fearful rumors about the edge. At last, from nowhere, welcome winged messengers appeared, signifying momentous success. [Christopher Columbus/He] knew he was right.

3. The procedure is quite simple. First you arrange everything into different groups. One pile is enough if you don't have much to do. Then you have to go somewhere else if you don't have a machine. You put them in the machine and turn it on. It is better not to put too many in at once. Then you sit and wait.* You have to stay there in case anything goes wrong. Then you put everything in another machine and watch it go around. When it stops, you take the things home and arrange them again. Then they can be put away in their usual places. Soon they will all be used again and you have to do it all over. [Doing your laundry/The whole thing] can be a pain.

21 Priming and the Passive/Active Model of Word Recognition

Donald E. Broadbent
Margaret H. P. Broadbent
Department of Experimental Psychology
University of Oxford
Oxford, England

ABSTRACT

A number of theories of word recognition suppose that two successive phases occur in the process. On one view, the first is passive, and the second is active; also the first is supposed to be the one primarily operative when gross word-shape cues are used. The second on the other hand is primarily operative when some letters are missing and some clearly visible.

The experiments show that contextual priming gives especially good performance in the missing letter case when the priming has been reliable and active use of it encouraged. With blurred word shapes, however, reliability of the cue is of no benefit. These results support the view just given.

INTRODUCTION

The experiments to be discussed are relevant to a number of similar but partly different theories, which might all be called *passive/active, multistage,* or *perceptual-cycle models.* Slightly different versions are given, for example, by Becker and Killion (1977), Broadbent (1977), Navon (1977), and Neisser (1967), and still others might be formulated. For purposes of exposition, the following account follows the lines of Broadbent (1977), without the supporting evidence quoted in that paper; but it should be remembered that some particular factors of the theory can be changed without invalidating the general class of theories.

A VERSION OF PASSIVE/ACTIVE THEORY

The key notion of this theory is that the process of identifying a word divides into two *phases*, which follow each other in time. The term *phase* is used rather than the more familiar *stage*, because the latter is commonly employed to describe different mechanisms within the person, with information being passed from one place to another. In the present theory, the same mechanisms may well be used, but they operate in one way during the earlier phase and in another way in the second later phase.

First Phase

This phase takes the original vast set of words that might be appropriate and reduces it to a moderately small set of possibilities that are then used as the start of the next phase. The phase has the following features.

Passive Character. This phase is driven by the stimulus pattern rather than certain words being tested against the input. Instead evidence about the presence or absence of all conceivable words is accumulated at an equal rate. The phase may indeed have biases in its functioning, such that some words are more likely than others to be included in the set of words in the final output. However, a word that has the advantage of this kind of bias does so regardless of the nature of the input stimulus and is, therefore, quite likely to be passed on to the next phase even though it was not objectively the stimulus. The phase is in general a system of *logogen* type.

False Alarms. Following the last point, any factor that makes a word more likely to go through this phase of the process produces an increase in false alarms as well as an increase in correct responses; in terms of signal detection theory, it gives an effect on β rather than d'. An example of a variable showing this effect and acting at this phase of the process is the frequency of a word in the language as a whole.

Global Analysis. This phase is viewed as acting on relatively global aspects of the stimulus such as the total shape of a word rather than local details such as letters or, still less, line segments. As a result, factors affecting this phase are especially likely to give measurable effects if one uses a visual stimulus that has been blurred by throwing a projected word out of focus or by typing through many thicknesses of carbon paper. Such a treatment leaves the word shape visible but obscures detail, where other degradations may destroy the shape but leave some details clear.

Second Phase

This phase acts on the relatively small set of words generated from the first phase and tests them against parts of the stimulus information that may not have been used in the first phase. The final output is then a word that passes this process of testing. The phase has the following features.

Active Testing.   This phase is system-driven rather than stimulus-driven, top-down rather than bottom-up. As a result, it may start first with particular prejudices or hypotheses about the nature of the environment and thus like the first phase be biased in favor of particular possibilities. However, because any hypothesis is actively tested, incorrect ones will not survive.

Absence of False Alarms.   As a result, any biases affecting this process will give a difference in the number of correct perceptions but should not give a difference in the number of false alarms; effects would be on d and not on β. Variables that are suspected of acting at this stage are word emotionality and letter-digram probability.

Local Detail.   The testing of the possible words is undertaken against specific local details of the stimulus input rather than generalized global features of the type that activate the first phase. Consequently, factors affecting this phase will only show themselves in experimental situations that leave some local detail available and allow the active process to test possibilities against this detail. For example, the display of words visually, with some letters completely degraded and other letters clearly visible, will meet these conditions.

Perceptual-Cycle Characteristics

This theory can be described as a *perceptual-cycle model,* because it supposes that the final choice of a word emerges from an alternating or cyclic operation. At the first phase the global features of the environment narrow down the possibilities, a process usefully termed "suggestion" by Navon (1977). At the next phase the possible words are tested against the input, which Navon, again usefully, calls "enquiry." The result of this test then acts back into the system, which may produce a further test, and so on. It is worth emphasizing the cyclic nature of the process, because it means that separation of the two phases is likely to be a theoretical ideal rather than something completely attainable in experimental practice. Although it may well be true that presentation of blurred words gives greater importance to the suggestion process and that presentation of a word without some letters gives greater emphasis to the enquiry process, there are doubtless some relics of both processes with either technique. The use of a tachistoscope will produce some compromise combination of the different phases, the exact balance depending on the duration of the exposure (Broadbent & Broadbent, 1977).

In reading or other natural tasks either phase may be important, depending on the strategy used by the person.

Relation to Other Theories

It may be helpful to consider ways in which other theories of the perceptual-cycle type could be produced by changing some of the specific features of the previous presentation. One might postulate merely a passive phase followed by an active phase, without particular links of either phase to global rather than local features. This would correspond to the original views of Neisser (1967). The association of global features with the first phase converts the view to that of Navon (1977), who does not however consider whether any properties, such as word frequency, affect one phase rather than the other. It would be logically possible to associate global feature detection with the second stage rather than the first. Although it is hard to find an author who gives such a view explicitly, it is perhaps implicit and presupposed in many theories that regard perception as starting with detection of illumination at points rather than regions. We have taken Navon's view because of his results and our own.

Conversely, Becker's view does not associate global or local features with either phase, but it does link the effects of frequency to the second phase rather than the first; the suggestion is that a small set of words is tested against the input in order of frequency, so that common words are identified most rapidly. We have adopted the opposite view because of the well-established effects of word frequency on false positives, which are hard to reconcile with a locus of the effect in an active phase.

All three views, and our own, regard the second phase as active, so that the top-down adoption of one hypothesis leads to testing it against the environment and, thus, to the prediction that the second phase will not allow false alarms. It would also be possible to hold that the second phase was passive, and once the hypothetical percept had been adopted, it was not tested against input. This is the "sophisticated guessing" view of bias in perception; again we have taken the opposite postulate because of our own earlier results.

In principle, there are at least 64 different two-phase theories that can be devised by different association of each stage with active processing, global features, or sensitivity to stimulus probability. Our particular combination has however some evidence in favor of each of its choices of assumption.

The Problem of Priming

Within this theoretical context, it becomes a problem to know whether contextual priming is supposed to act in the first phase or the second phase. On the one hand, Becker and Killion (1977) showed that the presentation of an associated word before a stimulus interacted with the effects of stimulus intensity; that is, a contextual prime made a big difference to performance if the stimulus intensity was low but not much difference when the stimulus intensity was high. For this reason they suggest that priming bypassed the first phase of the process and showed itself in the second or active phase. A high level of stimulus intensity was not therefore necessary.

On the other hand, it is also known that the effects of contextual priming alter with the reliability of the prime; that is, a word with the same degree of association with another word may prime it more effectively if, during the particular experiment, words have usually been followed by their associates. Priming is less effective if that has not been the case (Tweedy, Lapinski, & Schvaneveldt, 1977). Again, if a situation is employed in which subjects compare the similarity or difference of two letters, and if they are given a previous priming stimulus of a letter that is contained in the test display, then reaction to the test stimulus is faster. However, the exact nature of the effect depends on the reliability of the prime; if it is often absent from the test stimulus and thus unreliable, incorrect primes give performance no worse than the unprimed case. If, however, the prime is usually reliable, then the rare cases of an incorrect prime give a cost; reaction is slower than in the unprimed case (Posner & Snyder, 1975). The suspicion that these effects immediately create is that reliable primes act in a rather different way from unreliable primes: With the reliable prime a strategy is adopted of actively testing the suggested word against the stimulus input, whereas with the unreliable prime the process remains passive although conceivably biased. In other words, this variable may act in either of our two hypothetical phases.

It becomes immediately relevant to ask whether the effect of contextual priming is on β or on d' and whether there is any interaction between the reliability of a prime and the kind of stimulus degradation that is used in the experiment. The following results were intended to shed light on these points.

PRIMING AND BLURRED WORDS

In Experiments 1 and 2, the stimulus word was always a blurred word, and on 60% of occasions it was accompanied by some form of prime. If a prime was present, it was objectively appropriate on two-thirds of the trials and could therefore be regarded as reliable.

Method

Presentation of Stimuli. Each experiment tested 16 women drawn from the Oxford Subject Panel. Each subject was presented with 60 stimulus words, each of which was a Xerox copy of a word blurred in the following fashion. The list of stimuli was typed on an electric typewriter, in lowercase letters, through 12 layers of bond paper with a clean carbon between each of the last four layers. Sheet 11 was used to generate the version actually presented to the subject. The 60 stimuli were presented on eight display cards, each bearing 7 or 8 numbered stimuli arranged in a column with vertical spaces between each stimulus. Where context was given, a priming word or words was typed to the left of, but on the same level as, the corresponding stimulus. Each display card was presented together with a cardboard mask, containing a slot of size such that only one stimulus with its context (if any) was visible at any one time. The subject observed each stimulus in turn and wrote her response on the appropriately numbered line in a booklet with a page for each display card. As soon as she had recorded her response, she moved the slot down the card to display the next stimulus. After completion of the first 30 stimuli, she received a break of about two minutes before continuing with the remaining 30.

When context was present, it took the form of a single word, or of two words (Experiment 2 only), which were typed clear without any blurring. Subjects were instructed that they should look at each word in turn and try to identify it; they were also told that when clear words were present, they should look at them first because they were often but not always related to the blurred one and so might give them a clue.

Selection of Materials (Experiment 1). All stimuli were five-letter words, either nouns, adjectives, or verbs (not plurals), and had a word frequency above 25 occurrences per million. The 60 stimuli were divided from the experimenter's point of view into three categories: filler, target, and match words. The 12 filler items were simply words meeting the previous criteria, which were also known to occur as the primary response to some associative stimuli (Postman & Keppel, 1970). Indeed, in five cases the response was given by over 50% of the subjects for that associative stimulus, and the link was therefore very strong indeed. These items were included in the experiment merely to encourage the subject to rely on the primes; every subject therefore received these filler items, and in every case the associative stimulus was given as a prime word.

The 24 target words were similarly selected, except that associative strengths over 50% were avoided; each subject saw all target items but received the associative prime for only half of them.

Each of the 24 match words was derived from a target word by starting from a point in a list of words of the appropriate frequency class and searching for the first word which had two and only two letters in common with the target word and occurring in the same position and which was also the same part of speech as the target word. Words that had previously been included in the experimental design were of course excluded. The starting points for the search through the word-frequency list were at a series of points equally spaced through each frequency class by a distance sufficient to give the total number of match words required in that frequency class. Each subject saw all the match words, half of them being presented together with the associative stimulus appropriate to their corresponding target. For any one subject, the match words which were primed corresponded to targets which had not been primed for that subject and vice versa. Thus of the 60 stimulus words, the subject saw 24 without a context, of which 12 were in fact targets and 12 match words; out of the 36 primed words, 12 were fillers, 12 were target words, and 12 match words. It will be realized that the interest of the match words lay not so much in correct identifications of the words but in the occasions when they were mistaken for their corresponding target words.

Selection of Materials (Experiment 2).   In this case the set of target and filler items was slightly modified, so that each stimulus not only met the general characteristics just mentioned but also occurred as a common associate in the response lists of two different associative stimuli, which were not themselves associated with each other.[This last requirement was relaxed for some of the 12 filler items, as the number of suitable words in the Postman & Keppel (1970) lists was being exhausted.] For any one subject, then, half the primed items, whether filler, target, or match, were accompanied by both their prime stimuli, whereas the other half were accompanied only by one context word. In the latter case, the one prime was the word with a weaker association to the particular response word. All words appeared equally often in each condition of priming by counterbalancing over subjects. Two different orders of presentation were employed, although no particular differences appeared between them.

Results

The proportion of correct responses to targets and false alarms consisting of target-word responses to match words are shown in Table 21.1

In both experiments, the number of hits rises significantly with each increasing degree of priming, $p < .05$ by sign test. However, the increase in false alarms was equally significant with each increase in degree of priming. Thus the possibility arises that the effect of priming is purely by a biased

TABLE 21.1

	Experiment 1		Experiment 2	
	Hit Rate	False Alarm Rate[a]	Hit Rate	False Alarm Rate[a]
Unprimed	.224	.005	.193	.000
Single prime	.641	.109	.615	.104
Double prime	—	—	.729	.240

[a]Target response to match word.
Within each column, all pairwise differences between rows are significant.

passive process, with the rise in hits entirely explained by the rise in false alarms. Experiment 1 did not provide suitable data for checking measurements derived from signal detection theory; the number of false alarms was extremely low when unprimed match words were presented, most subjects giving no such responses at all. In order to enter the calculations of signal detection theory, one needs to assume that such a zero measurement represents a true rate that is greater than zero but presumably less than the minimum nonzero value possible in the experiment, which was of course just over .08. A common assumption is that the rate is half the minimum, in this case .04. For the data in Experiment 1, however, the results were so extreme that one could obtain flatly contradictory results by slightly changing the assumption about the handling of zero entries; on one assumption d' increased with priming, whereas on another it did not. This was in fact the reason for running Experiment 2, because the comparison of single-prime and double-prime conditions in that experiment allowed the false alarm rates to be higher and thus made the calculation less dependent on assumptions.

In fact for Experiment 2 a measure similar to d' shows eight subjects giving an increase and eight giving a decrease, when two primes are used rather than one. On the other hand, the measure comparable to β gives a significant difference between the two cases by sign test, $p = .022$. [The measures used were in fact those due to Luce (1959), which have the merit of ready calculation from any obtained probability rather than relying upon the data-fitting values available in tables.]

It should be noted, in view of the relatively small numbers of different words employed, that analyses across words give results broadly similar to those across subjects, except that the difference in false alarms between two primes and one, in Experiment 2, is not quite significant.

The implication of these results is that even reliable primes show no indication of producing their effect by an active testing mechanism but rather give a rise in false alarms that appears to be sufficient to account for the rise in correct detections; that is, it appears to be in the first rather than the second phase of the perceptual-cycle theory, much as the effect of word frequency is. However, these results are all obtained using blurred words; in view of the crucial part played in our version of perceptual-cycle theory by the nature of the stimulus degradation employed, it seemed necessary to go on to alternative forms of degradation.

EXPERIMENT 3: THE INTERACTION OF RELIABILITY AND STIMULUS DEGRADATION

In this experiment, exactly the same stimulus words and procedure for each subject were adopted as in Experiment 2. The exact words employed are given in Table 21.2. However, that experiment was essentially repeated four times, with the four possible combinations of reliable/unreliable primes and degradation by blurring/removal of stimulus letters. The details are as follows.

Types of degradation

For 32 subjects, the procedure of Experiment 2 was adopted, except that the stimulus words were not blurred but rather had the second, fourth, and fifth letters removed, leaving only the first and third.

For the other 32 subjects, blurred stimuli were employed, using the ninth rather than the eleventh sheet from the original typing. This change was to give a level of performance on unprimed words, which would be closely similar to that with the other form of degradation.

Reliability

For half the subjects receiving each form of degradation, the filler items were the same as in Experiment 2, and in the experience of those subjects therefore primes were reliable. For the other 32 subjects, however, the filler items were changed by reassignment of the clear words and the degraded stimulus words, so that the former ceased to be appropriate to the latter. In the experience of these subjects, therefore, primes were inappropriate in 24 of the 36 trials and could therefore be regarded as unreliable.

Results

Effects on Hit Rate. This measure gives the only results applicable to all conditions; it will be obvious that false alarms could only occur for words degraded by removing letters, if the surviving letters happened to be identical in the target and the match words. This would naturally happen only rarely; in fact the random procedure described previously for finding match words did

TABLE 21.2
Words Used in Experiments 2 and 3

Set	Second Prime	First Prime	Position in List	Target	Position in List	Match
a	bitter	sugar	2	sweet	45	great
	thirsty	river	24	water	32	offer
	home	cottage	47	house	28	sense
	eat	gin	39	drink	10	dress
	square	earth	14	round	53	south
	sharp	cut	60	knife	17	crime
b	grass	color	54	green	3	group
	chimney	cigarette	33	smoke	13	shade
	fruit	blossom	19	apple	37	title
	flute	minstrel	8	music	59	visit
	read	letters	30	write	49	guide
	wool	mutton	44	sheep	23	fleet
c	lamp	dark	50	light	29	first
	black	snow	4	white	34	third
	butter	rye	58	bread	9	speed
	war	justice	38	peace	18	least
	bill	accountant	25	money	42	mouth
	ceiling	rug	12	floor	55	cloud
d	long	tall	7	short	40	whole
	table	sit	20	chair	57	shape
	bath	dirt	27	clean	48	plain
	law	command	43	order	5	cover
	wish	sleep	35	dream	15	drive
	man	harem	52	woman	22	world
Filler Items						
	feet	leather	51	shoes		
	pencil	carbon	1	paper		
	people	mob	31	crowd		
	copper	iron	16	metal		
	tie	blouse	46	shirt		
	life	bomb	26	death		
		hand	21	glove		
		king	41	queen		
		lion	11	tiger		
		loud	36	noise		
		robber	56	thief		
		joy	6	happy		

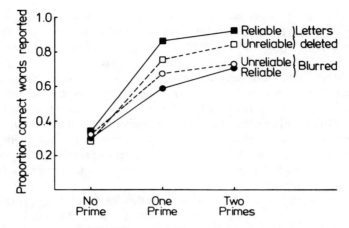

FIG. 21.1.   Results of Experiment 3: The interactions of priming, reliability of priming, and type of stimulus degradation. As reliability is varied by altering the priming of other filler items, all data for primed words are for cases of appropriate priming.

not produce any match word for which it was true, and there were therefore never any false alarms in conditions using degradation by removal of letters.

The hit rate in the various conditions is shown in Fig. 21.1; it is immediately apparent that the conditions interact; that is, priming has a smaller effect on blurred words than it does on those degraded by deleting letters (for the interaction $p < .001$ by analysis of variance tested against differences between subjects). Thus despite the comparable results obtained for the two methods of degradation in unprimed conditions, there is over the whole experiment an advantage for the words degraded by the removal of letters ($p < .001$). There is also of course the main effect of priming ($p < .001$).

Perhaps the most interesting result is the interaction of reliability and kind of degradation ($p < .05$); the reliability of the prime has a bigger beneficial effect when letters are missing. Numerically the effect is actually reversed with blurred words, and unreliable primes gave better results. Thus over the whole experiment there is no significant main effect of the reliability of the prime nor an interaction of the effect of priming with reliability. These results strongly support the notion that the action of priming is different for the two forms of stimulus degradation, the reliable primes introducing some process that is particularly appropriate for stimuli degraded by removing letters rather than blurring the whole word.

Measures from Signal Detection Theory

As already noted, no false alarms at all occur when letters are missing. If one were to calculate measures from signal detection theory for that degradation, one would have to conclude that all differences due to priming were differences of a d' type and, therefore, apparently due to active processing.

In the case of blurred words, where false alarms do occur, the number of subjects showing an increase in the quantity corresponding to d' with two primes rather than one is balanced by the number showing a decrease; p does not even fall below the .50 level for either the reliable or the unreliable group. The same applies if measurement is made across words rather than across subjects. On the other hand, the measure equivalent to β once again gives a significant difference between two primes and one for either group alone, when tested against subjects. Against words there are significantly more false alarms with primed than unprimed words, but the difference in β does not reach a significant level.

Thus once again there is no evidence that the beneficial effect of priming on blurred words is due to any active testing process; the improvement in identification of targets is always matched by an increase in incorrect identification of match words.

CONCLUSIONS AND PROBLEMS

The results given thus far make almost too satisfactory a story. They are consistent with the view that priming can work in two different ways. One mode of performance is active and is associated with reliable primes, with degradation by missing letters, and with an effect on hits that does not depend on the existence of false alarms. The other effect however is associated with blurred words, with unreliable primes, and with occurrence of false alarms; it appears therefore to be a more passive and stimulus-driven type of process. Because these results fit so tidily into the existing formulation, perhaps we should give certain cautions against oversimplification.

Active Processes With Blurring: Difference Between Words

In these results the major differences between blurring and removal of certain letters cannot be due to quantitative differences in the amount of degradation; performance on unprimed words was equal with the two forms of degradation. However, when this matching is not performed, quantitative as well as qualitative factors may intrude. It is clearly arbitrary to suppose that blurring removes all details that might be used for testing a perceptual hypothesis, and in particular it may well be that some words rather than others survive this treatment and still leave enough information to allow the testing of perceptual hypotheses. Although the major effects are, as just noted, significant when tested against words; it is clear that some words do differ quite substantially from the performance on the majority of words. An interesting test can be performed on the data from the "reliable blurred" condition of Experiment 3: That condition might be likely to encourage active processes, and yet the form of stimulus degradation was blurring. If we look at the performance on individual words and calculate Luce's parameter corresponding to d', we find that some words give an increase in this parameter when there are two primes rather than one, whereas other words give a decrease. When we look at these same words in unprimed conditions, we find that the proportion of correct identifications is .32 in the former case and only .13 in the latter; by U-test, the performances differ with $p = .05$. The matched words in each case give the same proportion of false alarms, namely .25. Thus it does not seem that the rise in d' when certain words are primed is merely chance; rather, these are the words that contain rather more detail even after blurring, so that they give better performance when seen without a context. This subset of words also responds to priming by showing an increase in hits greater than the increase in false alarms. Such a result confirms the warning given at the beginning of the chapter; it is too simple to suppose that blurring completely excludes active testing or that deletion of some letters excludes any passive processes.

The Question of Cost

In the paper by Posner and Snyder (1975), the two forms of priming were distinguished by considering effects on stimuli that had been inappropriately primed. If the general context was one of primes being reliable, these stimuli showed a cost; if primes were in general unreliable, these stimuli showed no cost. In terms of the present experiment, the appropriate analysis would seem to be the responses, to match words that were objectively correct rather than incorrect responses of the target word. One might well suppose that active priming might reduce such correct responses, whereas passive priming would not.

The data were shown in Table 21.3 and unfortunately do not really support such a view. On the whole, a match word does produce more correct responses when on its own than it does with two contextual primes; but this

TABLE 21.3
Proportion Correct Responses to Match Words in Experiment 3

		No prime	1 prime	2 primes
Missing letters	Reliable prime	.156	.104	.135
	Unreliable prime	.109	.125	.094
Blurred words	Reliable prime	.286	.281	.271
	Unreliable prime	.300	.375	.219

effect seems to be just about as great with blurring as with missing letters and with unreliable as with reliable primes. When there is only one prime present, there is really scarcely any cost at all, and although it is numerically greatest for reliable priming of the missing letter case, the differences are very tiny. The beautiful harmony of the results with the literature is not therefore quite complete, and some further elaboration is necessary.

One possibility that is worth a consideration is that Posner and Snyder (1975) were using latency of response as their measure, whereas in the present case all the data reported have been in terms of probability. One can well imagine that, if a prime suggests that a particular word be tested against the stimulus input, this will create a delay before that word is rejected as inappropriate and the process restarts from some other basis. It might well be however that the initial false start had no effect on the final probability of choosing a response. In other words, the costs of Posner and Snyder may be costs only in terms of time and not probability. Unfortunately, data on time were not collected throughout our own experiments, but when this point began to emerge, some rough data on latency were obtained from some of the subjects, by the primitive technique of the experimenter noting the time given on a stopwatch whenever the subject moved the slot from one stimulus to the next. For eight subjects in the "reliable missing letter" condition, every individual gave slower responses to a match word when primed with one irrelevant prime than when the match word appeared alone ($p = .01$). For six subjects in the "reliable blurred" condition, there was no such difference, $p > .05$. Both groups show, as might be expected, a beneficial effect of priming upon latency for the target words, $p < .05$. These results do at least support the suggestion that latency and probability are different in the extent to which they show costs of inappropriate active priming.

Passive Processes With Missing Letters: A Further Caution

A third complication should be mentioned, particularly for readers of earlier volumes in this series, because it affects the interpretation of one result published earlier (Broadbent & Broadbent, 1977). Although three of the experiments in that chapter were simply consistent with perceptual-cycle theory, the fourth was curious. In it, the missing letter technique was used for unpleasant words, there being always a neutral word that was also consistent with the surviving letters. For each such pair of words, subjects tended to pick one rather than the other; the preference being based on letter-digram probability rather than emotionality. If more letters were provided, however, the bias was greater and this appeared to require some extra complication of theory.

In two studies yet to be published, however, we have found that exactly the same stimuli give the *opposite* result when they are presented mixed with a number of other stimuli, none of these other stimuli being consistent with unpleasant words but only with neutral ones. Thus in a context of nasty words the effect of letter digrams becomes more important as the sensory evidence increases; in a context of neutral words it becomes less important. For the intermixed neutral stimuli, the bias increases with the number of letters just as it did for unpleasant words in the unpleasant context.

This effect deserves more examination elsewhere; but one way of interpreting it is that, even with the missing letter technique, a context of words from one category gives a passive bias in favor of that category. Only when many letters are supplied does the possibility of active testing override this bias. Thus, if this interpretation holds up, the missing letter technique may at low levels of evidence show passive effects just as we have earlier seen that the blurred word technique may at high levels give active effects.

General Conclusion

The foregoing cautions should avoid too simplistic a conclusion; nevertheless, the data are broadly consistent with a two-stage model, of global passive processes followed by active detailed testing of the environment.

ACKNOWLEDGMENT

The authors are employed and their research is supported by the Medical Research Council.

REFERENCES

Becker, C. A., & Killion, T. H. Interaction of visual and cognitive effects in word recognition. *Journal of Experimental Psychology: Human Perception and Performance,* 1977, *3,* 389–401.

Broadbent, D. E. The hidden pre-attentive processes. *American Psychologist,* 1977, *32,* 109–118.

Broadbent, D. E., & Broadbent, M. H. P. General shape and local detail in word perception. In S. Dornic (Ed.), *Attention and Performance VI.* Hillsdale, N.J.: Lawrence Erlbaum Associates, 1977.

Luce, R. D. *Individual choice behavior,* New York: Wiley, 1959.

Navon, D. Forests before trees: The precedence of global features in visual perception. *Cognitive Psychology,* 1977, *9,* 353–383.

Neisser, U. *Cognitive Psychology,* New York: Appleton-Century-Crofts, 1967.

Posner, M. I., & Snyder, C. R. R. Facilitation and inhibition in the processing of signals. In P. Rabbitt & S. Dornic (Eds.), *Attention and Performance V.* New York: Academic Press, 1975.

Postman, L., & Keppel, G. (Eds). *Norms of word association.* New York: Academic Press, 1970.

Tweedy, J. R., Lapinski, R. H., & Schvaneveldt, R. W. Semantic-context effects on word recognition: Influence of varying the proportion of items presented in an appropriate context. *Memory & Cognition,* 1977, *5,* 84–89.

22

Conscious and Preconscious Recognition of Polysemous Words: Locating the Selective Effects of Prior Verbal Context

Tony Marcel
Medical Research Council
Applied Psychology Unit,
Cambridge, England

ABSTRACT

This chapter addresses the following questions concerning the processing of words with more than one meaning. How many meanings are computed and in what manner? At what point and how does prior context have a selective effect? What role does consciousness play? It is proposed that all meanings are accessed in a first preconscious stage, irrespective of context. However context determines what interpretation will be represented in consciousness.

The criterial index of whether a particular meaning had been accessed was facilitation of lexical decision to a subsequent word related to that meaning. Three letter-strings (LSs) were presented successively. Lexical decision was required to LS1 and LS3. On critical trials LS2 was a polysemous word (e.g., PALM) and LS3 was related to one of its meanings (WRIST). LS1 was either related to the same meaning (HAND), a different meaning (TREE), or unrelated to the following words (CLOCK). Control conditions included association of only LS1 and LS3 and lack of any association. LS2 was (1) left unmasked to allow awareness; (2) pattern masked to prevent awareness but allow semantic access; or (3) energy masked to prevent both awareness and lexical processing.

When subjects were aware of LS2, prior context determined which meaning was chosen (indicated by facilitation of LS3 decision latency). But when LS2 was pattern-masked such that subjects were unaware of its presence, apparently both meanings were accessed, irrespective of context. It is argued that unconscious perception, including lexical/semantic access, is of unlimited capacity and precedes conscious perception, which is limited to one interpretation of an event at a time. Prior context is only used selectively after semantic access to determine what enters consciousness. This second stage of comprehension is constructive, and context is used inferentially as a consistency criterion. All semantic interpretations of a word accessed in the first stage automatically activate associated lexical entries. Once a conscious interpretation is arrived at, only entries associated with that interpretation receive activation; entries associated with incompatible interpretations receive inhibition.

INTRODUCTION

This chapter has two aims. One is to shed light on the processes involved in recognizing and comprehending words and how context enters into those processes. The other aim is to indicate the importance of distinguishing conscious from preconscious processes in both our investigations and our theories.

Lexical Polysemy

If every word in the language had a unique physical representation and a unique meaning and usage, the problems for theories of speech perception and language comprehension would be considerably simplified but still bad enough. But as Ziff (1967) has remarked, it appears that at least 50% of a reasonably adequate English lexicon is constituted of either homonymous or polysemous entries.[1]

Different approaches to word recognition and comprehension provide different accounts of the treatment of polysemy and how context affects it. In both the lexical and the semantic domains there are two broad classes of views, which will be very briefly outlined. One view is that access to lexical entries is achieved by a sequential search and matching of entries with the input; another view is that it is automatic and simultaneous. Forster (1976), who holds the former view, sees only one lexical entry being able to be matched against input at a time. Morton (1969) on the other hand sees several lexical entries as being accessed at the same time by one stimulus word, identification being the result of passive activation to a threshold. A difference exists among these points of view as to how prior semantic context acts to facilitate the recognition and processing of associated stimuli. Selective theories hold that prior context operates before lexical access of a target item to bias retrieval or interpretive mechanisms toward accessing a particular entry or interpretation (Forster) or selects a subset of entries for subse-

---

[1]Such words are often referred to as *homographs* or *ambiguous words*. First, the term homograph refers to any two words with the same spelling but whose pronunciation may differ. The words referred to here have different meanings with the same spelling and pronunciation. Second, psychologically speaking these words are not necessarily ambiguous; linguistically speaking they do have multiple meanings.

quent matching operations (Becker, 1976). Nonselective theories can either (a) see context as priming associated entries, so that they will be privileged in reaching a critical threshold of activation (Morton), or (b) assume that contextual information is used after lexical or semantic access to choose the appropriate candidate or discard irrelevant candidates. However, nonselectivity theorists do not see prior context as affecting which lexical or semantic entries are actually accessed in the first place. These views thus give different accounts of the understanding of polysemous words and how it is affected by prior context. According to the selective or serial encoding view, only one interpretation is ever accessed at one time (though in sentences it could turn out to be inconsistent with later context). According to a strong or unitary version (Schvaneveldt, Meyer, & Becker, 1976), the effect of prior semantic context is to ensure that only the lexical or semantic representation of the polysemous word appropriate to the prior context is accessed. According to a weaker version (Hogaboam & Perfetti, 1975), the meanings of a polysemous word are examined serially in order of frequency until one that matches context is encountered. According to the nonselective or parallel, multiple-encoding view, both (or all) lexical or semantic representations of the polysemous word are accessed and the effect of prior context is to select the appropriate entry *after* such access (Warren, Warren, Green, & Bresnick, 1978).

Recent reviews of ambiguity, its resolution, and the effects of context have invoked the theoretical distinction between preconscious and conscious processes (Clark & Clark, 1977; Levelt, 1978; MacKay, 1970). Thus, although we may only be aware of one meaning, it may be that multiple meanings have been computed nonconsciously. However, experimental investigations carried out so far have either relied on measures that are dependent on what the subject consciously understands the meaning to be (e.g., recall, sentence completion), or, when they have used measures that could be argued to be sensitive to early nonconscious stages (e.g., automatic associative effects, as in Conrad, 1974), have nonetheless taken no steps actually to *preclude* access to consciousness.

Elsewhere (Marcel, in press) I have indicated how great the differences between conscious and nonconscious representations may be. There is much evidence that what receives our attention and becomes conscious is only what is selected from alternative candidates. Indeed in perceiving words the available data (e.g., concerning unattended material) does suggest that more lexical and semantic representations are accessed unconsciously than those that achieve conscious representation. Moreover I have suggested in that paper how preconscious and conscious representations of an event may be *qualitatively* different and have qualitatively different effects.

In view of the foregoing it would seem desirable to do two things. First, one would like to determine what meanings are accessed automatically, but to use a measure that does not logically require the subject to access a semantic representation. One solution is to assess indirectly the meanings that are accessed by studying semantic effects upon some further task. Second, one would like to compare the effects of biasing context on the processing of polysemous words, both when the latter are nonconscious and when they are conscious. The following two sections explain how these manipulations are obtained.

The Lexical Decision Task as Evidence

In the lexical decision task the subject has to decide whether or not strings of letters are English words. Meyer and his co-workers have found reliable effects of semantic context on reaction times for words (Meyer, Schvaneveldt, & Ruddy, 1972). After a person has been presented with a word (e.g., DOCTOR), he is faster at deciding about an associated word (e.g., NURSE) than an unassociated word (e.g., BREAD). Meyer's experiments (Meyer, Schvaneveldt & Ruddy, 1972; Schvaneveldt & Meyer, 1973) taken together with the data of Marcel and Forrin (1974) and Neely (1977) suggest that the facilitation effect is best accounted for by associative activation that spreads at least partly in an automatic fashion to semantically related lexical entries and dies away over time. But the main point is that, however the effect occurs, and however the decision is made regarding the first word, the facilitation effect on subsequent associated words implies that the lexical, if not semantic, representation of the first word has been accessed.[2] Since the effect is obtained when the two words are not related in any other ways (e.g., graphically, phonologically), prelexical explanations are precluded.

Schvaneveldt, Meyer, and Becker (1976) have shown how this paradigm can be used to assess the way polysemous words are affected by prior context. Suppose that a polysemous word is followed by a word related to one of its meanings. If the decision about the second word is facilitated compared to when it is preceded by an unrelated word, then this suggests that the appropriate meaning of the polysemous word has been accessed. Since the association effect appears to be automatic upon lexical access, then if a word related to one of the meanings of a preceding polysemous word is not facilitated in its classification time, this would suggest that the appropriate meaning has not

---

[2]A distinction is drawn between lexical and semantic accounts of associative facilitation. If the internal lexicon is associatively organized as a thesaurus, then semantic interpretation need not be implicated. This is relevant in the present context, because Rubenstein, Garfield, and Millikan (1970) have suggested that polysemous words have multiple *lexical* representations. However, in models such as Morton's (1969), where the lexicon has no internal links, facilitation effects require semantic access. Because this issue is unsettled, in the rest of this chapter the term *lexical/semantic* representation or entry will be used, since the equivocation is not crucial for our present purposes.

been accessed. Suppose now that the polysemous word itself is preceded by a word that may or may not be related to one of its meanings. If the preceding and following words are related to the same meaning of the intervening polysemous word (HAND, PALM, WRIST)—the congruent case, then we should certainly expect facilitation of the third word. However, theoretical test cases are provided particularly by two other types of triple: (1) where the polysemous word is preceded by a totally unrelated word or a nonword (SPEED, PALM, WRIST)—the unbiased case; and (2) where it is preceded by a word related to a different meaning from that with which the third word is associated (TREE, PALM, WRIST)—the incongruent case. In the unbiased case the selective theory of lexical/semantic access predicts that facilitation of the third word will depend on which interpretation is given to the polysemous word, and will occur on less occasions than in the congruent case. The nonselective theory predicts that the unbiased case will yield facilitation as often as the congruent case. In the incongruent case, the selective theory predicts that no facilitation should accrue to the third word. The nonselective theory is less clear in its predictions about the unbiased and incongruent cases. In its strong form it predicts that facilitation should be received by the third word. In its weaker form it depends on whether postlexical inhibition affects associates. According to certain theorists (e.g., Shallice, 1972), conscious attention has just such an inhibitory effect on unattended or alternative stimuli or interpretations. We might then, according to this form of the nonselective theory, predict different effects on the processing of the third word according to whether the polysemous word is processed unconsciously but does not reach consciousness, or it does reach consciousness. Schvaneveldt, Meyer, and Becker (1976) have performed the experiment with the types of triples just described, as well as other control triples. Although supporting the selective access theory, their results are not totally clear-cut. More importantly for our present concerns, they omitted to make any manipulations to preclude conscious access of the polysemous word, which the present experiment purports to do. It is now necessary to describe that manipulation.

Criteria for Nonconscious Perception

So far the only procedure to address preconscious processes directly has made use of time. Neely (1977) examined the associative facilitation of a probe where the delay is too short to allow intentional processes but does allow automatic effects as opposed to where the probe delay does permit time for intentional processes to be mobilized. However, this procedure does not ensure that in the former case the stimulus event itself is not phenomenally conscious. What is required is a technique whereby access to conscious awareness is precluded. The procedure employed here aspires to exactly that.

Fuller descriptions of the technique appear in Marcel (in press) and Marcel and Patterson (1978). However, it is necessary to summarize the procedure and criteria here.

A word or a blank field is presented briefly, followed by a pattern mask. The stimulus-onset asynchrony (SOA) (i.e., onset–onset interval) is reduced until the subject can no longer guess above chance whether anything was presented before the mask. At this and lower SOAs subjects can still judge above chance which of two probe words is graphically or semantically more similar to the masked word. Words masked in this way also provide consistent semantic facilitation in a lexical decision task and interference in a color identification task, although subjects deny any knowledge of their presence. Words masked to the same criterion by peripheral, energy masking (as defined by Turvey, 1973) have no such effects (Marcel, in press, Experiments I, II, and III). The implication of this is that pattern masking prevents access to consciousness but does not affect lexical/semantic access. However, energy masking appears to reduce visual information such that no graphemic or lexical representation can be accessed. The definition of *nonconscious* used here is that a person denies having seen anything prior to the mask and cannot discriminate reliably, when forced to guess, between premask presentations which are blank and those which contain a word. The aim of the present experiment is to present the intervening polysemous word in word-triples as exemplified above (i.e., to replicate Schvaneveldt et al.'s study with appropriate stimuli), unmasked to allow awareness, pattern masked to prevent awareness but allow lexical/semantic access, and energy masked to prevent both awareness and lexical access.

METHOD[3]

Subjects

Twenty-four undergraduates at the University of Sussex were paid to act as subjects.

Apparatus

Stimuli were displayed as black-on-white slides. They were back-projected onto a ground-glass screen from three Kodak Carousel projectors via prisms. In front of each projector lens a solenoid-operated shutter was mounted to obtain accurate stimulus timing. Timing was controlled by specially built

---

[3]The design of the experiments closely follows Schvaneveldt et al. (1976). However, it does differ in some important and some trivial aspects.

circuitry. Brightness was adjusted by interposing neutral-density filters. The subject sat about 3 feet from the screen with a response button beneath each forefinger with which to make word/nonword judgments.

Procedure

The presentation procedure differed slightly for the three masking conditions, according to whether the second letter-string was (1) left unmasked; (2) pattern masked; or (3) energy masked. The presentation sequences for these conditions are illustrated in Fig. 22.1.

In the center of the ground-glass screen was drawn a rectangle 2.5 in. wide by 1 in. high. This served as a fixation area. Each trial consisted of three letter-strings being presented. The luminance of these fields was 5 ft L. Subjects were required to make word/nonword judgments as quickly as possible to letter-strings 1 and 3. One second before the first letter-string (LS1) an auditory warning signal was given, which was a loud click. LS1 was displayed until the subject responded by pressing one of the buttons. LS2 was presented 1.5 sec after offset of LS1. This display differed according to the masking condition (see following). LS3 was presented 1.5 sec after offset of LS2. This display was terminated by the subject's response. The next trial began 4 sec after this response. Reaction times were measured from the onset of a letter-string until the subject's response.

The second letter-string was displayed as follows. In the no-masking condition it remained on for .5 sec and was followed by a dark field until the third letter-string. In the pattern-masking condition, the second letter-string was displayed for 10 msec followed by a dark field and then a pattern mask of 5 ft L luminance that lasted 250 msec. The pattern mask was made of parts of letters dispersed randomly over the field. The onset asynchrony between the letter-string and the mask was determined individually for each subject as described in Marcel (in press). Essentially the experimental SOA was 5 msec beneath that at which that subject could no longer make presence–absence judgments above chance. In the energy-masking condition exactly the same procedure as in the pattern-masking condition was used except that the mask was a visual random-noise field as described by Laner, Morris, and Oldfield (1957) of 80 units per square centimeter when projected. Its luminance was 10 ft L. In all cases the fields intervening between stimuli were dark. The critical SOAs for the last two conditions were determined immediately before each testing session. Forty presence–absence trials were also given after each test session to check whether the subject's threshold SOA for detection had changed. In no case did it alter to a value beneath the SOA used for testing.

Since subjects could not see the second letter-string in the masked conditions, they were instructed not to respond to it in the nonmasked condition. They were told to use that letter-string, or the masks, as temporal cues for the following letter-string.

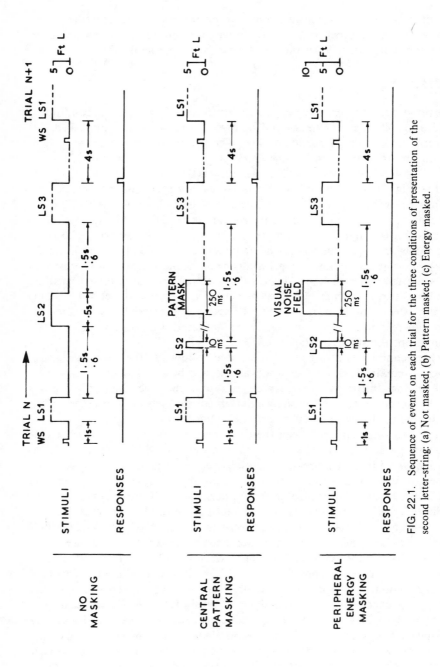

FIG. 22.1. Sequence of events on each trial for the three conditions of presentation of the second letter-string: (a) Not masked; (b) Pattern masked; (c) Energy masked.

Two experiments were conducted with different interstimulus intervals (ISIs). One employed 1.5-sec ISIs as described previously. The second employed .6-sec ISIs. These are both denoted in Fig. 22.1 The reason for this was as follows. Meyer et al. (1972) and Marcel and Forrin (1974) have shown that the priming effect of a stimulus word on an associate decreases over time. It is desirable to choose an ISI at which the first word has a measurable effect on the second and the second on the third, while any residual effect of the first on the third is not too contaminating. Since it is difficult to achieve a priori the optimal balance, the two ISIs were used. In addition, because effects are likely to be small and the error term large in an analysis of variance, given the number of critical cells, it was hoped that the 600-msec ISI would boost any associative effects.

Stimuli

Critical Trials. There were six types of critical trials. They were defined by the associative relations among the three words when all three letter-strings were words. They are exemplified in Table 22.1 as follows, where the names refer to the associative relationships:

1. *Congruent,* where the first word is related to the same meaning of the second word as is the third.
2. *Incongruent,* where the first word is related to a different meaning of the second word from the third.
3. *Unbiased,* where the third word is related to one meaning of the second, but the first word is not related to either word.
4. *Separated,* where the third word is an associate of the first but where neither is related to the second, polysemous word.
5. *Initial,* where the second word is related in one of its meanings to the first word but the third word is not related to either.
6. *Unassociated,* where none of the words is associated with the others.

TABLE 22.1
Examples of the Different Associative Relationships in All-Word Triples on
Critical Trials

Associative Relationships	*Examples*		
1. Congruent	Hand	– Palm	– Wrist
2. Incongruent	Tree	– Palm	– Wrist
3. Unbiased	Clock	– Palm	– Wrist
4. Separated	Hand	– Race	– Wrist
5. Initial	Speed	– Race	– Wrist
6. Unassociated	Clock	– Race	– Wrist

These six types of trial were chosen to provide evaluative controls. The base-line control condition is type (6), where the third word is not an associate of any preceding word and against which any other condition must be compared. Now all theoretical positions predict that compared to this, in condition (1), the third word will receive facilitation. However in neither condition (2) nor (3) can one infer to what extent the third word is primed by the second word unless one knows the effects of a related first word on the second and third words; that is, HAND may prime WRIST independently of PALM, and PALM may prime WRIST more strongly if it has been itself primed by HAND. Therefore condition (4) allows one to estimate the independent effect of HAND on WRIST, and condition (3) allows one to estimate the independent effect of PALM on an associate when it is not preceded by an associated word. Because any effect on the third word may be due not only to prior accessing of separate lexical entries but also to prior access to *associated* lexical entries per se, it is necessary to have the control provided by condition (5), where the third word is unrelated to the two preceding words, themselves associated.

List Design.   Thirty polysemous words were selected from those used by Schvaneveldt et al. (1976). They were selected on the basis of (1) equivalent meanings in British and American English; (2) roughly equivalent usage of the related words in British and American English; (3) equivalent spellings in British and American English. In each case two pairs of words were selected, one of each pair to precede and one to follow the polysemous word. The following word was an associate of one meaning of the polysemous word, the preceding word was chosen such that the polysemous word and the third word were associates of it. Each pair was related to a different meaning of the polysemous word. Where Schvaneveldt et al.'s stimuli were considered inadequate, stimuli were chosen from Cramer (1970), Kausler and Kamichoff (1970), or Kausler and Kollasch (1970). Examples of the stimuli are shown in Table 22.2.[4]

Samples from these words were used to construct the critical all-word trials. In addition, a population of 150 nonwords was constructed, from which trials containing nonwords were derived. Nonwords were between three and seven letters in length and obeyed the rules of English spelling (e.g., veath, nace).

There were 360 test trials per session. This was determined by balancing the response requirements of the first and third letter-string (LS). Thus there were

---

[4]Editorial constraints on space prevent displaying the total list of stimuli. The complete stimulus population can be obtained from the author.

TABLE 22.2
A Partial List of Items Used to Construct Critical Trials

Polysemous Words	Preceding	Following	Preceding	Following
Bail	Bucket	Boat	Jail	Court
Ball	Throw	Round	Dance	Gown
Bank	River	Shore	Money	Save
Bark	Tree	Birch	Dog	Howl
Bowl	Spoon	Soup	Cricket	Wicket

90 trials where LS1 was a nonword and LS3 was a nonword; 90 of LS1, a nonword and LS3, a word; 90 of LS1, a word and LS3, a nonword, 90 of LS1, a word and LS3, a word. The 90 trials where LS1 and LS3 were both words always had a polysemous word as the second letter-string and were made up of 15 trials of each of the six conditions exemplified in Table 22.1. However the second letter-string could not be used to predict the lexical status of the third letter-string because in the other three sets of 90 trials, nonwords, words, and polysemous words were equally distributed as the second letter-string.

Each masking condition was tested in two sessions. In the second session each subject received, in the equivalent trials of the six critical all-word triples, first and third letter-strings corresponding to the opposite meanings of the polysemous words as in the first session. Thus, if a subject had received THROW–BALL–ROUND in session 1, he would receive DANCE–BALL–GOWN in session 2.

Within a session subjects received each terminal word six times according to the six critical conditions. However the order of the conditions in which it appeared was randomized within a subject for the different terminal words and across subjects for particular terminal words. To counteract the effect of frequency of presentation the initial and second words were used as fillers on noncritical trials as many times each, to achieve equal total frequencies of presentation for each word. Sequences were generated with the constraint that no stimulus item could be repeated within seven trials. This was done to minimize the effects of repetition on lexical decision time.

Two equivalent sets of lists were generated, where the items in critical trials in set A were replaced in set B by equivalent items corresponding to the 15 polysemous words left unused in the first set of lists. Since each sample of polysemous words differed in set A, the balancing procedure allowed a test for the representativeness of the results for particular samples of the stimuli (Clark, 1973). The two sets of lists were used with different subjects. Each subject served in the two sessions for a masking condition on separate days of a week and served in each masking condition in separate weeks. The order of conditions was randomized over subjects.

RESULTS AND DISCUSSION

It should be pointed out that no subject was aware of the presence of the second word when it was masked by energy or by pattern. This aspect of the study, then, was successful.

The relevant data are the correct decision latencies to the third word on critical trials. For each ISI condition the three masking conditions were subjected to independent analyses of variance. Although we are interested in how different masking conditions affect the relations between critical trials, different masking conditions may (and do) have general effects on reaction time. Therefore overall analyses of variance might reveal main effects and interactions irrelevant to the main concerns and even obscure differences within a masking condition by taking account of irrelevant variance. For these reasons separate analyses were performed on each masking condition. Scheffé comparisons were performed on pairs of critical trial types.[5]

Figure 22.2 shows the mean reaction times for the third word in each critical trial type within each condition of masking and ISI. It also expresses these results as graphical comparisons between all other triples and the unassociated triple, (condition 6), which is taken as a base-line control. In the following discussion only those differences where Scheffé comparisons yielded *p* values of up to .05 are referred to as significant effects. When conditions are referred to as *faster* or *slower,* this indicates significant effects. Due to the complexity of the design, the data, and the theoretical predictions, the results are discussed to a certain extent at the same time as they are described. This is intended to help the reader encode the results in terms of the relevant contrasts.

Energy Masking. Let us consider the energy-masking conditions first, because it is assumed on the basis of Marcel (in press) that the second word does not gain lexical access and therefore has no effects on the following word. The only significant effects for 1.5-sec ISI are that both the congruent and the separated triples are faster than the unassociated and that the congruent is faster than the initial triple. For the 600-msec ISI both the congruent and the separated triples are faster than the unbiased, the initial, and the unassociated triples. Thus the only effects on the third word are when it is an associate of the first word. This is exactly what one would predict if effective energy masking indeed precludes lexical access of the second, masked word. This condition, then, provides us with a control with which to

---

[5]Analyses of variance were performed over both subjects and words for each stimulus list A and B. This was treated as a factor in a hierarchical analysis. Because stimuli differed between the lists, the overall error term on which Scheffé comparisons were based was derived from analysis over subjects only.

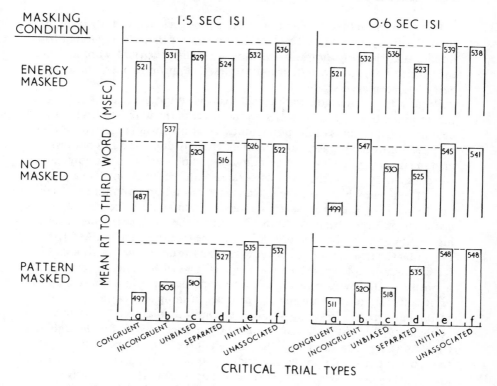

FIG. 22.2. Variation in mean positive RT to the third word in critical triples as a function of the associative relation among the three words.

evaluate the other two masking conditions, since it is as if no second, polysemous word had been presented. It is pertinent to note at this point that when the ISI was 1.5 sec, the facilitation of the third by the first word was slightly less than when the ISI was 600 msec. The total time elapsing between the first and third words was of the order of 3 sec in the first case and 1.2 sec in the second case. The difference in facilitation is consistent with the notion of decay of priming over time. However, if this account is correct, decay is apparently small between delays of 1.2 and 3 sec.

No Masking. Let us turn now to the conditions where no masking occurs and subjects are aware of the polysemous word. First, consider the two control conditions, initial and unassociated triples. With neither ISI is there any difference in RT between them. This replicates Schvaneveldt et al.'s (1976) finding, where the ISI was zero. However for reasons of conservatism, further comparisons take the relationship between the first two words into account as a control, as did Schvaneveldt et al.

For both ISI values the congruent triple produces significantly faster RTs than all other triple types. The fact that it is faster than the separated triple implies that the polysemous word itself is priming the third word and that, therefore, as expected on congruent triples, its appropriate lexical/semantic entry has been accessed.

What is to be inferred from the fact that the congruent triple is faster than the unbiased triple? This depends on the effect of the unbiased triple. It may be that both meanings of the polysemous word are always accessed, in which case the extra facilitation on congruent trials is due to additional residual priming from the first word. Alternatively, on unbiased trials the polysemous word may only access the entry associated with the third word on a proportion of trials, in which case the extra mean facilitation on congruent trials is due to ensuring that the appropriate lexical address, and hence priming, is achieved on every trial. At both ISI values, the unbiased triples produce higher (though nonsignificantly) RTs than the separated triples. At 600-msec ISI, unbiased triples produce faster RTs than the unassociated triples; at 1.5-sec ISI, they do not. These results are inconsistent with the nonselective access hypothesis. However, even the selective hypothesis predicts that the appropriate entry should be accessed and produce priming on a certain proportion of unbiased trials, lowering mean RT. One other aspect of the results is germane to this. At both ISI values the variance of RTs for the unbiased triples was significantly larger than for any other triple type.[6] This suggests that on some trials RT to the third word was facilitated and on others it was not, possibly even being delayed. This strongly supports the selective access hypothesis. We are also led to interpret the extra facilitation for congruent triples as due to the appropriate entry for the polysemous word being accessed on *all* such trials. However, since separated triples provide facilitation in the energy-masked condition and at 600-msec ISI in the nonmasked condition, it is probable that an additional source of facilitation on congruent trials is from residual priming from the first word.

While with 600-msec ISI incongruent associations produced RTs that were no different from either unassociated or initial associate triples, with 1.5-sec ISI they produced RTs that were significantly longer than the control conditions. The immediate implication of this is to support the selective theory and argue strongly against the nonselective theory. The fact that, with both ISIs, RTs to incongruent triples were longer than control RTs (though in one case nonsignificantly) makes it tempting to infer that incongruent associations produce an *interfering* effect; that is, access to one lexical/semantic entry of a polysemous word makes it harder to access entries associated with any other

---

[6]Homogeneity of variance was tested using the F max statistic (Winer, 1971). Variances for triples other than the unbiased did not show a deviation from homogeneity. That of the unbiased condition was then compared to the largest of the other conditions to obtain an F ratio. This showed the unbiased to have significantly larger variance ($p < .05$, one-tailed).

entries of the polysemous word. This would be consistent with the apparent combination of facilitative and interfering effects noted previously in the case of the unbiased triples. Whether or not this is the case, the results strongly suggest that the effect of prior context is to guide lexical access prior to that stage of representation.

In summary the results in the no-masking condition essentially replicate Schvaneveldt et al.'s findings. They are consistent with the strong version of a selective theory of the effect of prior context in word recognition. Facilitation only appears to accrue for words related to one meaning of a polysemous word, the meaning related to the prior context. However, let us turn now to the results obtained when the second word is pattern masked.

Pattern Masking.   The results when the polysemous word was pattern masked provide an entirely different and surprising picture. But let us start with the less controversial results. First, there was no difference between the initial and unassociated triples. Second, the separated triples at both ISIs produced faster RTs than the control conditions. This effect was somewhat greater with the 600-msec than the 1.5-sec ISI. Again, as with the energy-masking and no-masking conditions, this is exactly what one would expect with the decay of residual priming from the first word.

Let us now turn to the three conditions where the third word is an associate of the second. The first point to note is that although no subject was aware of the masked word, it had reliable effects upon an associated word following it. This confirms prior results and discussions of masking (Marcel, in press). The least controversial condition is the congruent one. Here extra facilitation of the third word, over and above that produced by the first word in the separated condition, was produced by the second word. The most important results are provided by the unbiased and the incongruent conditions. With both ISIs the unbiased condition produced faster RTs than even the separated condition. This is in marked contrast to results in the no-mask conditions. Facilitation in the separated condition supposedly derives from the first word each time it achieves lexical/semantic access. Since facilitation in the unbiased condition is even greater than that in the separated condition, it appears that the polysemous word accessed a lexical/semantic representation appropriate to the meaning of the following associate on each trial, even without appropriate prior context. It would thus appear that on each trial the polysemous word is accessing *both* lexical/ semantic entries. It is possible, however, to argue that this is not the case. An alternative proposal is that with unbiased triples the polysemous word accesses a single interpretation that on only some proportion of trials is the one associated with the third word. Priming received by the third word on those trials would be greater than that received from the first word of separated associates because less time had elapsed between the second and third words than between the first and third words. Thus the unbiased triples might yield shorter RTs to the third word than the separated triples. A simple test of this is to compare the facilitation in the unbiased condition at 1.5-sec ISI with the facilitation in the separated condition at 600-msec ISI. In the latter case the time between the first and third words is about 1200 msec and, therefore, less than that between the second and third words with 1.5-sec ISI. Our measure of facilitation is the difference in RT between the facilitating conditions and the unassociated condition. For the unbiased condition at 1.5-sec ISI the difference was 22 msec; for the separated at 600-msec ISI it was 13 msec. Therefore the unbiased still provides greater facilitation, supporting the nonselective access theory. Additional support comes from the fact that, in contrast to when the second word was not masked, in the pattern-masking condition no greater variance was associated with RTs to unbiased triples than with those for other triple types.

The most important difference between the no-masking and pattern-masking conditions is in the case of the incongruent triples. With pattern masking, incongruent triples also produce even greater facilitation than separated triples. This provides much greater support for the nonselective access theory than the effect of unbiased triples, because it indicates that polysemous words prime associates even when prior context indicates a different, inappropriate lexical/semantic representation. Before discussing this issue at greater length, it is worth attending to the different amounts of facilitation with different triples. Although the unbiased and incongruent triples produced facilitation, at neither ISI did the facilitation produced by these conditions differ significantly, nor was it as great as that produced by congruent triples. The most plausible reason for this is that additional priming accrues from the first, associated word in the congruent case.

To summarize the results in the pattern-masking condition, the reliable facilitation of responses to the third word in the incongruent and unbiased triples strongly supports the nonselective access theory. These data are inconsistent with and qualitatively different from those in the no-masking condition. When the polysemous word is not masked and the subject is aware of it, prior context seems to bias reliably its interpretation as judged by effects upon a subsequent word. When the polysemous word is pattern masked and the subject is unaware of it, it consistently affects a subsequent word, and prior context seems to have no effect upon its interpretation; that is, both lexical/semantic entries are accessed.

GENERAL DISCUSSION: CONSCIOUS AND NONCONSCIOUS PERCEPTION AND COMPREHENSION OF POLYSEMY

Dixon (1971) has proposed several empirical criteria that would operationally justify explanations in terms of nonconscious perception. The most important and stringent is "the occurrence of contingent responses, without reported awareness of the stimulus, that differ qualitatively from those elicted by the same stimuls when presented *above* the awareness threshold [p. 18]." The results of the present experiment show that not only do pattern masked stimuli, of which the subject is unaware, produce facilitative effects ("contingent responses"), they produce more facilitative effects than nonmasked stimuli, which moreover, are *qualitatively* different. The experiment thus appears to satisfy Dixon's criterion. It reinforces the conclusion of a prior article (Marcel, in press) in indicating that pattern masking mainly affects not visual analysis but conscious awareness. The implication of the qualitative difference is that to investigate perceptual processes it is inadequate and potentially misleading to examine only conscious perception. Nonconscious or preconscious perception should also be examined.

Let us return to the main concerns of this chapter—the nature and locus of the effects of prior context on lexical and semantic processing of polysemous words. The results of the experiment without masking suggest that prior context affects processing of the second word before its lexical/semantic representation is accessed. However, when the second word is pattern masked to prevent awareness, the results indicate that prior context does not determine which lexical or semantic representation is accessed. One solution to this paradox is to propose that prior context, insofar as it affects perception, operates only after lexical access to select what will enter consciousness.

Consider the following theoretical framework, which derives from and abbreviates the proposals in Marcel (in press). Perceptual analysis, including (in the case of words) lexical and semantic access, is automatic and unconscious. (Obviously when the physical information is itself degraded or ambiguous, as in blurred print, conscious processes may intercede, for example to decide just what letters or phonemes might be present. Here inferential processes are intentional, and we are aware of them.) Processes of perceptual analysis are of unlimited capacity, in that however much is presented that can be dealt with by peripheral sensors will be processed in parallel. Nor is there a limitation on how many lexical or semantic addresses may be activated *unconsciously*, at one time. Conscious representation follows unconscious representation. For a candidate interpretation to enter consciousness, a record of its modality-specific description (i.e., the results of perceptual analyses) is necessary and must be matched to automatically produced "hypotheses." Pattern masking interferes either with the availability or accessibility of this record or with the process of resynthesizing the records of information from separate systems specializing in the analysis of different aspects of environmental events. Conscious percepts, unitary and organized, require the *recovery* of such information and its *synthesis*. Not all information need be recovered for conscious representation; unrecovered unconscious information can guide and influence our behavior.

Conscious representation is of limited capacity in that only one representation or interpretation of an event can be entertained at a time. Thus, if a

Necker cube is seen consciously as a cube, only one three-dimensional interpretation can be seen at a time, although different interpretations may replace
on another sequentially. If conditions permit (e.g., by the masking delay) or if
an event is chosen to reach consciousness (e.g., by intentional allocation of
attention), a decision has to be made, in the case of multiple stimulus
articulations ([weltə] = "way to" or "waiter"?) or interpretations (palm = tree
or hand?), as to which of these one will be aware of. In certain cases, internal
consistency of interpretation will suffice for the resolution of ambiguity (see,
for example, those artificial intelligence attempts at scene analysis reviewed
by Mackworth, 1976). In other cases, if context is available it will be used at
that point. If context is not contradictory, then the interpretation with the
greatest a priori probability (frequency) will be chosen. In the case of single
words, if more than one lexical/semantic entry is activated and if no context is
available, then the most highly activated entry will be that which reaches
consciousness. Associative priming is here proposed to be an immediate
consequence of lexical/semantic access and its degree does not depend on nor
reflect the amount of activation of the source location. Thus in the case of the
congruent triples in the present experiment, the third word receives priming
from both the first and second words independently, but the additional
activation of the second word by the first does not itself transfer greater
activation from the second to the third word. Certain evidence (Marcel, in
press, Experiment IV, where repetition of a masked word did not facilitate its
detection but did increase its associative priming effect) suggests that priming
received by a lexical entry cannot by itself aid that entry to achieve consciousness. However, if that entry does achieve consciousness, then priming received by it will affect conscious decisions about the external stimulus event
that corresponds to it (e.g., lexical decision).

This framework permits a full account of the results in the conditions with
and without pattern masking. Preconscious perception is nonselective and
prior context does not affect it. Therefore the polysemous word accesses all
semantic interpretations and activates lexical entries associated with each
meaning, whatever precedes it. Conscious perception is selective and is affected by prior context. Therefore the polysemous word at this stage only
activates lexical entries associated with the meaning selected by context. Prior
context only operates after lexical/semantic identification. I wish to suggest
that the reason why lexical entries associated with meanings that are incongruent with the context do not continue to show the effects of activation once
the polysemous word is conscious is that they now receive inhibition. It is
interesting that when there was no masking and subjects were aware of the
polysemous word, the results suggested some degree of interference with the
processing of the third word when it was associated with a meaning of the
polysemous word other than that selected by the prior context. If lexical
access is in parallel and semantic facilitation is due to automatic activation,

then it is plausible that impeded lexical access is due to "negative priming" or inhibition. Indeed Shallice (1978) suggests that when two or more processes or representations within a single domain are activated that are behaviorally or cognitively incompatible, they exercise reciprocal inhibition, each to the degree of its activation. The fact that no interference is evident on incongruent triples in the pattern-masked condition suggests that inhibition is consequent upon or synchronous with conscious access, but not prior to it. Thus a decision mechanism that chooses what will become conscious (according to consistency, context, sensory information), itself applies inhibition to other candidates for conscious representation. Of course this inhibition would itself decay; otherwise we could not become sequentially conscious of alternative interpretations. It is noteworthy that Schvaneveldt et al. (1976), who did not employ masking, also obtained longer RTs to their incongruent triples than to appropriate control triples.

The present study suggests that the different approaches to word recognition outlined in the introduction apply to different aspects of the process. On the whole the nonselective theory applies to preconscious identification, whereas the selective theory applies to conscious perception. Both views of the locus of contextual effects can be accommodated, because although such effects precede and determine the conscious percept, they follow initial preconscious identification. It is instructive that, in previous research on polysemous words, those studies that have supported the nonselective view have tended to use indirect techniques, de-emphasising attention to the meaning of the polysemous word and assessing the fairly immediate effects of the stimulus (Conrad, 1974; Foss & Jenkins, 1973). Those studies that have supported the selective view have tended to direct conscious attention to the meaning of the polysemous word or to use memory techniques (Gartman & Johnson, 1972; Light & Carter-Sobell, 1970; Winograd & Conn, 1971). Thus the more the situation involves focal attention to polysemous words, the more it will tend to produce data consistent with selective access and vice versa.

Two Effects of Context

The processes addressed by the present study and preceding discussion may be placed in the wider context of comprehension of utterance and text. I have suggested that all the meanings of a word are accessed at a first nonconscious stage of comprehension. However this experiment has only examined two primary meanings and many words have multiple meanings and usages. More important, words can be used in new ways, metaphorically, ironically, or sarcastically or within indirect speech acts. In these cases the consciously perceived meaning seems much more to be *inferred from* the context rather than *selected by* context out of an already accessed array of candidates. Plainly it is necessary to distinguish word meanings from their situational interpretations. It may be best to think of this in terms of two stages of comprehension. In the first stage, which is unconscious, words access both core features of denotation (Katz & Fodor, 1963) and sets of typical scenario-like and associative knowledges including their affective connotations. The second stage, which I wish to associate with consciousness, involves constructing a unitary representation of the utterance or text. In this stage the relevant aspects out of the total set of accessed information are chosen by inference to permit an interpretation that is consistent with surrounding discourse, pragmatics, and the external situation (i.e., to make sense). Comprehension of metaphors (as opposed to idioms) usually requires the listener to focus on an aspect of the meaning of the word or phrase that is hardly ever central to the "literal" usage. Indeed, in Gricean terms (Grice, 1967), in order to understand irony, understatement, scarcasm, and metaphor, as well as indirect speech acts, listeners must infer what is being implied by realizing which maxim of communication (truthfulness, relevance, informativeness, clarity) is being violated.

Verbal context, then, plays an automatic and an inferential role at different stages.

1. Within the first stage of comprehension all aspects of each semantic interpretation which is accessed automatically prime associated lexical entries, such that any activity involving retrieval of that entry (conscious recognition, lexical decision, decomposing it for some purpose) will be facilitated. Once a conscious interpretation has been arrived at, only lexical entries associated with that interpretation continue to receive associative activation; entries associated with incompatible interpretations receive inhibition at that stage.

2. In order to arrive at a consistent conscious interpretation, verbal context is used along with extra-linguistic information in an inferential manner to account for the use of particular words and syntactic forms. This might lead the listener to focus on either a core or scenario feature or even to negate one. Elsewhere (Marcel, in press) I have proposed that conscious percepts are subject to our implicit notions of rationality. One of our ideas of rationality is to be able to account for events. The force of context at this stage is to bias our accounts of utterances by providing an extra criterion. Obviously the techniques used in the present study permit it to apply only to the first stage.

Selectivity in Perception and Action

It has been the contention of this chapter that prior to conscious attention perceptual computations are nonselective. Not only is the whole perceptual array analyzed, but multiple interpretations of each event in the array are computed. Prior context does not affect these computations. This view may appear counter to principles of preparation and anticipation. As a computational heuristic, it would seem to be a sound biological principle to utilize events at time T_1 to prepare for ecologically correlated events at time TI_2. Most descriptions of preparation or expectancy in the spheres of action and perception give a selective account (Requin, 1978); that is, preparation to deal with one event or action accordingly puts other events or actions, especially incompatible ones, at a computational disadvantage. Just as with actions, perceptually nonexpected events would take longer to process due to reorientation, resetting of analytic mechanisms, or recovery from inhibition. However it may be less useful and valid to apply such notions to perception than to action. Action is necessarily and by definition selective, in that any single action is categorical. Beyond the general effects of arousal, preparatory tuning of muscular synergies at some stage must be selective, due to both the organizational and mutually inhibitory nature of such synergies (see Turvey's 1977 review). But, except for the orientation of our receptors, how useful as regards categorical perception is the notion of selective preparation, in the sense of being effective early in processing and differential in its benefits? First, from a computational point of view, early selection is inefficient and potentially costly. If we examine the artificial intelligence attempts at scene analysis reviewed by Mackworth (1976), we find that in general they have found it preferable to compute all possible hypotheses of interpretation up to as high a level as possible before opting for one. Indeed over the course of these attempts they have become, if anything, less top-down. One reason for this is that mistaken hypotheses necessitate lengthy backtracking. Thus if a certain contextual cue suggests analysis of particular aspects or a particular segmentation or interpretation and this turns out to be inappropriate, then computations will have to be carried out again from that point in processing where the selection was made.

Second, in real-time systems, such as biological ones, the backtracking problems became more serious. With an ever-flowing environment, conserving the moment-to-moment records of either the sensory information or the results of successive processing stages is very uneconomical. Indeed, most of the human psychological literature suggests that such records are not kept for very long (for vision, see Coltheart, 1972; for audition, see Massaro, 1972). Of course this does not refer to the records of conscious percepts.

These arguments are functional ones. The implicit point here regarding the empirical literature is that those studies that have been taken as evidence of early selection have in fact relied on conscious behavior, which is a late stage, or have required the recovery of information as opposed to testing its representation indirectly (Marcel, in press).

To be speculative, let us suppose that the link between perception and action is in consciousness. This is not to deny that most of the processing in motor control is nonconscious, nor that nonconscious aspects of perception modulate the details and analogue aspects of actions. Rather it is to say that intentional actions are unitary in their goals (i.e., are *categorical*) and that the voluntary initiation of categorical actions must be based on an unequivocal representation of the environment. Thus perception without action can be infinitely ambiguous. It is when action is required that selection between alternatives must be made. It is this selection, which is the perceptual prerequisite for action, that is the goal of focal attention and thus consciousness.

REFERENCES

Becker, C. A. Allocation of attention during visual word recognition. *Journal of Experimental Psychology: Human Perception and Performance*, 1976, *2*, 556–566.

Clark, H. H. The Language-as-fixed-effect fallacy: A critique of language statistics in psychological research. *Journal of Verbal Learning and Verbal Behavior*, 1973, *12*, 335–359.

Clark, H. H., & Clark, E. V. *Psychology and language: An introduction to psycholinguistics.* New York: Harcourt, Brace, Jovanovich, Inc., 1977.

Coltheart, M. Visual information processing. In P. Dodwell (Ed.), *New horizons in psychology: 2*, New York: Penguin, 1972.

Conrad, C. Context effects in sentence comprehension: A study of the subjective lexicon. *Memory & Cognition*, 1974, *2*, 130–138.

Cramer, P. A. A study of homographs. In L. Postman & G. Keppel (Eds.), *Norms of word association*, New York: Academic Press, 1970.

Dixon, N. F. *Subliminal perception: The nature of a controversy.* London: McGraw-Hill, 1971.

Forster, K. I. Accessing the mental lexicon. In R. J. Wales & E. Walker (Eds.), *New approaches to language mechanisms*, Oxford: North-Holland Publ. Co., 1976.

Foss, D. J., & Jenkins, C. M. Some effects of context on the comprehension of ambiguous sentences. *Journal of Verbal Learning and Verbal Behavior*, 1973, *12*, 577–589.

Gartman, L. M., & Johnson, N. F. Massed versus distributed repetition of homographs: A test of the differential encoding hypothesis. *Journal of Verbal Learning and Verbal Behavior*, 1972, *11*, 801–808.

Grice, H. P. William James Lectures, Harvard University, 1967, published in part as "Logic and conversation." In P. Cole & J. L. Morgan (Eds.), *Syntax and semantics, Vol. 3: Speech acts.* New York: Seminar Press, 1975.

Hogaboam, T. W., & Perfetti, C. A. Lexical ambiguity and sentence comprehension. *Journal of Verbal Learning and Verbal Behavior*, 1975, *14*, 265–274.

Katz, J. J., & Fodor, J. A. The structure of a semantic theory. *Language*, 1963, *39*, 170–210.

Kausler, D. H., & Kamichoff, N. C. Free recall of homographs and their primary associates. *Journal of Verbal Learning and Verbal Behavior*, 1970, *9*, 79–83.

Kausler, D. H., & Kollasch, S. F. Word associations to homographs. *Journal of Verbal Learning and Verbal Behavior*, 1970, *9*, 444–449.

Laner, S., Morris, P., & Oldfield, R. C. A random pattern screen. *Quarterly Journal of Experimental Psychology*, 1957, *9*, 105–108.

Levelt, W. J. M. Studies in sentence perception: 1970–1976. In W. J. M. Levelt & G. B. Flores d'Arcais (Eds.), *Studies in the perception of language*, London: Wiley, 1978.

Light, L. L., & Carter-Sobell, L. I. Effects of changed semantic context on recognition memory. *Journal of Verbal Learning and Verbal Behavior*, 1970, *9*, 1–11.

MacKay, D. G. Mental diplopia: Towards a model of speech perception at the semantic level. In G. B. Flores d'Arcais & W. J. M. Levelt (Eds.), *Advances in psycholinguistics*, Amsterdam: North Holland Publ. Co., 1970.

Mackworth, A. K. Model-driven interpretation in intelligent vision systems. *Perception,* 1976, *5,* 349–370.

Marcel, A. J. Conscious and unconscious perception: Visual masking, word recognition, and an approach to consciousness. *Cognitive Psychology,* (in press).

Marcel, A. J., & Forrin, B. Naming latency and the repetition of stimulus categories. *Journal of Experimental Psychology,* 1974, *103,* 450–460.

Marcel, A. J., & Patterson, K. E. Word recognition and production: Reciprocity in clinical and normal studies. In J. Requin (Ed.), *Attention and performance VII.* Hillsdale, N. J.: Lawrence Erlbaum Associates, 1978.

Massaro, D. W. Perceptual images, processing time and perceptual units in auditory perception. *Psychological Review,* 1972, *79,* 124–145.

Meyer, D. E., Schvaneveldt, R. W., & Ruddy, M. G. *Activation of lexical memory.* Paper presented at the meeting of the Psychonomic Society, St. Louis, Mo., November, 1972.

Morton, J. Interaction of information in word-recognition. *Psychological Review,* 1969, *76,* 165–178.

Neely, J. H. Semantic priming and retrieval from lexical memory: Roles of inhibitionless spreading activation and limited capacity attention. *Journal of Experimental Psychology: General,* 1977, *106,* 226–254.

Requin, J. (Ed.), *Anticipation et comportement.* Paris: Editions du C. N. R. S., 1978.

Rubenstein, H., Garfield, L., & Millikan, J. A. Homographic entries in the internal lexicon. *Journal of Verbal Learning and Verbal Behavior,* 1970, *9,* 487–494.

Schvaneveldt, R. W., & Meyer, D. E. Retrieval and comparison processes in semantic memory. In S. Kornblum (Ed.), *Attention and performance IV,* New York: Academic Press, 1973.

Schvaneveldt, R. W., Meyer, D. E., & Becker, C. A. Lexical ambiguity, semantic context, and visual word recognition. *Journal of Experimental Psychology: Human Perception and Performance,* 1976, *2,* 243–256.

Shallice, T. Dual functions of consciousness. *Psychological Review,* 1972, *79,* 383–393.

Shallice, T. The dominant action system: An information-processing approach to consciousness. In K. S. Pope & J. L. Singer (Eds.), *The stream of consciousness: Scientific investigations into the flow of human experience.* New York: Plenum Press, 1978.

Turvey, M. T. Peripheral and central processes in vision. *Psychological Review,* 1973, *80,* 1–52.

Turvey, M. T. Preliminaries to a theory of action with reference to vision. In R. Shaw & J. Bransford (Eds.), *Perceiving, acting and knowing: Toward an ecological psychology,* Hillsdale, N.J.: Lawrence Erlbaum Associates, 1977.

Warren, R. E., Warren, N. T., Green, J. P., & Bresnick, J. H. Multiple semantic encoding of homophones and homographs in contexts biasing dominant or subordinate meanings. *Memory & Cognition,* 1978, *6,* 364–371.

Winer, B. J. *Statistical principles in experimental design* (2nd ed.), New York: McGraw-Hill Inc., 1971.

Winograd, E., & Conn, C. P. Evidence from recognition memory for the specific encoding of unmodulated homographs. *Journal of Verbal Learning and Verbal Behavior,* 1971, *10,* 702–706.

Ziff, P. Some comments on Mr. Harman's confabulations. *Foundations of Language,* 1967, *3,* 403–408.

23 Memory and Attention in Text Comprehension: The Problem of Reference

A. J. Sanford
S. Garrod
Department of Psychology
University of Glasgow
Glasgow, Scotland

ABSTRACT

In a text it is commonplace to refer to a given individual by different expressions as the text unfolds. This poses something of a problem for the text processor. A method is introduced for assessing some of the factors influencing the ease of comprehension of such (anaphoric) references, and some preliminary results are described. One problem of interest is the effect of the specificity of the expression used to introduce the individual has on the ease of subsequent integration. A number of alternative theories are outlined, and on the basis of an experiment it is suggested that an appropriately specific expression serves to call up from memory a specific representation (the scenario) that a more general one cannot. It is argued that such a scenario may facilitate the integration of subsequently encountered material. The scenario notion is discussed with respect to other studies designed to test its viability. Although tentative, it would appear to provide a potential lead into a number of aspects of text comprehension.

INTRODUCTION

One of the most important problems for text comprehension is understanding how the individual ideas in a text are extracted from the language input and are integrated into a coherent representation. Part of this general problem is how references to individuals (people, things, events) are made and integrated. It is with this reference problem that the present chapter is concerned.

It is typical of any text to find that an individual in it is referred to in more than one way. On various occasions a sea captain might be referred to as *a sailor, a man,* or *he,* for example. This fact alone raises a number of problems —for instance, what level of specificity do we choose to use as the name of an individual when it is first introduced? What levels do we use in subsequent (*anaphoric*) references? How do we make the connection between anaphors that are different lexical items? Following we discuss these issues and attempt to set them into an information-processing framework amenable to experimental investigation.

Anaphoric reference occurs when identical or related noun phrases are used to refer to a particular individual at different points in a text. An example is:

(1a) The carnation won the prize.
(1b) The flower was the biggest in the show.

In this case *flower* is an anaphor of *carnation*. Clearly in order to produce an integrated memory representation of set 1a and b, it is necessary to use our knowledge of the class membership relation holding between antecedent and anaphor. In fact, for an anaphoric relation to exist it is necessary that either the antecedent or anaphoric noun phrase denotes a member of the set of entities denoted by the other; that is, the two should be semantically coextensive (see Stenning, 1975).

One important issue is thus to track down the procedures by which the anaphoric bridge between the two critical individuals is made. Another important issue (which we concentrate on for the main part of this chapter) relates to the *order* of the lexical items themselves in examples like that just given. In sentence set 1, we begin with a relatively specific word (*carnation*) and subsequently refer to it by a more general term (*flower*). This is a more natural way of writing than making a transition from an initial general term to a subsequent specific term for the anaphor, as in set 2:

(2a) The flower was the biggest in the show.
(2b) The carnation won the prize.

Besides seeming somewhat awkward, this order is also in violation of Grice's (1975) maxim of quantity, in which a communicator is urged to be as informative as necessary without providing misleading details. In this way a progression from an initial specification which is optionally informative to subsequent references which are more general would seem to provide a formula in agreement with the maxim.

ANAPHORA: MEASURING THE
BRIDGING PROCESS

In order to establish the variables influencing the bridging process and thereby to provide a tool for the establishment of a process model of it, the authors devised a technique enabling measurements to be taken of the time subjects spend reading each and every sentence of a text. Subjects pace themselves by pressing the space bar of a teletype terminal in order to obtain a display of each sentence. Through the computer that controls the experiment, the time that the subject takes over each sentence can be recorded. The reading times obtained can be manipulated for any sentence of interest (the target sentence) by varying either the content of the sentence itself or the nature of the antecedent context. The assumption is that processing complexity or difficulty will be reflected in the reading times. Finally, in all our studies, after each passage has been read, the subject is asked a question about it to ensure that he always reads for meaning. After a certain amount of practice, subjects can perform the task without any apparent difficulty.

In order to investigate the processes underlying anaphoric reference, Garrod and Sanford (1977, 1978) capitalized on what is already known about class-membership evaluation. Consider sentence pair 3:

(3a) A bus/tank came trundling down the hill.
(3b) The vehicle almost hit a pedestrian.

In the first sentence of this pair, *bus* is a common (high dominance) member of the class *vehicle*, although *tank* is a less common (low dominance) member, as specified by the Battig and Montague (1969) production norms. Elsewhere it has been established that highly dominant class members are accepted more rapidly as members of their classes than low-dominance members (e.g., Rosch, 1973; Wilkins, 1971). Now it has to be argued that in order to establish a connection between the two sentences, we have to map *the vehicle* onto *a bus* or *a tank*. In order to do this we have to make use of the fact that *bus* or *tank* are members of the class *vehicle*. If the retrieval of this information takes longer with *tank* than *bus*, then this fact should be reflected in the reading time for the second sentences of the pairs like that previously given.

Just as we may expect to be able to detect differences in the time taken to perform anaphoric mapping as a function of the dominance as a class member, so we might be able to detect differences in integration time depending on the relative specificity of an antecedent and an anaphor. For example, the sequence shown in pair 3 seems much more natural than pair 4 as we have already intimated:

(4a) A vehicle came trundling round the bend.
(4b) The tank/bus almost hit a pedestrian.

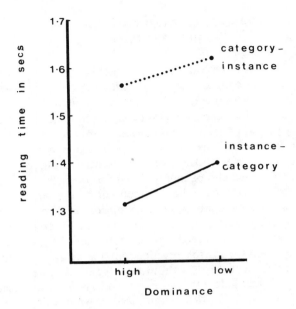

FIG. 23.1.   Mean reading time for target sentences as a function of dominance and antecedent-target specificity order. (After Garrod & Sanford, 1977.)

Half of the subjects in the experiment saw materials like set 3 (i.e., specific
antecedent) and half saw materials like set 4, with a general antecedent.

The pattern of results, shown in Fig. 23.1, revealed two substantial main
effects. First, high-dominance class members result in shorter reading times
for the target sentences, regardless of the order of specificity. Second, specific
antecedent–general target pairs produce more rapid target reading times than
do general antecedent-specific pairs.

In the case of the specific antecedent pairs, the target sentence is identical
for the two dominance conditions, and so the dominance effect results
entirely from the context. In the case of the general antecedent pairs, the
target sentences do differ, but only to the extent that they contain either a
high- or a low-dominance instance. An independent control used single
sentences followed by a question, and it was established that they did not
differ in reading time. So the dominance effect for both orders results from
and indicates the presence of the processes of retrieving class-membership
information from long-term memory.

In the case of the specificity effect, a control condition comparing reading
times for single sentences containing categories or exemplars showed that
sentences containing exemplars are in fact read reliably *faster* than sentences
containing categories. So specific target sentences are slower only in the
presence of the antecedent context containing a coreferential noun phrase.

One final point is that there was no reliable interaction between the specificity and dominance effects. The same mapping has to be made regardless of presentation order.

ANAPHORA: ORIGINS OF THE SPECIFICITY EFFECT

There are two main classes of theory that offer themselves as potential explanations for the specificity effect. The first would ascribe the latency difference to the information content of the target sentence; the second to the kind of representations set up by the specificity of the antecedent. Let us examine each class in turn.

An explanation based on the information content of the target sentence is based on the fact that the specific-to-general transition conveys no new information about the target individual when the target sentence is introduced. Calling a *tank* a *vehicle* tells us nothing new. On the other hand, calling a *vehicle* a *tank* does tell us something new, and it is quite plausible that the incorporation of this new information into the memory representation could be time-consuming and lead to the observed longer reading times in the general-to-specific condition. Indeed, this was the explanation that we emphasized in our original analysis of the results (Garrod & Sanford, 1977, 1978; Sanford & Garrod, in press).

An explanation based on antecedent specificity is very different. Suppose that when we use a noun phrase initially, a more specific phrase makes it somehow easier to integrate subsequent information that is coreferential than is the case when we use a less specified antecedent. In this case it would not be the introduction of extra information in the target sentence which produced the increased reading time but the specificity of the antecedent which mattered. The rationale for such an explanation could take several forms. For example, prior mention of a general term such as *vehicle* could be thought of as opening up a wide range of anaphors (e.g., *vehicle, it,* and all exemplars of the vehicle class), whereas the use of a more specific term (such as *tank*) might open up a correspondingly small class (*vehicle, it, all exemplars* of tanks). If part of the mapping process included a matching search between the potential anaphor set and the given anaphor, the process could take longer for the larger set. Indeed, in direct tests demanding the evaluation of class-membership statments, there is some evidence that larger classes lead to longer evaluation times (Landauer & Meyer, 1972).[1] Alternatively, we could enter-

---

[1] More recent research has suggested that the results originally presented in support of this argument may be handled by other explanations (Smith, E. E., Shoben, E. J., & Rips, L. J. Comparison processes in semantic memory. *Psychological Review*, 1974, *81*, 214–241). However, it still appears tenable in the present situation.

tain an explanation based on other ideas as to the nature of the representation of the initial sentence. For example, the sentence

(5) A tank came trundling down the hill.

could lead to some sort of mental *scenario* embodying default concepts about the behavior of tanks, the kinds of circumstances that might result in such a situation, etc. A sentence based on a less well-specified individual (e.g., vehicle) could lead to a more poorly defined scenario or even to no scenario at all, with the comprehender awaiting further information before forming one. We already have some evidence to suggest that specific and general terms differ in their effects on understanding—in isolation, sentences carrying specific terms are read more rapidly than those carrying general terms (possibly because a scenario is more easily found in long-term memory). If we further assume that a well-formed scenario facilitates integration, then we have a rationale for faster comprehension following from more highly specified antecedents.

In order to narrow the field of explanations, we carried out an experiment including general-to-general and specific-to-specific transitions. If *target specificity* is the critical variable, then the general-to-general transition should be faster than the general-to-specific transition, because in the former case no extra information is conveyed by the target. If *antecedent specificity* is the crtical variable, the general-to-general and the general-to-specific transition should be slower than specific-to-general and specific-to-specific transition.

AN EXPERIMENT ON SPECIFICITY

Method

Subjects.   Sixteen subjects, undergraduates at the University of Glasgow, took part in the experiment. They were paid £0.50 for a session of about 40 minutes, including practice time.

Materials.   Sixty-four sentence pairs were produced, each pair being expressed in four different forms: specific to specific, specific to general, general to general, general to specific. A question was added to each pair. Half of the questions to specific-to-general and general-to-specific pairs required integrated materials to be used, and half did not. Furthermore, half of each of these sets used a specific name in the question; half, a general name. Half of all the questions required a *yes* answer and half *no*. An example of the materials is shown in Table 23.1.

TABLE 23.1
Sample Materials Used in the Specificity Experiment and Mean
Reading Times for the Appropriate Targets in Milliseconds

Condition		Mean Target RT
S–S	The Lorry would not get up the hill.	
		1493
	The lorry was overloaded.	
	Was the lorry going down the hill?	
S–G	The lorry _____	
	The vehicle_____	1511
	Was the lorry_____?	
G–G	The vehicle_____	
	The vehicle_____	1567
	Was the vehicle _____?	
G–S	The vehicle_____	
	The lorry _____	1578
	Was the lorry_____?	

Four files of materials were produced on disk, each consisting of the 64 pairs, 16 in each of the four possible specificity configurations. In this way, over the four files the 64 pairs occurred in every possible configuration, but within a file each pair appeared only once. This arrangement was used so that each subject would see a particular set of materials once only. The files were arranged such that the 64 items were in random order for the first file, but the same order was preserved for the other files. Thus if in file 1 *tank to vehicle* occurred at, say, position 3, files 2, 3, and 4 had the tank–vehicle materials at position 3 also. This offers an opportunity to reduce materials-effect variance due to practice effects.

Procedure

The stimuli were presented using the self-paced reading paradigm. Every time the subject pressed the space bar of the VDU console, the next sentence appeared. The first sentence of any set consisted of the display *NEXT TRIAL*, the remainder being, in order, antecedent, target, and question. The subject sat so that he pressed the space bar with a thumb. When the question appeared, the subject pressed *Y* if he thought it required *yes* and *N* if it required *no*. He was instructed to read through the materials of any given set as quickly as he found comfortable and to answer the question as quickly and accurately as possible. Prior to the experimental test run, the subject received considerable practice with the self-paced reading task by working through two long passages; he then received some examples of short passages with questions to answer.

Each subject saw one file only of 64 materials.

Results

The overall mean reading times for the two types of target sentence under the two antecedent conditions are given in Table 23.1. One analysis of variance was carried out on the subjects' mean times, treating materials as a fixed effect, and another on mean times for materials, treating subjects as a fixed effect. This procedure enables the calculation of min F' (Clark, 1973) to be made.

The results of these analyses indicate that specific antecedents produce shorter reading times for the target sentence than general antecedents by about 71 msec, this being statistically reliable with min $F'(1, 77) = 4.17$; $p < .05$. Neither repetition nor the interaction of repetition with antecedent type approached significance (all F's by subjects and by materials less than 1). In other words, a general antecedent has a relative retarding effect on reading time for targets, regardless of whether the anaphor in the target is a *repeat* of the general noun phrase or a more specific noun phrase. Obviously these results cannot be explained in terms of the information content of the critical noun phrase in the target sentence. It is the specificity of the antecedent that is the important thing.

An illuminating post hoc analysis was carried out that we believe enables the field of explanations to be narrowed still further. If we are to assume that it is richness of a scenario that is at the root of the specificity effects, then we might speculate that certain entities in the scenario-retrieving sentence would be more instrumental in its selection than others. Specifically, it is widely recognized that a sentence can be thought of as having two components—a *topic* component and *a comment* component (Grimes, 1975; see also Halliday, 1967). The topic is the principal individual in the sentence, and the comment refers to information about that individual. Thus a sentence like

(6) The boy is petting the cat.

is judged to be "about" *a boy*, whereas

(7) The cat is being petted by the boy.

is judged to be "about" *a cat* (Hornby, 1974).

We suggest that a scenario is principally governed by the topic (or principal actor) and the action being described—other individuals playing a less central or supportive role. According to this line of argument we might expect the

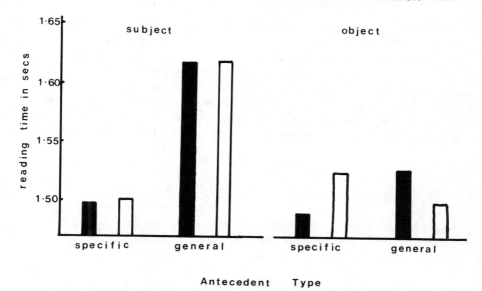

FIG. 23.2.   Mean reading time for target sentences as a function of antecedent type, following a split of the materials into those containing the critical noun phrase in the subject and object positions. Black bars—specific targets; white bars—general targets.

specificity effect to be greatest for antecedents that are the topic (i.e., in the subject position because the subject portrays the principal topic of discourse in these materials, as topic specification would lead to easier scenario selection). Indeed, scrutiny of the materials indicated that those materials not showing the effect had the noun phrase of interest in a nontopicalized position—for example:

(8) Mrs. Dupont dropped the *vegetable/cucumber*.

Fortunately, about half of the materials were topicalized and half not, and the average number of words and letters in the two sets of materials so formed were the same. By partitioning the materials in this way, the pattern of results shown in Fig. 23.2 was obtained. An analysis of variance was carried out including topicalization as a factor[2] and revealed a main effect of antecedent type [min $F'(1, 64) = 4.272$; $p < .05$] and some evidence for an interaction between topicalization and antecedent specificity—reliably by materials [$F(1,$

---

[2]In order to have an equal number of data entries for the subject and object position materials in the post hoc analysis, the number of each material type had to be reduced to 30 (losing only two items).

60) = 4.168; $p < .043$] but just missing by subjects [$F(1, 15) = 3.094$; $p < .096$]. All other main effects and interactions were unreliable by both subjects and materials. The interaction is sufficiently respectable to merit further consideration, and individual analyses carried out on topicalized and non-topicalized' sets show that for the topicalized set the antecedent effect is reliable [min $F'(1, 39) = 4.67$; $p < .05$], but no other effects approach significance, even by separate Fs. For the nontopicalized materials, no effect approaches reliability, even by separate Fs (all Fs < 1.5 for denominator dfs of 15 and 30).

DISCUSSION OF THE SPECIFICITY EFFECT

In our initial discussion of hypotheses for the specificity effect, we mentioned two that ascribed the results to the antecedent rather than to the target—the range-of-anaphors account and the scenario-richness account. We are in possession of two results that appear to rule out the first of these explanations. First, consider the results of the post hoc analysis of the previous experiment. The range of anaphors opened should be the same, regardless of whether the antecedent was topicalized or not, and consequently the specificity account should have occurred in both cases, which it did not. Furthermore, the implication is that the process of mapping one lexical item onto another is independent of the process producing the specificity effect, because mapping has to occur in both cases but the specificity effect is present in only one of them.

The second piece of evidence comes from a reconsideration of the relationship between specificity and dominance discussed earlier. The evidence we presented (Fig. 23.1) showed that these two factors were independent. Now a specific antecedent like *robin* or *goose* should give access to a range of anaphors, including *bird,* this being the sense in which they are interpreted. If a search was initiated in the anaphor set for *bird* when it was met, it seems unlikely that a dominance effect would result. However, the magnitude of the effect was about the same regardless of antecedent specificity. This casts further doubt on an explanation based on the range of anaphors and also supports the idea that lexical mapping processes and those producing the specificity effect are independent, at least with materials of the kind we have used.

At this stage we can only suggest lines along which an explanation of the specificity effect might go. As we have indicated, it seems likely that the kinds of representation produced by sentences containing specific and general topics differ in their richness. With a more specified item, we know much more about the properties of the individual concerned and the sort of actions into which it can enter. If we accept this idea, then a number of explanations for the antecedent specificity effect are possible. One view is that a specific topic can call on a preexisting modular memory structure which can be held in working memory more easily than could a general topic which had no preexisting modular structure. If integration time for the second sentence is a function of working memory load, then we could explain the slowness of integration engendered by a general antecedent. We would have to argue that modular structures are more likely to be pushed into working memory if their referents are in the topic position. Such an argument does rest on the idea that a complex (specified) structure is *easier* to retain than a simple (unspecified, merely named) structure. However, complexity does not necessarily imply that maintenance in memory should be more difficult—it could well be easier if the structure is well established and strongly integrated. A second view is that underspecified (general) topics set up processes explicitly *looking for* more specification. The most extreme example of this is found in the device of *cataphora*, where a new individual is introduced by means of a pronoun, for example. Thus:

(9) One still winter's night it appeared in the middle of the lawn.

uses *it* to introduce a new individual. There is nothing wrong with this; it appears to serve the function of emphasizing the new individual and promises that more will be divulged of the individual's nature at some later point in the text. Perhaps the search for greater specificity slows down the satisfactory conceptual integration of subsequent anaphoric material, whether it is specifying, as in the case of specific targets, or not, as in the case of general targets. Although these arguments are necessarily speculative, there is evidence that suggests they are worth pursuing. Sanford, Garrod, and Bell (1979) showed that sentences producing a specified scenario enable the integration of subsequent coreferential material to take place more quickly than sentences producing a less specified scenario. For example, antecedents like sentences 10a and 10b produce relatively fast integration of 10c in terms of reading time.

(10a) A weapon was protruding from the corpse.
(10b) There was blood all over the floor.
(10c) The weapon was covered with fingerprints.

On the other hand, pairs like sentences 10d and e produce a relatively slow integration when they are antecedent to 10c;

(10d) A weapon was bought from a shop in town.
(10e) It was the only one of its kind.

In a rating study, subjects reported that it was easier to produce a summary title for the 10a and b passage than the 10d and e passage—and it was also easier to produce a visual image.

Of course, the whole issue of specificity, concreteness, and imagery is something beyond the scope of this chapter, but we do appear to have a convergence on the idea that specificity aids integration. Rather than elaborate in a speculative way, let us return to one of the fundamental assumptions underlying the present discussion. This is the idea that the representation used in working memory during text comprehension is more than just the superficial propositional content of the antecedent materials, in which case specificity of antecedent could hardly influence subequent integration in the way it does. Rather, a more substantial and complex structure, the scenario, is implicated.

INTRODUCING NEW INDIVIDUALS

The idea of the scenario is that noun phrases and the actions in which they are involved can serve to call up from memory complex modular information structures that are based upon the readers experience of related (or identical) situations. In the cognitive science literature, such possibilities have been discussed as *frames* (Minsky, 1975), *Scripts* (Schank & Abelson, 1977), and *Schemata* (Rumelhart & Ortony, 1978). One of the features of such a system is, for any representation of a situation that is called up, that individuals not explicitly mentioned in the text may already be present in the resultant scenario-based working memory structure. This implies that individuals can be introduced into a text without the necessity of having to construct inferential bridges at the time they are introduced because the bridges are effectively already there at the time the new individual is introduced. This will only be true of individuals that are a built-in part of the scenario stereotype. Other individuals that are not part of the stereotype when introduced may have the potential to be related to the scenario structure, but this will involve on the spot bottom-up inference making at the time the sentence introducing the new individual is encountered. We may very well expect built-in individuals to be processed more rapidly than arbitrary individuals, and the speed of processing should be amenable to examination by the self-paced reading paradigm. Consider the following simple example, which relies upon the structure of the verb *to dress:*

(11a) Mary was dressing the baby.
(11b) The clothes were made of soft pink wool.

Although clothes have not been explicitly mentioned in sentence 11a, a link is easily formed between *clothes* and *dressing*. From our point of view, the interest lies in how this link is made. Either the representation of 11a would consist of a fairly full semantic structure embodying the fact that dress is equivalent to *transferring clothes* from the onset or it could consist of a simpler representation that has the potential to yield the implicature. [An example of differing degrees of representational complexity is given in Kintsch (1977), who argues that under circumstances only simple representations are generated.]

A test of these alternatives has been carried out using the reading time paradigm (Garrod & Sanford, in preparation; Sanford & Garrod, in press). The critical test involved comparing the time to read sentences like 11b when preceded by an antecedent in which the new individual is merely implied or one in which it is made explicit, as in sentence 11c:

(11c) Mary was putting the clothes on the baby.
(11b) The clothes were made of soft pink wool.

If the antecedent *clothes* is already represented in the implied antecedent condition, we would expect no differences in reading time for 11b in the two conditions. However, if *clothes* is not already in the representations, and a bridge has to be formed at the point when *the clothes* is encountered, then sentence 11b should take longer to process after the implied antecedent 11a than after the stated antecedent 11c.

There was no difference between the two conditions, from which we conclude that the transfer of clothes was already part of the representation set up by using the verb *was dressing*. This is strong evidence for the operation of top-down contextually motivated bridging in the case of verb-implied antecedents. We would say that clothes transfer is part of the *scenario* formed on encountering sentence 11a.

Parallel results can also be obtained with materials in which the freshly introduced individual is already implied on more general grounds. For instance, given a title like *A breakdown* and some sentences referring to *slamming the door*, it does not take any extra time to read a target introducing a new entity, *the car*, than it does if *car* had already been made explicit. On the other hand, with a title like *In a bad mood*, it does (Garrod & Sanford, in preparation). In other words, the title *A breakdown* serves to elicit a scenario containing information about car breakdowns, which in turn makes available information implicating individuals which have not been mentioned explicitly in the text. By contrast, although mention of a car can be fitted into the *bad mood* passage, *car* is not implied by it and will have no advance representation in working memory.

GENERAL CONCLUSION

The main point we wish to make in this chapter is that the specificity of a key-topicalized antecedent noun phrase influences the ease with which subsequent anaphoric material can be integrated. In our earlier work (Garrod & Sanford, 1977, 1978) the presence of a specificity effect was already established, but it was unclear whether its origin was in the greater amount of information conveyed by a specific anaphor noun phrase following on a more general antecedent or whether it lay in some facilitating power that could be attributed to a more specific antecedent. The present main study suggests the latter.

On the basis of the main and subsidiary analyses carried out, we are led to suggest that wherever possible the comprehension system seeks out a concrete or tangible representation of a given sentence and that this representation will contain default information not made explicit in the text. If this view is correct, it would seem inappropriate to consider accounts of text comprehension based essentially upon concatenating the propositional information contained in a text, with perhaps minimal recourse to long-term memory in order to make inferences where text-based propositions fail to provide predicator or argument repetitions as a means of achieving cohesion. The proposition-based view has been extensively studied by Kintsch and his colleagues (e.g., Kintsch, 1974) and has been expressed fairly fully in a recent paper (Kintsch & van Dijk, 1978). In their paper, although allowance is made for the modifying processes of *macrooperators,* the basis of text comprehension is still largely attributed to the propositional structure of what is on the page. Macro-operators serve to select out important propositions or to generalize propositions of similar meaning—in short, they serve an encoding function of influencing the probabilities of remembering propositions in a text base.

In contrast to this point of view, we would like to suggest that one of the key elements of text interpretation is that wherever possible a linguistic input addresses a knowledge structure in long-term memory and that this knowledge structure does some of the work involved in the integration process. The basic structure retrieved we have called the *scenario,* but the idea is similar to that put forward by proponents of artificial intelligence under the guise of *frames* and *scripts.* In the case of the specificity results, we assume that a scenario can be retrieved more readily when the sentence involves a specific noun. Indeed, we would suggest that this potential to retrieve a scenario is one of the reasons why Grice's (1975) maxim of informativeness is so important. Subsequent integration should be easier with a working memory representation involving a scenario because it will entail a constrained and concrete set of representataionl possibilites to produce an integrated configuration with later linguistic inputs.

Of course not all texts will necessarily be able to draw upon preexisting scenario structures, but they may still be intelligible at some level. For example, when a student first learns a new subject, he may have certain key summary propositions brought to his attention. From the point of view of his teacher, each of these propositions carries with it complete mental scenarios —networks of implications, unstated individuals, and associated scriptal or procedural elements. From the student's point of view, he is dealing with bald superficial propositions. In a real sense, his understanding probably consists of little more than being able to hold these propositions in memory and to be able to draw conclusions from them in a syllogistic sense. If we imagine a self-paced reading task in which the three sentences consist of abstract syllogisms, it seems probable that either reading times would be very long or memory, very poor. Furthermore, reading about a familiar topic is easier and faster than reading about an unfamiliar topic (e.g., Kintsch, Kozminsky, Stretby, McKoon, & Keenan, 1975). From the point of view we have been asserting, the problem is one of the ease with which parts of the text access related scenario structure in long-term memory. The notion that rich memory structures enable better text integration to take place than does a text-related propositional structure can be thought of as paralleling the observation that rich relational structures facilitate the learning and retention of otherwise simple materials, such as paired associates or word lists (Bower, 1972).

ACKNOWLEDGMENTS

We would like to thank Liz Bell, who carried out much of the experimental work described in this chapter, and members of the H. J. Watt Society, who have made numerous useful comments. The research was supported by a grant to the authors from the British Social Science Research Council.

REFERENCES

Battig, W. F., & Montague, W. E. Category norms for verbal items in 56 categories. A replication and extension of the Connecticut category norms. *Journal of Experimental Psychology Monograph*, 1969, *80*, 1–46.

Bower, G. H. Mental imagery and associative learning. In L. W. Gregg (Ed.), *Cognition in learning and memory*. New York: Wiley, 1972.

Clark, H. H. The language-as-fixed-effect fallacy: A critique of language statistics in psychological research. *Journal of Verbal Learning and Verbal Behavior*, 1973, *12*, 335–359.

Garrod, S., & Sanford, A. J. Interpreting anaphoric relations: The integration of semantic information while reading. *Journal of Verbal Learning and Verbal Behavior*, 1977, *16*, 77–90.

Garrod, S., & Sanford, A. J. Anaphora: A problem in text comprehension. In R. N. Campbell & P. T. Smith (Eds.), *Recent advances in the psychology of language*. London: Plenum Press, 1978.

Grice, H. P. Logic and conversation. In P. Cole & J. L. Morgan (Eds.), *Studies in syntax, III.* New York: Academic Press, 1975.

Grimes, J. E. *The thread of discourse.* The Hague: Mouton Janura Linguarum Minor, 1975.

Halliday, M. A. K. Notes on transitivity and theme in Engligh II. *Journal of Linguistics,* 1967, *3,* 199–244.

Hornby, P. A. Surface structure and presupposition. *Journal of Verbal Learning and Verbal Behavior,* 1974, *13,* 530–538.

Kintsch, W. *The representation of meaning in memory.* Hillsdale, N.J.: Lawrence Erlbaum Associates, 1974.

Kintsch, W. *Memory and cognition.* New York: Wiley, 1977.

Kintsch, W., & van Dijk, T. A. Toward a model of text comprehension and production. *Psychological Review,* 1978, *85,* 363–394.

Kintsch, W., Kozminsky, E., Stretby, W. J., McKoon, G., & Keenan, J. M. Comprehension and recall of text as a function of content variables. *Journal of Verbal Learning and Verbal Behavior,* 1975, *14,* 196–214.

Landauer, T. K., & Meyer, D. E. Category size and semantic-memory retrieval. *Journal of Verbal Learning and Verbal Behavior,* 1972, *11,* 539–544.

Minsky, M. A framework for representing knowledge. In P. H. Winston (Ed.), *The psychology of computer vision.* New York: McGraw-Hill, 1975.

Rosch, E. On the internal structure of perceptual and semantic categories. In I. E. Moore (Ed.), *Cognitive development and acquisition of language.* New York: Academic Press, 1973.

Rumelhart, D. E., & Ortony, A. The representation of knowledge in memory. In R. C. Anderson, R. J. Spiro, & W. E. Montague (Eds.), *Schooling and the acquisition of knowledge.* Hillsdale, N. J.: Lawrence Erlbaum Associates, 1978.

Sanford, A. J., & Garrod, S. Implicit information in comprehending discourse. In R. Drachman (Ed.), *Salzburg contributions to linguistics, 4,* in press.

Sanford, A. J., Garrod, S., & Bell, E. Aspects of memory dynamics in text comprehension. In M. M. Gruneberg, P. E., Morris, & R. N. Sykes (Eds.), *Practical aspects of memory: Proceedings of the International Conference.* London: Academic Press, 1979.

Schank, R., & Abelson, R. *Scripts, plans, goals, and understanding.* Hillsdale, N.J.: Lawrence Erlbaum Associates, 1977.

Stenning, K. *Understanding English Articles and Quantifiers.* Unpublished Ph.D. dissertation, Rockefeller University, 1975.

Wilkins, A. J. Conjoint frequency, category size and categorization time. *Journal of Verbal Learning and Verbal Behavior,* 1971, *10,* 382–385.

24
Speech as Eyes See It

Ronald A. Cole
Carnegie-Mellon University

Victor W. Zue
Massachusetts Institute of Technology

ABSTRACT

Three studies examined subjects' ability to identify phonetic information from speech spectrograms. In Experiment 1, five students (enrolled in a graduate course in speech communication that included some training in spectrogram reading) were asked to label phonetically spectrograms of five unknown sentences. On the first choice, the students correctly identified about 50% of all the segments and an additional 30% were identified on second and third choices. Experiments 2 and 3 examined the performance of a speech scientist who has had extensive practice in labeling spectrograms. In Experiment 2, the reader labeled 11 spectrograms as quickly as possible in a single pass from left to right. Labeling time decreased with practice from about 12 sec per segment to about 3 sec per segment. Labeling accuracy, about 85% correct including first, second, and third choices, was not correlated with reading time. Experiment 3 explored the reader's ability to name words in a known carrier phrase from spectrograms. On the first trial, 21 of the 25 words were correctly identified with a mean time per segment of about 2.3 sec. The implications of the results to the use of vision as a substitute communication channel for language were discussed.

A speech spectrogram provides a visual display of the energy in speech in terms of time—along the horizontal axis; frequency—along the vertical axis; and intensity—by the darkness of the markings. Spectrograms are relatively easy to produce, and they display most of the relevant acoustic characteristics of speech sounds. For this reason, the speech spectrogram has been the most widely used form of display in speech research over the past three decades. To be sure, a spectrogram sometimes introduces distortions to the acoustic structures of speech and often does not provide adequate information on

475

prosodic cues, such as stress and intonation. Nevertheless, a speech spectrogram gives a good description of the segmental acoustic properties of speech, and it has been an invaluable tool in the development of our understanding of speech production and perception.

Is it possible to learn to read a speech spectrogram? With sufficient practice, can one examine a spectrogram of an unknown utterance and determine what was said? The results of spectrogram reading experiments by Klatt and Stevens (1973), and Lindblom and Svensson (1973; see also Svensson, 1974) have shown that spectrogram reading is a difficult task.

In the Klatt and Stevens study, the authors attempted to label phonetically a set of 19 spectrograms of unknown utterances spoken by 5 unfamiliar male talkers. The spectrograms displayed questions that could be asked of a computer program designed to answer questions about moon rocks (e.g., "How many moon rocks do we have?"). In order to minimize the possibility of recognizing words on the spectrograms, the readers placed a mask over each spectrogram which allowed only 300 msec of speech to be visible at one time. Labeling was performed in a single pass as the mask was moved across the spectrogram from left to right.

DHK labeled 10 spectrograms. He correctly identified 41% of all segments and provided a correct partial transcription (e.g., "sonorant," "high front vowel") on an additional 31%. KNS labeled 9 spectrograms. He correctly identified 24% of all segments and provided a correct partial transcription on an additional 50%. Averaging across the two readers, 33% of all segments were correctly identified as either a first, second or third choice (first choice statistics were not presented), with a further 40% given a correct partial transcription.

On the basis of their results, Klatt and Stevens expressed doubt that the words in an unknown sentence could be recognized from a spectrographic display:

> While improved knowledge of acoustic phonetics and a more precise input representation of the acoustic signal might provide some increase in the initial transcription score, it is probable that the improvement will not be substantial. Any strategy that relies on direct analysis of the input signal and utilizes a system of rules that transforms the results of this analysis into a pattern of segments and features, will provide error-free specification of only a small fraction of the phonetic features in the kind of sentence material used in this study. It will be possible to identify only a few of the words based on this kind of information alone. (p. 216)

In a second part of the study, the investigators attempted to recognize the words displayed on each spectrogram by using the phonetic information derived from the spectrograms to ask questions of a computer program. The program contained information about the words in each of the sentences from which the spectrograms were made and would display word candidates consistent with a partial phonetic specification. For example, the investigator might ask the computer for all words in the sentence corpus "that begin with a /p/ or a /t/, followed by a nonlow front vowel, followed by zero or one sonorants, followed by an /s/." The computer would then print out all word candidates meeting these criteria, and the investigator could look at the spectrogram and decide upon the most likely candidate. Klatt and Stevens report that each question yielded an average of five word candidates, and the correct word was among these candidates only 25% of the time. However, when the correct word was present in the computer response, it was recognized in every case.

The strategy of using an interactive computer facility to evaluate word candidates from spectrographic data resulted in almost perfect word recognition. The final identification score for the words in the 19 sentences was 96%.

As part of a study of prosodic and grammatical influences on speech perception, Svensson (1974) had a group of subjects read spectrograms. Svensson's subjects consisted of workers at the Speech Transmission Laboratory of the Royal Institute of Technology in Stockholm and of students at Stockholm University who had participated in a spectrogram reading course. Thus, these subjects had a relatively high degree of sophistication in spectrogram interpretation.

In the first part of the study, the subjects were all presented with spectrograms of nonsense utterances, consisting of phonologically permissible nonsense words spoken with sentence intonation. The subjects were given written instructions on spectrogram interpretation, which included relevant acoustic data and a decision procedure for segment identification. Each subject was presented with nine spectrograms, an hour being allotted for reading each one. The participants were instructed to write down a single segment label for each segment identified on the spectrograms. The results, according to Svensson, were disappointing, with performance ranging from a low of 22% segments identified to a high of 51%. The average level was 38%. In the second part of the study, spectrograms of meaningful utterances were used. Performance on this material was almost identical to that in the first part of the study, despite the fact that the subjects knew that they were dealing with meaningful utterances generated from a restricted grammar and a limited lexicon.

In a subsequent experimental condition, Svensson (also reported in Lindblom and Svensson, 1974) constrained the spectogram reading task in a number of ways. Subjects were again presented with spectrograms of unknown utterances, but syllable stress and tonal accent were indicated on the spectrograms for each vowel (tonal accent, which has two levels—a rising or falling fundamental frequency contour—is phonemic in Swedish). The subjects were told that all spectrograms displayed declarative sentences having a particular grammatical structure, and restrictions were imposed on word choice so that long words, compound words and deviant forms were excluded. Finally, the subjects were taught a detailed decision strategy for interpreting spectrograms. When the task was constrained in this way, subjects correctly identified over 85% of all words and over 97% of all phonetic segments. Lindblom and Svensson [1974] conclude that "spectrograms of Swedish utterances can be read with great accuracy under nontrivial reading conditions."

A recent experiment by Cole, Rudnicky, Zue, and Reddy (1979) shows that, with sufficient practice, it is possible to learn to determine the phonetic content of an unknown utterance from a spectrographic display. They describe the performance of an expert spectrogram reader, VZ, who has spent between 2500 and 3000 hours studying spectrograms of fluent speech. In their experiment, VZ was asked to label phonetically 23 spectrograms of unknown utterances, including English sentences, semantically and syntactically anomalous sentences, and sequences of words and nonsense words spoken with sentence intonation.

In order to measure VZ's ability to identify and label phonetic segments from speech spectrograms, the phonetic transcriptions produced by VZ were compared to transcriptions produced by three phoneticians who listened to the utterances. According to the phoneticians, there were 499 segments in the 23 utterances, and VZ identified the existence of 485 of them, or slightly more than 97% of all segments. VZ produced the same segment label as at least one transcriber on 424 of the 499 segments, or 85%. This compares with an average agreement of about 90% between each pair of phoneticians. Perhaps most important, a linguist who examined VZ's transcriptions of the 15 normal English sentences was able to identify all but 5 of the words in the sentences.

Figure 24.1 displays a spectrogram of the utterance "The soldiers knew the battle was won," the first spectrogram presented to VZ. The transcription produced by VZ is shown directly under the spectrogram. Figure 24.2 compares the transcription produced by VZ to the transcriptions produced by the phoneticians.

A detailed analysis of VZ's performance (from videotapes and verbal protocols) revealed a number of insights into his methods. Perhaps most interesting, higher-order knowledge about the syntactic and semantic structure of English was rarely used to interpret spectrograms. Performance was slightly *better* on sequences of words and nonsense words (90%) than on English sentences (85%). Thus, phonetic segments were identified solely from visual information displayed on the spectrograms.

An important point to emerge from the analysis of VZ's performance was that phonetic segments were identified through the recognition of *characteristic visual patterns*. To be sure, VZ has an extensive knowledge of the effects of coarticulation on the acoustic realization of segments, and this knowledge

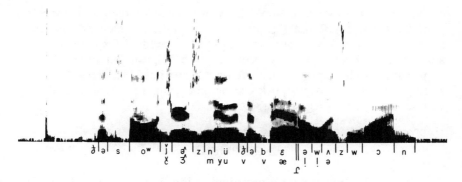

FIG. 24.1. Speech spectrogram of the utterance "The soldiers knew the battle was won."

was used to interpret spectrograms. For example, the occurrence of an /l/ modifies the formant frequencies of an adjacent vowel, and VZ compensates for this effect when identifying the vowel. But such cases were the exception rather than the rule; most phonetic segments were readily identified through the recognition of characteristic visual patterns.

The report by Cole et al. (1979) was offered as an existence proof, a demonstration that it is possible to determine the phonetic content of an unknown utterance from a spectrographic display. Having established this proof, our subsequent research has been directed to two additional questions. First, is VZ's skill teachable? Can a properly motivated student learn to label a spectrogram following, say, 50 hours of intensive study? Or, will future spectrogram readers have to emulate VZ and spend hundreds or thousands of hours studying spectrograms? Experiment 1 describes the performance of some of our students who have been learning to read speech spectrograms.

VZ:	ð ə	soʷ	ǰ ɚ z č ʒ	nü yu	ð ə v	bɛɾə væ l	wʌz lə	wɔn
T1:	ð ə	sol	ǰ ɚ z	nu	ð ə	bæɾl	wɨz	wʌn
T2:	ð ʌ	sol	ǰ ɚ z	nu	ð ə	bæɾl	wʌz	wɔn
T3:	·ð ə	sol	ǰ ɚ z	nu	ð ə	bæɾl	wəz	wʌn

FIG. 24.2. Transcriptions produced by VZ to a spectrogram and by three phoneticians who listened to the utterance from which the spectrogram was made.

The second question that we ask is: How fast can VZ read speech spectrograms? Experiments 2 and 3 investigate the manner in which VZ's performance is affected by instructions that emphasize speed. In Experiment 2, VZ attempted to label phonetically spectrograms of English sentences as quickly as possible in a single pass from left to right. Experiment 3 describes VZ's first attempt to name words as quickly as possible from a spectrogaphic display without first writing segment labels.

EXPERIMENT 1

Although VZ's ability to read spectrograms is a skill that many of us might like to learn, an investment of 2000 hours is likely to discourage all but the most enthusiastic students of speech. It would therefore be of considerable interest to demonstrate that spectrogram reading is a teachable skill and that it can be taught in a reasonable amount of time.

During the spring semester of 1978, VZ taught a course entitled "Speech Production and Perception" to five graduate students at Boston University. None of the students had previously taken a course in acoustic phonetics. The course met once a week for 3 hours for 13 weeks. For the first 10 weeks of the course, VZ lectured on the articulatory and acoustic correlates of phonetic segments, with emphasis on the segmental, or static, characteristics of speech sounds. During this period, the students made approximately 40 spectrograms of isolated consonant–vowel–consonant (CVC) syllables and had examined them from time to time. However, they were not exposed to spectrograms of fluent speech. During the final 3 weeks of the course, in an effort to synthesize the material presented earlier, VZ described the spectrographic representation of the sounds of English in natural continuous speech. The students were also exposed to a description of the rules governing the concatenation of speech sounds. In addition, the students were able to observe VZ read spectrograms and describe the strategies that he used. The members of the class, working as a group, were gradually given the responsibility of reading spectrograms, with VZ acting as a consultant. On the last day of the class, the students were given spectrograms of the five sentences shown in Table 24.1 and a set of generalized instructions summarizing the acoustic cues that might be helpful in reading spectrograms. Working as a group, the students were instructed to segment and label phonetically the spectrograms without help from VZ. The students were instructed to indicate the existence of each phonetic segment by placing small vertical lines directly below the spectrogram. Phonetic labels were then placed between those lines. When more than one label was postulated, the students usually rank ordered their choices in a vertical column. Unless otherwise indicated, the accuracy scores for phonetic labeling reported in the text include all choices, whereas details

TABLE 24.1
Students' Labeling Performance

Sentence	No. of Segments	No. of Guesses	Percent Correct
The lawyer tried to lose his case.	20	32	90
Cut the pie into large parts.	19	43	89
Always close the barn door tight.	20	40	85
Men strive but seldom get rich.	22	43	77
The hat brim was wide and too droopy.	23	41	74
TOTAL	104	199	83

of labeling accuracy—including performance for each choice—are reported in the tables.

The students' performance on these five spectrograms was compared to transcriptions produced by two experienced phoneticians who listened to the sentences. A segment was assumed to exist when both transcribers (Ts) produced a segment label. By this criterion, there were 104 segments, and the two Ts produced the same segment label on 99 of the 104 segments, or 95% of all labels. Three of the four disagreements occurred when one T indicated a reduced vowel followed by a nasal (in "seldom" "pie in" and "wide and") and the other T indicated a syllabic nasal. The other two disagreements were /e/ versus /ə/ in "always" and /z/ versus /s/ in "was."

The students identified the existence of 98 of the 104 segments, or 94% of the segments. Students' labeling performance on each spectrogram is summarized in Table 24.1, which shows the number of segments in each sentence, the number of segments postulated by the students for each utterance, and the percentage of segments correctly identified. The students produced the same segment label as either transcriber, as a first, second, or third choice, on 84 of 104 segments, or 83%. Table 24.2 shows the students' labeling performance on each class of sound. It can be seen that the students agreed with the label produced by either transcriber 85% of the time for both consonants and vowels and 78% of the time for "others" (/l/, /r/, /w/, /y/, /ɝ/, /ɚ/, /l/ and /n/) Averaging over the three classes of sounds, the students agreed with either of the transcribers on their first, second, and third choices, respectively, 51, 24, and 8% of the time.

Figure 24.3 shows the spectrogram of the sentence "The lawyer tried to lose his case," along with the phonetic transcription produced by the students. Although the students failed to identify the existence of two of the segments on this spectrogram, it is possible to recover the words in this sentence by reading the students' phonetic transcription from left to right.

There were, of course, important differences between the way in which the students and VZ read speech spectrograms. The students took more than 3

TABLE 24.2
Agreement Between Students and Either T

Choice	Consonants		Vowels		Others		All Segments	
	Proportion	(%)	Proportion	(%)	Proportion	(%)	Proportion	(%)
First	27/52	52	18/34	53	8/18	44	53/104	51
Second	12/52	23	8/34	23	5/18	28	25/104	24
Third	5/52	10	3/34	9	1/18	6	9/104	8
TOTAL	44/52	85	29/34	85	14/18	78	87/104	83

FIG. 24.3.   Phonetic transcription produced by five students to speech spectrogram of the utterance "The lawyer tried to lose his case."

hours to read the five spectrograms, whereas VZ rarely takes more than 3 or 4 minutes to interpret a single spectrogram. The students also produced more labels per segment than VZ. The students identified the existence of 98 segments and produced a total of 199 segment labels, or slightly more than two labels per segment. They produced a single segment label only 30% of the time and were correct on their first choice only 51% of the time. By contrast, VZ produced about 1.5 labels per segment, produced a single segment label over half of the time, and was correct on his first choice over 65% of the time.

To summarize, after a brief period of exposure to spectrogram reading, the students in VZ's class were able to pool their knowledge to identify 83% of the segments on speech spectrograms of unknown sentences. It appears that spectrogram reading is teachable.

EXPERIMENT 2

Experiment 2 was undertaken to determine how fast VZ can label a spectrogram of an English sentence. We further constrained the task by requiring VZ to label each spectrogram in a single pass from left to right.

Material and Procedure

The 11 English sentences that were presented to VZ on speech spectrograms were shown, in the order in which they were presented, in Table 24.3. The sentences were recorded onto magnetic tape by a male speaker and a spectrogram of each utterance was made on a Kay Sona-Graph.

TABLE 24.3
Summary of VZ's Performance on Eleven Spectrograms Read in Experiment 2

	No. of Segments	Reading Time (sec)	Time per Segment	Accuracy (%)
Do you eat Chinese food?	13	155	11.9	92
Rub two sticks together.	16	107	6.7	81
Do you have a square route?	15	109	7.3	73
Can you recognize Victor Zue?	19	100	5.3	68
Why do you eat so fast?	14	58	4.1	86
We loved your banquet.	14	72	5.4	50
Please listen to my story.	17	78	4.6	94
The rubber swan is mine.	15	82	5.5	87
Go dive in the lake.	11	69	6.3	91
I used to have a newspaper route.	20	77	3.8	80
The music was too loud.	16	42	2.6	100
MEAN =	15.4	86	5.7	82

The spectrograms were presented to VZ during a single session in September, 1978, at M.I.T. The experiment was performed in a sound-treated room and the session was recorded on magnetic tape. The experimenter randomly picked one of the spectrograms from the set of 11, placed it face down on a desk in front of VZ, and said "ready, get set, go." As soon as VZ turned over the spectrogram, the experimenter started a stopwatch. VZ then proceeded to label the spectrogram, and the experimenter stopped the stopwatch as soon as the last phonetic label was written. On three occasions when VZ seemed to be stuck on a difficult segment, the experimenter suggested that he move on to the next segment. Otherwise, the spectrograms were labeled without interruption. After each spectrogram was labeled, VZ was told the utterance.

Results

Two experienced phoneticians—different from those used in the previous study—listened to the 11 sentences and produced a phonetic transcription. The Ts produced the same label on 161 of the 170 segments, or 95% of all segments. The 9 disagreements included /ɾ/ versus /ð/ in "together"; /ɑ/ versus /ɔ/ in "swan"; /I/ versus /ə/ in "we"; /ʌ/ versus /ɔ/ in "loved"; /n/ versus /ŋ/ in "banquet"; /I/ versus /u/ in "do"; /n/ versus /n̩/ in "can"; /ə/ versus /ɚ/ in "Victor"; and /d/ versus /t/ in "loud".

VZ produced the same label as either transcriber, as first, second, and third choices, on 138 of 170 segments, or 81%. VZ's performance on each spectrogram is summarized in Table 24.3, and the percentage of agreements between VZ and the two Ts is shown in Table 24.4 for each class of segment. Table 24.4

TABLE 24.4
Agreement Between VZ and Either T in Experiment 2

Choice	Consonants		Vowels		Others		All Segments	
	Proportion	(%)	Proportion	(%)	Proportion	(%)	Proportion	(%)
First	49/78	63	41/63	65	20/29	69	110/170	65
Second	14/78	18	8/63	13	1/29	3	23/170	13
Third	3/78	4	2/63	3	—	—	5/170	3
TOTAL	66/78	83	51/63	81	21/29	72	138/170	81

reveals that averaging over the three classes of sounds, VZ agreed with either T on first, second, and third choices, respectively, 65, 13, and 3% of the time.

As Fig. 24.4 shows, VZ's labeling time decreased with practice from an average of 11.9 sec per segment on the first spectrogram labeled to an average of 2.6 sec per segment on the final spectrogram. This rather dramatic practice effect occurred within a total of 15.8 min spent on the 11 spectrograms.

Figure 24.4 also shows that the decrease in labeling time was not linear. VZ took almost twice as long to label the first spectrogram as any of the others. Labeling time stabilized at about 5.5 sec per segment on the fourth through

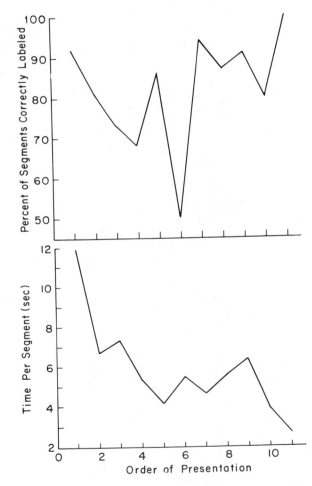

FIG. 24.4.   Accuracy and speed with which 11 spectrograms were labeled by VZ.

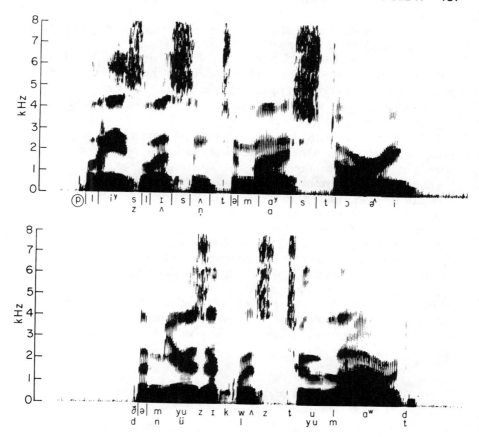

FIG. 24.5.   Upper panel: Speech spectrogram and transcription of seventh spectrogram labeled by VZ. Lower panel: Speech spectrogram and transcription of eleventh spectrogram labeled by VZ.

ninth spectrograms and decreased to an average of 3.2 sec per segment on the final 2 spectrograms. A Spearman rank-order correlation revealed a significant correlation between the time per segment on each spectrogram and its order of presentation (r_s = .719, p < .02).

Why did labeling time decrease during the course of the experiment? The slow labeling speed on the first spectrogram can probably be attributed to the fact that VZ verbalized throughout while reading this spectrogram. Following a suggestion by the experimenter, VZ did not verbalize on the remaining spectrograms. Examination of VZ's transcriptions revealed that as labeling time decreased, so did the number of labels postulated per segment. On the first 5 spectrograms, VZ provided 137 labels for 77 segments, or 1.8 labels per segment. On the last 5 spectrograms, VZ provided 116 labels for 79 segments, or 1.4 labels per segment. It appears that VZ became more confident in his choices as the experiment progressed. A second change in strategy involved the use of segment markers. On the first seven spectrograms, VZ placed a segment marker after each label. On the eighth through eleventh spectrograms, segment markers were used only occasionally. This strategy shift can be seen by comparing VZ's transcription of the two spectrograms shown in Fig. 24.5. The upper panel of Fig. 24.5 displays the seventh spectrogram that VZ labeled, the last spectrogram on which segment markers were consistently used. The spectrogram in the lower panel, in which only two segment markers were used, was the final (and the fastest) spectrogram labeled.

One of the most interesting (and encouraging) results of the experiment was that little tradeoff was observed between labeling time and accuracy. We fully expected that VZ would produce more errors when attempting to label spectrograms as fast as he could. But the overall accuracy in the present experiment was only about 4% less than that observed by Cole et al. (1979) for 23 spectrograms of normal and anomalous sentences. And in the present experiment, errors in labeling did not increase as labeling time decreased. In fact, a slight trend in the opposite direction was observed; VZ identified 80% of the segments on the first 5 spectrograms labeled and 90% of the segments on the last 5 spectrograms. And the most accurate identification performance of all—100% segment identification—was observed on the fastest spectrogram labeled.

EXPERIMENT 3

The labeling times observed with spectrograms of fluent speech cannot be regarded as a direct measure of reading speed, because VZ spent some portion of his time writing segment labels. Experiment 3 was performed in order to obtain a measure of reading times when VZ was not required to write the segment labels. Accordingly, in the present experiment, VZ was presented with spectrograms of words in a known carrier phrase and was asked to say each word as quickly as possible.

Stimuli and Procedure

The stimuli were spectrograms of 25 words in the carrier phrase "Say _____again". The words, shown in Table 24.5, formed five sets of five words each. The five two-syllable words were presented first, followed in order by the two-segment, three-segment, four-segment, and five-segment words.

Because VZ had never before attempted to read spectrograms without writing the segment labels, 15 practice trials were administered before naming latencies were measured. The practice trials consisted of the presentation of

TABLE 24.5
Reading Time for Words in a Carrier Phrase

Two-Segment Words			Three-Segment Words			Four-Segment Words		
Word	VZ	Time	Word	VZ	Time	Word	VZ	Time
Too	Too	3.8	Man	Man	6	Most	Must*	6
By	By	3	Such	Such	12.5	Years	Years	7
She	See (she)	3 (4.5)	Good	Got (good)	6.5 (14)	State	State	7
May	Me (may)	3 (7)	Days	Days	6	Great	Great	11
Zoo	Zoo	7	Church	Church	3.1	School	Score (school)	8 (11)
MEAN TIME PER SEGMENT		2.0			2.3			1.95

Five-Segment Words			Two-Syllable Words		
Word	VZ	Time	Word	VZ	Time
States	States	10	Number	Number	11
Plant	Plant	31.5	Always	Always	13
Trust	Crust*	15	Modern	Madder (modern)	8 (20)
Street	Scrape*	19	Record	Worker*	7
Scroll	Scroll	12	Simply	Simply	6.5
MEAN TIME PER SEGMENT		3.5			1.9

five two-segment, five three-segment, and five four-segment words in a carrier phrase. During the experimental trials, the experimenter randomly picked one of the spectrograms from the set of five currently being read, placed it face down on a desk in front of VZ, and said "ready, get set, go." VZ then turned over the spectrogram and said the word as quickly as he could. After naming the word, the experimenter determined the current identity of the word from a code number on the spectrogram and told VZ the answer. As the experimenter looked up the correct word, VZ continued to inspect each spectrogram, and in five cases he changed his guess.

The entire session was recorded on magnetic tape. Naming latencies were measured after the experimental session. The sound of VZ turning over each spectrogram was clearly audible on the recording tape, and naming latencies were measured from the onset of this sound to the onset of the verbal response. In those cases in which VZ changed his guess, response times were measured for both guesses.

Results

The results are shown for each word in Table 24.5. VZ correctly named 16 of the 25 words on his first guess. An additional 5 words were correctly identified on a second guess. (Second guesses and naming latencies to second guesses are shown in parentheses in Table 24.5.) If we do not give VZ credit for a correct second guess, then he correctly identified 80 of the 97 segments in the 25 words, or 82% of all segments. If credit is given for a correct second guess, then 90 of the 97 segments were correctly identified, or 93%.

The average time to name a word (correct or incorrect) was 4 sec for two-segment words, 6.8 sec for three-segment words, 7.8 sec for four-segment words, 17.5 sec for five-segment words, and 9.1 sec for two-syllable words (mean = 5.2 segments). It can be seen that response times increased with the number of segments in the word. The increase in naming latencies as a function of the number of segments in a word was approximately linear, except for the rather long naming latencies to five-segment words (due largely to the fact that it took VZ 31.5 sec to name the word "plant"). The results suggest that VZ was reading the words segment by segment.

Table 24.5 shows that the time per segment was remarkably similar for two-, three-, and four-segment words and words with two syllables. VZ averaged about 2.3 sec per segment over all words. If we consider only correct first guesses, the mean time per segment was 2.5 sec, and if we include correct second guesses, the mean time per segment was 2.7 sec. Because segment durations in fluent speech average about 100 msec, VZ performed at about 25 times real time.

DISCUSSION

On Teaching About Speech

Over 15 years ago, Fant (1962) advocated spectrogram reading as an excellent way to learn about the acoustic structure of speech. In his words, "speech researchers would ... benefit greatly from going through this learning process." The performance of our students in Experiment 1 and the enthusiasm they showed while learning to interpret spectrograms clearly supports Fant's recommendation.

To be sure, spectrogram reading is no substitute for a course in acoustic phonetics. A thorough understanding of speech requires more than the singular ability to match visual patterns to phonemes. It is, for example, just as important to understand the articulatory basis of the visual patterns displayed on a spectrogram. However, spectrogram reading provides the student with an ideal opportunity to apply theory to data. It is a classic case in which learning is accomplished by *doing*. We therefore recommend spectrogram reading as an important supplement to a course in speech perception or acoustic phonetics.

Visual Speech: A Substitute for Spoken Language

Can a spectrographic display be read in real time? According to Nickerson (1978), who has considered this problem at length:

> There are two conclusions to be drawn from ... considerations of the ability of the visual system to discriminate ordered stimuli such as those encountered in speech. First, it is not clear that the eye is very much worse than the ear in this regard. In particular, it is not clear that, given a proper visual coding scheme, the eye could not learn to distinguish among real-time visual analogs of the acoustic representations of words. Second, vision has an advantage over audition in that differences that are difficult to resolve temporally can be represented, and readily distinguished, spatially. The usual convention in representing time-varying variables visually is to represent time by one spatial dimension on a display. An advantage of such a representation is that it provides a memory, of sorts, of the time-varying event; consequently, features that could not be detected as they occurred may be perceived after the fact by examining the display [p. 120].

Thus, on theoretical grounds, there seems to be no reason to exclude vision as a substitute channel for speech perception.

The issue, of course, is not a theoretical one but an empirical one. The only attempt to learn on-line spectrogram reading was reported by Potter, Kopp, and Green (1947). The subjects in this study attempted to read the output of the newly invented Direct Translator, a device that produced a real-time spectrogram within a telephonelike bandwidth of 300 to 3600 Hz. The subjects, a small group of Bell Laboratories employees, spent about 90 hours learning to recognize visual patterns of individual words as they were spoken by members of the group. During the study, pairs of subjects attempted to communicate with each other without sound using the Direct Translator. According to Potter et al. (1947),

> . . . The visible speech class members were able to converse satisfactorily among themselves by talking clearly and at a fairly slow rate. Within the limits of their vocabularies they were able to carry on conversations with about the same facility as a similarly advanced class in some foreign language. When new and entirely unfamiliar words were discovered on the translator screen, the more experienced students usually were able to read the words after a few repetitions.

Despite these rather encouraging results, the Direct Translator did not find much use outside of speech laboratories. The original hope of the Bell Laboratories project was to produce a device that would allow the deaf to communicate by means of the telephone. Apparently, the investigators concluded that this goal was not feasible, although the reasons for this decision (e.g., economic, technological, or behavioral) are not clear. Since the Potter et al., (1947) study, there have been no further published attempts to teach on-line spectrogram reading.

A major problem in evaluating the results of the Potter et al. (1947) study is that the participants attempted to identify visual patterns corresponding to words. Although recognition of patterns for common words is likely to be helpful when reading spectrograms, it is well-known that words lose their patternlike character in natural continuous speech (Cole & Jakimik, 1978; Klatt, 1977; Klatt & Stevens, 1973; Reddy, 1976). Thus, a word-level pattern recognition approach to on-line spectrogram reading is doomed to fail when applied to conversational speech. A subject who has learned the visual pattern for "what" may be able to recognize its prototype pattern in an utterance like "What are you doing?," but recognition is likely to fail in productions like "Whacha doing?" or "Whadaya doing?"

In many cases, words are only partially specified by their acoustic structure and are partially specified by the context in which they occur. A number of experiments have shown that word recognition occurs through the interaction of these two sources of constraint (Cole & Jakimik, 1978; Marslen-Wilson & Welsh, 1978; Morton & Long, 1976; Pickett & Pollack, 1963). It seems likely that real-time perception of speech using a spectrographic display will also require the efficient and rapid use of both phonetic information (provided, perhaps, by the automatic recognition of syllable-sized visual patterns) and higher-order linguistic knowledge.

Our research has shown that the phonetic information in a spoken sentence can be decoded from a spectrographic display. But can this information be extracted rapidly enough to read a spectrographic display in real time? In Experiment 2, VZ performed at about 2.6 sec per segment on the best spectrogram read. Even if we assign half of his time to the process of writing segment labels, performance is still about 10 to 12 times real time (because the average duration of a phonetic segment in our corpus is about 100 msec). At present, we do not have enough data to determine whether 10 times real time is an encouraging or discouraging result. It is well to remember, however, that Experiment 2 represents VZ's first attempt to label spectrograms quickly. Labeling time decreased on successive spectrograms during the experiment, and it is almost certain that performance will improve, perhaps dramatically, with intensive practice at spectrogram reading (VZ's practice has been extensive, not intensive), with practice at recognizing syllable-sized visual patterns, and with practice at using higher-order linguistic and pragmatic knowledge to interpret these patterns.

Despite the problems involved, we believe that real-time comprehension of visible speech is humanly possible. The research reported in this chapter provides some cause for cautious optimism. We are encouraged by the success of our students in learning to interpret spectrograms and by the fact that VZ's labeling performance did not suffer—and actually showed some improvement in both accuracy and speed during the course of the experiment—under novel reading conditions.

REFERENCES

Cole, R. A., & Jakimik, J. Understanding speech: How words are heard. In G. Underwood (Ed.), *Information processing strategies*. London: Academic Press, 1978.

Cole, R. A., Rudnicky, A. I., Zue, V. W., & Reddy, D. R. Speech as patterns on paper. In R. Cole (Ed.), *Perception and production of fluent speech*. Hillsdale, N.J.: Lawrence Erlbaum Associates, 1979.

Fant, G. Descriptive analysis of the acoustic aspects of speech. *Logos, 5,* 3–17, 1962.

Klatt, D. H., & Stevens, K. N. On the automatic recognition of continuous speech: Implications from a spectrogram-reading experiment. *IEEE Transactions on Audio and Electroacoustics, AU-21* (3) June, 1973, 210–217.

Klatt, D. H., Review of the ARPA speech understanding project, *Journal of the Acoustical Society of America,* 1977, *62,* 1345–1366.

Lindblom, B. E. F., & Svensson, S. G. Interaction between segmental and non-segmental factors in speech recognition. *IEEE Transactions on Audio and Electroacoustics,* 1973, *AU-21,* 536–545.

Marslen-Wilson, W. D., & Welsh, A. Processing interactions and lexical access during word recognition in continuous speech. *Cognitive Psychology,* 1978, *10,* 29–63.

Morton, J., & Long, J. Effect of word transitional probability on phoneme identification. *Journal of Verbal Learning and Verbal Behavior,* 1976, *15,* 43–51.

Nickerson, R. S. On the role of vision in language acquisition by deaf children. In *Deaf Children: Developmental Perspectives,* Academic Press, New York, 1978.

Pickett, J. M., & Pollack, I. Intelligibility of excerpts from conversation. *Language and Speech,* 1963, *6,* 165–171.

Potter, R., Kopp, G., & Green, H. *Visible speech,* New York: van Nostrand, 1947.

Reddy, D. R. Speech recognition by machine: A review. *Proceedings of the IEEE,* 1976, *64,* 501–531.

Svensson, S. G. Prosody and grammar in speech perception. *Monographs from the Institute of Linguistics, University of Stockholm* (MILOS), 1974, *2,* Stockholm.

VI SHORT-TERM MEMORY

25

Short-Term Recognition Memory

Bennet B. Murdock, Jr.
University of Toronto
Ontario, Canada

ABSTRACT

This chapter is a review of data and theories in the area of short-term recognition memory. The data covered are signal-detection analysis, encoding time, forgetting and lag, latency functions, interrelationships among accuracy and latency and confidence, latency distributions, and changes in the parameters of the latency distributions with list length. The theories covered are the conveyor belt model of Murdock (1974); the resonance retrieval theory of Ratcliff (1978); and CADAM, the distributed memory model of Liepa (1977).

INTRODUCTION

In this chapter I would like to consider short-term recognition memory. There are two main parts. The first covers data, whereas the second covers theories. I shall restrict the coverage to item information and shall not deal with either associative information or serial-order information. It is however necessary to consider encoding, storage, and retrieval processes, for one cannot have a complete analysis without all three.

For the most part I am concerned with tasks where both accuracy and latency data are collected, and accuracy is less than perfect. Any adequate theory must be able to explain both accuracy data and latency data (Aubé & Murdock, 1974). When both accuracy and latency vary with experimental conditions, one can then make powerful tests of the theory. Confidence judgments, when available, may even carry the analysis one step further.

The two main experimental paradigms I refer to are the study-test procedure and the continuous recognition memory task. Generally, in the study–test procedure (to my knowledge first used by Strong, 1912) one presents a list of *n* study items followed by 2 *n* test items, the test items being in random order. Subjects are to report *yes* or *no* (perhaps augmented by a confidence judgment) according to whether or not the test item had been present in the study list. In the continuous recognition memory task, as introduced by Shepard and Teghtsoonian (1961), there is simply one long continuous list with the initial presentation of (new) items interleaved with the first (or second, or third, . . .) testing of old items. The customary independent variables are output position and lag. Output position is the location of each item in the test list, whereas lag is the number of items intervening between study and test. New items have no lag, so one must use test or output position. The main dependent variables are accuracy, latency, and confidence.

BASIC EMPIRICAL EFFECTS

Signal-Detection Analysis

A signal-detection analysis of data is often used. A plot of hits as a function of false alarms is shown in Fig. 25.1, and the best-fitting straight line is the familiar ROC (receiver operating characteristic) curve. These data are actually the results from one subject in a study–test confidence–judgment procedure where the data from old and new items have been pooled over lag and output position. The straight line is a reasonable fit to the data, and d' (the conventional signal-detection measure) serves as a convenient summary statistic.

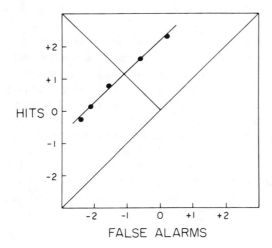

FIG. 25.1. Receiver operating characteristic (ROC) curve for the data of one subject from a confidence–judgment study-test procedure. The axes are standard scores. (Figure 2.9 from Murdock, 1974.)

There are data suggesting the equivalence of different experimental procedures. Green and Moses (1966) found that a confidence-judgment and a forced-choice procedure gave equivalent results. Murdock and Dufty (1972) found that a confidence-judgment and a yes-no procedure gave equivalent results.

It seems to be generally true that recognition-memory data satisfy the basic assumptions of signal-detection theory. Such findings do not provide strong support for the theory because rather different theoretical positions can make similar predictions (Lockhart & Murdock, 1970). However, they do mean that the use of the d' measure is justified, because the assumptions underlying its use are met.

Encoding Time

The longer the presentation time, the more time there is available for encoding, and memory benefits accordingly. This relationship is shown in the left-hand panel of Fig. 25.2, where the dependent variable plotted is d'. Much of the data on which this figure is based comes from Loftus (1974) who varied presentation duration from 25 to 500 msec in a study-test procedure. He presents data for individual subjects that are, of course, somewhat variable. However, the variability is not too great, so the smooth curve shown in Fig. 25.2 is probably a reasonable approximation.

Forgetting and Lag

The right-hand panel of Fig. 25.2 shows that d' decreases as lag increases. In other words, forgetting occurs. It is a reasonable approximation to say that d' decreases exponentially with lag (Wickelgren & Norman, 1966), although the

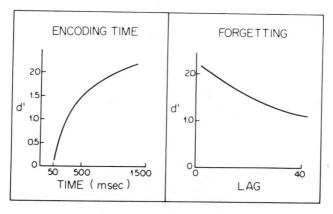

FIG. 25.2. The left-hand panel shows how d' increases as the duration of the encoding time increases. The right-hand panel shows forgetting: The decrease in d', as lag increases.

numerical values of the parameters depend on the experimental conditions. Again, note that the dependent variable is d'. Probability values may not show large changes, but d' is quite a sensitive measure when one is working in the tails of the distribution. This could be another reason for the popularity of d' as a measure of memory-trace strength.

Lag, the independent variable, is an interference measure and not a decay measure. One could probably use an unfilled retention interval to find a purer measure of decay as a function of time, but some picture–memory data by Nickerson (1968) indicate one might have to wait as long as a year to obtain comparable forgetting.

Latency Functions

The latency functions are somewhat different, depending on whether the ensemble size is below or above memory span. The classical results for subspan lists are shown in Fig. 25.3, where mean reaction time (or latency) is plotted as a function of set size. These data are from Sternberg (1969), and in this case positive and negative (old and new) probes give rise to the same linear function. Often old and new items will both be linear functions with the same slope but different intercepts, the intercept being higher for negative than positive probes. The parallel linear functions have given rise to a scanning interpretation; by this view, the subject does an exhaustive item-by-item comparison or scan through the positive set.

A comparable analysis for supraspan lists is shown in Fig. 25.4. The data show mean reaction time for old items as a function of lag. A study–test procedure with 15-item lists was used, and lag was therefore a mixture of study and test items. Reaction times are again a linear function, but this time

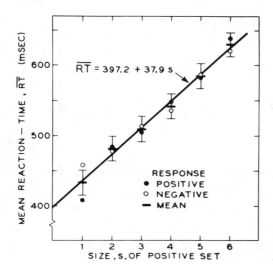

FIG. 25.3.   Mean reaction time as a function of set size for positive and negative probes. (Figure 4 from Sternberg, 1969.)

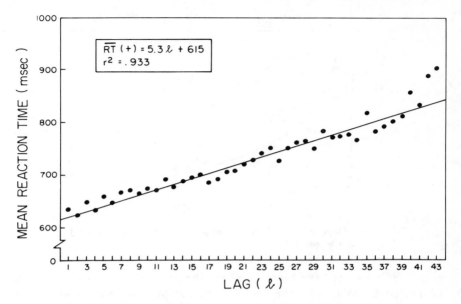

FIG. 25.4. Mean reaction time as a function of lag for high-confident *yes* responses to old items. (Figure 5 from Murdock & Anderson, 1975.)

the independent variable is lag rather than set size. For supraspan lists, it is probably unwise to use set size as the independent variable because this necessitates collapsing over lag (or output position). On the other hand, for subspan lists, lag or output position can be mapped into set size by using the notion of functional set size. In a study–test procedure, functional set size is the number of items that could be tested at any ouput position. In one study (Murdock & Anderson, 1974) the study–test procedure gave comparable results to those shown in Fig. 25.3 when functional set size was used as the independent variable. Thus, the difference in the abscissas of Fig. 25.3 and 25.4 does not necessarily weaken the contrast between subspan and supraspan lists.

However, the different slopes may be another matter. By now it seems quite clear that the slope is less for supraspan than for subspan lists. For average values, a slope of about 35 msec per item is reasonable for subspan lists, whereas a slope of about 5 msec per item is reasonable for supraspan lists. If one thinks of the slope as a measure of scanning rate (or comparison time per item), this means that the scan is slower for lists below memory span than for lists above memory span.

This difference is 7:1, or almost an order of magnitude, so it is a big effect. It is probably not due to the use of different paradigms. As noted previously, the Sternberg paradigm and the study–test paradigm give converging results below memory span when functional set size is used. Above memory span,

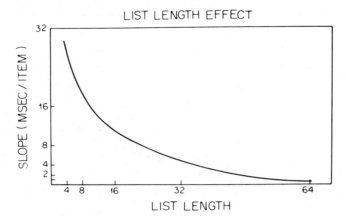

FIG. 25.5.   Slope of the lag–latency or output position–latency function as a function of list length.

comparable results have been found for the prememorized lists paradigm (Atkinson & Juola, 1973), the study–test paradigm (Murdock, 1974), and the continuous recognition-memory paradigm (Hockley, 1980).

Murdock and Anderson (1974) suggested that the slope difference between subspan and supraspan lists might be a function of a speed–accuracy tradeoff. When supraspan lists are compared to subspan lists, speed (comparison time per item) is higher but accuracy (d' or hits) is lower. However, when it is considered that accuracy is very high in the prememorized-lists paradigm and yet there is still the same low slope, this interpretation seems unlikely. This slope effect has been found for both words (Burrows & Okada, 1975) and for pictures (Banks & Fariello, 1974), so it does not seem to be specific to the type of stimulus material used in the experiment.

Although the slope difference may be dichotomous (Burrows & Okada, 1975), some data reported in Murdock & Anderson (1974) suggest that the slope change with ensemble size may be graded. Figure 25.5 shows a very provisional relationship; the slope of the scanning function decreases from 35 msec per item with 4-item lists to 1 msec per item at 64-item lists. There is not enough data available yet to claim that this figure represents the true state of affairs, but in terms of what we know now it is at least a possibility.

Interrelationships

Latency and Confidence Judgments.   The general relationship between latency and confidence judgment is shown in Fig. 25.6. The high-confident responses are the fastest, whereas the low-confident responses are the slowest, and each step down in the confidence–judgement scale adds about 250 msec

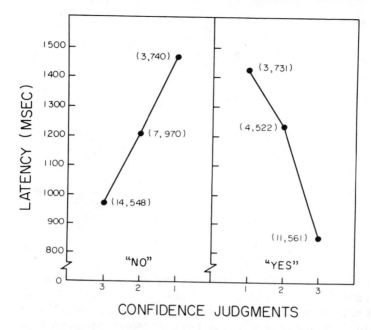

FIG. 25.6.   Mean latency for high (3), medium (2), and low (1) confidence judgments for *no* and *yes* responses. (Figure 2 from Murdock & Dufty, 1972.)

to the mean reaction time. These particular data (from Murdock & Dufty, 1972) were obtained in a situation where the subject had to respond on a six-point scale. Essentially the same result occurs if subjects first make a binary yes–no response and then give a subsequent confidence judgment at their leisure (Mandler & Boeck, 1974).

Accuracy and Confidence Judgments.   The general relationship between accuracy and confidence judgment is shown in Fig. 25.7. Here a posteriori probability is plotted as a function of confidence judgment. A posteriori probability is the probability, or relative frequency, that an item given a particular confidence judgment was an old item. For a confidence judgment of +++, perfect performance would approach 1.0, whereas, for a confidence judgment of ---, perfect performance would approach 0. Not only did this happen, but even the lowest confidence judgments (+ and –) each differed from chance (.50).

Accuracy and Latency.   The general relationship between accuracy and latency is shown in Fig. 25.8. These data come from a continuous recognition memory task (Hockley, 1980) where lags on the second presentation (2*P*

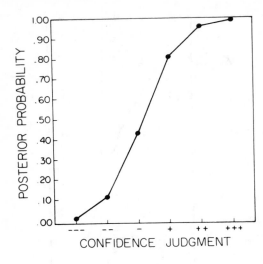

FIG. 25.7. *A posteriori* probability as a function of confidence judgment for the same data shown in Fig. 25.1. (Figure 2.11 from Murdock, 1974.)

items) and lags on the third presentation (3*P*) each varied from 0–40. The points could lie on a single function, but separate curves for 2*P* and 3*P* items would not be unreasonable either. Although Fig. 25.6 and 25.7 seem characteristic of a fair amount of data, I am somewhat less confident about Fig. 25.8. Whereas these particular data certainly seem clear enough, they are the first such data I have seen, so I have no way of knowing how typical this finding will turn out to be.

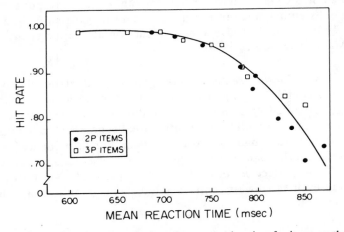

FIG. 25.8. Hit rate as a function of mean reaction time for items on their second presentation (2*P*) and their third presentation (3*P*). (Data from Hockley, 1980.)

Latency Distributions

The latency distributions for recognition memory data seem to be well characterized as the convolution of a normal and an exponential distribution (Ratcliff & Murdock, 1976). The convolution would result if there were two successive and independent stages, one normally distributed with parameters μ and σ and the other exponentially distributed with parameter τ. Then the sum of these two stages, or the convolution of the two density functions, would be a positively skewed distribution with parameters μ, σ, and τ.

Some relevant data are shown in Fig. 25.9. The histograms are the obtained results, and the dots indicate the best-fitting convolution. The first column shows hits for input positions 1-8 at output positions (in a study–test paradigm) 1-8, 9-16, 17-24, and 25-32. The second column shows the same for input positions 9-16; the third and fourth columns show correct rejections and misses. Goodness of fit is indicated by χ^2. All things considered the fits seem quite good, so we have a way of characterizing the reaction-time distributions for correct responses and errors at different study and test positions in terms of a simple three parameter function.

Parameter Functions

There are two aspects of the parameter functions to consider here. First, there is the question of how the parameters of the covolution model change with lag or output position. Because σ stays essentially constant at a value generally in the 50–80 msec range, the two parameters we are concerned with are μ and τ. The functions for μ and τ are shown in Fig. 25.10. For each list length, both the function for μ and the function for τ are reasonably linear. In this figure, note that output position is divided into four (equal-size) blocks. This is a scale factor, so the absolute position would differ according to list length.

Because these functions are reasonably linear, each function has a slope and an intercept. The second aspect to consider is how these slopes and intercepts change with list length. This is shown in Fig. 25.11. The slopes decrease in roughly exponential fashion as list length increases. The intercepts increase in roughly linear fashion as list length increases. These data have been obtained by doing the convolution analysis (to determine the values of μ, σ, and τ) separately for each subject at each of the four output position blocks for each list length shown in Fig. 25.10. Then, the parameters were averaged across subjects and a standard least-squares analysis was done to obtain the list-length slope and intercept values plotted in Fig. 25.11.

The exponential slope functions have the same rate constant, and the linear intercept functions are parallel. Consequently, it requires six parameters to construct the curves of Fig. 25.11. With these six parameters it is then possible to generate the latency distributions for any given output position at any

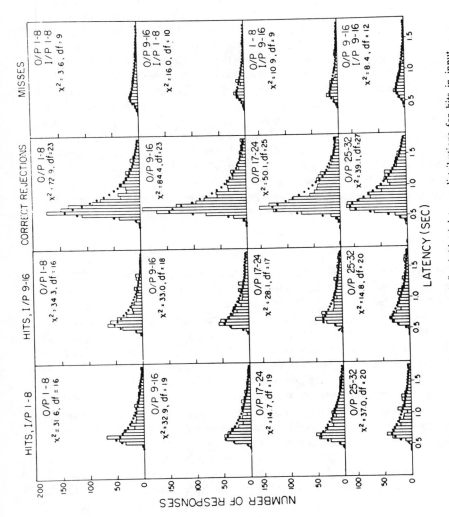

FIG. 25.9. Empirical (rectangle) and fitted (dots) latency distributions for hits in input positions 1–8 and 9–16, also correct rejections and misses. The horizontal panels in the table are for output positions 1–8, 9–16, 17–24, and 25–32. (Figure 9 from Ratcliff & Murdock, 1976.)

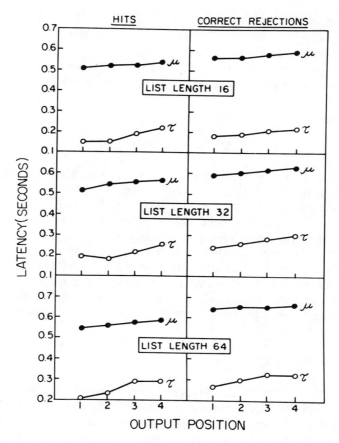

FIG. 25.10. Distribution parameters μ and τ for hits and correct rejections as a function of output position (in blocks) for three different list lengths (Figure 12 from Ratcliff & Murdock, 1976.)

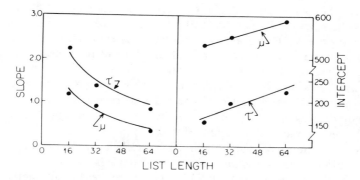

FIG. 25.11. Effect of list length on the slope (left side) and intercept (right side) of the linear functions for μ and τ shown in Fig. 25.10.

given list length. Even though this is simply an empirical analysis, still it provides a powerful method of characterizing latency data under a variety of conditions. Of course, to what extent these results apply beyond the limits tested is an open question.

MODELS AND THEORIES

To date, there are three models or theories which have been developed which can explain these data at a quantitative level. They are the conveyor belt model (Murdock, 1974), the resonance retrieval theory (Ratcliff, 1978), and the distributed memory model CADAM (Liepa, 1977). Models for memory scanning of the Sternberg variety, of which there are many, would have to be extended to deal with situations where accuracy is considerably less than perfect, so they are not included here. Accounting for all these data in fine-grain detail is a rather formidable undertaking, and none of these three models is completely successful. However, each has enough merit to warrant inclusion here. Also, they tend to complement each other; the strengths of one may be the weakness of another.

Conveyor Belt Model

Description.   This model, as suggested by Murdock (1974) and Murdock and Anderson (1975), is based on the metaphor of a conveyor belt. Items are encoded one at a time and stored in memory in temporal order much like baggage on a continuously moving ramp or conveyor belt. Just as baggage contains personal effects, so items in memory may be composed of features. To retrieve an item, one must engage in a high-speed backward self-terminating comparison process. Items are examined, one by one, until the scan finds a match or the beginning of the list is reached. The order is backward in that the most recent item is examined first; the scan goes backward in time. Accuracy reflects the success of the scan, and an interference process is assumed to account for the fact that d' decreases with lag. Latency reflects the number of items the probe is compared with, and the slope of the (linear) lag–latency function gives the per item comparison time. Confidence judgments reflect the number of scans. If the outcome of a scan is uncertain, the criteria for a successful match may be lowered and the scan repeated.

The model was developed to explain the data shown in Fig. 25.2, 25.4, and 25.6, so one cannot claim support for the model from these findings. The effect of repetition is consistent with the model. When an item is repeated, the scan should stop when the most recent occurrence is encountered. Thus, the slope of $1P$ (once presented) and $2P$ (twice presented) items should be the same. Results reported in Murdock, Hockley, and Muter (1977) suggest they are. Also, the model can handle forced-choice data quite well. In *m*-alternative forced choice, each test consists of one old item and *m* − 1 new items. The lag–latency function is still linear, with slope and intercept each approximately *m* times the value for single-item tests (Murdock & Anderson, 1974). Finally, latency in two alternative judgments of recency seem to depend strongly on the recency of the later item but not at all on the recency of the earlier item (Muter, 1979), another finding consistent with the conveyor belt model.

Problems. There are four main problems for the conveyor belt model. The first problem is the list-length effect. Why should the scan become faster as list length increases? It is one thing to posit different comparison rates for subspan and supraspan lists, but it is somewhat puzzling to find 5-msec slopes for 16-item lists but 1-msec slopes for 64-item lists.

This same problem occurs in the latency data from a continuous recognition paradigm. Figure 25.12 shows the lag–latency curves for 2*P* and 3*P* items, and the curves are negatively accelerated (Hockley, 1980). In the Sternberg study–test, or prememorized lists paradigms the subjects know the ensemble size before testing begins, so they could adjust their scan rate in

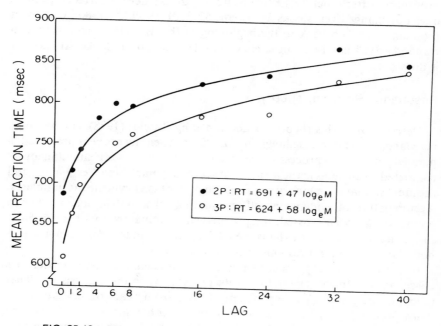

FIG. 25.12. Mean reaction time as a function of lag for the second (2*P*) and third (3*P*) presentation of items in a continuous recognition memory paradigm. (Data from Hockley, 1980.)

advance. In a continuous task, however, short, medium, and long lags are thoroughly intermixed so it is not clear how these negatively accelerated functions could occur. (One could argue that the scan speeds up, but then why does this not happen in a study–test procedure?)

The second problem is scanning residue. If there were scanning, then perhaps there might be some aftereffect of scanning, or residue. This could show up in either accuracy or latency. Two attempts (Murdock et al., 1977; Muter & Murdock 1977) have failed to find any scanning residue. Of course, there is no requirement that there be any, so such results are not a serious disconfirmation of the model. However, so far all the evidence for scanning has been inferential, and it would be nice to obtain some direct evidence that scanning does in fact occur.

The third problem for the conveyor belt model is the distributional analysis. As argued in Ratcliff and Murdock (1976), scanning effects should show up primarily, if not exclusively, in μ but not in τ. As shown in Fig. 25.10, exactly the opposite occurs. Of the 5-msec slope, roughly 4 msec is accounted for by τ but only 1 msec by μ. This point is also discussed in Murdock et al. (1977).

The fourth (and most serious) problem comes from the continuous task procedure. After Block 1 (the first 64 items), the latency for correct rejections does not change over Blocks 2–5 (items 65–320) (Hockley, 1980). Clearly, if the scan has to go back to the beginning of the list before the subject can respond *no* to a new item, the latency should increase over blocks. Apparently it does not.

Resonance Retrieval Theory

Description.   This theory, as developed by Ratcliff (1978), is based on a resonance metaphor. As shown in Fig. 25.13, when the probe is presented, a parallel comparison process is assumed to occur. The probe is simultaneously compared to all items in the memory or search set. Each item "resonates," and the more similar the memory and probe item, the faster evidence accumulates. Accumulation of evidence is self-terminating for a match; once the match boundary has been crossed, the process will terminate with a *yes* response. For a nonmatch, it is exhaustive. All processes must cross a nonmatch boundary before a *no* response can be given.

As shown in the top panel of Fig. 25.14, the accumulation of evidence is based on a diffusion or random walk process. As in the analysis by Feller (1968) of the gambler's ruin problem, starting from z each observation leads (with probability p) to one step up or (with probability $1 - p$) to one step down. The top and bottom boundaries are a and 0, and first-passage time distributions are also indicated. The middle panel shows the relatedness distributions for old and new items, with u the mean relatedness of old items

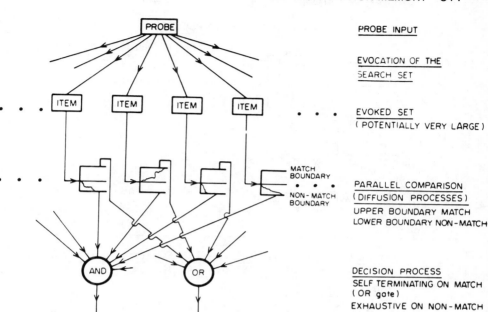

PROBE INPUT

EVOCATION OF THE
SEARCH SET

EVOKED SET
(POTENTIALLY VERY LARGE)

MATCH BOUNDARY

NON - MATCH BOUNDARY

PARALLEL COMPARISON
(DIFFUSION PROCESSES)
UPPER BOUNDARY MATCH
LOWER BOUNDARY NON - MATCH

DECISION PROCESS
SELF TERMINATING ON MATCH
(OR gate)
EXHAUSTIVE ON NON - MATCH
(AND gate)

RESPONSE OUTPUT

FIG. 25.13. An overview of the resonance retrieval theory. (Figure 1 from Ratcliff, 1978.)

and v the mean relatedness of new items. Expected reaction-time distributions are shown in the bottom panel of Fig. 25.14, with the continuous diffusion process (with u now the angle of drift) replacing the discrete gambler's ruin random walk.

The theory can handle not only accuracy and mean latency but also the reaction-time distributions. This point is illustrated in Fig. 25.15, which shows how the relatedness distribution maps into a reaction-time distribution. Relatedness determines the angle of drift. With high relatedness, there is a rapid approach toward the match boundary and only slightly skewing in the reaction-time distribution. As relatedness decreases, so does the angle of drift of the diffusion process, and the skewness in the reaction-time distribution increases. This illustrates the basis for the greater increase in τ than in μ as lag or output position increases.

This theory has seven parameters: u and v, the mean relatedness for old and new items; η, the standard deviation of the relatedness distributions; s, the standard deviation of the drift of the diffusion process; z and a, the starting point and match boundary for the random walk; and T_{ER}, the "time-for-encoding-and-response" parameter. Some parameters stay fixed in estimat-

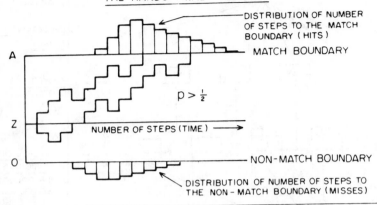

THE RANDOM WALK PROCESS

DISTRIBUTION OF NUMBER OF STEPS TO THE MATCH BOUNDARY (HITS)

MATCH BOUNDARY

A

$p > \frac{1}{2}$

NUMBER OF STEPS (TIME) ⟶

Z

NON-MATCH BOUNDARY

O

DISTRIBUTION OF NUMBER OF STEPS TO THE NON-MATCH BOUNDARY (MISSES)

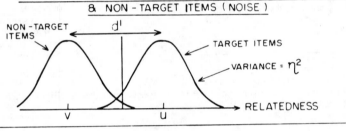

RELATEDNESS DISTRIBUTIONS FOR TARGET ITEMS (SIGNAL) & NON-TARGET ITEMS (NOISE)

NON-TARGET ITEMS

d'

TARGET ITEMS

VARIANCE = η^2

RELATEDNESS

V   U

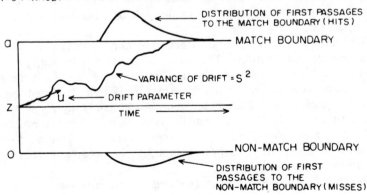

THE DIFFUSION PROCESS

(FOR TARGET ITEMS WITH RELATEDNESS DISTRIBUTION MEAN u + VARIANCE η^2)

DISTRIBUTION OF FIRST PASSAGES TO THE MATCH BOUNDARY (HITS)

a

MATCH BOUNDARY

VARIANCE OF DRIFT = S^2

u   DRIFT PARAMETER

Z   TIME ⟶

NON-MATCH BOUNDARY

O

DISTRIBUTION OF FIRST PASSAGES TO THE NON-MATCH BOUNDARY (MISSES)

FIG. 25.14. An illustration of the random walk and diffusion process, together with relatedness distributions that drive the diffusion process. (Figure 3 from Ratcliff, 1978.)

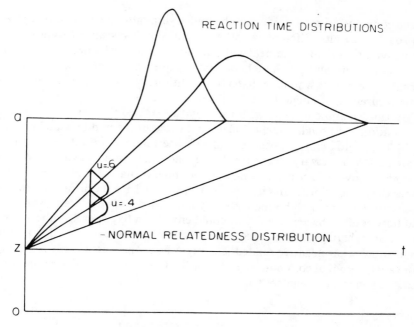

FIG. 25.15. A geometrical illustration of the mapping from a normal relatedness distribution to a skewed reaction-time distribution. (Figure 4 from Ratcliff, 1978.)

ing various conditions of an experiment, so the degrees of freedom are somewhat less. The theory can account for accuracy and latency data, including the distributions. Even more impressive, the theory can be applied to data from a variety of different experimental paradigms (Sternberg, study-test, prememorized lists, the continuous recognition memory task, even speed–accuracy tradeoff studies). Its ability to cope with data from all these different paradigms is one of its strongest features.

Comments. I would make three comments about this theory. First, it says nothing about encoding or storage processes. The items are simply assumed to exist in memory; it is a theory of retrieval only. This of course is simply a matter of incompleteness. The resonance retrieval theory could perhaps be coupled to some storage model (e.g., the conveyor belt model) to provide a more complete picture of the processes involved in recognition memory.

Second, it does not neatly map into the convolution model. The convolution model enters as a step in the parameter-estimation procedure, but although the theory can obviously cope with the reaction-time distributions, there is nothing in the resonance retrieval theory that corresponds to μ and τ

in the convolution model. Indeed, the underlying rationale behind these two approaches is quite different. Another way to say this is simply to note that the convolution model can deal with the latency data with fewer free parameters. (The convolution model, of course, does not predict accuracy, so perhaps a rejoinder would be that a few additional parameters to encompass both accuracy and latency is a small price to pay.)

My third comment deals with the negative relatedness for the new-item distribution. Although not specifically indicated in the middle panel of Fig. 25.14, u (for old items) is positive, and v (for new items) is negative. Negative relatedness is necessary to ensure that the accumulation of evidence drives new items down to zero, the nonmatch boundary; that is, relatedness determines the angle of drift, and it must be negative to drive the diffusion process from z to the nonmatch boundary. But what does negative relatedness mean, and how could it be achieved? One could envision a fixed-set Sternberg-type procedure where positive and negative relatedness made sense. I don't quite understand what negative relatedness might be if one were simply sampling from a large pool of common English words. How and when are nonpresented items assigned this negative value?

CADAM

Description. CADAM, an acronym for "content addressable distributed associative memory" was developed by Liepa (1977) and is also briefly outlined in Murdock (1979). It is very similar to models propósed by Anderson and his colleagues (Anderson, 1968, 1973; Anderson, Silverstein, Ritz, & Jones, 1977) and Kohonen and his colleagues (Kohonen, 1977). However, CADAM can explain item information, associative information, and serial-order information. Only item information is considered here.

The basic features of CADAM are illustrated in Fig. 25.16. Items are represented as vectors in multidimensional space or, in more common terminology, an item is a vector of attributes (Bower, 1967; Underwood, 1969). These attributes are random variables with symmetric (perhaps normal or uniform) distributions. These distributions must be centered on zero, but their variance is a possible parameter of the model. There must be a memory vector **M** for storage, and each item $\mathbf{f}_i$ is added to **M** when it is encoded. Thus, the memory vector is simply the sum of all presented items. To account for forgetting, one possibility is given by the difference equation:

$$\mathbf{M}_i = k\mathbf{M}_{i-1} + \mathbf{f}_i \tag{1}$$

for $k \leq 1$; that is, each element in the memory vector is multiplied by a constant k before a new item is added to memory. The parameter k would then determine the amount of forgetting. Retrieval consists simply of com-

CADAM

ITEMS : $f_i = (\text{...}, f_{-1}, f_0, f_1, \text{...})$

ELEMENTS :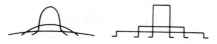

ENCODING : $M_i = k\,M_{i-1} + f_i$

RETRIEVAL : $f \cdot M = \left\{ \begin{array}{ll} d', & \text{PROBE} = \text{OLD} \\ o, & \text{PROBE} = \text{NEW} \end{array} \right\}$

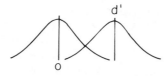

LATENCY : ? ? ?

FIG. 25.16.   CADAM in outline form. The items are vectors of attributes; the elements of the vectors are symmetric random variables centered on zero; encoding involves adding items to a common memory store; and retrieval involves computing the dot product of the probe and the memory vector.

puting the dot product $f \cdot M$. When summed over items this dot product will have a new-item distribution centered on zero and an old-item distribution centered on d'. (If the vectors are normalized to 1, then the expected value of d' will also be 1).

Some of the advantages of this type of model have been discussed by Anderson et al. (1977) and by Murdock (1979). Storage and retrieval processes are distributed or global rather than compartmentalized or local. Parallel rather than serial processing is implied, and there is no search or scan process to locate target information. A signal-detection analysis is derived from underlying assumptions, not simply assumed ad hoc.

Imperfect recognition is a natural consequence of this approach, and similarity effects are probably self-evident. Also, of the three models discussed in this section, CADAM is probably the best suited to account for some of the higher-level effects of recognition memory. These include context effects and encoding specificity (Tulving & Thomson, 1973), the false recognition effect (Underwood, 1965), repetition and spacing effects (Hintzman, 1976), recognition failure of recallable words (Flexser & Tulving, 1978), and the "levels" effect associated with depth of processing (Craik & Lockhart, 1972). Whether CADAM can explain all these effects consistently and parsimoniously, of course, remains to be seen.

A problem for CADAM would seem to be the ahistorical nature of the memory trace. In this regard it is clearly a type of strength theory, and Anderson & Bower (1972) have discussed some of the problems. In particular, it is not clear how this class of theory can handle list discrimination or judgments of frequency and recency of multiply presented items. However, CADAM is more than a theory of item recognition; it has associative and serial-order components too. Perhaps these must be incorporated into the simple version discussed here to accommodate these empirical effects.

Comments.   At this point, CADAM seems to have considerable potential, but much remains to be done. In particular, how can we explain latency data? What is the mechanism, or mechanisms, that generate these effects? Let me suggest three possibilities.

The first possibility is to use a strength–theory approach to latency. This is illustrated in Fig. 25.17. The strength distributions are a natural concomitant of CADAM, but the additional assumption is made that latency is a function of distance from the criterion. An exponential function is a reasonable

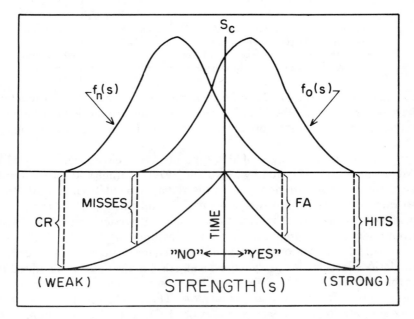

FIG. 25.17.   The relationship between strength and latency for old (o) and new (n) items. Latency (time) is shown as an exponential function of distance from the criterion. (Figure 3.3 from Murdock, 1974.)

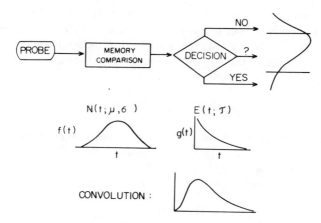

FIG. 25.18. A simple two-stage memory-decision model. The time for memory comparison is normally distributed; the decision stage has an exponential or waiting-time distribution; and the resulting reaction-time distribution is the convolution of these two stages.

transfer function to map strength into latency. A discussion and criticism of this approach may be found in Murdock (1974, pp. 282–283), but the reader should be warned that the matter is somewhat more complicated than indicated there.

A second possibility is indicated in Fig. 25.18. Perhaps there is a two-stage process, memory comparison (wherein the dot product $\mathbf{f} \cdot \mathbf{M}$ is computed) followed by a decision process. The time for the memory-comparison process would be normally distributed, whereas the time for the decision process would be exponentially distributed. There are three possible outputs from the decision stage. These are *no, uncertain,* or *yes.* This is where confidence judgments could come in. This model is similar to that suggested by Hohle (1965) and, of course, dovetails with the convolution model described earlier.

A third possibility would be to concatanate the CADAM retrieval operation with a random walk process. Perhaps the dot product involves a self-terminating summation process, going toward the top boundary to produce a *yes* response or toward the bottom boundary to produce a *no* response. One could perhaps combine the encoding and storage features of CADAM with Ratcliff's resonance retrieval theory.

CONCLUSION

It is obvious that we now have a wealth of data on short-term recognition memory. One could not ask for much more; the effects are reliable, regular, and easy to describe. Further, the theories, even if not completely correct, have scored some modest successes and are neither trivial nor simplistic. Although the end is not yet in sight, we do seem to have made considerable progress. We probably have a firmer grip, both empirically and theoretically, on recognition memory than on most other areas in the human memory field.

ACKNOWLEDGMENT

This work was supported by Research Grant APA 146 from the National Research Council of Canada. I would like to thank Roger Ratcliff, Paul Muter, and Bill Hockley for helpful comments on the manuscript.

REFERENCES

Anderson, J. A. A memory storage model utilizing spatial correlation functions. *Kybernetik*, 1968, *5*, 113–119.

Anderson, J. A. A theory for the recognition of items from short memorized lists. *Psychological Review*, 1973, *80*, 417–438.

Anderson, J. A., Silverstein, J. W., Ritz, S. A., & Jones, R. S. Distinctive features, categorical perception, and probability learning: Some applications of a neural model. *Psychological Review*, 1977, *84*, 413–451.

Anderson, J. R., & Bower, G. H. Recognition and retrieval processes in free recall. *Psychological Review*, 1972, *79*, 97–123.

Atkinson, R. C., & Juola, J. F. Factors influencing speed and accuracy of word recognition. In S. Kornblum (Ed.), *Attention and performance IV*. New York: Academic Press, 1973.

Aubé, M., & Murdock, B. B., Jr. Sensory stores and high-speed scanning. *Memory & Cognition*, 1974, *2*, 27–33.

Banks, W. P., & Fariello, G. R. Memory load and latency in recognition of pictures. *Memory & Cognition*, 1974, *2*, 144–148.

Bower, G. H. A multicomponent theory of the memory trace. In K. W. Spence & J. T. Spence (Eds.), *The psychology of learning and motivation: Advances in research and theory* (Vol. 1). New York: Academic Press, 1967.

Burrows, D., & Okada, R. Memory retrieval from long and short lists. *Science*, 1975, *188*, 1031–1033.

Craik, F. I. M., & Lockhart, R. S. Levels of processing: A framework for memory research. *Journal of Verbal Learning and Verbal Behavior*, 1972, *11*, 671–684.

Feller, W. *An introduction to probability theory and its applications* (Vol. I) (3rd ed.). New York: Wiley, 1968.

Flexser, A. J., & Tulving, E. Retrieval independence in recognition and recall. *Psychological Review*, 1978, *85*, 153–171.

Green, D. M., & Moses, F. L. On the equivalence of two recognition measures of short-term memory. *Psychological Bulletin*, 1966, *66*, 228–234.

Hintzman, D. L. Repetition and memory. In G. H. Bower (Ed.), *The psychology of learning and motivation: Advances in research and theory* (Vol. 10). New York: Academic Press, 1976.

Hockley, W. E. *Recognition performance under steady-state conditions*. Unpublished doctoral dissertation, University of Toronto, 1980.

Hohle, R. H. Inferred components of reaction times as functions of foreperiod duration. *Journal of Experimental Psychology*, 1965, *69*, 382–386.

Kohonen, T. *Associative memory: A system-theoretical approach.* Berlin: Springer-Verlag, 1977.

Liepa, P. *Models of content addressable distributed associative memory (CADAM).* Unpublished manuscript, University of Toronto, 1977.

Lockhart, R. S., & Murdock, B. B., Jr. Memory and the theory of signal detection. *Psychological Bulletin,* 1970, *74,* 100–109.

Loftus, G. R. Acquisition of information from rapidly presented verbal and nonverbal stimuli. *Memory & Cognition,* 1974, *2,* 545–548.

Mandler, G., & Boeck, W. J. Retrieval processes in recognition. *Memory & Cognition,* 1974, *2,* 613–615.

Murdock, B. B., Jr. *Human memory: Theory and data.* Potomac, Md.: Lawrence Erlbaum Associates, 1974.

Murdock, B. B., Jr. Convolution and correlation in perception and memory. In L-G. Nilsson (Ed.), *Perspectives in memory research: Essays in honor of Uppsala University's 500th Anniversary.* Hillsdale, N.J.: Lawrence Erlbaum Associates, 1979.

Murdock, B. B., Jr., & Anderson, R. E. *Retrieval of item information from subspan and supraspan lists.* Paper presented at the meeting of the Psychonomic Society, Boston, November 1974.

Murdock, B. B., Jr., & Anderson, R. E. Encoding, storage, and retrieval of item information. In R. L. Solso (Ed.), *Information processing and cognition: The Loyola symposium.* Hillsdale, N.J.: Lawrence Erlbaum Associates, 1975.

Murdock, B. B., Jr., & Dufty, P. O. Strength theory and recognition memory. *Journal of Experimental Psychology,* 1972, *94,* 284–290.

Murdock, B. B., Jr., Hockley, W. E., & Muter, P. Two tests of the conveyor-belt model for item recognition. *Canadian Journal of Psychology,* 1977, *31,* 71–89.

Muter, P. Response latencies in discriminations of recency. *Journal of Experimental Psychology: Human Learning and Memory.* 1979, *5,* 160–169.

Muter, P., & Murdock, B. B., Jr. A search for scanning residue in recognition memory. *Bulletin of the Psychonomic Society,* 1977, *10,* 66–68.

Nickerson, R. S. A note on long-term recognition memory for pictorial material. *Psychonomic Science,* 1968, *11,* 58.

Ratcliff, R. A theory of memory retrieval. *Psychological Review,* 1978, *85,* 59–108.

Ratcliff, R., & Murdock, B. B., Jr. Retrieval processes in recognition memory. *Psychological Review,* 1976, *83,* 190–214.

Shepard, R. N., & Teghtsoonian, M. Retention of information under conditions approaching a steady state. *Journal of Experimental Psychology,* 1961, *62,* 302–309.

Sternberg, S. Memory-scanning: Mental processes revealed by reaction-time experiments. *American Scientist,* 1969, *57,* 421–457.

Strong, E. K., Jr. The effect of length of series upon recognition memory. *Psychological Review,* 1912, *19,* 447–462.

Tulving, E., & Thompson, D. M. Encoding specificity and retrieval processes in episodic memory. *Psychological Review,* 1973, *80,* 352–373.

Underwood, B. J. False recognition produced by implicit verbal responses. *Journal of Experimental Psychology,* 1965, *70,* 122–129.

Underwood, B. J. Attributes of memory. *Psychological Review,* 1969, *76,* 559–573.

Wickelgren, W. A., & Norman, D. A. Strength models and serial position in short-term recognition memory. *Journal of Mathematical Psychology,* 1966, *3,* 316–347.

26 Spatial Working Memory

A. D. Baddeley
Medical Research Council
Applied Psychology Unit
Cambridge England

K. Lieberman
Department of Psychology,
Stirling University
Stirling, Scotland

ABSTRACT

The role of imagery in verbal memory is explored using the framework of a working memory system comprising a central executive and two hypothetical "slave" systems, an articulatory loop and a visuo-spatial "scratch pad." Experiments 1 and 2 suggest that the scratch pad is sensitive to disruption by concurrent spatial rather than visual activity. It is further shown that a concurrent spatial task, pursuit tracking, interferes with the utilization of a visual imagery mnemonic for remembering word lists. Comparable disruption does not occur in the case of a mnemonic based on alphabetic order rather than imagery. Some broader implications of the assumption of a spatial working memory system are discussed.

INTRODUCTION

Following a series of experiments exploring the role of memory in reasoning, learning, and comprehension, Baddeley and Hitch (1974) proposed that the concept of short-term memory should be modified. The alternative proposed was termed *working memory* and comprised a central executive component that was assumed to be responsible for control processes and at least two supplementary "slave" systems, an articulatory loop and a visuo-spatial temporary store or "scratch pad." The articulatory loop was assumed to allow speech-based material to be maintained using subvocalization, a process making comparatively light demands on the central executive and being particularly appropriate for maintaining serial order. The articulatory loop was assumed to be responsible for the speechlike characteristics of performance in many short-term memory tasks, including the phonemic similarity effect (Conrad, 1964) and the word-length effect (Baddeley, Thomson, & Buchanan, 1975a), both of which can be eliminated if the material is presented visually and vocalization suppressed.

The present study is concerned with the second hypothetical slave system, the visuo-spatial scratch pad. This was discussed only briefly by Baddeley and Hitch (1974) but began to be explored in a series of studies by Baddeley, Grant, Wight, & Thomson (1975b). The experiments that follow are a continuation of this series. The experiments utilized the technique pioneered by Lee Brooks (1967, 1968) whereby the process of imaging is disrupted by a concurrent visuo-spatial task. Our previous study demonstrated that a concurrent tracking task using a pursuit rotor dramatically impaired the subject's memory performance on a task that Brooks had previously shown to depend on imagery, whereas no such decrement occurred on a task relying on verbal encoding. We were also able to show that the memory task based on imagery impaired tracking performance, whereas the verbal memory task did not.

Having established that pursuit tracking was a suitable task for disrupting the use of visuo-spatial imagery, we then used tracking to study the encoding of verbal material of high- or low-rated concreteness/imageability (Baddeley et al, 1975b). Subjects performed a paired-associate task involving concrete nouns and highly imageable adjectives such as *strawberry—ripe* and *bullet—grey* or pairs involving abstract nouns and low-imageability adjectives such as *gratitude—infinite* and *mood—cheerful*. There is abundant evidence (Paivio, 1971) that concrete and imageable material is remembered very much better than abstract material of low imageability, an effect that is usually attributed to the subject's strategy of actively forming and using visual images in order to assist his learning. If this were the case we argued, it should be possible to disrupt the process by means of a concurrent visuo-spatial task. The effect of this should be to reduce the advantage enjoyed by concrete over abstract material. We therefore required our subjects to learn both types of material either unencumbered by a supplementary task or while pursuit tracking. Tracking caused a small overall impairment in performance; despite the absence of instructions to use imagery there was a massive difference between the abstract and concrete material, but there was no trace of the predicted interaction. On the basis of these results it was suggested that a distinction should be drawn between the abstract–concrete distinction and imagery as a control process whereby material is manipulated in a visuo-spatial working memory. The former, it was suggested, represents the manner in which a given type of material is registered in semantic memory. Its manner of registration will influence performance whether or not the control process of visuo-spatial imagery is employed in learning or recall.

The experiments to be described represent a continuation of this study. More specifically we try to answer three questions: (1) Does the system involved in the control process of imagery employ *visual* or *spatial* coding? (2) Is the system limited to the type of immediate memory task studied by both Brooks and ourselves, or is it also involved, as we predicted, in the use of imagery in mnemonics? (3) What is the relationship between this subsystem and the rest of working memory on the one hand and semantic memory on the other?

VISUAL OR SPATIAL WORKING MEMORY?

In presenting our previous results at the Attention and Performance meeting, I referred throughout to their implication for a *visual* working memory system. In the discussion, Daniel Kahneman raised the issue of whether the evidence necessarily implied a visual as opposed to a spatial system, and it became obvious that our data would not allow us to choose between these possibilities. Experiments 1 and 2 therefore aim to answer this question. In the first experiment, the influence of a spatial but nonvisual task on imagery is studied, whereas in the second the disrupting effect of a task involving visual but nonspatial processing is examined.

EXPERIMENT 1

In this study subjects were required to perform the immediate memory tasks that had previously been shown by Brooks (1967) and Baddeley *et al* (1975b) to emphasize either visuo-spatial or verbal coding. Subjects are required to perform both tasks alone and while performing an auditory tracking task that involves pointing to a moving sound source while blindfolded. The task has a clear spatial component, but it does not depend on visual input.

Apparatus

The subject was seated in front of a pendulum made from a 6-ft 4-in. light metal rod attached to the ceiling at a height of 9 ft 6 in. above the floor and 3 ft 11 in. from either wall. The bob of the pendulum contained a sound-emitting device, a 2½-in. 35-ohm loud speaker and a photocell. The sound emitter produced a continuous tone under ambient illumination, and a sequence of higher-pitched bleeps when light was shone on the photocell. The subject held a flashlight in his hand and attempted to keep the beam of the light on the photocell; when he did so, the emitted sound became intermittent, providing feedback.

Material

This comprised the memory-span material used by Brooks (1967) and Baddeley *et al* (1975, Experiment 2). Two types of sequence were used, one easily visualized and termed the *spatial material;* the other formally equivalent but not easily visualized termed the *nonsense material.* The subject is told to imagine a 4 × 4 matrix and is taught that one particular square (the second square in the second row) will be designated the *starting square.* Each message described the location of the digits 1 to 8 within the matrix, and in each case the digit 1 was in the starting square and successive digits appear in adjacent squares. Because the message is always presented in the sequence 1 to 8, it is possible to remember it in terms of a path through the matrix, with each successive digit being located as above, below, to the right, or to the left of the previous location (e.g., in the starting square, put a 1; in the next square to the right, put a 2; in the next square up, put a 3; etc.). The nonsense messages are formally equivalent except that the words *up* and *down* are replaced by *good* and *bad,* whereas the words *left* and *right* are replaced by *slow* and *quick* (e.g., in the starting square, put a 1; in the next square to the quick, put a 2; in the next square to the good, put a 3; etc.). Both we and Brooks find that the nonsense sequences are more difficult than the spatial but that reducing them from eight to six items gives an approximately equivalent probability of correct reproduction. Throughout therefore we use eight-digit messages for the spatial material and six-digit sequences for the nonsense material.

Design

All subjects were tested on four conditions comprising the two types of material tested with and without concurrent auditory tracking. Subjects received eight messages in each of the four conditions. Eight research students served as subjects and were paid £2.00 for participating in Experiments 1 and 2. Half began with Experiment 1 and half with Experiment 2. The order of conditions was determined by a Greco–Latin square within which the two spatial and the two nonsense conditions were blocked so as to minimize disruption of strategy by change of memory task.

Procedure

Subjects were first trained on the auditory tracking task up to a point at which they were able to achieve a score of at least 80% time on target over two successive 30-sec runs. Subjects were then given practice on the spatial memory task. Here they were given six practice trials, unless they reached a criterion of two successive perfect runs in less than six trials. They were then given practice on combining the two tasks until the subject had reached a level of skill whereby the tracking task was not substantially lowered by the memory task, and the memory task did not produce a large number of hestitations. The nonsense task was then practiced to the same criterion, and subjects were finally practiced at combining the nonsense task and tracking, again to the same criterion. They were then tested on the four conditions in the appropriate order. In the dual-task conditions, subjects tracked during both presentation and recall.

Results

Performance was scored in terms of number of sequences in which reproduction was perfect, for which the maximum is eight in each condition. Because the number of observations is small and scores are not normally distributed, the data were analyzed using nonparametric tests. There was a clear tendency for tracking to disrupt recall on the spatial task, with mean number of correct sequences dropping from 6.75 to 3.14, a decrement being shown by all subjects ($p < .005$, sign test). In the case of the nonsense task, mean memory performance dropped from 6.50 to 5.14 sequences correct during tracking. A decrement was present for five of the eight subjects but was not significant statistically. For seven of the eight subjects, tracking led to a greater recall decrement on the spatial task than on the nonsense task ($p < .05$, sign test).

Tracking performance was slightly poorer when doing the spatial task (80.1% time on target) than during the nonsense task (84.8%), an effect that was shown by seven of the subjects ($p < .05$, sign test). In general, however, the fact that not only was the spatial task more vulnerable to tracking but also that tracking itself was more vulnerable to the effect of the spatial task combine to rule out a speed error tradeoff interpretation of our results. Our data are clearly consistent with the assumption that the memory task relying on imagery has a spatial component that does not depend on direct visual input. It may of course have a purely visual component in addition to the spatial component; this possibility was explored in Experiment 2.

EXPERIMENT 2

In this study we used the same spatial and nonsense memory tasks, but this time we attempted to disrupt performance using a concurrent visual task, brightness judgment, for which the spatial demands were minimal.

Procedure

The material and experimental design were identical with Experiment 1, but, instead of the auditory tracking task, subjects were required to judge the brightness of a series of light patches on a screen. These were provided by a Carousel projector loaded with slides, each containing either two or three layers of tracing paper. The subjects were seated about 1 meter in front of a screen that was totally illuminated by the projector. The room was in darkness except for a low level of ambient illumination provided by a flashlight, so as to allow the experimenter to record the subject's responses. Stimuli were presented at a rate of 1 every 2.5 sec. In order to minimize any spatial component in the response, subjects were given only a single key that they were instructed to press whenever they saw a bright stimulus. Half the stimuli were bright, and half were dim.

Subjects commenced the session by practicing on the brightness discrimination task. They were given a minimum of 30 practice slides and continued to practice until they had reached a consistent level of performance of at least 90% correct responses. Subjects then received training on the memory tasks and on combining the memory and supplementary tasks, as in Experiment 1. Subjects were then tested on eight sequences in each of the four conditions, the order of conditions for any given subject being equivalent to that experienced in Experiment 1. In the dual-task conditions, subjects began the brightness judgment task before the presentation of the first sequence and continued performing the task until that condition was completed.

Results

Considering first the number of sequences correct, the pattern of Experiment 1 was reversed, with the retention of nonsense sequences being significantly disrupted by the concurrent task (from a control mean of 7.25 to an interference mean of 4.14 sequences), an effect that occurred with all eight subjects ($p < .005$, sign test). The disruption effect was not significant for the spatial memory task (from 5.75 to 4.72), where it was shown by only five of the eight subjects. Comparing the two conditions, seven of the eight subjects showed a greater degree of disruption on the nonsense than on the spatial tasks ($p < .05$, sign test). Subjects were successful in maintaining their discrimination performance at around the 90% mark, and there were no differences between the performance of subjects doing the two types of memory task, with three doing better while processing spatial messages, three doing the opposite, and two showing no difference.

Discussion

It is clear form Experiment 2 that the concurrent visual task of judging brightness was sufficient to cause a significant decrement in performance on the memory task, but that this was not specific to the spatial condition. Indeed, the evidence suggests that the disruption was rather less on the spatial than the nonsense conditions.

The combined results of the two experiments allow us to reject two rival interpretations to that of a spatial working memory. The first of these argues that the decrement shown in Experiment 1 and in Baddeley *et al* (1975) simply reflects the greater vulnerability of the spatial task, possibly stemming from its comprising longer sequences. The greater disruption of recall in the nonsense condition of Experiment 2 rules this out. The second is the hypothesis that a modality-specific visual memory system is involved. The fact that a spatial task disrupts performance in the imagery condition whereas a visual task does not implies spatial rather than visual coding.

SPATIAL MEMORY AND IMAGERY MNEMONICS

In our previous paper (Baddeley et al., 1975b) we suggested distinguishing between the control process of imagery that represents the manipulation of visuo-spatial information in some form of working memory and the variable of rated imageability/concreteness, representing the way in which material is registered in semantic memory. It was suggested that it is this latter characteristic of material that accounted for the powerful effect of rated concreteness on memory performance. It was suggested on the other hand however that imagery mnemonics do rely on spatial working memory. As Bower (1972) has pointed out, for an imagery mnemonic to be successful, the two items visualized must be made to interact in some way; if the plausible assumption is made that the items are held and manipulated in a spatial working memory, then it follows that a concurrent tracking task should interfere with the use of an imagery mnemonic. Experiments 3 and 4 test this prediction.

EXPERIMENT 3

Subjects were instructed to use either rote memory or a pegword mnemonic employing visual imagery to remember lists of 10 words, each of which was paired with a digit from 1 to 10. On half the trials subjects were required to track on a pursuit rotor, whereas on the other half they were free to concentrate on the memory task. It was predicted that tracking would differentially disrupt performance based on the imagery mnemonic.

Materials

These compised eight lists of 10 words of which half were high in rated concreteness (> 6.5) and half were low (< 2.0), as rated in the Paivio, Yuille, and Madigan (1968) norms. The two types of material were matched for Thorndike–Lorge frequency, with all words having a frequency of at least 20 per million.

Design and Subjects

The design involved two types of learning instruction, visual imagery and rote, which were combined with the presence or absence of a concurrent tracking task to produce four conditions. Subjects were tested on two lists in each condition, with each list containing five abstract and five concrete words presented in random order. The two lists in any given condition were blocked, but the order of the four conditions was determined by a Latin square. Subjects were 28 Stirling University undergraduates, with seven subjects being assigned at random to each row of the Latin square.

Procedure

Subjects were first trained to perform the pursuit rotor task. This involved tracking a circular path with a stylus on a Lafayette pursuit rotor. During this initial phase the rotor was adjusted to a point at which subjects were able to achieve a tracking performance of 80–90% time on target over three successive 30-sec practice trials. This was typically within the range of 20–30 rpm.

They were then taught the one-is-a-bun pegword mnemonic (Paivio, 1971) to a criterion of two successive perfect recalls. They were then instructed to use the mnemonic by creating a visual image of each word and integrating it with the image of the item associated with the pegword. For example, if the pair was *one—ship*, the subject was to associate the number *one* with the word *bun* and form an interacting image of a ship and a bun, perhaps of a ship sailing into a huge floating bun. Subjects were then given a practice list of 10 number–word pairs in ascending order and were tested by being presented with the numbers 1–10 in random order and required to call out the word that had been associated with that particular number in that list. It was then pointed out that for half the lists this strategy should be used; for the other half the pairs would be presented much more rapidly and the subject was instructed to repeat each pair to himself and avoid attempting to form visual images. The test then began with pairs of items in the visual imagery condition being presented at a rate of 6 sec per pair, whereas the rote condition involved presenting each pair three times at a rate of 2 sec per pair. In both cases recall was at a rate of 6 sec per item. In half the conditions subjects were required to track during both presentation and recall, whereas in the remaining conditions no supplementary task was required. They were instructed to regard the tracking task as primary, using the analogy of driving a car while listening to the radio.

Results

Under control conditions the imagery mnemonic was effective giving a mean 67.3% correct pairs compared with 50.0% under rote learning instructions. Concurrent tracking reduced performance in the imagery condition to a level of 57.5%, whereas rote performance was unaffected at 49.5% correct. Analysis of variance showed significant effects of instructions (F 1, 27 = 21.63, $p < .001$) indicating that the imagery mnemonic was proving helpful. There was also an overall effect of concurrent tracking (F 1, 27 = 4.76, $p < .05$), but this was modified by an interaction with instructions (F 1, 27 = 5.33, $p < .05$) indicating as predicted that the spatial concurrent task disrupted performance *only* when subjects were using the visual imagery mnemonic. There was a tendency for concrete words to be better recalled than abstract (F 1, 27 = 8.33, $p < .01$). The concreteness/imageability effect interacted with learning instruction (F 1, 27 = 7.45, $p < .05$) but not with tracking (F 1, 27 < 1.0).

Subjects were successful in maintaining their tracking performance at the 80% level, with no differences appearing across conditions.

Discussion

The results of Experiment 3 are consistent with the hypothesis that the spatial working memory system is involved in the pegword imagery mnemonic, because the advantage provided by the imagery mnemonic is abolished by the spatial tracking task. At the same time, the lack of an interaction between suppression by tracking and rated concreteness supports our previous conclusion (Baddeley et al., 1975b) that concreteness does not depend for its effect on the operation of the spatial working memory system. It does however appear to be sensitive to either presentation rate or encoding instructions, because when subjects were instructed to use a rote rehearsal strategy and material was presented rapidly, the effect of concreteness disappeared. It is tempting to suggest that under these conditions subjects were relying on a relatively shallow phonemically based code that was hence unaffected by the semantic characteristics of the remembered material (Baddeley, 1966).

Taken overall therefore, the results of Experiment 3 conform closely to predictions. The effects were however much weaker than those obtained in earlier experiments in the series. One possible reason for this is suggested by Experiments 1 and 2, which imply that the crucial factor about the tracking task is its *spatial* component. Although the pegword mnemonic involves manipulating visual images so as to make them interact spatially, it could be argued that the degree of spatial precision necessary is relatively slight. We therefore decided to study the influence of tracking on a mnemonic that we chose as having a much clearer and more important spatial component than the pegword mnemonic. For this we employed a version of the classical location mnemonic in which we instructed our subjects to imagine a walk through the University of Stirling campus. A sequence of 10 locations along this walk was selected, and subjects were instructed to remember the various items by imagining them located at the appropriate point along the walk.

EXPERIMENT 4

Procedure

The material and experimental design followed that used in Experiment 3, with the exception that only 12 subjects were tested, three being assigned at random to each row of the Latin square. Once again Stirling University undergraduates participated in the experiment for course credit. In place of the pegword mnemonic they were taught a location mnemonic based on a path through the University campus that contained 10 well-known and easily discriminable locations. They were told to imagine themselves following the route and the 10 locations were pointed out, the procedure being repeated until they successfully reported the correct locations themselves in the appropriate order on two successive trials. The second major difference from previous experiments was in requiring serial recall rather than associating each item with a digit. Hence in the mnemnic condition the subjects were presented with the 10 words at a rate of one every 6 sec and were instructed to associate an image of each successive item with the appropriate location along the walk. In the rote learning condition the items were presented at a rate of one every 2 sec with the subjects instructed to avoid the use of imagery. In order to keep total presentation time constant, the whole sequence was repeated three times in the rote conditions.

Results

Mean recall scores for the various conditions are shown in Fig. 26.1. There was a significant overall effect of tracking (F 1, 11 = 18.87, $p < .01$). The overall effect of the imagery mnemonic failed to reach significance, (F 1, 11 = 1.93, $p > .05$) but the predicted interaction occurred between imagery

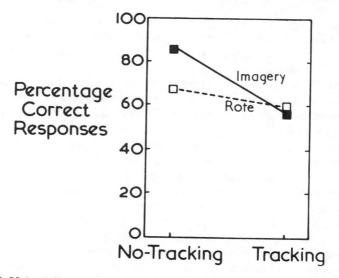

FIG. 26.1. Influence of pursuit tracking on serial verbal recall based on either rote learning or a location mnemonic.

mnemonic and tracking (F 1, 11 = 15.62, $p < .01$). There was no effect of the abstractness of the material (F 1, 11 < 1), and none of the further interactions achieved statistical significance. In the unloaded control condition the imagery strategy led to significantly better recall than the rote strategy (t = 2.44, $p < .05$). The difference between the two conditions was however abolished by the addition of the tracking task, with the imagery and tracking condition in fact being nonsignficantly worse than the rote condition while tracking (t = 0.13, $p > .05$). The effect of tracking on learning using imagery was very consistent, being shown by all 12 subjects tested (t = 4.91, $p < .001$), whereas the effect of pursuit tracking on rote learning failed to reach significance (t = 1.99, $p > .05$).

Once again subjects maintained their tracking performance at the recommended level, achieving 84.9% time on target for the imagery condition and 86.1% for the rote, with six subjects tracking better under imagery and six under rote conditions.

Discussion

Experiment 4 broadly replicates the effects shown in previous experiments. Once again, a visuo-spatial tracking task is found to interfere with the use of an imagery mnemonic, although having no comparable effect on the rote learning strategy. In contrast to the previous study, the effect is shown clearly by all 12 subjects tested, hence lending further support to the suggestion that tracking will have a particularly clear effect on a mnemonic making heavy demands on precise spatial coding.

Unlike the previous study where there was an effect of the concreteness of material, provided the subject was using the imagery mnemonic, in this experiment we found no effect of type of material on recall. This is consistent with Paivio and Csapo's (1969) suggestion that visuo-spatial coding is much less appropriate in serial recall than in free recall or paired-associate learning. The fact that an imagery mnemonic may nevertheless work very effectively in serial recall provides yet another example of the need to distinguish between the control process of imagery and its use in mnemonics on the one hand and the variable of rated concreteness or imageability on the other.

So far, our experiments appear to fit our predictions reasonably accurately. In discussing them, however Patrick Rabbitt pointed out that our results could equally well be explained by the simple generalization that organized learning is more easily disrupted by a secondary task than rote learning. In all cases, the task that is disrupted by tracking is that in which the subject uses the more complex organizational strategy, and it can plausibly be argued that anything that occupies processing capacity will be particularly detrimental to complex learning strategies such as those involved in the two mnemonics. Experiment 5 attempts to test this interpretation by studying the influence of pursuit tracking on a first-letter alphabetic mnemonic. If pursuit tracking has a general effect on the subject's organizational skills, we should observe a similar decrement.

EXPERIMENT 5

Design and Material

The basic design was the same as that used in Experiment 4 with the exception that the location mnemonic was replaced by a mnemonic based on the initial letter of the words to be recalled. This necessitated changing the material. Two types of lists were created; both comprised items from a single semantic category such as *foreign cities* or *reading material*. The items were selected such that one item started with each of the first 10 letters of the alphabet. In the mnemonic condition, the order of the items was determined by their initial letter, *A* through to *J*, (e.g., *Amsterdam, Berlin, Chicago, Durban, . . . , Jerusalem*). Half the lists were alphabetically ordered, whereas the remainder also comprised items beginning with each of the first 10 letters of the alphabet but were presented in random order. Finally, for each condition, half of the categories were selected as concrete items and half as abstract; this latter distinction was based on the experimenter's judgment, because standardized ratings were not available for many of the items used. The lists were balanced for word frequency. Lists were balanced across subjects such that any given category appeared equally frequently as an alphabetically ordered and unordered list. Subjects were tested on two abstract and two concrete lists in each of the four conditions produced by combining two types of list, alphabetic and random, and two load conditions, with and without tracking. A total of 16 women from the Applied Psychology Unit Subject Panel were tested, four being assigned at random to each row of a Latin square.

Procedure

Subjects were first trained on the pursuit rotor up to a level of 75–80% time on target. This took between five and ten 20-sec trials. They were then given instruction on the two memory tasks in which the subject was first given a cue as to whether an alphabetical or random list was involved, followed by the 10 items each preceded by the relevant number (e.g., *Foreign Cities, Alphabetical—One—Amsterdam, Two—Berlin, Three—Chicago*, etc). Recall was cued by presenting the digits *One, Two, Three*, etc. in ascending order. Rate of presentation and recall was 8 sec per word, a rate that was found to yield approximately the same overall recall score as was obtained in the previous study using a location mnemonic.

Results

The mnemonic worked, with subjects recalling a mean of 9.17 items as compared with 6.58 in the rote condition. With concurrent tracking these scores fell to 8.92 and 5.81, respectively. Analysis of variance indicated a highly significant effect of alphabetic ordering (F 1, 15 = 49.24, $p < .001$), a significant effect of tracking (F 1, 15 = 5.77, $p < .05$), but no significant effect of level of concreteness (F 1, 15 < 1) and no statistically significant interactions. This result seems to rule out the simple generalization that tracking differentially interferes with memory organization. We obtained a mnemonic effect that is very close in magnitude to that obtained using the location mnemonic. There is however no evidence to suggest that the mnemonic condition here is particularly susceptible to interference, indeed the trend if anything is in the opposite direction. As in the previous study we find no evidence for an abstract versus concrete difference; although too much emphasis should not be placed on this because the materials were not standardized, it nevertheless reinforces the previous suggestion that serial learning does not appear to be very sensitive to the degree of concreteness of the material being learned.

IMPLICATIONS FOR THE STRUCTURE
OF THE MEMORY SYSTEM

Is There a Separate Visuo-Spatial Memory?

In this and the previous study (Baddeley et al., 1975), we have consistently argued for a separate visuo-spatial working memory system. Such an interpretation was suggested by Brooks (1967, 1968), and it has been widely accepted since that time (e.g., Bower, 1972). Our results suggest that the system relies on spatial rather than visual coding because it can be disrupted by a spatial task that is free from visual input and is relatively resistant to disruption by a visual task that makes only a slight spatial processing demand. This conclusion is consistent with that of Byrne (1974) who observed that a spatially incompatible pointing task disrupted the use of imagery in recall.[1]

Further evidence for a spatial working memory system is provided by the mental rotation task first studied by Shepard and Metzler (1971). Although early studies with this have all used visual stimuli, a recent study by Carpenter and Eisenberg (1978) has shown similar effects with haptic stimuli explored tactually by blindfolded normal or congenitally blind subjects.

In a paper published since the completion of the present experimental series, Phillips and Christie (1977a) have argued that the evidence at present available forces the assumption of at least two components in tasks relying on imagery but does not force the conclusion that one of these is visuo-spatial in nature. Using a working memory framework, it is possible, for example, to explain all the data in terms of a general-purpose central executive and an articulatory loop. Although we would contend that it is difficult to give a plausible interpretation of all the available data in these terms, none of the available experiments logically forces the assumption of three separate processes. The problem of designing such a study presents an interesting technical challenge.

---

[1]Subsequent to the performance of Experiment 1, a somewhat less Gothic means of disrupting spatial coding has been developed by Ian Moar at the Applied Psychology Unit (Moar, 1978). This involves a matrix of buttons that are hidden from the subject by a cover. He is required to press the buttons one after the other following a boustrophedal path through the array, up one row and back down the next. Although the path is entirely predictable, the subject must maintain a reasonably accurate representation of his location if he is to avoid missing buttons as he moves along, and this appears to be sufficient to cause a clear decrement in tasks involving visuo-spatial imagery. Because it is easier to instrument than our auditory tracking, it is a preferable means of disrupting imagery, particularly because we found our auditory tracking task extremely difficult for some undergraduate subjects tested in a pilot study.

Neuropsychological Evidence for Separate Systems

Further evidence for both long- and short-term visual and spatial memory systems comes from the clinical literature and, in particular, from the work of De Renzi and his co-workers. For example, De Renzi and Nichelli (1975) have contrasted verbal and spatial memory span. Verbal memory span is measured using either a conventional digit span or a modified version wherein the subject points to a series of digits so as to avoid any potential difficulties due to possible limitations in speech. The spatial memory span was measured using a task devised by Corsi (quoted by Milner, 1971) in which the subject has placed in front of him a board containing nine randomly spaced cubes. The experimenter taps a sequence of from two to eight cubes, and the subject is required to reproduce the sequence of taps. Verbal memory span was a clearly separable function that tended to be associated with left-hemisphere damage. Impaired spatial memory span on the other hand was associated with posterior lesions in either hemisphere. In a subsequent study, De Renzi, Faglioni, and Preveidi (1977) drew a further distinction between spatial memory-span performance, which again they found to be impaired following damage to the posterior part of either hemisphere, and long-term visual memory, which was disrupted only by right-hemisphere damage. The distinction is further supported by a number of more detailed case histories of patients showing grossly impaired spatial learning while having a normal spatial memory span. De Renzi and Nichelli (1975) cite examples of the converse, namely patients who are grossly defective on spatial memory span but who show no difficulty in learning a visual maze and show no evidence for topographical disorientation in the real world. Such results are consistent with the concept of a spatial working memory system that is used for the Corsi block tapping test but is separate from the long-term visuo-spatial memory system necessary for geographical orientation.

The neuropsychological evidence we have discussed so far has been largely confined to spatial memory; imagery may of course be involved but the evidence for this is at present far from clear. A more direct involvement of imagery is however suggested by an intriguing recent observation by Bisiach and Luzzatti (1978) who describe the performance of two patients suffering from posterior right-hemisphere lesions following stroke. In both cases the patient had a hemianopia in the left visual field together with unilateral neglect, a tendency to ignore items presented to the left of the midline, although such items could be reported if requested. The patients were asked to imagine themselves in the Cathedral Square of their home city of Milan. They were asked to imagine themselves standing outside the cathedral and to describe the scene. In both cases subjects successfully described buildings that would have been in their right visual field but completely ignored buildings on the left. They were then asked to imagine that they had crossed the square and were pointing in the opposite direction and were asked to repeat the exercise. They then described the buildings that had previously been in their neglected hemifield perfectly adequately, presumably because performance was now dependent on the intact right hemifield. Those buildings that had previously been described perfectly adequately were not omitted, presumably because report relied on the operation of the neglected hemifield. Although only two cases are reported, it appears that this is by no means an uncommon phenomenon. It appears to imply a very close relationship between some of the processes involved in visual perception and those involved in imagery. Although it would be premature to suggest that such patients have a defect that is associated with spatial working memory, this clearly presents a hypothesis that is worth further exploration. For example, using the simple analogy of the visuo-spatial scratch pad as a screen on which spatial information may be represented, one might conclude either than part of the screen was inoperative or that the process of scanning the screen was defective, in each case allowing only part of the system to be used.

One Central Executive or Two?

Bearing in mind the evidnece from both normal and neuropsychological sources, there would appear to be a good case for assuming a separate spatial working memory system. Baddeley and Hitch (1974) tentatively suggested a system comprising a central executive served by two slave systems, an articulatory loop and a spatial scratch pad. The evidence we have discussed is so far consistent with such a notion. It is however also consistent with an alternative version assuming completely parallel and separate visual and spatial working memory systems. Fortunately, Phillips and Christie (1977a, b) have provided some very compelling evidence for a single central executive. Their task required the subject to remember a 4 × 4 or 5 × 5 matrix of calls, any one of which had a 0.5 probability of being filled. An initial study (Phillips and Christie, 1977a) showed that subjects are able to maintain one such stimulus pattern reasonably accurately over a matter of seconds. If a series of such patterns is presented, performance on all but the last item drops to a common asymptotic level. In their second study Phillips and Christie (1977b) studied the factors that disrupt performance. In a series of five experiments they showed very clearly that the most crucial factor is not the *visual* similarity between a subsequent event and the pattern being retained but rather the extent to which the interpolated task demands central processing capacity. Hence, retention of the matrix is far better following the reading of a series of visually presented digits than it is following the addition of visual or auditory digits. They argue convincingly that maintenance of such a spatial representation is crucially dependent on general processing capacity. Phillips and

Christie's results suggest therefore that the maintenance of a precise and detailed visual representation may make very heavy general processing demands, implying a single central executive for both visuo-spatial and verbal tasks.

Is There a Nonspatial Visual Memory?

We have so far argued strongly for a spatially based working memory system. The existence of such a system does not of course preclude the occurrence of a parallel system or component concerned with pictorial or nonspatial visual representation. Indeed, work on animals has suggested just such a distinction between a spatial component of visual perception concerned with *where* an object is seen and a feature system concerned with what is seen. Neurological evidence from goldfish (Ingle, 1967) and golden hamsters (Schneider, 1967, 1969) suggests that locational information is mediated by the superior colliculi of the optic tectum, whereas pattern discrimination involves a cortical system. Although exactly equivalent data are not available for man, Weiskrantz, Warrington, Sanders, and Marshall (1974) have shown that certain patients may be able to respond by pointing to the location of an object despite the fact that it is not consciously perceived, due to cortical damge. Such "blindsight" is again compatible with two separate visual systems, one cortically mediated and the other relying on neurologically separate pathways.

Probably the best evidence for a nonspatial component to visual imagery is presented by Janssen (1976a, b, c). He describes a series of experiments following up the report by Atwood (1971) that memory for high imagery phrases such as *nudist devouring bird* is disrupted if followed by a task requiring the subject to process a visually presented digit in contrast to abstract phrases such as *the intellect of Einstein was a miracle,* which are more disrupted by the processing of an auditory digit. We ourselves found difficulty in replicating Atwood's result, as have a number of other investigators (see Baddeley *et al,* 1975b). Janssen succeeds in producing the Atwood effect consistently over several experiments and argues that other failures to replicate, including our own, stem from using an interfering task that is spatial rather than visual. His results and those of Atwood therefore do seem to point quite strongly toward a visual component that differs from the spatial component studied in our own experiments in a number of respects. In particular, Janssen's effect interacts with type of material, with visual disruption present for imageable material but not for material of low imageability, even though the subject is attempting to use an imagery strategy. This contrasts with our own results that suggest that the nature of the material is of minimal importance, with spatial interference being present for both abstract and concrete material, provided the subject is attempting to use an imagery strategy.

Understanding the relation between spatial working memory and the more visual system suggested by Janssen's work presents an important but difficult problem. A related and perhaps even more important problem concerns the nature of rated concreteness/imageability. How do these powerful variables have their effect, and why do their effects differ, with concreteness tending to be more important in learning (Richardson, 1975a, b) and imageability in perception (Marcel and Patterson, 1978)?

In conclusion, the evidence seems to suggest the existence first of a visuo-spatial working memory system that is used both in immediate memory and in long-term verbal memory when a spatial mnemonic is employed. The work of Phillips and Christie (1977b) suggests that such a system is probably also heavily dependent on a central processor of limited capacity. There appears in addition to be evidence for a nonspatial system or possibly a component of a more complex system that is used for maintaining highly imageable material and may be disrupted by a very simple visual processing task (Janssen 1975a, b, c). These systems are in turn dependent on a semantic memory system that is sensitive to separable effects of both concreteness and imageability.

ACKNOWLEDGMENTS

We are grateful to the Medical Research Council and Social Science Research Council for financial support; to Graham Hitch, Karalyn Patterson, and Bill Phillips for discussion and comments; and to Mark Roberts, who ran Experiment 5.

REFERENCES

Atwood, G. E. An experimental study of visual imagination and memory. *Cognitive Psychology*, 1971, *2*, 290–299.

Baddeley, A. D. The influence of acoustic and semantic similarity on long-term memory for word sequences. *Quarterly Journal of Experimental Psychology*, 1966, *18*, 302–309.

Baddeley, A. D., & Hitch, G. J. Working memory. In G. Bower (Ed.), *Recent advances in learning and motivation 8*, New York: Academic Press, 1974.

Baddeley, A. D., Thomson, N., & Buchanan, M. Word length and the structure of short-term memory. *Journal of Verbal Learning and Verbal Behavior*, 1975, *14*, 575–589. (a)

Baddeley, A. D., Grant, S., Wight, E., & Thomson, N. Imagery and visual working memory. In P. M. A. Rabbitt & S. Dornic (Eds.), *Attention and performance V*. London: Academic Press, 1975. (b)

Bisiach, E., & Luzzatti, C. Unilateral neglect of representational space. *Cortex*, 1978, *14*, 129–133.

Bower, G. H. Mental imagery and associative learning. In L. W. Gregg (Ed.), *Cognition in learning and memory*. New York: Wiley, 1972.

Brooks, L. R. The suppression of visualization by reading. *Quarterly Journal of Experimental Psychology*, 1967, *19*, 289–299.

Brooks, L. R. Spatial and verbal components in the act of recall. *Canadian Journal of Psychology*, 1968, *22*, 349–368.

Byrne, B. Item concreteness versus spatial organization as predictors of visual imagery. *Memory & Cognition*, 1974, *2*, 53–59.

Carpenter, P. A., & Eisenberg, P. Mental rotation and the frame of reference in blind and sighted individuals. *Perception & Psychophysics*, 1978, *23*, 117–124.

Conrad, R. Acoustic confusion in immediate memory. *British Journal of Psychology*, 1964, *55*, 75–84.

De Renzi, E., Faglioni, P., & Previdi, P. Spatial memory and hemispheric locus of lesion. *Cortex*, 1977, *13*, 424–433.

De Renzi, E., & Nichelli, P. Verbal and non-verbal short-term memory impairment following hemispheric damage. *Cortex*, 1975, *11*, 341–354.

Ingle, D. Two visual mechanisms underlying the behavior of fish. *Psychologische Forschung*, 1967, *31*, 44–51.

Janssen, W. H. Selective interference in paired-associate and free recall learning: Messing up the image. *Acta Psychologica*, 1976, *40*, 35–48. (a)

Janssen, W. H. Selective interference during the retrieval of visual images. *Quarterly Journal of Experimental Psychology*, 1976, *28*, 535–539. (b)

Janssen, W. H. *On the nature of the mental image.* Soesterberg, The Netherlands: Institute for Perception TNO, 1976. (c)

Marcel, A. J., & Patterson, K. E. Word recognition and production: reciprocity in clinical and normal studies. In J. Requin (Ed.), *Attention and performance VII*. Hillsdale, N.J.: Lawrence Erlbaum Associates, 1978.

Milner, B. Interhemispheric differences in the localization of psychological processes in man. *British Medical Bulletin*, 1971, *27*, 272–277.

Moar, I. T. *Mental triangulation and the nature of internal representations of space.* Unpublished PhD thesis, University of Cambridge, 1978.

Paivio, A. *Imagery and verbal processes.* New York: Holt, Rinehart & Winston, 1971.

Paivio, A., & Csapo, K. Concrete-image and verbal memory codes. *Journal of Experimental Psychology*, 1969, *80*, 279–285.

Paivio, A., Yuille, J. C., & Madigan, S. Concreteness imagery and meaningfulness values for 925 nouns. *Journal of Experimental Psychology Monograph Supplement*, 1968, *76*(1, Pt. 2).

Phillips, W. A., & Christie, D. F. M. Components of visual memory. *Quarterly Journal of Experimental Psychology*, 1977, *29*, 117–133. (a)

Phillips, W. A., & Christie, D. F. M. Interference with visualization. *Quarterly Journal of Experimental Psychology*, 1977, *29*, 637–650. (b)

Richardson, J. T. E. Imagery and deep structure in the recall of English nominalizations. *British Journal of Psychology*, 1975, *66*, 333–339. (a)

Richardson, J. T. E. Concreteness and imageability. *Quarterly Journal of Experimental Psychology*, 1975, *27*, 235–250. (b)

Schneider, G. E. Contrasting visuo-motor functions of tectum and cortex in the golden hamster. *Psychologische Forschung*, 1967, *31*, 52–62.

Schneider, G. E. Two visual systems. *Science*, 1969, *163*, 895–902.

Shepard, R. N., & Metzler, J. Mental rotation of three-dimensional objects. *Science*, 1971, *171*, 701–703.

Weiskrantz, L., Warrington, E. K., Sanders, M. D., & Marshall, J. Visual capacity in the hemianopic field following a restricted occipital ablation. *Brain*, 1974, *97*, 709–728.

27 Short-Term Recall of Linear and Curvilinear Movements by Blind and Sighted Subjects

V. K. Kool
Indian Institute of Technology
Bombay, India

ABSTRACT

The main purpose of this chapter is to report how blind subjects differ from blindfolded sighted subjects in their estimation of short and long targets while making linear and curvilinear movements. These differences were studied on the basis of the implications of a motor program theory that holds that short movements are programmed and long ones depend on feedback. Two experiments were conducted to examine if a visual reference system helps sighted individuals in performing better than blind individuals on short targets. The difference between the two groups was studied using location, distance, and simple reproduction cues. It was found that errors of the sighted group were less than those of the blind group on simple reproduction and location cues. However, errors of the sighted group increased on long targets of the distance task. It was also found that on long targets blind subjects performed better than sighted subjects who, in contrast, were better on short targets, irrespective of the effects of cues. It was also shown how errors of blind and sighted groups were found equal for the curvilinear movements with distance cues.

INTRODUCTION

It is generally agreed that human beings receive information from a wide variety of sense modalities and that all the available information is transformed into some internal code. When a blindfolded individual is asked to make a movement, his internal code is mainly based on kinesthetic information coming from muscles or joints of the body. Thus, a record of motor outflow is stored in the brain that could be reproduced later when required. In terms of motor program theory (Keele, 1968; Keele & Summers, 1976) it would be explained as a set of prestructured movement commands that contain all the details of the movement (e.g., amount of contraction of muscles, its duration and magnitude).

A necessary condition for a rigid motor program theory is the absence of feedback control. However, a current synthesized motor program model shows four essential components: a movement generator or motor program system, a template or comparison center, an efferent copy, and feedback (Keele & Summers, 1976). A motor program center generates a pattern of neural outflow to the musculature. This results in kinesthetic feedback, but some other sensory features may be involved also. To judge the accuracy of this feedback a template of ideal feedback is proposed. The efferent copy helps in relating the program center with the template and establishes which template or part of a template is relevant at any time. The program continues if the feedback matches the template; otherwise corrections are issued.

After examining the implications of a motor program concept, Klapp (1975) suggested that very short movements could be programmed and executed without feedback control, whereas long movements remain under feedback control. Because it has been reported that short targets are overshot and long targets are undershot (Hermelin & O'Connor, 1975; Pepper & Herman, 1970; Stelmach & Wilson, 1970), this difference may be attributed to programming and feedback in the execution of a response. Earlier Posner and Keele (1969) have also suggested that short movements require more attention during execution and storage and thereby place higher demands for central processing than long movements.

Because sighted individuals are predominantly in the habit of relying on visual cues, a central problem raised in this chapter is: How does a visual reference system affect retention of movements of sighted individuals, particularly in those conditions in which kinesthetic information alone is crucial? The answer to this question is sought by comparing sighted with congenitally blind individuals who have been without vision since birth. Two experiments are reported in this chapter to focus on this issue. In Experiment 1 simple reproduction of the linear and curvilinear movements of the bilnd and sighted subjects were studied. It is proposed in this experiment that in simple reproduction of movements the sighted subjects would recall better than the blind subjects. It is also proposed that the blind subjects would overshoot short targets with greater magnitude than their sighted counterparts.

The second experiment deals with the effects of location and distance cues. The location cue is one in which the target point is the same as on the standard trials but the starting point is somewhere midway. The distance cue requires a movement of the same extent as on the standard trial but the starting point is different. Several studies have been conducted to show that the coding of information in these two types of tasks is different [i.e., location is centrally coded although distance is dependent on a kinesthetic memory code that is subject to spontaneous decay (Laabs, 1973; Stelmach, 1974)].. The results of these experiments show that location cues are well retained unless information-processing activity is introduced during the retention interval. In contrast, distance cues are poorly recalled and show rapid forgetting over short periods of time without any processing activity.

It is hypothesized in Experiment 2 that if short movements are programmed, blindfolded sighted subjects would do better than blind subjects not only on recall of the location cues but also on the distance cues. However, performance of blind subjects is proposed to improve with increase in the target length because they can effectively use their kinesthetic codes based on feedback.

It is also proposed that the type of movement would affect the magnitude of the difference between blind and sighted subjects. A comparison of linear and curvilinear movements shows that the linear movement involves movement in one direction only, whereas the direction of movement on an angular apparatus changes continuously. This means that spatiotemporal cues involved in these two movements are not identical. In other words, if the speed of movement is held constant, total time taken in reaching a point on a linear movement is less than when the same point is reached through a curvilinear path. Given this argument, it is hypothesized in Experiment 2 that reproduction of a curvilinear movement based on the distance cues would be a mismatch to the original movement format and hence deprive blind subjects of the advantage of kinesthetic information that they were able to use effectively on the horizontal task.

EXPERIMENT 1

Method

Experimental Design and Procedure. Each subject was blindfolded before the experiment started. Both blind and sighted subjects were placed in a standard position at the apparatus, which was fixed almost halfway between their shoulders and hips. The subjects were asked to move a lever to a target and subsequently to return it to the starting position. Recall was taken after the subject returned to the starting point.

The experiment was conducted on the linear and curvilinear tasks. Each subject performed under all the three retention interval conditions, 5, 20, and 90 sec on 10-, 20-, 30-, and 40-cm targets in the horizontal task and on 30°, 50°, 120° and 140° targets in the curvilinear task. Twelve randomly arranged trials were given to each subject in this experiment.

Two separate three-way analyses of variance tests (2 × 3 × 4) having blind/sighted (groups), retention intervals, and target positions as the main variables were used to examine accuracy of kinesthetic recall on the linear and curvilinear tasks.

Materials.   A linear slide as reported by Adams and Dijkstra (1966) was used for the horizontal task. It was 55 cm in length mounted with a starting lever and a stop peg. Sliding the lever gave nearly frictionless movement, and it could be stopped by the experimenter at any desired target by fixing the stop peg.

For studying curvilinear movement, a D-shaped apparatus as reported by Stelmach (1969) was used. The radius of the semicircle was 22.5 cm and each angle was separated by a gap of 4 mm. A stop peg was used to stop movement at any target as the subject moved along the arc.

Subjects.   In this experiment, 18 congenitally blind and 18 sighted adults volunteered as subjects. Blind subjects had been sightless since birth and they were staying or working in a local workshop for the blind. Both blind and sighted subjects were matched on educational attainments and intelligence. Only right-handed subjects were included in the sample.

Results and Discussion

Horizontal Task.   Table 27.1 shows average absolute error scores of blind and sighted subjects. An analysis of the variance test revealed significant effects of two main varaibles [i.e., groups, $F(1, 34) = 17.96$, $p < .01$, and

TABLE 27.1
Means and S.D. for Absolute Errors of Blind and Sighted Groups on the
Horizontal Task

Targets (cm)	Recall Intervals (sec)	Sighted Group		Blind Group	
		Mean	S.D.	Mean	S.D.
10	5	2.63	1.74	5.81	6.68
	20	2.82	1.62	6.48	6.15
	90	2.93	2.67	10.70	10.01
20	5	2.08	1.61	3.31	3.90
	20	2.22	2.02	7.41	7.29
	90	3.78	3.26	7.06	4.79
30	5	2.44	1.75	4.67	3.78
	20	3.99	3.35	3.91	2.69
	90	4.02	4.28	4.25	3.96
40	5	2.05	1.30	3.77	2.56
	20	2.34	2.25	3.97	4.06
	90	3.97	2.82	6.98	6.03

TABLE 27.2
Means and S.D. for Algebraic Errors of Blind and Sighted Groups on the
Horizontal Task

Targets (cm)	Recall Intervals (sec)	Sighted Group		Blind Group	
		Mean	S.D.	Mean	S.D.
10	5	1.16	3.02	5.81	6.68
	20	1.78	2.78	6.26	6.39
	90	2.28	3.28	10.20	10.55
20	5	0.31	2.67	3.02	4.14
	20	−1.28	2.75	6.19	8.41
	90	0.24	5.07	4.84	7.14
30	5	−0.86	2.93	2.93	5.32
	20	−0.46	5.28	1.39	4.62
	90	1.10	5.85	2.19	5.45
40	5	−1.10	2.20	1.71	4.30
	20	−1.11	3.10	−1.62	5.48
	90	−2.70	4.12	1.02	9.32

recall intervals, $F(2, 68) = 6.09, p < .01$], but the target effect was not significant. Recall intervals × targets was the only first-order interaction that was significant: $F(6, 204) = 6.06, p < .01$. The most interesting result of this analysis was obtained in the second-order effect: $F(6, 204 = 10.21, p < .01$, which revealed the conjoint effect of the three variables in this experiment. This result indicates that there was a difference between recall accuracy of blind and sighted subjects when they estimated near and far target lengths at different recall intervals.

Further confirmation of the results was obtained in the analysis of algebraic errors of blind and sighted subjects. These errors for both groups are reported in Table 27.2. Identical ANOVA tests as computed for absolute errors revealed a significant difference between blind and sighted groups: $F(1, 34) = 16.48, p < .01$. The effect of targets was also significant: $F(3, 102) = 7.80, p < .01$, and this finding shows that near targets were overestimated and far targets underestimated. Another interesting feature of this analysis is that the second-order effect was again found significant: $F(6, 204) = 5.96, p < .01$.

Curvilinear Task. Average absolute errors of blind and sighted subjects are shown in Table 27.3. An analysis of variance tests yielded significant effects of two main variables: groups, $F(1, 34) = 16.48, p < .01$; and recall intervals, $F(2, 68) = 6.09, p < .01$. As obtained in the analysis of absolute errors of the horizontal task, target length did not affect the results significantly.

Besides the significant effect of recall intervals × targets, $F(6, 204) = 3.58, p < .01$, the groups × targets effect was also found significant: $F(1, 34) = 16.48, p < .01$. This latter finding on the curvilinear task that was not

TABLE 27.3

Means and S.D. for Absolute Errors of Blind and Sighted Groups on the
Curvilinear Task

Targets (°)	Recall Intervals (sec)	Sighted Group		Blind Group	
		Mean	S.D.	Mean	S.D.
30	5	4.66	3.18	16.66	27.40
	20	6.00	3.02	20.22	25.81
	90	8.61	7.06	48.94	52.34
50	5	4.55	3.41	13.38	14.68
	20	4.33	3.78	19.33	17.72
	90	15.66	16.21	35.00	35.93
120	5	8.38	8.28	12.88	9.57
	20	8.11	7.51	14.16	13.32
	90	15.66	16.56	17.22	12.87
140	5	6.66	5.45	8.33	6.48
	20	6.16	5.47	8.83	6.11
	90	14.44	13.18	19.33	19.79

obtained with the horizontal task indicates that the extent of absolute errors on this task decreased among blind subjects with increase in the length of targets, but this was not so in the case of sighted subjects. However, the significant second-order interaction, $F(6, 204) = 10.21, p < .01$, available in this analysis bears resemblance to the results obtained in the horizontal task.

Mean algebraic errors obtained in the curvilinear task are reported in Table 27.4. An analysis of variance tests on this data yielded significant differences for groups: $F(1, 34) = 12.42, p < .01$; targets, $F(3, 102) = 7.71, p < .01$; and recall intervals, $F(2, 78) = 4.22, p < .01$. As was the case in the horizontal task ANOVA, groups × targets intervals was significant; $F(2, 68) = 4.68, p < .01$. This indicates that sighted subjects did not show much variation in overshooting or undershooting with lapse of time, in contrast to blind subjects who tended to overshoot particularly short targets more, with increase in the recall intervals. A further interesting picture of this analysis was obtained in the second-order significant interaction consisting of groups × recall intervals × targets [$F(6, 204) = 3.40, p < .01$], which shows that the overshooting tendency of blind subjects tended to decline with increase in target length and recall intervals, whereas the sighted group did not show this tendency to any remarkable extent.

A very interesting common result in both horizontal and curvilinear tasks is that blind and sighted subjects differed in interaction with targets and recall intervals. The difference between these two groups is most conspicuous when their performance is compared at the 90-sec delay in recall at the nearest target. The results support the hypothesis that sighted subjects preprogram their movements for the short targets by deriving support from their visual reference system. On the other hand, in the absence of any visual reference

TABLE 27.4
Means and S.D. for Algebraic Errors of Blind and Sighted Groups on the
Curvilinear Task

Targets (°)	Recall Intervals (sec)	Sighted Group		Blind Group	
		Mean	S.D.	Mean	S.D.
30	5	0.77	5.70	16.33	27.61
	20	5.11	4.43	19.88	26.08
	90	7.83	7.99	48.94	52.34
50	5	2.88	4.98	9.94	17.34
	20	0.00	5.85	15.11	21.63
	90	11.66	19.46	24.55	37.36
120	5	0.27	11.95	0.22	16.35
	20	1.33	11.14	5.83	18.81
	90	−10.77	20.27	7.00	20.68
140	5	3.11	8.15	5.77	8.96
	20	0.50	8.36	−2.27	10.70
	90	−2.88	19.64	5.88	27.40

system, blind subjects depend on their memory for movement alone, and this is susceptible to decay at longer recall intervals. Therefore, it is not surprising that the difference between blind and sighted groups was highest at the 90-sec interval.

The question that remains unanswered is: Why do blind and sighted groups fail to differ with the same magnitude at long targets as compared to their difference at short targets? In fact, the available data indicate that blind subjects even gave better performance than sighted subjects on long targets. One explanation for this result is that with the increase in length of targets the movements of subjects in both groups were guided by feedback and this probably undermined the relative advantage of the visual reference system available to the sighted group.

EXPERIMENT 2

Method

Experimental Design and Procedure. A $2 \times 2 \times 3 \times 5$ analysis of variance design (within subjects) having blind and sighted subjects (groups), location, and distance (cues); 5-, 20-, 90-sec recall intervals; and 10-, 15-, 20-, 25-, and 50-cm target positions for the horizontal task or 30°, 50°, 70°, 90° and 110° target positions for the curvilinear task as main variables was employed. Each subject was given 15 trials randomly arranged with respect to target positions and recall intervals.

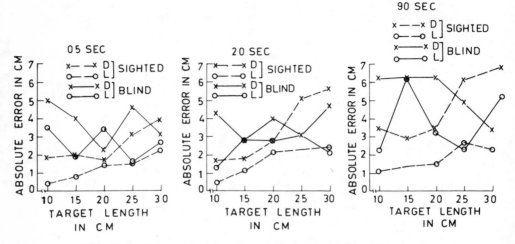

FIG. 27.1. Average absolute errors of blind and sighted subjects on the horizontal task.

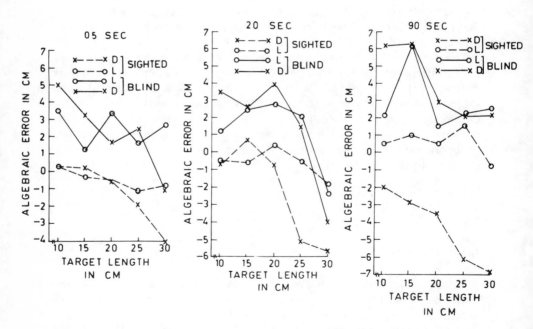

FIG. 27.2. Average algebraic errors of blind and sighted subjects on the horizontal task.

The procedure of this experiment is identical to Experiment 1 except that the subjects were tested on the location or distance cues. In a location task, the subject, after having made a standard movement up to a target point and returned to the starting point soon after, was asked to reach the same target point from a starting point that was halfway between the end point and the stopper. In a distance task, a movement of the same extent as on the standard trial was requested from a starting point that was halfway between the end point and the stopper.

Materials.   Materials were the same as described in Experiment 1.

Subjects.   Twenty subjects, 10 congenitally blind and 10 sighted, participated in each experiment—horizontal and curvilinear. Subjects were matched with respect to age, sex, intelligence, and academic record.

Results and Discussion

Horizontal Task.   Absolute and algebraic errors of subjects obtained in this experiment are shown in Fig. 27.1 and 27.2, respectively. Analysis of absolute errors showed groups $[F(1, 16) = 17.48, p < .01]$, cues $[F(1, 16) = 38.85, p < .01]$, and recall intervals $[F(2, 32) = 10.03, p < .01]$ as significant. Among first-order interactions only groups × targets was significant $[F(4, 64) = 4.94, p < .01]$. Separate analyses of the location and distance tasks based on simple main effects yielded some useful information. In the location task, blind and sighted subjects were found significantly different at shorter targets only. This supported the hypothesis that sighted subjects would do better than blind subjects on shorter targets. Analysis of the distance task has revealed an even more interesting result for these two groups. Although the performance of blind subjects was poorer than sighted at shorter targets in much as on the location task, at longer targets their performance became superior, particularly with delay in recall, to that of sighted subjects. Analysis of algebraic errors based on an ANOVA test similar to one used for absolute errors support this conclusion much more clearly. In this analysis the sighted group was consistently found superior to the blind group on short targets irrespective of delay in recall, but as length of target increased, their performance became significantly inferior to that of the blind group $[F(1, 16) = 24.80, p < .01]$. This result strongly supports the hypothesis that blind subjects utilize their movement cues more effectively than sighted subjects.[1] To verify

---

[1]To check the consistency of the horizontal task data, a comparison between blind and sighted groups was also made on the vertical task following an experimental design similar to one used for the horizontal task. A striking resemblance between the two tasks was recorded. The two groups differed on the vertical task in much the same way as they did on the horizontal task. To save space and avoid repetition, the analysis of this task is not reported in this chapter. However, figures and the analyses of data on the vertical task are available from the author upon request.

this finding, an identical experiment involving curvilinear movements was conducted.

Curvilinear Task. Figures 27.3 and 27.4 show absolute and algebraic errors of this experiment. The results of absolute error analysis yielded significant effects of all the main factors: groups [$F(1, 16) = 33.49, p < .01$]; cues [$F(1, 16) = 93.46, p < .01$]; recall intervals [$F(2, 32) = 6.03, p < .01$]; and targets [$F(4, 64) = 10.90, p < .01$]. The interaction effects were insignificant. The computation of simple main effects separately for the distance and location data revealed some different results in contrast to linear task analysis. The most interesting finding for the location task was that blind and sighted groups did not differ from each other at short recall intervals (i.e., 5 and 20 sec), but they did differ at a delayed recall interval (i.e., 90 sec). This finding is also supported in the analysis of algebraic errors for 90-sec delay at short targets. These results show that on a curvilinear task blind subjects make effective use of their kinesthetic cues and perform almost equally as well as their sighted counterparts. However, it was only at the 90-sec recall interval when much of the movement information is lost that sighted subjects were found superior. Analysis of absolute errors of the distance task did not reveal any significant difference between the two groups at the 5-sec recall interval but differed at short targets upon delay in recall.

Analysis of algebraic errors did not yield any significant difference between the two groups. This is in sharp contrast to the finding reported for the horizontal task on which blind and sighted subjects differed to a very great extent. This finding, therefore, supports the hypothesis that blind subjects fail to take advantage of their kinesthetic cues owing to a mismatch between their standard and test movements.

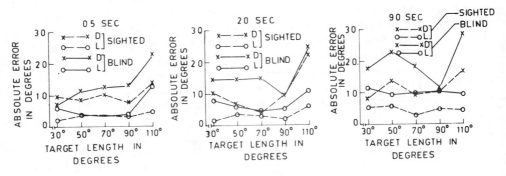

FIG. 27.3. Average absolute errors of blind and sighted subjects on the curvilinear task.

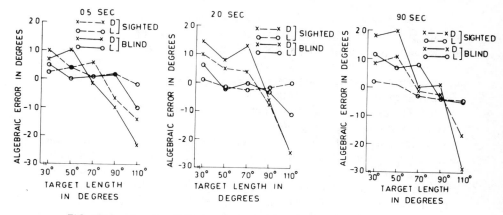

FIG. 27.4. Average algebraic errors of blind and sighted subjects on the curvilinear task.

GENERAL DISCUSSION AND CONCLUSIONS

The findings reported here show consistently that blind subjects were poorer than sighted subject in their recall accuracy of short targets involving simple reproduction of movements. The results of this study imply that sighted subjects did derive benefit from their visual reference system in producing a response that matched the standard movement more accurately than blind subjects did. These results also indicate that although movement involves kinesthetic feedback, a visual reference system can integrate with the kinesthetic system to guide a response. On the other hand, the differences between these two groups narrowed, or even reversed, with the increase in length of targets. If long movements operate under feedback control, the superior performance of the blind group is obviously expected because of their greater dependence on kinesthetic information.

The results obtained on the location and distance cues extend these findings. Because sighted subjects showed less errors than blind subjects in recalling short targets of the horizontal task, the advantage of the visual reference system alone can be considered responsible for this difference. On the other hand, the curvilinear movements of both blind and sighted groups were not significantly different on the same location task. The results are even more interesting for the distance task. Although blind and sighted groups did not differ on the curvilinear movements, they differed on the horizontal task; the performance of the blind group was superior to the sighted group on long targets and vice versa.

A plausible explanation can be given for these findings. It seems that sighted subjects are unable to derive benefits from their visual reference system while making a curvilinear movement. In other words, integration of kinesthetic information with information arising from the visual reference system provides an important clue that explains superior performance of the sighted group on short targets of the horizontal task, irrespective of the location or distance cues. Conversely, when kinesthetic cues alone are relied upon in the distance task, sighted subjects perform poorer than blind subjects on long targets of the horizontal task.

This interpretation is strongly supported by the absence of a difference between blind and sighted groups in their use of the distance cue in making curvilinear movements. Due to a mismatch between the standard movement and the test movement both the groups perform in the same way, particularly at long targets. However, this explanation does not account for the difference between blind and sighted groups with the location cue, for this task invovles partial use of the original format of movement and no mismatch exists between the standard and test movements. Another reason may be that the location task with a curvilinear movement facilitates organization of movement (Diewart & Stelmach, 1977). It is well established that some points in the curvilinear task (e.g., 90° point) cause spatial coding (Stelmach 1970). The upward or downward movement on an angular task itself may become a strong cue. However, a word of caution is added here regarding this interpretation. Because horizontal and curvilinear movements cannot be compared simultaneously owing to difficulty in defining the exact length of movements on these two types of tasks in an identical way, this conclusion remains tentative.

There is also evidence that blind subjects consistently estimated both near and far targets longer than their sighted counterparts. Previous researchers reported that short targets are overestimated and long targets underestimated. By and large, this trend was observed in both groups of this study, but the longer responses of the blind group compared with the sighted group in almost all the conditions show the behavioral characteristic of this group. It seems that in the absence of a visual reference system their responses are not firmly controlled by a motor program, but tend to be guided by feedback control. This interpretation receives support from a recent study by Miller (1977). She reported that blind subjects rely on movement sequences, whereas sighted subjects can use some form of spatial layout.

Taking a clue from the aforementioned results, it is worthwhile to examine some of the implications of the motor program theory for this study. First, an attempt is made to link the differences between blind and sighted groups on short targets with the difference in the nature of their programming, which is guided in the sighted group predominantly by the visual reference system and in the blind group by the kinesthetic source. However, no attempt is made to answer how feedback control as well as programming may operate for short movements. Second, given that long movements operate under feedback, it is not surprising to find blind subjects performing better than sighted subjects because they use and depend on kinesthetic cues to a great extent. Finally, to produce a response, the unit that evaluates feedback, namely the template or comparison center, must receive matching information, for if any mismatch is introduced, as in case of the curvilinear movements with distance cues, the relative advantages would be lost. The lack of difference between blind and sighted groups in such a case bears testimony to it.

ACKNOWLEDGMENTS

This study is supported by a grant from the Department of Social Welfare, Government of India. The author would like to express his gratitude to Mr. S. Singh, Ms. M. Rana, and Mr. K. Pathak for their work in collection and analyses of data. The author is also grateful to Dr. O. B. Sayeed for analyzing data on the computer.

REFERENCES

Adams, J. A., & Dijkstra, S. Short-term memory for motor responses. *Journal of Experimental Psychology*, 1966, *71*, 314–318.

Diewert, G. L., & Stelmach, G. E. *Perceptual organization in motor learning.* Unpublished report, Motor Behavior Laboratory, University of Wisconsin, Madison, Wis., 1977.

Hermelin, B., & O'Connor, N. Location and distance estimates by blind and sighted children. *Quarterly Journal of Experimental Psychology*, 1975, *27*, 295–301.

Keele, S. W. Movement control in skilled motor performance. *Psychological Bulletin*, 1968, *70*, 387–403.

Keele, S. W., & Summers, J. J. The structure of motor programs. In G. E. Stelmach (Ed.), *Motor control: Issues and trends.* New York: Academic Press, 1976.

Klapp, S. T. Feedback versus motor programming in the control of aimed movements. *Journal of Experimental Psychology: Human Perception and Performance*, 1975, *104*, 147–153.

Laabs, G. J. Retention characteristics of different reproduction cues in motor short-term memory. *Journal of Experimental Psychology*, 1973, *100*, 168–177.

Miller, S. Spatial representation by blind and sighted children. In G. Butterworth (Ed.), *The child's representation of the world.* New York and London: Plenum Press, 1977.

Pepper, R. L., & Herman, L. M. Decay and interference effects in the short-term retention of a discrete motor act. *Journal of Experimental Psychology*, 1970, *83*, 1–18.

Posner, M. I., & Keele, S. W. Attention demands of movements. *Proceedings of the XVIth international congress of applied psychology*, Amsterdam, Swets & Zeittinzer, 1969, 418–422.

Stelmach, G. E. Short-term motor retention as a function of response-similarity. *Journal of Motor Behavior*, 1969, *1*, 37–44.

Stelmach, G. E. Kinesthetic recall and information reduction activity. *Journal of Motor Behavior*, 1970, *3*, 183–194.

Stelmach, G. E. Retention of motor skills. *Exercise and Sport Sciences Reviews*, 1974, *2*, 1–26.

Stelmach, G. E., & Wilson, M. Kinesthetic retention, movement extent, and information processing. *Journal of Experimental Psychology*, 1970, *85*, 425–430.

28 Repeated Negatives in Item Recognition: Nonmonotonic Lag Functions

Roger Ratcliff
Dartmouth College
New Hampshire, United States

William E. Hockley
University of Toronto
Canada

ABSTRACT

The interaction of two different types of information used in item recognition is examined in three experiments using a study–test procedure. On each trial, the subject studies 16 words presented singly. The test list consists of single words to which the subject has to respond *old* or *new* by pressing either of two buttons. Both old and new words in the test list may be tested once or twice. The data of main interest are reaction time and accuracy for the second test of new words as a function of lag between the first and second tests. At lag 0, reaction time is short and accuracy high; at lags 2, 3, and 4, reaction time is long and accuracy, low; at longer lags, reaction time decreases and accuracy improves. This non-monotonicity is inconsistent with unelaborated versions of several models of memory retrieval and forces the addition of a process that allows a response to a test word to be based on the subject's memory of the previous response to the word. A three-boundary random walk model is proposed to explain the data, and the relation of this model to other current models in the item recognition literature is considered.

INTRODUCTION

An item in memory may have stored with it information about past occurrences of the item. In this chapter, we investigate the interaction of two different kinds of such information. One kind of information may indicate that the item was recently encountered. We call this *recency information;* it has been modeled by concepts such as strength (Wickelgren & Norman,

1966), short-term memory (Atkinson & Shiffrin 1968), and list markers (Anderson & Bower, 1972). A second kind of information that may be stored with the internal representation of an item is information that allows the subject to remember what response has been made to an earlier test of the item. This can be called *response information* (Theios, *et al.,* 1973).

The interaction between response information and recency information in memory retrieval has been neglected in recent research. Several models make no explicit provision for the use of response information (Atkinson & Juola, 1973; Wickelgren & Norman, 1966). In these models, processing an item changes only its recency (strength or familiarity); no information is stored in memory as to the response made to the item. This chapter demonstrates the inadequacy of such models by showing that response information interacts in a significant way with recency information to determine speed and accuracy of recognition.

Three experiments are presented in this chapter. In each, a study–test procedure was used. Subjects were presented with a 16-word study list followed by a test list of either 32 or 52 words, presented one at a time. For each test word, subjects were required to respond *old* if the test word had appeared in the study list and *new* if it had not. Some of both the old and the new words in the test list were repeated; the data of main theoretical interest are the accuracy and latency of the responses to these repeated words as a function of the lag between repetitions.

The hypothesis tested by these experiments is that a response to the first presentation of a test word in the test list leaves two kinds of information available in memory: response information and recency information. If the response was correct, then the response information in memory will serve to make the response to a second presentation of the same test item faster and more likely to be accurate. Recency information, on the other hand, may aid recognition on the second presentation of a repeated old word but hinder performance on the second presentation of a repeated new word. A further hypothesis is that the decay characteristics of response information and recency information are not the same; thus, whether response or recency information dominates when a word is presented for a second test may depend on the lag between the first and second tests. When recency information dominates, correct responses to the second tests of repeated old words should be faster and more accurate than correct responses to the second tests of repeated new words.

EXPERIMENT 1

Experiment 1 was performed to investigate reaction time and accuracy for the second presentation in the test list of old and new words as a function of the lag between the first and second presentations.

Method

Subjects. Four University of Toronto undergraduates served as subjects and were paid for their participation. All subjects completed 1 practice and 12 experimental sessions.

Apparatus. List generation, display, and response recording were controlled by a PDP-12A laboratory computer. The subjects responded on a six-key response panel connected to the computer via six sense lines. For each response, the key pressed and the latency of the response (measured from the onset of the test word to the key press) were recorded. The measurements of latency were accurate to 5 msec.

Procedure. Each session was made up of 40 study–test trials. Each trial consisted of the presentation of 16 study words followed by 32 test words. The test list was composed of 10 study words (selected randomly) of which 6 were presented twice and 10 new words of which 6 were presented twice. Thus the test list was composed of half old and half new words.

The study words were presented in an unrestricted random order. Test words were presented in a random order with the following restriction: Of the 12 test words to be repeated, two old words and two new words were randomly selected. For each of these words, a lag (the number of intervening words between each presentation of a repeated word) between 0 and 7 was randomly selected. Then one old and one new word were positioned in the first half of the test list and one old and one new word were positioned in the second half of each test list; then their repetitions were positioned to satisfy the lag determined by the random draw. This procedure guaranteed extra numbers of short lags (0–7) in both halves of the test lists. Finally, the remaining test words (both repeated and nonrepeated) were randomly placed in the empty positions of the test list. Lags longer than 7 were obtained by this random placement.

For each session, words were selected randomly without replacement from the Toronto Word Pool, a collection of 1080 common two-syllable English words not more than eight letters long with homophones, contractions, archaic words, and proper nouns deleted. The study words were shown individually for 750 msec per item with a 250-msec blank interval between words. The presentation of the test words was self-paced with the next word appearing 500 msec after a response. A row of question marks presented for 1.5 sec separated the study and test lists. The subject initiated each study trial.

The subject's task was to respond *old* if a word had been a member of the study list and *new* if the word had not been in the study list regardless of whether or not the word had been repeated in the test list. The subjects responded on the six-key response panel where the keys indicated, from left to right, *sure new, probably new, maybe new, maybe old, probably old,* and *sure old.*

The subjects were instructed to respond both as accurately and as quickly as possible, but the emphasis was placed on accuracy. After each session, subjects were given feedback on the accuracy of their performance. Each session took less than one hour to complete and no subject did more than one session per day.

Results

Figure 28.1 shows accuracy and latency as a function of test position for high-confidence (sure) responses to once-presented (1P) old and new words. These results are similar to results usually obtained in the study–test paradigm (Murdock, 1974; Murdock & Anderson, 1975; Ratcliff & Murdock, 1976),

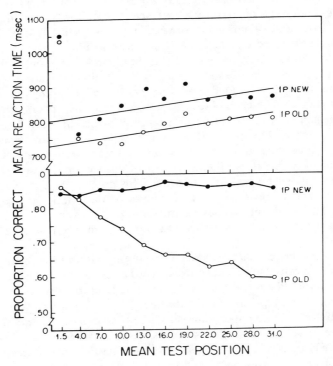

FIG. 28.1.   Mean reaction time and proportion of correct high-confidence responses of 1P items as a function of mean test position for Experiment 1. (Best-fitting linear functions derived from means excluding first and second test positions. For 1P new, RT = 805.13 + 2.79X; for 1P old, RT = 731.52 + 2.95X.)

which suggests that processing has not been radically altered by the addition to the test list of repeated words. (Note that the slow response latencies at the first and second test positions are the result of some inertia on the part of the subject in switching from the study to the test phase, see Murdock & Anderson, 1975.)

Figure 28. 2 shows the results of interest; accuracy and latency for high-confidence responses to the second presentation (2P) of twice-presented old and new words (for which the response on the first presentation was correct) as a function of lag from the first presentation. For 2P new words, the lag function is nonmonotonic in both accuracy and latency. At 0 lag, accuracy is high and latency is fast; at intermediate lags 2, 3, and 4, accuracy is relatively low and latency, slow; and as lag becomes very long, 8 to 32, accuracy becomes somewhat higher and latency, somewhat faster. The implications of these data are discussed after presentation of Experiment 2.

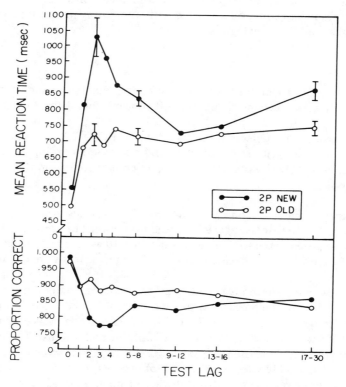

FIG. 28.2. Mean reaction time and proportion of correct high-confidence responses to 2P items conditionalized on correct first presentation responses as a function of test lag for Experiment 1. Longer test lags are blocked as indicated. The bars indicate representative standard errors for the reaction-time means. The standard errors of the proportions are all less than .02.

There were very few lower-confidence responses (less than 7% of the responses were not high confidence) and the proportion of lower-confidence responses as a function of lag was approximately constant, except at lag 0 where there were very few such responses. Thus the use of the confidence-judgment procedure gave little additional information.

EXPERIMENT 2

Experiment 2 was designed to replicate Experiment 1. The only differences were that selection of lags for repeated words was more strictly controlled so that accuracy and latency at a particular lag could be obtained (instead of an average over several lag values as in Experiment 1) and that a yes/no response procedure was used instead of a confidence–judgment procedure so that error responses and correct 2P responses conditionalized on incorrect first presentation responses could be inspected without needing to take into account the various confidence categories.

Method

Subjects.   Four University of Toronto undergraduates served as subjects and were paid for their participation. All subjects completed 13 sessions.

Apparatus.   The subjects were tested on the PDP-12A computer. As in Experiment 1, list generation, display, and response recording were under computer control. All word lists were again constructed from the Toronto Word Pool.

Procedure.   Each session was made up of 32 study–test trials. Each study list consisted of 16 words and was followed by a test list of 52 words. The test list was composed of the 16 study words of which 10 were repeated and 16 new words of which 10 were repeated. Thus half the test words were old and half were new.

The study words were presented in an unrestricted random order. In the test list, the lags of the repeated words were carefully controlled. There were 10 possible lags: 0, 1, 2, 3, 4, 8, 12, 16, 24, and 32. Each lag was used for one repeated old word and one repeated new word in each test list. The test lists were constructed by the following procedure: First, 10 old words and 10 new words were randomly selected. For each of these words, a lag was randomly selected without replacement from the set of possible lags. This was done independently for old and new words. Then each of these words was fitted into the test list in a random position and each repetition was fitted into the list according to the lag selected. If the second word (the repetition) was to be positioned past the end of the test list, a new random position was chosen and the cycle repeated. This procedure was continued until all 20 words and their repetitions were fitted into the test list. Then the remainder of the old and new words were randomly selected and positioned in the remaining unfilled positions of the test list.

The study list words were presented individually for 750 msec per word with a 250-msec blank interval between words. The presentation of test words was self-paced with the next word appearing 250 msec after a response. Subjects were required to respond *yes* if the test word was in the study list and *no* otherwise.

In all other respects, Experiment 2 was identical to Experiment 1.

Results

Figure 28.3 shows accuracy and latency as a function of test position for 1P words. These results replicate those shown in Fig. 28.1. Figure 28.4 shows the lag functions for 2P old and new words; these are similar to those shown in

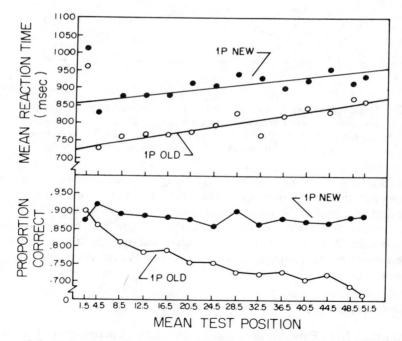

FIG. 28.3.   Mean reaction time and proportion correct of 1P items as a function of mean test position for Experiment 2. (Best fitting linear functions derived from means excluding first and second test positions. For 1P new, RT = 856.55 + 1.81X; for 1P old, RT = 721.34 + 2.76X.)

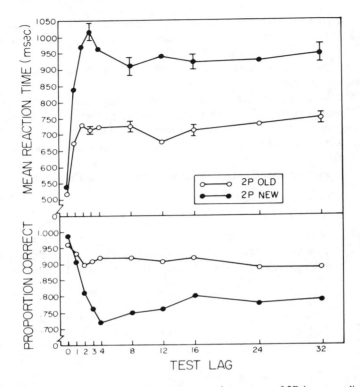

FIG. 28.4.   Mean reaction time and proportion correct of 2P items conditionalized on correct first presentation responses as a function of test lag for
Experiment 2. The bars indicate representative standard errors for the reaction
time means. The standard errors of the proportions are all less than .02.

Fig. 28.2. The function for 2P new words is again nonmonotonic. Figure 28.5
shows accuracy for 2P responses conditionalized on an incorrect response to
the first presentation. Accuracy increases from a relatively low value at lag 0
to a moderate value at longer lags, but the function does not appear nonmonotonic. (Note that with the relatively small number of responses contributing to the measured accuracy, there is not enough sensitivity to detect
nonmonotonicity if it were there.)

Discussion

The results from Experiments 1 and 2 show that both accuracy and latency as
a function of lag are nonmonotonic for 2P new words. This nonmonotonicity
suggests the operation of two opposing factors, one dominating over short
lags, 0, 1, and 2, using information about the response to the first presentation, and the other dominating over intermediate and longer lags using

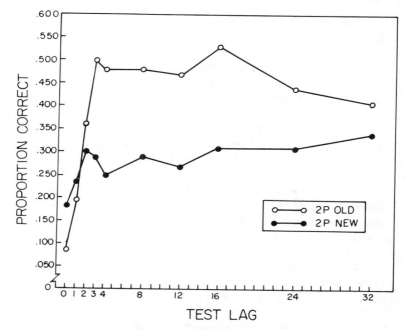

FIG. 28.5.   Proportion correct of 2P items conditionalized on incorrect first presentation responses as a function of test lag for Experiment 2. The standard errors of the proportions are all less than .04.

recency information. At very short lags, response information is available; this information leads to fast and accurate responses (given that the response to the first presentation was correct). At intermediate lags, response information has been forgotten and recency information competes, leading to slower and less accurate responses for 2P new items (for 2P old items both response information and recency work together). At longer lags, recency information has been lost and latency and accuracy both improve a little. Thus, we can explain the nonmonotonic lag function in terms of fast decaying response information and more slowly decaying recency information.

This two-factor explanation for the nonmonotonic lag function gains support from the data for correct responses to 2P items conditionalized on an incorrect first presentation response. We assume that at short lags the subject is using response information. Then, if the subject made an incorrect first presentation response, he should be more likely to make an incorrect 2P response. At longer lags, the subject should have lost the response information and accuracy should improve. This is just what is shown in Fig. 28.5.

If we accept the hypothesis that there are two factors giving rise to the nonmonotonic function, then the simplest kind of model is one that asssumes a probability mixture of two processes. Suppose that there is one fast process based on response information that produces fast reaction times (e.g., 500 msec; see Fig. 28.2) at short lags and a second, slower process based on recency information that competes at intermediate lags producing slower reaction times. As the recency information is forgotten, reaction times speed up again slightly. Thus the nonmonotonic lag function is composed of a high proportion of fast processes at short lags and a high proportion of slow processes at intermediate and long lags.

There is an easy way to test the assumption of a probability mixture of two processes if the two individual processes are stationary and the only change in reaction time as a function of lag is a change in the relative proportion of the two distributions. This assumption predicts that reaction distributions for responses at each lag will be bimodal. In fact, it can be seen by inspection that the reaction-time distributions are unimodal. Table 28.1 shows parameter averages across subjects for the convolution of normal and exponential distributions fitted to observed reaction-time distributions for Experiment 2. This convolution model (Ratcliff, 1978; Ratcliff, 1979; Ratcliff & Murdock, 1976) has been used as an empirical summary of the reaction-time distributions found in memory retrieval paradigms. In the model, there are three parameters: μ and σ are the mean and standard deviation, respectively, of the normal distribution, and τ is the mean of the exponential distribution. Changes in the parameter μ reflect changes in the leading edge or mode of the distribution; changes in τ represent spread in the tail of the distribution. In the previous case (two stationary processes), bimodality at lags 1 and 2 would show up as no change in μ between lags 0, 1, and 2. In Table 28.1, this pattern is not observed; both μ and τ increase (τ faster than μ) and σ increases a little

TABLE 28.1

Parameter Values (averaged across subjects) for Fits of
the Distribution that Is the Convolution of Normal and
Exponential Distributions to the Observed Reaction-
Time Distributions for 2P (twice-presented) New Items
in Experiment 2

Test Lag	μ	σ	τ
0	406	34	135
1	484	60	340
2	517	70	429
3	530	73	433
4	538	78	403
8	506	59	363
12	487	51	410
16	518	57	374
24	491	53	385
32	496	62	390

Note: μ, σ, and τ are measured in milliseconds.

as a function of lag (cf. Ratcliff & Murdock, 1976). (Note that chi-square values for goodness of fit of the convolution model range from 4.7 with 10 degrees of freedom for the best fit to 34.4 with 9 degrees of freedom for the worst fit. These fits are somewhat better than those displayed in Ratcliff, 1979, Fig. 3.) Thus, the hypothesis that the nonmonotonic lag function for 2P new items is the result of a probability mixture of two processes, each process stationary as a function of lag, and changes in reaction time resulting from a change in the proportion of the two processes, can be dismissed.

Let us now describe an alternative two-factor view using the retrieval model proposed by Ratcliff (1978). In that model, a test item makes contact with the representation of each study item in memory. We shall further assume that the test item also makes contact with the representations of test items presented earlier in the list (an assumption left implicit in Ratcliff, 1978, p. 65; see Crowder, 1976, chap. 9). In Ratcliff's model, evidence as to whether the test item matches one of the items contacted in memory is accumulated by a random walk process. If a match occurs, processing immediately terminates with a *yes* response. If none of the comparisons terminates with a match, then, when the last nonmatch terminates, a *no* response is initiated. This model is not able to account for the very fast *no* responses for 2P items at lag 0. This is because the model assumes processing to be exhaustive for nonmatch comparisons; one fast finishing nonmatch comparison cannot speed up the other slower nonmatch comparisons that all must terminate before a *no* response can be made.

To overcome this problem, we propose a generalization of Ratcliff's model that is consistent with the data presented in this chapter (and other data providing similar problems that are discussed later). The *no* responses to 2P new items at zero lag appear to have a strong nondefault character; information about the previous response seems to be used in making the decision. This suggests a comparison process in which there are two nondefault matches (yes and no) and a default nonmatch: a three-boundary random walk (see Audley & Pike, 1965; Laming, 1968). (Note that a similar argument could be made for the existence of two types of *yes* responses, one based on response information and one based on recency information. The resulting four-boundary random walk would not produce any important changes in the qualitative discussion of the three-boundary random walk that follows.)

The three-boundary random walk can be conceptualized as three counters accumulating information: one counter for information leading to a positive response (recency and positive response information), a second counter for negative response information, and a third default counter. A decision is made when the information accumulated in one counter first exceeds the information in the maximum of the other two by some criterial amount. This is a relative stopping criterion and should not be confused with an absolute stopping criterion (Audley & Pike, 1965). The usual two-boundary random walk model with an absolute criterion (starting point, C, and boundaries, A and $-A$) is formally equivalent to a counter model with two counters, one starting with an advantage of C counts, that accumulate information until one counter exceeds the other by the criterial amount ($2A$) (Audley & Pike, 1965; Pike, 1973).

To model the pattern of results obtained in Experiments 1 and 2 with the three-boundary random walk model, it is necessary to make some assumptions about how response information and recency information vary as a function of lag. The assumptions are the same as those made earlier, namely, that response information, available at short lags, decays very quickly and that recency information decays more slowly and so is available at intermediate lags. Given these assumptions, the three-boundary random walk model can account for the nonmonotonic lag functions for 2P words quite simply. At very short lags, response information accumulates quickly in the nondefault negative counter; at intermediate lags, recency information accumulating in the positive counter dominates information accumulating in both the nondefault and default negative counters; finally, at long lags, neither the response nor the recency information dominates. This account of the 2P lag functions is consistent with the shape of the reaction-time distribution as it changes with lag; increases in mean reaction time are mainly due to spread in the distribution, with a smaller increase in reaction time of the fastest responses. This account is also consistent with the result that accuracy increases as the rate of accumulation of information increases.

The major problem with the three-boundary random walk model is that there are far too many parameters and so far too much model freedom. Thus the model cannot make quantitative predictions about data. This does not, however, reduce the usefulness of the model as a metaphor nor detract from the fact that the model can account adequately for both changes in mean reaction times and accuracy and changes in the shape of the reaction-time distribution.

EXPERIMENT 3

Characterizing the retrieval process in terms of three counters suggests that there are at least three separate responses that the subject could make: old; new, first presentation; and new, second presentation. In Experiment 3, subjects were asked to make these responses explicitly; there were three response keys: one for old responses; one for new, first presentation; and one for new, second presentation. By using these three keys, we hope to separate the default and nondefault components in 2P new responses and thus to separate response and recency information.

We could also have separated the responses to first and second presentation old words. We did not do this because we wanted to keep Experiment 3 as analogous as possible to Experiments 1 and 2 and because we wanted to reduce the probability that the subjects would view the task as judgment of frequency.

Method

Experiment 3 is the same as Experiment 2 except that subjects responded by pressing one of three (instead of two) response buttons. The three buttons were placed at positions equidistant from a resting position and the subject responded by moving his index finger from the resting position and depressing the response key. Four subjects were each tested for eight sessions plus one practice session.

Results

The main results are shown in Fig. 28.6 and 28.7. Figure 28.6 shows accuracy and latency as a function of lag for 2P old and 2P new words conditionalized on a first presentation correct response. The interesting result is that the nonmonotonicity found for 2P new words in Experiments 1 and 2 has moved to 2P old words. Otherwise, results are the same as in Experiments 1 and 2; overall reaction time is longer and accuracy is lower for 2P new words compared with 1P new words, and reaction time is shorter and accuracy is higher for 2P old words compared with 1P old words.

There is a further nonmonotonic accuracy function shown in Fig. 28.7, where 2P new words conditionalized on an incorrect first presentation response have a very low probability of being correct at lag 0. The probability increases to a maximum at lag 3 and then decreases again as lag increases further.

The nonmonotonic hit and false alarm rates shown in Fig. 28.6 and 28.7 also lead to nonmonotonic d' functions.

Discussion

In Experiment 3, we added a third response key for responses for the second presentations of new words. Addition of a special response category for 2P new words might have changed the subject's perceived task to a combination of recognition, frequency judgment, and recency judgment. However, the pattern of results for Experiment 3 is much the same as the pattern of results for Experiments 1 and 2. The main exception is that the nonmonotonic lag function that appeared for 2P new word responses in Experiments 1 and 2 appeared for 2P old word responses in Experiment 3.

A clue to the reason for the switch of nonmonotonicity from 2P new words to 2P old words can be found by examining 2P new responses to old words. There is a marked nonmonotonic trend in the proportion of these errors. It is

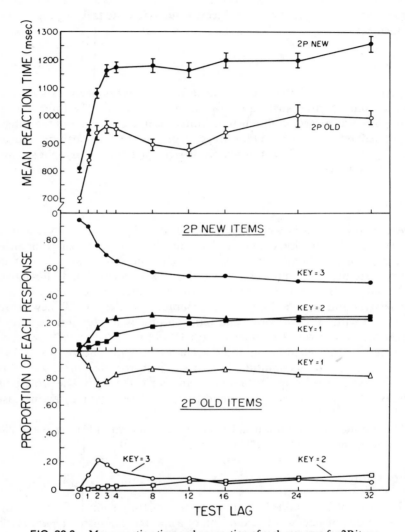

FIG. 28.6. Mean reaction time and proportion of each response for 2P items conditionalized on 1P correct responses as a function of test lag for Experiment 3. The bars indicate standard errors of the reaction-time means. The standard errors of the proportions are all less than .02. (Key = 1 indicates an old response, Key = 2 indicates a 1P new response, and Key = 3 indicates a 2P new response.)

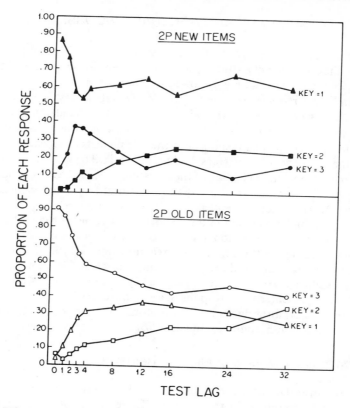

FIG. 28.7.   Proportion of each response to 2P items conditionalized on first presentation incorrect responses as a function of test lag for Experiment 3. The standard errors of the proportions are all less than .05. (Key = 1 indicates an old response, Key = 2 indicates a 1P new response, and Key = 3 indicates a 2P new response.)

as though the subject has decided to respond 2P new if he is sure that the test word is a repetition but not sure whether the word is old or new. In Experiments 1 and 2, if subjects were sure they had seen a test item recently, then they may have been biased toward responding *old* because they viewed the task as detecting old words among new. When a special category for 2P new items was added in Experiment 3, the emphasis shifted to the 2P–1P new discrimination and subjects may have been biased to respond 2P new for words they had seen recently. This can be translated into the three-counter random walk model postulated earlier as follows: Suppose that, for the second test of a repeated test word, recency is very strong but response information is missing. Then, in the two-key procedure in Experiments 1 and 2, criteria are set so that evidence is accumulated toward an old response. On the other hand, in the three-key procedure in Experiment 3, criteria are set so that evidence is accumulated toward a new response.

SUMMARY AND GENERAL DISCUSSION

We performed three experiments that investigated the effect of repeating test items in the test phase of a study–test procedure. Subjects were presented with 16 study words (one at a time) followed by a test list, presented one word at a time, and were required to respond *yes* (or *old*) if the test word was in the study list and *no* (or *new*) otherwise. Some of the old and some of the new words were repeated through the test list. The functional relationships of major interest concerned responses to the second tests of repeated words for which the response to the first test had been correct. The interesting questions were how latency and accuracy of these responses varied as a function of the lag between the two tests of a word. In the first two experiments, the lag function of 2P (twice presented) new items was nonmonotonic. At lag 0, accuracy was high and reaction time, short. At intermediate lags (2, 3, and 4), accuracy was low and reaction time was longer; at longer lags (12, 16, and 24), accuracy became a little higher and reaction time a little shorter than at intermediate lags. In the third experiment, a three-key response panel was used and subjects were required to hit one key for old responses, a second key for 1P (once presented) new responses, and a third key for 2P new responses. It was found that although the nonmonotonic lag function for 2P new items vanished, a nonmonotonic lag function for 2P old items appeared.

Implications for Models of Memory Retrieval

There are several models of memory retrieval that appear inadequate in light of the results presented in this chapter. These are models that employ the concept of strength or familiarity: for example, the Atkinson and Joula model (Atkinson & Juola, 1973; Atkinson, Herrmann, & Wescourt, 1974) and strength theory (Wickelgren & Norman, 1966). Neither of these models is capable of accounting for the fast 2P new responses at 0 lag. Both models would have to predict that reaction times for these responses would be very long and that conditional accuracy (conditional on a correct 1P response) would be very low. They would have to make these predictions because when the word is first tested, strength or familiarity should be very significantly increased and this should lead subjects to respond old when the word is presented for a second test, or at least to respond new very slowly. The thrust of this argument against strength theory is very much in line with the argument presented by Anderson and Bower (1972) who show that a strength theory is incapable of accounting for the levels of list discrimination they obtain in their experiments.

To account for the fast and accurate 2P new responses, it is necessary to postulate an additional process that allows subjects to access and use information stored about the previous response made to that item. To account for the nonmonotonic lag function, it is also necessary to assume that response information is lost much more quickly than strength (recency information). The forgetting function for response information seems remarkably similar in decay rate to the forgetting function for associative information (see Murdock, 1974). This may indicate that the relation between the test word and the response to the test word is associative.

The random walk model for memory retrieval proposed by Ratcliff (1978) also cannot explain the fast 2P new responses at zero lag. This is not because relatedness is assumed to increase in the same way as strength in simple strength theory (Wickelgren & Norman, 1966) because Ratcliff (1978) explicitly notes that relatedness is the product of a mapping from a complex memory representation to a single dimensioned variable and it is certainly possible for response information to contribute to relatedness. Rather, the problem lies in the assumption that processing of negatives is parallel and exhaustive. This means that one fast finishing process cannot influence the overall negative reaction time because all other comparisons must terminate. Ratcliff's model can be extended to account for the nonmonotonic lag functions in the following way. The nature of the 2P new response at zero lag does not seem to have the default character of the negative responses in Ratcliff's original model; rather it seems to have a positive (self-terminating) character. To model this, we can move to a three-boundary random walk (Audley & Pike, 1965) where there is a default negative boundary, a positive boundary, and a nondefault negative boundary. This model is capable of explaining the patterns of results found in the experiments presented in this chapter.

Some Relationships Between the Multiboundary Random Walk and Other Models

The three-boundary random walk has interesting properties that relate it to other theoretical views. First, consider the model of Schneider and Shiffrin (1977) for memory scanning tasks. It has two components: controlled and automatic processing. Ratcliff's (1978) model is able to account for the controlled processing component by assuming that processing is parallel and modeling the processing by a two-boundary random walk with positive and default negative boundaries. In moving from controlled to automatic processing, subjects are assumed to learn the appropriate response (see Shiffrin & Schneider, 1977, Fig. 11) to the stimulus. This can be modeled by a three-boundary random walk with a positive, a default negative, and a nondefault negative boundary. Subjects in the controlled processing mode accumulate little evidence in the nondefault counter, and the decision is made on the basis of the positive and default negative counters; this is identical to Ratcliff's (1978) model. On the other hand, when subjects are in the automatic mode, they accumulate little evidence in the default negative counter and the decision is made on the basis of the positive and nondefault negative counters. These two self-terminating processes would be capable of dealing with the relative lack of set size effects found by Shiffrin and Schneider (1977) because, under conditions where the memory set is very well learned, similar amounts of learning would be expected whether the memory set was 1 or 4. Note that as yet we have not considered the visual search component of the Schneider and Shiffrin model.

Second, consider a Sternberg varied set experiment in which the digit 6 whenever presented is always a negative probe (the subject may be explicitly instructed beforehand). It is not difficult to see that reaction time to the digit 6 would decrease and accuracy increase, again leading to problems with the exhaustive processing assumption used in Ratcliff's (1978) model. If we invoke the three-boundary model, then again it is easy to see that the fast responses to the digit 6 can be modeled by the nondefault negative comparison process.

Third, the three-boundary random walk model described earlier can be viewed as a restricted relative of Morton's (1969; 1970) logogen model. The logogen model is concerned with word recognition phenomena and supposes that evidence is accumulated toward a particular word as a response. The evidence boundary for response is a fixed criterion so that as soon as one of the word logogens accumulates enough evidence, a response is made. In contrast the three-boundary random walk uses a relative criterion: The evidence in one counter must exceed the evidence in the maximum of the other counters by a fixed amount before a response can be made.

From these three examples we can see that the three-boundary random walks offers the possibility for some interesting extensions and some interesting comparisons and contrasts with other models.

To conclude, we have shown in this chapter that several models of memory retrieval are inconsistent with the nonmonotonic lag functions for repeated test items that have been presented in this chapter. It is necessary to elaborate the models to include a process that allows the subject to access and use response information in making the decision about list membership.

ACKNOWLEDGMENTS

This research was supported by research grants APA 146 from the National Research Council of Canada and OMHF 164 from the Ontario Mental Health Foundation to B. B. Murdock, Jr.

We would like to acknowledge the help and criticism of Ben Murdock and Gail McKoon.

REFERENCES

Anderson, J. R., & Bower, G. H. Recognition and retrieval processes in free recall. *Psychological Review*, 1972, *79*, 97–123.

Atkinson, R. C., Herrmann, D. J., & Wescourt, K. T. Search processes in recognition memory. In R. L. Solso (Ed.), *Theories in cognitive psychology: The Loyola Symposium*. Hillsdale, N.J.: Lawrence Erlbaum Associates, 1974.

Atkinson, R. C., & Juola, J. F. Factors influencing speed and accuracy of word recognition. In S. Kornblum (Ed.), *Attention and performance IV*. New York: Academic Press, 1973.

Atkinson, R. C., & Shiffrin, R. M. Human memory: A proposed system and its control processes. In K. W. Spence & J. T. Spence (Eds.), *The psychology of learning and motivation: Advances in research and theory* (vol. 2). New York: Academic Press, 1968.

Audley, R. J., & Pike, A. R. Some alternative stochastic models of choice. *British Journal of Mathematical and Statistical Psychology*, 1965, *18*, 207–225.

Crowder, R. G. *Principles of learning and memory*. Hillsdale, N.J.: Lawrence Erlbaum Associates, 1976.

Laming, D. R. *Information theory of choice reaction time*. New York: Wiley, 1968.

Morton, J. The interaction of information in word recognition. *Psychological Review*, 1969, *76*, 165–178.

Morton, J. A functional model for memory. In D. Norman (Ed.), *Models of human memory*. New York: Academic Press, 1970.

Murdock, B. B., Jr. *Human memory: Theory and data*. Potomac, Md.: Lawrence Erlbaum Associates, 1974.

Murdock, B. B., Jr., & Anderson, R. E. Encoding, storage, and retrieval of item information. In R. L. Solso (Ed.), *Theories in cognitive psychology: The Loyola Symposium*. Hillsdale, N.J.: Lawrence Erlbaum Associates, 1975.

Pike, R. Response latency models for signal detection. *Psychological Review*, 1973, *80*, 53–68.

Ratcliff, R. A theory of memory retrieval. *Psychological Review*, 1978, *85*, 59–108.

Ratcliff, R. Group reaction time distributions and an analysis of distribution statistics. *Psychological Bulletin*, 1979, *86*, 446–461.

Ratcliff, R., & Murdock, B. B., Jr. Retrieval processes in recognition memory. *Psychological Review*, 1976, *83*, 190–214.

Schneider, W., & Shiffrin, R. M. Controlled and automatic human information processing. *Psychological Review*, 1977, *86*, 1–66.

Shiffrin, R. M., & Schneider, W. Controlled and automatic human information processing: II. Perceptual learning, automatic attending, and a general theory. *Psychological Review*, 1977, *84*, 127–190.

Theios, J., Smith, P. G., Haviland, S. E., Traupman, J., & Moy, M. C. Memory scanning as a serial self-terminating process. *Journal of Experimental Psychology*, 1973, *97*, 323–336.

Wickelgren, W. A., & Norman, D. A. Strength models and serial position in short-term recognition memory. *Journal of Mathematical Psychology*, 1966, *3*, 316–347.

29

The Octave Illusion and the What–Where Connection

Diana Deutsch
Center for Human Information Processing
University of California, San Diego
La Jolla, California
United States

ABSTRACT

The effects of delivering two sequences of sine wave tones simultaneously, one to each ear, are explored. Where pitch perception is concerned, given certain sequential configurations, the frequencies followed are those presented to one ear rather than to the other; yet given other configurations, following on the basis of frequency proximity or contour occurs instead. The decision as to which following principle is adopted depends on the frequency relationships between the tones as they occur in sequence at the two ears, and this is true even when time intervals of several seconds intervene between successive tones. Where localization is concerned, there is a strong tendency under certain conditions to localize each tone toward the ear receiving the higher-frequency signal, regardless of whether the higher or the lower frequency is perceived.

The experiments show that selection between acoustic stimuli may take place during a stage where these stimuli are fragmented into their separate attributes and that these selection processes can occur according to independent and even contradictory criteria. As a result, given certain configurations, we end up perceiving a stimulus that does not exist. A model is advanced which explains these illusory phenomena and which also explains how we generally manage to arrive at veridical rather than illusory percepts.

INTRODUCTION

This chapter explores the perceptual consequences of delivering two simultaneous streams of sine wave tones, one to each ear. Striking illusions are readily produced by this method. These demonstrate that acoustic stimuli are at some stage fragmented into their separate attributes, that selection processes take place during this stage, and that they can occur in parallel according to independent and in some cases even contradictory criteria. Given this stage of perceptual fragmentation, we must assume that an additional mechanism later operates to recombine these attribute values in such a way as to maximize the probability of veridical perception.

THE OCTAVE ILLUSION

When a pure tone of 400 Hz is presented continuously to one ear and simultaneously a pure tone of 800 Hz is presented at equal amplitude to the other ear, most listeners will perceive both tones and localize them correctly. However, when these same 400- and 800-Hz tones are repetitively presented in alternation, such that when one ear receives 400 Hz, the other ear receives 800 Hz, a very strange phenomenon emerges. Almost no one can guess what this simple stimulus is (at least without prolonged listening), and instead a variety of illusory percepts are obtained (Deutsch, 1974). The most common illusion is that of a single tone that switches from ear to ear, and as it switches, its pitch simultaneously shifts back and forth from high to low; that is, the listener hears a single high tone in one ear alternating with a single low tone in the other ear. The stimulus configuration and this percept are illustrated in Fig. 29.1

It was hypothesized that this illusion results from the operation of two different selection mechanisms underlying the pitch and the localization percepts. To provide the perceived sequence of pitches, the frequencies arriving at one ear are attended to, and those arriving at the other ear are suppressed. But to provide the perceived localizations, each tone is localized in the ear that receives the higher-frequency signal, regardless of whether the higher or the lower frequency is perceived. Thus given a listener who follows the frequencies presented to the right ear, when a high tone is delivered to the right ear and a low tone to the left, this listener hears a high tone because this is the tone delivered to his right ear. Further, he localizes the tone in his right ear, because this ear is receiving the higher-frequency signal. But when a high tone is delivered to the left ear and a low tone to the right, the listener now hears a low tone because this is the tone delivered to his right ear; but he localizes the tone in his left ear, because this ear is receiving the higher-frequency signal. So the entire sequence is heard as a high tone to the right alternating with a low tone to the left. However, given a listener who follows the sequence of frequencies delivered to his left ear instead, keeping the localization rule constant, the same sequence is perceived as a high tone to the

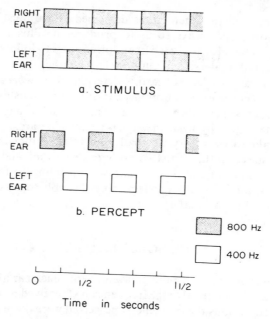

FIG. 29.1.   a. Representation of the stimulus pattern used in Deutsch (1974). Filled boxes represent tones of 800 Hz, and unfilled boxes represent tones of 400 Hz. This pattern was repetitively presented for 20 sec without pause. b. Representation of the illusory percept most commonly obtained (adapted from Deutsch, 1974).

left alternating with a low tone to the right (Deutsch, 1975a). This hypothesis was confirmed in a further study (Deutsch & Roll, 1976).

The question then arises as to whether the interactions underlying these localization and frequency suppression effects take place between pathways relaying information from the two ears or whether instead pathways conveying information from different regions of auditory space are involved. To investigate this issue, the configuration was presented to listeners through spatially separated loudspeakers rather than earphones (Deutsch, 1975a). It was found that the illusion was obtained under these conditions also, even though both sequences were now presented to both ears, with only localization cues to distinguish them. This shows that the octave illusion must have a very complex basis. In order for it to occur with speakers, the listener must first identify, for each simultaneous tone pair, which speaker is emitting the high tone and which, the low. These correct assignments having been made, the information must then travel along pathways that are specific to region in auditory space, and the interactions described above must occur between such second-order pathways so as to produce the illusory percepts. The mechanism responsible for pitch perception chooses to follow the frequencies that are presented to one side of auditory space rather than to the other; that is, the decision as to *what* is heard is determined by *where* the signals are coming from. Yet the localization mechanism chooses instead to follow the higher-frequency signal; that is, the decision as to *where* the stimulus is located is determined by *what* the signal frequencies are.

(For the sake of simplicity we shall refer to the following of the signal presented to one ear rather than to the other as 'ear dominance'. However, the reader should bear in mind that the pathways responsible for this effect are specific to position in auditory space, and not simply to ear of input, and we shall return to this point later).

THE SCALE ILLUSION

In the sequence giving rise to the octave illusion, each ear always received a frequency that was identical to the frequency just received by the opposite ear. Under these conditions the frequencies perceived were those presented to one ear rather than to the other. However, using a different dichotic tonal sequence, Deutsch (1975b) found no ear dominance. Listeners were presented with a major scale, with successive tones alternating from ear to ear. This scale was played simultaneously in both ascending and descending form, such that when a component of the ascending scale was in the right ear, a component of the descending scale was in the left ear and vice versa. The majority of listeners perceived the correct sequence of frequencies, but as two separate melodies; one corresponding to the higher sequence of tones, and the other to the lower sequence. Other listeners perceived instead only a single melody, which corresponded to the higher sequence of tones, and they heard little or nothing of the lower sequence. This illusion is described in detail elsewhere (Deutsch, 1975a, 1975b). However, it should here be noted that, in sharp contrast to the results with the octave sequence, no ear dominance was produced here; instead, following always occurred on the basis of frequency proximity (Bregman, 1978; Dowling, 1973). When only one melody was heard, this corresponded to the higher frequencies and not the lower, regardless of ear of input. Moreover for most listeners, both members of each simultaneous tone pair were perceived and neither was suppressed. This experiment therefore demonstrates that ear dominance cannot be regarded simply in terms of simultaneous interactions but depends on sequential relationships also. A series of experiments was performed to obtain a better understanding of the sequential conditions for producing this effect.

PARAMETRIC STUDIES OF EAR DOMINANCE

Apparatus

Tones were generated as sine waves by two Wavetek function generators (Model No. 155) controlled by a PDP-8 computer. The output was passed through a Crown amplifier and presented to subjects in sound-insulated booths through matched headphones (Grason-Stadler Model No. TDH-49).

Experiment 1

This experiment was designed to test the hypothesis that ear dominance occurs in sequences where the two ears receive the same frequencies in succession, but not otherwise. The experiment employed two conditions. In each condition subjects were presented with sequences consisting of 20 dichotic chords, each 250 msec in duration, with no gaps between them.

The experiment employed the two basic patterns shown in Fig. 29.2. The basic pattern in Condition 1 consisted of the repetitive presentation of a single chord, whose components stood in octave relation and alternated from ear to ear such that when the high tone was in the right ear, the low tone was in the left ear and vice versa. It can be seen that here the two ears did indeed receive the same frequencies in succession. On half the trials the sequence presented

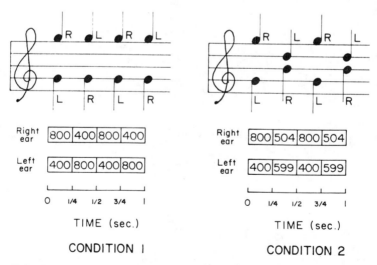

FIG. 29.2. Examples of stimulus configurations used in the two conditions of Experiment 1. Numbers in boxes indicate tonal frequencies. Musical notation is approximate.

to the right ear began with the low tone and ended with the high tone; on the other half this order was reversed. Subjects judged for each sequence whether it began with the high tone and ended with the low tone or whether it began with the low tone and ended with the high tone, and from these judgments it was inferred which ear was being followed for pitch.

The basic pattern in Condition 2 consisted of the repetitive presentation of two dichotic chords in alternation, the first forming an octave and the second a minor third, so that the entire four-tone combination constituted a major triad. It can be seen that here the two ears did not receive the same frequencies in succession. On half the trials the right ear received the upper component of the first chord and the lower component of the last chord; and on the other half this order was reversed.

To evaluate the strength of ear dominance under these two conditions, the amplitude relationships between the tones at the two ears were systematically varied, and the extent to which each ear was followed was plotted as a function of these amplitude relationships. The results, averaged over four subjects, are shown in Fig. 29.3. It can be seen that in Condition 1 the frequencies presented to the dominant ear were followed until a critical level of amplitude relationship was reached, and the nondominant ear was followed beyond this level. So a clear following on the basis of ear of input occurred, and clear ear dominance was obtained. But no such following occurred in Condition 2. Not only was there no ear dominance, but a simple

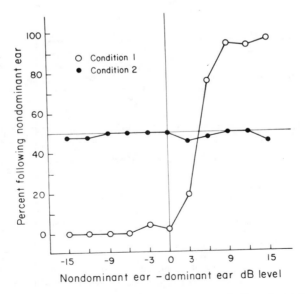

FIG. 29.3.   Percent following of nondominant ear in Experiment 1 as a function of amplitude differences at the two ears. ° Condition 1, and ● Condition 2.

following on the basis of amplitude did not occur either. However, hypothesizing that the subjects were following this sequence on the basis of frequency proximity (Bregman, 1978; Dowling, 1973), a very consistent pattern emerged. All subjects showed consistent following of either the higher frequencies or the lower frequencies, regardless of ear of input or of relative amplitude. Three subjects consistently followed the lower frequencies, and one consistently followed the higher frequencies.

This experiment therefore provides strong evidence that ear dominance occurs in sequences where the two ears receive the same frequencies in succession, but not otherwise.

Experiment 2

This experiment was performed as a further test of the hypothesis. Two conditions were again employed. Here all sequences consisted of two dichotic chords. As shown in Fig. 29.4, the basic pattern in Condition 1 consisted of two presentations of the identical chord, whose components formed an octave, such that one ear received first the high tone and then the low tone, while simultaneously the other ear received first the low tone and then the high tone. The basic pattern in Condition 2 consisted of two chords, each of which formed an octave but which were composed of different frequencies. The combinations shown in Fig. 29.4 were presented in strict alternation.

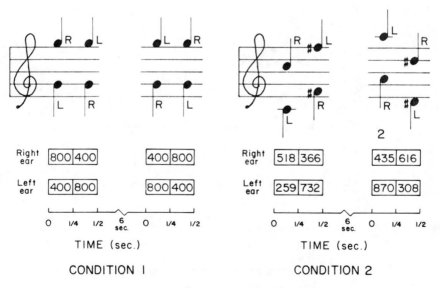

FIG. 29.4.   Examples of stimulus configurations used in the two conditions of Experiment 2. Numbers in boxes indicate tonal frequencies. Musical notation is approximate.

Thus any given frequency combination was repeated only after a substantial time period during which several other frequency combinations were interpolated.

The results of this experiment, averaged over four subjects, are shown in Fig. 29.5. It can be seen that, as expected, clear ear dominance occurred in Condition 1. But there was again a total absence of ear dominance in Condition 2. And, just as in Experiment 1, following by amplitude did not occur either. Assuming, however, that the subjects were responding in this condition on the basis of overall contour, a very consistent result was obtained. Patterns of response always indicated an ascending sequence when the second chord was higher than the first and a descending sequence when the second chord was lower than the first. This always occurred even in the face of substantial amplitude differences between the tones at the two ears.

These two experiments show, therefore, that ear dominance effects occur when the two ears receive the same frequency in succession (or, rather, when the same frequency emanates successively from two different regions of auditory space). When this condition was not fulfilled, following occurred on other lines. We can therefore suggest that ear dominance effects are based on forward inhibitory interactions between elements underlying the same frequency but different spatial locations.

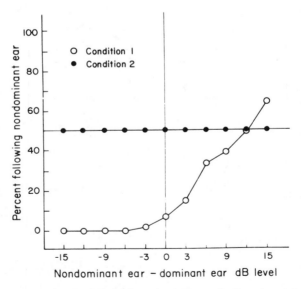

FIG. 29.5.   Percent following of nondominant ear in Experiment 2 as a function of amplitude differences at the two ears: ° Condition 1 and ● Condition 2.

Experiment 3

We now turn to the question of whether the absence of ear dominance found in the second conditions of Experiments 1 and 2 was due simply to the delay between successive presentations of the same frequencies at the two ears or whether this was due to the interpolation of tones of different frequencies or whether both these factors were involved. Experiment 3 explored the effect on ear dominance of interpolating a single tone of different frequency between two dichotic chords of identical frequencies, holding the delay between these chords constant.

The experiment employed the two conditions shown in Fig. 29.6. It can be seen that these conditions were identical except that in Condition 2 a single tone was interpolated during the interval between the dichotic chords. This tone was presented simultaneously to both ears.

The results of the experiment, averaged over four subjects, are shown in Fig. 29.7. It can be seen that a single interpolated tone did indeed reduce the size of the ear dominance effect. This reduction was highly consistent in three of the subjects, and the fourth showed only a small effect in this direction.

Experiment 4

This experiment was performed to evaluate the behavior of ear dominance as a function of time delay between onsets and offsets of successive chords of identical frequencies. Informal studies had indicated that the effect was

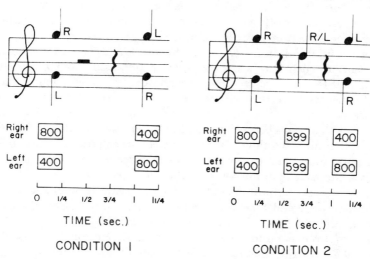

FIG. 29.6. Examples of stimulus configurations used in the two conditions of Experiment 3. Numbers in boxes indicate tonal frequencies. Musical notation is approximate.

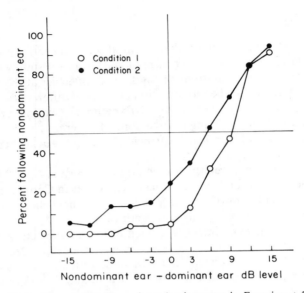

FIG. 29.7.   Percent following of nondominant ear in Experiment 3 as a function of amplitude differences at the two ears: ° Condition 1 and • Condition 2.

strongest when such chords were presented in rapid repetitive sequence and that it was attenuated when a delay was incorporated between successive chords. A further question explored was whether the critical factor here was the delay between the offset of one chord and the onset on the next or whether it was the delay between successive onsets.

In all conditions of the experiment, tones of 400 and 800 Hz were presented in alternation, such that when the right ear received 400 Hz the left ear received 800 Hz and vice versa. Four conditions were compared; in each of these, sequences were separated by a 10-sec intertrial interval. The basic sequence in Condition 1 consisted of 20 dichotic chords, each 250 msec in duration, with no gaps between them. Condition 2 was identical to Condition 1, except that only two chords were presented on each trial. Condition 3 was identical to Condition 2, except that a gap of 2¾ sec was interpolated between these two chords. Condition 4 was identical to Condition 3, except that both chords were 3 sec in duration, and there were no gaps between these chords. So in Conditions 3 and 4 the delays between onsets of successive chords were identical, although these chords differed considerably in duration.

The strengths of ear dominance under these different conditions are shown in Fig. 29.8. A highly significant effect of conditions was found [$F(3, 9)$ = 11.59, $p < .01$]. It can be seen that the strongest effect did indeed occur in Condition 1, where 20 chords were presented in rapid repetitive sequence

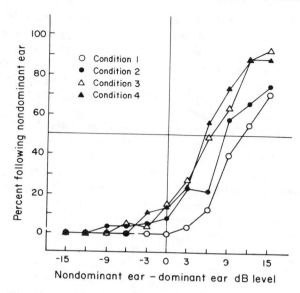

FIG. 29.8. Percent following of nondominant ear in Experiment 4 as a function of amplitude differences at the two ears.

before the 10-sec intertrial interval. The next strongest effect occurred in Condition 2, where two dichotic chords were presented in rapid sequence, but successive pairs of chords were separated by intervals of 10-sec duration (i.e., the intertrial interval). The weakest effects occurred in Conditions 3 and 4 where, in addition to the intertrial interval, 3-sec delays intervened between onsets of the two dichotic chords within each trial.

It is of particular interest to note that the strengths of effect in Conditions 3 and 4 were closely matched, even though chords of very different durations were employed. It will be recalled that the delays between onsets of the two chords in these conditions were identical. So it seems that the strength of inhibitory interaction underlying ear dominance is determined by the time interval between onsets of the successive tones. The durations of the tones themselves do not appear of importance and neither does the time interval between the offset of one tone and the onset of its successor.

Discussion

Given this set of experiments, we can propose that the mechanism underlying ear dominance has the following characteristics. First, elements underlying the same frequency but which convey information from different regions of auditory space are linked in mutual inhibitory interaction. From Experiment 4 we conclude that the inhibition exerted by one element on another acts over relatively long time periods, that is, over periods characteristic of short-term memory. We can also conclude that the inhibition exerted by one element on another cumulates with repetitive stimulation and cumulates more rapidly as repetition rate increases. The duration of the stimulus itself appears of little importance in determining the amount of such inhibition. And from Experiments 1, 2, and 3 we also conclude that disinhibition occurs when elements responding to different frequencies are activated.

We may next ask why such a system should have developed, that is, what the usefulness of such a system might be. One possibility is that this mechanism enables us to follow new, ongoing information with a minimum of interference from echoes or reverberation. In normal listening situations, when the same frequency emanates successively from two different regions of auditory space, the second occurrence may well be due to an echo. This is made more probable as the delay between these two occurrences is shortened. But if other frequencies are interpolated between two such occurrences of the same frequency, an explanation in terms of echoing is rendered less likely. If this interpretation is correct, then the present phenomenon falls into the class of mechanisms (such as those underlying the precedence effect) that operate to counteract misleading effects of echoes and reverberation (Haas, 1951; Wallach, Newman, & Rosenzweig, 1949).

LOCALIZATION BY FREQUENCY

The last section was concerned with only one component of the octave illusion, that is, the mechanism that determines what pattern of frequencies is followed. But it will be recalled that patterns of localization obey a different rule: Each tone is localized in the ear that receives the higher-frequency signal, regardless of whether the higher or the lower frequency is perceived.

This effect has also been studied as a function of amplitude relationships between simultaneous tones (Deutsch, 1978). In this case, the amplitude of the high tone was varied relative to the low tone in each sequence. It was found that with long repetitive sequences a localization toward the higher-frequency signal occurred even when the lower frequency was substantially higher in amplitude. But with short sequences consisting of only two dichotic chords, localization patterns followed patterns of relative loudness closely. This localization by frequency effect was also found to be very robust in terms of onset and offset disparities between the high and low tones, when long repetitive sequences were used. Varying the onset of the low tone relative to the high tone by 5 msec in either direction did not affect the localization toward the higher-frequency signal (Deutsch, in press).

A PROPOSED WHAT-WHERE CONNECTION

We have discussed in some detail the mechanism determining *what* frequencies we hear under these conditions and also rather briefly the mechanism determining *where* the sounds appear to be coming from. We have seen that these *what* and *where* mechanisms operate at some stage so independently that we can end up perceiving a stimulus that does not exist, that is, with its pitch taken from one source and its location from another. This brings us to the very thorny question of how the *what* and *where* information gets put back together once it has been pulled apart so as to produce an integrated percept. We do not perceive a disembodied location, together with a pitch floating in a void; rather we perceive a pitch *at* a location. If we were concerned only with explaining the illusion at this point, we could simply assume that the outputs of the *what* and *where* decision mechanisms become linked together. But unfortunately this simple solution will not work. In normal listening we are presented with sounds from several sources, and we do generally manage to recombine the different attribute values so as to arrive at a correct set of simultaneous auditory descriptions. This would not be possible if the *what* and *where* mechanisms each simply produced a set of outputs, because we would not know which output from the *what* mechanism to link with which output from the *where* mechanism.

The following solution is here proposed. As shown in Fig. 29.9, we may hypothesize two equivalent arrays. In each of these arrays individual elements are sensitive both to a specific value of frequency and also to a specific value of spatial location; that is, they are sensitive to a specific conjunction of attribute values. [Evidence for such elements has been obtained at various levels in the auditory system: for instance, by Goldberg and Brown (1967) and Moushegian, Rupert, and Langford (1967) at the superior olivary complex; by Rose, Gross, Geisler, and Hind (1966) and Geisler, Rhode, and Hazelton (1969) at the inferior colliculus; and by Brugge, Dubrovsky, Aitkin, and Anderson (1969) at the auditory cortex.] We assume that these two arrays are identical in organization as far as input is concerned; however the output of one array signals pitch and the output of the other array signals localization. We may further assume that, depending on the precise stimulus parameters (including very importantly the sequential setting), specific patterns of interaction take place within these arrays. These patterns were presumably evolved to take care of specific stimulus conditions, and in normal listening they probably function to counteract misleading effects in the environment.

What we have depicted on these arrays are the projections resulting from a high tone to the left and a low tone to the right. In this case let us assume that there are no inhibitory interactions within these arrays, and the two stimuli

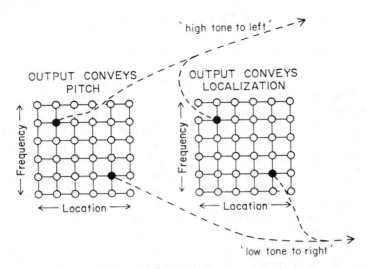

FIG. 29.9.   Hypothesized arrays mediating selection of pitch and localization values. This figure displays outputs and their linkages where two simultaneous tones are veridically perceived. See text for details.

are veridically perceived. This would be the case, for instance, when steady tones of long duration are present. We can explain this outcome by assuming that there is a linkage together between the outputs of those activated elements that are in analogous positions on these two arrays. If there are no outputs from elements in strictly analogous positions, we can assume that outputs from elements in the most proximal positions are linked together.

In Fig. 29.10 we have the situation in the alternating octave sequence, where interactions within the array that conveys pitch results in the signaling only of a low tone, and interactions within the array that conveys localization results in the signaling only of a localization to source of the higher frequency. There is therefore only one output from the pitch array and only one output from the localization array. Because there are no outputs from elements situated in more proximal positions along these two arrays, these two outputs are linked together. As a result we hear a low tone to the left, which was not in fact presented. And so the octave illusion results.

DISCUSSION

Another powerful demonstration of the influence of spatial information in determining what frequencies are followed has been provided by Kubovy, Cutting, and McGuire (1974). They presented a set of simultaneous and continuous sine wave tones to both ears and phase-shifted one of these relative to its counterpart in the opposite ear. The phase-shifted tone thus

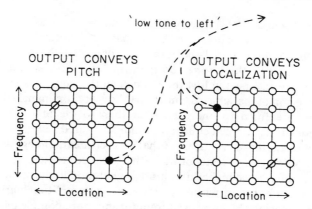

FIG. 29.10.   Hypothesized arrays mediating selection of pitch and localization values. It is assumed that the same two tones are presented as in Fig. 29.9 but under sequential conditions giving rise to the octave illusion. This figure displays outputs and their linkages under these conditions. ϕ indicates inhibited elements. See text for details.

appeared to occupy a different position in space. When these tones were shifted in sequence, a melody was clearly heard whose components corresponded to the shifted tones. However this melody was undetectable when heard with either ear alone (Kubovy, in press; Kubovy & Howard, 1976).

Other studies have provided evidence for dissociations between the mechanisms processing *what* and *where* information in both the auditory and the visual systems. Poljak (1926) hypothesized on neuroanatomical grounds that the early stages of the auditory pathway involve a ventral route, subserving localization and orientation functions, and a dorsal route, subserving discriminatory functions. Recently Evans and his colleagues have provided neurophysiological support for this hypothesis (Evans, 1974). For the visual system, Schneider (1967) found that ablation of the visual cortex in hamsters produced an inability to discriminate visual patterns, while producing little decrement in the ability to localize objects in space. Yet when the superior colliculus was ablated instead, there resulted a complete inability to orient to a visual stimulus, while pattern discrimination remained excellent.

At the behavioral level, several studies have shown dissociations between *what* and *where* mechanisms in audition. Odenthal (1963) presented subjects with a dichotic chord that was followed after a silent period by a comparison tone. When the frequency difference between the components of the dichotic chord was very small, subjects heard a single pitch, which Odenthal termed an *intertone*. It was found that the pitch of this intertone did not change with changes in the relative amplitudes of the components of chord; however these changes produced a lateralization of the intertone toward the ear receiving the higher-amplitude signal.

Efron and Yund (1974) also obtained a dissociation using the following paradigm. Subjects were presented with a pair of dichotic chords, which were separated by an interval of 1-sec duration. For each dichotic chord pair, one ear received first the high tone and then the low, while simultaneously the other ear received first the low tone and then the high. It was found that a large proportion of the subjects tended to follow predominantly the pattern of frequencies presented to one ear rather than to the other. Yet when the simultaneous tones were at equal amplitude, the fused sound was heard as in the center of the head. As in Odenthal's experiment, changing the relative amplitude of the components of the dichotic chord resulted in a localization to the ear receiving the higher-amplitude signal though the pitch of the sound often remained constant within a wide range of amplitude variation.

Similar dissociations have been found using more complex stimuli. Carlson, Fant, and Grandstrom (1975) presented different formants from a synthetic vowel sound to different ears. They found that varying the relative formant amplitudes produced little effect on the perception of vowel quality, while producing a strong effect on lateralization.

For the visual system, what–where dissociations may be obtained by simultaneous manipulation of depth and pattern perception. An elegant demonstration of this nature is provided in Kaufman (1974).

Various theorists have been concerned with the general question of how attribute values, once pulled apart, are recombined so as to produce a correct set of simultaneous percepts. For instance, assuming that the processing mechanisms for color and form are at some stage separate, how is it that when presented with a red circle and a green square we see the circle as red and the square as green? Attneave (1974) has suggested that such correct conjunctions are achieved by the tagging of attribute values to placemarkers (i.e., "that where is the glue that holds quite different what-properties together. [p. 109]). Triesman, Sykes, and Gelade (1977) independently reached a similar conclusion. They further suggested that we process serially stimuli in different spatial locations, so that integration of a single perceptual object is achieved by linking together those attribute values that are identified during any one temporal interval. The mechanism proposed here for the integration of pitch and localization values to form simultaneous unitary percepts bears some similarity to these proposals for the case of vision, because it assumes that both the pitch and the localization mechanisms are composed of elements that are tagged to specific spatial locations.

CONCLUSION

In our natural environment, we are constantly presented with simultaneous streams of sound that emanate from different positions in space. These sounds are superimposed on each other before they reach our ears, and in analyzing them we are confronted with two basic tasks. First, we must decide *what* sequences of sounds are being emitted, and, second, we must decide *where* each sound is coming from.

This chapter has been concerned with the mechanisms whereby such multiple auditory descriptions are arrived at. We have been concerned only with the case where two streams of sine wave tones are presented, one to each ear, and have not even considered how we manage to reconstruct simultaneously presented complex waveforms. Yet although very simple stimulus parameters have been used, we have seen that, in most of the stimulus situations explored, the percepts that emerge are typically wildly wrong. However, the ways in which they go wrong have provided some insights into the mechanisms that our auditory system employs as it generally arrives at the right conclusions. It is clear that these mechanisms are very complex; but this is hardly surprising, for we are dealing with a very complex auditory environment.

ACKNOWLEDGMENTS

This research was supported by U.S. Public Health Service Grant MH-21001. A more extensive description of the findings reported here together with related phenomena may be found in Deutsch (in press). I am particularly indebted to F. H. C. Crick for discussions concerning perceptual organization.

REFERENCES

Attneave, F. Apparent movement and the what–where connection. *Psychologia—An International Journal of Psychology in the Orient,* 1974, *17,* 108–120.

Bregman, A. S. The formation of auditory streams. In J. Requin (Ed.), *Attention and performance VII,* Hillsdale, N.J.: Lawrence Erlbaum Associates, 1978.

Brugge, J. F., Dubrovsky, N. A., Aitkin, L. M., & Anderson, D. J. Sensitivity of single neurons in auditory cortex of cat to binaural tonal stimulation: Effects of varying interaural time and intensity. *Journal of Neurophysiology,* 1969, *32,* 1005–1024.

Carlson, R., Fant, C. G. M., & Grandstrom, B. Two-formant models, pitch and vowel perception. In C. G. M. Fant & B. Lindblom (Eds.), *Auditory analysis and perception of speech. Proceedings of the 1973 Leningrad Symposium.* London: Academic Press, 1975.

Deutsch, D. An auditory illusion. *Nature,* 1974, *251,* 307–309.

Deutsch, D. Musical illusions. *Scientific American,* 1975, *233*(4), 92–104. (a)

Deutsch, D. Two-channel listening to musical scales. *Journal of the Acoustical Society of America,* 1975, *57,* 1156–1160. (b)

Deutsch, D. Lateralization by frequency for repeating sequences of dichotic 400- and 800-Hz tones. *Journal of the Acoustical Society of America,* 1978, *63,* 184–186.

Deutsch, D. The octave illusion and auditory perceptual integration. In J. V. Tobias & E. D. Shubert (Eds.), *Hearing research and theory.* New York: Academic Press (in press).

Deutsch, D., & Roll, P. L. Separate "what" and "where" decision mechanisms in processing a dichotic tonal sequence. *Journal of Experimental Psychology: Human Perception and Performance,* 1976, *2,* 23–29.

Dowling, W. J. The perception of interleaved melodies. *Cognitive Psychology*, 1973, *5*, 322–337.

Efron, R., & Yund, E. W. Dichotic competition of simultaneous tone bursts of different frequency. *Neuropsychologia*, 1974, *12*, 249–256.

Evans, E. F. Neural processes for the detection of acoustic patterns and for sound localization. In F. O. Schmitt & F. T. Worden (Eds.), *The neurosciences, third study program*. Cambridge, Mass.: MIT Press, 1974.

Geisler, C. D., Rhode, W. S., & Hazelton, D. W. Responses of inferior colliculus neurons in the cat to binaural acoustic stimuli having wide band spectra. *Journal of Neurophysiology*, 1969, *32*, 960–974.

Goldberg, J. M., & Brown, P. B. Response of binaural neurons of dog superior olivary complex to dichotic tonal stimuli. Some physiological mechanisms of sound localization. *Journal of Neurophysiology*, 1967, *32*, 613–636.

Haas, H. Über den Einfluss eines Einfachechos auf die Horsamkeit von Sprache. *Acustica*, 1951, *1*, 49–52.

Kaufman, L. *Sight and mind*. New York: Oxford University Press, 1974.

Kubovy, M. Concurrent pitch-segregation and the theory of indispensable attributes. In M. Kubovy & J. Pomerantz (Eds.), *Perceptual organization*. Hillsdale, N.J.: Lawrence Erlbaum Associates, in press.

Kubovy, M., Cutting, J. E., & McGuire, R. M. Hearing with the third ear: Dichotic perception of a melody without monaural familiarity cues. *Science*, 1974, *186*, 272–274.

Kubovy, M., & Howard, F. P. Persistence of a pitch-segregating echoic memory. *Journal of Experimental Psychology: Human Perception and Performance*, 1976, *2*, 531–537.

Moushegian, G., Rupert, A. L., & Langford, T. L. Stimulus coding by medial superior olivary neurons. *Journal of Neurophysiology*, 1967, *30*, !239–1261.

Odenthal, D. W. Perception and neural representation of simultaneous dichotic pure tone stimuli. *Acta Physiologica Pharmacologica Neerlandic*, 1963, *12*, 453–496.

Poljak, S. The connections of the acoustic nerve. *Journal of Anatomy*, 1926, *60*, 465–469.

Rose, J. E., Gross, N. B., Geisler, C. D., & Hind, J. E. Some neural mechanisms in the inferior colliculus which may be relevant to localization of a sound source. *Journal of Neurophysiology*, 1966, *29*, 288–314.

Schneider, G. E. Contrasting visuomotor functions of tectum and cortex in the golden hamster. *Psychologische Forschung*, 1967, *31*, 52–62.

Treisman, A. M., Sykes, M., & Gelade, G. Selective attention and stimulus integration. In S. Dornic (Ed.), *Attention and performance VI*. Hillsdale, N.J.: Lawrence Erlbaum Associates, 1977.

Wallach, H., Newman, E. B., & Rosenzweig, M. R. The precedence effect in sound localization. *American Journal of Psychology*, 1949, *62*, 315–336.

VII SEMANTIC MEMORY

30 Semantic Memory: A Tutorial

Walter Kintsch
University of Colorado
United States

> *Perhaps we overestimate situational independence; perhaps we underestimate the fact that every linguistic representation of some circumstance is in principle incomplete and must be supplemented from our knowledge about the circumstance.*
> Karl Bühler (1934, p. 255)

ABSTRACT

The data and theoretical issues on semantic memory are briefly outlined. It is concluded that in spite of some very definite achievements the approach taken is no longer fruitful today. A historical analysis attempts to show why the field of semantic memory has developed as it did. Finally, some suggestions are made about how the study of semantic memory could be redirected along more promising lines.

INTRODUCTION

As to the domain of semantic memory, I shall adhere strictly to the distinction introduced in 1972 by Tulving. Episodic memory, according to Tulving, contains spatially and temporally marked information about episodes or events. It has an autobiographical reference: "It happened to me" is always implied, and how and when something happened rather than what happened is often the most significant portion of a memory episode. Thus, when a subject in a psychological laboratory learns to recall a list of words, he is not learning the words themselves (he already knows those), but he learns to associate the words with a particular experimental context. Episodic memory is context-dependent, in the sense that it is available only in the presence of rather specific contextual retrieval cues. On the other hand, semantic memory refers to general knowledge. The original context of acquisition, and hence the personal reference, is no longer of any significance, because general knowledge can be retrieved and used in a wide variety of contexts. Word meanings are an important part of this general knowledge store, but I shall argue that attempts to equate semantic memory with word meanings only, that is, with the "subjective lexicon," are misguided and are doomed to failure. Semantic memory is our whole-world knowledge—including what we know about robins, $7 \times 4 = 28$, what to do in a restaurant, and the history of the Civil War, to cite some prominent examples.

Obviously, semantic and episodic memory are not always cleanly separable. They are, rather, end points on a continuum reaching from completely context-dependent episodes to truly general knowledge, but this in no way impairs the usefulness of the distinction. The term *semantic memory* is, however, sometimes used in a much more general way, as a synonym for all meaningful memory. Thus, memory for a story is termed *semantic memory*, whereas memory for a word list is called *episodic*. This is a deplorable tendency, because by thus broadening the meaning of the term *semantic memory* it is successfully drained of its substance and degenerates into an empty catch phrase.

Modern interest in semantic memory, as thus defined, is quite recent. Indeed, we are today celebrating the tenth birthday of the field: Quillian published his dissertation in 1968 as a chapter entitled "Semantic Memory" in a book edited by Minsky. It is no exaggeration to claim that the immediate origins of the research area that I am reviewing here today lie in this publication.

My task is made easy by the availability of a number of excellent and current reviews of the work on semantic memory: The basic experimental procedures and findings were summarized by Smith, Rips, and Shoben in 1974—not much has happened since—and the theoretical issues are discussed by Collins and Loftus (1975), McCloskey and Glucksberg (1979) and Smith (1978). Indeed, these sources are so good, current, and comprehensive, that I see no need to duplicate them here. I shall only briefly outline the data and theoretical issues that characterize the modern work on semantic memory, referring you to the reviews I mentioned for all the details and merely pointing out how the area has developed during the last 10 years in rough outlines.

TEN YEARS OF SEMANTIC MEMORY: DATA, MODELS, AND ISSUES

What do psychologists actually do when they study semantic memory? In his 1978 review, Smith gives us the ground rules for this activity. First you are concerned with word meanings; then you combine these word meanings to obtain a sentence meaning; that sentence meaning can then be related to some real-world situation so that you can find out whether it is true or false; and finally you may draw permissible inferences from your sentence meaning. That, indeed, appears to be very much the program that everyone has adhered to in those last 10 years, starting at the beginning, with the word meanings. Indeed, the last three problems have as yet received very little study. There has been some concern with inferences; not so much within the semantic memory tradition proper but more from a standpoint of text processing. The relation between semantics and perception has only recently been investigated, in the pioneering work of Miller & Johnson-Laird (1976). The combinatorial rules that are needed to obtain sentence meanings from word meanings are also largely unexplored at this time, though a recent paper by Rips, Smith, and Shoben (1978) attacks this problem in a very interesting way. But without doubt, the bulk of the work on semantic memory deals with word meanings, particularly with the structure of concrete nouns and their organization in the subjective lexicon. Since that is where the action has been, that is what I shall have to review.

The basic paradigm in the study of semantic memory has been a sentence verification task. Sentences of the form "*S is a P*" (e.g., *A robin is a bird*) are shown to subjects who have to respond as rapidly as they can whether the sentence is *true* or *false;* the mean reaction times to true and false sentences are the dependent variables of interest. The results from these studies can be summarized succinctly: Subjects are consistently faster to verify true sentences when the subject and predicate are more closely related semantically (e.g., *robin, sparrow*) than when they are less strongly related (e.g., *goose, chicken*). This has variously been termed the typicality effect, the semantic distance, or semantic relatedness effect. Conversely, for false sentences, semantic relatedness slows down response times. Thus, subjects are faster to respond *false* to *A robin is a car* than to *A robin is a mammal*. True reaction times decrease with the semantic relatedness between the subject and predicate of a sentence. False reaction times increase with semantic relatedness. Figure 30.1 shows a typical result.

This result is robust and quite general. It holds for verification of property statements (*A canary can sing, A canary has gills*—e.g., Collins & Quillian, 1969), as well as for same–different decisions (*eagle–hawk* versus *eagle–lion*—

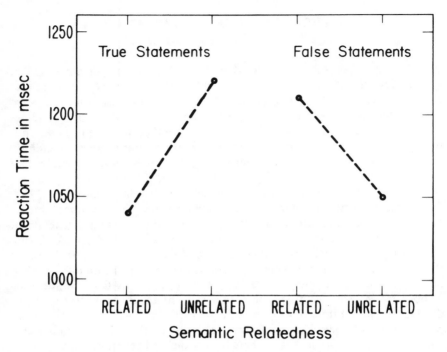

FIG. 30.1.   Average latencies of true–false judgments as a function of semantic relatedness for true and false sentences (after Kintsch, 1974, Fig. 10.3,
Exp. a).

e.g., Schaeffer & Wallace, 1969). If subjects are given a category name plus a
property and are asked to produce an appropriate response, response time
will again be shorter when the response is closely related semantically to the
prescribed category (e.g., *fruit–starts with letter a*) than when it is not (e.g.,
fruit–starts with letter k) (Loftus, 1974). Analogous results have been obtained in sentence generation and sentence completion tasks by Rosch (1974,
1975). Rips (1975a) has observed the same typicality effect in an inductive
reasoning task: Subjects who learned that a typical species possessed some
property (e.g., an unknown disease) were likely to generalize this property to
other species, but they did not do so when the same fact was learned about an
atypical species. Thus, when *robins* suffered from the mysterious disease,
more species of *birds* were judged to be affected than when the disease
pertained to *ostriches*. In a rather different task, namely a Sternberg scan for
presence or absence of words in a category, semantic relatedness affected
reaction times in much the same way as in a verification task, leading Homa
and Omohundro (1977) to conclude that similar decision processes are involved in both tasks. Finally, Guenther and Klatzky's (1977) study should be

mentioned here, reporting a semantic relatedness effect for pictures as well as words.

At various times, researchers have reported other phenomena about semantic memory, such as a category size effect (Landauer & Meyer, 1972), an imagery effect (Jorgensen & Kintsch, 1973), or a frequency effect (Conrad, 1972). However, in every case a confounding with semantic relatedness exists, which accounts for either all or most of these effects (Smith, Rips, & Shoben, 1974).

The semantic relatedness effect is, then, by far the most salient phenomenon observed in all of these studies. There are, however, some task variables that have been shown to interact with this effect in determining reaction times. First, there are priming effects, in that the repetition of related stimuli in an experiment has been shown to reduce judgment times (Collins & Quillian, 1972). This has been explained either as a residual activation (Collins and Loftus, 1975) or as a reorganization of the semantic structure (Hopf-Weichel, 1977). Then there are important list effects, as reported by Rips (1975b) and McCloskey and Glucksberg (1979).

It makes a significant difference for the verification of true sentences whether the false sentences in the list are semantically related (as in *All birds are sparrows, All birds are geese*) or unrelated (as in *All birds are diamonds, All birds are forgeries*). True reaction times are considerably faster when the sentences are embedded in a list with unrelated–false items, though in both cases a semantic relatedness effect was still present. Finally, there are some studies which demonstrate that the semantic relatedness effect is not always observed but that there are experimental conditions which modify the subjects' decision strategies in such a way that the typical effects of semantic relatedness are no longer obtained. This happens, for instance, with contradictory test sentences where Holyoak and Glass (1975) have reported that sentences of the type *All fruits are vegetables* are rejected faster than sentences of the type *All fruits are flowers* (but see McCloskey and Glucksberg, 1979, for some rather different findings). Lorch (1978) also shows that with explicit quantified sentences (*All S are P*) factors beyond mere relatedness may determine reaction times. Thus, although semantic relatedness effects are certainly dominant in these experiments, subjects can be made to assume strategies that do not lead to these effects.

Indeed, if one views semantic relatedness as a special instance of a similarity relation, effects similar to those observed in the domain of semantic memory have been reported in several other areas, including pattern recognition (Posner & Keele, 1968) and a perceptual judgment (Egeth, 1966). Quite generally, positive decisions are facilitated when the items to be compared are similar, whereas negative decisions are slowed down.

But let us return to semantic memory. What sort of theories have been constructed to explain the effects outlined above? Again, for an in-depth

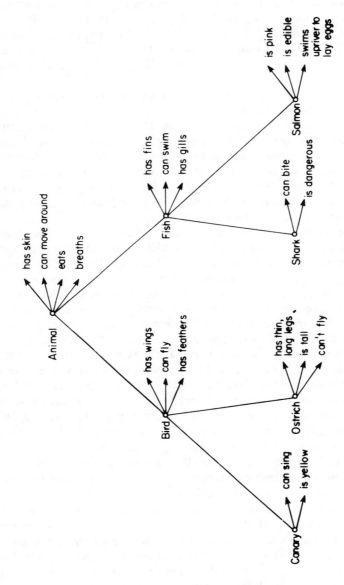

FIG. 30.2.   A hypothetical memory structure after Collins and Quillian (1969).

answer to this question, the reader is referred to Smith (1978). I shall only sketch the main features of some of the more familiar models. It has generally been assumed that the semantic relatedness effect reflects something about the dynamics of the process of retrieving information from semantic memory. Recently, this assumption has been questioned (Corbett & Wickelgren, 1978), but the main theories to be considered here are retrieval theories. Figure 30.2 shows a semantic net as originally conceived by Collins and Quillian (1969). In this model, semantic memory is organized as a hierarchy of superset relations. Properties of concepts are stored only with the highest superset to which they apply. In their model, sentences were verified by searching this net: *A canary can sing* is immediately verifiable because the predicate is stored directly as a property with the *canary*-node; *A canary has skin,* on the other hand, requires a search of the *canary, bird,* as well as *animal* nodes (and hence takes longer). The marker search model of Glass and Holyoak (1974/75) can be regarded as an updated version of a network search model. The main competition to search models has come from the feature comparison model of Smith, Shoben, and Rips (1974), which is illustrated in Fig. 30.3. Instead of searching a hierarchical network, the semantic features of the subject and predicate are compared in a two-stage decision process: If the overall similarity of the two feature sets is above some criterion value, a positive response is made; if it is below some acceptable value, a negative response is made; if it is indeterminate (i.e., the similarity index falls between the two decision criteria),

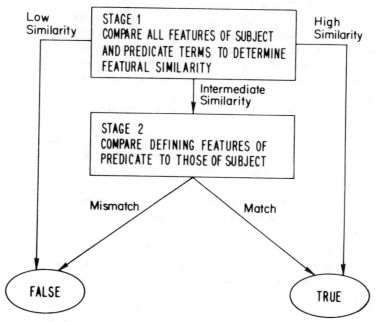

FIG. 30.3.   The feature comparison model (after Smith, 1978).

the process enters into its second stage, where the "defining" features of the two terms are compared in more detail. It is worth noting that this model is formally similar to the model of recognition memory developed by Atkinson & Juola (1974) as well as to some models of perceptual judgment (Hawkins & Shipley, 1972).

The semantic memory model to end all models is that of Collins and Loftus (1975), which combines aspects from both feature comparison and network search models, replacing the network search with a spreading activation process. It allows for a number of different response strategies and, as Smith (1978) puts it, "does a good job of accounting for empirical findings." But our authority then goes on to complain that a model that has everything and does everything is simply not much fun.

At the other extreme is a supersimple model recently proposed by McCloskey and Glucksberg (1979): It is a feature comparison model that accounts for the empirical findings of verification experiments in the most parsimonious manner: a probabilistic comparison of unstructured feature sets, with no frills.

What are all these models good for, or more precisely, what are the issues that people want to decide with all this apparatus? Originally, the whole enterprise started out as a contest between *network* versus *feature* models, but Hollan's (1975) demonstration of the mathematical equivalence of the two took much of the interest away from this question. It is still an important issue, however, because, as has often been remarked, the use of a felicitous or infelicitous notation is not at all irrelevant for the progress of a science.

Smith (1978) identifies *storage* versus *computation* as the main issue of current interest. In feature models, subset relations must be computed, whereas the Collins and Quillian (1969) network model stores these relationships directly. This is certainly an important issue, but it cannot be phrased in terms of mutually exclusive alternatives. We have to store something before anything can be computed, and, conversely, we can hardly do without any computational facility: To repeat a slightly stale example from my 1974 book, to assume that information like *Napoleon had toes* is stored in semantic memory is a bit preposterous. So the question is *what* is stored, *what* is computed—which is not a problem for which any of the extant models are particularly helpful.

Another contrast is that between *directed search* processes and *spreading activation* processes. Again, this is a perfectly valid question—but at the present stage of development of memory models we can dismiss it as merely a preference for one language over another. In most formulations the two are probably equivalent. Precise quantitative models from which differential predictions could be derived are as yet lacking.

Another issue that Smith identifies in his 1978 review concerns the distinction between a *dictionary* and an *encyclopedia* that is incorporated into most semantic memory models. For instance, in the Smith et al. model the distinction between features that define the meaning of a word versus those that are only characteristic is a basic one. In the model of McCloskey and Glucksberg, on the other hand, this distinction is lacking, and I shall argue that this distinction is not a helpful one.

Finally, there is the issue of *decomposition* in semantic memory. Is our knowledge about the meaning of words, and indeed about the world at large, stored in terms of semantic elements, or do we operate with larger units? In other words, is the decomposition of a concept into its semantic elements an obligatory aspect of semantic processing, or is it performed only when a particular task demands it? Note that the question is not whether decomposition is possible. Because everyone of us can decompose many complex semantic concepts when asked to do so, decomposition is certainly possible. The question is whether it is obligatory (as, for instance in the model of language comprehension proposed by Schank, 1972). Feature models, of course, require decomposition, at least to some degree. Network models usually operate with larger chunks as units. A number of people have argued that decomposition is not obligatory [e.g., Hayes-Roth & Hayes-Roth (1977); Holyoak, Glass, & Mah (1976); Kintsch (1974).] However, the precise conditions under which decomposition does or does not occur are still poorly understood. This is an issue of some significance—but semantic memory experiments, or the present crop of models, have not contributed much to its elucidation, at least so far.

So where are we after 10 years of semantic memory? We have an important and well-established experimental phenomenon, the semantic relatedness effect, plus a number of other observations of secondary significance. We have a number of theories that are based on rather different assumptions, but which all explain the experimental phenomena reasonably well (or could be extended in what their authors would claim to be minor ways to do so). However, in terms of the issues that really have motivated this research, we have so far not received any clear answers. The impression is unavoidable that questions have been asked in the context of a research paradigm that was simply not rich enough to provide definitive answers. The data from the experiments discussed here do not provide enough constraints to enable us to decide the issues that everyone is interested in. Just as a provocation, but not totally unreasonably, let me suggest that the sentence verification data of the last 10 years have told us precisely nothing about the structure of semantic memory. Most likely, the semantic relatedness effect merely reflects some very general properties of human decision processes, as attested by the parallel effects that have been observed in studies of memory, perceptual judgment, and pattern matching. The verification latencies can be taken as a measure of the similarity of the terms that are being compared, but they are not informative when it comes to the nature of that similarity or the details of the comparison processes. Similarly, priming effects in reaction-time experiments are ubiquitous and have told us little that specifically pertains to semantic structure. Finally, the list context effects of McCloskey and Glucksberg have a familiar analogue in recognition memory experiments: Unrelated distractor items in a list induce rather different response strategies in subjects than related ones, a distinction that has been around for a while under such labels as class versus item recognition processes. Thus, once more, we may be dealing here with rather general characteristics of decision processes, which have only very weak implications for the aspects of semantic structure and semantic processes that we really want to investigate.

Others have of course noted this dilemma before, and some rather different responses to it can be distinguished. The first one is common among hardcore experimental psychologists. Basically, this is the tack taken by Smith, and its consequences are most clearly demonstrated by McCloskey and Glucksberg. If you want to stick with the sentence verification paradigm, they are saying, you might as well forget about the broader questions concerning semantic processes and structures and focus only on the experimental procedure at hand; let's devise the most elegant, most parsimonious model for these data and be done with it; the details of the model are important only in the context of the specific data it was designed to handle. Apart from the fact that the model they actually design is in my opinion the nicest one yet, I have little appreciation for this sort of retreat. I don't care about sentence verification data per se (and I don't suppose McCloskey and Glucksberg care either)—I want to know about semantic memory!

The other reaction, well argued by Breuker (1976) and exemplified in the work of Miller and Johnson-Laird (1976), is to forget about the experiments and follow the lead of artificial intelligence, linguistics, and philosophy. If we take our intuitions as data, we immediately have available an enormously rich base upon which we can construct practically endless speculations. However, intuition and the methods of artificial intelligence alone cannot possibly let us decide among such issues as computation versus storage and decomposition versus chunking in any more definitive manner than sentence verification experiments could. These are simply questions of psychological fact, quite apart from what intuition tells us or questions of computational feasibility.

We need the experimental method, but not merely to produce an impoverished data base. We need broad, general theories of cognitive processes that speak to the important issues—but then we need to design experiments that allow us to test such theories. Collins and Loftus' (1975) theory has often been criticized as too broad and vague, and, indeed, it is too powerful for the domain of sentence verification experiments. The problem lies, however, not in the generality of the theory but in the manner of evaluating it. It needs a much broader, richer data base. Not one experiment, nor a single experimental paradigm, but several converging experimental approaches might succeed where sentence verification alone failed.

At this point it might be useful to step outside the strict limits of the semantic memory tradition of the last 10 years and try to see whether we can find some useful hints about where to go from a consideration of the historical context of this work.

Roots

Let us reconsider the ground rules for semantic memory research, as they were described by Smith (1978). I have already mentioned that, so far, all the participants have respected those ground rules. As you will remember, you start with the definition of words. Just about all the work reviewed here has been concerned with the structure of word definitions and the way such definitions are accessed and used. Later, the plan is to put these word definitions together so that the meaning of a sentence can be computed from the definitions of the words in it, plus the syntactic relations among them. And even later, one may be concerned about the role of this sentence in a real-world context and about the inferences that can be derived from it. But none of these further issues are really acute until the structure of word meanings has been explored, because at least some information about that structure is a precondition for the further stages of research.

The purpose of my discussion here is to undermine as much as possible this research program, which I think has led semantic memory research into avenues of investigation that are barren and lead nowhere. Others have made similar arguments, particularly Hörmann (1976) whose penetrating review of modern psycholinguistics contains a very good discussion of the issues raised here.

It will not be easy to undermine this program. These ideas are firmly established in modern linguistics and philosophy, as well as in psychology. Furthermore they have a long and prominent history. In modern times, their clearest expression, from which the psychological work is quite directly derived, is found in the work of Katz and Fodor (1963). But the key ideas of Katz and Fodor are deeply rooted in philosophical thought, going back through Locke and the scholastics to Aristotle.

Aristotle, in *Topica,* was concerned with the proper definition of words from a logical standpoint. He wanted to make sure that errors in reasoning are avoided that are due to unclear word meanings or, more specifically, to the improper use of word meanings in logical arguments. He introduced what is today called a *semantic classification hierarchy* where each class (genus) is subdivided into two or more subclasses (species). A genus is a class in which things that are in some essential way alike but that differ in other character-istics are combined [p. 101]. He even suggests an operational definition of genus: The answer to the question "What is the object before you?" identifies the genus to which the object belongs; thus, if the object in question were a *man,* this answer should be, "He is an animal [p. 102]." The essence of an object is its genus, but there are other characteristics that must be considered in a definition [p. 102]. First, there are the properties of an object, which are predicates that do not indicate its essence but yet belong to that thing alone. For instance, *man* has the property "capable of learning grammar." On the other hand, the attribute "sleeps" does not belong to man alone and is only a temporary property, whereas "biped" is only a relative property (e.g., to distinguish *man* from *ox*). Finally, there are accidental attributes, which belong (or may belong) to an object merely by accident, such as "sitting posture." Apparently, Aristotle did not envision a sharp dividing line among relative, temporal, and accidental properties, because he explicitly mentions that accidents may turn into relative properties [p. 102]. I have in Fig. 30.4 put together Aristotle's own examples in a contemporary form as a semantic hierarchy. The point that I want to make is simply that from Aristotle to the present semantic memory models there has been very little change in the way we conceive of word meanings.

Aristotle also makes a number of other observations that are worth noting for their modern counterparts. He is greatly concerned with upholding the distinction between class (genus) and the defining characteristic of the class (differentia) [p. 120]. Each differentia induces its own genus, so that from the property of *walking* we obtain the class of *walking animals,* but he emphasize the danger of confusing genus and differentia [p. 144].

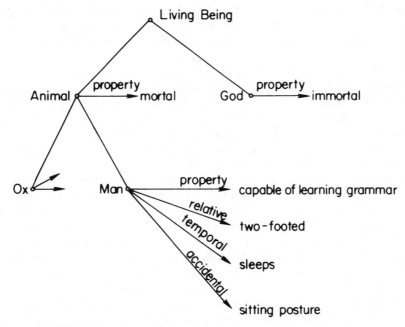

FIG. 30.4.   A semantic structure (genus–species) after Aristotle.

The same thing may belong to more than one genus [p. 123]. This idea predates the modern emphasis on cross-classifications in semantic hierarchies. Thomas Aquinas, who took over this Aristotelian framework wholesale, attributed special importance to the fact that distinctions must be examined and maintained within the framework in which they were worked out. A new context may require quite a different classification schema (Chenu, 1964, p. 176).

In one interesting respect Aristotle's semantic memory model, as shown in Fig. 30.4, was quite different than, say, a Collins and Quillian type network. Collins and Quillian would verify "Man is mortal" via the inference chain "man is an animal" and "animals are mortal" ("mortal" is the differentia of the genus "animal" that distinguishes it from the immortal gods). Thus, the subordinate assumes a property of the superordinate. Aristotle sees it the other way around [p. 120]. Whatever properties belong to the various species of a genus also belong to the genus but not vice versa. Thus, the genus *animal* has the properties "rational," "irrational," "biped," "quadruped," etc. (and hence contradictory attributes may belong to the same thing!), but there is no necessity that all the attributes that belong to a genus also belong to each species (*animal* has the properties "flying" and "quadruped," whereas *man* does not). Of couse, it is not all the same thing to say that "An animal is a quadruped" and "the genus animal possesses the property quadruped"!

Aristotle's schema was a logical one and not a psychological, or even a linguistic one. But it could not be contained in the philosophy books. John Locke, through his work on ideas, transferred the Aristotelean classification system directly into the mind, and today it dominates in practically unaltered form both psychology and linguistics. Figure 30.5 shows a modern semantic hierarchy, the famous "bachelor" example from Katz and Fodor (1963). At the top of this hierarchy, we have the word's syntactic form class. Particular meanings are obtained through such semantic markers as (human), (male), and eventually via a semantic distinguisher, for example, (who has never married), a property that "belongs to the thing alone." We define via essence-plus-property, neglecting temporary and accidental attributes. Note that although Aristotle (or Collins and Quillian) orders objects in a network, Katz and Fodor give us a hierarchically ordered feature set; but one can easily turn one into the other.

Figure 30.6, where we shift back from "man" and "bachelor" to dear old "robin," exhibits the same scheme after Smith, Shoben, and Rips (1974). Like Aristotle, Smith et al. think of definingness (their term, not mine) as a continuum rather than in terms of well-defined, necessary, and sufficient criteria. In both cases this assumption of a continuum appears to be motivated by an inability to specify strict criteria. (It is like admitting that you can't do it but will do it anyway.)

The fact that our thinking about the structure of word meanings is very much the same today as it was 2000 years ago has, of course, nothing to do

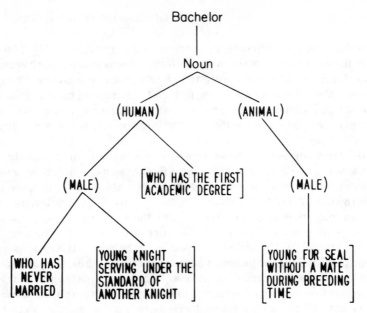

FIG. 30.5. A semantic structure after Katz and Fodor (1963). Markers are found in round brackets; distinguishers, in square brackets.

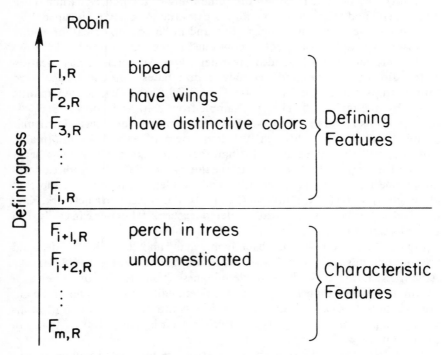

FIG. 30.6. Defining and characteristic features for "Robin" after Smith, Shoben, & Rips, 1974.

with either its correctness or its usefulness. It merely indicates that the whole framework within which modern semantic memory models are conceived is a very old one and that it initially derives from logical considerations. What is good for logic is not necessarily appropriate for psychology or linguistics. Logicians since Frege and Russell have valiantly and perhaps rightly insisted on the independence of their discipline from psychological intrusions. Psychologists as well as linguistics, on the other hand, have taken the relevance of logic in their own disciplines for granted,[1] perhaps because of the far greater prestige that logic enjoys. In linguistics, semantics has become nice and clean by distinguishing between the concepts of lexicon and encyclopedia. The former contains the defining properties of words, and it alone is important for the calculus of meaning elements that constitutes linguistic semantics. The encyclopedia, on the other hand, is for the nondefinitional information about word meanings, including general world knowledge; it is a hopeless mess and not a proper subject for linguistic inquiry. The lexicon is relatively simple and all we need to know for the study of semantics. Semantic memory has become for the psychologist what the lexicon is for the linguist. Indeed, the term *subjective lexicon* is often used as a synonym or partial synonym for semantic memory, and more than one psychologist has deplored the fact that it is apparently not very well possible to keep the dreadful mess of "world knowledge" out of his neat subjective lexicon.

It is of course easy to understand why Aristotle's logical scheme has exerted such an attraction upon both linguists and psychologists. It held the promise of simplifying the study of semantics by some orders of magnitude. But it is possible that by thus simplifying the task we have maneuvered ourselves into a corner from where some of the psychologically interesting problems of semantics have become inaccessible. Complaints about too great a reliance on logical commonplaces in the study of meaning are almost as old as the practice itself. Around the middle of the 13th century, an angry Albertus Magnus wrote: "They made no other investigation about things except a logical one.... For my part, I abhor such conclusions based on logic in the sciences that deal with things" (Metaphysics I, tr. 1, c. 2). We shall need to investigate the reasons for these complaints.

Problems

Discovery Procedures. Let us consider Fig. 30.5 again, the lexical entry for "bachelor" as it was suggested by Katz and Fodor, (1963). A number of

---

[1]Also at issue is the relevance of linguistics for psychology. In commenting on this chapter, Jan Keenan expressed her puzzlement over why a descriptional system for language (Chomsky, Katz, & Fodor) should be regarded as relevant to how people acquire or use language, whereas a descriptional system of mathematics (Russell & Whitehead) is never regarded as relevant to how people do mathematics or how children acquire mathematical knowledge.

authors (Bolinger, 1965; Hörmann, 1976) have pointed out an apparent arbitrariness in the construction of the semantic markers. Why, for instance, did Katz and Fodor not introduce an additional marker (young) in the definitions of the *knight-* and *seal-bachelor?* What are the criteria that determine the number of markers and, thereby, the extent to which subcategorization is introduced?

What we need are discovery procedures for markers, and, indeed, linguists have tried to develop such procedures. In structural linguistics, for instance, a technique called *componential analysis* was introduced for this purpose (Lounsbury, 1964), and the basic principles of componential analysis were taken over by generative grammarians (Katz, 1967): List sets of words to derive what is common to the meaning of the words and what distinguishes them from other sets of words. Thus, we might contrast, *man, woman,* and *child* with *steer, cow,* and *calf* to derive the marker (human), or *man, woman, steer,* and *cow* could be compared with *child* and *calf* to yield (adult), and so on. But obviously this is not a serious discovery procedure, because you have to know beforehand which words to put together in order to discover your differentia! At most, such a procedure can justify the elevation of some attribute to marker status, but we certainly cannot discover anything with it.

If the criteria for marker selection are not to be found within linguistics, they may perhaps be found outside linguistics. Bierwisch (1970) took his clue from the universal nature of semantic markers. He argued that markers are universal because all people, whatever their language, are alike in terms of their basic cognitive processes. Because there are certain constants in the way we perceive the world around us and interact with it, an adequate semantic description must be based upon these constants. Universal semantic markers are the direct consequence of the genetically determined cognitive characteristics of the human organism. Hörmann (1976) points out that this is a rather important advance beyond the original conception of Katz and Fodor: A semantic marker is no longer abstracted from an appropriate grouping of objects; rather we group these objects because our apperceptive apparatus responds to these objects in the same way [p. 87]. Thus we then need to identify the cognitive and perceptual properties that determine the marker system in our language.

This was attempted by Miller and Johnson-Laird in 1976. Miller and Johnson-Laird have collected a list of basic perceptual predicates from which the procedures can be formulated that people use in verifying sentences. They distinguished 82 basic perceptual predicates. The arguments of these predicates are objects and attributes (denoted $x, y, \ldots$) as well as time and event indexes (t, e). Some examples are Above (x, y), Inline (x, y, z). Permit (e, e'), and Time (e, t). Miller and Johnson-Laird intend these perceptual predicates to form one component upon which the semantic analysis is to be based. However, in actual practice, when they reach the semantic analysis, they pretty much forget about the perceptual basics. In any case, it would not help us very much for our problem of determining objectively what is a semantic marker, because their analysis merely shifts the level from linguistics to psychology: The problem is, now, what is a basic perceptual predicate? There are no explicit criteria for the inclusion of predicates in Miller and Johnson-Laird's list, other than that the "perceptual impressions are sufficiently direct and immediate." We might as well rely on Katz and Fodor's linguistic intuition as on Miller and Johnson-Laird's psychological intuition. We also have no assurance that their list is complete, nor do we know how incomplete it may be. Miller and Johnson-Laird have constructed their list of basic perceptual predicates in the time-honored but highly suspect manner of armchair psychology. Is it possible to bring the body of existing research in perception to bear on this problem? Can one devise experimental procedures to identify a set of basic perceptual operators? Linguistis like Bierwisch and theoretical psychologists like Miller and Johnson-Laird as well as computer scientists interested in artificial intelligence (Winston, 1975) have taken the lead and identified a promising research field. Experimental psychologists have some exciting opportunities here.

Context. Markers are context-dependent: Thus *love* is more (+pleasant) than *cordiality,* but if *cordiality* is contrasted with *hostility,* it is (+pleasant) (Perfetti, 1972). Markers are also task-dependent: A lot more markers are needed to define *whale* than merely to decide whether *whale* is an *animal* (Bolinger, 1965; Hörmann, 1976). Smith (1978) has argued that this task and context dependence does not per se make feature or marker systems unworkable, and that is quite correct. This matter was perhaps best put some time ago by Weinreich (1966). Weinreich introduced the notion of transfer features to deal with the obvious context dependency of word meanings. Take, for instance, the phrase *the pretty bus driver; bus driver* is unspecified as to (+male), but the word *pretty* itself specifies it as (−male). Or, consider Anderson and Ortony's clever examples, *The container held the apples* and *The container held the cola* (Anderson & Ortony, 1975). In the first sentence, the "feature" (contained in baskets, boxes,...) is transferred from *apples* to *container,* specifying it as a *basket* or *box;* in the second example, the *cola* transfers its feature (contained in bottles, cans,...) to *container,* which thereby is understood by people as a *bottle* or a *can.* Or, alternatively, one could construct a somewhat more elegant model, where the feature (+liquid), which is part of the meaning of *cola,* modifies the existing features of *container* in such a way as to produce *bottle.* I suspect that many linguists (and psychologists!) might greatly prefer this second version, because it looks clean and logical and avoids introducing such obvious bits of world knowledge in the guise of features as (+contained in bottles). But that is just another piece of self-deception, because there is no way around the world knowledge in our example: We can't produce *bottle* merely from (+liquid), for we are equally likely to obtain *barrel* as a container of liquids, or *pipeline*, which would be quite appropriate if the liquid were *wine* or *oil*, respectively, but which is not the way people understand *The container held the cola.*

In principle, however, I can see nothing wrong per se with the idea of specifying word meanings via features. Note also the popularity of the feature concepts in the related field of memory studies, where Bower's multicomponent theory of the memory trace and Underwood's attribute conception of memory have proved very influential (Bower, 1967; Underwood, 1969). Where semantic memory theorists (as well as their linguistic companions) have gone wrong is in trying to construct a neat logical, Aristotelian system, for the definition of word meanings from features. As Smith points out, this trend is present to some extent in every current semantic memory model (with the exception of the recent McCloskey and Glucksberg model). Without an untenable lexicon–encyclopedia distinction, feature systems remain a viable theoretical alternative, that is, if one is willing to accept such awkward features as (+heavy iron skillet) that Lehrer (1974) needs for the lexical entry of *sauté* or (+contained in bottle) for which I argued previously. Some authors prefer to characterize word meanings through complex propositional expressions instead of trying to mask the complexity of these expressions (Quillian, 1968; Kintsch, 1974, p. 35). But this is of course merely an issue of notational preference.

Semantic Space.   The same logical conception of semantics against which I have just been arguing is also behind another main current in the study of semantic memory. That is the repeated effort to scale semantic space. Examples include the semantic differential of Osgood, Suci, and Tannenbaum (1957), the early work of Miller (1969) on word clustering, the ambitious and comprehensive projects of Fillenbaum and Rapaport (1971), and several later offshoots thereof. The trouble with this work is that although there are a small number of stable semantic subspaces (e.g., kinship, color, and animal names), the "bulk of the vocabulary is loosely structured and full of components unique to single pairs or small numbers of pairs [Weinreich, 1963, p. 149]." Worse, even where there are stable dimensional structures, they are task- and context-dependent. There is no hope of ever identifying n semantic dimensions, such that the meaning of each semantic concept could be characterized by values on each of these dimensions. The meaning of *love* is rendered just as incompletely by three values on the dimensions of evaluation, activity, and potency as the meaning of *bear* is by two values specifying its value on a size and predatoriness dimension. As if one would rescale *bear* in the context of Kipling's *Jungle Books*, undoubtedly some rather different dimensions would emerge. Semantic memory as a static structure independent of context and specific uses just won't do. This is of course in no way an indictment of the use of scaling methods in the study of semantic memory. Such techniques are useful for many purposes, as when the semantic relations determined in one task context are to be compared with those from another domain (Rips, Shoben, & Smith, 1973, where a structure based on similarity ratings is used to predict sentence verification times). But there is little value in scaling "the" semantic structure.

Beyond the Lexicon

So far, I have stressed two main themes. First, that the sentence verification experiment "A robin is a bird—True/False?" has ceased to be useful. The data obtained from such experiments do not sufficiently constrain theoretical alternatives. They do not permit us to decide among such psychologically important issues as whether semantic memory should be modeled by network or feature theories where storage ends and computation begins and what role semantic primitives play in the system, whether a dictionary versus encyclopedia distinction is required, or whether the basic operations in semantic memory are pattern matching and comparison, search processes, or spreading activation processes. As McCloskey and Glucksberg have demonstrated, it is possible to account for the findings of typical sentence verification experiments without ever touching on any of these issues. In other words, "A robin is a bird" tells us little of interest about semantic memory. The sentence verification paradigm is not, after all, the "road into the mental dictionary" that many had hoped it was (Smith, 1978).

My second point was that our conception of this "mental dictionary" was an overly narrow one. It is basically a logical rather than a psychological conception, and I have argued that psychology (and for that matter, linguistics, too) has been impeded by this carryover from philosophy (see also Hörmann, 1976; Chafe, 1971). It seems that the whole concept of mental dictionary or subjective lexicon was a mistake when it comes to the study of semantic structures and that we ought to concern ourselves with questions about the representation and structure of knowledge instead.

Such a reorientation holds great promise for semantic memory research. Because of space limitations, I can do no more here than sketch some alternative directions that semantic memory research might take. I have been critical of the past record of research in this area, but I am optimistic and confident about its future. It could be a rich and rewarding field, if we learn from the mistakes of the past.

Semantic memory research may obtain the results that have eluded it so far when structures larger than the word are considered as its units of analysis. There are two very promising current attempts to explore such units. One is the work of Miller and Johnson-Laird (1976) on semantic fields, and the other is frame theory in one of its many versions. The former is still oriented toward the traditional concept of a lexicon, whereas with frame theory we finally manage to leave these old constraints behind.

The strength of Miller and Johnson-Laird's work is that whereas other work on semantic memory had a too narrow focus, Miller and Johnson-Laird have opted for a comprehensive approach. Sentence verification is not the only important task to be considered. One also needs to perform an action, to satisfy a request made by a sentence, or to find information to answer a question. A semantic memory model must be able to deal with all of these tasks.

Miller and Johnson-Laird use a procedural semantics that enables them to deal with the inherent fuzziness of concepts. The boundaries of concepts are fuzzy and context-dependent (Rosch, 1975), which ever since Aristotle has been a major obstacle in attempts to define words. Smith et al. (1974), following Aristotle, have attempted to overcome this problem by distinguishing between definitional and accidental properties. Miller and Johnson-Laird propose a model of the subjective lexicon in which functional information supplements the traditional attribute-oriented word definitions in an important way, permitting them to deal more successfully with the inherent lack of precision in the meaning of concepts. Furthermore, they can handle the problem of contextual constraints and shifts in meaning by resurrecting the notion of a semantic field. They did not invent this concept (like other field theories, it goes back to prewar Germany, e.g., Trier, 1931), but Miller and Johnson-Laird are the first to have successfully made use of this concept in the study of semantic memory. Fields were introduced into semantics for a very different reason than componential analysis, semantic markers, or defining features: not to analyze a semantic concept into its elements but to specify subtle differences in meaning through field contrasts. Thus, the analytical, context-free, logical definitions of word meaning that we inherited from Aristotle are replaced here by an emphasis on larger units. The meaning of a word is specified not per se but by its relationship to its context, which in this case is a semantic word field.

In a field theory, concept or word definitions do not stand alone but are supported by control processes that determine the use of the word definitions in various tasks and situations. To determine what the field characteristics are and how they depend on task demands and context may be more promising research questions than the concern with the structure of word concepts. Fields are shifting and interlocking, with each context, each task, demanding its own field analysis. Of course, these context effects cannot be arbitrary. As Bühler pointed out forcefully, "Meinen kann ich schliesslich alles mit allem— I can mean anything with anything—would be the surest means to make any language communication impossible, an end effect in which even the freest of the free is not interested [Bühler, 1934, p. 231]."

The other proposal for dealing with supraword units in the investigation of semantic memory structures is frame theory (Minsky, 1975; Schank & Abelson, 1977). The step from semantic fields to frames and schemata is an important one, because it finally takes us beyond the lexicon and lets us face squarely the problems of the representation of knowledge. But it is also a step from a reasonably well-worked-out theory with an interesting technical development (Miller and Johnson-Laird's use of decision tables) into the realm of programmatic ideas and terminological confusion.

Considerable terminological clarification could be achieved, if the field would choose to accept some suggestions made by Nelson (1977). She distinguishes between *concepts* (the kind of word concepts with which we have been concerned here, *robins* as well as *birds*), *event structures* (the relations and functions into which a concept enters, e.g., the concept *face* pertains to the event structure *wash your face*), *scripts* or *frames* (which contain several event structures and several concepts, organized by a goal, e.g., Schank's restaurant script), and *categories* (which are general and context-free structures, defining logical not physical relations). What we have here is a progression in unit size from concepts to event structures to scripts/categories. However, these units may vary in the extent to which they are context bound. Categories are abstract and by necessity context free, but concepts, event structures, and even scripts may or may not be context free. Nelson gives the example of a child whose concept of *face* is still context bound: at 18 months, the child understood "Wash your face," and "Where is your nose?" but not "Where is your face?". The concept *face* for that child was not yet freed from the particular event structure "Wash your face." Similarly, event structures as well as scripts may be context bound (e.g., in the case of the child that performs a certain action or action sequence well in a specific context but cannot do so outside that context). It is the context-bound–context-free dimension rather than the complexity dimension per se, which is relevant to the episodic–semantic memory distinction, according to Tulving's definition that I have used here. General knowledge, that is, semantic memory, is context free, whether it is about concepts or scripts.

There is another consideration here that must not be neglected, and that is a dimension of generality. Concepts may be specific (*robin*) or general (*bird*); frames or scripts too range from specific (the nature of *piggy bank* in Charniak, 1972) to general (the nature of *space* in Minsky, 1975). Categories may also be specific (e.g., a particular taxonomic hierarchy) or general, where they become principles for the organization of knowledge. Some authors would like to reserve the term *schema* for general categories. Schemata are thus structural entities for organizing knowledge (e.g., Beaugrande, 1979; Kintsch & van Dijk, 1978).

Of great interest to students of semantic memory are, of course, the appropriate conditions that transform a context-specific memory episode into an item of general knowledge that is usable in a wide variety of contexts. Or perhaps one should say that these conditions ought to be of much interest to students of semantic memory, because so far very little work has been done concerning this rather crucial problem. There are two obvious approaches. The first one is to study the acquisition of knowledge in young children; there has been a tradition of work in this area and much current interest (see the review by Nelson, 1977). Where psychologists have really been amiss is in the study of knowledge acquisition by adults or school-age children. This is a rich and fertile field awaiting psychologists with ideas. As Tulving said in 1972, we know a great deal about the learning and retention of episodic information, but what determines knowledge acquisition and retention? Nelson suggests that it is not a question of repetition or even deep levels of processing but a departure from prior expectations. A quality of surprise and disconfirmed predictions may be crucial. This suggests that in order to learn one must already know something, because without some prior knowledge there can be no predictions to be disconfirmed. Classical notions about apperception and the apperceptive mass offer themselves for study.

Knowledge use presents another set of important problems. Once a schema has been acquired, what controls the selection of the right kind of schema? In the current literature the schema, frame, or script often comes to the rescue like the *deus ex machina* in classical tragedy. But how do we know when to call up this script or that? What is involved in schema use?

We cannot consider these questions here. But this is perhaps enough to indicate that the semantic memory area provides rich research opportunities, if we manage to free ourselves from the traditional constraints that have hampered progress in this area. You may remember those pernicious ground rules that Smith described for semantic memory research. They were essentially a psychological restatement of Katz and Fodor's program for an interpretative semantics, which we have seen is an outgrowth of logical thinking, alien to both linguistics and psychology. Katz and Fodor's program is reasonable as long as one accepts their basic premise: that the meaning of a sentence can be calculated from the meaning of its constituent words plus syntactic structure. If so, then it indeed makes sense to concentrate on word meanings first and then to worry about the combination rules, putting off other issues altogether. The lexicon thus becomes the crucial component of semantics, in fact, almost the sole component. As Hörmann rather bitingly puts it "The lexicon in generative linguistics was the bag in which syntax carried along semantics, which it could not entirely forego [Hörmann, 1976, p. 117]."

But the premise may be rejected. It is not necessarily true that sentence meanings must be constructed from stored word meanings guided only by syntax. Everything I have said here leads to the conclusion that, in fact, such a program is not workable. Certainly, the idea of a lexicon containing word definitions with variable doses of accidental world knowledge mixed in has not been notably successful so far. Perhaps the structure that we have been looking for is not at the level of words at all but in higher-order units—fields, scripts, and schemata. Perhaps one cannot define a word except with reference to such higher-order units. This view is not new. Wittgenstein's philosophical writings provided the groundwork for this position (Wittgenstein, 1953). Wittgenstein pointed to the lack of clear boundaries between classes, explicitly rejecting a lexicon with class structure. His notion of the "language game" was an important stimulus for the rethinking of the relationship between language and psychology that is now in progress. Instead of a conception of meaning in terms of reference or structure, Wittgenstein's dictum that meaning is the use of language is being taken seriously by psychologists. Use is to be understood here in a broad sense, with linguistic as well as extralinguistic aspects, as Bühler had advocated some time ago. Hörmann claims that in order to know what a word means one must understand the sentence in which it is used. Sentences, on the other hand, can only be understood in a concrete speaker–hearer context. In order to comprehend the sentence, the Wittgensteinian comprehender must be able to know or guess what it means in the first place. Words obtain their meaning from the sentences in which they are used; they stand to sentences in a figure–ground relationship. I would amend Hörmann's scenario slightly because we are not so much concerned with sentences here as with semantic memory. Words obtain their meaning from the scripts, categories, and schemata in which they participate. It is the relatively stable structure of semantic memory that provides a basis for the semantics of words. These larger units ought to be the main concern of semantic memory research.

ACKNOWLEDGMENT

The comments of a number of colleagues, including Sam Glucksberg, Jan Keenan, and Ed Smith, have been very valuable to me in preparing this chapter. The opinions and evaluations offered here are, of course, strictly my own.

REFERENCES

Alberti Magni opera omnia. Cura et labore A. Borgnet, Vol. VI, Paris: 1890.

Anderson, R. C., & Ortony, A. On putting apples into bottles—A problem of polysemy. *Cognitive Psychology,* 1975, *7,* 167–180.

Aristotle, *Topica.* In W. D. Ross (Ed.), *The works of Aristotle* (Vol. 1). Oxford: Clarendon Press, 1928.

Atkinson, R. C., & Juola, J. F. Search and decision processes in recognition memory. In D. H. Krantz, R. C. Atkinson, R. D. Luce, & P. Suppes (Eds.), *Contemporary developments in mathematical psychology* (Vol. 1), San Francisco: Freeman, 1974.

Beaugrande, R. A. de. Toward a general theory of creativity. *Poetics,* 1979, *8,* 269–306.

Bierwisch, M. Semantics. In J. Lyons (Ed.), *New Horizons in Linguistics.* Harmonsworth, England, 1970.

Bolinger, D. L. The atomization of meaning. *Language,* 1965, *41,* 555–573.

Bower, G. H. A multicomponent theory of the memory trace. In K. W. Spence & J. T. Spence (Eds.), *The psychology of learning and motivation* (Vol. 1). New York: Academic Press, 1967.

Breuker, J. A. Semantic memory. *Nederlands Tijdschrift voor de Psychologie en haar Grensgebieden,* 1976, *31,* 131–151.

Bühler, K. *Sprachtheorie.* Jena: Rischer Verlag, 1934.

Chafe, W. L. Directionality and paraphrase. *Language,* 1971, *47,* 1–26.

Charniak, E. Toward a model of children's story comprehension. Cambridge, Mass.: MIT dissertation, 1972.

Chenu, M. D. *Toward understanding Saint Thomas.* Chicago: Henry Regnery, 1964.

Collins, A. N., & Loftus, E. F. A spreading activation theory of semantic processing. *Psychological Review,* 1975, *82,* 407–428.

Collins, A. M., & Quillian, M. R. Retrieval time from semantic memory. *Journal of Verbal Learning and Verbal Behavior,* 1969, *8,* 240–248.

Collins, A. M., & Quillian, M. R. Experiments on semantic memory and language comprehension. In L. Gregg (Ed.), *Cognition in learning and memory.* New York: Wiley, 1972.

Conrad, C. E. H. Cognitive economy in semantic memory. *Journal of Experimental Psychology,* 1972, *92,* 149–154.

Corbett, A. T., & Wickelgren, W. A. Semantic memory retrieval: Analysis of speed–accuracy tradeoff functions. *Quarterly Journal of Experimental Psychology,* 1978, *30,* 1–15.

Egeth, H. E. Parallel versus serial processes in multidimensional stimulus discrimination. *Perception & Psychophysics,* 1966, *1,* 245–252.

Fillenbaum, S., & Rapaport, A. *Structures in the subjective Lexicon.* New York: Academic Press, 1971.

Glass, A. L., & Holyoak, K. J. Alternative conceptions of semantic memory. *Cognition,* 1974/75, *3,* 313–339.

Guenther, R. K., & Klatzky, R. L. Semantic classification of pictures and words. *Journal of Experimental Psychology: Human Learning and Memory,* 1977, *3,* 498–514.

Hawkins, H. L., & Shipley, R. H. Irrelevant information and processing mode in speeded discrimination. *Journal of Experimental Psychology,* 1972, *96,* 389–395.

Hayes-Roth, B., & Hayes-Roth, F. The prominence of lexical information in memory representations of meaning. *Journal of Verbal Learning and Verbal Behavior,* 1977, *16,* 119–136.

Hollan, J. D. Features and semantic memory: Set-theoretic or network model? *Psychological Review,* 1975, *82,* 154–155.

Holyoak, K. J., & Glass, A. L. The role of contradictions and counterexamples in the rejection of false sentences. *Journal of Verbal Learning and Verbal Behavior,* 1975, *14,* 215–239.

Holyoak, K. J., Glass, A. L., & Mah, W. A. Morphological structure and semantic retrieval. *Journal of Verbal Learning and Verbal Behavior,* 1976, *15,* 235–247.

Homa, D., & Omohundro, J. Search and decision processes in semantic memory. *Journal of Verbal Learning and Verbal Behavior,* 1977, *16,* 383–394.

Hörmann, H. *Meinen und Verstehen.* Frankfurt, A. M.: Suhrkamp, 1976.

Hopf-Weichel, R. Reorganization in semantic memory. *Journal of Verbal Learning and Verbal Behavior,* 1977, *16,* 383–394.

Jorgensen, C. C., & Kintsch, W. The role of imagery in the evaluation of sentences. *Cognitive Psychology,* 1973, *4,* 110–116.

Katz, J. J. Recent issues in semantic theory. *Foundations of Language,* 1967, *3,* 123–194.

Katz, J. J., & Fodor, F. The structure of semantic theory. *Language,* 1963, *39,* 170–210.

Kintsch, W. *The representation of meaning in memory.* Hillsdale, N.J.: Lawrence Erlbaum Associates, 1974.

Kintsch, W., & van Dijk, T. A. Toward a model of text comprehension and production. *Psychological Review,* 1978, *85,* 363–394.

Landauer, T. K., & Meyer, D. E. Category size and semantic memory retrieval. *Journal of Verbal Learning and Verbal Behavior,* 1972, *11,* 539–549.

Lehrer, A. *Semantic fields and lexical structure.* Amsterdam: North Holland, 1974.

Loftus, E. F. Activation of semantic memory. *American Journal of Psychology,* 1974, *86,* 331–337.

Lorch, R. F. The role of two types of semantic information in the processing of false sentences. *Journal of Verbal Learning and Verbal Behavior,* 1978, *17,* 523–537.

Lounsbury, F. G. The structural analysis of kinship semantics. In H. G. Lund (Ed.), *Proceedings of the 9th International Congress of Linguistics.* London, 1964, 1073–1093.

McCloskey, M., & Glucksberg, S. Decision processes in verifying category membership statements: Implications for models of semantic memory. *Cognitive Psychology,* 1979, *11,* 1–37.

Miller, G. A. A psychological method to investigate verbal concepts. *Journal of Mathematical Psychology,* 1969, *6,* 169–191.

Miller, G. A., & Johnson-Laird, P. N. *Language and perception.* Cambridge, Mass.: Harvard University Press, 1976.

Minsky, M. A framework for representing knowledge. In P. H. Winston (Ed.), *The psychology of computer vision.* New York: McGraw-Hill, 1975.

Nelson, K. Cognitive development and the acquisition of concepts. In R. C. Anderson, R. J. Spiro, & W. E. Montague (Eds.), *Schooling and the acquisition of knowledge.* Hillsdale, N.J.: Lawrence Erlbaum Associates, 1977.

Osgood, C. E., Suci, G. J., & Tannenbaum, P. H. *The measurement of meaning.* Urbana, Ill.: University of Illinois Press, 1957.

Perfetti, C. A. Psychosemantics. *Psychological Bulletin,* 1972, *78,* 241–259.

Posner, M. I., & Keele, S. W. On the genesis of abstract ideas. *Journal of Experimental Psychology,* 1968, *77,* 353–363.

Quillian, M. R. Semantic memory. In M. Minsky (Ed.), *Semantic information processing.* Cambridge, Mass.: MIT Press, 1968.

Rips, L. J. Inductive judgments about natural categories. *Journal of Verbal Learning and Verbal Behavior,* 1975, *14,* 665–681. (a)

Rips, L. J. Quantification and semantic memory. *Cognitive Psychology,* 1975, *7,* 307–340. (b)

Rips, L. J., Shoben, E. J., & Smith, E. E. Semantic distance and verification of semantic relations. *Journal of Verbal Learning and Verbal Behavior,* 1973, *12,* 1–20.

Rips, L. J., Smith, E. E., & Shoben, E. J. Semantic composition in sentence verification. *Journal of Verbal Learning and Verbal Behavior,* 1978, *17,* 375–402.

Rosch, E. Universals and culture specifics in human categorization. In R. Breslin, W. Lonner, & S. Bochner (Eds.), *Cross-cultural perspectives on learning.* London: Sage Press, 1974.

Rosch, E. Cognitive reference points. *Cognitive Psychology,* 1975, *7,* 532–547.

Schaeffer, B., & Wallace, R. Semantic similarity and the comparison of word meanings. *Journal of Experimental Psychology,* 1969, *82,* 343–346.

Schank, R. C. Conceptual dependency: A theory of natural langauge understanding. *Cognitive psychology,* 1972, *3,* 552–631.

Schank, R. C., & Abelson, R. *Scripts, plans, goals, and understanding.* Hillsdale, N.J.: Lawrence Erlbaum Associates, 1977.

Smith, E. E. Theories of semantic memory. In W. K. Estes (Ed.), *Handbook of learning and cognitive processes* (Vol. 6). Hillsdale, N.J.: Lawrence Erlbaum Associates, 1978.

Smith, E. E., Rips, L. J., & Shoben, E. J. Semantic memory and psychological semantics. In G. H. Bower (Ed.), *The psychology of learning and motivation* (Vol. 8). New York: Academic press, 1974.

Smith, E. E., Shoben, E. J., & Rips, L. J. Structure and process in semantic memory: A featural model for semantic decisions. *Psychological Review,* 1974, *81,* 214–241.

Trier, J. *Der deutsche Wortschatz im Sinnbezirk des Verstandes.* Heidelberg: 1931.

Tulving, E. Episodic and semantic memory. In E. Tulving & W. Donaldson (Eds.), *Organization of memory.* New York: Academic Press, 1972.

Underwood, B. J. Attributes of memory. *Psychological Review,* 1969, *76,* 559–573.

Weinreich, U. On the semantic structure of language. In Greenberg, J. H. (Ed.), *Universals of language.* Cambridge, Mass.: M.I.T. Press, 1963.

Weinreich, U. Explorations in semantic theory. In T. A. Sebeok (Ed.), *Current trends in linguistics.* The Hague:Mouton, 1966.

Winston, P. H. The psychology of computer vision. New York: McGraw-Hill, 1975.

Wittgenstein, L. *Philosophical investigations.* New York: Macmillan, 1953.

31

Some Characteristics of Word Sequences Retrieved from Specified Categories

Tarow Indow
*Keio University, Mita Minato-ku
Tokyo, Japan**

ABSTRACT

The retrieval of words belonging to a specified category is a Poisson process. When a natural category that is not highly structured (i.e., flowers) is given, the subject makes a more or less random search through long-term memory. When an artificially created category is used (i.e., common nouns with a given sound in a specified position), the retrieval process either is the same as with natural categories or changes its pattern. When the search path is prescribed, words are retrieved at a constant rate. When retrieval from the same category is repeated a number of times, then the total number of retrieved words tends to increase and also the pattern of retrieval gradually changes. Some quantitative characteristics of these phenomena are described. It never happens that irrelevant words are retrieved, and it is rare that the same word is retrieved more than once in a sequence. The results are described from experiments that were designed to make explicit the mode of monitoring whether items selected in search are relevant and new. A model of search and monitoring is presented and an analogy between memory retrieval and visual search in pattern recognition is presented with some experimental data.

INTRODUCTION

When a subject is asked to list all words belonging to a given category, such as flowers, cumulative totals of retrieved words $n(t)$ as a function of time exhibit a smooth curve with negative acceleration. The phenomenon was first reported

---

*The author is now at the University of California, Irvine, United States.

by Bousfield and Sedgewick (1944) for group data, but it is usually the case that each single retrieval sequence by an individual subject is stable enough to be treated quantitatively (Johnson, Johnson, & Mark, 1951). Hence, discussions to follow are focused, as far as possible, upon data in which no averaging over subjects is involved. It cannot be claimed that the psychological mechanism in this type of retrieval is the same as the one underlying consecutive retrieval of appropriate words under natural conditions of human life. In the normal course of talking or conversation, words are retrieved so smoothly that we hardly feel any effort to search, at least on a conscious level. Only in case of the "tip of the tongue" state (Brown & MacNeill, 1966) are we aware of being engaged in some kind of scanning through our "archival memory" (Nickerson, 1977) or "lexical store" (Atkinson & Juola, 1974). In the course of dumping all words belonging to a specified category, however, one experiences a definite feeling of search from the beginning, and analysis of the results will reveal something about the organization of words in long-term memory (LTM), search or scanning processes through LTM, and also monitoring mechanisms during retrieval.

GENERAL PROPERTIES OF CUMULTATIVE TIME COURSE CURVE: $n(t)$

In almost all cases, the curve is approximately of the form

$$n(t) = n(\infty)(1 - e^{-\lambda t}), \qquad \lambda > 0 \tag{1}$$

and the two parameters, $n(\infty)$ and λ, are negatively related. The asymptote $n(\infty)$ represents the total number of relevant words available to the subject at that retrieval process, and λ is related to the rate of retrieval in the sense that

$$\frac{dn(t)}{dt} = \lambda[n(\infty) - n(t)]. \tag{2}$$

When retrieval from the same category is repeated a number of times, either in immediate succession or at moderately long (e.g., 2-week) intervals, $n(\infty)$ tends to increase and λ to be proportional to $1/n(\infty)$ (Indow & Togano, 1970). However, if a category is given in which words are sequentially organized and a search path is prescribed (e.g., cities in Japan from north to south), then $n(t)$ is linear up to $n(\infty)$:

$$n(t) = \lambda t, \qquad 0 \leq n(t) \leq n(\infty). \tag{3}$$

Hence, the fact that Equation 1 holds for natural categories such as flowers, mammals, family names, or one-syllable English nouns (for Japanese students) implies that words in these categories are not uniformly organized along some path in LTM and the subject has to make a random scan to some extent. Of course, the order of words in sequence is not completely independent from one retrieval to the next when retrieval from the same category is repeated. In terms of Kendall's rank correlation τ, the concordance is on the order of .10–.20. If retrieval is repeated more than four times in immediate succession, the order tends to be more stabilized (Indow & Togano, 1970). Also clustering of associated words in a single sequence is observed (Bousfield, 1953). However, the aforementioned low correlation suggests that clustering is not very stable over repeated retrievals.

Instead of categories that naturally exist, categories artificially created can also be used. Quite often, $n(t)$ is still of the form of Equation 1. Two examples are given in Fig. 31.1; Japanese common nouns having *nu* as the first sound or

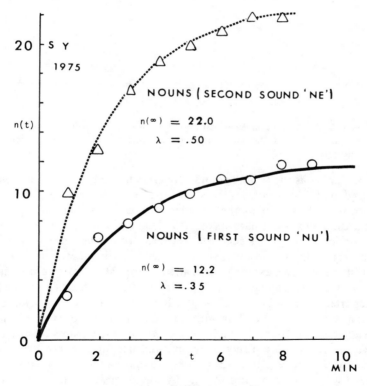

FIG. 31.1. Two examples of retrieval of a subject from artifically created categories of which the time course curve is the same with that for natural categories.

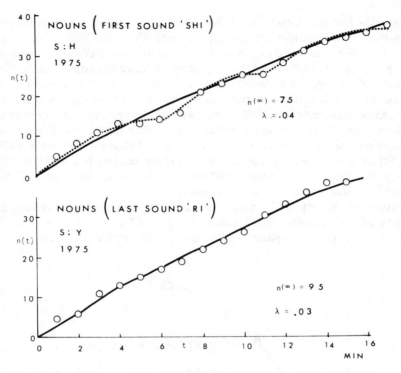

FIG. 31.2.   Two examples of retrieval of a subject from artificially created categories of which the time course curve is different from that for natural categories.

those having *ne* as the second sound.[1] It is very unlikely that words are being organized in LTM according to such criteria. In these cases, there is no difference at all, insofar as the cumulative time course curve is concerned, whether the category is natural or artificially defined. However, if an artificially defined category is such that retrieval from it becomes very difficult for the subject, then λ becomes small and the negative acceleration becomes less conspicuous. Two examples are shown in Fig. 31.2. Both are still fitted by Equation 1 but the change of mode will be clear. Th subject (Y) of the lower plot reported that he has to think of a few words, at each retrieval, before finding a relevant word ending with *ri* among them. If this is called *indirect* retrieval, then, in cases in which Equation 1 holds, all subjects admit that retrieval is much more *direct* in nature and usually it is not necessary to conceive of any irrelevant words in order to make a relevant word available. Relevant words seem to pop up one by one directly. In fact, intrusion of

---

[1]An unpublished experiment made by H. Suzuki in 1975.

irrelevant words in the retrieved sequence has never been observed except in cases in which the subject misunderstands the word. The upper plot in Fig. 31.2 shows a wiggling result and the subject (H) reported that she used the strategy of searching separate sets of common nouns one by one: animals, utensils, foods, or words with respective Chinese characters, and so on. Logically, the same strategy is applicable in natural categories too; for example, flowers can be separately searched according to season, color, and so forth. Nevertheless, retrieval is usually much more random according to both retrospection of subjects and the objective records of word sequences. In other words, it is generally the case that, when retrieving from natural categories, the subject does not try to make good use of subcategories that must exist. As shown in Fig. 31.3, the same type of wiggling of $n(t)$ is also noticed when retrieving is continued over a long period of time. However, this is not ascribed to the retrieval strategy under discussion but to the fact that the search effort fluctuates because the subject cannot maintain the effort to search at a constant level over 20 minutes, for example.

As mentioned before, $n(\infty)$ cannot be regarded as the absolute total number of words that the subject knows of a given category. If the retrieval is repeated, $n(\infty)$ tends to increase, which suggests that the subject fails to retrieve some relevant words in a single sequence (*miss*, or *omission*), but those missed words in LTM tend to be activated during that sequence so as to

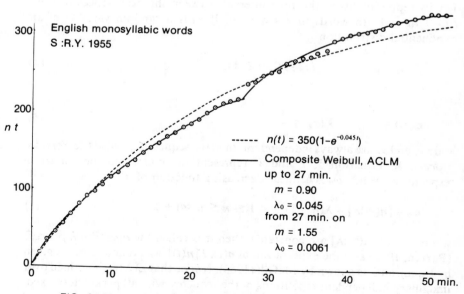

FIG. 31.3. An example of long retrieval sequence. The task was to list monosyllabic English words (by a Japanese student).

become available in subsequent retrievals. As also mentioned before, the probability of another kind of error (i.e., retrieving irrelevant words) is practically zero. There is one more kind of error, namely reproducing the same word more than once in a single sequence. The frequency with which this *repetition error* is made depends on whether the sequence is written by the subject or verbally produced and tape-recorded. Obviously, the error rate is slightly higher in the latter case. How to define and evaluate the rate of repetition error is not obvious because the probability of the error depends at each moment of retrieval on both $n(t)$ and the total number of relevant words in LTM. When a repetition error occurred, only the first retrieval was counted in $n(t)$ and repeated occurrence of the same word was not included in all the data reported here. Generally speaking, in the case of $n(\infty) = 60$, for example, duplications are at most 4 and usually on the order of 1 or 2, if any. According to reports of subjects, it happens rather frequently, especially at the later stage of a sequence, that words that have already been retrieved come to mind and are consciously discarded. Hence, there must be an efficient monitoring mechanism that discriminates *new* items from *old* items in each retrieval; some monitoring activity is conscious, but there may be preconscious monitoring as well.

RETRIEVAL SEQUENCE AS A POISSON PROCESS

Let us represent by τ_n the time interval between the occurrences of the $(n - 1)$th and nth words in a sequence. If τ_n is a random variable of an exponential distribution

$$f(\tau_n) = \omega_n e^{-\omega_n \tau_n} \qquad (\tau_n \geq 0, n \geq 1), \tag{4}$$

$$E(\tau_n) = \frac{1}{\omega_n}, \qquad V(\tau_n) = \frac{1}{\omega_n} \tag{5}$$

and τ_{n-1} and τ_n are always independent, then the sequence is called the *Poisson process*. In Equation 5, E and V represent the mean and the variance, respectively. When ω_n is a linear decreasing function of n,

$$\omega_n = [n(\infty)\lambda] - \lambda(n - 1), \qquad 1 \leq n \leq n(\infty) + 1 \tag{6}$$

where λ and $[n(\infty)\lambda]$ are constants, then it is called the *pure-death process* (Parzen, 1962) and the expectation of $n(t)$, $E[n(t)]$, as a function of t is given by Equation 1 as shown by McGill (1963). Notice that $E[N(t)]$ is defined over imaginary independent repetitions of the sequence with all parameters fixed. Probably this is a reason that each single retrieval sequence by an individual subject can be well fitted by Equation 1. Notice also that, on the average,

$$\frac{dn(t)}{dt} = \frac{1}{E(\tau_{n+1})} = \omega_{n+1}$$

and, when Equation 1 holds, Equations 2 and 6 imply the same thing. To use the cumulative time course curve $n(t)$ and to describe it by Equation 1 is useful for making explicit the fundamental property of retrieval processes under discussion. However, originally independent observations have to be converted to a nonindependent variable $n(t)$. As an alternative approach, the following simple procedure was tried. A retrieved sequence was divided into blocks, $(2k + 1)$ words in each. Then, according to Equation 5, empirical values of ω_n could be obtained by

$$\omega_n = (2k + 1) \ (t_{n+k} - t_{n-k-1})^{-1}, \tag{7}$$

where t_n represents the time at which the nth word was retrieved. Figure 31.4 shows ω_n thus estimated ($k = 1, 2$) for the two examples given in Fig. 1 of Indow and Togano (1970). As to the fit of Equation 1, these examples are of

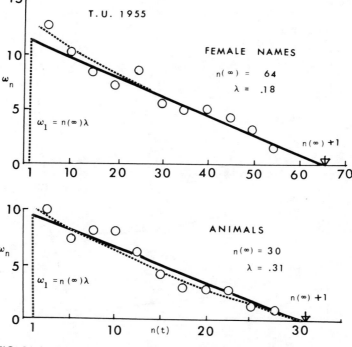

FIG. 31.4. Two examples of such a change of parameter ω_n in a Poisson process as a function of cumulative totals of retrieved words that is described by Equation 1 (the time course curves in Fig. 1 in Indow & Togano, 1970).

the same degree of goodness as the examples in Fig. 31.1 in the present chapter. As expected, the results can be fitted by Equation 6. However, as indicated by the dotted curve, slight curvilinearity being concave upward seems to exist. This phenomenon corresponds to what was called the *initial divergence* by Bousfield and Sedgewick of their group data (1944). However, it was almost undetectable in Fig. 1 of Indow and Togano, which suggests that ω_n is more sensitive in revealing the real features of the sequence. The curvilinearity is more obvious in Fig. 31.5 in which the data in Fig. 6 of Indow and Togano were reanalyzed in the following way.

Each of nine subjects repeated retrieval of flower names five times in immediate succession. For each sequence a figure like those in Fig. 31.4 was constructed ($k = 2$). Then nine curves in each repetition were Vincentized with regard to the abscissa by putting individual values of $n(\infty)$ equal to the

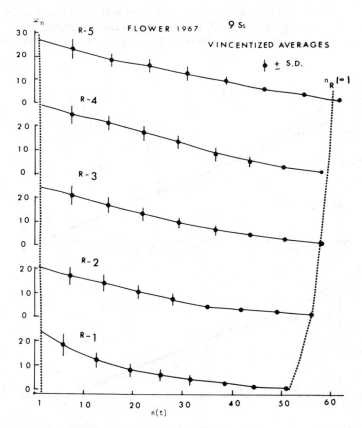

FIG. 31.5. Changes of curves of parameter ω_n in a Poisson process and of asymptote $n(\infty)$ according to repetition of retrieval in immediate succession (the time course curves in Fig. 6, Indow & Togano, 1970).

average value of $n(\infty)$ and then averages of nine curves were taken. As shown by vertical bars in Fig. 31.5, individual differences were rather small. Interestingly enough, the trend becomes less curved with repetition, which is rather contradictory to what is expected from Fig. 6 of Indow and Togano (1970) in which individual time course curves in each repetition were Vincentized with regard to the ordinate $n(t)$ and then averaged. By this procedure, larger individual differences in the earlier part of the sequence become more influential from $R - 3$ on, which makes the fit of Equation 1 to the average curves less satisfactory.

It seems to the author very natural to regard the retrieval sequence as a Poisson process. Hence, a psychologically meaningful question is why does ω_n decrease as a function of n approximately linearly or with negative acceleration as shown in Fig. 31.4 and 31.5? A possible reason would be the elimination of once retrieved words by the monitoring mechanism, at the conscious level or at a preconscious level, that has to take place more and more often as $n(t)$ increases (Indow & Togano, 1970; Kaplan, Carvellas, & Metlay, 1969). Should it be the only cause, though this seems rather unlikely to the author, then it implies that the scanning through LTM is serial and exhaustive and the distribution of relevant words in LTM is uniform when Equation 6 holds. The slight curvilinearity of ω_n as a function of n suggested in Fig. 31.4 and 31.5 implies that there may be some minor deviations from this model in the mode of scanning and/or in the structure of data base in LTM.

Although it may not be the only cause, it seems plausible that a monitoring mechanism is in operation that prevents intrusion of *old* words into the sequence. Hence, three experiments were conducted in which the monitoring mechanism was deliberately called for. The reports of these experiments are made elsewhere (Indow & Takada, 1979) and only the implications are discussed briefly in the next section.

ON THE MONITORING MECHANISM

When $n(t)$ reached a prescribed level n_i in a retrieval sequence, the following recognition test was made either immediately or with an interval of time T. In the recognition test, several probe words were presented one at a time and the subject had to decide for each word whether it had already been retrieved (Y) or not. The latter response consisted of two kinds: N to a probe word of the same category and N' to a probe word of a different category (e.g., "dog" when flower names are being retrieved). The recognition test is similar to the procedure used in the well-known experiments on short-term memory (STM) by Sternberg (1966, 1969, 1975). In the Sternberg case, however, the list in STM is given by the experimenter, whereas in the present case the list is generated by the subject. If the monitoring during retrieval process is being done through the serial and exhaustive scanning of the list of already retrieved words, decisions in the recognition test would also be made in a similar way. If so, the mean reaction time $\overline{Rt}(n)$ is expected to be a linear function of $n(t)$, the number of words of the self-generated list in STM,

$$\overline{Rt}(n) = \alpha + \beta n \tag{8}$$

and the slope β to be the same positive value for Y and N responses, and almost zero for N' responses (Indow & Murase, 1973). Sternberg's results consistently showed that β is about 38 msec for Y as well as N responses. The prescribed level n_i was changed in several steps and, in the case of immediate recognition tests $(T = 0)$, the retrieval process was resumed right after each recognition test. It was shown that the insertion of recognition tests did not disturb the retrieval process at all and $n(t)$ was again of the form of Equation 1. In cases with an interval $T > 0$, the retrieval was terminated at $n(t) = n_i$ and the subject was called for the recognition test when T had elapsed. The interval T was varied from 4 hours to 28 days. For recognition tests during the retrieval process $(T = 0)$, a set of $\overline{Rt}(n)$ was obtained for each subject and for the recognition test at $T(> 0)$, comparison of $\overline{Rt}(n)$ can be made only on group data.

The results clearly indicate that $\overline{Rt}(n)$ is not an increasing function of n for the three responses at all values of T. An example, the recognition test during the retrieval of flower names $(T = 0)$, is shown in Fig. 31.6 in which $n_i = 10$, 20, . . . , 80. For example, points farthest left represent means of reactive time of 14 subjects at $n(t) = 10$ for Y, N, and N', respectively. As subjects whose $n(\infty)$ is less than n_i cannot be included, the number of subjects upon which means are based, $N(n)$, becomes smaller than 14 when n_i is large. For N' $\beta = 0$ is not surprising, because no scanning is necessary. However, the same was true for Y and N, and β tends to be even negative, though slightly. Values of the slope β when $T = 4$ hours and 2 days for four categories based upon 24 subjects were as follows in terms of milliseconds.

	4 hours	2 days
Y	–2.3	1.3
N	–1.8	–1.4
N'	–2.4	–1.3

According to auxiliary experiments, the finding cannot be ascribed to uncontrollable factors such as differences in familiarity of words at different positions in a sequence. Consequently, the results suggest that decisions in the recognition test for self-generated lists are accomplished differently than in Sternberg's paradigm with lists given by the experimenter. That will also suggest that the monitoring during retreival process, the discrimination of

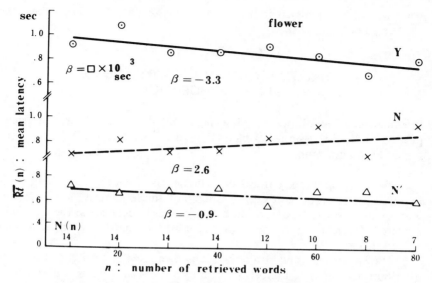

FIG. 31.6.   Results of recognition experiments inserted in retrieval sequences (flower names for 14 subjects).

new words from old ones, is supported by some other mechanism than scanning through the list of old words in STM.

Then, the following model for the monitoring seems to be most plausible. To each word in memory, there may be a list of attributes that constitutes its meaning. For each word belonging to a natural category, at least one tag indicating the category will be inherent in the list of attributes. For example, rose, chrysanthemum, and so on may all be tagged so as to indicate that these are flowers, and such tags would be useful in making these words susceptible to retrieval when flower is specified as the category. The monitoring during the retrieval as to whether a word is relevant or not will be done by means of these tags. When an artificially defined category is given, there will be no single tag representing the given category for any word. However, a set of relevant attributes (e.g., common name or having a specified sound at a specified position) will play the same role. The monitoring during the retrieval as to whether a word is new or old will be done in a similar way if a tag is attached to the list of attributes whenever a word is once retrieved. In the recognition test described previously, when a probe word is given, the subject understands its meaning, which means that the list of attributes is available to the subject at that moment. If there is a tag indicating that the word has been retrieved, the subject will respond Y. If the decision is made in this way, the reaction time may depend on the length of attribute list but must be independent of $n(t)$, the number of words already retrieved. Why β tends to be negative will be discussed in a report (Indow & Takada, 1979) where the whole results are described.

DIRECT ACCESS IN MEMORY AND IN
VISUAL PERCEPTION

In conclusion, the following analogy is presented as a model for the retrieval process under discussion. Let us imagine that each word in LTM is represented by a light bulb.

1. When a category, natural or artificial, is specified, most light bulbs representing relevant words are "turned on" simultaneously. Some relevant words may be missed, but that probability tends to decrease as the retrieval is repeated. It practically never happens, however, that irrelevant words are turned on.

2. Words are retrieved by a serial scanning guided by the lights. Either the distribution of lights is almost uniform over LTM or there are differences in density in different areas in LTM. In the latter case, scanning begins with the most densely populated areas.

3. The scanning will be nonexhaustive if the light is turned off whenever a word is retrieved, whereas the scanning will be exhaustive if there is no such mechanism. However, when a word is retrieved, no matter whether the light is left on or turned off, the bulb is tagged to indicate that the word has been retrieved. By means of the tag, the word is discarded when it is selected again in the exhaustive scanning.

4. If a parallel scanning, instead of a serial one, is assumed in 2, the monitoring as to whether selected words are new or old is not necessary. However, the result of the recognition test during the retrieval suggests that the bulb is still being tagged after a word is retrieved, though the tag is not used in the retrieval process.

5. The pattern of the distribution of lights in LTM and the mode of scanning through lights must be such that the combination accounts for the change of ω_n as shown in Figs. 31.4 and 31.5.

Under the assumption of parallel scanning, each word has its latency for being retrieved and Equation 1 implies that the distribution of latencies over the set of relevant words is exponential with the parameter λ, which corresponds to ω_n in Equation 4. At first, it seemed plausible to the author that the stability of Equation 1 is due to the robustness of the equation. It became clear by a computer simulation,[2] however, that a relatively small deviation from the

---

[2]An unpublished experiment made by H. Komiya in 1975.

exponential distribution is effective enough to make the cumulative time course curve detectably different from Equation 1.

As we do not know anything about underlying physiological mechanisms, presenting a model like this is analogous to writing a computer program in a higher-level symbolic language without paying any attention to internal processes in a computer. From this point of view, the author feels less difficulty in talking about the serial scanning process in 2, the process of attaching tags, and the monitoring mechanism in 3, but much difficulty in assuming the mechanism mentioned in 1 and 3—the (simultaneous) direct access to relevant words. The same type of mechanism was assumed in a recent model of retrieval from STM (Ratcliff, 1978). Without this assumption, we have to think of scanning over the entire domain of LTM, and this assumption seems to be inevitable to understand the consecutive retrieval of appropriate words in the natural course of talk or conversation. In the case of retrieval, almost all relevant words in a specified category are assumed to be turned on; in the natural course of talk, only one word most appropriate under a given context is usually turned on. Analogous direct access may or may not be involved in visual pattern recognition. Koehler and Restorff (1935) pointed out that the spontaneous pairing of two identical figures embedded in a group of several figures of different types is analogous to retrieval from memory, and the ease of pairing or of retrieval depends on the degree of dissimilarity between the particular item and the rest of the items in the visual field or in memory. The same argument will apply to detection of a given single target in visual search. Under ordinary conditions, visual scanning is serial and self-terminating, and very slow compared with memory scanning (Indow & Murase, 1973).

Experiments are under progress that are designed to test whether there is detection without search of a target or of a pair of the same items in visually presented figures, and the first study[3] failed to reveal the operation of such a process. A visual stimulus consisted of a number of meaningless figures randomly scattered in a plane. A few examples of the figures are shown in the inserts of Fig. 31.7 and 31.8. It will be clear that the figures within each of the four groups are relatively similar to each other and that there is a different degree of similarity between groups. The degree of similarity was scaled in two auxiliary experiments. In one of the main experiments, a target figure was given (triangle in the insert of Figure 31.7) and then a stimulus consisting of several figures was presented. The subject had to response Y or N according to whether or not the target figure was in the stimulus. In the other experiment, a stimulus consisting of several figures was presented and the subject had to respond Y or N depending on whether or not the stimulus contained a pair of identical figures (triangles in the insert of Fig. 31.8). In both inserts each circle

---

[3]An unpublished experiment made by Omiya in 1976.

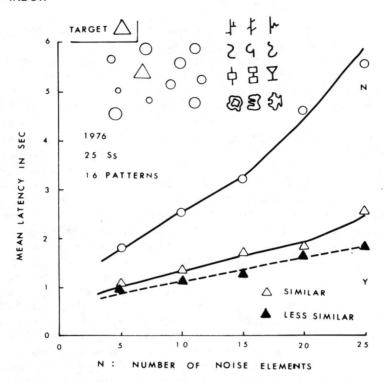

FIG. 31.7. Visual detection of a given target figure, embedded in more or less similar *n* figures.

represents a more or less different figure of the same type, and the degree of similarity between the figure represented by triangle and distractors represented by circles was varied in three steps. Insofar as figures used in this experiment are concerned, even when figures of greatest difference in pattern were used, latency of Y response was still an increasing function of the number of distractors (filled triangles in the plots in figure 31.7 and 31.8), which seems to suggest that a serial search underlies a task of the kind under discussion. It is of interest to determine the degree of dissimilarity at which the detection or pairing becomes completely independent of the number of distractors. It is easier in visual search experiments than in memory search experiments (especially LTM search) to control the structure of the data base on such aspects as number and distribution of items and similarity among items. Hence, in order to throw light upon the somewhat mysterious process of direct access in memory retrieval, what we might profitably do is to establish firm correspondences between analogous phenomena in memory retrieval and in visual search.

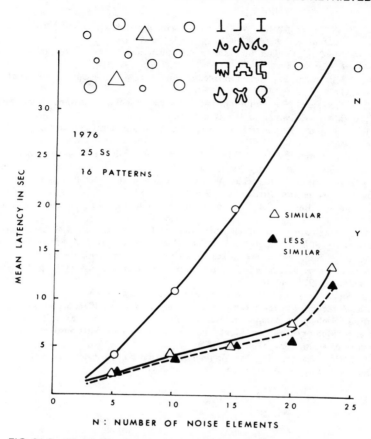

FIG. 31.8. Visual detection of a pair of identical figures embedded in more or
less similar *n* figures.

ACKNOWLEDGMENT

The study was partially supported by Grant No. 362 from Electrical Communication
Laboratories, NTT.

REFERENCES

Atkinson, R. C., & Juola, J. F. Search and decision processes in recognition memory. In D. K.
    Krantz, R. C. Atkinson, R. D. Luce, & R. Suppes (Eds.), *Contemporary developments in
    mathematical psychology* (Vol. 7). San Francisco; Freeman, 1974.
Bousfield, W. A. The occurrence of clustering in the recall of randomly arranged associates.
    Journal of General Psychology, 1953, *49,* 229–240.

Bousfield, W. A., & Sedgewick, H. W. An analysis of sequences of restricted associative responses. *Journal of General Psychology,* 1944, *30,* 149–165.

Brown, R., & MacNeill, D. The "tip of the tongue" phenomenon. *Journal of Verbal Learning and Verbal Behavior,* 1966, *4,* 325–337.

Indow, T.,. & Murase, A. Experiments on memory and visual scanning. *Japanese Psychological Research,* 1973, *15,* 136–146.

Indow, T., & Takada, H. Recognition memory of retrieved sequence of words. Submitted for publication, *Acta Psychologica,* September, 1979.

Indow, T., & Togano, K. On retrieving sequence from long-term memory. *Psychological Review,* 1970, 317–331.

Johnson, D. M., Johnson, R. C., & Mark, A. L. A mathematical analysis of verbal fluency. *Journal of General Psychology,* 1951, *44,* 121–128.

Kaplan, I. T., Carvellas, T., & Metlay, W. Searching for words in letter sets of varying size. *Journal of Experimental Psychology,* 1969, *82,* 377–380.

Koehler, W., & von Restorff, H. Zur Theorie der Reproduktion, *Psychologische Forschung,* 1935, *21,* 56–112.

McGill, W. J. Stochastic latency mechanisms. In R. D. Luce, R. R. Bush, & E. Galanter (Eds.), *Handbook of mathematical psychology* (Vol. 1), chap. 6. New York: Academic Press, 1963.

Nickerson, R. S. Some comments on human archival memory as a large data base. In *Proceedings, very large data bases,* Third International Conference on Very Large Data Bases, Tokyo, Japan, 1977, 159–168.

Parzen, E. *Stochastic processes.* San Francisco: Holden-Day, 1962.

Ratcliff, R. A theory of memory retrieval. *Psychological Review,* 1978, *85,* 59–108.

Sternberg, S. High-speed scanning in human memory. *Science,* 1966, *153,* 652–654.

Sternberg, S. Memory-scanning: Mental processes revealed by reaction-time experiments. *American Scientist,* 1969, *57*(4), 421–457.

Sternberg, S. Memory-scanning: New findings and current controversies. *Quarterly Journal of Experimental Psychology,* 1975, *27,* 1–32.

32

Interaction of Intrinsic and Extrinsic Knowledge in Sentence Recall

Gregory V. Jones
University of Oxford
England

ABSTRACT

A model is described that distinguishes between intrinsic knowledge (concerning the occurrence of a particular event) and extrinsic knowledge (concerning the location of that event within one's store of knowledge as a whole). The distinction is associated with one between direct-access and generation-recognition routes in retrieval. According to the model, configural (or gestalt) effects in recall are expected to arise only when generative processes utilizing extrinsic knowledge occur at both encoding and retrieval. The results of a sentence recall experiment that is reported provide support for this view.

INTRODUCTION

This chapter is concerned with what are hypothesized to be two functionally different types of knowledge, *intrinsic* and *extrinsic,* and with their roles in sentence recall. Suppose that one is first informed that *The player served the ball* and then subsequently is asked the question *What did the player serve?* There are two ways in which this question may be answered. First, one may simply recall the particular information conveyed by the event itself (intrinsic knowledge): in this case that it was the ball that was served. Second, one may use extraneous information (extrinsic knowledge) to infer that a player is most likely to have served a missile such as a ball. Indeed, this inference could of course be drawn even by a second person who had never heard the original sentence. Thus it is suggested that extrinsic knowledge may play a generative role in retrieval. In addition, extrinsic knowledge may play a similar role at the encoding stage; that is, the perceiver of a sentence may encode not only the verbatim stimulus presented but also further related information, for example, that the sentence refers to tennis.

The major purpose of this chapter is to investigate how these two types of knowledge, intrinsic and extrinsic, interact in sentence processing and specifically to test a particular explanation of the observation of configural effects in multiple-cued recall. First, however, some existing evidence concerning the interaction of intrinsic and extrinsic knowledge in the recall not of sentences but instead of simple word pairs is reviewed.

Consider a pair of weakly related words such as *cloth* and *SHEEP*. Suppose that, as for example in the experiments of Watkins and Tulving (1975), a person is first shown such a pair and subsequently tested for recall in two different ways. The person first is asked whether or not they recognize the word *SHEEP,* and second is provided with *cloth* as a cue with which to attempt to recall *SHEEP.* A considerable number of experiments of this general form have been carried out and have yielded the interesting finding that items may frequently be recalled although they cannot be recognized. Indeed, the level of recall may even be higher overall than that of recognition (Tulving & Thomson, 1973; Watkins & Tulving, 1975). Furthermore, Tulving and Wiseman (1975) have gathered together the results of a large number of such experiments and shown that there is a considerable regularity in them, with recognition and recall empirically related in such a way that

$$P(\text{Rn}|\text{Rc}) = P(\text{Rn}) + c[P(\text{Rn}) - P(\text{Rn})^2], \tag{1}$$

where $P(\text{Rn})$ is the probability of correct recognition, $P(\text{Rn}|\text{Rc})$ is the probability of correct recognition given that correct recall has occurred, and the value of c is approximately constant at $\frac{1}{2}$.

Recently, Flexser and Tulving (1978) have proposed that the partial independence of recognition and recall expressed by Equation 1 arises because the recall and recognition processes are independent at the retrieval stage but covary with goodness of item encoding. In contrast, the view is taken here that in retrieval *cloth* may lead to *SHEEP* in two different ways. First, *cloth* may access directly the intrinsic knowledge of its co-occurrence with SHEEP, whereas, second, extrinsic knowledge may be used to generate a series of words related to *cloth* until one of them, *SHEEP,* is correctly recognized (as proposed by Bahrick, 1970, 1979). It was shown by Jones (1978a) that if it is assumed that these two processes operate independently, then Equation 1 (initially formulated empirically by Tulving & Wiseman, 1975) may also be obtained theoretically. In this case the value of c is given by $P(\text{G})[1 - P(\text{E})]/P(\text{Rc})$, where $P(\text{G})$ is the probability of generating *SHEEP* from *cloth* using extrinsic knowledge and $P(\text{E})$ is the probability of utilizing encoded intrinsic knowledge concerning the co-occurrence of *cloth* and *SHEEP.*

This theory makes three predictions. The first is that the empirical values of c and of $P(\text{Rc})$ should be inversely correlated. The second is that, for constant conditions of encoding, values of $cP(\text{Rc})$ should be positively related to the degree of association between cue and target [i.e., $P(\text{G})$]. The third is that, for a constant degree of association between cue and target, values of $cP(\text{Rc})$ should be negatively related to the degree to which cue and target are encoded together [i.e., $P(\text{E})$]. Relevant data support the first two predictions (see Jones, 1978a), and as yet are not available in relation to the third. Thus direct evidence exists for the utility of the distinction between intrinsic and extrinsic knowledge.

DIRECT-ACCESS RETRIEVAL

Following Bower (1967, 1977), it is assumed that the memory trace that remains after the occurrence of an event may be conceptualized as a bundle of attributes or components that to some extent at least may function independently; for example, individual attributes may be forgotten separately (Bregman, 1968; Jones, 1979). A specific form of this view has been termed the *fragmentation hypothesis* by Jones (1976, 1978b). According to this view, recall of a multicomponent memory trace (or *fragment* of an original event) is rendered possible only as a result of the occurrence of a retrieval cue whose own content overlaps with that of the trace. A similar view has been expressed by Tulving and Bower (1974) and Tulving and Watkins (1975), but the present model goes further by postulating that the direct-access retrieval process can succeed if and only if there is content overlap between retrieval cue and trace.

One way in which to investigate the recall of sentential intrinsic knowledge is to use sentences in which the key words are selected at random (subject to certain weak semantic and syntactic selection rules), for example *The player saw the chair.* Here extrinsic knowledge cannot generally be used in the way that it could for a highly redundant sentence such as *The player served the ball* to generate one part of the sentence from another part used as cue. Such generative processes are inherently directional and, hence, are expected to cause the different words of redundant sentences to differ in their efficacies as retrieval cues (Horowitz & Prytulak, 1969; Wright, 1969), though Perfetti and Goldman (1974) only obtained such differences for sentences presented with prior thematizing contexts. For nonredundant sentences, on the other hand, the finding for reflexive comparisons (i.e., $P(a|b)$ against $P(b|a)$) has in general been one of symmetry (Adams, 1978, Exp. 3, 4; Wilhite, 1980). Similarly, Anderson and Bower (1973, chap. 10) have reported the results of a series of detailed, large-scale experiments using randomly constituted sentences such as *In the kitchen the policeman interviewed the celebrity,* and these have been shown by Jones (1978b) to accord closely with the predictions of the fragmentation hypothesis. The results of several other related sets of experiments investigating the multiple cuing of simple SVO (subject–verb–object) sentences (viz., those of Anderson, 1976, chap. 10, of Anderson & Bower, 1972, and of Foss & Harwood, 1975) are open to a wider range of interpretation, however. In particular, they suggest that memory may be organized not only associatively (as assumed by the unelaborated fragmentation hypothesis) but also configurally, and they are considered in more detail below.

CONFIGURAL EFFECTS IN MEMORY

The general philosophical issue of whether memory can better be accounted for on an associative or on a configural or gestalt basis has received excellent discussion from Anderson and Bower (1973, chap. 1–3). An important line of empirical work investigating this issue, originated by Anderson and Bower (1972), is relevant to the present work. Anderson and Bower proposed a particular form of associative model (subsequently incorporated into the larger HAM model as described by Anderson & Bower, 1973, chap. 11) in which a sentence is represented in memory by a particular propositional structure composed of nodes and associative links. All three major constituents of an SVO sentence in memory are postulated to be linked separately to a particular propositional node, P, and a characteristic probability with which excitation traverses each of the associative links in recall is assumed: A from S to P, B from V to P, and C from P to O. Thus it can be seen that according to this model

$$P(O|S) = AC, \quad P(O|V) = BC, \quad \text{and} \quad P(O|SV) = AC + BC - ABC.$$

Substituting,

$$P(O|SV) = P(O|S) + P(O|V) - P(O|S)P(O|V)/C,$$
$$P(O|SV) \leq P(O|S) + P(O|V) - P(O|S)P(O|V);$$

that is, according to Anderson and Bower's hypothesis the efficacy of two cues in inducing recall is less than or equal to that which would be expected if the two cues acted independently (the value of the latter expectation could in practice be reduced by correlations over subjects or items). If each sentence were encoded as a gestalt, however, it might be expected that the efficacy of the two cues would be greater than that which would be expected if they acted independently, because the original encoding would be more nearly reinstated by the double cue.

Anderson (1976) has reviewed several sets of experimental results in this area and concluded that they are consistent with Anderson and Bower's associative model when subjects are given no special instructions on how to process the sentences to be remembered but that configural effects are observed when subjects are given instructions that encourage them to process the sentences as meaningful entities: instructions to generate continuations to the sentences (Anderson & Bower, 1972, Exp. 3, 4) or to rate the meaningfulness of each sentence (Foss & Harwood, 1975).

The situation is complicated, however, by the fact that Anderson and Bower's is only one possible version of the associative hypothesis. The fragmentation hypothesis version, on the other hand, allows for considerably higher levels of double-cued recall. According to this model the characteristic probabilities of occurrence of three different types of trace are relevant. These may be denoted as j, the probability of occurrence of a full SVO trace; l, the probability of an SO trace; and m, the probability of a VO trace. It can be seen that the posited feature-overlap retrieval process should yield

$$P(O|S) = j + l, \qquad P(O|V) = j + m, \quad \text{and} \quad P(O|SV) = j + l + m.$$

Substituting,

$$P(O|SV) = P(O|S) + P(O|V) - j, \quad \text{or} \quad P(O|SV) \leq P(O|S) + P(O|V);$$

that is, according to the fragmentation hypothesis the efficacy of a double cue may be as high only as that to be expected if the two cues exerted their effects without any redundancy of action at all. Foss and Harwood (1975) have in fact proposed that this upper bound is the extreme value allowed by any associative theory. The results of the majority of multiple-cuing experiments have conformed to this upper bound (see Jones, 1978b). For three sets of results the bound has been exceeded but in each case not significantly so (Anderson, 1976, chap. 10, Exp. 1; Foss & Harwood, 1975, Exp. 1, 2). Thus investigation of the effects of multiple cuing at present does not appear to provide conclusive evidence for the existence of gestalt mnemonic processing.

It should be noted, however, that the conformation of existing data to the predicted double-cued limit cannot be taken as strong evidence in favor of the unelaborated fragmentation hypothesis. This is because there are many possible patterns of data arising from configural processing that could nevertheless remain within the theoretical bounds. In particular, the previous derivation of the fragmentation upper bound shows that it should be reached only when $j = 0$, that is, where there are no SVO traces at all in existence at the time of recall. This condition is unlikely to obtain in practice, however, because it is noticeable that sentences are most frequently recalled either completely (i.e., via SVO traces) or not at all (Anderson & Bower, 1973; Horowitz & Prytulak, 1969). Consequently, the expected efficacy of a multiple cue is usually considerably less than that dictated by the theoretical upper bound. Configural enhancement of the expected level of recall might still be insufficient to cause it to exceed the bound. It is desirable, therefore, to devise a more sensitive test for the occurrence of a configural effect.

Consider an experiment using SVO sentences in which recall is cued not only by S, V, and SV but also by O, SO, and VO. Then the fragmentation hypothesis predicts that the average probabilities of failing to produce any correct recall should be the same for single and for double cues. This perhaps counterintuitive prediction follows from consideration of the expected probabilities of no recall for each of the types of cue in terms of the relevant types of trace. Five types of trace are relevant here (three of which were introduced previously) and may be denoted as $j = P(\text{SVO})$, $k = P(\text{SV})$, $l = P(\text{SO})$, $m = P(\text{VO})$, and $n = P(\text{null})$, where a null trace is one that is not of use in cued recall (through having lost either all or all but one of its relevant components). For the cue types S, V, O, SV, SO, and VO, the expected probabilities of no recall are $(m + n)$, $(l + n)$, $(k + n)$, $(k + n)$, $(l + n)$, and $(m + n)$, respectively. It may be noted that the model of Anderson and Bower (1972, 1973) would make a similar prediction if it were modified by making the assumption that all links are symmetric; for example, the expected probability of no recall would be $(1 - AB - AC + ABC)$ for cuing with VO as well as with S.

The predicted symmetry of the single- and double-cued no recalls should be disrupted by any configural processing that, in raising the probability of correct recall to a double cue, should concomitantly produce a larger degree of absence of recall for single than for double cues. It can be seen that the present associative prediction is open to a considerably more sensitive empirical test than that considered earlier, for it takes the form of specifying an equality rather than an inequality. Such a test is reported below.

GENERATIVE PROCESSES AT ENCODING AND RETRIEVAL

It is apparent from the foregoing that there is suggestive (though, it is argued, not conclusive) evidence from multiple-cuing experiments for the configural recall of sentences that a person has been instructed to process meaningfully. Such a phenomenon might be expected to result from subjects interpreting such instructions as encouraging the utilization of extrinsic knowledge. In particular, when a subject is asked to judge the likelihood of a sentence, it is plausible that the success with which it is possible to use extrinsic knowledge to generate an element that is related to two or more components of that sentence may be used as an index of its likelihood. Subsequently, configural effects in recall will arise if the relevant two or more components when provided as retrieval cues are successful in again generating the same element as was encoded at presentation, which may then function as an additional direct-access retrieval cue. It follows from this explanation that the magnitude of any observed configural effect should be positively related to the degree of relation between the different components of a stimulus and, thus, to its rated likelihood. An experimental test of this prediction was carried out as follows.

Method

The 24 subjects in this experiment, who were paid for their participation, were all members of the Oxford Subject Panel and aged between 18 and 30 years; 16 were female and 8, male.

A set of 108 simple SVO sentences (e.g., *The miner won the pipe*) was formed by randomly combining 108 human nouns, 108 transitive verbs, and 108 nonhuman object nouns. Verbs with strong semantic selection rules (e.g., *drank*) were not included, so as to avoid the occurrence of severe semantic anomaly.

Sentences were presented in three sets of 36 each. Each sentence was printed on a separate page of a booklet, which the subject studied (in time with an auditory bleep) for 10 sec each. During this period the subject had to underline one of the words *unlikely/possible/likely,* which were printed underneath each sentence. The order of presentation of sentences was balanced over subjects. The 36 sentence pages were followed by 36 question pages arranged in the same order. Each question consisted of an earlier sentence with either one or two of its key words omitted. The subject had 15 sec in each case in which to attempt to recall the missing word(s). The six different types of question (S, V, O, SV, SO, VO cues) each occurred six times in each set, at intervals arranged so that the average question serial position for each type of question was the same.

Results

The judgments made concerning the likelihood of each sentence proved to be quite consistent, the average value of the 24 correlations between individual subjects' rankings of the set of sentences and rankings averaged over subjects being 0.66. Sentences were rated as *unlikely, possible,* and *likely* on 34.2, 43.6, and 22.2% of occasions, respectively. As examples, all subjects rated *The archer painted the dust* as *unlikely;* subjects on average rated *The judge jerked the bowl* as *possible* (i.e., it received equal numbers of *likely* and *unlikely* ratings in addition to *possible* ones), and all subjects rated *The artist raised the pencil* as *likely.* The recall data corresponding to individual sentential rankings of *unlikely, possible,* and *likely* were analyzed separately.

Table 32.1 shows the overall probability of correctly recalling the object when cued by subject and verb either singly or together. It can be seen that

TABLE 32.1
Probabilities of Recall of Objects (O) Given Subjects (S) and Verbs (V), Together With
Theoretical Double-Cued Upper Limits

Sentence Type	$O\|S$	$O\|V$	$O\|SV$	$(O\|S + O\|V - O\|S \cdot O\|V)$	$(O\|S + O\|V)$
Unlikely	.361	.293	.443	.548	.654
Possible	.421	.332	.500	.613	.753
Likely	.396	.386	.687	.629	.782

none of the observed double-cued probabilities exceeds the fragmentation nonredundant-cues upper bound [viz., $P(O|S) + P(O|V)$] although the Anderson and Bower independent-cues upper bound [viz., $P(O|S) + P(O|V) - P(O|S)P(O|V)$] is exceeded for *likely* sentences. It may be noted that the overall magnitude of the configural tendency appears smaller than in the comparable experiments of Anderson (1976, chap. 10, Exp. 1) and of Foss and Harwood (1975, Exp. 1, 2). This perhaps resulted from the use here of a different orienting task and also the use of a greater variety of cues, which may have caused configural encoding to be less specifically related to potential S and V cues alone.

The fragmentation hypothesis prediction that the average probabilities of no correct recall to single and to double cues should be equal was tested using the results shown in Table 32.2. Any configural effect should be manifest as an excess incidence of no-correct recall for single cuing. Examination of Table 32.2 indicates that such an excess occurred for each of the three levels of rating, its magnitude constituting 1.6, 4.1, and 13.9% for *unlikely, possible,* and *likely* sentences, respectively. Sign tests indicated that the effect was reliable only in the case of *likely* sentences, for which it was displayed by 18 subjects out of 24, $p < .01$. It may also be noted that even for the *unlikely* sentences the specific symmetries predicted by the simple fragmentation hypothesis did not hold well: V was the least effective single cue, but the

TABLE 32.2
Percentage Occurrences of Complete Recall Failure for Each Type of
Cue

Sentence Type	Cue Type					
	S	V	O	SV	SO	VO
Unlikely	58.2	64.2	46.6	55.7	52.1	56.5
Possible	51.9	63.5	53.5	50.0	55.9	50.8
Likely	52.8	52.5	36.9	31.3	39.5	29.8

Note: S = subject, V = verb, O = object.

corresponding SO cue was the most rather than the least effective double cue. The reason for this is unclear.

Discussion

It was proposed that configural effects in multiply cued recall are observed when a subject is able to generate using extrinsic knowledge the same element related to two or more stimulus components at both presentation and retrieval. It was found that, consistent with this proposal, the experimentally estimated magnitude of such an effect was positively related to the rated likelihood of the stimulus material, which was taken as a measure of the ease with which such an element could be generated.

It can be seen from the single-cued data of Tables 32.1 and 32.2 that the base level of (nonconfigural) recall also increased with rated sentence likelihood. This finding is consistent with an elaboration of the original dual-mechanism model of recall. In that model (Jones, 1978a) it was assumed that $P(E)$ (the probability of directly accessing encoded knowledge) and $P(G)$ (the probability of generating the correct candidate at retrieval) were independent of each other. According to the present view, however, the two quantities may be expected to exhibit some degree of positive correlation. This follows from the positing of a generative process at encoding as well as at retrieval and, thus, the possibility of facilitatory mediation. In the case considered previously, for example, the probability of *cloth* and *SHEEP* being encoded in the same memory trace might be enhanced by the formation of an encoding corresponding to, say, *cloth*–wool–*SHEEP*. According to this view, varying the degree of association between cue and target should affect not only the generation-recognition route but also, as in the present experiment, the direct-access route in retrieval.

Direct evidence of the nonindependence of the two retrieval routes comes from reanalysis of the recognition and recall data which were considered by Jones (1978a). Instead of couching predictions in terms of the Tulving–Wiseman constant, c, it is possible to estimate values for the $P(E)$ and $P(G)$ parameters directly.[1] When recognition fails, recall can occur only by means of direct accessing, and thus the value of the $P(E)$ parameter can be estimated as the probability of correct recall conditionalized on recognition failure [i.e., $P(E) = P(Rc|\overline{Rn})$]. The value of the $P(G)$ parameter can then be obtained by rewriting Equation 2 of Jones (1978a) as

$$P(G) = \frac{P(Rc) - P(E)}{P(Rn)[1 - P(E)]} . \tag{2}$$

---

[1]The author is grateful to Arthur J. Flexser for pointing out that direct estimation of these parameters is possible.

For the corpus of data examined by Jones (1978a), comparison of the two sets of parameter values indicates, as anticipated, a significant positive correlation, $r(103) = .45, p < .001$. The existence of this correlation has several interesting implications.

First, it is of course consistent with the view that generative processes are of importance at encoding as well as at retrieval. Second, the bootstrapping logic that allows the empirical values of the two sets of estimates to demonstrate that one of the underlying assumptions of their derivation is not strictly correct and, hence, that the estimates themselves may not be strictly correct either may be remarked upon. It can be seen that the existence of a positive correlation between $P(E)$ and $P(G)$ does not in fact affect the correctness of $P(Rc|\overline{Rn})$ as an estimator for $P(E)$, because recognition failure means that the associated value of $P(G)$ is irrelevant to the probability of recall. On the other hand, for cases of *correct* recognition the correlation will tend to make the operation of the two retrieval routes redundant, lowering the overall level of recall; conversely, for an observed level of recall, Equation 2 here will tend to underestimate the correct value of $P(G)$. Third, it was assumed by Jones (1978a) not only that $P(E)$ and $P(G)$ were independent of each other but also that they were both independent of $P(Rn)$. Using the direct estimates given earlier, this assumption also was investigated. It was found that there was not significant evidence of a relationship between $P(Rn)$ and $P(G)$, $r(103) = -.09$ but that there was between $P(Rn)$ and $P(E)$, $r(103) = -.24, p < .05$. The latter negative correlation perhaps reflects a tendency for subjects to concentrate during stimulus presentation either on the potential target alone, which would facilitate $P(Rn)$, or else on both the potential cue and target, which would facilitate $P(E)$; in any case, the correlation seems unlikely to affect quantitative values of parameter estimates greatly. Finally, it is apparent that it is possible to test predictions concerning hypothesized generative or encoding effects using direct estimates of $P(G)$ or $P(E)$ rather than by means of the expression $cP(Rc)$ together with the assumption of otherwise constant variables (as in the latter two of the three predictions listed on p. 639). When this was carried out for the five sets of data considered by Jones (1978a, Table 1), for example, it was found that there was perfect agreement between objective degrees of cue–target association and corresponding estimated values of $P(G)$ for all but 1 of the 12 experimental conditions.

The present model is closely related to those proposed by Kintsch (1974) and by Anderson (1976). Kintsch proposed that the particular combination of elemental features encoded to represent a verbal item is a function of the context of that item and that subsequent recognition of the item is dependent on a sufficiently close reinstatement of that particular coding. Using the terms of Tulving (1972), semantic memory is postulated to be utilized in the feature selection process at both presentation and recall, although the resulting encoding is postulated in both cases to reside in the separate episodic store.

The account of Anderson (1976), like that proposed here, does not require a distinction to be made between episodic and semantic memory but instead proposes that the contexts of presentation and of recall determine the selection either of a set of propositions that may be elaborated concerning the item to be remembered or else of particular senses of the relevant words (Reder, Anderson, & Bjork, 1974). At recall, a multiple cue is more likely to reinstate the original elaborations or senses and thus to lead to configural effects. The explanation of configural effects proposed here is closely similar to Anderson's elaboration explanation, differing principally in that it is not assumed that elaboration is of a propositional nature. This less restrictive explanation appears to have some intuitive plausibility (e.g., subjectively the sentence *The shop sells bread* may produce the isolated elaboration *baker* rather than a proposition corresponding to, say, *The shop is owned by a baker*), but it is difficult to envisage how the two explanations might be differentiated experimentally.

A notable feature of the present treatment of memory for sentences is its nonlinguistic nature. This reflects an underlying assumption that this level of analysis is an appropriate one at which to study many aspects of memory for language (cf. Bower, 1978). It is not denied that at least some of the principles that govern what is to form the *content* of memories derived from language and from other materials will differ. Nevertheless, it appears economical to suppose that the basic *structure* of mnemonic processing will be common to the two cases. If this is so, then it appears advisable at this structural level to formulate models that may be applied with indifference to memory for language and for other materials. Like all theories, such models will in effect define their own problems with which to deal. As an example, consider the apparently ineluctable question (Anderson, 1978) of whether the effects of imagery upon memory are exerted via propositional or via analogue representations. One possible solution (Jones, 1978b) is to cut this Gordian knot by demonstrating that imaged and nonimaged materials are processed isomorphically in memory. Thus the mnemonic consequence of imagery need not be represented either propositionally or analogically but instead as a set of quantitative changes in the contents of memory. Within the terms of this view, further progress would be represented by obtaining an understanding of the numerical values of these changes.

Finally, the model adopted here should be related to a similar one examined recently by Till (1977). Till presented subjects with sentences such as *The proofreader circled the dates* and subsequently provided an extralist retrieval cue such as *manuscript*. If the sentences are conceptualized as composed of two halves, subjects and predicates, then (ignoring configural encoding for the present) complete recall should be possible in two different ways. In the present terms these are as follows. First, extrinsic knowledge might allow both sentence components to be generated and recognized.

Second, only one sentence component might be recalled in this way, but it might then directly access intrinsic knowledge relating it to the other component. Till (1977) obtained empirical estimates of the probabilities of success of each of these constituent processes together with that of overall recall. He found that, in accord with the view espoused here, the level of recall predicted by the aforementioned analysis was in each case highly correlated over sentences with the actual level of recall and in some cases did not differ significantly from it but that under certain circumstances it was necessary to postulate the existence of a configural element, accessible to the extrinsic cue, that was derived from the sentence as a whole.

REFERENCES

Adams, R. G. *Retrieval from remembered sentences.* Unpublished doctoral dissertation, Council for National Academic Awards (North East London Polytechnic), 1978.

Anderson, J. R. *Language, memory, and thought.* Hillsdale, N.J.: Lawrence Erlbaum Associates, 1976.

Anderson, J. R. Arguments concerning representations for mental imagery. *Psychological Review,* 1978, *85,* 249–277.

Anderson, J. R., & Bower, G. H. Configural properties in sentence memory. *Journal of Verbal Learning and Verbal Behavior,* 1972, *11,* 594–605.

Anderson, J. R., & Bower, G. H. *Human associative memory.* Washington, D.C.: Winston, 1973.

Bahrick, H. P. Two-phase model for prompted recall. *Psychological Review,* 1970, *77,* 215–222.

Bahrick, H. P. Broader methods and narrower theories for memory research: Comments on the papers by Eysenck and Cermak. In L. S. Cermak & F. I. M. Craik (Eds.), *Levels of processing in human memory.* Hillsdale, N.J.: Lawrence Erlbaum Associates, 1979.

Bower, G. H. A multicomponent theory of the memory trace. In K. W. Spence & J. T. Spence (Eds.), *The psychology of learning and motivation: Advances in research and theory* (Vol. 1). New York: Academic Press, 1967.

Bower, G. H. Commentary on the multicomponent theory of the memory trace. In G. H. Bower (Ed.), *Human memory: Basic processes.* New York: Academic Press, 1977.

Bower, G. H. Interference paradigms for meaningful propositional memory. *American Journal of Psychology,* 1978, *91,* 575–585.

Bregman, A. S. Forgetting curves with semantic, phonetic, graphic, and contiguity cues. *Journal of Experimental Psychology,* 1968, *78,* 539–546.

Flexser, A. J., & Tulving, E. Retrieval independence in recognition and recall. *Psychological Review,* 1978, *85,* 153–171.

Foss, D. J., & Harwood, D. A. Memory for sentences: Implications for human associative memory. *Journal of Verbal Learning and Verbal Behavior,* 1975, *14,* 1–16.

Horowitz, L. M., & Prytulak, L. S. Redintegrative memory. *Psychological Review,* 1969, *76,* 519–532.

Jones, G. V. A fragmentation hypothesis of memory: Cued recall of pictures and of sequential position. *Journal of Experimental Psychology: General,* 1976, *105,* 277–293.

Jones, G. V. Recognition failure and dual mechanisms in recall. *Psychological Review,* 1978, *85,* 464–469. (a)

Jones, G. V. Tests of a structural theory of the memory trace. *British Journal of Psychology,* 1978, *69,* 351–367. (b)

Jones, G. V. Multirate forgetting. *Journal of Experimental Psychology: Human Learning and Memory,* 1979, *5,* 98–114.

Kintsch, W. *The representation of meaning in memory.* Potomac, Md.: Lawrence Erlbaum Associates, 1974.

Perfetti, C. A., & Goldman, S. R. Thematization and sentence retrieval. *Journal of Verbal Learning and Verbal Behavior,* 1974, *13,* 70–79.

Reder, L. M., Anderson, J. R., & Bjork, R. A. A semantic interpretation of encoding specificity. *Journal of Experimental Psychology,* 1974, *102,* 648–656.

Till, R. E. Sentence memory prompted with inferential recall cues. *Journal of Experimental Psychology: Human Learning and Memory.* 1977, *3,* 129–141.

Tulving, E. Episodic and semantic memory. In E. Tulving & W. Donaldson (Eds.), *Organization of memory.* New York: Academic Press, 1972.

Tulving, E., & Bower, G. H. The logic of memory representations. In G. H. Bower (Ed.), *The psychology of learning and motivation: Advances in research and theory* (Vol. 8). New York: Academic Press, 1974.

Tulving, E., & Thomson, D. M. Encoding specificity and retrieval processes in episodic memory. *Psychological Review,* 1973, *80,* 352–373.

Tulving, E., & Watkins, M. J. Structure of memory traces. *Psychological Review,* 1975, *82,* 261–275.

Tulving, E., & Wiseman, S. Relation between recognition and recognition failure of recallable words. *Bulletin of the Psychonomic Society,* 1975, *6,* 79–82.

Watkins, M. J., & Tulving, E. Episodic memory: When recognition fails. *Journal of Experimental Psychology: General,* 1975, *104,* 5–29.

Wilhite, S. C. *Cued recall of sentences: A general structural account.* Unpublished doctoral dissertation, University of Oxford, 1980.

Wright, P. Transformations and the understanding of sentences. *Language and Speech,* 1969, *12,* 156–166.

33

Memory for Personally and Socially Significant Events

Janice M. Keenan
Susan D. Baillet
University of Denver
Denver, Colorado
United States

ABSTRACT

The high memorability of personally and socially significant events can be accounted for within a cognitive framework that assumes that events concerning the self and personally significant others undergo a high degree of elaboration during encoding because of the richness of the conceptual structures they reference; the richer the conceptual structure, the more elaborate the encoding and, thus, the more memorable the event. Two experiments are presented exploring these assumptions. It is found that a continuum of contexts (specific people or cities) rated in terms of the subject's knowledge about them produces an inverse relationship between decision time and later recognition when the decision involves personal evaluation; specifically, the richer the conceptual structure, the faster the decision and the better the memory. When the decision is factual, decision time is again correlated with amount of knowledge, but memory is not related to decision time or knowledge. These results are consistent with the cognitive framework; they do not, however, preclude a motivational account.

INTRODUCTION

In our casual observations of memory performance in day-to-day situations, we have been continually impressed by the fact that people tend to remember things much better, or more easily, when those things concern either themselves or people they know well. This seems to hold both for episodic and semantic memory. Consider the retention of praise, insults, or gossip. Memory for details of the occurrences of these events—who said it and when and where it was said—seems to far surpass memory for verbal events that lack the personal or social force of these statements. Similarly, incorporating new facts about the world, such as theories of neurosis, seems to be facilitated when they can be related to oneself or one's acquaintances.

Observations such as these date back to the work of Bartlett (1932) who reported that when a face or some detail in a story reminded subjects of themselves or someone they knew, retention was particularly good. Yet, to date, we know very little beyond these observations about the role of personal and social relevance in memory processing.

In the quest to understand what is remembered and why, current researchers have paid relatively little attention to personal and social relevance as a factor in memory performance. In fact, the materials used in much memory research suggest that researchers have deliberately chosen to avoid the topic. This may have been a wise choice for the initial stages of investigation because, unlike other stimulus characteristics, personal and social significance cannot be defined across subjects but depend on the individual. However, now that memory research has reached a stage where there is a wealth of data and a number of highly sophisticated, quantitative models to account for these data, it seems appropriate to begin investigations into the messier factors. Certainly, such investigations are necessary if we hope to be able to generalize our models of memory functioning to everyday behavior.

In recent years there have been a small number of studies concerned with memory for personally and socially significant events. The results of these studies are consistent with the more casual observations that these events are particularly memorable. For example, Rogers, Kuiper, and Kirker (1977), using a levels-of-processing paradigm (Craik & Tulving, 1975), had subjects rate adjectives under four different encoding tasks: structural, rhyme, semantic, and self-reference. Results of a subsequent, incidental recall test for the adjectives showed that those encoded with respect to the self were recalled much better than the others.

Events can be personally significant either because they are perceived as related to the self or because they are brought about or initiated by the self. The data of Rogers et al. (1977) show that memory performance is facilitated by the first type of personally significant events; studies by Brenner (1973) and Jarvella and Collas (1974) show that memory performance is also facilitated by the second type. Brenner had college students each perform a simple verbal task in a group setting and found that they remembered the contents of their own performances much better than anyone else's. Jarvella and Collas (1974) had pairs of subjects act out a dialogue and found that subjects later recognized their own statements better than those of their partners.

Besides this evidence demonstrating superior retention for information concerning the self, there is some experimental evidence supporting the notion that information concerning socially significant others is also well remembered. For example, in a study of natural conversation, Keenan, MacWhinney, & Mayhew (1977) found that statements which conveyed information about the speaker–listener interaction (i.e., statements that carried socially significant information) were remembered far better than statements which did not contain such interactionally significant information. Also, Brenner (1976) using the same paradigm as he had used in his earlier work, but this time with a large group of married or dating couples, found that although subjects again remembered their own performances the best, they recalled their mates' performances better than any of the others. Finally, a questionnaire study by Brown and Kulik (1977) provides evidence suggesting that the more socially significant the event, the better the memory. They asked subjects to recall the circumstances in which they first heard of nine surprising political events, such as the murders of President Kennedy, Martin Luther King, Bobby Kennedy, and Malcolm X. They found that subjects' memories for some of these events were quite vivid and detailed. For example, almost everyone could recall where they were when they heard, what they were doing at the time, and who told them, when the event was President Kennedy's assassination. More important for our purposes was the finding that the frequency with which people reported such vivid memories was a function of the social significance of the event. Thus, the number of Black Americans recalling the circumstances under which they heard of Martin Luther King's assassination was more than twice that of the White Americans; the difference was even larger for figures such as Malcolm X and Medgar Evers.

The results of these few studies, when taken together, provide fairly compelling evidence for the personal or social significance of information as a powerful determinant of memory performance. The question we now need to address is *why*. Why do people have such good memories for information concerning themselves and, to a lesser extent, people they know well?

Existing principles of memory operation (Craik & Tulving, 1975) state that highly memorable events are those that have undergone a high degree of elaboration in the initial encoding and have been integrated with existing knowledge structures. Such events are said to be less subject to interference and to be accessible by more retrieval cues than events with more impoverished encodings. Personally and socially significant events, therefore, must be events that have undergone a high degree of elaboration in the initial encoding.

But what induces the high degree of elaboration of these events? To date, only the orienting task has been studied as a governing factor. But the orienting task in many of the studies just reviewed was the same for both information that was personally or socially significant and information that was not. There must, therefore, be additional factors that govern the degree of elaboration an event will receive.

We propose that the semantic structure to which an event is encoded can also determine amount of elaboration. Specifically, the richer the encoding schema, the more elaboration the event can receive. It seems reasonable to assume that one knows more about oneself than anybody or anything else; that is, the self is the richest schema in memory. Similarly, the schemata for one's family members and friends can be assumed to be typically among the richest in memory. Thus, personally and socially significant events undergo a high degree of elaboration and, consequently, are particularly memorable, because of the richness of the schemata to which they are encoded.

If this account of the memorability of personally and socially significant events is accurate, it ought to be possible to demonstrate a systematic relationship between the degree of personal significance and memory performance. Specifically, the more significant a person is to one, the more knowledge one will have of that person to bear on the encoding of events concerning that person and, thus, the more memorable those events will be. Experiment 1 attempts to provide this demonstration.

EXPERIMENT 1

A levels-of-processing-type paradigm, consisting of an initial encoding phase for word items followed by an unexpected recognition test for the word events, was employed. This paradigm was chosen because it assesses memory performance under incidental or nonstrategic encoding conditions and, thus, permits experimental control over the encoding operations. We assume that encoding operations are a function of the orienting or encoding task and the richness of the conceptual structure referenced by the task. In this experiment the encoding task was always the same—an evaluative judgment concerning whether or not an adjective describes someone's personality; what varied was the significance or richness of the person schema referenced by the task. Thus, any observed differences in memory performance can be attributed to differences in significance among the person schemata.

Method

In the encoding phase of the experiment, subjects were presented with questions. Following each question, an adjective was presented, and the subject had to respond *yes* or *no*. The encoding questions were of the form *Describes X?*, where *X* refers to a person. We selected seven person categories to fall on a continuum of how much we expected our subjects to know about each; they were, from best-known to least well-known: yourself, your best friend, one of your parents, a friend who is not your best friend, your teacher or boss, your favorite TV character, and Jimmy Carter. (The experiment was run in the fall of 1977, Carter's first year in office.) Each subject chose one person who fit each of the categories other than self and Jimmy Carter and wrote down the names to ensure that the same individual would be referred to each time the encoding question was presented.

In addition to these seven person-reference encoding questions, we also used a semantic question that is commonly used in levels-of-processing experiments. The question was, *Means the same as_____?*, where the blank contained a word that was or was not synonymous with the adjective that followed. This question was included simply as a basis for comparison with the person-reference questions. It is well known that this encoding question induces processing that leads to fairly good memory performance; and we were curious to see if the person-reference questions would lead to better or worse memory performance than this semantic question.

Forty-eight adjectives selected from norms provided by Kirby and Gardner (1972) were used. Approximately one-third of these represented fairly favorable characteristics (kind), another third were less favorable (rude), and the final third were not easily classified as either positive or negative (curious).

All stimuli were displayed on a CRT connected to a PDP-11/10 computer. Responses were made by pressing buttons labeled *yes* and *no* on a button box in front of the subject. Each encoding question was presented for 2 sec, which was plenty of time to read the question and think about the person it referenced. The question was then replaced by an adjective, and the subject responded *yes* or *no* as to whether the adjective described the person named in the question, or, in the case of the semantic question, if it meant the same as the word in the question. Encoding times were measured from the onset of the adjective to the subject's response; consequently, the time to access the person schema is not involved in the encoding times. Forty-eight encoding trials were presented; each of the eight questions was presented six times, in random order, each time with a different adjective. Across all subjects, the 48 adjectives were paired equally often with each of the eight encoding questions.

After the encoding trials, the subject participated in an unrelated experiment for 10 min. Then an unexpected recognition test, consisting of the 48 adjectives from the encoding phase plus 48 adjective distractors, was given. The distractors were chosen from the same pool as the encoding items. Each of the test items was presented one at a time on the screen and the subject was required to respond *old* or *new* to each item. After the recognition test, the subject ranked the seven people used in the encoding task in terms of how well they knew each one and in terms of how well they liked each one.

Forty-eight people from the University of Denver community participated in the experiment and were paid for their services. Initial instructions led them to believe that the purpose of the experiment was to examine reaction times to personality judgments.

Results

Figures 33.1 and 33.2 present the mean proportion correct and encoding times for each of the eight types of encoding questions. For both of these figures, the order of the seven people reflects their average rank ordering across all subjects, both in terms of how well they were known and how much they were liked. *Yourself* represents the highest rank (best-known and best-liked), whereas *Jimmy Carter* has the lowest rank (least-known and least-liked).

Recognition. In analyzing the recognition data, we first looked at possible differences between items that had received a *yes* response in the encoding phase and items that had received a *no* response. More adjectives received a *yes* response than a *no* response (28.3 versus 19.6), so the data were converted to proportions of those rated *yes* or *no* that were recognized. By using proportions, the differences in memory performance across the person categories cannot be attributed to, say, more *yes* responses for well-known categories and a tendency to remember *yes* responses better than *no* responses. In fact, there was no effect of the type of response on memory; the mean proportion of words rated *yes* that were recognized was .77 and that of words rated *no* was .76. Nor did the type of response interact with the encoding questions. Figure 33.1 therefore shows the mean recognition scores collapsed over *yes* and *no* encoding decisions.

As Fig. 33.1 clearly depicts, recognition performance is indeed a function of the relative significance of the person to which the items were encoded. Specifically, the more one knows about a person and, in this case, the more one likes a person, the more likely one is to recognize events encoded with respect to that person, $F(7, 280) = 15.02, p < .001$. A trend analysis across the person categories yielded a highly significant linear trend, $F(1, 280) = 95.74, p < .001$.

The order of the seven people in Fig. 33.1 reflects their average rank order, calculated across all subjects. However, not everyone ranked the people in exactly the same way. As a matter of fact, a few of our subjects felt that they knew more about Jimmy Carter than their parents, and a few liked him or their favorite TV character more than their parents. We therefore analyzed the recognition data again, this time as a function of the subjects' own rank orderings of the poeple. Rank 1 was always *yourself*, but all the other ranks represented a mixture of the person categories. Regardless of whether the data are viewed in terms of rank order on knowing or liking, the results using individual rank orderings are very similar to those using the average rank orderings. There is a significant effect of the rank order of the persons on both dimensions [$F(6, 222) = 12.86, p < .001$ for knowing and $F(6, 222) = 11.10, p < .001$ for liking], and the linear trend is again highly significant, $F(1, 222) = 81.54, p < .001$.

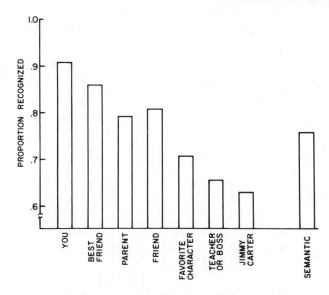

FIG. 33.1.   Proportion correctly recognized as a function of encoding question for Experiment 1. The people are ordered according to how well-known and how well-liked they are (average rank across subjects), with Jimmy Carter representing the lowest rank.

The semantic encoding question was included as an example of a question generally leading to good memory, to compare to the person-reference questions. Items encoded with respect to yourself and your best friend were recognized significantly better than items encoded under the semantic question, but items encoded in relation to teacher or boss and Jimmy Carter were significantly worse ($p < .05$ using Newman–Keuls test). Thus it is not the case that all person-reference questions result in better memory than the typical semantic question; rather, the effectiveness of an encoding question depends on the richness of the conceptual framework referenced by the question.

Encoding Times.   No specific predictions were made for the encoding times; yet, as can be seen in Fig. 33.2, encoding times were also systematically related to the relative significance of the person categories. But, contrary to the usual finding in levels of processing tasks (Craik & Tulving, 1975), here we find that the categories associated with more elaborate encodings and better memory performance are the ones that received the least amount of encoding time. In general, the more significant the person, in terms of knowing and liking, the faster the response, $F(7, 280) = 3.86, p < .001$.

We also found that *yes* responses were significantly faster than *no* responses, $F(1, 40) = 9.02, p < .01$; the average response time for *yes* responses was 2.147 sec, whereas that for *no* responses was 2.314. This finding is

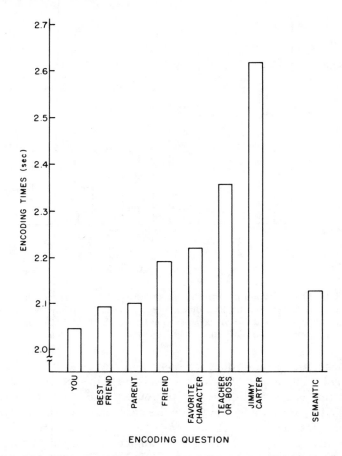

FIG. 33.2.   Mean encoding times as a function of encoding question for
Experiment 1.

consistent with other research utilizing questions that require semantic processing (Craik & Tulving, 1975). Finally, the interaction of response with type
of encoding question was not significant, $F(7, 280) = 1.01$.

Discussion

We proposed that one of the reasons why personally and socially significant
events are so memorable is because of the amount of elaborative processing
they undergo as a consequence of the rich conceptual schemata to which they
are encoded. The results of this experiment support this notion in that
recognition memory performance was found to be a positively increasing
function of the rated knowledge of the person schemata used in encoding. We

also found that decision times, too, are related to one's rated knowledge of a person. Surprisingly, this relationship is just the opposite of that observed for memory performance. In this section we discuss possible explanations for this inverse relationship between decision time and later recognition.

There are three possible hypotheses for the processes underlying the time it takes to evaluate an adjective with respect to a person schema. One is that all the decisions are accomplished by a fact-retrieval mechanism. Another is that all the decisions are computed from existing knowledge. The third possibility is that some decisions are based on fact retrieval and others must be computed. We examine each in turn.

The fact-retrieval hypothesis assumes that all the adjectives or their meanings are already stored in memory, prior to the experiment, as associated descriptors of each person schema. Determining whether or not an adjective describes a person involves scanning the descriptors of the person schema until the adjective's meaning or its opposite is found. This scanning could be similar to the fact-retrieval mechanism first proposed by Anderson and Bower (1973). The main problem with this hypothesis is that it is highly unlikely that all the adjective meanings would be associated with all the person schemata prior to the experiment. Also, certain formulations of this fact-retrieval process would give rise to a pattern of latencies that is just the opposite of what we observed. Specifically, response times would increase with the amount of information associated with a concept because there is more information to be scanned—what Anderson and Bower (1973) called the "fanning effect."

The computation hypothesis assumes that instead of simply scanning and retrieving adjective descriptors, one must compute the appropriateness of the adjective by evaluating information associated with the person schema. According to this account, latencies for person schemata that are rich in information should be faster than those for schemata that are less rich because of the higher likelihood that information relevant to the computation is available. For example, when determining if one's best friend is patient or kind, it is likely that there are several instances of behavior stored in memory that are amenable to this classification and that can be utilized in determining the response (e.g., the time he spent 3 days debugging my program). The quantity and quality of these relevant memory traces will determine the speed of response, such that the more available and the more appropriate they are to the classification, the faster the response. On the other hand, when determining if Jimmy Carter is patient or kind, it is less likely that information specifically relevant to the classification is available. One must, therefore, derive an answer from more general notions (e.g., the types of people that become politicians); it seems reasonable that such a derivation should require more time.

The third hypothesis is a hybrid of the first two and states that, if possible, decisions will be made by the fact-retrieval mechanism previously outlined; if that fails, however, the decision will be computed. This hypothesis assumes that the more well-known the person, the more likely the schema includes specific evaluations, such as kind or patient, in addition to the particular events that led to the evaluation. Thus, the more well-known the person, the more likely fact retrieval can operate. The less well-known the person, the less likely one has thought about specific evaluations of the person and, thus, the more likely the answer must be computed. Because computation is more time-consuming than fact retrieval, decision times should increase for lesser-known people.

The computation hypothesis and the hybrid hypothesis both offer plausible accounts of the encoding times. In order to decide between them, one needs to examine their implications for memory performance.

Like many others (Craik & Lockhart, 1972; Jacoby, 1978; Tulving & Thomson, 1973), we assume that the memory trace of an adjective event consists not only of the adjective itself but of all the information that was utilized in evaluating its fit to the person schema. Given this assumption, it follows that the episodic memory representation of adjectives whose encodings involved computation should be more elaborate and, thus, more easily retrieved than those whose encodings involved simple fact retrieval (Jacoby, 1978). According to this reasoning, the hybrid model would predict that adjectives encoded to less well-known persons would be more memorable than those encoded to well-known persons because more computation was involved in their encodings. Because the results of this experiment were just the opposite of these predictions, we can reject this model.

The computation hypothesis is able to account for observed memory performance just as well as decision times. According to this hypothesis, memory traces resulting from adjectives encoded with respect to well-known persons will be more elaborate and, thus, more easily retrieved than those of adjectives encoded with respect to less well-known persons, because the rich conceptual schemata associated with well-known persons can provide more relevant information to the computation than the more impoverished schemata associated with less well-known persons.

The hybrid model could be modified so that it, too, could accommodate the memory results. In particular, one could assume that when a specific evaluation is already stored with a person schema, its storage is so intimately connected to the particular information from which it was derived that access of the evaluation automatically causes this supporting information to also be activated. In this case, the episodic memory representation of the adjective would be just as rich as if it had been newly computed. Although there is currently no way to decide between this modified hybrid hypothesis and the computation hypothesis, it is important to keep in mind that what leads to high memorability is the overall complexity of the encoding.

To this point, we have attributed the memorability of personally and socially significant events to the richness of the conceptual schemata associated with the self and personally significant others. We have thus provided a strictly cognitive account of the findings. It is worth noting, however, that an account in terms of motivational factors is also possible. As stated earlier, the obtained ratings of how much one knows about a person and how much one likes a person were very highly correlated. Thus, it is possible to conclude from this study that the stronger one's positive feelings for a person, the more likely one can recognize events encoded with respect to that person.

EXPERIMENT 2

It is difficult to decide which is the more appropriate theoretical framework—cognitive or motivational—for viewing these results. The present data do not favor one over the other. Experiment 2 attempts to examine the importance of emotional involvement by comparing performance when the encoding schemata are places to that when the encoding schemata are persons. Places were selected because emotional or noncognitive factors seem much less involved in events concerning them than in events concerning people; in other words, the personal significance of places seems well characterized by how much one knows about them. If the results obtained for places are similar to those for persons, we can feel more comfortable about characterizing personal significance in terms of amount of knowledge. If, on the other hand, the results for places are different than those for people, it would compel us to characterize personal significance in motivational terms such as emotional involvement, arousal, and interest.

To test further the hypothesis that it is the amount of encoding elaboration that determines memory performance, this experiment employs factual judgments as well as evaluative judgments. Factual judgments differ from evaluative judgments in that they do not require an assessment of the schema as a whole or a large subset of it. Therefore, they should not result in the kind of elaborate memory traces previously described for evaluative judgments and thus are not expected to show any effects of the richness of the encoding framework on memory performance. Richness is a property of the schema as a whole, not of individual nodes within the schema; so we should not expect effects of richness when only a single node is being accessed.

If factual judgments for person categories do show the same effects of richness as evaluative judgments, then a motivational account would be favored. Specifically, we would need to assume that any time a significant person schema is accessed, emotional arousal is produced in proportion to the significance of that person; and the more arousal produced, the more memorable the event.

Method

The procedure was the same as that in Experiment 1: first, an encoding phase, consisting of questions and words; next, an unrelated filler task; and, finally, an unexpected recognition task. The two types of judgments (evaluative and factual) were crossed with the two areas of knowledge (persons and places) to yield four types of questions: an evaluative question about a person (e.g., *Describes you?*), a factual question about a person (*Do you have...*), an evaluative question about a location (*Describes the city you identify with?*), and a factual question about a location (*Found in the city you identify with?*). For each type of question, four people and four cities were chosen to fall on a continuum from well-known to little-known. Thus, there were 16 different questions. These, and examples of the words, are shown in Table 33.1. The people selected for the encoding questions were yourself, your parent, your favorite TV character, and Jimmy Carter. The places were restricted to continental United States cities and were the city you identify with, such as your hometown; a city you have been to and know pretty well; a city you have been to and do not know very well; and a city you have never been to and do not know much about. Each subject chose one city to fit each category and

TABLE 33.1
Questions and Sample Words for Experiment 2

Describes you?	
Describes your parent?	Curious
Describes your favorite character?	Rude
Describes Jimmy Carter?	
Do you have...	
Does your parent have...	Cheeks
Does your favorite character have...	Gills
Does Jimmy Carter have...	
Describes the city you identify with?	
Describes the city you know pretty well?	Exciting
Describes the city you don't know very well?	Peaceful
Describes the city you've never been to?	
Found in the city you identify with?	
Found in the city you know pretty well?	Streets
Found in the city you don't know very well?	Equator
Found in the city you've never been to?	

chose a parent and TV character and wrote the names down to ensure that the same name would be used each time the question appeared.

The adjectives for the person-evaluative questions were a subset of those used in Experiment 1. A second, nonoverlapping set of adjectives from Experiment 1 was used to constitute some of the words in the place evaluative condition; the remainder were generated by the experimenters. The nouns in the person-factual condition were parts of a body—human body for positive response items and animal bodies for negative response items. The nouns in the place-factual condition included things that are found in every American city, things that are found in no American city, and things that may or may not be found in an American city.

Each encoding question was presented for 3 sec and was then replaced by an adjective, for the evaluative questions, or a noun, for the factual questions, to which the subject responded *yes* or *no*. One hundred and sixty such encoding trials were presented; each of the 16 questions was presented 10 times, in random order, each time with a different target word. Across all subjects, the 40 words for each question type were paired equally often with each of the four people or places. After the encoding trials, the subject participated in an unrelated experiment for 10 min. Then there was a recognition test consisting of the 160 words from the encoding phase plus 160 distractors. The distractors were chosen from the same pool as the target items. After the recognition test, the subjects ranked the person categories in terms of how well they knew each one.

Forty people from the University of Denver community were paid for their participation. As in Experiment 1, they were not aware of the memory test but instead thought that the experiment concerned the speed of decision making.

Results

Recognition. The recognition data are shown in Table 33.2. Note that each subject's own rank ordering of the categories was used to calculate the results; the self always received the highest rank and is represented by Level 1 (best-known).

Overall, there is a significant main effect of level, with better memory for words concerning better-known or more personally significant categories, $F(3, 108) = 3.49, p < .02$. However, this main effect is attenuated by a highly significant interaction of level with type of judgment, $F(3, 108) = 8.53, p < .001$. This interaction reflects the fact that the effect of level of personal significance is found only in the evaluative judgments, not in the factual judgments. This is true for both people and places: The three-way interaction was not significant, $F(3, 108) = .64$. So, for evaluative judgments, the more significant the schema referenced in encoding, the better the memory for the

TABLE 33.2
Mean Proportion Recognized as a Function of Each Individual's
Rank Order of the Person and Place Categories in Experiment 2

		Level			
		1	2	3	4
Evaluative judgment	People[a]	.76	.72	.62	.67
	Places	.74	.72	.64	.66
Factual judgment	People[a]	.79	.80	.81	.82
	Places	.76	.72	.76	.75

[a]Rank 1 is always *yourself*.

encoded event. For factual judgments, however, memory performance bears little relation to the significance of the encoding schema.

Factual items had a significantly higher hit rate (.77) than evaluative items (.69), $F(1, 36) = 26.37$, $p < .001$; however, their false alarm rates were not significantly different, .12 for factual items and .11 for evaluative items. The difference in memorability of factual and evaluative items can probably be attributed to the fact that factual items are concrete nouns whereas the evaluative items are adjectives.

Under evaluative judgments, person and place items had identical hit rates (.69) and nearly identical false alarm rates (.10 for persons and .12 for places). Under factual judgments, person items had a higher hit rate (.81) than place items (.75), but they also had a higher false alarm rate (.14 for persons and .10 for places).

Within the person evaluative condition, the relation between the polarity of the adjective and the level of significance of the person was examined. We expected that positive adjectives, such as *kind,* would be more memorable when encoded in relation to the self or the next most significant person and that memory for negative adjectives, such as *rude*, would decrease for the more significant persons. We examined a subset of the words: eight which had been rated by 50 new subjects as unanimously positive and eight which had been rated as unanimously negative. Surprisingly, there was no interaction between polarity and level. Negative adjectives were remembered slightly better (77%) than positive adjectives (72%), and this held at each level. For negative adjectives, the percent recognition across the four levels from most significant to least was: .93, .79, .65, and .70; for positive adjectives, the percent recognition across the four levels was: .85, .73, .61, and .69.

Encoding Times. As in Experiment 1, we again found that the more one knows about something or the more personally significant it is, the faster one can make a judgment about it, $F(3, 108) = 10.91, p < .001$. This was true for both persons and places. Surprisingly, in light of the recognition data, this relationship held for factual items as well as evaluative items; so, for example, subjects were significantly faster in verifying that they had arms than in verifying that Jimmy Carter had an arm. Collapsing over type of category and type of judgment, the average encoding times (in seconds) for the four levels from most significant to least were: 1.114, 1.152, 1.209, and 1.227. A trend analysis showed this to be a significant linear trend, $F(1, 108) = 3.97, p < .05$.

Questions involving evaluative judgments took significantly longer (1.296) to answer than those involving factual judgments (1.055), for both people and places, $F(1, 36) = 105.30, p < .001$. Questions about people were answered more quickly (.980) than those about places (1.129) only for factual judgments, $F(1, 36) = 24.94, p < .01$. For evaluative judgments, the difference in latencies between people and places was not significant, $F(1, 36) = 2.06$, $p = .16$, though the direction was the same as for factual judgments (1.276 versus 1.316). Again, *yes* responses were significantly faster than *no* responses, 1.098 versus 1.253, $F(1, 36) = 28.37, p < .001$; this was true for both types of judgments and for place categories as well as person categories.

As with the recognition data, we examined the relation between the polarity of an adjective and the level of significance within the person evaluative condition. We expected positive adjectives to be responded to more quickly when they concerned the self or a highly significant other and that negative adjectives would be responded to more slowly when they concerned the self or a highly significant other. No such relationship was found. Positive adjectives were responded to slightly faster (1.13) than negative adjectives (1.26), and this held for all levels of significance. For positive adjectives, the mean encoding times across the four levels from most to least significant were: .982, 1.048, 1.181, and 1.302. For negative adjectives, the mean encoding times were: 1.171, 1.288, 1.261, and 1.335.

Discussion

The results of this experiment are consistent with an account of memory for personally and socially significant information in terms of the relative richness of the encoding framework. For both people and places, a richer conceptual framework led to better memory performance. However, this was only true for items encoded under evaluative judgments; for items encoded under factual judgments, the richness of the conceptual framework had no effect. The reason for this is that evaluative judgments demand that an item be encoded in relation to much of the information in the schema; factual judgments require only access of a single node in the schema and, thus, do not involve the richness of the schema in the memory trace of the item.

There was one unexpected finding in this experiment; namely, that encoding times for factual judgments, like those for evaluative judgments, were inversely related to the amount of knowledge associated with the encoding framework. Certainly, this result requires a different explanation than what was offered for evaluative judgments because memory performance, which is intricately tied to the encoding process, showed no effect of the richness of the encoding framework for factual judgments but did show an effect for evaluative judgments.

One possible way subjects could have answered the factual questions used in this experiment, especially those pertaining to persons, is the following. When a body part, such as arm, was presented, they could have determined whether or not it was a human body part; if so, they would respond *yes*; if not, they would respond *no*. This strategy does not utilize any information about the person named in the encoding question. For this reason, it easily explains the failure of level of significance to effect memory performance: Richness of the schema has no effect because the schema plays no role in the encoding of the item. But, if the schemata play no role in encoding, then why are encoding times inversely related to their significance? It seems that in order to explain the encoding times, one must assume that the particular person and place schemata, not just generic schemata, were utilized in encoding.

It is likely that the effects of significance of the schemata on factual encoding times were due, at least in part, to the strength of association between items and the encoding schemata. It is well-known that the stronger the association or relatedness between two items, the faster one can affirm the association. Thus, we need only assume that association strengths between items and schemata were positively correlated with the significance of the schemata in this experiment to explain the encoding times.

The assumptions that parts of the body are more highly associated with one's self-concept than one's concept of Jimmy Carter and that properties of a city, such as a bank, are more associated with the city in which one lives than a city which one has never visited seem quite reasonable. To illustrate, body parts should be most central to our self-concept because they constitute our appearance, and appearance is an important part of self-image; also we use the various parts of our bodies and depend on them to interact with the world. Body parts should be next most important to our concept of parents because we have physical contact with them as well as knowledge of their appearance. Body parts should be less important to a favorite TV character because, though we are exposed to their appearance, we do not physically interact with them. Finally, body parts are least important to our concept of Jimmy Carter because appearance (except perhaps those aspects of it that lend themselves to caricature) has relatively little importance for one's memory representation of a political figure; also, of the four person categories, we probably have had the least amount of exposure to his appearance. Similarly, for places, a bank should be more highly associated with the city with which we identify than a city we have never visited because we actually use a bank in the city with which we identify.

One final comment should be made about the encoding times. For both factual and evaluative judgments, we found that the more information associated with a schema, the faster the response. This is just the opposite of what John Anderson has observed in several studies of what he calls the "fanning" effect (Anderson, 1974, 1976; Anderson & Bower, 1973; Lewis & Anderson, 1976), where the more facts that are stored with a concept the slower one is to verify any of them. Recent evidence by Smith, Adams, and Schorr (1978) suggests that the fanning effect only occurs when there is a lack of integration among the facts stored with the concept. Assuming that the self and the other conceptual categories used in this experiment are well-integrated structures, the present encoding times can be viewed as further support for Smith et al.'s position.

CONCLUSIONS

We have proposed that memory for personally and socially significant events can be explained within either a cognitive or a motivational framework. We focused primarily on the cognitive account in designing these experiments because the language of cognition, unlike that of motivation, provides a rich set of constructs with which to develop a mechanistic explanation of the results; the language of motivation, as it currently stands, permits only a descriptive account. Although the cognitive framework permits a mechanistic account, it was not obvious that it would be sufficient to account for memory for personally and socially significant events; because existing principles of memory operation derive from experiments that used tasks and materials that had little personal significance, we thought it necessary to assess the generality of these principles.

It is important to note that, in developing the cognitive account, we found it necessary to add to existing principles of memory operation. Specifically, we needed to assume that elaboration of a memory trace depends not only on the encoding task (Craik & Tulving, 1975) and the meaningfulness of the event (Seamon & Murray, 1976) but also on the richness of the semantic structure to which the event is encoded. We suggest that the richness of the conceptual structure to which an event is encoded may provide a more general definition of encoding elaboration than has been offered to date (Craik & Tulving, 1975, Experiment 7), because it applies across a wide range of semantic encoding tasks and it can be determined ahead of time rather than post hoc.

Although the present results can be explained within a cognitive framework, they raise the possibility of a motivational account. According to this account, the crucial dimension underlying memory is not what the subject knows or the amount of knowledge that is used in encoding the item but rather what the subject feels about what he knows. If we assume that these feelings are evoked only when the judgment is one of personal opinion, such as evaluative judgments, and that the intensity of these feelings increases with the familiarity of the person, we can then predict the levels of significance effect on memory for items encoded under evaluative judgments.

Many of the great early writers on the subject of mental processing, such as Bacon, Hobbes, Spinoza, Locke, and Hume, considered the emotions to play a very significant, if not primary, role in determining memory processing (Rapaport, 1942). Such views have had little bearing on current memory models, probably because the amount of emotional involvement in materials and tasks used in most research is negligible. As research into memory for personally and socially significant events proceeds, however, it may be that the data will call for models which echo these earlier conceptions; that is, models which incorporate the constructs of motivational psychology into the mechanistic process models of cognition. For now, however, the data can be adequately explained using only cognitive constructs; they may raise the possibility of a motivational account, but they do not compel one.

ACKNOWLEDGMENTS

This research was funded by a Biomedical research grant from the University of Denver to the first author. We thank Gail McKoon, Richard Olson, and George Potts for their helpful comments.

REFERENCES

Anderson, J. R. Retrieval of propositional information from long-term memory. *Cognitive Psychology,* 1974, *5,* 451–474.

Anderson, J. R. *Language, memory, and thought.* Hillsdale, N.J.: Lawrence Erlbaum Associates, 1976.

Anderson, J. R., & Bower, G. H. *Human associative memory.* Washington, D.C.: Winston, 1973.

Bartlett, F. C. *Remembering: A study in experimental and social psychology.* Cambridge, England: Cambridge University Press, 1932.

Brenner, M. The next-in-line effect. *Journal of Verbal Learning and Verbal Behavior,* 1973, *12,* 320–323.

Brenner, M. *Memory and interpersonal relations.* Unpublished doctoral dissertation, University of Michigan, 1976.

Brown, R., & Kulik, J. Flashbulb memories. *Cognition,* 1977, *5,* 73–99.

Craik, F. I. M., & Lockhart, R. S. Levels of processing: A framework for memory research. *Journal of Verbal Learning and Verbal Behavior,* 1972, *11,* 671–684.

Craik, F. I. M., & Tulving, E. Depth of processing and the retention of words in episodic memory. *Journal of Experimental Psychology: General*, 1975, *104*, 268–294.

Jacoby, L. L. On interpreting the effects of repetition: Solving a problem versus remembering a solution. *Journal of Verbal Learning and Verbal Behavior*, 1978, *17*, 649–668.

Jarvella, R. J., & Collas, J. G. Memory for the intentions of sentences. *Memory & Cognition*, 1974, *2*, 185–188.

Keenan, J. M., MacWhinney, B., & Mayhew, D. Pragmatics in memory: A study of natural conversation. *Journal of Verbal Learning and Verbal Behavior*, 1977, *16*, 549–560.

Kirby, D. M., & Gardner, R. C. Ethnic stereotypes: Norms on 208 words typically used in their assessment. *Canadian Journal of Psychology*, 1972, *26*, 140–154.

Lewis, C. H., & Anderson, J. R. Interference with real world knowledge. *Cognitive Psychology*, 1976, *8*, 311–335.

Rapaport, D. *Emotions and memory*. Baltimore: Williams & Wilkins Co., 1942.

Rogers, T. B., Kuiper, N. A., & Kirker, W. S. Self-reference and the encoding of personal information. *Journal of Personality and Social Psychology*, 1977, *35*, 677–688.

Seamon, J. G., & Murray, P. Depth of processing in recall and recognition memory: Differential effects of serial position and stimulus meaningfulness. *Journal of Experimental Psychology: Human Learning and Memory*, 1976, *2*, 680–687.

Smith, E. E., Adams, N., & Schorr, D. Fact retrieval and the paradox of interference. *Cognitive Psychology*, 1978, *10*, 438–464.

Tulving, E., & Thomson, D. M. Encoding specificity and retrieval processes in episodic memory. *Psychological Review*, 1973, *80*, 352–373.

34

Method for Exploring Retrieval Processes Using Verbal Protocols

Michael David Williams
Stephanie Santos-Williams
Navy Personnel Research and Development Center
San Diego, California
United States

ABSTRACT

A method has been developed for analyzing complex verbal protocols from subjects thinking aloud during difficult retrieval tasks. Previous work with subjects thinking aloud while attempting to recall the names of high school classmates has identified a number of recurrent phenomena and systematic search strategies. By applying our analysis to a portion of the same data base we are able to derive a set of equations that formally define a number of the recurrent phenomena; in particular, partial recall, extended retrieval, overshoot, systematic hypothesizing, and contextual retrieval. In addition, the analysis provides the basis for a systematic examination of the search strategies. In applying the analysis to the locations strategy, we noted three characteristics of the strategy: (1) nonveridical representation of the space being searched; (2) flexible focus on a number of "levels" in the spatial representation; and (3) opportunistic excursions from the primary search strategy. Our effort demonstrates the possibilities of conducting useful quantitative analysis of lengthy and complex verbal protocols in order to examine the process of retrieval.

INTRODUCTION

The primary purpose of this chapter is to report on our progress in developing a methodology for exploring the problem-solving character of the retrieval process. The methodology is based on formalizing protocols from subjects thinking aloud while attempting a difficult retrieval task. We mean the term *difficult retrieval task* to refer to those complex and convoluted searches that result when the answer to a memory query is not immediate. Some common examples would be trying to recall the names of an acquaintance from the distant past, trying to recall an algebraic equation not used since college, or an experimental recall situation in which the cues have been deliberately minimized. In such situations, the retrieval process is often lengthy. A process of "intentional remembering" (as it is called by Flavell & Wellman, 1977; Kenisten & Flavell, 1978; and others) seems to come to the foreground. The retrieval process seems slowed; incidental recollections abound; systematic search processes seem evident.

Consider the following example. The subject was asked to think aloud while attempting to recall the names of classmates from high school:

Protocol 1

Prop No.	Symbol	Text	About
1	*s*	if I keep going down	
2	*rlo*	Silvergate	
3	*rco*	there is	
4	*rpc*	someone who lived on the	
5	*rlo*	corner house,	
6	*rco*	it had a	[5]
7	*rob*	purple door,	
8	*rco*	it is a	[5]
9	*rob*	grey house with a	
10	*rob*	lavender purple door, and	
11	*rco*	he was in my grade,	[4]
12	*pq*	what's his name...	[4]
13	*rin*	I remember he was	[4]
14	*rph*	Jewish because they	[4]
15	*rlo*	always had a	
16	*rob*	menorah in the window	
17	*pc*	and he had a humm,	
18	*.mm 19		
19	*pq*	what was his name,	[4]
20	*rph*	he had dark hair,	[4]
21	*rph*	sort of tall and	[4]
22	*rph*	thin,	[4]
23	*?*	he reminded me of	[4]
24	*rfn*	Nevin Hammer but[1]	
25	*me*	it is not him, um, hmm	[24]
26	*pc*	I can't really think of his name,	[4]
27	*pc*	maybe I'll come back to it,	
28	*pc*	let me see,	

The goal of the methodology we are developing is to make the many levels of structure that are evident in the raw protocols from these difficult retrieval

---

[1]All names, except those of public figures and a few cases where the phonetics of the name are at issue, have been changed in the protocols presented in this chapter.

tasks objective and quantifiable. It is intended that these quantifiable verbal protocols will form the basis of a broader theoretical effort in the analysis of remembering as a problem-solving process.

THE EXPERIMENT

In Williams (1978), four subjects were directed to think aloud while attempting to remember the names of all their classmates in high school. The subjects were from 4 to 19 years out of high school. The experimenter had copies of the appropriate yearbooks to verify the accuracy of the names recalled. Subjects were run from 4 to 10 hours in sessions of approximately 1 hour, one session per day.[2] A portion of the general results are presented in Fig. 34.1. Two primary things noted at that time were the large number of names recalled (both correct and incorrect) and that subjects could apparently recall new names correctly for an indefinite period of time. The subject above recalled five new correct names during the tenth hour. In addition, a variety of recurrent phenomena were observed. These phenomena included:

1. Extended retrievals: where the subject recalled part of a target name, or a partial description of a target person, and then proceeded to recall substantial amounts of incidental information about the target person, in an apparent attempt to construct a complete picture of the person, from which a name could be found.

2. Partial recalls: where subjects recalled part of a name, a first name only, or the first letter of one of the names (e.g., it started with a p.)

3. Contextual retrieval: where subjects used locations, activities, and other schemes as contexts from which to recover information.

4. Systematic hypothesizing: where subjects systematically guessed possible information under some constraint looking for something that "fits." For example, "His name began with a P: Peter, Paul, Perry, ..."

Other phenomena included overshoots, distractions, self-corrections, and the systematic application of an array of search strategies (such as the location strategy, where subjects scanned a mental map, locating peoples' homes, from which people were derived and subsequently named). These phenomena are described at length in Williams (1978).

All of these observations fit within a characterization of the retrieval process as largely a problem solving process. According to Williams (1978):

---

[2]All subjects found this task quite tiring and complained vigorously if the experimenter tried to keep them at the task much over 1 hour per day.

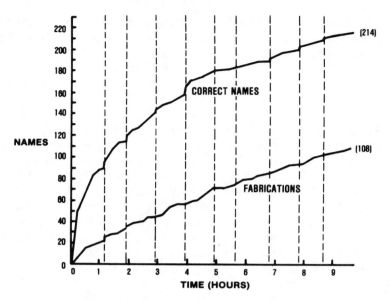

FIG. 34.1.   Cumulative correct names and fabrications recalled by S1 over time (from Williams, 1978). Dotted lines indicate session boundaries.

The characterization of the search process is substantially that of a reconstructive retrieval process. Information about the target item is used to construct a description of some aspect of the item. The description is used to recover a fragment of information about the item which is added to what is known. From this information a new description can be formed to retrieve still more information, until the particular piece of information sought can be recovered. The three stages are FIND A CONTEXT, in which a proper environment for conducting a search is recovered, SEARCH, in which bits and pieces of information appropriate to the context are recovered until an adequate description can be formed within the search context, and VERIFY, in which the record recovered is checked to confirm that it is about the target item. Each of the three stages has embedded within it one or more recursive calls to the retrieval process.

This characterization is based, in part, on the notion of descriptive retrieval presented in Norman and Bobrow (1979), and Williams and Norman (1976) and is related to the model of search presented by Shiffrin (1970).

A problem in this earlier work is that all the strategies and recurrent phenomena are identified only in terms of sample protocols. There is no objective specification of the phenomena or their parameters. In addition, the list of phenomena and simple cumulative counts of names over time seemed too sparse a representation of the rich and convoluted structure of the protocols themselves.

The remainder of this paper is a report on our efforts to formalize the analysis of the first 7 hours of verbal procotol from S1, the first subject in Williams (1978). The major objective is to convert the initial subjective observations into countable, quantifiable objects and to permit a quantitative description of the rich structures evident from even a casual reading of the protocols.

S1 is a female, 5 years out of high school. She has lived in San Diego in the same house for her entire life. She attended only one high school for 2½ years, graduating 6 months ahead of her class. Most of the subject's classmates from junior high also went to high school with her. Her graduating class had 609 members listed in the senior yearbook.

Basic Analysis

To begin, S1's protocol was transcribed into data files readable by a computer. This permitted us to use the power of a line-oriented text editor to segment and annotate the transcript. In addition, powerful character string search and selection operators could now be used to search and summarize various aspects of the files.

Subjects' protocols can be broken down into a finite set of propositions. For this particular task we found that each proposition could be placed into one of five major categories, each of which can be in turn subdivided into subcategories. In all, we have identified approximately 30 subcategories useful in our analysis of S1.

Five Major Categories

The five major categories are: strategy comments, processing comments, metamemory comments, recalls, and excursions.

1. Strategy Comments. Strategy comments are propositions where subjects attempt to explain how they are searching their memories. Some examples are: "I'm trying to think of the people that sat around me [in English class]." "I'm trying to think of the sports we played and who's on which team."

2. Processing Comments. Processing comments are propositions that key some change in processing. Usually they are summarylike comments, suggesting a sequence of retrievals or retrieval attempts. One example is a negative processing comment, where the subject reports a failure to retrieve additional information in a given context; "I can't remember anyone else in that class." "I don't know anyone on the swim team."

3. Metamemory Comments.   Metamemory comments are subjects' statements about, or evaluations of, specific recalls. One example is a metamemory reoccurrence comment, where the subject recalls that some particular piece of information has been previously recalled. For example, "I already named her," "... who I already named."

4. Recalls.   Recalls are propositions that represent what a subject has recalled. Some examples are recall of a name (Sam Jones), some physical characteristic of a person, (she had red hair), or a location (Catalina Street).

5. Excursions.   Excursions are the portions of the protocol generated from the experimenter's intrusions or from the initial protocol at the beginning of each session in which subjects reported inadvertent recollections that occurred between sessions. For example, occasionally the subject would mistakenly infer that the expreimenter's comment "What are you thinking now?" was intended to provoke a strategylike statement (rather than just a prod to verbalize). In such cases, all statements made by the subject that appeared to be a direct response to the inferred question rather than a simple verbalization of on-going process, were classified as excursions.

Three of the major categories (processing comments, metamemory comments, and recalls) contain a number of subcategories. Names and symbols for each subcategory are listed in Appendix A.[3]

In the first 7 hours of S1's protocol there are over 10,000 propositions. Some propositions can contain others, much in the manner of predicates in the predicate calculus. For example, the recall fact or comment (symbol rco) "He was in my 10th grade art class" contains location/activity (symbol rla) "10th grade art class."

On occasion, subjects make a large number of comments *about* a particular person or object. Protocol 1 provides an example. We try to capture this reference to a common object (or person) by appending to the proposition the number of the first proposition that references the object. We commonly refer to this relation by saying, for example, that proposition 11 is "about" proposition 4.

A second relation that can occur is when the subject refers to a succession of locations, activities, or descriptions each more specific that the last. Thus, in the following sample protocol, S1, while trying to generate likely names, goes through an alphabetic generation scheme. In such a case, the items that fit within the letter-set context *W–A–R* are a subset of the items that fit within

---

[3]Space limitations preclude the addition of formal definitions and examples for each of the subcategories. A complete listing of the subcategories including definitions and examples is available upon request from Mike Williams at Navy Personnel Research and Development Center, San Diego, CA, 92152.

W–A, which items are in turn a subset of the items within the *W* context. We code this by appending to the more *specific* proposition the number of the proposition within which it is "embedded."[4]

Protocol 2
Sample of Embedded Notation: S1

Prop No.	Symbol	Text	About	Embedded
1113	*rls*	'W',		
1114	*pc*	ok there's, um,		
1115	*s*	start out with		
1116	*rls*	'WA',		{1114}
1117	*rgl*	Wally		{1116}
1118	*pn*	I didn't know any Wallys		
		.... >		
1154	*rls*	'WAN'		{1116}
1155	*rfn*	Peggy Wand		{1154}
1156	*mr*	I already named,	[1155]	
1158	*rls*	'WAR'		{1116}
1159	*rfn*	there's Julia Wardlow and		{1158}
1160	*mr*	I already named her,	[1159]	

Formal Definitions of Recurrent Phenomena

One of the things we can do with this basic analysis is formalize some of the complex patterns of events in S1's protocol. This permits us to create objective definitions of some of the recurrent phenomena. The primary advantage of these definitions is the formalization of the phenomena to the extent that we can objectively identify when a phenomenon occurs (and therefore can count it), specify some parameters of the phenomenon (such as the length), and state the precise relationships between certain of the phenomena (such as that extended retrievals often begin with a partial recall).

Partial Recalls

A partial recall is the case in which a subject can remember only a fragment of the information being sought.[5] Our categorization scheme is set up in a manner that allows us to identify partial recall of names. There are four categories of partial names: phonetic, semantic, first name only, and last

---

[4]*Embedded* number references are distinguished from *about* number references by bracketing conventions (see protocol 2).

[5]Because of the nature of the task set for S1, the only partial recalls we can identify are partial recalls of names. In the case of physical descriptions and other incidental information the "unit" of information to be specified is not well specified enough to define a fragment of that unit.

name only. We use braces to indicate the necessary selection of one of the events (in this case one of the four possible categories) and symbols from Appendix A to represent the propositions.

$$
(1) \quad \text{partial recall} = \quad \begin{Bmatrix} \text{rnl} \\ \text{rnl} \\ \text{rns} \\ \text{rnp} \end{Bmatrix}
$$

S1 made 1020 partial recalls in the first seven sessions. There were 780 partial recalls of first names only (rnl), 202 partial recalls of last names only (rnl), 18 partial recalls of semantic constraints on a name (rns), and 20 partial recalls of phonetic or orthographic constraints on a name (rnp). One difficulty with this scoring method is that S1 often recalls a previously identified person by first or last name alone, implying that the rest of the name is available though not mentioned. For example, "I already mentioned Gay." Thus, the total number of partial recalls is probably severely distorted by this referential use of first and last names.

Extended Retrieval

An extended retrieval is when a subject introduces a candidate person without a full name (i.e., with a partial name or pronoun and limited description) followed by a number of descriptive pieces of information about the person. The extended retrieval sometimes concludes with the recovery of a full name. Expanding the previous notation used, a plus sign (+) is used to indicate concatenation of events, parentheses indicate the optional insertion of an event, and the star (*) operator indicates one or more cycles of the event in parentheses. We can now express the pattern of extended retrievals as per the equation in Fig. 34.2a. The question mark indicates the possible intrusion of retrieval activity not directly associated with the extended retrieval, and the arrows labled *about* indicate that the propositions pointed from must refer back to the proposition pointed to.

Procotol 1 is an example of an extended retrieval. In this case, proposition 4 is a person–candidate recall ("someone who lived . . . .", rpc). This event is followed by a number of statements that describe the house in which the person lived (propositions 5 through 10). Propositions 11 through 14 are a collection of facts (rco), physical characteristics (rph), processing queries (pq), and inferences (rin) about the candidate person mentioned in statement 4. Some additional bits and pieces of information are mentioned that are a part of the inference though not precisely *about* the candidate person. Some

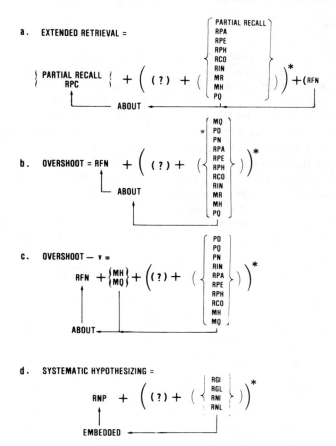

FIG. 34.2. Equations that express the formal definitions of some of the recurrent phenomena observed in subjects' verbal protocols. Two- and three-letter codes refer to proposition subcategories listed in Appendix A.

additional information about the candidate is then recalled, propositions 19 through 23. In this particular case, the extended retrieval does not end in the recall of a full name.

There were 118 extended retrievals in the first 7 hours of S1's protocol.[6] Twenty-three of these extended retrievals ended in the retrieval of a full name.

---

[6]Thirty-two of the 118 extended retrievals observed are so brief (just two or three propositions long) that, though they meet the formal requirements of our definition of an extended retrieval, they violate the "spirit" of the notion. The origin of these brief extended retrievals could be argued to be the result of an output problem. If three pieces of information are recalled in the same instant, the subject might choose to output them in a variety of orders. Note that one of the advantages of our formal definitions is that we can readily set a length criterion to filter out any extended retrievals we feel are inadequate.

Overshoot

An overshoot is the case in which a subject recalls a full name and then continues to recall additional descriptive information about the person named. An equation formalizing this definition is presented in Fig. 34.2b.

Several reasons for the phenomenon of overshoot have been suggested by Williams (1978). Among the possibilities are the verification of the retrieved name, the search for new retrieval contexts to find new names, and incidental demand characteristics of the retrieval task given.

Support for overshoot as a verification process can be found when the subject expresses uncertainty in a name recalled followed by an overshoot. Such evidence would be a metamemory hedge ("I think that is right.") or a metamemory query ("Is that right?") that refers to the name recovered. We can define a particular type of overshoot pattern, say an overshoot-v, in which such evidence is present. Figure 34.2c is a formal specification of this type of overshoot.

The following protocol provides an example of a verification overshoot.

Protocol 3
Sample of Verification Overshoot: S1

Prop No.	Symbol	Text	About
945	*rfn*	Nancy Miller	
946	*mh*	I think that's her name,	[945]
947	*rph*	she had long blond hair and	[945]
948	*rph*	she was real short,	[945]
949	*rph*	she had a cute shape	[945]
950	*rph*	but she had buck teeth,	[945]
951	*mh*	I think,	[950]
952	*rco*	she got	[945]
953	*rph*	braces in her senior year, umm,	[945]
945	*rfn*	Nancy Miller, hmm ok,	[945]
955	*pc*	let me see,	

In the first 7 hours of S1's protocol we can identify 395 overshoot events, of which 29 are of the overshoot-v variety.

Systematic Hypothesizing

Another recurrent phenomenon observed in all subjects is systematic hypothesizing. Although there are an array of different types of systematic hypothesizing that can be observed in S1's protocols, the particular categorization scheme we have used gives us the ability to identify only a limited number of these types. In particular, the cases in which S1 guesses first or last names given some partial recall (of either phonetic or semantic nature). Figure 34.2d specifies the pattern of events that define the occurrence of systematic hypothesizing. The protocol below gives an example of systematic hypothesizing by S1.

Protocol 4
Systematic Hypothesizing: S1

Prop No.	Symbol	Text	About	Embedded
1158	*rco*	there's another		
1159	*rpc*	girl [in the context of a dance group]		
1160	*pq*	what was her name?, last name was..		
1161	*rnp*	began with an 'r'	[1159]	
1162	*rgl*	Reese, or	[1159]	
1163	*rgl*	Race, and	[1159] {1161}	
1164	*rph*	she was short and	[1159] {1161}	
1165	*rph*	she had dark brown hair,	[1159]	

This scheme misses systematic hypothesizing by the subject when the hypothesizing is about things such as probable classes in high school or other incidental retrieval efforts. There are six systematic hypothesizing events (concerning name generation) in the first 7 hours of S1's protocol.

Contexts

There are several levels at which we can gather evidence about the use of search contexts by S1 given the analysis techniques at our disposal.

The most straightforward type of evidence is simply the number of times and the rate of recall of information that can be classified as contextual. In particular, any time S1 recalls a location, activity, or letter-set constraint we can argue that these pieces of information can be used as a context to guide the retrieval process.

A second level of evidence is that often S1 will recall a sequence of contexts that are *embedded* in one another. The retrieval of letter sets in protocol 2 is an example of this structural relationship between contexts retrieved.

Accuracy of Classification

We have made an attempt to determine the accuracy of our coding scheme by having an independent judge classify samples of S1's protocol from a variety of sessions. We used listings which were already segmented (to simplify our scoring) but which had the classifications removed. Agreement between judges averaged about 85%. Over categories, agreement ranged from as low as 20% for the S category (what the first judge classified as S, the second judge classified as pd) to as high as 100% for the rfn, rph, rpe, mr, and other categories. Fortunately, most patterns in which we are interested are judged in terms of the propositions that are the most reliably classified.

THE LOCATIONS STRATEGY

To give an idea of how we can use the analysis to examine some of the global aspects of the retrieval protocols, we discuss some of our observations about S1's use of the locations strategy. Williams (1978) observed that subjects used a variety of systematic search strategies over the course of their recall attempts. One of those strategies was the location strategy. The locations strategy is the case where a subject systematically searches a mental map where target items are likely to be recalled. An example of the use of this strategy is the following:

Protocol 5

Mental Map: S1

Prop No.	Symbol	Text
771	*rco*	no one lives on
772	*rlo*	Ladera,
773	*rco*	that's the very end street,
773a	*pd*	they were all younger, okay
774	*s*	if I go over one,
775	*rlo*	that's Carmelo, um,
775a	*pn*	no one lived on that one,
776	*rco*	the next one is
777	*rlo*	Brindizzi, and
778	*pn*	no one I knew lived on that one, next one is
779	*rlo*	Algesiras, .su
780	*.mm 39	
781	*rco*	there were
782	*pn*	two people but they were both a year younger than me, that lived on that street,
783	*s*	I'll go over to the next one is
784	*rlo*	Monaco, I think and, that,
785	*rco*	oh
786	*rpn*	she was a year yonger than me too, ok, now if I go over to
787	*rco*	the next one's
788	*rlo*	Marseille,
789	*rpa*	he was a year younger and
790	*rpa*	the other one was two years older and

We can use the information collected in the basic analysis to chart out the overall time course of S1's use of locations strategy simply by noticing the rate

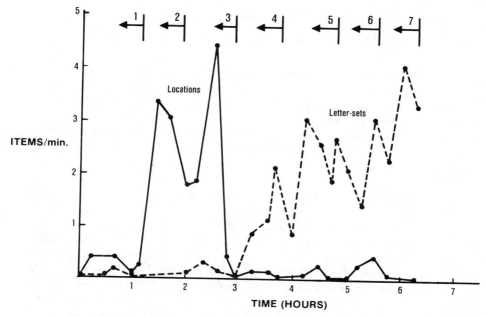

FIG. 34.3.   Recalls per minute of locations (rlo) and letter sets (rls) over time. The use of location information is indicative of use of the locations strategy. Letter-set information is indicative of another search strategy and is plotted here for comparison purposes only.

of locations recalled. Figure 34.3 plots number of locations per minute recalled by S1 during her first seven sessions. The numbered arrows at the top of the graph indicate the session boundaries. Letter-set recalls (indicative of another search strategy, name generation) per minute are also plotted to give some indication of how we can pull out the use of one strategy from another using this technique. All that is really important to notice is that we can provide objective indication of the onset, offset, and duration of various search strategies by the simple expedient of plotting the rate of retrieval of certain types of information over time. In this case, we see that S1 used the location strategy extensively during the second and third sessions.

We have available a map of the region the subject is searching. In addition, from debriefings with S1 we have S1's estimates of where each of the people she named, during the use of the locations strategy, actually lived (to the best of S1's knowledge). These two additional sources of information, along with the basic analysis we have already done, permit us to make a set of observations about S1's use of this particular strategy.

Structure of the Locations Strategy

We noted three things when examining S1's use of locations strategy.

1. S1 does not have a veridical mental map of the region.
2. S1 showed signs of what we call flexible focus; that is, she was able to retrieve names from a number of what appeared to be hierarchical representations of the same region.
3. S1 made brief switches out of the systematic search strategy she was using to follow what appeared to be promising leads useful with alternative search strategies.

Nonveridical Map.   On several occasions, S1's protocol indicated that the mental map she was using was flawed. An example of these flaws is shown in Fig. 34.4 derived from the segment of S1's in protocol 5.

We can note that the map we have constructed from S1's description is missing one street and has inverted the order of another pair. There are several instances in S1 protocol of such flaws. We are uncertain at this time of precisely how to quantify them, the primary problem being that many of S1's descriptions are brief and it is difficult to determine exactly how many possibilities for error S1 has given us in her protocol, how many errors of omission are due to a bad map, etc.

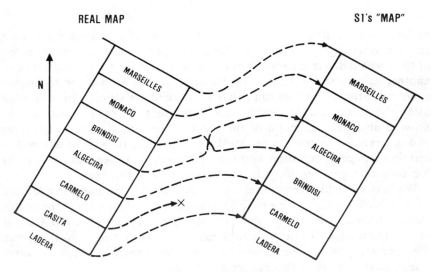

FIG. 34.4.   A comparison of a section of a real map of the region being searched by S1 and a map constructed from S1's description.

Flexible Focus. On occasion, S1 is able to recall new names just using global information about a region or neighborhood, whereas at other times it seems fruitful to examine a neighborhood street by street (and at times corner by corner). This ability to conduct useful searches while focusing on any of a variety of levels in the mental representation is called *flexible focus*.

Evidence supporting this observation comes from subject self-report and the subject's inability during debriefing to identify where certain of the people named lived beyond a general neighborhood specification. The following are protocols from S1 contrasting the levels from which information can be retrieved.

Protocol 6

Flexible Focus, Neighborhood: S1

Prop No.	Symbol	Text
600	*s*	okay if I go back beyond those streets
601	*rco*	I don't know them very well .su
602	*rco*	but I did know some people that lived
603	*rlo*	back there,
604	*rnl*	Ernie and
605	*rfn*	Don Boom
606	*rco*	he lived
607	*rlo*	back in there and

Protocol 7

Flexible Focus, Local: S1

Prop No.	Symbol	Text
182	*s*	if I cross the street on
183	*rfn*	Randy Moore's street the
184	*rlo*	cul-de-sac and this
185	*rpc*	one girl used to live there but
186	*rco*	she moved away and then there was
187	*rpc*	a girl that lived
188	*rlo*	at the end of the cul-de-sac but
189	*rco*	she was year younger than me and
190	*rco*	I used to
191	*rat*	baby sit for the
192	*rpn*	people that lived
193	*rlo*	next door to her, turn around,
194	*rpn*	the
195	*rlo*	guy that lived on the corner
196	*rco*	um he was a year older,

During debriefing S1 was able to identify (on a map of the region she reported surveying) street locations for 81% of the people she named. For 15 % she was able to identify only a neighborhood. Although neither pieces of this evidence are conclusive (because S1 cannot identify where a person lived given the name does not mean that she could not recall the name given the location), they are consistent with, and support the notion of, flexible focus.

Opportunism.   Frequently S1 will abandon the locations strategy for brief instances, retrieve some names or information with another strategy, and then return to the locations strategy. This brief strategy shift often seems stimulated by the retrieval of some information that would be particularly useful in the context of the new strategy. We refer to this behavior as *opportunism.*

Using a map of the region we can follow S1's search pattern. Comparing this pattern to the locations S1 specified for individuals during debriefing, we can observe deviations from the basic search strategy. The following protocol shows such deviations as well as comments from S1 suggesting the source of the deviations.

Protocol 8
Opportunism: S1

Prop No.	Symbol	Text	About
1	*rfn*	Shelly [Lutz], [recalled using locations strategy]	
2	*mr*	I already named her,	[1]
3	*rfn*	Helena Heffner [lives in region outside that being searched]	
4	*.mm 25		
5	*pi*	I remembered her because	[3]
6	*rco*	I used to know her in the	[3]
7	*rla*	7th grade,	
8	*rco*	she used to hang around	[3]
9	*rfn*	Shelly Lutz and I in	
10	*rla*	7th grade	
11	*pn*	but I never knew, recall her past	[3]
12	*rla*	7th grade	
13	*rco*	but I remember she did	[3]
14	*rev*	graduate with our class.	
15	*rco*	that reminded me of	
16	*rnl*	Helena	[3]
17	*pd*		
18	*rnl*	Helena reminds me of	
19	*rfn*	Liz Brackman and [lives in region outside that being searched]	
20	*rev*	she also graduated with our class,	[19]
21	*rph*	they sort of looked alike,	[3]
22	*rpe*	sort of acted alike too, ok,	[3]
23	*rco*		[19]
24	*rfn*	Liz Brackman lives down in	
25	*rlo*	La Playa	
26	*?*	but I missed her as I was going through there ok, um,	

The locations of the target names (in square brackets) were obtained in debriefing sessions with S1.

Conclusion

The primary intent of this paper has been to give an overview of the methods we have developed to examine complex verbal protocols from subjects thinking aloud while attempting difficult retrieval tasks. We are looking at difficult retrieval tasks in order to gain some insight into the *processes* of retrieval. The specific data base we are using is from a subject thinking aloud for over 7 hours while attempting to recall the names of classmates. The goal of the methodology is to provide mechanisms for building formal and quantitative descriptions of the rich procedural structures apparent in the verbal protocols.

The basic form of analysis we introduced is to break down the protocol into propositions, each of which can be classified into one of about 30 categories. From the basic analysis, along with information available from subject debriefings, we are able to describe substantial portions of the structure of the subject's protocol at a variety of levels.

At the most detailed level of analysis, we were able to write "equations" that are formal definitions of an array of recurrent phenomena. The phenomena so defined included partial recall, extended retrieval, two types of overshoot, systematic hypothesizing, and contextual retrieval. These phenomena are for the first time quantifiable objectively defined events.

At the most global level of analysis, we were able to display a number of the systematic search strategies used by the subject over the course of hours. For example, we can identify the 2-hour course of one subject's consistent use of the locations search strategy.

At an intermediate level of analysis, we were able to pull apart some of the structural characteristics of the locations-search strategy. In particular, we noted three characteristics of the locations strategy (beyond its highly systematic nature). We noted that the subject's mental map was flawed, that the subject successfully used several distinct levels of spatial representation, and that the subject briefly switched strategies in the midst of the systematic application of the locations strategy.

Space limitations prohibit any substantial discussion of the theoretical implications of the phenomena we have observed. Such a discussion is available in Williams (1978). We can state, however, that our ultimate goal is to build a theory of retrieval as a recursive, reconstructive, problem-solving process. The effort in this chapter is one of building tools. Our fundamental conclusion is that we now have one of the tools necessary to move the theory we are building from semianecdotal evidence to objective empirical demonstration.

ACKNOWLEDGMENTS

The data base used in this work comes from research performed at the University of California, at San Diego (see Williams, 1978). Research support for Michael David Williams for the analysis techniques discussed in this chapter was provided by the Navy Personnel Research and Development Center under the independent research program project number 042.06.03.01. We would like to thank Jim Hollan and Naomi Miyake for their useful comments during the development of this work. Jim has contributed substantially to our thinking on the directions our analysis should go as well as providing motive force to the effort. Naomi showed us how to get the protocol analysis off the ground and provided some key ideas to speed the process. We must also thank Barbara Hayes-Roth for stimulating us to notice the "opportunistic" behavior of our subject.

Opinions or assertions contained herein are those of the authors and are not to be construed as official or reflecting the views of the Department of the Navy.

APPENDIX A
Strategy Comments

Name: Strategy :: *Symbol:* S

Metamemory Comments
Name: Metamemory Hedge :: *Symbol:* mh
Name: Metamemory Query :: *Symbol:* mq
Name: Metamemory Evaluation :: *Symbol:* me
Name: Metamemory Reoccurrence :: *Symbol:* mr

Processing Comments
Name: Negative Processing Comment :: *Symbol:* pn
Name: Processing Description Comment :: *Symbol:* pd
Name: Processing Query :: *Symbol:* pq
Name: Processing Chatter :: *Symbol:* pc

RECALLS
Name: Full Name :: *Symbol:* rfn
Name: Partial recall—first name :: *Symbol:* rnl
Name: Partial recall—last name :: *Symbol:* rnl
Name: Person—Candidate Recall :: *Symbol:* rpc
Name: Person—Noncandidate Recall :: *Symbol:* rpn
Name: Physical Characteristic Recall :: *Symbol:* rph
Name: Personality Characteristic Recall :: *Symbol:* rpe
Name: Letter-Set Recall :: *Symbol:* rls

Name: Partial Recall—phonetic :: *Symbol:* rnp
Name: Semantic Recall :: *Symbol:* rns
Name: Recalled Object :: *Symbol:* rob
Name: Recalled Event :: *Symbol:* rev
Name: Recalled Activity :: *Symbol:* rat
Name: Recalled Location :: *Symbol:* rlo
Name: Recalled Location Activity :: *Symbol:* rla
Name: Recalls Concerned with Persons Age :: *Symbol:* rpa
Name: Recall Inference :: *Symbol:* rin
Name: Recall Comment or Fact :: *Symbol:* rco

REFERENCES

Flavell, J. H., & Wellman, H. M. In R. V. Kail & J. W. Hagen (Eds.), *Perspectives on the development of memory and cognition.* Hillsdale, N.J.: Lawrence Erlbaum Associates, 1977.

Keniston, A., & Flavell, J. H. *The nature and development of intelligent retrieval.* Unpublished manuscript, 1978.

Norman, D. A., & Bobrow, D. G. Descriptions: An intermediate stage in memory retrieval. *Cognitive Psychology,* 1979, *11,* 107–123.

Shiffrin, R. M. Memory search. In D. A. Norman (Ed.), *Models of human memory.* New York: Academic Press, 1970.

Williams, M. D. *The process of retrieval from very long term memory.* Unpublished Dissertation, University of California, San Diego, 1978.

Williams, M. D., & Norman, D. A. *Some characteristics of retrieval from very long term memory.* Paper presented at the meeting of the Psychonomics Society, ST. Louis, Mo., 1976.

VIII REASONING, PROBLEM SOLVING, AND DECISION PROCESSES

35

Reasoning, Problem Solving, and Decision Processes: The Problem Space as a Fundamental Category

Allen Newell
Department of Computer Science
Carnegie-Mellon University
Pittsburgh, Pennsylvania
United States

ABSTRACT

The notion of a problem space is well known in the area of problem solving research, both in cognitive psychology and artificial intelligence. The *Problem Space Hypothesis* is enunciated that the scope of problem spaces is to be extended to all symbolic cognitive activity. The chapter is devoted to explaining the nature of this hypothesis and describing some of its potential implications, with no attempt at a critical marshalling of the evidence pro and con. Two examples are used, one a typical problem solving activity (the Tower of Hanoi) and the other syllogistic reasoning. The latter is an example where the search behavior typical of problem spaces is not clearly in evidence, so it provides a useful area to explore the extension of the concept. A focal issue used in the chapter is the origin of the numerous flow diagrams that serve as theories of how subjects behave in tasks in the psychological laboratory. On the Problem Space Hypothesis these flow diagrams derive from the interaction of the task environment and the problem space.

INTRODUCTION

I am concerned with human goal-oriented cognition: what humans do when they bring to bear what they know to attain some end. I take my title from the session in which I have been invited to give an opening presentation, because it exhibits a particular feature of cognitive psychology's current state that I can use as a starting point.

Substantial areas of psychological study exist in *reasoning* (Falmagne, 1975, Revlin & Mayer, 1978, Wason & Johnson-Laird, 1972); *problem solving*

(Greeno, 1977, Newell & Simon, 1972); and *decision processes* (Slovic, Fisch-hoff, & Lichtenstein, 1977). Yet, in looking at any of these fields it is hard to detect the existence of the others. These three areas must in most ways be the same: problematic situations presented verbally to be dealt with by cognition and decision. Indeed, we often use the same term in all three areas. We "decide" which of two probabilistic bets to take (much studied in the area of decision processes); "decide" what chess move to make (much studied in the area of problem solving); and "decide" which conclusion follows from a syllogism (much studied in the area of reasoning). Similar semantic games could be played with the other terms. However, studies of each of these areas rarely give more than lip service to the results and theories from the others. What should be a unified scientific endeavor seems fragmented.

Multiple diagnoses for this fragmentation are possible. Deny the symptom. Argue, along with Voltaire's Dr. Pangloss, that it reflects a perfectly appro-priate state for a developing science. Note that the areas have distinct intellec-tual roots, and mutter that history explains (and excuses) all. Grasp the nettle and assert the three psychological domains to be genuinely distinct. However, I do not wish to argue the case in detail here. I do wish to assume that enough others share my unease to let me use this issue of fragmentation as a point of entry to what fundamental category of cognition might help resolve it.

Consider the tasks used by psychologists to study cognition. Traveling through them yields a distinct impression of just one damn task after another: Maier's two-string problem, Edward's book-bag and poker-chip task, R. Sternberg's analogies task, Restle's Tangled Tale sentence, Wertheimer's parallelograms, Revlin and company's classical syllogisms, and Newell and Simon's cryptarithmetic. The world of all tasks seems like a zoo formed from a medieval bestiary—far from random, lots of odd structure, perhaps bias (too many toy tasks?), but without essential orderliness.

Repeat that trip, stopping at tasks where some theorizing has occurred. For much of the best, we find a *flow diagram* presented, such as the one in Fig. 35.1 (Revlin & Leirer, 1978), with control flowing between boxes that carry labels such as *encode* and *compare*. These flow diagrams constitute the framework of the theory of each task.

Figure 35.1 is taken from the area of reasoning. Analogous diagrams could be found in abundance in all three areas. I assume such diagrams are familiar enough not to require further illustration. It is not uncommon to criticize flow diagrams, questioning their usefulness as a theoretical language; I have been known to do so myself (Newell, 1973). However, my question here is different. I am willing to accept that these flow diagrams acquire additional rules and data associated with the boxes, even equations and simulation programs. My question is: *Where* did those flow diagrams originally come from? They are different for every task, though they all surely bear a family resemblance. Theorists seem simply to write a different theory for each task. Details get

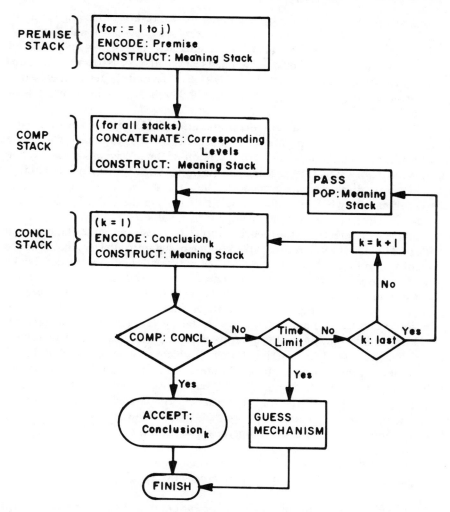

FIG. 35.1. Typical flow diagram: Conversion model of formal reasoning (Revlin & Leirer, 1978).

filled in experimentally, but the frameworks (i.e., the flow diagrams) are just written down.

The diversity of these flow diagrams is connected to the fragmentation of cognitive studies. Diversity per se does not cause the trouble, for the tasks themselves are indeed diverse and the theories must reflect that. The difficulty lies in the emergence of each of the microtheories full blown from the theorist's pen. There is no way to relate them and thus they help ensure the division of the study of human cognition into qualitatively isolated areas.

The difficulties in finding communality do not rest just in giving common technical content to the terms in the boxes, such as *encode* and *compare,* though these surely pose problems. They emerge with each flow diagram, and equally without essential discipline. They seem weak vessels to try to shore up, though some are trying (Sternberg, 1979). But beyond the terms themselves the structure of the flow diagrams also embodies the theory and must be dealt with as well.

The diversity of these flow diagrams arises in large part because these diagram theories incorporate the detailed structure of each task within the very fiber of the theory. They are a version of the magician's trick—by the time the theory emerges, the scientific magic has already taken place. Though the theorist does not have a theory of how the subject would do a task, he himself can do what the subject does (i.e., analyze the task); hence, he can create each theory separately out of his own subjective analysis.

I have no quarrel with the theorist's direct analysis as a source of theoretical ideas. The difficulty stems from the volume of separate analyses that produce a corresponding volume of distinct flow diagrams. The prescription I take from this is the need to understand where these flow diagrams come from— not to understand where theorists get them but to understand where subjects get them. Given that humans are cognitively integrated, how does this organization occur. Can we understand how the task gives rise to the flow diagram?

I propose a solution to this in terms of *problem spaces,* a concept already familiar in the study of search in human problem solving (Erickson & Jones, 1978) and applied widely there (Simon & Lea, 1974). It was introduced formally in Newell & Simon (1972), but derives from extensive work in artificial intelligence, where all programs characterized as *heuristic search* provide prototypic examples of problem spaces. The central proposition of this chapter is to extend the scope of this concept:

> *Problem Space Hypothesis:* The fundamental organizational unit of all human goal-oriented symbolic activity is the *problem space.*

In general terms this proposition is clear enough. There are things called *problem spaces,* which humans have or develop when they engage in goal-oriented activity. To understand such activity is to discover what problem spaces a human is using. From these flow the descriptions and predictions of interest, especially those concerned with how behavior is organized to accomplish tasks. The proposition is inclusive, claiming coverage of all symbolic goal-oriented activity, but hedges on whether all cognitive activity is symbolic. [The notion of *symbolic* (Newell & Simon, 1976) is ultimately central to the hypothesis but doesn't enter explicitly into this chapter.] It is an empirical hypothesis about the nature of human behavior. It is clearly of more general import than just where flow diagrams come from; that issue is just an entry point. In the words of the title, the hypothesis claims the problem space to be a fundamental category of cognition.

This chapter attempts to make this proposition intelligible. It does not present the case for it critically. There is no space for that. We avoid formalism as much as possible to concentrate on the central notions. We lay out quickly and oversimply the notion of a problem space, using the Tower of Hanoi task as an example, where the notion has already been applied. Then we pick another example, syllogistic reasoning, to develop what the hypothesis means in areas other than problem solving. Again, space permits only one such example, though the hypothesis is intended much more broadly. However, this provides enough of an illustration to discuss some general issues.

PROBLEM SPACES AND PROBLEMS

The Tower of Hanoi puzzle provides a convenient initial example to make the notion of a problem space concrete. It is normally considered to be a problem-solving task (Nilsson, 1971, Simon, 1975) and has been analyzed in essentially problem space terms.

We start with informal definitions:

Problem Space: A problem space consists of a set of symbolic structures (the *states* of the space) and a set of *operators* over the space. Each operator takes a state as input and produces a state as output, although there may be other inputs and outputs as well. The operators may be partial (i.e., not defined for all states). Sequences of operators define *paths* that thread their way through sequences of states.

Problem: A problem in a problem space consists of a set of *initial* states, a set of *goal* states, and a set of *path constraints.* The problem is to find a path through the space that starts at any initial state, passes only along paths that satisfy the path constraints, and ends at any goal state.

A problem space is a set of symbolic structures within which to move around, an arena wherein many specific problems can be posed and attempted. A problem space and problem are mental constructs (i.e., mental operators and states), though they may lead to external actions. A subject *has* a problem space if he can mentally represent the states of the space and carry out the operations. He *has* a problem in a problem space if: (1) he has the space; (2) he can obtain representations of the initial states, recognize paths that satisfy the path constraints, and recognize the goal states; and (3) his behavior is controlled so as to attempt the problem in the space.

The task and one possible problem space for the Tower of Hanoi are given in Fig. 35.2. The states are all the configurations of a fixed set of disks on three

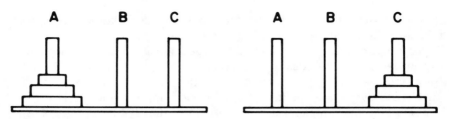

Task and Problem Statement

A board has three pegs, A, B and C (as shown at left). On Peg A are N disks of different sizes (3 in the diagram), in order with the largest at the bottom. The task is to get all the disks on Peg C in the same order (as shown at right). A disk may be moved from any peg to another, providing (1) that it is the top disk on its peg and (2) that it cannot be put on top of a disk smaller than itself.

Problem Space
Στ *States:* Arbitrary configurations of the N disks on the three pegs.
Operators:
Move a disk by removing it from a peg and putting it on another peg.
Recognize a configuration as an instance of a pattern.

Problem
Initial state: The configuration shown in the diagram at left.
Goal state: The configuration shown in the diagram at right.
Path constraint: No disk may be placed on a smaller disk.

FIG. 35.2.   Tower of Hanoi: Problem space.

pegs. There are two operators. One takes an arbitrary disk and peg as input and moves the disk to the peg (a new state). The other produces a symbolic expression asserting that a given configuration fits a given pattern. Possible patterns include concrete configurations, such as the two in the figure, and also patterns such as "peg P is empty" and "the disks are not in order on peg P". The problem statement specifically asserts this space to be the arena in which action takes place. It gives both initial and goal states explicitly. It imposes a path constraint; this is necessary because the space itself consists of *all* configurations of disks. It is not difficult to see that the Tower of Hanoi puzzle can be expressed in problem space form. Normal adults have the ability to create the space of configurations of Fig. 35.2 and perform the moves and recognitions. Thus, they can *have* the space of Fig. 35.2 in the manner called for—select and apply operators, test for results, etc.

Other problem spaces are possible for the Tower of Hanoi problem. Indeed, any problem space that contains this one works fine. For instance, the basic operators might be pick up a disk, move the hand, and deposit the disk. Then the move operator described as unitary in Fig. 35.2 becomes composite. Additional path constraints become necessary: A disk can be set down only on a peg; and only one disk can be moved at a time. Without these, one hand could hold a disk in mid-flight while another is moved.

Smaller spaces may also be possible. The states could be limited to ordered stacks of blocks and the move operator could apply only where the disk on the receiving peg was larger than the disk being moved. This space incorporates the path constraint as part of the operator. Whether this problem space is possible for a given subject depends on whether the subject's behavior can become organized so that the test for legality of a move is reliably incorporated within the move itself. If a move must actually be considered and the result viewed to see if it is legal, then the subject can have the space of Fig. 35.2 but cannot have this smaller space.

Each problem space provides a possible way to represent a task so as possibly to obtain a solution. It describes an ability of the subject to confine behavior to the problem space. It describes the units of behavior (i.e., the operators) the subject will use in working on a task.

Resource and capacity limits exist on processing. In problem spaces these take the form of two principles.

Serial Action: At most one problem space operator can be performed at a time.

Thus, at any point in time the subject is located at a single *current state* to which a *current operator* is being applied to yield a *current result* (i.e., a new state). Seriality specifically refers to this action. More than one problem or problem space may be active [e.g., to apply an operator in one problem space may require passing into another problem space (concerned with the mechanics of the operator), thus working in two problem spaces at once, though of course doing only one operator].

Finite Stock: The subject has a limited set of states (the stock) available to become the current state.

This is a memory and access limitation. However, the stock is not identical with short-term memory; some states may exist in long-term memory or be available perceptually as external memory. The actual size of the stock is variable in the same way as the size of human short memory, depending on the complexity of the state, the external memories used, etc.

In the Tower of Hanoi problem these two principles mean that a subject can consider only one move at a time (in thought, not just in the external world) and, after having considered a move, there will be only a few new states possible: the new state resulting from the move; the state from which the move was just considered; the state that is set up in the external world (if that is different); the original initial state; possibly another remembered one.

Given a problem in a problem space, the only way a subject can solve the problem is by *searching* in the space: working out from the current state by applying operators, adding new states to the stock to be used at new points of search, evaluating whether the results help, etc. To accomplish this search requires performing repeatedly a fixed set of functions:

> *Search Control:* The following functions determine the behavior in a problem space while working on a given problem.
>
> > Decide to quit the problem.
> > Decide if a goal state has been produced.
> > Select a state from the stock to be the current state.
> > Select an operator to be the current operator.
> > Decide to save the new state just produced by an operator.

These functions operate within a cycle consisting of repeating the following three steps:

1. Select a state; select an operator.
2. Apply operator to state, producing new state.
3. Decide if a goal state; decide to quit; decide to save the new state.

The subject has a mechanism (the *architecture*) for carrying out this control cycle. It is a fixed mechanism that works for all problem spaces: bringing the selected operator and state in contact, so the new state can be produced; bringing the decision processes in contact with this new state, so goal attainment can be determined; and so on. Its exact properties are important, including memory management for the limited stock and basic error detection, though we do not discuss the architecture further.

More than one function can be performed at some steps: the two selections in step 1 and the three decisions in step 3. Within a step no process takes priority over any other. In what order the selection of an operator and of a state takes place depends on the content of the selection processes. Likewise, depending on the particular situation, the decisions could be made in any order.

Control over the search depends on the knowledge of these functions that the subject has *immediately available*. This restriction to immediate availability arises as follows. All knowledge about a task is obtained by taking steps in a problem space; that is what it means to be working in a problem space. Hence, choosing what step to take cannot itself be an extended deliberation that considers and reasons about the problem—that would involve taking steps in the problem space, contra assumption. What the control processes of selection and decision can involve is applying stored knowledge available in the subject's long-term memory. But there is a limit to how much can be done without thinking a new thought about the task itself (i.e., without moving in the problem space).

The restriction implies that subjects cannot normally take too long to make a step, though no strict temporal limit exists. Subjects take steps in a problem space every few seconds (Newell & Simon, 1972). Where the time per state is fairly long (10–15 sec), either the state is relatively complex, taking time to assimilate, or the operators take time to apply. Unlike the search control, the application of an operator need not be immediate but can involve going into a different problem space. A typical example is applying an unfamiliar complex formal rule, as in algebra.

The restriction that search control involves only bringing to bear immediately available knowledge is important, because it limits the complexity of the search control process. It lets us think of the search control primarily in terms of the knowledge it embodies rather than the processes for making that knowledge effective.

A subject can attempt to solve a problem in a problem space with *any* body of search control knowledge: from none at all, yielding undirected search, to knowledge that completely specifies all choices correctly, yielding the solution directly. Thus, to have a problem space is already to have relevant ways of behaving in a task situation, though the larger the space and the less effective the control knowledge, the smaller the chance of success. For instance, if a subject has only the knowledge represented in Fig. 35.2 (i.e., no special search control knowledge at all), the problem can still be attempted. A combinatorial search problem then occurs, which can be analyzed in terms of the branching factor of the search (three) and the depth to solution ($2^N - 1$ for N disks) (Nilsson, 1971).

Subjects of course are never this ignorant; they have some effective knowledge for controlling the search. Figure 35.3 gives some examples. In accordance with the previous remarks, it is sufficient to express the search control just by the knowledge involved, without explicit characterization of the processing. K1 to K3 simply provide minimal knowledge for their respective control functions. K4 says to move forward with each step; it induces a depth-first strategy. K5 is the most obvious means-ends principle. The Tower of Hanoi is problematic just because K5 does not suffice (i.e., disks cannot simply be moved to the desired peg). It is a puzzle just because K6, the obvious means-ends knowledge to avoid difficulties, is ineffective with more than two disks.

K7–K9 reflect a general avoidance of duplicate and redundant activity. K7 cuts down the branching factor from 3 to 2. K8 cuts it to 1 on every other move, giving an effective branching factor of 1.4. Finally, K9 is a slightly more penetrating formulation to avoid looping, reducing the branching to 1 (except at the initial position). However, if K9 is to be implemented, the subject must remember the peg from which the smallest disk came, which is a minor augmentation of the problem space state. Thus, adding K7–K9 completely

Decide to quit the problem
　　K1. Quit if succeed.
　　K2. Quit when told by experimenter.

Decide if goal state has been produced
　　K3. A state is a goal state if it is the exact pattern desired.

Select a state from the stock to be the current state
　　K4. Make new state the current state.

Select an operator to be the current operator
　　K5. Move a disk to the peg specified by a goal state.
　　K6. Move an obstructing disk to another peg.
　　K7. Do not move back to just prior position.
　　K8. Do not move a disk twice in a row.
　　K9. Do not move smallest disk back to its just prior peg.

Decide to save a new state just produced by an operator
　　K10. Add newly produced state to the stock.

FIG. 35.3.　Tower of Hanoi: Search control knowledge.

determines the course of problem solving. It leaves open only the (fateful) choice on the very first move. Subjects do exist who proceed in exactly this fashion (Anzai & Simon, 1979); upon discovering they have made the wrong initial choice, they recall the initial move, chose the alternate one, and then proceed according to the same heuristics to solve the problem.

K10 goes hand in hand with K4. It would lead to remembering the entire path, except that short-term memory is limited. Additional control knowledge would be needed to determine which states to retain if some have to be abandoned. We haven't shown such knowledge, because its form depends on the nature of the architecture (i.e., what aspects of short-term memory can actually be controlled by the subject). Moreover, with the other search control knowledge of Fig. 35.3, the subject never goes back to a deliberately remembered state but simply always pushes forward.

Various means exist for organizing search control knowledge. One is to create new problems (i.e., subgoals), attempt them, and incorporate the results in the further search. For simplicity we cast the basic functions of search control to be those required, assuming the problem to be fixed. But the subject also selects problems and problem spaces. Though not requiring additional capabilities, except for memory management, much additional power and complexity accrues thereby, namely, the goal hierarchy. For instance, organizations of subgoals and search control knowledge can be fashioned into *methods*, which coordinate the selection and actions in various useful ways. A number of these methods, which have shown up repeatedly in *artificial intelligence* investigations of problem solving and elsewhere, have acquired familiar names:

Generate and Test: Generate in any way possible (e.g., systematically or haphazardly) a sequence of candidate states, testing each for whether it is the desired state.

Heuristic Search: Apply heuristics to reject possible operators from the current state and to reject newly produced states; remember the states with untried operators in some systematic way (different schemes yield search strategies, such as *depth first, breadth first, progressive deepening,* and *best first*).

Hill Climbing: Generate and apply operators from the current state; select one that produces a state with an improved evaluation and move to it.

Means-Ends Analysis: Compare the current state with the desired state to detect any difference; use that difference to select an operator that reduces or eliminates it; otherwise proceed as in heuristic search.

Operator Subgoaling: If an operator cannot be applied to a current state, set up a subgoal to find a state in which the operator can be applied; otherwise proceed as in heuristic search or means-ends analysis.

Planning: Abstract from the present state (by processing only selected information throughout) and proceed to solve the simplified problem; use what is remembered of the path as a guide to solving the unabstracted problem.

These are often called the *weak methods,* because they can be relevant when little is known about the task, though, when so evoked, they are not very powerful. However, they often suffice to solve a problem, if the space is not large or if extensive search is undertaken. These methods are simply organizations of search control knowledge, though it is beyond the scope of this chapter to lay this out. Functions, such as *evaluate* (hill climbing) and *detect differences* (means-ends analysis) can be performed within search control if sufficiently simple (i.e., sufficiently like a recognition). Complex versions would require search control to evoke subgoals to accomplish them in some problem space. The methods also are *open,* in that they do not specify completely all the functions and hence admit the addition of more search control knowledge (e.g., about differences in means-ends analysis).

The first two methods, generate-and-test and heuristic search, occur automatically in a problem space (indeed, heuristic search gave rise to the notion of the problem space). They are identified as distinct methods, because they are normally realized within control structures (standard programming languages) where they must be constructed and deliberately evoked, just like any other method. The other methods all require the task to have some additional characteristics (the weak conditions) that are known to the subject: Hill climbing requires evaluation of states; mean-ends analysis requires differences; operator subgoaling requires the conditions of operator applicability to be symbolizable; etc.

Let us add a single item of control knowledge for the Tower of Hanoi:

K11. Get an obstructing disk on the other-peg.

K11 expresses operator subgoaling, because the construct of obstruction derives from inapplicable operators. This differs from K6 only in setting a subgoal (*get*) rather than selecting an actual operator (*move*). With K11 some problems can be solved without stringent knowledge about avoiding duplicate paths (K8 or K9). The architecture is assumed to manage the resulting stack of subgoals that builds up as the knowledge is used repeatedly and recursively. The limits to subgoal management set limits to the effectiveness of solving Tower of Hanoi problems with just K11.

Subjects not only show problem-solving behavior in the Tower of Hanoi, they ultimately show skilled behavior, proceeding to solve each puzzle in a direct way that takes time but does not exhibit search. Simon (1975) has provided an analysis of four distinct, complete strategies for skilled behavior in the Tower of Hanoi. Three of the strategies arise by adding more search control knowledge to what we have assembled so far. The *goal-recursion strategy* simply expands K11 to apply to pyramids of disks rather than just disks, its key notion being the invention of the concept of pyramid by the subject. The *simple perceptual strategy* expands K11, not by the pyramid but by the less powerful notion of the largest obstructing disk (on the source peg). The *sophisticated perceptual strategy* adds to this latter an item that extends the notion of obstructions to the target peg as well as the source peg. (The fourth strategy, *move pattern,* raises issues about mimicing external behavior sequences that lie outside our illustration.)

The problem space hypothesis asserts that skilled, routine behavior is organized within the problem space by the accumulation of search control knowledge. This is just what we see in these three strategies. Though how the accumulation occurs is not given, the final result consists simply of the addition of search control knowledge. There is no fundamental difference between problem solving and routine behavior in control organization, except in completeness and adequacy of search control knowledge.

Simon (1975) embodies the various strategies in a *production system,* a species of pattern-directed rule-oriented programming system (Newell & Simon, 1972). This can be seen as an operational realization of the search control knowledge, and in fact such systems are active candidates for the underlying architecture of human cognition (Newell, 1973; 1980).

THE CATEGORICAL SYLLOGISM:
A REASONING TASK

There is a long history of research into human performance on classical Aristotelian syllogisms. Its fascination arises from the basic clash in our civilization between rationality and irrationality, and its projection to the clash between logic and psychology. Should humans behave according to the dictates of formal logic? Do they have their own "psychologic"? Are they simply "irrational"? Formal syllogisms provide ample evidence that people in fact cannot reason very well. They make lots of mistakes in answering (say) "All A are B; some C are not B; are some A not C necessarily?" The tone for research was set many years ago by Woodworth & Sells (1935), whose hypothesis of an *atmosphere* effect describes one form of illogic (or at least superficiality) whereby subjects respond according to the affirmative or negative tenor of the syllogism.

Current research is constructing information-processing theories of how people perform syllogisms, decomposing the task into various stages (e.g., encoding, comparing, responding) and finding experimental demonstrations of which stages seem responsible for various aspects of performance (Falmagne, 1975; Revlin & Mayer, 1978). It forms a useful example for us, because though research is active and current, there is little contact between its processing models and those in problem solving and decision making, as a glance at the two recent books just cited shows. Thus, we can see what analysis in terms of problem spaces might add.

Standard syllogistic reasoning tasks are formed from three terms (e.g., A, B, C), combined into two assertions (the major and minor premise) involving pairs of terms (A and B; B and C), from which some assertions (the conclusion) about the third pair (A and C) may or may not follow. Four logical assertions are possible from the two quantifiers (*all, some*), negation (*no/not*), and the copula of implication (*are*):

| Major Premise: | All A are B |
| Minor Premise: | Some B are C |

Conclusion:	All A are C	Which of the list follow?
	No A are C	
	Some A are C	
	Some A are not C	
	Nothing follows	

Both abstract syllogisms (above) and concrete syllogisms (No Senators belong to the Harem Club; some sheiks belong to the Harem Club; therefore no sheiks are Senators) are used.

Current theory can be typified by the flow diagram shown earlier (Fig. 35.1) from Revlin and Leirer (1978). Its stages permit focusing on whether the difficulty lies in encoding (how sentences are interpreted) or in inferencing; and on whether the difficulty lies with the givens or the conclusion. Typical of recent work is the hypothesis (Revlin's conversion model) that subjects apply conversion operations that take "All A are B" into "All B are A," thus producing errors in the encoding stage, and the hypothesis (Erickson, 1978) that subjects solve the problem by constructing internal Venn diagrams but fail to construct all possibilities.

The problem space hypothesis implies that subjects solve syllogistic reasoning tasks by working in a problem space. They have a representation for the possible states of knowledge about the syllogism plus operators for generating and manipulating that knowledge. If their search control knowledge is sufficient, they will go directly to an answer; when faced with difficulties, they will search in this space (i.e., try different manipulations in attempting to solve the problem). They do not have simply an algorithm or method, as in Fig. 35.1. If such a flow diagram describes their behavior, then it is the resultant of the problem space and the task environment.

Let's look at one possible problem space for syllogistic reasoning.

Abstract Object Problem Space

Figure 35.4 shows a problem space based on positing objects that have the attributes, A, B, C mentioned in a syllogism. These objects are abstract: They can be either *necessary* or only *possible;* and they can have only some of the attributes mentioned in the syllogism. Thus, they represent various situations of partial knowledge, which the subject is to flesh out by moving in the space.

This space is a natural one. It corresponds to attempting to imagine the things that are being talked about in the syllogism, as in the following monologue about the syllogism: All A are B; no C are B; therefore necessarily some A are not C.

"OK, there are some things that have A and also have B.
Though some things that don't have A could also exist, and they could have B or not.

But things that have C cannot also have B.
Though things that don't have C could have B or not.

Now, does that force some things that have A to not have C?

Well, those things that have A, have B...
and having B they can't have C.

States: Set of abstract objects with various properties

[Possible A+ B–]	=	Possible object with attribute A and without B
		Nonoccurring attributes are not yet examined
[Necessary C–]	=	Object without attribute C necessarily exists
[Possible A+ open-B–]	=	B– is an open attribute for the object

All possible object are instances of objects already in the state

Encoding Operators

E1.	All X are Y	=> [Necessary X+ Y+], [Possible X– Y+], [Possible X– Y–]
E2.	No X are Y	=> [Necessary X+ Y–], [Possible X– Y+], [Possible X– Y–]
E3.	Some X are Y	=> [Necessary X+ Y+], [Possible X+ Y–],
		[Possible X– Y+], [Possible X– Y–]
E4.	Some X are not Y	=> [Necessary X+ Y–], [Possible X+ Y+],
		[Possible X– Y+], [Possible X– Y–]

Production Operators

Q1.	[Any X Y], [Any X Z] => [Possible X Y Z] if attributes agree, else nothing
Q2.	[Necessary X Y], [Possible X Y Z] => [Possible X Y open-Z]
Q3.	[Possible X Y open-Z], no [Any OK-X OK-Y op-Z] => [Necessary X Y Z]
	[Possible X Y Z] if find

R1. [Any X Y . . .] is an instance of [Any X Y] if occurring attributes agree

FIG. 35.4.   Abstract object problem space for syllogisms.

And, OK, there isn't any thing that has B that has C.

So there are some things that surely have A and haven't C."

An example of an object in a state is [Possible A+ C–], which has attribute A, does not have attribute C, and is only known possibly to exist. That the attribute B does not occur means that no knowledge is yet availabe on it. Relevant partial knowledge may be acquired about whether a possible object is in fact necessary, namely, that an object with some of its attributes is already necessary. Those attributes for which it is still unknown are called *open.*

Consider the encoding operator E1, which produces a new state in the space by taking as input (along with the state) an externally given assertion and adding the indicated objects. From "All X are Y" is known: (1) some objects with attribute X necessarily exist and they also have Y (hence [Necessary X+ Y+]); (2) some objects possibly exist without attribute X and either with or without attribute Y (hence [Possible X– Y+] and [Possible X– Y–]). E1 adds all three of these objects to produce the new state. The objects in a state represent *all* the objects that can exist; hence, E1 expresses that [X+ Y–] is not possible simply by not adding it to the state. The encoding operators embody assumptions about language. For instance, subjects see [X+ Y+] as necessary rather than just possible, because they do not make the logician's interpretation of quantification, which admits vacuous cases.

Operator Q1 produces abstract objects with the combined attributes of two other objects (which are therefore instances of the input objects). Suppose one was [Any X+ Y+] and the other was [Any X+ Z–] (where *any* means either *necessary* or *possible*); Q1 produces [Possible X+ Y+ Z–]. In words: if some things that have X have Y and some things that have X don't have Z, then it's possible that some things that have X both have Y and don't have Z. Q1 can be applied only if all the common attributes agree in sign (e.g., [X+ Z+] and [X– W+] can't possibly refer to the same object, because it couldn't both have X and not have X). The results of Q1 can never be known for sure to exist, so it is always only *possible* (e.g., in the previous example with [X+ Y+ Z–], all the [X+ Y+]s might actually be [X+ Y+ Z+] and the [X+ Z+]s might be [X+ Z+ Y–], so no common object would in fact exist). The role of Q1 is to generate candidate inferences.

Q2 is part of showing that a possible object is necessary. The grounds for such an inference comes from: If [X+ Y+] is necessary, then for any additional attribute, Z, either [X+ Y+ Z+] or [X+ Y+ Z–] (or both) must exist. Hence, if [X+ Y+ Z–] is not possible, then [X+ Y+ Z+] must be necessary. Q2 records the existence of a necessary object and identifies the attribute to be used to make the inference. This is the *open* attribute—where it is not known whether objects with the complementary sense of the attribute can exist. There may be more than one way to identify an open attribute in a possible object and hence more than one way to infer that it is actually necessary.

Q3 finishes the job of inferring that a possible object is necessary. It searches the state for the complementary object (i.e., the one with the opposite sense of the open attribute). This object must also be compatible with the other attributes of the object. In the figure we express this as OK-X: either the attribute agrees in sense with the one in the input object or it is missing entirely (in which case it could be either sense). If such an object cannot be found, then the inference to necessity can be made; if the object can be found, then the object remains only possible. For example, suppose Q2 had produced [Possible X+ Y– open-Z+], because [Necessary X+ Y–] was in the state. If an object such as [Possible X+ Y– Z–] occurred, no inference could be made that [Possible X+ Y– open-Z+] was necessary; if no such object was around, then Q3 could produce [Necessary X+ Y– Z+]. [Possible Y– Z–] would also be sufficient to deny the inference, so there need not be an identity match. Note that Q3 depends on an object *not* existing in the state. By representing nonpossibility by absence, this particular problem space is vulnerable to errors of omission.

Finally, besides operators that produce new objects, there must also be a recognition operator, R1, that sees that one object is an instance of another (e.g., that [Possible X+ Y+] is an instance of [Possible X+]).

P1.   All A are B
P2.   No C are B

C1.   Some A are not C

1.	E1(P1)	=> I1:	[Necessary A+ B+], [Possible A– B+], [Possible A– B–]
2.	E2(P2)	=> I2:	[Necessary C+ B–], [Possible C– B+], [Possible C– B–],
			[Necessary A+ B+], [Possible A– B+], [Possible A– B–]
3.	E4(C1)	=> G:	[Necessary A+ C–]
4.	Q1(I2)	=> I3:	[Possible A+ B+ C–], [Necessary C+ B–],...
5.	Q2(I3)	=> I4:	[Possible A+ B+ open-C–], [Necessary C+ B–],...
6.	Q3(I4)	=> I5:	[Necessary A+ B+ C–], [Necessary C+ B–],...
7.	R1(I4,G)	=> I6:	(This state is an instance of G), [Necessary A+ B+ C–],...

FIG. 35.5.   Example of solving a syllogism in abstract object space.

Figure 35.5 shows how reasoning would go in this space. Starting with a state with no objects, the first three steps translate the problem into an internal state. Step 4 applies Q1 to [Necessary A+ B+] and [Necessary B+ C–] to produce a possible inference, [Possible A+ B+ C–]. In step 5, Q2 uses [Necessary A+ B+] to identify C– as open. This permits Q3 to make the inference to [Necessary A+ B+ C–], because nothing of the form [Necessary OK-A+ OK-B+ C+] exists. All the objects with C+ have B–, so don't apply to an object with B+. The final step is by R1 which detects that [Necessary A+ B+ C–] is an instance of [Necessary A+ C–] in the goal state.

Figure 35.5 gives a direct route to the solution. How could it be found? Though by no means large, the space itself contains a number of paths [e.g., Q1 can be applied to any pair of the objects (nine cases) and will be successful in four cases, each of which can be the target for upgrading to necessary]. Elementary search control is in fact sufficient. Means-ends analysis says to apply operators that produce necessary objects with A+ and C–. Thus Q1 is selected with [Necessary A+ B+] or [Necessary C+ B–] for one of the inputs, say [Necessary A+ B+], to be concrete. Operator subgoaling obtains the other inputs, say [Necessary C– B+] (that is, the lack of an input is a failure of the operator to apply, which leads to a subgoal of getting the input). Once [Possible A+ B+ C–] is in hand, means-ends analysis selects Q2 to make it necessary. There is again a need for a second input, and operator subgoaling selects [Necessary A+ B+]. Q3 follows directly by the attempt to make the output necessary.

The point is not that this is terribly difficult problem solving—precisely the opposite. Whereas completely random behavior is not satisfactory (one can rattle around even in a space of less than 10 elements), just a little elementary search control is enough to dictate reasonably focused behavior. No extra apparatus is required to create appropriate task-directed behavior. The elementary search control does not always completely dictate the path. In the present case, the initial path could have followed Q1 to [Necessary B+ C–]

instead of [Necessary A+ B+]; it would have generated the alternative legitimate inference of no C are A but would have led to backtracking to make contact with some A are not C.

What Problem Spaces Say About Syllogistic Reasoning

We now can see what problem spaces suggest about the nature of syllogistic reasoning and how it should be studied.

Where Do Flow Diagrams Come From?   Flow diagrams are essentially the trace of the operators under search control regimes. The path of Fig. 35.5 is *encode,* then *compare* (it lacks a *respond,* because we didn't bother to define a task output). Such a path, of course, is only a single path through the flow diagram. However, if we merge several such paths over a set of tasks, we will get the full-blown flow diagram. The decision boxes represent the places where operator or state selection goes one way or another, for different tasks. Whether decision boxes and separate paths exist in the flow diagram depend on how much is aggregated under the terms *encode, compare,* etc. In our example, *compare* comprises Q1, Q2, and Q3.

Obvious flow diagrams (i.e., obvious to use in their logic) are ones where, given the problem space, it requires only *obvious* control (e.g., means-ends analysis) to determine the sequence of operators to solve the problem.

As the subject acquires skill in this task, there will occur both development of the problem space itself and growth of search control knowledge. Special features of the task will be recognized and incorporated, well beyond the elementary organizational schemes we have focused on here. They will have the character of unique domain-dependent knowledge, not general methods. What the hypothesis then prescribes is the general form that the theory will take (i.e., an accumulation of search control knowledge and predominantly a further specification of the more general methods).

Avoidance of the Fixed-Method Fallacy.   Much current work in syllogistic reasoning proceeds by positing a particular representation and/or method, the flow diagram of Revlin and Leirer again being a good example, but not the only one. Erickson (1978) posits that all subjects encode into (multiple) Venn diagrams. These studies commit the *fixed-method fallacy,* which attributes to all subjects (on all occasions) the same method without any attempt to ascertain either that all subjects indeed follow the specified method or that the consequences derived are invariant over different possible methods. They take as indicative of the model's success that it generates results in reasonable agreement with group data on percent correct.

Many of these results, however, are not unique to the method but flow from disparate methods defined for different problem spaces. To pick a central issue, whether errors occur during encoding or inference, the conversion hypothesis posits an encoding error that transforms "All A is B" to an internal code for "All B is A," proceeding afterward with flawless logic. The model of Revlin and Leirer embodies this hypothesis and from its success these authors conclude for the "human's are logical" position. But in other problem spaces what is encoding conversion in the Revlin and Leirer model is either short-term memory error and/or inference error. For instance, consider conversion in the abstract object problem space:

"All A are B" = [Necessary A+ B+], [Possible A– B–], [Possible A– B+]
"All B are A" = [Necessary B+ A+], [Possible B– A–], [Possible B– A+]

The difference lies not in the focal object (where the knowledge is strongest) but in a secondary object. This latter could certainly be misconstructed by the encoding operator. However, it could also be transformed by short-term memory errors during reasoning. Further, the role of these objects in reasoning is either to inhibit Q3 from concluding necessity (by being the complementary expression) or to be the input to Q1 in producing an alternative that reduces an "all" inference to a "some" inference. In both, retrieval failure masquerades for encoding failure, because the result is that Q1 or Q3, respectively, doesn't obtain an input that does the job.

The point is not that the example problem space is right and Revlin and Leirer, wrong. The point is that problem spaces imply that ranges of possible behaviors are there to be explored. They make clear that the same subject on repeated occasions will exhibit a range of behavior, even though working in the same space. They offer suggestions (which have not been exploited yet) of how to characterize ranges of variability by variation in search control knowledge. Positing a single method or flow diagram provides a much more constrained basis to consider individual variations and continually seduces into the fixed-method fallacy.

Extension and Task Variation.   A problem space provides an arena for a class of problems (one of its essential notions). Whether the problem is one of making an inference, validating an inference, or choosing inferences by multiple choice, the tasks all occur in the same problem space by a change in goals, though they may evoke different search control knowledge. Extending the task, while keeping within the problem space, should still elicit appropriate behavior, with much of the original search control knowledge still applicable (though perhaps less effective). For example, more entities can occur: "All A are B; No A are C; Some B are D; All C are D; Is it true necessarily that some A are not D?" Flow diagrams, by being an amalgam of task and control, have difficulty dealing with famillies of related tasks. Information-processing models built to handle just the classical two-premise syllogism require serious augmentation and modification for such extensions.

Multiple Problem Spaces.   Several qualitatively distinct problem spaces are possible for reasoning about categorical syllogisms. We can get spaces corresponding to the first-order predicate calculus, various concrete models of the syllogisms (e.g., Venn diagrams), relations between terms, and even natural language—all in addition to the abstract or prototypic object space used here for illustration. There are variations within a given type of space. For instance, a variant of the abstract object space is to admit explicit objects that are *not possible* rather than relying on the absence of objects in the state.

The general grounds of these different spaces are not necessarily foreign to existing work. Venn diagrams are used as the explicit basis for some models (Erickson, 1978). Johnson-Laird (1975, Johnson-Laird & Steedman, 1978) has developed a model based on a representation with similarities to the abstract objects; he creates multiple individuals corresponding to each abstract object. However, the point here is not that one problem space is right. Humans can reason about syllogisms in many different ways; and the same individual can use different problem spaces on different occasions, possibly even within the same experiment. The point is that reasoning is the (more or less) knowledgable exploration of an area, not just the following of a given procedure.

DISCUSSION

We have used a single task domain to illustrate and make concrete what the problem space hypothesis means outside its original area of problem solving search. Let us now state more generally some consequences that flow from the hypothesis.

Predicting the Control Structure for a Task.   The hypothesis implies that the problem space structure is common ground for all symbolic cognition. Analysis of a cognitive task involves first specifying the problem space and then specifying the search control knowledge used within that problem space. Elementary search control knowledge is also common, namely, subgoals, weak methods, obvious loop avoidance, and obvious waste motion avoidance. Thus the problem space, with its standard complement of control knowledge, provides the starting point in looking for specific theories for a task.

Under some conditions the problem space and elementary search control knowledge can be sufficient to obtain a basic theory of the subject's behavior in the task (i.e., the structure corresponding to the flow diagrams). We saw this in the syllogistic reasoning task. This is what satisfies the initial goal of this chapter to explain where the idiosyncratic yet obvious flow diagrams come from that grace so much of our current cognitive theorizing. They come from the problem space. They are obvious, because the only knowledge used is elmentary search control knowledge, which is "obvious" to us all, as participating human beings. They are idiosyncratic to each task, because the structure of the tasks is idiosyncratic—a reflection of the oft-quoted parable of the ant whose complex path results from the contours of the sand grains and not from complex internal mechanisms (Simon, 1969).

Two conditions at least permit the structure of behavior for a task to be obtained from just the general problem space structure. In one, the task is simple and transparent, relative to the cognitive ability of the subject. Then elementary search control knowledge suffices. This is the situation in the syllogistic reasoning tasks. In the other, the situation is novel, so that the subject does not have much prior knowledge and does not have time to extract much new specific knowledge. Then the subject must rely on elementary knowledge. This condition produces novice problem-solving behavior.

Experience with a task leads to the growth of search control knowledge. Behavior increasingly reflects this knowledge, so that the mechanisms implied by the elementary search control knowledge no longer suffice for determining behavior. However, this additional knowledge still serves the basic functions of control and the problem space remains the control framework within which behavior is generated. Furthermore, if the situation shifts outside the reach of the subject's specific knowledge, then again behavior is generated by more elementary search control knowledge—which is all the subject knows that is relevant.

Experience leads to the growth of new problem spaces and not just to the growth of search control knowledge within a problem space. Dramatic change of space occurs, as in seeing that a verbal problem can be reformulated as an algebraic equation. But evolution of a space also occurs, with new data structures being added to the state and new operators to the repertoire. Such changes can occur concurrently with changes in search control, because they are not necessarily incompatible.

Is the Hypothesis Disprovable?   The hypothesis as stated is empirical, asserting how humans process information and behave thereby. However, the flexibility of the concept (pick any states, any operators, any search control knowledge) suggests that for any behavior there might be some problem space (or several) that yield it. If so, the usual uncomfortableness at having gotten a tautology in tow might follow. There is a genuine issue here, though not one that is insurmountable.

The set of problem spaces is universal relative to its architecture; that is, there exists a problem space that produces any behavior stream compatible with the architecture. It is important that this be so, to meet the human's need to shape behavior in whatever way is necessary to meet the demands of an unpredictable environment. Moreover, this is important for whatever control structure might exist to guide human behavior, whether a problem space or some other kind. Conceivably, no universal control might be possible—any control scheme would have some deficiency (i.e., some way in which it restricts the possible behaviors of the subject), with different schemes having characteristic deficiencies. Then it would be possible, in principle, to determine subject's control schemes by observing these deficiencies. In fact, we know that universal computational schemes are possible—that is what the theory of universal Turing machines is all about. Whatever one universal control scheme can do, another can imitate. Thus, if the question is posed right, in a technical sense one can never disprove the basic problem space hypothesis from performance (Anderson, 1976)—nor disprove its competitors.

The issue is not insurmountable, because tests of control structure are not forced to consider only the qualitative (in the sense of time-independent) aspects of the behavior stream, which is where the universality is guaranteed. Even putting to one side physiological and evolutionary data as too remote, there is the timing of behavior, the acquisition and modification of the control structure, and errors—to name just the more obvious sources of data that can penetrate the masquerade of one universal control system by another. However, the ability for all control schemes to produce flexible behavior to the point of mutual imitation still makes the issues of testing indirect, complex, and difficult, to say the least.

Let us note briefly some consequences of the problem space hypothesis that make it potentially vulnerable to disproof.

1. In novel situations problem spaces must be created by the subject. Because the subject has no special knowledge, the space must be constructed in terms of the surface features of the external environment. Thus, there are places where it is possible to predict what the problem space will be. Work on novel tasks (with underlying structure isomorphic to the Tower of Hanoi) gives some evidence for this already (Hayes & Simon, 1976).

2. Many events can throw the subject off a straight and narrow path, wherein the search control knowledge was adequate (e.g., external interruptions and memory errors). Such events leave the subject engaged in a wider search in the problem space, using more elementary search control knowledge. These error and recovery behaviors should be *systematic,* in reflecting the same space; that is, the subject's behavior when errors occur should appear rule governed in ways appropriate to being in a particular problem space.

3. The subject's movement toward skilled behavior should be continuous, in that change occurs by accretion of search control knowledge within a fixed space. Unfortunately, other forms of procedural learning may be sufficiently

hard to distinguish so that testing the hypothesis in this fashion is especially difficult [e.g., learning by successive invention of new methods (which surely occurs) and learning by compiling the experience obtained in the problem space into some other procedural language].

4. The problem space has strong implications for the transfer of skill. Indeed, the assertion about the universal availability of the elementary search control (e.g., the weak methods) is an assertion about transfer. If a subject maps a task into an existing problem space, then the transfer of this knowledge to the new task is implied (as transformed by the encoding of the task, of course).

5. Last, but not least for this chapter, is the use of the problem space hypothesis to predict flow diagrams. Failure to predict the actual control organizations, as derived in the usual way by informal analysis, would count against the hypothesis.

Banishment of (Half) the Homunculus.   A major item on the agenda of cognitive psychology is to banish the homunculus [i.e., the assumption of an intelligent agent (little man) residing elsewhere in the system, usually off stage, who does all the marvelous things that need to be done actually to generate the total behavior of the subject]. It is the homunculus that actually performs the control processes in Atkinson & Shiffrin's (1968) famous memory model, who still does all the controlled processing (including determining the strategies) in the more recent proposal of Shiffrin & Schneider (1977), who makes all the confidence judgments, who analyzes all the payoff matrices and adjusts the behavior appropriately, who is renamed the "executive" in many models (clearly a promotion), and who decides on and builds all those flow diagrams.

The universal organization in terms of problem spaces solves half of the problem of the homunculus. It provides the top-level executive organization that is used for all cognitive behavior. At the top, it claims, is a search effort in terms of the operators of the current space. No intelligent agent is required to run this search, because it runs in any event, even with no search control knowledge, and it runs automatically with whatever search control knowledge it happens to have.

The claim on the simplicity of the top-level executive is double-barreled, for it will not do to banish the homunculus from performance, only to have him show up arranging for the intelligent creation of problem spaces. But much of problem space creation is a symbolic cognitive task and hence must be performed by the subject by means of a problem space (or so the hypothesis claims). But then the elementary character of the highest-level space applies to this aspect of behavior as well.

In any event, the problem space only solves half the problem. The other half of banishing the homunculus resides with the architecture, which closes the gap between the problem space and complete mechanism. The claim that the architecture is also nonintelligent (i.e., not a homunculus) is also plausible, given that the architecture primarily carries out housekeeping functions; but discussion is outside the bounds of this chapter.

CONCLUSION

We have laid out in this chapter a proposal for a fundamental category of all symbolic cognitive activity—the problem space, wherein the human always is embedded in an *ensemble* of possible behaviors, to be realized by selective search. We have claimed that it provides grounds for understanding where all the diverse flow diagrams come from and, further, that it has the potential for helping to make cognition whole again. But, though important, these two claims simply provided an orientation for the presentation. The basic point is the hypothesis that this is the way human cognition is.

This chapter has lived within many constraints. It has been limited to an exposition of the hypothesis, neither assembling the evidence pro and con nor contrasting it with alternative control structures. It has been limited to exploring a single example that bears on extending the problem space from the domain of its initial formulation (problem solving) to other areas of cognition. The title contains both the terms *reasoning* and *decision processes*. Though taken from the title of the section, they are intended to indicate the breadth of the hypothesis, namely to all cognition. There is indeed nothing special about the area of reasoning nor about the categorical syllogism. Thus, it seems important to leave *decision processes* in the title, though it remains purely a promissory note.

Finally, the chapter has been limited to the central issue of performance in a problem space and has not dealt with the acquisition of problem spaces or their dynamic modification. This perhaps laid too much stress on the role played by the search control knowledge, in contradistinction to the operators or the representational structure of the states. This seems justified because of the unfamiliarity of the control structure and the need to exhibit how it welds the problem space into a functioning unit. But the tilt should be made explicit.

Still, with all the limitations stated, enough has been said, I hope, to convey the potential of the hypothesis and to recommend it for your consideration. The presentation obviously forms an implicit argument for the hypothesis. But there should be little difficulty separating the general and illustrative sorts of evidence presented here from the detailed demonstrations that are still necessary.

ACKNOWLEDGMENTS

This research was sponsored in part by the Palo Alto Research Center of Xerox and in part by the Defense Advanced Research Projects Agency (DOD) ARPA Order No. 3597, monitored by the Air Force Avionics Laboratory under Contract F33615-78-C-1551.

The views and conclusions contained in this document are those of the author and should not be interpreted as representing the official policies, either expressed or implied, of the Defense Advanced Research Projects Agency or the U.S. Government.

I wish to acknowledge Stu Card and Tom Moran who helped immensely in the development of this theory, as we struggled together to find a way of constructing a useful taxonomy of tasks. To Herb Simon, as always, must go credit for many of the underlying ideas.

REFERENCES

Anderson, J. R. *Language, memory, and thought.* Hillsdale, N.J.: Lawrence Erlbaum Associates, 1976.

Anzai, Y., & Simon, H. A. The theory of learning by doing. *Psychological Review,* 1979, *86,* 124–140.

Atkinson, R. C., & Shiffrin, R. M. Human memory: A proposed system and its control processes. In K. W. Spence & J. T. Spence (Eds.), *The psychology of learning and motivation.* New York: Academic Press, 1968.

Erickson, J. R. Models of formal reasoning. In R. Revlin & R. E. Mayer (Eds.), *Human reasoning.* Washington, D.C.: Winston, 1978.

Erickson, J. R., & Jones, M. R. Thinking. *Annual Review of Psychology,* 1978, *29,* 61–90.

Falmagne, R. J. (Ed.). *Reasoning: Representation and process.* Hillsdale, N.J.: Lawrence Erlbaum Associates, 1975.

Greeno, J. Nature of problem solving abilities. In W. K. Estes (Ed.), *Handbook of learning and cognition.* New York: Wiley, 1977.

Hayes, J. R., & Simon, H. A. Understanding complex task instruction. In D. Klahr, (Ed.), *Cognition and instruction,* Hillsdale, N.J.: Lawrence Erlbaum Associates, 1976.

Johnson-Laird, P. N. Models of deduction. In R. J. Falmagne (Ed.), *Reasoning: Representation and process.* Hillsdale, N.J.: Lawrence Erlbaum Associates, 1975.

Johnson-Laird, P. N., & Steedman, M. The psychology of syllogisms. *Cognitive Psychology,* 1978, *10,* 64–99.

Newell, A. Production systems: Models of control structures. In W. Chase (Ed.), *Visual information processing.* New York: Academic, 1973.

Newell, A. Harpy production systems and human cognition. In R. Cole (Ed.), *Perception and production of fluent speech.* Hillsdale, N.J.: Lawrence Erlbaum Associates, 1980.

Newell, A., & Simon, H. A. *Human problem solving.* Englewood Cliffs, N.J.: Prentice-Hall, 1972.

Newell, A., & Simon, H. A. Computer science as empirical inquiry: Symbols and search. *Communications of the ACM,* 1976, *19,* 113–126.

Nilsson, N. *Problem-solving methods in artificial intelligence.* New York: McGraw-Hill, 1971.

Revlin, R. Two models of syllogistic reasoning: Feature selection and conversion. *Journal of Verbal Learning and Verbal Behavior*, 1975, *14*, 180–195.

Revlin, R., & Leirer, V. O. The effect of personal biases on syllogistic reasoning: Rational decisions from personalized representations. In R. Revlin & E. Mayer (Eds.), *Human reasoning*, Washington, D.C.: Winston, 1978.

Revlin, R., & Mayer, R. E. *Human reasoning*. Washington, D.C.: Winston, 1978.

Shiffrin, R. M., & Schneider, W. Controlled and automatic human information processing: II. Perceptual learning, automatic attending and a general theory. *Psychological Review*, 1977, *84*, 127–190.

Simon, H. A. *The artificial sciences*. Cambridge: MIT Press 1969.

Simon, H. A. The functional equivalence of problem solving skills. *Cognitive Psychology*, 1975, *7*, 268–288.

Simon, H. A., & Lea, G. Problem solving and rule induction: A unified view. In L. Gregg (Ed.), *Knowledge and cognition*. Hillsdale, N.J.: Lawrence Erlbaum Associates, 1974.

Slovic, P., Fischhoff, B., & Lichtenstein, S. Behavioral decision theory. *Annual Review of Psychology*, 1977, *28*, 1–39.

Sternberg, R. The nature of mental abilities. *American Psychologist*, 1979, *34*, 214–230.

Wason, P. C., & Johnson-Laird, P. N. *Psychology of reasoning: Structure and content*. Cambridge: Harvard University Press, 1972.

Woodworth, R. S., & Sells, S. B. An atmosphere effect in formal syllogistic reasoning. *Journal of Experimental Psychology*, 1935, *18*, 451–460.

36

A Proposed Resolution of Curious Conflicts in the Literature on Linear Syllogisms

Robert J. Sternberg
Yale University
New Haven, Connecticut
United States

ABSTRACT

Students of reasoning have engaged in a vigorous debate regarding the representations and processes used by subjects solving linear syllogisms. Meaningful communication between proponents of the various positions has been hampered by the appearance of curious conflicts in reported data sets for the linear syllogism problems. The present experiment was intended to isolate the source of these conflicts in the literature. Eighteen adult subjects received linear syllogisms under instructions designed to yield speeds commensurate with error rates of about 10%. Latency and error data were analyzed both separately (via multiple regression) and jointly (via canonical regression). These data were also analyzed via pseudodeadlines, according to which responses were counted as correct if they were correct and fell below a given pseudodeadline and were counted as erroneous if they were incorrect or fell above a given pseudodeadline. The analyses revealed that the source of the conflicts in the literature is the failure of researchers to appreciate the complex interrelationships between latency and error rate. When these interrelationships are taken into account, the conflicts disappear.

INTRODUCTION

In a linear syllogism, an individual is presented with two premises, each describing a relation between two terms. One of the terms overlaps between premises. The individual's task is to use this overlap to infer the relations among the three terms of the linear syllogism and then to answer a question about one or more of these relations. A typical linear syllogism is:

> Jon is taller than Bob.
> Sam is shorter than Bob.
> Who is tallest?

Psychologists have been investigating the representations and processes people use in solving linear syllogisms since Burt's (1919) adoption of the problem for one of his tests of mental ability. In recent years, a vigorous debate has arisen regarding whether subjects' representations of the relations among terms are spatial (DeSoto, London, & Handel, 1965; Huttenlocher, 1968; Huttenlocher & Higgins, 1971), linguistic (Clark, 1969a, b), or a mixture of both (Sternberg, in 1980a,b). Data recently collected from four experiments in my laboratory make a strong case for a proposed mixture model (Sternberg, 1980b). These data fail to resolve the debate, however, because of surprising inconsistencies across data sets collected in different laboratories. In particular, whereas my own data and those of Potts and Scholz (1975) and of Hunter (1957) support the mixed model, data collected by Clark (1969a, b) and by Keating and Caramazza (1975) support a linguistic model (see Sternberg, 1980b).

This chapter seeks to resolve these inconsistencies and, in so doing, to advance our understanding of how linear syllogisms are solved. In the next section, the three alternative models of linear syllogistic reasoning are briefly described. (A more detailed description of each model can be found in Sternberg, 1980b.) Then possible sources of conflict in data testing these models are described. Finally, an experiment is presented that seeks to resolve the conflicts regarding which model is best. The results of the experiment may be of interest to experimental psychologists engaged in modeling thought processes in tasks other than linear syllogisms, because the results call into question our often cavalier ways of dealing (or failing to deal) with the relationships between response time and error rate.

MODELS OF LINEAR SYLLOGISTIC REASONING

In this section, three alternative models of linear syllogistic reasoning—a spatial model (based upon the accounts of DeSoto et al., 1965; Huttenlocher, 1968; Huttenlocher & Higgins, 1971), a linguistic model (based upon the account of Clark, 1969b), and a mixed model (based upon the account of Sternberg, 1980b)—are described briefly and compared. An example of a linear syllogism, "C is not as tall as B; A is not as short as B; Who is shortest?" will be used to facilitate comparison.

Spatial Model

In the proposed spatial model, the terms of the syllogism are arranged into an imaginal, linear spatial array that is an analogue of a physical, linear array. Thus, the terms of the example problem will be arranged into an imagined array in which A is at the top, B is in the middle, and C is at the bottom.

The subject must first read the terms of the problem. The terms in each premise are first arranged in a two-item array. The initial arrangement disregards the negation, if one is present. Thus, the first pair of terms is arranged as C/B and the second pair as B/A. Arrangement of terms from the top down (as is done when the adjective *tall* or *taller* appears in the premise) is easier and hence faster than arrangement of terms from the bottom up (as is done when the adjective *short* or *shorter* appears in the premise). Next, if a negation appears in a premise, a new array is constructed in which the terms of the old array are flipped around in space. In the example, two new arrays, B/C and A/B, are constructed.

The subject next attempts to integrate the two arrays. This integration will be easier if the subject worked from the ends of the larger array inward rather than from the middle outward in constructing the two smaller arrays. A possible reason for this directional effect is that working from the ends inward brings one to the pivot, or middle term, of the series. If one ends up on the middle term, then it is immediately available for use as the pivot of the larger array. If one does not end up on the middle term, one must search for it, taking additional time. In an affirmative problem, this means that the preferred order of terms in a premise is the outermost term followed by the middle term. In a negative equative problem (such as the example problem), the preferred order is reversed, for the flipping of terms reverses the last term to be encoded in working memory.

Just as it was easier to work from the top down within each of the two two-item arrays, it is easier to work from the top down across the two two-item arrays, so that processing is facilitated if the first premise consists of the A and B (top two) terms of the array rather than the C and B terms, as in the example. The subject integrates the two arrays into a single array, $A/B/C$, reads the question, and then seeks the answer to the question in the array. In the example, the correct answer is C.

Linguistic Model

In the proposed linguistic model, the terms of the syllogism are stored by way of functional relations that represent the relation between them at the level of linguistic deep structure: (B is tall+; C is tall); (B is short+; A is short). In the linguistic model, unlike in the spatial model, information from the two premises is left unintegrated.

The subject begins solution by encoding the surface structural strings into linguistic deep structures of the kind shown previously. Marked adjectives (such as *short* and *shorter*) are assumed to be stored in more complex form than unmarked adjectives (such as *tall* and *taller*) and hence are assumed to take longer to encode. The initial encoding disregards the negation, if one is present. Thus, the first pair of terms is arranged as (*C* is tall+; *B* is tall) and (*A* is short+; *B* is short). Upon encountering the negations, the subject effects a linguistic transformation that brings the propositional strings to the form shown in the preceding paragraph.

It is assumed in this model that in order to conserve space in working memory, the encoding of the first premise is compressed, so that only the first relation, in the example, (*B* is tall+), remains in working memory. Because *B* is the middle term, the pivot of the three-item relation is retained in working memory, and locating it does not present a problem. But if the first premise had been "*B* is not as short as *C*," only (*C* is short+) would have been retained in working memory, resulting in the subject's needing to search long-term memory for the missing pivot term (*B*). This search for the pivot consumes additional time.

Having found the pivot, the subject reads the question. If the question contains a marked adjective, additional time is spent encoding it. In the example, the subject seeks the individual who is shortest. All propositional information is now made available for the final search. Solving the problem requires finding the individual who is short+ relative to the pivot, but no such individual is found in the example. The reason no such individual is found is that the form of the question is incongruent with the way in which the answer term has been encoded. Whereas the shortest term, *C*, was previously encoded as tall (relative to the tall+ *B*), the question asks for the person who is shortest. The subject must therefore make the question congruent with the problem terms as encoded. He or she does so by looking for the least tall individual— someone is tall− relative to a tall pivot, or tall relative to a tall+ pivot. The subject can now respond with the correct answer, *C*.

Linguistic–Spatial Mixed Model

In the proposed mixed model, the terms of the syllogism are first decoded into linguistic deep-structural propositions (as in the linguistic model) and are then encoded into spatial arrays (as in the spatial model). However, the mixed model involves only a subset of the processes used in the spatial and linguistic models and adds some processes appearing in neither of the other two models.

The subject begins solution by decoding the surface-structural strings into linguistic deep structures. These linguistic deep structures then form the basis for the construction of spatial arrays, one for each premise. Marked adjectives are assumed to increase processing time, both through increased linguistic decoding time and through increased spatial encoding time. Negations are handled as in the spatial model, with new arrays constructed from the original arrays by flipping the elements of the original arrays in space.

In order for the subject to combine the terms of the premises into a single spatial array, the subject needs the pivot available. Either the pivot is immediately available from the spatial encoding of the premises or else it must be located. The pivot is immediately available in all: (1) affirmative problems; and (2) negative equative problems in which the second premise begins with the pivot (see Sternberg, 1980b, for a description of the mechanism of pivot search). In the example problem, the second negative equative premise does not begin with the pivot but with an end term, so that the pivot must be located as the term that overlaps between the two two-item spatial arrays. Once the pivot has been located, the subject seriates the terms from the two two-item spatial arrays into a single three-item spatial array. In forming the array, the subject starts with the terms of the first premise and ends with those of the second premise. The subject's mental location after seriation, therefore, is in that half of the array described by the second premise (which is the top half in the example). The subject next reads the question. If there is a marked adjective in the question, the subject will take longer to decode the adjective linguistically and to seek the response to the problem at the nonpreferred (usually bottom) end of the array. The response may or may not be immediately available. If the correct answer is in the half of the array where the subject just completed seriation (his or her active location in the array), then the response will be immediately available. If the question requires an answer from the other half of the array, however, the subject will have to search for the response, mentally traversing the array from one half to the other and thereby consuming additional time. In the example, the subject ends up in the the top half of the array but is asked a question about the bottom half of the array ("Who is shortest?"), requiring search for the response.

Under certain circumstances (see Sternberg, 1980b), the subject checks the linguistic form of the proposed response against the form of the adjective in the question. If the two forms are congruent, the subject responds with the designated answer. If not, the subject first makes sure that congruence can be established and then responds. In the example, congruence must be established, because the shortest term, C, has previously been decoded in terms of the adjective *tall*. Once congruence has been established, C can be recognized as the correct answer to the example problem.

Summary

The models all agree that some form of encoding, negation, marking, and response contribute to response latency, and although the models in some cases disagree as to the exact form each operation takes, mathematical parameters corresponding to the durations of these operations are estimated from the same independent variables for each model. Each model also contains a pivot search operation, although the parameter corresponding to the duration of this operation is estimated in a different way for each model. The spatial model further contains a premise order parameter, and the mixed model further contains a response search parameter. The linguistic model further contains a noncongruence parameter, which appears only under special circumstances in the mixed model (including the circumstances of the experiment to be described in this chapter).

CONFLICTS IN DATA SETS
TESTING THE MODELS

The data from previous research reveal curious conflicts. Except for the data set of Clark (1969b),[1] the data sets appear to be reliable, and so the inconsistencies among data sets seem likely to be due to factors other than chance. What factor or factors might be responsible for the inconsistencies? Two possibilities are considered in this chapter. First, there may be a difference in speed–accuracy tradeoff between subjects in the experiments supporting the mixed model and subjects in the experiments supporting the linguistic model. The error rate in each of the Sternberg (1980b) experiments was 1%; in the Potts and Scholz (1975) experiment (Experiment 1, Group 1), the error rate was 7%; Hunter (1957) did not report error rates. The error rate in the Clark (1969b) experiment was 7%; it was 30% in the Clark (1969a) experiment, and 22% in the Keating and Caramazza (1975) experiment. These last two experiments used a procedure different from that of the other experiments, where standard latency measurements for solving individual items were taken. In these two experiments, subjects were given 10 sec to solve each problem. An error was counted if the subject either responded incorrectly or failed to respond at all in the 10 sec. The deadline procedure used by Clark (1969a) and by Keating and Caramazza (1975) would seem to encourage subjects to emphasize speed at the expense of accuracy, because any response taking longer than 10 sec, whether right or wrong, was counted as an error. Support in these experiments for the linguistic model may thus have been due to the higher error rates obtained. Second, the procedure used in these two experiments may itself have been responsible for the conflicts in the data. If we ignore the probably unreliable data of Clark (1969b), we find that data obtained under standard response-time procedures tend to support the mixed

---

[1]The models were fitted to geometric mean latencies for 32 data points. The quality of the data are suspect, however, because: (1) there were only 13 subjects, with three observations per subject; (2) the longest latency for each subject for each item (33% of the observations) was discarded; (3) and error responses were also discarded (7% of the observations).

model, whereas data obtained under the deadline procedure tend to support the linguistic model. If experimental procedure is the factor responsible for the difference in model fits, then two subfactors need to be distinguished. First, the use of a deadline may in and of itself lead to a linguistic strategy. Second, the modeling of errors (in the deadline procedure) rather than latencies (in the standard procedure) may lead to the apparent superiority of the linguistic model. The research to be described was intended to distinguish among these possible explanations of the conflicts among data sets.

EXPERIMENT

A single experiment proved sufficient to distinguish among the hypotheses considered previously regarding the conflicts among data sets and to discover the responsible factor. In this experiment, subjects solved linear syllogisms under the standard conditions, with as long as they needed to solve each item. However, subjects were strongly encouraged to solve items as rapidly as they could, and a bonus was paid to reward fast performance accompanied by only a moderate degree of accuracy.

Method

Subjects

Subjects were 18 undergraduates attending the Yale summer term. Of these subjects, 10 were women and 8 were men.

Materials

Stimuli were two-term series problems and three-term series problems (linear syllogisms). The 32 types of three-term series problems varied dichotomously along five dimensions: (1) whether the first premise adjective was marked or unmarked; (2) whether the second premise adjective was marked or unmarked; (3) whether the question adjective was marked or unmarked; (4) whether the premises were affirmative or negative; and (5) whether the correct answer was in the first or second premise. The 8 types of two-term series problems varied dichotomously along three dimensions: (1) whether the premise adjective was marked or unmarked; (2) whether the question adjective was marked or unmarked; and (3) whether the premise was affirmative or negative. There were three replications of each item type, one using the adjective pair *taller-shorter,* one using the adjective pair *better-worse,* and one using the adjective pair *faster-slower.*

Apparatus

Two- and three-term series problems were administered via a Gerbrands two-field tachistoscope with an attached centisecond clock.

Design

The design of the experiment was completely within subject: Each subject received each item type three times, once with each adjective. The dependent measures of interest were response time and error rate.

Procedure

Subjects were first shown examples of typical two- and three-term series problems and were told that their task was to solve items of these types. These items, and the practice items given later, used the adjective pair *older–younger,* which was not used in the actual test items. Instructions to subjects indicated that the subjects should solve problems at a rate that would allow about 10% errors and that a monetary bonus would be paid for fast performance at an error rate of about 10%. In fact, the bonus was computed strictly on the basis of error rate. A bonus of 50¢ was paid for four errors (out of 40 items), 35¢ for three or five errors, 15¢ for two or six errors, 10¢ for one or seven errors, and 0¢ for zero or eight or more errors. Subjects were told after each third of the items was completed what their bonus for the preceding 40 items was and what their maximum bonus could have been (50¢). Subjects were then told to speed up if their error rate was under 10% or to slow down if their error rate was over 10%.

All testing was done in one session. Testing began with the administration of eight practice items. Next, subjects received 120 stimulus items. Items were blocked by number of terms (two or three) and by adjective pair (*taller–shorter, better–worse, faster–slower*), with order of blocks counterbalanced across subjects.

Results

The results of the experiment are presented in four parts. In the first, the success of the speed–accuracy tradeoff manipulation is evaluated. In the second, comparability of the present data set to previous ones, as measured by standard data-analytic techniques, is assessed. In the third, latency and error data are analyzed as though various deadlines had been used in presenting the stimulus items. The data are partitioned on the bases of pseudodeadlines of 2, 4, 6, 8, 10, 12, 14, 16, and ∞ sec. In the fourth, the latency and error data are considered simultaneously as joint dependent variables. This analysis shows the serious consequences of failing to take into account both solution latency and error rate, as well as the relationships between them.

Success of the Speed–Accuracy Tradeoff Manipulation

The first issue that needs to be addressed is whether the speed–accuracy tradeoff manipulation in the instructions to subjects was successful. The mean solution latency for the three-term series problems in this experiment was 5922 ± 128 msec. Respective means for Experiments 1–4 of Sternberg (1980b) were 7285 ± 177, 7489 ± 188, 7002 ± 170, and 7069 ± 161 msec. The mean response time in the present experiment was therefore more than one second faster than the mean response time in any of the earlier experiments, indicating that the instructions in the present experiment were successful in speeding up subjects. The mean error rate in the present experiment was 7%, compared to 1% in each of the earlier experiments, indicating that the insructions were also successful in increasing error rates. The speed–accuracy tradeoff manipulation may therefore be viewed as having succeeded.

Comparability of Present Data to Previous Data

Intercorrelations of Data Sets. The present data set is highly similar to those presented in Sternberg (1980b). The median intercorrelation across data sets from the four experiments presented in Sternberg (1980b) was .84, whereas the median intercorrelation between the present data set and these four previous data sets was .86. Because the split-halves reliability of the present data set was also .86[2] and because the previous data had a median split-halves reliability of .89, the correlations between the present and previous data sets were about as high as the reliabilities of the data would allow.

Qualitative Fits of the Models to the Latency Data. Five-way analyses of variance were conducted on the observed solution latencies and on the predicted soultion latencies for each model. The five factors in the analyses were the same ones that generated the $2^5 = 32$ linear syllogism types in the experiment (see "Materials" section). Each cell of the 2^5 design contained three observations, namely, the means over subjects of the solution latencies for a given adjective pair.

The results of the analyses of variance replicated those of Sternberg (1980b). The major findings were these:

---

[2]Reliabiity of the latency data for the three-term series problems was computed by arbitrarily dividing the subjects into two halves, correlating the two sets of latencies across the 32-item types and correcting the resulting correlation by the Spearman–Brown formula.

1. The effect of marked adjectives was highly significant for both premises, $F(1, 64) = 47.95$, $p < .001$ for premise 1 and $F(1, 64) = 7.38$, $p < .01$ for premise 2, but only marginally significant for the question, $F(1, 64) = 3.63$, $p < .10$. All three models predicted a marking effect of 35 csec for both premises and question, although the observed effects were 63, 25, and 17 csec, respectively. The models were therefore successful in predicting an effect but unsuccessful in predicting the differential effect of where the marked adjective occurred.

2. The observed effect of negation, 65 csec for the two premises combined, was highly significant, $F(1, 64) = 50.75$, $p < .001$, and equal in magnitude to the effect predicted by each of the three models.

3. Items with the correct answer in the first premise were significantly harder than items with the correct answer in the second premise, $F(1, 64) = 28.28$, $p < .001$. The mixed model correctly predicted this effect and its duration, 49 csec. This latency reflects the need of the subject to search for the response in items where the response is not immediately available. The linguistic and spatial models, lacking a response search operation, failed to predict this effect.

4. The observed data showed five statistically significant interactions. The mixed model correctly predicted four; the linguistic model, three; and the spatial model, two of these interactions. The mixed and spatial models each predicted one spurious interaction; the linguistic model predicted two.

Quantitative Fits of the Models to the Latency Data.   Each of the three models was fitted separately to group latency data for three-term series problems only, for two- and three-term series problems together, and for three-term series problems for each adjective considered separately. Table 36.1 shows the means and standard errors of the latency data, plus the values of R^2 obtained in predicting the latency data from the independent variables specified by each of the three models (and described in detail in Sternberg, 1980b). The higher values of R^2 for the two- and three-term series problems in combination are due to the separation of the encoding component in these analyses; this component is confounded with the response component in the analyses of three-term series problems only. In general, the results closely replicate those of Sternberg (1980b), except for the faster latencies obtained due to the speed–accuracy tradeoff manipulation.

The mixed model performed considerably better than did either the linguistic or spatial model: The value of R^2 for the mixed model was .251 higher than that for the linguistic model and .237 higher than that for the spatial model. Even with the optional noncongruence parameter deleted, R^2 for the mixed model, .761, was still .155 better than that for the next best model. Deletion of this parameter is of doubtful theoretical justification, however, because the mixed model specifes that the full set of parameters is necessary to account for

TABLE 36.1
Quantitative Fits of the Models to the Latency Data

Data Set Three-Term Series	Item Latencies		R^2 for Model		
	$\bar{X}$	$S\bar{x}$	Mixed	Linguistic	Spatial
All adjectives	5922	128	.843[a]	.592[a]	.606[a]
Taller–Shorter	5824	138	.690[a]	.528[a]	.563[a]
Better–Worse	5964	139	.692[a]	.468[a]	.396[a]
Faster–Slower	5964	153	.683[a]	.586[a]	.576[a]
Two- and Three-Term Series					
All adjectives	5245	240	.966[a]	.921[a]	.924[a]

Note: Response latencies are presented in milliseconds.
[a]$p < .01$

subjects' performance under these circumstances (see Sternberg, 1980b). Each subject's data were also analyzed individually, and the results of the individual model fitting also supported the mixed model. Although the mixed model is superior to the alternative models, it is not the true model: The residual variance was highly significant ($p < .001$), indicating that systematic variance was still left unaccounted for.[3]

Although the present data set is highly correlated with the preceding (Sternberg, 1980b) data sets, leading to comparable patterns of model fits, there was a large difference between mean latencies in the present versus the preceding tasks. By decomposing response time into components and then comparing latency parameter estimates across data sets, it is possible to localize the effect of the speed–accuracy tradeoff manipulation upon information processing. Table 36.2 presents parameter estimates from the present experiment and two previous experiments (from Sternberg, 1980b) that were highly comparable to the present experiment except for the emphasis upon accuracy in the instructions. A comparison of the parameter estimates for the various experiments shows a general decrease in the latencies of the various component processes under the speed condition. But the decrease is not uniform: It is due primarily to more rapid encoding, that is, construction of the spatial array showing the relationships among terms of the problem. Rapid construction of this array would seem likely to increase subjects' susceptibility to errors and, indeed, a decrease in overall latency of 1 sec was bought at the cost of a sevenfold increase in error rate.

---

[3]Significance of the residual variance was determined by computing residuals of the observed from the predicted latencies for each of two arbitrarily chosen groups of subjects, correlating the residuals, and correcting the resulting correlation by the Spearman–Brown formula.

TABLE 36.2
Latency Parameter Estimates for Present Experiment and Two Previous Experiments:
Mixed Model

| | Estimated Latency | | |
| | Speed Emphasis | Accuracy Emphasis | |
Latency Parameter	Present Experiment	Experiment 3[a]	Experiment 4[a]
Encoding	1354[c]	2986[c]	3124[c]
	(70)	(184)	(152)
Negation	143[b]	184[b]	244[c]
	(65)	(86)	(71)
Marking	327[c]	307[c]	380[c]
	(58)	(73)	(63)
Pivot search	788[c]	1154[c]	1008[c]
	(159)	(226)	(174)
Response search	485[c]	522[c]	656[c]
	(108)	(163)	(118)
Noncongruence	395[c]	538[c]	396[c]
	(102)	(119)	(111)
Response	1944	2517	2353

Note: Standard errors of parameter estimates are shown in parentheses below the appropriate estimates. All latencies are in milliseconds.
[a]Data from Sternberg, 1980a,b.
[b]$p < .05$
[c]$p < .01$

So far, the data have not revealed why the linguistic model performs better than the mixed model under certain circumstances. They have shown, however, that the difference in model performance cannot be attributed merely to a difference between speed–accuracy tradeoff conditions in the various experiments. The first suggested explanation of the conflict among data sets in the literature on linear syllogisms is therefore shown to be incorrect.

Reanalysis of Data with Pseudodeadlines

The second suggested explanation of the conflict in the literature was based upon the use of a deadline procedure in the reliable data sets supporting the linguistic model, but of a standard unlimited-time procedure in the reliable data sets supporting the mixed model: The difference in relative model fits might be due to a difference in procedures. Ideally, one would want to test this hypothesis by testing multiple groups of subjects under various deadlines. The limiting case of these deadlines would be infinite time, which would be equivalent to the standard unlimited-time procedure. An experiment with a large number of different deadlines is impractical, however. An exploratory procedure was therefore used in which the data were partitioned by means of pseudodeadlines. In this procedure, the data were reanalyzed as if each of a sequence of increasing deadlines had been used. As a first pseudodeadline, all correct responses with latencies of 2 sec or less were counted as "corrects;" all error responses and responses with latencies of over 2 sec were counted as "errors." The pseudodeadline procedure was then repeated for simulated deadlines of 4, 6, 8, 10, 12, 14, 16, and ∞ sec. In this last case, only genuine error responses were treated as errors, for, of course, all latencies were finite.

Error Rates. Means and standard errors of the proportions of errors, as well as fits of the models to proportions of errors, are shown in Table 36.3. Modeling of logarithms of numbers of correct responses yielded comparable results. Keep in mind that in the present method of analysis, each subject receives a score of 0 (correct) or 1 (error) on a given item; the data become approximately continuous only when averaged across subjects.

The data reveal a most interesting pattern: For pseudodeadlines of under 10 sec, the performance of the mixed model is clearly superior to the performance of any of the other models. At 10 sec, however, the relative performances of the models change dramatically. Although the predictive power of all the models is reduced, the predictive power of the mixed model is reduced to a far greater extent than that of either of the other two models. The linguistic model now becomes slightly superior to the mixed model, and this superiority holds up at 14, 16, and ∞ sec (where only genuine error responses are modeled). Thus, a cutoff of 10 sec, that which happened to have been used by Clark (1969a) and by Keating and Caramazza (1975), turns out to be a crossing point in the relative performances of the mixed and linguistic models. At this cutoff, there is a sharp decrease in the variance of error rates across

TABLE 36.3
Quantitative Fits of the Models to the Error Data Partitioned by Pseudodeadlines

Pseudodeadline	Proportion of Errors		R^2 for Model		
(sec)	$\bar{X}$	$S_{\bar{x}}$	Mixed	Linguistic	Spatial
2	.998	.001	.053	.031	.027
4	.779	.018	.774[b]	.487[b]	.419[b]
6	.432	.021	.722[b]	.576[b]	.476[b]
8	.222	.018	.804[b]	.652[b]	.687[b]
10	.131	.012	.454[b]	.498[b]	.417[b]
12	.098	.009	.440[b]	.428[b]	.417[b]
14	.080	.009	.395[b]	.446[b]	.405[b]
16	.076	.009	.334[a]	.407[b]	.339[b]
∞	.069	.008	.263	.387[b]	.276

Note: Model fits are for three-term series, all adjectives combined.
[a] $p < .05$
[b] $p < .01$

items (as can be inferred from the large drop in standard error as shown in the table), and only 13% of the responses are being counted as errors. It therefore appears that the interpretation and modeling of error rates from the deadline (or pseudodeadline) procedure is somehow responsible for the crossover in relative model fits, although the mechanism behind the crossover remains to be explained.

Some understanding of why the crossover happens can be gleaned by examining the standardized regression coefficients (beta weights) for each of the parameters of each model at the various pseudodeadlines. These coefficients are shown in Table 36.4. In order to provide a base line for comparison, standardized regression coefficients are also shown for response times as modeled in the preceding section.

Consider first the standardized coefficients for the mixed model. All coefficients were statistically significant in predicting response times but not in predicting error rates as analyzed under the pseudodeadline procedure. In particular, the coefficients for pivot search and response search, the two parameters unique to the mixed model, were statistically significant up to 8 sec, but they were nonsignificant thereafter (except for pivot search at 12 sec). The standardized coefficient for noncongruence also started off significant and became nonsignificant, although not until a pseudodeadline of 16 sec. The steep decrease in R^2 for the mixed model at 10 sec can thus be understood in terms of the failure of pivot search and response search to distinguish between *correct* and *error* responses at this and subsequent pseudodeadlines.

Consider next the standardized coefficients for the linguistic model. Of greatest interest was the pattern of coefficients for linguistic pivot search. This parameter did not contribute significantly to prediction of response time, but it did contribute significantly to prediction of error rates from the 6-sec cutoff to the cutoff of ∞ sec. This pattern of significant prediction of error rate coupled with nonsignificant prediction of response time is most unusual, because response time is often viewed as a more sensitive measure of the same thing measured by error rate. Discussion of this unusual finding is deferred until p. 740. The pattern of loadings indicates that the drop in predictive power of the linguistic model at 10 sec is attributable to only a single parameter, negation, as opposed to two parameters, pivot search and response search, in the mixed model. It is therefore not surprising that the drop for the linguistic model was smaller than that for the mixed model.

Finally, consider the standardized coefficients for the spatial model. An examination of these coefficients reveals that the drop in predictive power at 10 sec is due to the reduction in predictive power of the negation parameter, as in the linguistic model.

To summarize, the analyses of error rates modeled under the pseudodeadline procedure show that the linguistic model becomes superior to the mixed model in predictive power when the variance across items in error rates

TABLE 36.4
Standardized Parameter Estimates for Error Data Partitioned by Pseudodeadlines and for Latency Data

Pseudodeadline (sec)	Mixed Model		Mixed Pivot Search		
	Marking	Negation	Search	Noncongruence	Response Search
2	−.06	.20	−.16	−.06	.11
4	.40^b	.16	.40^b	.25^b	.48^b
6	.43^b	.20	.29^a	.32^b	.44^b
8	.52^b	.03	.45^b	.37^b	.28^b
10	.48^b	.01	.23	.29^b	.23
12	.41^b	−.16	.33^a	.29^a	.23
14	.43^b	−.19	.26	.30^a	.17
16	.42^b	−.20	.26	.23	.16
∞	.38^a	−.15	.12	.23	.19
Latencies	.43^b	.18^a	.48^b	.31^b	.34^b

Pseudodeadline (sec)	Linguistic Model		Linguistic Pivot Search	
	Marking	Negation	Pivot Search	Noncongruence
2	−.06	.11	−.06	−.11
4	.40^b	.39^b	.19	.37^b
6	.43^b	.36^b	.31^b	.40^b
8	.52^b	.29^b	.21^a	.50^b
10	.48^b	.14	.36^b	.35^b
12	.41^b	.03	.33^a	.39^b
14	.43^b	−.03	.35^a	.38^b
16	.42^b	−.05	.38^b	.30^a
∞	.38^b	−.09	.41^b	.26^a
Latencies	.43^b	.46^b	.11	.44^b

Pseudodeadline (sec)	Spatial Model		Spatial Pivot Search	
	Marking	Negation	Search	Premise Order
2	−.06	.11	.00	.11
4	.40^b	.39^b	.32^a	−.06
6	.43^b	.36^b	.37^b	.14
8	.52^b	.29^b	.57^b	.00
10	.48^b	.14	.41^b	.04
12	.41^b	.03	.48^b	.10
14	.43^b	−.03	.47^b	.06
16	.42^b	−.05	.39^b	.09
∞	.38^a	−.09	.33^a	.11
Latencies	.43^b	.46^b	.46^b	.00

Note: Model fits are for the three-term series, all adjectives combined.
$^a p < .05$
$^b p < .01$

becomes very small. In the present data (and very likely in previous data as well), a sharp decrease in variance occurs at a pseudodeadline of 10 sec. At this point, only 13% of responses are counted as errors. Both the mixed and linguistic models show decreases in predictive power at the 10-sec cutoff, but the decrease is much more pronounced for the mixed model than for the linguistic model. This is because two parameters in the mixed model—pivot search and response search—become useless in predicting errors at this point. In the linguistic model, only negation loses its predictive power at this point.

Response Times. The analyses just presented suggest that something about the deadline or pseudodeadline procedures leads to conclusions different from those drawn when standard unlimited-time procedures are used. It is not clear yet, however, what this "something" is. As noted earlier, it may be the deadline or pseudodeadline procedures themselves; or it may be the modeling of error data, irrespective of the use or nonuse of deadlines or pseudodeadlines. Note in this regard that modeling of error rates in the limiting pseudodeadline condition (∞ sec) results in superior prediction for the linguistic model over the mixed model. In order to distinguish between these two possibilities, each of the three models was fitted to latency data analyzed via pseudodeadlines. In one set of analyses, the models were fitted to latencies *above* each of the pseudodeadlines. Latencies below the cutoffs were treated as missing data. In a second set of analyses, the models were fitted to latencies *below* each of the pseudodeadlines. Latencies above the cutoffs were treated as missing data. If the mere use of pseudodeadlines (or deadlines) accounts for the conflicts in the data, then the mixed model should perform better than the linguistic model at some cutoffs but not at others. If, however, it is modeling of error data that is responsible for the conflicts, then the mixed model should be superior to the linguistic model, irrespective of the particular cutoff used.

Means, standard errors, and model fits for latencies above and below the cutoffs are shown in Table 36.5. Note that not every item type had any observations above or below every possible pseudodeadline. For example, only 13- of the 32-item types had any observations with latencies of greater than 14 sec; no item types had any observations with latencies of less than 2 sec. The interpretation of the data in Table 36.5 is unequivocal. For all pseudodeadlines under or over which there was statistically significant prediction, the mixed model was clearly superior to either the linguistic or the spatial model. Thus, it was not the use of deadlines per se that resulted in the superiority of the linguistic model: If latencies are modeled under the pseudodeadline procedure, the mixed model is always better. Rather, it was the use of error rate as a basis for modeling that resulted in the conflict. The mixed model better predicts latencies; the linguistic model better predicts error rates. The probable reason for the crossover in performance of the

TABLE 36.5
Quantitative Fits of the Models to the Latency Data Partitioned by Pseudodeadlines

Pseudodeadline (sec)	Item Latencies			R^2 for Model		
	$\bar{X}$	$S\bar{x}$	N^a	Mixed	Linguistic	Spatial
Latencies Above Pseudodeadline						
2	5930	129	32	.846[c]	.607[c]	.606[c]
4	6680	98	32	.680[c]	.546[c]	.591[c]
6	8321	124	32	.452[c]	.339[c]	.435[c]
8	10,414	160	32	.081	.066	.054
10	12,912	508	30	.271	.122	.203
12	14,937	584	25	.247	.225	.238
14	17,740	592	13	.367	.280	.060
16	19,122	538	10	.224	.400	.141
∞	—	—	0	—	—	—
Latencies Below Pseudodeadline						
2	—	—	0	—	—	—
4	3332	30	32	.454[c]	.356[b]	.377[b]
6	4356	46	32	.711[c]	.378[b]	.424[c]
8	5038	63	32	.747[c]	.488[c]	.400[c]
10	5434	91	32	.844[c]	.585[c]	.551[c]
12	5644	103	32	.824[c]	.643[c]	.577[c]
14	5776	112	32	.795[c]	.593[c]	.545[c]
16	5813	117	32	.793[c]	.597[c]	.555[c]
∞	5922	128	32	.843[c]	.592[c]	.606[c]

Note: All latencies are expressed in milliseconds. Modeling was of the 32 three-term series item types.
[a] N refers to number of item types (out of 32) for which there were any observations (nonmissing data) above or below pseudodeadline.
[b] $p < .05$
[c] $p < .01$

models at the 10-sec cutoff is that, at this point, almost all the countable errors were actually errors rather than long solution latencies.

Modeling of Latency and Error Data Simultaneously

Model Fitting by Canonical Regression. The analyses just described suggest that complete understanding of linear syllogistic reasoning requires simultaneous consideration of both solution latency and error rate as dependent variables. This simultaneous analysis was done here by canonical regression (Cooley & Lohnes, 1971; Sternberg, 1977b; Tatsuoka, 1971). In the present use of canonical regression, solution latency and error rate were considered jointly as dependent variables, with the independent variables the same as in each of the models as previously described. Canonical weights (analogous to beta weights in regression) are derived by least squares for each dependent and independent variable to maximize the canonical correlation between the two sets of variables. As in factor analysis (but not in simple or multiple regression), it is possible to have more than one set of weights, with each subsequent set of weights orthogonal to all previous ones and describing different aspects of the relationship between dependent and independent variables.

Mixed, Linguistic, and Spatial Canonical Models. Table 36.6 shows the fits of the mixed, linguistic, and spatial canonical models to the latency and error data, as well as the standardized parameter estimates (canonical weights) for each of the dependent and independent variables.

The first canonical variate was statistically significant for each model. The mixed model clearly gave the best account of the first canonical variate. Indeed, the value of canonical R^2 for the mixed model, .849, was only trivially higher than the value of multiple R^2 for the mixed model (for latencies considered alone), .843 (see Table 36.1). The increments in R^2 for the other models were also trivially small. The standardized parameter estimates for the dependent variables on the first variate reveal that solution latency was the main contributor to the variate, and the standardized parameter estimates for the independent variables on the first variate closely resemble those of the independent variables in predicting solution latency alone (see Table 36.4). The first variate, therefore, seems very closely to resemble solution latency considered in isolation from error rate.

The second canonical variate was statistically significant only for the linguistic model. The weights for the dependent variables reveal that error rate makes a large contribution to this variate and that the contribution of solution latency is negative. This negative weight suppresses the variance in solution latency that is correlated with error rate. This suppression is needed in order to make the second canonical variate orthogonal to the first. The second canonical variate, then, apparently represents that part of error rate that is orthogonal to solution latency. Linguistic pivot search, which is unique to the linguistic model, makes the strongest positive contribution toward the prediction of this variate.

Full Canonical Model. The results obtained so far suggest that the mixed model is best in predicting solution latencies (which are represented by the first canonical variate) and that the linguistic model is best in predicting error rates, and, in particular, that portion of error rate that is uncorrelated with solution latency (which is represented by the second canonical variate). These results suggest that some combination of the mixed and linguistic models may

TABLE 36.6
Quantitative Fits and Standardized Parameter Estimates of the Canonical Models to the Latency and Error Data

	Variate	
	1	*2*

Canonical R^2

Mixed model	.849[b]	.142
Linguistic model	.632[b]	.268[a]
Spatial model	.622[b]	.160

Standardized Parameter Estimates for Dependent Variables

Mixed model		
Latency	.96	—
Error rate	.10	—
Linguistic model		
Latency	.87	−.60
Error rate	.29	1.02
Spatial model		
Latency	.92	—
Error rate	.20	—

Standardized Parameter Estimates for Independent Variables

Mixed model		
Marking	.49	—
Negation	.17	—
Pivot search (mixed)	.52	—
Noncongruence	.34	—
Response search	.37	—
Linguistic model		
Marking	.61	.24
Negation	.47	−.70
Pivot search (linguistic)	.27	.67
Noncongruence	.58	−.01
Spatial model		
Marking	.60	—
Negation	.51	—
Pivot search (spatial)	.62	—
Premise order	.03	—

Note: All model fitting was done on the 32 three-term series item types.

[a]$p < .05$
[b]$p < .01$

give a superior account of solution latency and error rate considered jointly to that given by either model alone. In order to investigate this possibility, a fully exploratory analysis was conducted in which a full model was tested that included all parameters of the three models previously considered. The results of fitting this full model are shown in table 36.7.

The value of canonical R^2 for the first variate, .858, is only trivially higher than that value of canonical R^2 for the first variate when the mixed model is fit alone, .849. Even combining the parameters of the three models, therefore, one cannot do any better than the mixed model in predicting the latency-based first variate. The value of canonical R^2 for the second variate, .432, represents a noticeable increase over the value of .268 for the linguistic model alone. As in the linguistic model alone, however, the linguistic pivot search parameter appears to be the truly powerful predictor of performance, with spatial pivot search making a secondary contribution.

TABLE 36.7
Quantitative Fit and Standardized Parameter Estimates
of the Full Canonical Model to the Latency and Error
Data

	Variate	
	1	2
Canonical R^2		
Full Model	.858[b]	.432[a]
Standardized Parameter Estimates for Dependent Variables		
Latency	.94	−.48
Error rate	.15	1.05
Standardized Parameter Estimates for Independent Variables		
Marking	.50	.29
Negation	.20	.04
Mixed pivot search	.43	−.88
Response search	.37	.05
Noncongruence	.25	−.10
Linguistic pivot search	.04	.86
Premise order	.02	.17
Spatial pivot search	.17	.62

Note: All model fitting was doine on the 32 three-term series item types.
[a]$p < .05$
[b]$p < .01$

Experience with canonical regression has shown that the standardized parameter estimates are often less readily interpretable than the correlations of the original variables with canonical variate scores (see Sternberg, 1977b). These scores are computed for each observation simply by summing the product of each standardized independent or dependent variable times its corresponding standardized weight. Correlations between the canonical variate scores and the original variables are presented in Table 36.8.

Solution latency is very highly correlated with both the dependent and independent variate scores. Error rate is also fairly highly correlated with scores on the first variate. This pattern of correlations is to be expected if error rate is a less precise measure than solution latency of whatever it is that solution latency measures. In one aspect, therefore, error rate is an imperfect substitute for solution latency. But, in another aspect, error rate measures something solution latency does not measure (as expressed in the second canonical variate). This pattern is not unique to linear syllogisms: It appears for analogies as well (Sternberg, 1977b).

Turning to the correlations for the independent variables, one can see that all the independent variables of the mixed model are significantly correlated with both the dependent and independent variate scores, except in one instance, response search. Of all the parameters, only linguistic pivot search shows significant and substantial correlations with both the dependent and independent second-variate scores. Thus, it is indeed this operation that is responsible for the superiority of the linguistic model in accounting for error rate.

TABLE 36.8
Correlations of Canonical Variate Scores with Original Variables

Original Variable	Variate 1		Variate 2	
Dependent	Dependent	Independent	Dependent	Independent
Latency	$.99^c$	$.92^c$	$-.14$	$-.09$
Error rate	$.45^b$	$.42^b$	$.89^c$	$.59^c$
Independent				
Marking	$.46^b$	$.50^b$	$.19$	$.29$
Negation	$.42^b$	$.45^b$	$-.31$	$-.47^b$
Mixed pivot search	$.65^c$	$.70^c$	$-.23$	$-.34$
Response search	$.35$	$.37^a$	$.03$	$.05$
Noncongruence	$.46^b$	$.49^b$	$.06$	$.09$
Linguistic pivot search	$.17$	$.18$	$.37^a$	$.57^c$
Premise order	$.02$	$.02$	$.11$	$.17$
Spatial pivot search	$.48^b$	$.52^b$	$.13$	$.19$

$^a p < .05$
$^b p < .01$
$^c p < .001$

Discussion

The significant correlation of the linguistic pivot search variable with error rate but not solution latency initially seems perplexing. How is it possible for a variable to contribute to error rate but not to solution latency? A plausible explanation (Schustack, 1977) is that the linguistic pivot search operation is always executed, but it takes a constant amount of time across item types and hence does not appear as a separate latency parameter. Instead, its latency is absorbed into the global constant (used in the models of linear syllogistic reasoning to estimate response component time). By this explanation, subjects always compress the first premise of a linear syllogism and later retrieve from long-term memory the term that was temporarily deleted from working memory. However, the linguistic pivot search operation leads to errors in solution only in cases where the term that is temporarily deleted in compression is also the pivot term. In these cases, an error in the operation will result in selection of an incorrect pivot and, hence, an error in solution. In cases where the temporarily deleted term is not the pivot, the value of this term does not lead to selection of an erroneous pivot and, hence, does not lead to an error in solution.

Subjects are generally not aware of the pitfalls posed by structural variables that contribute differentially to error rate but uniformly to solution latency. Consider, for example, a variant of a problem that is a classic in puzzle books: A plane traveling from the United States to Canada crashes directly on the border between the two countries. In what country will the survivors be buried? Most people unfamiliar with the problem respond quickly with either "the United States," "Canada," or "either country." The printed solution, however, will usually be that "survivors aren't buried" (at least, not immediately)! Suppose, though, the problem had been stated in this way: A plane traveling from the United States to Canada crashed directly on the border between the two countries. In what country will the deceased be buried? Readers who are tripped up by the first version of the problem would generally encode this second version of the problem in the same way as they would encode the first version, responding in approximately the same amount of time. Yet, they would be far more likely to respond with an "acceptable" answer to the second version. Because the source of difficulty in the first version of the problem is not recognized as such, it does not contribute differentially to solution latency. The true nature of the problem is misapprehended. Such misapprehensions are common in ability-testing situations. Subjects who score relatively poorly may perceive themselves as scoring well because they solve problems that are different from and easier than the ones actually posed. In multiple-choice tests distractors are presented that capitalize upon the subjects' misapprehensions of the problems. The subjects thus never become aware of their misapprehensions.

The results of the present experiment show the importance of modeling both solution latencies and error rates jointly (Sternberg, 1977b) as well as separately (Sternberg, 1977a, b). Pachella (1974) has shown that differential error rates across conditions can drastically affect interpretation of latency outcomes, and the present results seem to indicate that the appearance of curious conflicts in the literature can arise simply from the failure to consider solution latency and error rate as conveying overlapping but by no means identical information. The conflict resided not in the data but in our inadequate interpretations of them. It is tempting in research on reasoning and other cognitive processes to deal with either solution latency or error rate to the exclusion of the other. Few studies give serious consideration to both. Most often, the inattention to one or the other dependent variable is not justified; sometimes, it is justified by an author's pointing to the high correlation between latencies and errors across conditions. This justification is unacceptable. On the one hand, interpretation of solution latency by itself is inadequate, because the unexplained variance in error rate may be both statistically significant and of signal importance in obtaining a complete understanding of the problem-solving process. On the other hand, interpretation of error rate by itself is inadequate, because error rate may be a complex variable comprising two kinds of errors that can be disentangled and thereby separately understood only in the context of solution latency. The present work shows this complexity in error rates for linear syllogism problems, and previous work shows it in error rates for the only other kind of problem that has been similarly analyzed, analogies (Sternberg, 1977b). Understanding of cognitive processes seems to require that serious attention be paid to both latencies and errors.

ACKNOWLEDGMENTS

I am grateful to Martin Guyote for assistance in stimulus preparation, data collection, and data analysis. Preparation of this report was supported by ONR Contract N0001478C0025 to Robert Sternberg. The research was supported by NSF Grant BNS-76-05311 to Robert Sternberg. Requests for reprints should be sent to Robert J. Sternberg, Department of Psychology, Box 11A Yale Station, Yale University, New Haven, Conn. 06520.

APPENDIX

Observed and predicted latencies for the linear syllogisms are shown in Table A. A complete listing of the independent variables used in parameter estimation can be found in Table 2 of Sternberg (1980b). The listing is available

Observed and Predicted Latencies for Linear Syllogisms

Item No.	Code[a]	Observed Latency	Predicted Latencies		
			Mixed Model	Linguistic Model	Spatial Model
1	00001	5223	5085	4882	5059
2	00100	5096	5394	5875	5416
3	00000	4630	4600	4696	5064
4	00101	5568	5878	5689	5421
5	11000	5481	5750	6232	5778
6	11101	6337	6155	5953	6135
7	11001	6159	6235	6046	5773
8	11100	5888	5670	5767	6130
9	01001	5184	5442	5053	4951
10	01100	4927	5313	5410	5308
11	10000	5581	4957	5053	4956
12	10101	5601	5798	5410	5313
13	10001	6296	5878	5689	5881
14	10100	5991	5750	6046	6238
15	01000	5234	5394	5689	5886
16	01101	6336	6235	6046	6243
17	11011	6860	6488	6698	6425
18	11110	5452	5923	6419	6782
19	11010	7219	6800	6884	6430
20	11111	7110	7204	6605	6787
21	00010	5080	4853	5348	5716
22	00111	5719	6132	6341	6073
23	00011	5835	6135	5534	5711
24	00110	6188	6443	6527	6068
25	10011	7406	6928	6341	6533
26	10110	6904	6800	6698	6890
27	01010	6308	6443	6341	6538
28	01111	7067	7285	6698	6895
29	01011	5635	5695	5705	5603
30	01110	5664	5267	6062	5960
31	10010	5222	5210	5705	5608
32	10111	6288	6051	6062	5965
RMSD			292	449	449

Note: All latencies are presented in milliseconds.

[a]Five-digit code represents item type. For code abcde,

a—First premise adjective marked? (0 = no, 1 = yes)

b—Second premise adjective marked? (0 = no, 1 = yes)

c—Question adjective marked? (0 = no, 1 = yes)

d—Premises negated? (0 = no, 1 = yes)

e—Answer to problem in first premise? (0 = no, 1 = yes)

upon request. Parameter estimates used in computing predictions were as follows:

Mixed Model. Marking, 357 ± 64 msec; negation, 127 ± 70 msec; pivot search, 796 ± 168 msec; response search, 485 ± 111 msec; noncongruence, 437 ± 119 msec; encoding + response, 4600 msec. (These parameter estimates differ slightly from those presented in Table 36.2 because they are based upon only the 32 linear syllogisms, exclusive of the eight two-term series problems).

Linguistic Model. Marking, 357 ± 100 msec; negation, 326 ± 87 msec; noncongruence, 636 ± 173 msec; linguistic pivot search, 186 ± 200 msec; encoding + response, 4696 msec.

Spatial Model. Marking, 357 ± 100 msec; negation, 326 ± 86 msec; premise order, 5 ± 173 msec; spatial pivot search, 465 ± 122 msec; encoding + response, 4594 msec.

REFERENCES

Burt, C. The development of reasoning in school children. *Journal of Experimental Pedagogy,* 1919, *5,* 68–77.

Clark, H. H. The influence of language in solving three-term series problems. *Journal of Experimental Psychology,* 1969, *82,* 205–215. (a)

Clark, H. H. Linguistic processes in deductive reasoning. *Psychological Review,* 1969, *76,* 387–404. (b)

Cooley, W. W., & Lohnes, P. R. *Multivariate data analysis.* New York: Wiley, 1971.

DeSoto, C. B., London, M., & Handel, S. Social reasoning and spatial paralogic. *Journal of Personality and Social Psychology,* 1965, *2,* 513–521.

Hunter, I. M. L. The solving of three-term series problems. *British Journal of Psychology,* 1957, *48,* 286–298.

Huttenlocher, J. Constructing spatial images: A strategy in reasoning. *Psychological Review,* 1968, *75,* 550–560.

Huttenlocher, J., & Higgins, E. T. Adjectives, comparatives, and syllogisms. *Psychological Review,* 1971, *78,* 487–504.

Keating, D. P., & Caramazza, A. Effects of age and ability on syllogistic reasoning in early adolescence. *Developmental Psychology,* 1975, *11,* 837–842.

Pachella, R. G. The interpretation of reaction time in information processing research. In B. Kantowitz (Ed.), *Human information processing: Tutorials in performance and cognition.* Hillsdale, N.J.: Lawrence Erlbaum Associates, 1974.

Potts, G. R., & Scholz, K. W. The internal representation of a three-term series problem. *Journal of Verbal Learning and Verbal Behavior,* 1975, *14,* 439–452.

Schustack, M. W. Personal communication, August 1977.

Sternberg, R. J. Component processes in analogical reasoning. *Psychological Review,* 1977, *84,* 353–378. (a)

Sternberg, R. J. *Intelligence, information processing, and analogical reasoning: The componential analysis of human abilities.* Hillsdale, N.J.: Lawrence Erlbaum Associates, 1977. (b)

Sternberg, R. J. The development of linear syllogistic reasoning. *Journal of Experimental Child Psychology,* 1980, *29,* 340–356. (a)

Sternberg, R. J. Representation and process in linear syllogistic reasoning. *Journal of Experimental Psychology: General,* 1980, *109,* 119–159. (b)

Tatsuoka, M. M. *Multivariate analysis: Techniques for educational and psychological research.* New York: Wiley, 1971.

37 Inductive Deductions and Deductive Inductions

Marilyn Jager Adams
Bolt Beranek and Newman Inc.
Cambridge, Massachusetts
United States

ABSTRACT

Different syllogistic forms are analyzed with respect to the set relationships that must hold between the terms in their premises in order for them to be valid syntactically and semantically at once. It is argued that much of our seeming illogic can be attributed to conflict between relationships semantically entailed by the terms of the argument and those described through its syntactic structure. To test this hypothesis, people were asked to judge the validity of syllogisms whose semantic implications were consistent, conflicting, or moot with respect to their syntactic implications. The results indicate, in keeping with our hypothesis, that people's inferences are strongly influenced by the semantic constraints of an argument. The discussion focuses on problems involved in communicating logical relations through natural langauge.

INTRODUCTION

Among the classic controversies that psychology has inherited from philosophy is that of whether human thought adheres to the laws of logic. On one side is the conviction that somehow it must. Reasoning is, after all, the only means we have for extending our knowledge beyond what we have learned explicitly. If we were insensitive to the laws of logic, we would have no basis, save empirical, for evaluating the necessity of our conclusions. Through inferences, we would eventually come to "know" all nature of erroneous and tenuous conjectures. Over the long run, reasoning would not serve to increase our sense of reality so much as to distort or overwrite it.

745

The other side of the controversy rests on the simple fact that it has been exceedingly difficult to produce convincing evidence that we do possess an inherent appreciation of logic. The major problem in this endeavor is that of ensuring that the acceptance or rejection of a conclusion will be the product of reasoning as opposed to prior knowledge or beliefs about its truth. Formal logic would seem to offer a solution to this problem as it offers a means of determining the validity of an argument strictly in terms of its structure. By substituting arbitrary terms into the logicians' formal arguments, one ought to be able to remove or neutralize semantic factors so as to obtain unconfounded measures of people's formal logical capacity.

As it happens, when arguments are built around arbitrary rather than meaningful terms, people are generally worse, not better, at distinguishing whether or not they are valid (Revlin & Leirer, 1978; Staudenmayer, 1975; Wason & Johnson-Laird, 1972; Wilkins, 1928). Indeed, if performance on unmeaningful arguments is taken as a pure index of our logical capacity, the implication is that that capacity is meager. The thesis of this chapter is, however, that such arguments do not provide adequate control over semantic factors and, therefore, that the quality of performance that they typically elicit may not be so condemning.

In particular, this chapter is focused on people's comprehension of the hypothetical syllogism. This syllogism has two valid forms:

[1]   If it is P, then it must be Q
         It is P
         _____

         Therefore, it must be Q.

[2]   If it is P, then it must be Q
         It is not Q
         _____

         Therefore, it must not be P.

These two forms are respectively referred to as *modus ponens* and *modus tollens*. The proposition in the *if* clause of the first premise is the *antecedent;* the proposition in the *then* clause is called the *consequent.*

There are also two especially seductive but invalid forms of the syllogism:

[3]   If it is P, then it must be Q
         It is Q
         _____

         Therefore, it must be P.

[4]   If it is P, then it must be Q
         It is not P
         _____

         Therefore, it must not be Q.

Both of these forms are named after the assumptions made by their second premises: form [3] is called the fallacy of *affirming the consequent;* form [4] is called the fallacy of *denying the antecedent.*

All arguments in the forms of the *modus ponens* and *modus tollens* will be valid. No arguments in the two fallacious forms can be valid. It is easier to understand why from the Euler diagram in Fig. 37.1. (In these diagrams, the set *U* symbolizes all other things in the universe that *it* could be.) The first premise of the argument asserts that everything that is subsumed by the antecedent term must be subsumed by the consequent or, in other words, that the antecedent must be a subset of the consequent. The *modus ponens* therefore asserts that anything that is member of the subset, *P*, must be member of its superset, *Q*. The *modus tollens* asserts that anything that is not member of *Q*, the superset, cannot be member of *P*, the subset. In view of the set relations between the antecedent and consequent, both of these are clearly sound, deductive arguments.

MODUS PONENS

IF IT IS P, THEN IT MUST BE Q

IT IS P
_____

IT MUST BE Q

AFFIRMATION OF THE CONSEQUENT

IF IT IS P, THEN IT MUST BE Q

IT IS Q
_____

IT MUST BE P

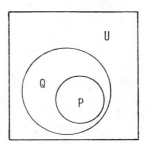

DENIAL OF THE ANTECEDENT

IF IT IS P, THEN IT MUST BE Q

IT IS NOT P
_____

IT MUST NOT BE Q

MODUS TOLLENS

IF IT IS P, THEN IT MUST BE Q

IF IT IS NOT Q
_____

IT MUST NOT BE P

FIG. 37.1.   The relation between the antecedent and consequent sets for hypothetical premises of the form "If it is *P*, then it is *Q*."

The two fallacious arguments, however, are not deductive, but inductive. The diagram makes obvious the uncertainty involved in arguing that something must be a member of the subset because it is a member of the superset (affirming the consequent) or that it must not be a member of the superset because it is not a member of the subset (denying the antecedent). Such inductive conclusions may be good guesses depending on the relative sizes of the subset and superset, but they are not compelling. They are equivalent to such arguments as that something must be a poodle because it is a dog or that something cannot be a dog because it is not a poodle.

In short, the first premise of the hypothetical syllogism may be seen as a description of the set relations that exist between the terms of the argument. Although this makes clear why two of these forms are valid and two are invalid, it also points out why the substitution of arbitrary terms into the premises may not result in a fair test of people's logical abilities; that is, if the set relation described by the hypothetical premise is incompatible with the relation that is already known to hold between the terms, then a conflict situation is defined. Which set relation should reasoners use to constrain their inferences? If they attend to the relation suggested by the semantics of the argument, then their conclusions will be at variance with those prescribed by its form. With respect to the syntactic structure of the argument, they will appear to be illogical even though, in terms of the set relations from which they are reasoning, their conclusions may be perfectly logical.

In Tables 37.1 and 37.2 are some examples illustrating how the semantic and syntactic constraints of an argument may interact. The semantic relation between the terms of the arguments in Table 37.1 are compatible with those described by the hypothetical premise: The premise asserts that the antecedent is a subset of the consequent and, indeed turkeys are a subset of birds. The reader should find the distinction between valid and invalid arguments in Table 37.1 relatively transparent. In Table 37.2, however, the semantic and syntactic constraints of the arguments are in conflict. Although the hypothetical premise asserts that bird, the antecedent, must be a subset of turkeys, the consequent, it is a matter of common knowledge that just the opposite is true. Distinctions between the valid and invalid forms in this table are consequently more difficult as they require the reasoner to concentrate on the structure of the arguments and to ignore the content.

EXPERIMENT I

The purpose of this study was to evaluate the extent to which people's reasoning is influenced by the set relations entailed by the terms of an argument. To this end, we asked subjects to judge the validity of syllogisms whose semantic constraints were consistent, in opposition, or moot with

TABLE 37.1

Examples of Syllogisms in Which the Set Relations
Described by the Hypothetical Premise Are Compatible
With Those Entailed by the Antecedent and Consequent
Terms

MODUS PONENS
> If it is a turkey, then it must be a bird
> It is a turkey

> It must be a bird

AFFIRMATION OF THE CONSEQUENT
> If it is a turkey, then it must be a bird
> It is a bird

> It must be a turkey

DENIAL OF THE ANTECEDENT
> If it is a turkey, then it must be a bird
> It is not a turkey

> It must not be a bird

MODUS TOLLENS
> If it is a turkey, then it must be a bird
> It is not a bird

> It must not be a turkey

TABLE 37.2

Examples of Syllogisms in Which the Set Relations
Described by the Hypothetical Premise
Are Incompatible With Those Entailed by the
Antecedent and Consequent Terms.

MODUS PONENS
> If it is a bird, then it must be a turkey
> It is a bird

> It must be a turkey

AFFIRMATION OF THE CONSEQUENT
> If it is a bird, then it must be a turkey
> It is a turkey

> It must be a bird

DENIAL OF THE ANTECEDENT
> If it is a bird, then it must be a turkey
> It is not a bird

> It must not be a turkey

MODUS TOLLENS
> If it is a bird, then it must be a turkey
> It is not a turkey

> It must not be a bird

---

respect to their syntactic or formal constraints. Because we were specifically interested in how the semantic constraints affected people's inferential tendencies, we wanted to control the temptation to accept or reject conclusions according to prior knowledge of their truth or falsity. We therefore could not use nominative sets and supersets (like turkey and bird or poodle and dog) as the terms in our experimental arguments, because semantically valid and invalid assertions would then correspond to necessarily and not necessarily true assertions, as in Tables 37.1 and 37.2, respectively. Instead, we needed a way of selecting terms such that they entailed the appropriate set relations but the truth or falsity of any particular conclusion was not predefined.

This was done by using nominative or adjective phrases as the antecedent and consequent, such that the hypothetical premise was of the form:

$$
\text{If it is} \begin{Bmatrix} \text{ADJECTIVE} \\ \text{or} \\ \text{NOUN} \end{Bmatrix}, \text{then it is} \begin{Bmatrix} \text{ADJECTIVE} \\ \text{or} \\ \text{NOUN} \end{Bmatrix}.
$$

The rationale was that although an object's properties may be *deduced* from knowledge of its identity, an object's identity can only be uncertainly *induced* from knowledge of any proper subset of its properties. Or, more formally, because decreasing intension defines increasing extension, any class of objects or events must be subsumed by a class defined by only one of the properties in its intension. For example, *canaries* corresponds to that set of things that is intensionally defined as living, flying, feathered, yellow, singing, etc., but canaries are only a *subset* of that class defined by the single property, living.

Thus, when the antecedent of a hypothetical premise is nominative and the consequent is adjectival, the semantic and syntactic constraints of the syllogism will correspond to one another; when the antecedent is adjectival and the consequent is nominative, they will be in opposition. To the extent that the semantically entailed constraints do influence people's reasoning, distinctions between valid and invalid arguments with nominative antecedents and adjectival consequents should be easier than distinctions between those with adjectival antecedents and nominative consequents.

We generated eight conditional statements for each of the four possible combinations of nominative and adjectival antecedents and consequents. The specific pairs of nouns and adjectives were selected to yield plausible, but not particularly familiar, descriptions: when the hypothetical premise consisted of an adjective phrase and a noun phrase, the former could not refer to characteristic or defining properties of the latter; when the premise consisted of two noun phrases or two adjective phrases, the antecedent and consequent terms could not be frequent associates or natural super/subsets of one another. An example of each of the adjective (A) and noun (N) combinations is given in Table 37.3.

TABLE 37.3

Examples of the Four Types of Nominative (N) and
Adjectival (A) Antecedent/Consequent Combinations

N/A	If it is a *flower*, it must be *white*.
N/N	If it is a *puppet*, it must be a *monkey*.
A/A	If it is *big*, it must be *dirty*.
A/N	If it is *new*, it must be a *pencil*.

Four sets of 32 syllogisms were generated from the conditional statements. Within each of the four sets, each type of antecedent/consequent combination was used equally often in each of the four syntactic forms of the argument. For example, of the eight adjective/adjective conditionals, two were used for the premises of the *modus ponens,* two for the *modus tollens,* two for the *affirmation of the consequent,* and two for the *denial of the antecedent.* Across the four sets of syllogisms, each of the conditional statements was used once in each of the four argument forms; this was done to cancel effects of whatever semantic associations there were between the words in the premises. Finally, half of the hypothetical premises read, "If it is a *Q*, then it must be a *Q*," and half read, "It must be a *Q* if it is a *P*"; this variable was counterbalanced across argument types and antecedent/consequent pairs both within and between the sets of syllogisms. The four sets of syllogisms were evenly distributed to 24 undergraduate subjects, whose task was to decide, for each syllogism, whether the conclusion followed necessarily from its premise. Although all the subjects were purportedly naive with respect to formal logic, the data from three were discarded because they made no errors.

The results are summarized in Table 37.4 in terms of the percentages of formally correct resposnes: For the *modus ponens* and the *modus tollens,* the figures correspond to the percentage of correct acceptances of the conclusions; for the two fallacious forms, they correspond to the percentage of correct rejections of the conclusions. The significance of the semantic structure of the arguments was confirmed through a two-way Friedman multi-

TABLE 37.4

Percentage of Formally Correct Responses by Type of Argument and Form
Class of the Antecedent and Consequent for Experiment 1
(A = adjective, N = noun)

	AN	*NN*	*AA*	*NA*	*Mean*
Modus ponens	83	83	87	98	88
Affirmation of consequent	71	69	75	79	73
Denial of antecedent	58	65	65	73	65
Modus tollens	29	56	48	67	50
Mean	60	68	69	79	69

sample test [$\chi^2(3)$ = 17.2, $p < 0.01$] (Bradley, 1968, pp. 138–140). This effect was almost entirely attributable to the noun/adjective and adjective/noun conditions. For 20 subjects, performance was more accurate on syllogisms with nominative antecedents and adjectival consequents than with the converse arrangement; for 3 subjects, the reverse was true; for 1 subject there was no difference. The probability that as many as 20 of 24 subjects would be biased toward either of these types of arguments by chance alone is less than .0003. In contrast, there was virtually no difference between adjective/adjective and noun/noun arguments: For 9 subjects, performance was better on the former; for 10 subjects, it was better on the latter; for 5 subjects, there was no difference. The suggestion is that subjects' inferences were influenced by the nature of neither the antecedent nor the consequent term alone but by the relation between them.

It is also worth noting that performance was generally above chance, which indicates that subjects were not insensitive to the syntactic constraints of the arguments. Although the Friedman test indicated that the differences in response accuracy across the four argument forms were significant [$\chi^2(3)$ = 24.2, $p < 0.01$], they did not interact with the combinations of terms [$\chi^2(9)$ = 14.9, $p > 0.05$].

EXPERIMENT II

In short, the results of Experiment I were entirely consistent with the notion that people are attuned to the semantic constraints of arguments. However, an alternative explanation might be that conditional statements are easier to interpret when the condition corresponds to the identity of some class of objects or events and its entailment corresponds to some property of that class. To assess this possibility, 24 different subjects were asked to evaluate a second set of syllogisms.

This second set of syllogisms was exactly like the first except that *both* terms of the hypothetical premise were negated. As is shown in Fig. 37.2, the effect of negating both terms is one of reversing the set relationship that must hold between them in order for the argument to be syntactically and semantically sound at once. With neither term negated, the hypothetical premise asserts that the antecedent must be a subset of the consequent; with both terms negated, it asserts that the antecedent must be a superset of the consequent. It follows that if the pattern of results of the first experiment reflected people's sensitivity to the semantic constraints of the arguments, then these syllogisms should have evoked just the opposite pattern of results.

As is shown in Table 37.5, that is exactly what happened. In contrast with the first experiment, performance on these syllogisms was most accurate with adjectival antecedents and nominative consequents and least accurate with

MODUS PONENS

Iꜰ ɪᴛ ɪꜱ ɴᴏᴛ P, ᴛʜᴇɴ ɪᴛ ᴍᴜꜱᴛ ɴᴏᴛ ʙᴇ Q

Iᴛ ɪꜱ ɴᴏᴛ P

Iᴛ ᴍᴜꜱᴛ ɴᴏᴛ ʙᴇ Q

AFFIRMATION OF THE CONSEQUENT

Iꜰ ɪᴛ ɪꜱ ɴᴏᴛ P, ᴛʜᴇɴ ɪᴛ ᴍᴜꜱᴛ ɴᴏᴛ ʙᴇ Q

Iᴛ ɪꜱ ɴᴏᴛ Q

Iᴛ ᴍᴜꜱᴛ ɴᴏᴛ ʙᴇ P

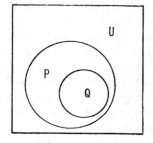

DENIAL OF THE ANTECEDENT

Iꜰ ɪᴛ ɪꜱ ɴᴏᴛ P, ᴛʜᴇɴ ɪᴛ ᴍᴜꜱᴛ ɴᴏᴛ ʙᴇ Q

Iᴛ ɪꜱ P

Iᴛ ᴍᴜꜱᴛ ʙᴇ Q

MODUS TOLLENS

Iꜰ ɪᴛ ɪꜱ ɴᴏᴛ P, ᴛʜᴇɴ ɪᴛ ᴍᴜꜱᴛ ɴᴏᴛ ʙᴇ Q

Iᴛ ɪꜱ Q

Iᴛ ᴍᴜꜱᴛ ʙᴇ P

FIG. 37.2. The relation between the antecedent and consequent sets for hypothetical premises of the form "If it is not P, then it is not Q."

TABLE 37.5
Percentages of Formally Correct Responses by Type of Argument and Form
Class of the Antecedent and Consequent for Experiment 2
(A = adjective, N = noun)

	AN	*NN*	*AA*	*NA*	*Mean*
Modus ponens	83	79	83	79	81
Affirmation of consequent	56	58	52	42	52
Denial of antecedent	81	75	73	50	70
Modus tollens	58	37	35	40	43
Mean	70	62	61	53	61

the converse arrangement. Again, the effect of the semantic structure of the argument was significant according to the Friedman test [$\chi^2(3) = 8.85, p <$ 0.05] and was almost entirely attributable to the adjective/noun and noun/ adjective conditions. For 17 of the 24 subjects, performance was more accurate with adjectival antecedents and nominative consequents than with the converse; for 4 subjects, the reverse was true; for 2 subjects, response accuracy did not differ between the two arrangements $\{p[(n \geq 17)/24] < .025\}$. There was no difference between the response distributions for adjective/adjective and noun/noun arguments.

Overall, performance was slightly less accurate than in the first experiment, but it was still generally above chance, suggesting again that subjects were not altogether insensitive to the inferential constraints carried by the syntactic structure of the argument. And, again, response accuracy differed significantly across the four argument forms [$\chi^2(3) = 25.3, p < 0.01$] but did not interact with the effect of terms [$\chi^2(9) = 11.9, p > 0.05$].

DISCUSSION

Taken together, the results of these experiments clearly indicate that the certainty that people attach to an inference is influenced by its semantic structure. Moreover, the effect demonstrated through these experiments does not depend on the established truth of the premises or the conclusion but instead on the logical constraints entailed by the semantic relationships between the terms of the argument.

The most important practical implication of these results is that, as intuitive logicians, people are more competent than has often been supposed. Given the set relations among the terms of an argument, they are attuned to the soundness of the inferences that follow. At least with simple arguments, like those studied here, we can therefore expect them to reason productively providing that they are reasoning directly in terms of the concepts themselves. The most frequent exceptions should be the products of ignorance rather than illogic, as when the reasoner is confused about the relations between the terms of an argument (e.g., if s/he believes that Communist is a superset of protestors). The demonstration that the semantic influences pivot on the logical constraints rather than the truth or falsity of the relations between the terms removes the paradox from the findings that meaningful arguments are easier to follow than nonmeaningful arguments whether or not their assertions conform to the reasoner's beliefs (Wason & Johnson-Laird, 1972; Wilkens, 1928). Its practical significance is that the effect of semantics will not be one of transforming lies to truths in the interpreter's mind but nonsense to sense.

Indeed, it is probably the reasoner's efforts to make sense of the conditional premise that are responsible for the semantic effect. The content and structure of a linguistic statement normally work together to determine its meaning.

The words evoke corresponding concepts together with their established interrelationships and their potential interrelationships as defined by their semantic features. The syntax specifies which of these interrelationships was intended. The problem with a statement like "If it's a dog, then it's a poodle" is that the interrelationships anticipated by its semantic content are incompatible with those specified by its syntax. To construct a coherent representation of its meaning, therefore, the interpreter must find a way to overcome this conflict. To this end, s/he has three options.

The first option is one of ignoring the semantic relationships and coordinating the terms as prescribed by the syntax of the premise. This is the only option that will consistently yield formally correct conclusions to the syllogism.

The second option is one of ignoring the syntactically defined relationship, or at least the direction of that relationship, and creating a representation that is consistent with the semantic underpinnings of the premise. For statements in which the syntactic and semantic constraints conflict, this option is tantamount to converting the premises. When exercised, it will convert the validity status of the syllogism as well: The *modus ponens* and *modus tollens* will beocme invalid inductive arguments, and the *affirmation of the consequent* and the *denial of the antecedent* will become valid deductive arguments.

The third option is one of interpreting the statement as meaning, "The only dogs in question are poodles." If the statement, "If it is a dog, then it's a poodle," occurred in a normal language context, this would almost certainly be the intended interpretation. Moreover, it is the only interpretation that violates neither the syntactic nor the semantic constraints of the premise: The sets corresponding to the antecedent and consequent terms are construed as equivalent and, therefore, as subsets of one another. This option does, however, alter the logical significance of the premise, transforming it from a conditional to a biconditional. The biconditional is not a misinterpretation so much as an overinterpretation of the conditional premise. The set relationship described by the biconditional will always be among those described by the conditional, but it will be the most extreme relationship for which the conditional could be true. Because of this, a biconditional interpretation of the hypothetical premise will not affect the validity of the *modus ponens* or the *modus tollens*. However, it will render the *affirmation of the consequent* and the *denial of the antecedent* valid as well.

Although the second and third options should generate well-defined and distinctly different patterns of errors, the individual data from these experiments are too sparse to afford direct statistical support of either. On the other hand, the existing literature on syllogistic reasoning provides support for both.

Chapman and Chapman (1959) suggested both options under the single title of "illicit conversion" as an explanation for errors on categorical syllogisms. As the psychological impetus for such errors, they cited not only the reasoner's real-world knowledge but also a tendency to interpret the copula in statements of the form "All A are B" as meaning "equivalent to" rather than "included in." A more general explanation for this tendency—one that could additionally account for analogous misconstruals of categorical premises in other moods and of conditionals as biconditionals—is that people will, on occasion, interpret the express relationship of A to B as reciprocative. Because Chapman and Chapman only tested subjects on invalid syllogisms, their data also provide no distinct evidence for either of the two options.

Direct evidence for the third option has been reported by Erickson (1978). He found that when subjects were asked to draw Venn diagrams to represent *universal affirmative* assertions, like "All A are B," nearly half drew set-identity rather than set-inclusion figures. Further, Bucci (1978), whose subjects ranged from 6 years old to adult, found that the probability of interpreting the *universal affirmative* as an assertion of set equivalence rather than set inclusion generally decreased with age but that for all age groups the tendency toward equivalence interpretations varied with the semantic content of the assertion. Virtually all of her adult subjects interpreted statements with relatively broad predicates, such as "All bears are *dangerous,*" as set inclusion assertions. In contrast, for statements with narrow predicates, such as "All oak trees have *acorns,*" roughly 20% turned to set equivalence interpretations; for abstract statements, such as "All the square blocks are purple," roughly 50% did so. Taplin, Staudenmayer, and Taddonio (1974) have found that the tendency to interpret affirmative hypothetical premises (e.g., "If P, then Q") as conditional, or set inclusion, assertions also increases developmentally. However, they have repeatedly demonstrated that for premises with neutral semantic content even adults tend most strongly toward biconditional interpretations (Staudenmayer, 1975; Taplin, 1971, Taplin & Staudenmayer, 1973; Taplin et al., 1974). As with categorical assertions, this tendency is sensitive to the semantic or pragmatic constraints of the assertion; Staudenmayer (1975), using causal hypothetical syllogisms, found that the percentage of subjects preferring conditional to biconditional interpretations was greater when the antecedent was merely sufficient ("If I turn the switch on, then the light will go on") as opposed to necessary ("If the switch is turned on, then the light will go on").

In support of the second option described above, Staudenmayer (1975) also identified a sizable group of subjects who consistently reversed the truth functional value of abstract hypothetical premises. Further, Revlis (1975) and Revlin and Leirer (1978) have cogently demonstrated the reality of the second option and, in particular, its responsiveness to the semantic content of the syllogism. Finally, the availability of both of these options to reasoners could explain the frequent finding that more errors are made in evaluating invalid than valid syllogisms: For invalid syllogisms, either conversion or the biconditional (reciprocative) interpretation of the premise will alter the "correct" conclusion; but, for valid syllogisms, only conversion will do so.

There are two more syntactic frames for the hypothetical syllogism corresponding to whether only the antecedent term or only the consequent term is negated. Again, if the interpretation of the hypothetical premise is viewed as a joint product of the set relations described by its syntax and those entailed by its semantics, we may gain some insight into the factors that render these frames more or less difficult to follow.

Let us first consider the case in which only the consequent is negated. People tend to be especially successful at distinguishing valid from invalid syllogisms with hypothetical premises of this form (Evans, 1972, 1977; Wason & Johnson-Laird, 1972). The diagram in Fig. 37.3 suggests a plausible explanation of why this is so. The hypothetical premise asserts nothing more than that the antecedent and consequent terms are distinctly different from one another. It thus stands as a conceptually sound description of the relation

MODUS PONENS

IF IT IS P, THEN IT MUST NOT BE Q

IT IS P
_____

IT MUST NOT BE Q

AFFIRMATION OF THE CONSEQUENT

IF IT IS P, THEN IT MUST NOT BE Q

IT IS NOT Q
_____

IT MUST BE P

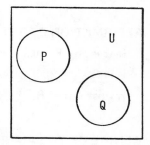

DENIAL OF THE ANTECEDENT

IF IT IS P, THEN IT MUST NOT BE Q

IT IS NOT P
_____

IT MUST BE Q

MODUS TOLLENS

IF IT IS P, THEN IT MUST NOT BE Q

IT IS Q
_____

IT MUST NOT BE P

FIG. 37.3. The relation between the antecedent and consequent sets for hypothetical premises of the form "If it is P, then it is not Q."

between most arbitrary pairs of terms. For most situations, the biconditional interpretation will only provide a less appropriate description, because it carries the additional implication that the antecedent and consequent terms conjointly exhaust the universe of possible identities for *it*. Nor will conversion improve the description: An exchange of the terms alone will not alter its meaning at all, because the express relation between them is reciprocative; an exchange of the terms *with* the negative qualifier will only complicate its meaning as discussed in the following.

The remaining version of the syllogism, in which only the antecedent of the hypothetical premise is negated, has proved to be especially difficult for people to follow in both natural and experimental langauge situations. As shown in Fig. 37.4, the hypothetical premise asserts that the sets referred to by the antecedent and consequent terms may overlap and must exhaust the

MODUS PONENS

IF IT IS NOT P, THEN IT MUST BE Q

IT IS NOT P

IT MUST BE Q

AFFIRMATION OF THE CONSEQUENT

IF IT IS NOT P, THEN IT MUST BE Q

IT IS Q

IT MUST NOT BE P

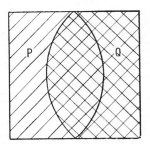

DENIAL OF THE ANTECEDENT

IF IT IS NOT P, THEN IT MUST BE Q

IT IS P

IT MUST NOT BE Q

MODUS TOLLENS

IF IT IS NOT P, THEN IT MUST BE Q

IT IS NOT Q

IT MUST BE P

FIG. 37.4.   The relation between the antecedent and consequent sets for hypothetical premises of the form "If it is not *P*, then it is *Q*."

relevant universe. In contrast, Wason and Johnson-Laird (1972, pp. 61–62) have remarked that, in natural language situations, statements of this form seem quite compellingly to mean, "It has to be either P or Q, but it cannot be both." In other words, the conditional is interpreted as a biconditional, thereby denying the possibility that the antecedent and consequent terms intersect. Within the present framework, this interpretation is easily attributed to the semantic content of the assertions: There are relatively few concepts that can overlap in the manner described by the conditional premise. For such statements as "If it is not on my desk, it is in my car" and "If it is not John, it is his brother," the possibility of *its* being both is pragmatically precluded. It should be noted that when the premise *is* built around suitably overlappable concepts, it regains its formal significance. Thus, the assertion, "If he is not stupid, he is lazy," carries the ready undestanding that he may in fact be both.

In experimental as opposed to natural language situations the predominant misconstrual of these premises seems not to be the biconditional but the conversion of the antecedent and the negated consequent; that is, the syllogisms in Fig. 37.4 tend to be interpreted as though they referred to the set relations shown in Fig. 37.3 (Evans, 1972, 1977). The explanation for this tendency may lie in the difficulty of conceiving of any two of an experimental set of arbitrary terms as exhausting the relevant universe. In natural language situations this aspect of the premise's meaning is readily assumed. Indeed, in most natural contexts, it could properly be termed deceitful to say, "If it's not on my desk, it's in my briefcase," while knowing *it* might well be someplace else. But the conviction that the antecedent and consequent terms exhaust the relevant possibilities is patently unrealistic in the typical experimental situation where the identity of *it* has been repeatedly redefined in terms of pairs of some finite set of alphanumeric characters or colors.

The more general point to be drawn from this discussion is that although such distortions of the premises will often lead to the rejection of the formally prescribed conclusion of a syllogism, they would seem to reflect the reasoner's respect rather than disregard for the laws of logic. It is, after all, the set relationships between the terms of an assertion that determine the certainty of the inferences that may follow. The validity of a syllogistic form is owed not to its syntactic structure per se but to the relationships implied by that structure. When the relationships that are known to exist between the terms of an argument conflict with those described by its syntax, it seems at least as rational to base one's inferences on the former as on the latter. Moreover, the biconditional interpretation, as it combines the syntactic and semantic constraints into a single coherent representation of the relationships under discussion, may be viewed as the most rational solution of all.

The problem of knowing whether what is said is what is meant has plagued not only reasoners but those who reason about reasoners as well. When Aristotle discussed deductive reasoning, he freely interchanged locutions like

"All A are B," "A is included in B," "B is predicated of all A," and "B belongs to all A." For this he has been charged with neglecting the use–mention distinction—with failing to make clear whether or when his variables stood for words as opposed to their conceptual referents. From the perspective of this study, one cannot help but wonder whether Aristotle's free exchange of these locutions was quite purposeful in that he was never really discussing language except as a means of describing possible configurations of conceptual sets.

If such were indeed Aristotle's intention, it might also explain the mystery of the figures. Aristotle pointed out that in order to infer anything about the relation of one set (A) to another (B), it is necessary to establish a third set (C) that can be related to both. This could be done, he claimed, in exactly three ways: (1) by predicating A of C and C of B; (2) by predicating C of both A and B; or (3) by predicating both A and B of C. It was not long before someone, inspired no doubt by the apparent symmetry between the second and third figures, suggested a fourth: predicating C of A and B of C.

The question of whether Aristotle omitted this figure as the result of some theoretical consideration or by oversight has never been answered. If one draws the Euler diagrams corresponding to the second and third figures, one will see that the set relations they admit are quite different from one another. If one draws the diagrams corresponding to Aristotle's first figure and the later suggested fourth, one will see that they are identical except in whether the most inclusive set is labeled as A or B. An alternative demonstration of this point is that for every argument in the first figure, there is an equivalent argument in the fourth figure but with the order of the terms and the premises reversed. Thus, AA1 arguments are equivalent to AA4 arguments, EI1 to IE4, AI1 to IA4, and so on. Given the abstract nature of the terms, A and B, it can therefore be argued that the first and fourth figures describe indistinguishable set relations. This, in turn, suggests that Aristotle may well have omitted the fourth on purpose.

Although the four figures were developed in the context of categorical syllogisms, the set relations each of them admits can be compared to those described by the four types of hypothetical premises. When this is done, the relations between the sets A and B that are suggested by universal affirmative arguments in the first and fourth figures turn out to be the same as those described by the hypothetical premises of the forms "If it is B, then it is A" and "If it is not B, then it is not A"; the set relations suggested by the second figure correspond to those described by the premise "If it is B, then it is not A"; whereas the set relations suggested by the third figure correspond to those described by the premise "If it is not B, then it is A." In view of this isomorphism, it is interesting that categorical and hypothetical syllogisms are generally discussed in separate chapters of textbooks on logic. Again the message is that we should take care in conceptually separating logical relations from the language in which they are expressed. In the end it seems that we, not Aristotle, have been guilty of the more serious abuse of the use–mention distinction in our determination to interpret the syllogistic forms as the laws of thought rather than as descriptions of those laws.

ACKNOWLEDGMENTS

This research was supported by contract number MDA 903-77-C-0025 from the Cybernetics Technology Office of the Advanced Research Projects Agency. I would like to thank Sarah Odell for her help in generating the stimuli, Brenda J. Starr for taking charge of the data collection logistics, and Joan Hirschkorn and Mary Tiernan for their help in preparing the manuscript.

REFERENCES

Bradley, J. V. _Distribution-free statistical tests._ Englewood Cliffs, N.J.: Prentice-Hall, 1968.
Bucci, W. The interpretation of universal affirmative propositions. _Cognition,_ 1978, _6,_ 55–77.
Chapman, L. J., & Chapman, J. P. Atmosphere effect re-examined. _Journal of Experimental Psychology,_ 1959, _58,_ 220–226.
Erickson, J. R. Research on syllogistic reasoning. In R. Revlin & R. E. Mayer (Eds.), _Human reasoning._ New York: Wiley, 1978.
Evans, J. St. B. T. Reasoning with negatives. _British Journal of Psychology,_ 1972, _63,_ 213–219.
Evans, J. St. B. T. Linguistic factors in reasoning. _Quarterly Journal of Experimental Psychology,_ 1977, _29,_ 297–306.
Revlin, R., & Leirer, V. O. The effect of personal biases on syllogistic reasoning: Rational decisions from personalized representations. In R. Revlin & R. E. Mayer (Eds.), _Human reasoning._ New York: Wiley, 1978.
Revlis, R. Syllogistic reasoning: Logical decisions from a complex data base. In R. J. Falmagne (Ed.), _Reasoning: Representation and process._ Hillsdale, N.J.: Lawrence Erlbaum Associates, 1975.
Staudenmayer, H. Understanding conditional reasoning with meaningful propositions. In R. J. Falmagne (Ed.), _Reasoning: Representation and process._ Hillsdale, N.J.: Lawrence Erlbaum Associates, 1975.
Taplin, J. E. Reasoning with conditional sentences. _Journal of Verbal Learning and Verbal Behavior,_ 1971, _10,_ 218–225.
Taplin, J. E., & Staudenmayer, H. Interpretation of abstract conditional sentences in deductive reasoning. _Journal of Verbal Learning & Verbal Behavior,_ 1973, _12,_ 530–542.
Taplin, J. E., Staudenmayer, H., & Taddonio, J. L. Developmental changes in conditional reasoning: Linguistic or logical? _Journal of Experimental Child Psychology,_ 1974, _17,_ 360–373.
Wason, P. C., & Johnson-Laird, P. N. _Psychology of reasoning: Structure and content._ Cambridge, Mass.: Harvard University Press, 1972.
Wilkins, M. C. The effect of changed material on ability to do formal syllogistic reasoning. _Archives of Psychology,_ 1928, _16,_ No. 102.

38 Individual Differences in General Abilities Useful in Solving Problems

Jonathan Baron
Jennifer Freyd
Judith Stewart
University of Pennsylvania
Philadelphia, Pennsylvania
United States

ABSTRACT

We report some experiments designed to identify the components of general problem-solving ability, both capacities and strategies. The first experiment looked for group differences in a possible capacity, the ability to use weak retrieval cues of the sort provided by acrostic puzzles, an ability of general value in problem solving. Graduate students (good problem solvers, we assume) and a control group read words aloud and were then unexpectedly tested for memory of the words. The students were more able than the controls to use weak cues consisting of a few letters from each word but less able to recognize the words themselves. The group differences in recognition are ascribed to greater familiarity of all words to students. An attempt to equate effective frequency eliminated the group difference in recognition, a result suggesting that the groups do not differ in incidental-learning ability. The last two experiments look for group differences in strategies useful in discovery of rules or principles, such as spelling sound rules. Students are more likely to modify their own proposed rules on the basis of counterexamples and more likely to state principles spontaneously.

INTRODUCTION

Data from I.Q. tests (e.g., Thurstone, 1938) and other sources indicate that people who are good at solving one type of problem are generally good at solving other types of problems. These correlations have been ascribed to general intelligence. But to date, the concept *general intelligence* remains primarily a psychometric construct rather than a description of mental processes used more often or more quickly by good problem solvers than by less good problem solvers. The present chapter is a preliminary attempt to test some hypotheses about what these processes might be.

Following Baron (1978), we hypothesize that good problem solvers are characterized not only by less restrictive biological limits on information processing (capacities) but also by a greater probability of use of certain highly general strategies. Our strategy here is to seek direct measures of these strategies and capacities and then to look for differences between groups likely to differ in the abilities (strategies and capacities) in question. If the groups differ, we can conclude that there are individual differences in the abilities in question and that these abilities have something to do with the criteria by which the groups were selected (for whatever reason). (For example, motivational differences may be the cause of measured ability differences. If so, the differences are still of interest to the extent to which the same motivivations work outside the laboratory.) This research strategy, and its problems, are discussed further by Baron (1978) and Baron and Treiman (1980).

In the first experiment we report, we seek such group differences in the ability to retrieve information from memory using weak retrieval cues—quite possibly a capacity. We argue that this ability is crucial in problem solving of all sorts, from acrostic puzzles to philosophy. The next two experiments look for group differences in strategies useful in the discovery of general rules. The second experiment looks at the strategy of proposing a candidate rule, testing the rule by seeking examples and counterexamples, and modifying the rule when counterexamples are found. The third experiment examines a strategy somewhat more primitive than the second, the strategy of overtly stating (to one's self, at least) a principle, when solving a problem where a principle or rule needs to be found. (This strategy is part of the strategy examined by the second experiment.)

The subjects used in the present studies were drawn from two groups. One group consisted of graduate students in psychology, mathematics, and anthropology (one subject), at the University of Pennsylvania. These students were selected in part because they were good problem solvers, we assume, although many other criteria were surely involved. The control group consisted of people from a part-time employment service, matched roughly in age and sex to the students. All subjects were between 22 and 30 years of age. Three of the eight students and four of the nine controls were female. Some subjects were not used in some tasks, as we point out later. As a rough check on the validity of our selection with respect to differences in problem-solving abilities, each subject was given 10 problems from the Raven's Progressive Matrices. The students all solved at least 8 problems, and the controls at most

5 (except for one control subject who solved 8 of a different selection of problems used for this subject only).

EXPERIMENT 1:
INCIDENTAL LEARNING AND WEAK-CUE RETRIEVAL

The ability to use weak cues for retrieval seems to be an essential part of problem solving (Nickerson, 1977). When we do a crossword puzzle, we try to retrieve a word, given a couple of letters and some associate of the word (often not previously perceived as an associate). When solving a problem such as Duncker's (1945) tumor problem, we must retrieve ideas, such as the idea of rotation (of the source of rays) when cued only with the problem of focusing the rays on the tumor. (Often such ideas must be modified before they are applied, a fact that makes their retrieval even more mysterious.) In such problems as the Progressive Matrices, the items retrieved are often rather general ideas or "frames" such as the idea of addition or of rotation. For a more realistic example, one of the authors solved the problem of how to remove 10-year-old stickers from some recently opened wedding presents by first trying to think of an organic solvent in the house and then retrieving the memory that there was some charcoal lighter fluid in the back hall; the interesting fact here is that lighter fluid was (apparently) never before encoded as an organic solvent.

The present experiment is based on a type of problem in which weak-cue retrieval is introspectively prominent, the type of problem found in acrostic or crossword puzzles. In essence, we ask whether the students are better than the controls at solving problems of this sort in part because the students are better at retrieving words they know, given the weak cues provided by the puzzle. The main alternative hypothesis is that the students are better just because they know more words or because their memory traces for the words they know are stronger.

We first presented words to subjects in a way designed to equate (depth of) encoding as much as possible. The subjects were asked simply to read the words aloud five times, without being told that their memory for the words would be tested. We then tested recognition memory for the words by presenting (whole) words that either had been previously presented or had not. In addition to our presenting these strong retrieval cues (as Tulving, 1974, might call them), we also presented weak cues in the form of words with most of the letters replaced by dashes (e.g., C--------A as a cue for CALIFORNIA). Again, half of these cues were parts of previously presented words and half were not. Subjects were asked to decide whether a word fitting the frame had been presented and to guess what the word was, if possible, whether or not they thought it had been presented. Our main hypothesis is that the controls, relative to the students, will show a greater deficit in recognition of the weak cues than of the strong cues and a greater deficit in recall of the words than in strong-cue recognition.

One possible confounding variable in studies of group (including developmental) differences is effective familiarity with stimuli, which may affect performance (Baron & Treiman, 1980). A solution to this problem would be to use entirely novel material. But it is not clear what that would be, because all stimuli are somewhat similar to stimuli we have experienced, and prior experience might make the greatest difference when the similarity is low. In the present experiment, we measured the effect of familiarity on our tasks, by varying the frequency of the words presented, hoping that it would have equal effects on all major tasks. The words were separated into five lists, each list drawn from one-fifth of the frequency rank list of Carroll, Davies, and Richman (1971). As an additional measure of effective frequency for individual subjects, subjects were asked, at the end of the experiment, to indicate which presented words they did not know the meaning of. These words can be assumed to have the same effective frequency for all subjects.

In the recognition experiment, subjects were asked to give confidence ratings: one (very sure the word was presented), two (think it was), three (think it wasn't), or four (very sure it wasn't). Use of this measure with both strong and weak cues ensures that measures of performance will be based on the same response scale. (Tulving, 1974, and others who compare different kinds of retrieval cues by comparing recognition and recall, have not achieved this sort of comparability.)

The design also allows us to gather preliminary data relevant to other questions. First, we can ask whether our groups differ in learning ability. The groups did show large differences in an intentional learning task. However, such differences in intentional learning may be due to differences in the strategies used to encode the stimuli. It is thus of interest to examine incidental learning, where such encoding differences are minimized (as done by Cermak & Reale, 1978, for example, in a study of chronic alcoholics).

Second, we can ask whether the groups differed in reading speed, for we timed the list reading. Lists were read in order of decreasing frequency, five times through all lists. The words were all of three or more syllables, selected so as to be ambiguous in stress or pronunciation if read according to spelling-sound rules alone. Thus, initial reading time could be used as a rough measure of familiarity, whereas asymptotic reading time could be used to estimate a subject's reading speed.

In summary, each subject was asked to read five lists of 20 words each, in order of decreasing frequency, five times through the lists. Subjects were told that the task was a measure of reading speed. Then a few minutes were taken to explain the (unexpected) memory tests. In these tests, subjects were shown five lists of 40 words each, in order corresponding tot he original lists, with distractors from the same frequency range as the targets. Alternate words in each list had most letters replaced by dashes. The subject was to indicate confidence that each item (or a word containing the given letters, for weak-cue items) had been presented. The weak cues were chosen to be equally "good" across frequency classes (as is verified in the data). Finally, subjects indicated which words they did not know the meaning of. Three of nine control subjects could read so few of the words that the experiment was halted immediately. This left six controls and eight students.

Retrieval Results

The measure of retrieval was the point biserial correlation between the subject's confidence rating and whether the item was presented. This measure resembles d' in that it attempts to remove influences of response bias. However, because it approaches an asymptote of 1.0, as performance improves, it resembles *hits minus false alarms* in its scaling properties.

Figure 38.1 shows retrieval as a function of cue type, group, and word frequency. Lower frequency yields higher performance (as found in all previous studies we know); for each cue type there is a significant negative correlation ($p < .05$, 3 df) between frequency and performance. This effect, as measured by the slope of the best fitting line, was if anything greater for weak cues than for strong cues.

As hypothesized, the students were more accurate than the controls with the weak cues ($p < .025$). This is not due to stronger memories of the stimuli, it appears, because they were less accurate with the strong cues ($p < .025$, 1 tailed). Lower performance with strong cues would be expected if the familiarity of the words was greater for the students than the controls, for familiarity impairs recognition. (Possibly the students read the words more quickly and thus encoded them less strongly, however.) But the students' superior performance with the weak cues is great enough to overcome this deficit, even though frequency itself has a negative effect on weak-cue retrieval as well as strong-cue retrieval.

We can ask whether students were more able to fill in a word that had been presented, on the basis of a weak cue. The students filled in a mean of 14.0 words; the controls, a mean of 6.8 [omitting one control who filled in no items at all, $t(11) = 2.74$, $p < .01$]. Because this difference could result if the students were simply more likely to fill in words, regardless of whether a word had been presented, we counted the number of filled-in words that had not been presented and that had the correct number of letters. The students filled in a mean of 18.5 of these; the controls, a mean 8.8. This difference was not significant [$t(11) = 1.2$]. To ask whether there was an interaction between

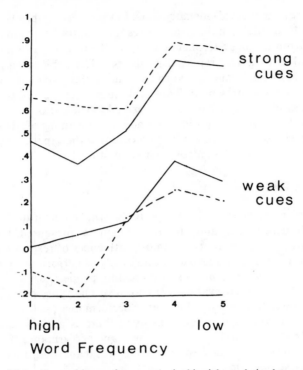

FIG. 38.1.   Recognition performance (point biserial correlation between whether the stimulus had been presented and the subject's confidence rating) as a
function of word frequency, for students (solid line) and controls (dashed line)
for the two cue types.

group and presented versus nonpresented in these scores, we computed the
correlation between group membership and each of the scores. (The scores
cannot be compared directly, because there is a greater opportunity to fill in a
nonpresented word—nonpresented words can be filled in for weak cues for
presented words.) The correlation between group membership and the number of presented words filled in (0.64) was in fact significantly higher [$t(10)$ =
2.10, $p < .05$] than the correlation for nonpresented words (0.31), given a
correlation of 0.77 between these two scores across all subjects. (This analysis
assumed that the nonpresented score is as reliable as the presented score, a
safe assumption given the greater range of the former.)

The result for filled-in words shows that the probability of filling in a word
is affected both by group membership and by whether the word had been
presented. This result rules out a simple explanation in terms of group
differences in motivation. It also rules out a model in which subjects generate
possible words, consistent with each weak cue, and then check each generated

word as if it were a strong-cue item. By this model, the students might perform better simply because they were better at generating possible words. But the group difference in filling in presented words is larger than that in filling in nonpresented words, so differences in the latter ability cannot account entirely for the former. (We assume that both groups followed the instructions to fill in even nonpresented words. In fact, this part of the task was emphasized to all subjects.) Note that in the model we just rejected the generation of words is unaffected (or equally affected for both groups) by whether the generated word had been presented. If we assume that the students were particularly prone to generate words that had been presented, the results are consistent with a less restrictive generate-and-test model.

As an additional check on the possibility that the group differences are due to differences in word knowledge, which would allow the students to generate more posssible words, a separate analysis was done of the recognition data for only the words each subject did not know the meaning of. Again, the students were more accurate with weak cues and less accurate with strong cues. Neither result was significant by itself, but the interaction between group and cue type was significant at the 0.025 level. (The measure of accuracy was the mean difference in ratings between each unknown presented word and the mean rating of all the unpresented words of the same cue type in the same list. The interaction was determined from the difference between dependent correlations between group and this measure for the two cue types. The relevant measures were: students—strong, 2.0; controls—strong, 2.5; students—weak, 0.8; controls—weak, 0.2.)

There are two possible artifactual explanations of our major results, one having to do with the quality of the weak cues as a function of frequency and the other with possible group differences in stimulus encoding. By the first account, the weak cues were more useful for low-frequency words than for high-frequency words (despite our efforts to prevent this); if the cues were equally useful, weak-cue recognition would actually be positively correlated with word frequency, and the group differences could then be explained in terms of differential effects of frequency on the two measures. To test this account, we defined cue effectiveness as the conditional probability of filling in the word from which each weak cue had been derived, given that a guess was made. For words that had not been presented, the cues were if anything more effective for the two higher-frequency lists (.52 and .42) than for the two lower-frequency lists (.36 and .31). This suggests that our efforts to make cues equally effective were successful. (Note that the words presented were chosen at random from the list of 40 test items for each list. Note also that although cues were apparently more effective for low-frequency presented words than for high-frequency presented words—.63 and .67 versus .84 and .79, respectively—this result simply reflects the negative effect of frequency on weak-cue recognition, as shown in Fig. 38.1.)

The second possible artifact is that the groups might have encoded words differently. For example, the students might have relied more heavily on phonetic representations, and this might have made the weak cues more effective for them. We cannot rule all hypotheses of this sort, and further tests of the generality of our findings are in order. However, a post hoc analysis suggests that the groups did not differ in semantic versus phonetic encoding. We selected five distractors that were semantically related to some presented item (e.g., government—Washington) and five that were phonetically (and possibly graphemically) related (e.g., experience—ebullience). Items in each of these sets were more likely to lead to false positive responses than were unrelated items ($p < 0.005$ for semantic, 0.05 for phonetic). The students falsely recognized 13 semantic distractors and 9 phonetic ones, and the controls falsely recognized 4 of each type. Thus, there is no evidence that the students were more prone to encode the words phonetically. Further evidence against the involvement of encoding differences is provided by the analysis of words that subjects did not know the meaning of, which could not, we assume, be encoded semantically very well. Recall that the major group differences were found for these items alone.

In sum, our results indicate a group difference in ability to retrieve with weak cues. This result is not due to differences in knowledge of words nor to differences in strength of encoding of words presented nor to other kinds of knowledge that might affect ability to generate words. The group difference is most easily ascribed to some more general ability. It is possible that the students are more prone to use a generate-and-test strategy, possibly because they are more motivated. It is also possible that the difference represents a less modifable capacity difference, possibly a capacity to retrieve with weak cues and possibly a more general capacity such as the amount of mental energy available. Further research must be directed at the generality of this sort of group difference, as well as its nature. (Note that even motivational differences are of interest if they are sufficiently general.)

Reading Times

An analysis of the reading times might serve two purposes. First, we might obtain a measure of asymptotic reading speed. Second, we might use times for first reading to estimate the familiarity of each list to each subject. By plotting strong-cue recognition accuracy against this measure, we can ask whether the groups differ in incidental learning, with word knowledge and encoding roughly equated.

We assumed, as a first approximation, that reading time approaches an asymptote by a constant proportion on each trial. This assumption yields an exponential practice curve, $R(i) = B[\exp(-Ci)] + A$, where $R(i)$ is the time for the ith trial, A is the asymptote, B represents the point at which practice

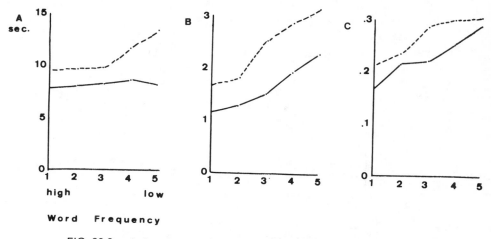

FIG. 38.2. *A, B,* and *C* parameters of the best-fitting exponential practice curve for students (solid line) and controls (dashed line).

started, and *C* represents the rate of improvement with practice. We use *B* as our estimate of list familiarity. *A, B,* and *C* were estimated for each list for each subject, using a program that minimized squared deviations of $\log[R(i)]$ from predicted values.

The mean parameter values for the two groups are shown in Fig. 38.2. The most encouraging result is that *A* is independent of frequency, as it should be, for the students and for all but the least frequent words (containing many unknown words) for the controls.

The group difference in *A* was significant ($p < 0.01$). [However, for the three highest-frequency classes, where *A* was unaffected by frequency, the difference was not quite significant: $t(12) = 1.75$.] Although there are many possible explanations of this result, it does suggest that it is possible to measure group differences in mental abilities in a way that removes confounding effects of familiarity with stimulus materials.

Figure 38.3 shows group means in strong-cue accuracy for each list as a function of $\ln(B)$. Arguably, the points lie along the same curve. If they really do, it would appear that there are no group differences in incidental learning when effective frequency (*B*) is held constant. We also found the best fitting line, for each subject, for strong-cue accuracy as a function of $\log(B)$. We then found the intercept of each line for $\log(B) = 2$, a point within the range of values for six subjects in each group. For these subjects, the strong-cue accuracy of the students was slightly lower than that of the controls. For all subjects, the accuracy at the intercept was nonsignificantly higher for the students [0.72 versus 0.69, $t(12) = 0.38$]. These results suggest that there are no differences in incidental learning between two rather extreme groups.

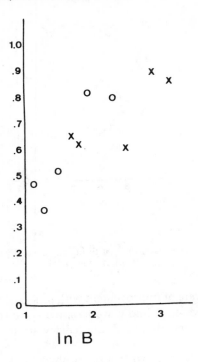

FIG. 38.3. Performance in recognition with strong cues (same measure as Fig. 1) as a function of the *B* parameter for the practice curves (used as a measure of familiarity). Each point represents a subject. The O's are students; the X's are controls.

Further evidence is needed, however, both on the generality of this result and on the validity of *B* as a measure of effective frequency.

EXPERIMENT 2: THE DISCOVERY OF RULES

In the next experiment, subjects were asked to discover spelling-sound correspondence rules. For example, they were asked to give a rule for when the letter *a* is pronounced as in *mate*. This task is similar to other members of a large class of problems that require the strategies of proposing principles or rules, testing the rules by trying to think of examples or counterexamples, and modifying the rules when the examples do not fit. Our task involves the sort of reasoning done in linguistics, which can serve as a model for scientific and philosophical reasoning in general. (For experimental purposes, linguistic tasks have the advantage that most speakers are familiar with the data to be accounted for by the rules sought.) The same kinds of strategies, involving formulation and tests of hypotheses, are undoubtedly useful in solving problems of other sorts, from debugging a computer program to buying a car.

The subjects used in Experiment 1 were used here as well. Three of the controls were eliminated because they did not know that spelling-sound rules existed. (They believed that they read by words or syllables only.) This left 8 students and 5 controls. The idea of rules was first explained to each subject, using the example of *r* (where the rule is very simple) and *g* (where the rule is complex). The rule for *g* as a function of the next letter and of position in the word was explained with examples. Subjects were asked to discover the conditions under which each letter was pronounced as in the following words: o—go, got; *i*—bit, bite; *a*—rat, rate; *t*—with, nation, native; *c*—cent, can't. Subjects were asked to talk aloud while working, and the experimenter asked questions freely, to elicit information about the strategies used. Subjects were told that the experimenter would help them think of examples if they asked. No subject gave a fully adequate rule for any item. But the purpose of the experiment was to assess strategies, and this assessment was easily made.

Written transcripts (and tapes when needed) of the interviews were scored for presence of certain strategies by Baron and Stewart. Seven of 13 were scored independently to check reliability, which was 84%. All disagreements were resolved by discussion, and the rest of the interviews were scored by both judges together.

The scoring categories used were the following:

Rule Statement.   A stated rule had to specify that a letter was pronounced in a certain way (in a context more general than one word) or that no rule was possible for choice between two pronunciations. Veracity was irrelevant.

No Hypothesis.   This represented absence of rule statement, for example, in cases in which a subject responded only by giving examples.

Rule Transfer.   A parallel between two rules (e.g., the three vowels, or *C* and *G*) was mentioned.

Example.   The subject gave an example before stating a rule (as if trying to use the example to arrive at a rule) or asked the experimenter for an example.

Confirming Example.   An example was given after a rule statement, the example obeying the rule stated. Confirming examples were scored + (plus) if the example met a condition specified by the rule. For example, "*C* is pronounced hard at the end of a word, like *TIC*." Confirming examples were scored − (minus) if the condition was not met and the pronunciation was not given (e.g., *lace* for the rule just given). Although + was used 27 times, −was used only once (by a student).

Disconfirming Example (Counterexample).   A counterexample can also be +; when the condition is met and the pronunciation is not given, or −, when the condition is not met and the pronunciation is given. For the final-*C* rule stated, *tick* is − and *bosc* is +. [Wason & Johnson-Laird, 1972, seem to use "confirming" to mean + (meeting the condition) and "disconfirming" to mean −. We find that our terms clarify their findings if not ours.] Positive counterexamples may be real exceptions, of course.

Unused Counterexample. A counterexample was given, either by the subject or the experimenter, but was not accounted for. If the subject said that something was an exception, we used this category only when the subject was blatantly wrong (to avoid the need to set a criterion for true exceptions).

Changed Rule. This category was used for changes in rules already stated (often to account for counterexamples) but not for new statements of disjunctive conditions for a certain pronunciation of a letter; a changed rule had to alter the pronunciation of some examples dealt with by the old rule.

Implicit Rule. This category was used when a stated rule contained a subcondition apparently designed to account for a small set of counterexamples. For example, a few subjects said that *th* is pronounced as in *with* except when the two letters are parts of different words, as in *pothole*. This kind of statement suggests that the subject had already thought of a counterexample and changed the rule to account for it.

Each category was coded at most once per letter (to avoid decisions about what was the same instance and to minimize effects of subject verbosity).

If students are better problem solvers, they ought to use optimal strategies more consistently. In particular, they ought to be more likely to use *changed rule* and *implicit rule* and less likely to use *unused counterexample*. Students were in fact more likely to change rules (1.9 out of 5 letters versus 1.0) and to give implicit rules (0.5 versus 0.0) and less likely to give unused counterexamples (0.5 versus 1.0). Other means are, for students and controls, respectively: rule statement, 4.0, 3.6; no hypothesis, 0.1, 0.6; rule transfer, 1.8, 0.8; example, 0.5, 0.2; confirming example, 1.9, 2.6; disconfirming example, 1.5, 1.6. Although significance tests are inappropriate for a study of this scope in which so many comparisons may be made, it does appear that the students were more likely to use strategies that a linguist should use. Whereas we would like to argue that the controls have a remediable deficiency in tendency to use optimal strategies, it is also possible that the controls were unable to think of rules to account for counterexamples even when they tried.

The following quotations illustrate the different styles of the two groups. The first is from a student; the second from a control:

1. *A* is generally long when it's by itself or when it comprises the initial syllable of a word. Is this true? Are there examples? Abate. No, forget that one. (Experimenter offers *appraise*.) Appraise, abate. No, it's short. Alphabet. No, *A*'s at the beginning of words generally seem to be short. (Coded as: rule statement, disconfirming example, changed rule.)

2. In *with* you don't have a *t* sound, you have a *t, h* sound. So really the *t* is not heard. . . . In *nation* you don't hear the *t* also. You hear an *s, h* sound. . . . In *native* you do hear the *t*. . . . Don't know why you do hear the *t* . . . (Experimenter: Why don't you hear it in *nation?*) Well, *tion* is a sound by itself. (Coded as: rule statement.)

Another finding of possible interest is that five of the eight students and none of the controls dealt with the three vowels as examples of a single general rule. This might indicate a greater tendency to try to generalize rules, a useful strategy not included in our scoring.

In sum, these preliminary results show that strategies for rule abstraction can be studied in a naturalistic (for academics) task. They suggest that groups differ in the tendency to use optimal strategies. Whether these tendencies are easily modifed is best determined by studies of training and transfer.

EXPERIMENT 3: STATEMENTS OF PRINCIPLES IN EVERYDAY PROBLEMS

The discovery of spelling-sound rules *requires* that the subjects state principles, so the data did not allow us to discover group differences in the tendency to state principles spontaneously. Spontaneous statements of principle (if only to one's self) may aid in the recognition of problems, in the discovery of general rules and, more generally, in the discovery of order in the world (Baron, 1978). In the present experiment, we look for group differences in the tendency to state principles in an open-ended interview. Subjects were asked questions about familiar topics, picked so that appropriate answers might or might not include principles: (1) what factors determine how fast a hot liquid will cool? For example, if you make some hot soup, what kind of things could you do to make it cool faster? (2) How could you compare foods to find out if you are getting the most nutritional value for the money? What do you have to consider? (3) When it is right or wrong to say something false about yourself? Suppose an adolescent asked you this. What would you say?

Subjects were encouraged to introspect and to say all they had to say about each problem. The experimenter frequently asked what the subjects were thinking, during silences, or what the reasoning had been behind an unclear statement.

After the subject answered the questions, the experimenter asked the subject to go through the problems again and to state a rule or principle for each problem. The questions were restated one by one for this purpose (e.g., can you state a general principle that accounts for the rate of cooling?). Subjects were told that they could give a number of rules instead of a single rule and that they could say they had already stated a principle in the first part instead of repeating it. Subjects seemed to understand these instructions, as every subject succeeded in giving at least one rule in this part, and most recognized when they had already stated a rule in the first part. The purpose of this second part was to find out whether any failure to give a rule in the first part was due to inability to arrive at a rule or to failure to make the attempt to do so. The latter possibility is implied by the claim that principle statement is a general strategy used more frequently by good problem solvers. Thus, we hypothesize that students will be less likely than controls to state principles only when asked to do so.

As judged by the experimenter (on the basis of notes and, when needed, tapes), five students states rules for all three problems in both parts and three stated rules for two problems, again in both parts. Thus, no student stated a rule only in the second part. Five of the seven controls, however, stated rules in the second part but not the first for at least one problem. The difference between groups (five out of seven versus zero out of three, three being those students not at ceiling on the first part) is significant ($p < 0.05$) by Fisher's exact test. Thus, it does seem that students are more prone to state rules (at least overtly) in situations in which rules are not explicitly required.

Other findings of possible interest are: (1) Six of the eight students as opposed to two of the controls changed the statement of a rule at least once (and two students did this twice). Although this difference is not significant, it is consistent with the findings of the last experiment, where students were more prone to try to improve their own rules. (2) Five of the eight students and one of the controls mentioned the impossibility of solving the second (food) problem (a problem formulated poorly with the intention of eliciting this strategy). Although not significant, this result suggests that students are more prone to use the strategy of converting an apparently impossible problem into a manageable one.

SUMMARY AND CONCLUSIONS

In the first experiment, we found that students were less able than controls to recognize words when given strong cues consisting of the words themselves but more able to recognize words with weak cues. The controls seem to have a differential deficit in retrieval with at least the sort of weak cue we used, whatever the ultimate source of this deficit. This experiment also suggested that the groups differ in reading speed, with the effects of word familiarity removed. Finally, the groups do not seem to differ in incidental learning (tested with strong-cue recognition), where group differences in encoding strategies are minimized. In looking for this difference, we attempted to remove the effects of effective frequency of the stimuli for each subject. Because our groups do differe dramatically in an (unreported) paired-associate learning task, this result suggests that individual differences in learning ability may be due largely to encoding strategies (and retrieval abilities).

The second and third experiments sought group differences in strategies useful at least in problems involving the discovery of rules or principles. Such strategies might be sufficiently general in their usefulness to constitute part of general intelligence in the sense discussed by Baron (1978). In the second experiment, subjects were asked to discover spelling-sound rules. Students were more prone to try to improve their initial statements of rules by thinking of counterexamples and then changing their rules to account for the counterexamples. In the third experiment, students were more likely to state principles spontaneously in response to open-ended questions that did not call for such statements. Controls were, however, able to state principles when asked— a result suggesting that principle statement is a teachable strategy (Baron, 1978).

The last two experiments are properly conceived as exploratory studies, because we have not tried to rule out the sorts of familiarity artifacts addressed in the first experiment. Further, these apparent strategy differences may be entirely the result of less modifiable capacity dfferences, such as available mental energy or weak-cue retrieval ability (if that is not itself the result of a strategy). The most optimistic interpretation of these results is that they represent differences in the probability of use of general strategies and that these differences result from differences in education (broadly or narrowly conceived). If so, it ought to be possible to improve people's problem-solving abilities through education.

ACKNOWLEDGMENTS

The work was supported by N.I.H. Grant MH 29453 (Baron, principal investigator). We thank D. G. Kemler for helpful discussion.

REFERENCES

Baron, J. Intelligence and general strategies. In G. Underwood (Ed.), *Strategies in information processing*. London: Academic Press, 1978.

Baron, J., & Treiman, R. Some problems in the study of differences in cognitive processes. *Memory and Cognition,* 1980, in press.

Carroll, J. B., Davies, P., & Richman, B. *American heritage word frequency book*. New York: American Heritage, 1971.

Cermak, L. S., & Reale, L. Depth of processing and retention of words by alcoholic Korsakoff patients. *Journal of Experimental Psychology: Human Learning and Memory,* 1978, *4*, 165–174.

Duncker, K. On problem solving. *Psychological Monographs,* 1945, *58,* Whole No. 270.

Nickerson, R. Crossword puzzles and lexical memory. In S. Dornic (Ed.), *Attention and performance VI.* Hillsdale, N.J.: Lawrence Erlbaum Associates, 1977.

Thurstone, L. L. *Primary mental abilities.* Chicago: University of Chicago Press, 1938.

Tulving, E. Cue-dependent forgetting. *American Scientist,* 1974, *62,* 74–82.

Wason, P. C., & Johnson-Laird, P. N. *Psychology of reasoning: Structure and content.* Cambridge: Harvard University Press, 1972.

39 A Little Learning...: Confidence in Multicue Judgment Tasks

Baruch Fischhoff
Paul Slovic
Decision Research
A Branch of Perceptronics
Eugene, Oregon
United States

The human understanding is of its own nature prone to suppose the existence of more order and regularity in the world than it finds. And though there be many things in nature which are singular and unmatched, yet it devises for them parallels and conjugates and relatives which do not exist.

Francis Bacon

ABSTRACT

A variety of discrimination tasks using complex, multifaceted stimuli were presented to subjects either with or without the opportunity to study a number of labeled examples. These tasks included deciding whether handwriting samples were produced by an American or a European, whether an ulcer was benign or malignant, and which of three horses was a winner of a race at Aqueduct in 1969. Complex stimuli were chosen so that there would be a high probability that in the labeled study examples diligent subjects could find some cue(s) highly correlated with the labels. Such capitalization on chance correlations has often been cited as a source of scientists' unwarranted confidence in their theories. As anticipated, subjects who studied labeled examples were consistently overconfident. However, subjects who studied unlabeled examples or no examples at all were equally overconfident. Some reasons for the independence of confidence from immediate experience are discussed.

INTRODUCTION

Many tasks we face in life may be described as multicue discriminations. Using information from a number of variables, we make judgments such as adequate–inadequate, malignant–benign, fast–slow, or Democratic–Republican. What determines our confidence in our ability to make a particular kind of discrimination? One important cue is likely to be how well we seem to have been able to make such discriminations in the past. How well do we ascertain that ability? We should have the most realistic appraisal when we have gone through a concentrated series of trials in each of which we first make the required discrimination and then receive accurate outcome feedback, perhaps with instruction in why we did well or poorly (Hammond & Summers, 1972).

Such ideal conditions are, in most people's lives, quite rare. Typically, trials are so spread out that it is difficult to extract general discriminatory principles; feedback is ambiguous or so long in coming that we cannot remember exactly what our judgment was or how we made it; no one is around to instruct us; and so on. The opportunities for extracting the wrong amount of confidence, either too much or too little, are enormous.

One seemingly minor deviation from these ideal conditions is having concentrated trials with stimuli and correct classifications presented simultaneously. For example, we might be presented a set of clinical profiles labeled *neurotic* or *psychotic* or race horses labeled *won* or *lost* or stocks labeled *rose* or *fell*. We are to study these sets in order to determine how differently labeled cases differ and to assess our ability to make that discrimination when faced in the future with unlabeled cases.

The present experiments examine the appropriateness of assessments of discriminatory ability derived under such conditions. All subjects received sets of learning trials in which experience was concentrated and stimuli were presented in a clear, common format. For some subjects, the study stimuli were labeled (e.g., malignant or benign); for others, they were unlabeled. At first glance, it might seem as though subjects receiving labeled stimuli would be in the best position to appraise their discriminatory ability. We predicted, however, that provision of labels would mislead and produce unwarranted confidence in one's judgments.

At least three lines of evidence pointed in this direction. Fischhoff (1975, 1977) has found that when people are told the outcomes to historical events, they exaggerate the likelihood that they would have been able to predict those outcomes had they not been told; when told the answers to general knowledge questions, they exaggerate how much they knew before being told. In a discrimination task, such a "knew-it-all-along" effect would lead people who have seen labeled trials to believe that they would have made more correct discriminations than would have been the case. It might also lead them to overestimate their ability to make such discriminations in the future.

The second line of evidence is anecdotal and may be found in methodological discussions of "correlational overkill" (Kunce, Cook, & Miller, 1975) or the "degrees of freedom" problem (Campbell, 1975). Given a set of labeled cases and a sufficiently large set of characterizing attributes, one can always devise a rule predicting the labels from the attributes to any desired level of proficiency. In regression terms, by expanding the set of independent variables one can always find a set of predictors (or even one predictor) with any desired correlation with the independent variable. The price one pays for overfitting is, of course, shrinkage, failure of the predictive (or discrimatory) rule to "work" on a new sample of cases. The frequency and vehemence of the methodological warnings suggest that correlational overkill is a bias that is quite resistant to even extended professional training (Armstrong, 1975; Crask & Perreault, 1977; Hamner, 1975; Lewis-Beck, 1978).[1] Overconfidence in future discrimination tasks would arise if judges did not realize the extent to which they may have capitalized on chance when explaining the labels in the study sample.

Third, the opportunity to study labeled examples may lead to overconfidence in one's ability to make future discriminations by enhancing an illusion of control. Langer (1975, 1977) argued that people overestimate their future success at tasks perceived to be dependent on skill (rather than luck). Furthermore, they tend to see an element of skill in situations that are governed by chance. Studying labeled examples might be expected to evoke undue feelings of skill (and control).

In order to see whether provision of labels with study examples induces overconfidence, we used a relatively small number of study examples (10–12), each of which was characterized by many attributes. Subjects' task was always to make a dichotomous discrimination on a subsequent set of unlabeled examples and indicate the probability of their choice being correct. The tasks were designed to appear difficult but to be impossible.

EXPERIMENT 1—HANDWRITING ANALYSIS

The task in Experiment 1 involved categorizing short handwriting samples as being written by either a European or an American. We predicted that allowing people to study a number of correctly labeled samples would in-

---

[1]O'Leary, Coplin, Shapiro, and Dean (1974), in a study of the explanatory protocols used by U. S. Department of State foreign affairs analysts, found that analysts relied on mulitvariate, explanatory models using discrete variables with nonlinear, time-lagged relationships between them. They observed that "the kinds of relationships found in the majority of [State Department] analyses represent such complexity that no single quantitative work in the social sciences could even begin to test their validity [p. 228]."

crease their confidence in being able to make future discriminations without actually improving their ability. Control groups studying the same samples without labels should be equally proficient but less confident.

Method

Design. In Part I, every subject studied 10 handwriting specimens, 5 written by Americans and 5 by Europeans, for a period of 5 minutes. For the *labels* group, these specimens were labeled according to continent of origin. For the *no-labels* groups, the specimens were unlabeled. In Part II, all subjects were given 10 additional specimens. For each, they were asked to make a best guess at the country of origin and to assess the probability that their guess was correct, using a probability from .50 to 1.00.

Stimuli. The 20 specimens used (10 European and 10 American) were selected from a set of 100 (50 European) collected by Dr. Lewis Goldberg in Eugene, Oregon, and in The Netherlands. The criterion for inclusion was being correctly identified by between 40 and 60% of a sample of 20 student subjects in Eugene (mean percent correct = 52.3%). We believed that discrimination was impossible for these specimens and unlikely to improve with the minimal opportunity for learning offered the labels group. In Part I 10 specimens were studied; in Part II 10 different specimens were judged. The 20 specimens were randomly sorted eight times into two sets of 10 (5 European, 5 American) for judgment by different subjects.

Instructions. In Part II, after choosing the appropriate continent, subjects were told to:

> Decide what the probability is that your answer is correct. This probability can be any number from .5 to 1.0. It can be interpreted as your degree of certainty about the correctness of your answer. For example, if you respond that the probability is .6, it means that you believe that there are about 6 chances out of 10 that your answer is correct. A response of 1.0 means that you are absolutely certain that your answer is correct. A response of .5 means that your best guess is as likely to be right as wrong. Don't estimate any probability below .5, because you should always be picking the alternative that you think is more likely to be correct. Write your probability on the space provided on the answer sheet.
> To repeat, this probability is a measure of your degree of certainty that your chosen alternative is the correct alternative. It is a number from .5 to 1.0 where .5 means complete uncertainty and 1.0 means complete certainty.

Subjects. A total of 52 paid subjects were recruited through an advertisement in the University of Oregon student paper. They were assigned to the two groups according to their preference for the time at which the groups were scheduled. Subjects in subsequent experiments were recruited and assigned in the same way.

Results and Discussion

Table 39.1 presents the mean percent correct and mean probability judgment for subjects in each group. Subjects who saw the labels in Part I were more confident than subjects who did not (mean probability of .745 versus .645). Unfortunately for the evaluation of our hypothesis, this increased confidence was highly justified. The minimal learning opportunity they received enabled labels subjects to identify correctly three-quarters of the test specimens. Subjects without that little learning did little better than chance (53% correct) in Part II.

If subjects use the probability scale correctly (i.e., if they are "perfectly calibrated," see Lichtenstein & Fischhoff, 1977, or Lichtenstein, Fischhoff, & Phillips, 1977), then their mean probability judgment should equal their percentage correct. By this criterion, the level of confidence of subjects in the labels condition was much more appropriate to their abilities than was that of the no-labels condition, which showed considerable overconfidence. Thus, the labels group both knew more and had a better appreciation of how much they knew. This result fits a pattern reported by Lichtenstein and Fischhoff (1977) who found that the appropriateness of probability responses increases as percent correct increases from 50% to about 75% (above which it decreases).

The inappropriateness of no-labels subjects' confidence judgments is even more apparent when one looks at the percentages of correct answers associated wtih different probability responses. There was, in fact, no systematic relation between probability judgment and percent correct. Subjects were correct about 50% of the time regardless of whether they said .5, .7 or 1.0.[2]

EXPERIMENT 2—ULCERS

Clearly, Experiment 1 did not provide an adequate test of the hypothesis that a worthless opportunity to learn an impossible task will lead people to be overconfident. The opportunity provided to labels subjects in Part I of Experiment 1 was much more useful than we imagined it would be.

Experiment 2 was designed to provide subjects with a completely unfamiliar and unlearnable task, diagnosing ulcers as malignant or benign on the basis of a smaller number of diagnostic signs. Cases were drawn from a

---

[2]These data are presented in detail in Fig. 3 of Lichtenstein and Fischhoff (1977). Similar independence of confidence and correctness was observed with other instances of overconfidence described below, although the details are omitted for lack of space.

TABLE 39.1

Performance (Percentage Correct) and Confidence (Mean Probability) in Part II

Experiment		Labels				No-Labels			
No.	Name	% Correct	Mean Probab.	Over/Under Confidence[a]	N	% Correct	Mean Probab.	Over/Under Confidence[a]	N
1	Handwriting	77.0	.745	-.025	22	53.3	.645	.112	30
2	Ulcers	76.3	.702	-.061	33	58.5	.599	.014	38
3	Stocks	49.3	.643	.150	38	44.0	.671	.231	25
4	Horse racing	41.5	.603	.188	46	39.1	.651	.260	42
5	Children's drawings	54.1	.667	.126	47	52.3	.677	.154	45
6	Children's drawings (discouraging instructions)	57.7	.631	.054	40	45.6	.627	.171	36

[a]Equals difference between mean probability and proportion correct. Negative sign indicates underconfidence.

study by Slovic, Rorer, and Hoffman (1971), which discovered, among other things, substantial disagreement among the expert radiologists who served as subjects.

The seven diagnostic signs were the size of the ulcer (larger or smaller than 2 cm), its location (on or off the greater curvature), and the presence or absence of "extraluminality," "associated filling defect," "a regular contour," "a rugal pattern (i.e., radiating folds)" and "associated duodenal ulcer." No further explication of these signs was provided. Subjects saw eight examples in each of Part I and Part II. Those seen in Part I either were labeled benign or malignant or were unlabeled. A total of 16 cases was used, divided into two sets each of which appeared in Part I for half the subjects. These were not actual cases, but artificial ones originally designed to be believable to a practicing radiologist. They did, however, have signs that in reality point overwhelmingly toward one diagnosis (that used as the label).

Results

Much to our surprise (and chagrin), the pattern of Experiment 1 was repeated. As shown in Table 39.1, subjects who saw eight labeled cases learned enough from them to make 76.3% correct discriminations in Part II, many more than the no-labels group (58.5%). Their confidence was also higher but with considerable justification. Again, subjects' learning ability thwarted our test of the hypothesis.

EXPERIMENT 3—STOCKS

Experiment 3 replicated Experiments 1 and 2 with a task chosen to be truly impossible: predicting whether each of 12 common stocks had increased or decreased in price over the period from Februrary 14, 1975, to March 19, 1975. The basis of these predictions was the stock market price and volume charts produced by Standard and Poor's Trendline division for the period July 12, 1974 to February 14, 1975. Subjects first learned how to read the major features of such charts and then in Part I were allowed to study four charts of stocks, two of which had increased and two of which had decreased over the period. The labels group was told how these four stocks had performed; the no-labels group was not.

We had no reason to believe that this rudimentary training would enable people to predict market fluctuations (we would be in the wrong business if it did). Performance charts also appeared to be an attractive stimulus because many investors seem to stay in the market only because of their ability to create an illusion of explicability. Indeed, their explanatory processes seem to exemplify those described in our hypothesis. Analysts draw upon an enor-

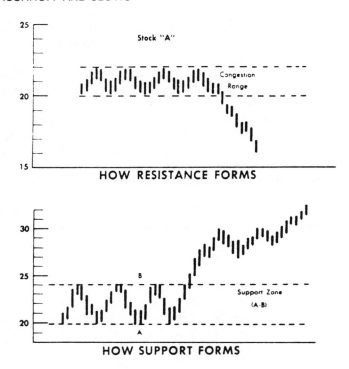

FIG. 39.1.   Ambiguity in diagnostic signs (Source: Jiler, 1962).

mous set of explanatory variables.[3] Not only is this set large enough to fit virtually any data, with a little ingenuity, but it contains contradictory explanatory rules. For example, if the market rises following good economic news, it is said to be responding to the news; if it falls, that is explained by saying that the good news had already been discounted. Figure 39.1 shows how two contradictory rules can be used, in hindsight, to show how a nondescript undulation in price foretold a subsequent increase or decrease in price (continued undulation, presumably, could be accounted for by a third rule).[4]

Whereas Fama (1965) has forcefully argued that market fluctuations are best understood as reflecting a random walk process, analysts' propensity for

[3]One of the authors once took a course in reading stock charts from a local broker. Each session involved the teaching of 10-12 new cues. When the course ended, 8 sessions and 83 cues later, the instructor was far from exhausting his supply.

[4]Exploitation of the ambiguity of such signs to make contradictory forecasts may be seen in the following quote from *Business Week*. "[A well-known economist] translates these pressures into an inflation rate of 8% to 9% by the final quarter of this year. And those numbers are springs on a bear trap, unless Wall Street has once again decided that inflation is good for stock prices [May 8, 1978, p. 28]."

overexplaining is such that they seem to deny any random component in stock prices. Perhaps the best evidence of this is their reliance on the ultimate fudge factor for explaining random variations, the "technical adjustment."

Method

Four alternative sets of stimuli were created in the following manner: All 618 stocks appearing in *Trendline* for February 14, 1975, were sorted into those that were at least one point ($1) higher on March 19, 1975, those that were at least a point lower on March 19, and those that were relatively unchanged. For each of the four sets, two stocks showing increases were chosen at random to serve as study stimuli (Part I) and six more were chosen as test stimuli (Part II); two and six stocks showing decreases were also chosen. A typical stimulus is shown in Fig. 39.2

A half-hour explanation of how to read the *Trendline* charts was presented to the subjects. Questions were encouraged and answered to the group as a whole before proceeding to Parts I and II, which were analogous to the

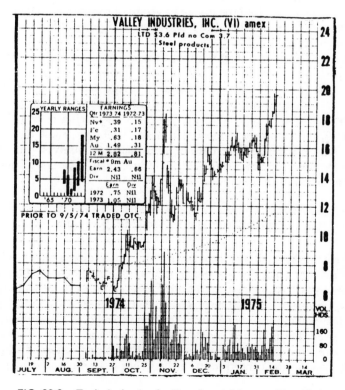

FIG. 39.2.   Typical stimulus for Experiment 3 (source: Trendline)

comparable sections of Experiment 1. A post-experiment questionnaire asked subjects about the strategies they had used.

Results

As hoped, labels subjects were unable to learn how to make the required discrimination. On Part II, they got only 49.3% correct. As predicted, they were substantially overconfident (mean probability = .643). Unfortunately for the hypothesis, no-labels subjects were just as confident (mean probability = .671) and, if anything, even more overconfident without the "benefit" of labeled charts in Part I.

Discussion

The most dramatic result of Experiment 3 was the gross overconfidence of the no-labels subjects. Apparently, with only a brief explanation of how to read charts, these people believed that they were able to predict the direction of price movement for a variety of stocks. Given this initial overconfidence (which also characterized the no-labels group of Experiment 1), our manipulation would have had to have been extremely powerful to have had any appreciable effect.

In the post-experiment questionnaires, subjects in both groups reported basing their predictions on fairly elaborate rules, some drawn from their own intuitive theories of finance and others derived from study of the charts themselves. At least some of them explicitly generated their own labeled study trials by attempting to predict the February 14 closing price from that of January 9, the February 13 closing from that of January 8, and so on. Given the amount of training information in the charts themselves, providing four March 19 closing prices to the labels group, may have constituted a very minor addition.

EXPERIMENT 4—HORSE RACING

The stock market task failed to test the "illusion of discriminability" hypothesis for two reasons: (1) no-labels subjects' undue confidence in their ability to perform an impossible task; and (2) the labels implicit in the stimuli given to no-labels subjects. Experiment 4 used a task chosen to avoid these two problems: picking the winner from the first three horses in parimutuel races. We believed that no-labels subjects would see this as a task with a very large luck and a very small skill component, whereas possession of labels would lead subjects in the other group to the hypothesized overconfidence.

Europe   **Asia**

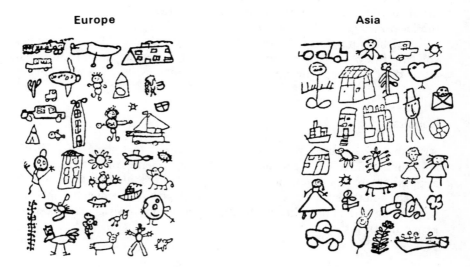

FIG. 39.3. Unlabeled (top) and labeled (bottom) study examples for Experiments 5 and 6 (source: Kellogg, 1970).

discriminations. Indeed, looking over the right-hand columns of Table 39.1, it appears that no-labels subjects gave a mean probability response of about .65 regardless of the task and their ability to perform it.

Before concluding that this "65" rule is a cultural universal, it is worth considering the possibility that this overconfidence was induced, at least in part, by the instructions or experimental setting. In Experiments 1–5, care was taken to avoid any intimation that the task was possible so that the instructions would not be blamed for the anticipated overconfidence of labels subjects. Nonetheless, perhaps people believe that any task set before them in an experiment must be possible. Experiment 6 was designed to reduce this possibility through the use of instructions stating explicitly that the children's drawings task might be impossible.

EXPERIMENT 6—DISCOURAGING INSTRUCTIONS

Method

The instructions used in Experiment 5 were prefaced with "Many people have claimed that the art of small children is the same in all cultural settings; others disagree." A final sentence was added stating that "All drawings were taken from the Child Art Collection of Dr. Rhoda Kellogg, a leading proponent of the theory that children from different countries and cultures make very similar drawings." To the Part II instructions was appended "Remember, it may well be impossible to make this sort of discrimination. Try to do the best you can. But if, in the extreme, you feel totally uncertain about the origin of all of these drawings, do not hesitate to respond with .5 for every one of them."

Results

As Table 39.1 shows, the change in instructions had some effect in the appropriate direction, reducing the mean confidence of both groups by approximately .05. Both, however, were still overconfident. Only 6 of 76 subjects (4 in the labels group, 2 in the no-labels group) accepted the option of responding with .5 to all items (about the same proportion as in the previous experiment).

EXPERIMENT 7—BELLWETHER PRECINCTS

So far, we've learned more about the dangers of no learning than about the dangers of a little learning. Before abandoning our hypothesis, we reviewed the tasks we had used to see whether, for all their variety, they might have shared some feature that kept labels subjects from capitalizing on chance correlations between independent variables and the dependent variable. One such common feature is the fact that the stimuli in all tasks were arranged by cases rather than by variables. To see if, for example, "number of days since last race" was a valid predictor of winning horse, a subject would have to flip through 10 pages of races and keep a running tally of the correlation between that predictor (number of days) and the criterion. Keeping track of 26 such correlations and their relative strengths may have confused labels subjects and reduced confidence. What would happen if our stimuli were organized by variables rather than cases or equally organized by both criteria?

Because none of our existing tasks lent themselves to such reorganization, we devised a new task allowing the stimuli to be organized either by cases or by predictors. In it, subjects were presented with fictitious voting records for a number of precincts (4 or 8) over a number of elections (8 or 20) for one office. For each election and precinct, subjects were told which of the two parties running (D or R) was favored and by how much. Their task after studying the records was to predict the winning party in the next election on the basis of a preelection poll of the precincts. The additional information given to labels subjects was who won each of the 8 or 20 study elections. In this task the precincts are potential predictors and the election results are the criterion. Both the past election and preelection poll results were generated randomly, so that there would, in fact, be no useful information for subjects to discern.

Method

Party preferences were generated using random normal deviates with a mean of 50 and a standard deviation of 12. The resulting numbers were treated as the percentage of voters favoring party D in each election. Numbers greater than 90 were treated as 90; those less than 10 were treated as 10. The results were presented in the form "party of preference, margin of victory." For example, a randomly generated number of 68 was interpreted as a vote of 68% D–32% R; it was presented to subjects as D-36 (= 68 – 32). The election results were also generated randomly, with equal likelihood for both parties. All the election results were presented on one page of computer printout in one large matrix (see Fig. 39.4). Election results (for labels subjects) appeared in separate lines above and below the matrix. Different sujects received different, independently generated matrices. Labels and no-labels subjects were yoked, each receiving the same matrix with preelection poll results. However, only labels subjects saw the election results. Three matrix sizes were used: (1) 8 elections and 20 precincts; (2) 4 elections and 20 precincts; and (3) 4 elections and 8 precincts.

After studying the election history matrix, subjects were presented preelection poll results for that next election and were asked to: (1) predict the winner of that election; and (2) indicate their confidence in having picked the winner. Confidence was elicited in odds rather than probabilities. In other experiments (Fischhoff, Slovic, & Lichtenstein, 1977), we had found that odds judgments are less likely than probability judgments to be rounded to a few stereotypic responses (.50, .60, .70, etc.). We hoped that using odds would provide greater sensitivity.

SUBJECT #2

```
                    E L E C T I O N

                    1        2        3        4
        Winner      D        D        R        R
```

Precinct #

1	R 37	R 13	R 5	D 3
2	R 23	R 41	R 12	R 27
3	D 12	R 59	D 15	D 38
4	D 1	R 2	R 14	R 39
5	R 13	R 17	D 12	D 4
6	R 6	D 13	R 41	R 17
7	R 27	D 8	R 23	D 29
8	R 14	R 23	D 25	R 43

FIG. 39.4. Typical study example for Experiment 7.

Results and Discussion

As Table 39.3 shows, there was no consistent pattern of results. For the [8 elections, 20 precincts] condition, the labels group gave greater median odds that their predictions were correct; for the 4 × 8 condition, they gave smaller median odds; for the 4 × 20 condition, the median odds for the groups were about equal. None of these differences was statistically significant (median

TABLE 39.3
Bellwether Precincts—Experiment 7 Median Odds of Being Correct

No. of elections	4	4	8
No. of precincts	8	20	20
No-labels group	5	2.5	2
	(56)	(28)	(35)
Labels group	2	2	3
	(59)	(33)	(38)

Note: Number of subjects appears in parentheses.

test; alpha = .05). Analyses done in terms of yoked labels and no-labels subjects (who saw the same randomly generated matrix and election poll results) also showed no consistent differences.[5] Of course, all of these medians were well above the chance response of 1:1 appropriate for an impossible task.

What went wrong this time? The most parsimonious explanation (in light of the earlier results) is that the labels manipulation paled before the confidence all subjects felt as soon as they were confronted with the task. To complicate matters, at least one quarter of the no-labels subjects created their own labels by totaling the results in the precincts presented on the study elections and treating those as total election results. In addition, a portion of subjects apparently found the task of poring over a large matrix of numbers quite frustrating and "gave up."

EXPERIMENT 8—AMOUNT OF STUDY

Two aspects of these results need explaining: (1) Why are no-labels subjects so confident? (2) Why doesn't the addition of labels induce even more confidence?

People's overconfidence in their general knowledge and intellectual ability is apparently a widespread and robust tendency (Fischhoff, Slovic, & Lichtenstein, 1977; Slovic, Fischhoff, & Lichtenstein, 1977, pp. 5–6, 14–17). When called upon to answer a particular question, people seem unaware of the tenuousness of their reasoning and assumptions or of the contrary evidence they have overlooked. When confronted with a series of similar tasks, many people may also generate an inappropriate global feeling of confidence: "Here's a task I can handle." This feeling may come from personal experience with a related task ("I've done quite a bit of handwriting analysis in the past") or from a culturally shared belief that the task (any task?) is tractable given the proper information (e.g., "One can win at the races with proper research" or "There are bellwether precincts to be found if one looks hard enough"). Although we tried not to encourage such expectations (especially in Experiment 6), nothing short of telling subjects that the task is impossible may be adequate.

One reason why the addition of labeled feedback may not augment this overconfidence is the fairly large number of study trials with which subjects were confronted. Finding one cue or a combination of cues that discriminate

---

[5]Not only are these results disappointing, the weak interaction exhibited in Table 39.3 actually goes somewhat in the opposite direction from what one might expect. Reducing the number of elections from 8 to 4 (while holding the number of precincts constant at 20) increases the probability of there being at least one bellwether precinct (predicting the results of all elections correctly) from .07 to .33. In addition, reducing the numer of elections made the whole task considerably easier, increasing labels subjects' chances of finding a bellwether precinct if one were present. Nonetheless, labels subjects were somewhat less confident in the 4 × 20 condition than in the 8 × 20 condition.

the two sets of stimuli for each of 10 to 12 trials may not be easy. Depending on how quickly they complete the search, subjects might realize the element of luck in their success or, more likely, just feel that the task was harder than it looked. For example, they may discover that cues that a priori they would have expected to discriminate do not. The reduction in confidence arising from discovering such difficulties may cancel the increase in confidence arising from discovery of a rule. Experiment 8 attempted to eliminate this possibility by severely reducing the number of study trials, which should increase the likelihood that some cues will be perfectly consistent discriminators.

In both Experiment 3 (stocks) and Experiment 7 (bellwether precincts), some subjects in the no-labels groups, quite obviously and ingeniously, produced their own labels. We suspect that some form of self-generated feedback may be quite common. For example, no-labels subjects might decide that some handwriting samples look American whereas others look European and then set out to figure out why. In doing so, they may not only be converting their task to that of labels subjects but doing so in a way that makes finding a good discriminatory rule quite easy: For one, they may be considering a reduced set of trial samples (those that appear clear-cut examples of one category or the other). In addition, their validation process may be circular. They may start out with one or several cues that seem a priori to be valid, use them to pick clear-cut cases, and then validate the cues by how well they work on the selected cases. In such a situation, a cue seems valid if it can be applied. Eliminating such self-generated cue validation would seem to be quite difficult. Experiment 8 tries to do so by eliminating the study session entirely. No-labels subjects went directly to the test examples of Part II.

Method

Two new versions were created for four of the tasks used in previous experiments. One version contained a minimal number of labeled study examples; the other contained no study section at all. The test examples of these tasks were identical to those used earlier. The tasks used were handwriting (Experiment 1), ulcers (Experiment 2), horse racing (Experiment 4), and children's drawings (discouraging instructions version—Experiment 6). Stocks and bellwether precincts were not used again because of the implicit feedback that was noted and exploited by some subjects. Handwriting and ulcers were used with some trepidation because the labels subjects in Experiments 1 and 2 were able to improve their performance on the basis of what they learned in the study section. We hoped that the abbreviated study session given the present labels group would not provide such an opportunity for learning.

The abbreviated study sessions (Part I) presented to labels subjects included one European and one American handwriting sample, one benign and one malignant ulcer, two horse races, and five European and five Asian drawings for the respective tasks.

Results

No-Study Session. As the right half of Table 39.4 shows, eliminating the study session entirely had no systematic effect on no-labels subjects. With handwriting, horse racing, and children's drawings, mean confidence and percent correct were virtually the same for the present subjects and those shown 10 unlabeled examples. With ulcers, percent correct went down somewhat and confidence increased, suggesting that the absence of overconfidence in Experiment 2 was only a chance result.

Abbreviated Labeled Study Sessions. Remarkably, seeing one pair of labeled examples enabled both handwriting and ulcer subjects to perform somewhat better than chance. They were more confident than the corresponding no-labels subjects (who did no better than chance), but this increased confidence was justified. The horse racing and children's drawing groups provide a better test of the effect of worthless study on confidence, because the few labeled examples they saw did not improve their performance. Their mean confidence was indistinguishable from that of subjects who studied 10 labeled examples. [6]

CONCLUDING DISCUSSION

Using a variety of tasks, instructions, and study sessions, these experiments have confirmed the most robust result of previous work on confidence (Einhorn & Hogarth, 1978; Fischhoff, Slovic, & Lichtenstein, 1977; Lichtenstein, Fischhoff, & Phillips, 1977): People are consistently overconfident in their ability to perform difficult or impossible tasks with which they have some minimal familiarity. As performance improves, overconfidence decreases.

Our attempts to manipulate confidence through the provision of useless study examples were humbled by this imported overconfidence. The fact that subjects were just as confident in the absence of study sessions (Experiment 8) as with them suggests that mere exposure to a comprehensible task leads people to feel that they have some competence to perform it. Some possible reasons for this illusion of competence were discussed earlier. Perhaps the

---

[6]A horse racing group that saw two unlabeled examples was also conducted ($N = 44$). They showed about the same percentage correct (37.3%), mean confidence (.623), and overconfidence (.250) as the other horse racing groups.

TABLE 39.4
Experiment 8: Amount of Study

Number of cases studied	Labels				No Labels			
	Percent Correct	Mean probab.	Over/under confidence[a]	N	Percent Correct	mean probab.	Over/under confidence[a]	N
Handwriting								
10 (Exp.1)								
2	77.0	.745	−.025	22	53.3	.645	.112	30
0	62.9	.705	.076	45	56.8	.641	.073	40
Ulcers								
8 (Exp.2)								
2	76.3	.702	−.061	33	58.5	.599	.014	38
0	70.5	.673	−.033	42	50.0	.643	.143	39
Horse Racing								
10 (Exp.4)								
2	41.5	.603	.188	46	39.1	.651	.260	42
0	40.7	.624	.217	44	40.0	.621	.221	38
Children's Drawings (Discouraging Instructions)								
60 (Exp.6)								
10	57.7	.631	.054	40	45.6	.627	.171	36
0	51.9	.651	.132	44	51.1	.650	.139	41

[a] Equals difference between mean probability and percent correct. Negative sign indicates underconfidence.

most interesting explanation to receive support from these studies is that confidence may be relatively independent of immediate experience. It would seem as though the very ability to generate an applicable rule for discrimination carries with it a conviction that the rule has some validity. Because it is almost always possible to generate some rule (e.g., "'rugal pattern' sounds malignant to me") overconfidence should then be the rule rather than the exception.

Once generated, confidence may be very difficult to dispel, for it is unusual to receive a concentrated set of clearly labeled examples of the sort needed to test one's rules (Goldberg, 1968). More typically, such feedback as we receive is late (so that we forget or misremember our predictions), spread over time (so that its cumulative impact is lost), or ambiguous (so that we can explain away our mistakes). All these characteristics of our experience could tend to leave our confidence unshaken by experience. And, on those rare occasions when feedback is prompt and precise, we may not know how to use it to assess discriminability (Einhorn & Hogarth, 1978; Fischhoff, in press; Wason & Johnson-Laird, 1972).

Flawed as it was, the opportunity for learning afforded by the labels conditions may actually be something of an antidote to the power of self-generated feedback, either by improving performance (as with ulcers and handwriting) or by showing that it's not all that easy to come up with a discriminating cue for a large set of study examples.

How has the present concentrated, immediate, and unambiguous experience affected our confidence in the hypothesis that motivated this enterprise? Rather little. We still believe that capitalization on chance patterns can generate undue confidence in erroneous theories. What has changed is our belief in the prevalence of looking for patterns as a mode of learning and determining confidence. Although an effective path to overconfidence, capitalization upon chance may not be a necessary one.

ACKNOWLEDGMENTS

Our thanks to Barbara Combs, Michael Enbar, Solomon Fulero, Gerry Hanson, and Mark Layman for help in conducting these experiments; to Nancy Collins and Peggy Roecker for typing and clerical assistance. We also thank Sarah Lichtenstein, Ray Nickerson, and two anonymous reviewers for their comments on earlier drafts.

This research was supported by the Advanced Research Projects Agency of the Department of Defense and was monitored by Office of Naval Research under Contract N00014-78-C-0100 (ARPA Order No. 3469) under Subcontract 78-072-0722 from Decisions and Designs, Inc. to Perceptronics, Inc. Correspondence may be addressed to either author at Decision Research, A Branch of Perceptronics, 1201 Oak Street, Eugene, Oregon 97401.

REFERENCES

Armstrong, J. S. Tom Swift and his electric regression analysis machine: 1973. *Psychological Reports*, 1975, *36*, 806.

Campbell, D. T. Degrees of freedom and the case study. *Comparative Political Studies*, 1975, *8*, 178–193.

Crask, M. R., & Perreault, W. D., Jr. Validation of discriminant analysis in marketing research. *Journal of Marketing Research*, 1977, *14*, 60–68.

Einhorn, J. H., & Hogarth, R. M. Confidence in judgment: Persistence of the illusion of validity. *Psychological Review*, 1978, *85*, 395–416.

Fama, E. F. Random walks in stock market prices. *Financial Analysts Journal*, 1965, *21*, 55–60.

Fischhoff, B. Hindsight ≠ foresight: The effect of outcome knowledge on judgment under uncertainty. *Journal of Experimental Psychology: Human Perception and Performance*, 1975, *1*, 288–299.

Fischhoff, B. Perceived informativeness of facts. *Journal of Experimental Psychology: Human Perception and Performance*, 1977, *3*, 349–358.

Fischhoff, B. For those condemned to study the past: Reflections on historical judgment. In R. A. Shweder & D. W. Fiske (Ed.), *New Directions for Methodology of Behavioral Science: Fallible Judgment in Behavioral Research*. San Francisco: Jossey-Bass, in press.

Fischhoff, B., Slovic, P., & Lichtenstein, S. Knowing with certainty: The appropriateness of extreme confidence. *Journal of Experimental Psychology: Human Perception and Performance*, 1977, *3*, 552–564.

Goldberg, L. R. Simple models or simple processes? Some research on clinical judgments. *American Psychologist*, 1968, *23*, 483–496.

Hammond, K. R., & Summers, D. A. Cognitive control. *Psychological Review*, 1972, *79*, 58–67.

Hamner, W. C. The importance of sample size, cut-off technique, and cross validation in multiple regression analysis. Paper presented at annual meeting of *American Institute of Decision Sciences*, 1975.

Jiler, W. *How charts can help you in the stock market*. New York: Trendline, 1962.

Kellogg, R. *Analyzing children's art*. Palo Alto, Calif.: National Press, 1970.

Kunce, J. T., Cook, D. W., & Miller, D. E. Random variables and correlational overkill. *Educational and Psychological Measurement*, 1975, *35*, 529–534.

Langer, E. J. The illusion of control. *Journal of Personality and Social Psychology*, 1975, *32*, 311–328.

Langer, E. J. The psychology of chance. *Journal for the Theory of Social Behavior*, 1977, *7*, 185–208.

Lewis-Beck, M. S. Stepwise regression: A caution. *Political Methodology*, 1978, *5*, 213–240.

Lichtenstein, S., & Fischhoff, B. Do those who know more also know more about how much they know? The calibration of probability judgments. *Organizational Behavior and Human Performance*, 1977, *20*, 159–183.

Lichtenstein, S., Fischhoff, B., & Phillips, L. D. Calibration of probabilities: The state of the art. In H. Jungermann & G. deZeeuw (Eds.), *Decision making and change in human affairs*. Amsterdam: D. Reidel, 1977.

O'Leary, M. K., Coplin, W. D., Shapiro, H. B., & Dean, D. The quest for relevance. *International Studies Quarterly*, 1974, *18*, 211–237.

Slovic, P., Fischhoff, B., & Lichtenstein, S. Behavioral decision theory. *Annual Review of Psychology*, 1977, *28*, 1–39.

Slovic, P., Rorer, L., & Hoffman, P. J. Analyzing the use of diagnostic signs. *Investigative Radiology*, 1971, *6*, 18–26.

Wason, P. C., & Johnson-Laird, P. N. *Psychology of reasoning: Structure and content*. London: D. T. Batsford, 1972.

Author Index

Klein, R. M., 45, 46, *56,* 61, 73, *74,* 124, *125,* 260, 263, 264, *275*
Klemmer, E. T., 41, 43, *56,* 101, 105
Kline, P., 400, *416*
Knight, Jr. J. L., 46, *55,* 240, 241, 243, *255, 256,* 298, 306, *314*
Knoll, R. L., 30, 42, 44, *57,* 95, 97, 103, *106,* 123, *125*
Knott, J. R., 79, 88, *90*
Knowles, W. B., 240, *255*
Koehler, W., 633, *636*
Koerner, E., 262, *275*
Koffka, K., 323, *343*
Kohonen, T., 514, *519*
Kollasch, S. F., 444, *456*
Koopman, B. O., 234, *237*
Kopp, G., 491, 492, *494*
Kornblum, S., 195, *196*
Kornhuber, H. H., 33, *56,* 75, 80, *89, 90*
Kosslyn, S. M., 322, *343,* 382, *391, 392*
Kozminsky, E., 411, *417,* 473, *474*
Krantz, D. H., 22, *25,* 367, *380*
Krashen, S. D., 253, *255*
Kristofferson, A. B., 100, *106,* 359, *360*
Kroll, J. F., 397, 398, 399, 408, 414, *417*
Kroll, N., *255*
Kubovy, M., 588, 589, *592*
Kuiper, N. A., 652, *669*
Kulik, J., 653, *658*
Külpe, O., 200, 208, *209*
Kunce, J. T., 781, *800*
Kutas, M., 80, 88, *90*
Kuypers, H., 32, 33, *53, 54*

L

Laabs, G. J., 543, *553*
LaBerge, D., 9, *25,* 215, *237*
Lachman, R., 401, 403, *416*
Lagasse, P. P., 43, *56*
Laming, D. R., 61, *74,* 356, *360, 564, 573*
Landauer, T. K., 463, *474,* 599, *619*
Lane, D. M., 298, 304, *314*
Laner, S., 441, *456*
Lang, P. J., 86, *90*
Langer, E. J., 781, *800*
Langford, T .L., 587, *592*
Lansman, M., *255*
Lapinski, R. H., 423, *433*

Lappin, J. S., 21, *25,* 73, *74*
Larkin, W., 180, *196*
Larsen, A., 17, *25*
Lashley, K. S., 108, *125*
Lea, G., 696, *718*
Lee, W., 161, *178,* 180, *196*
Lehrer, A., 612, *619*
Lehtiö, P. K., 381, 389, *392*
Leifer, L. J., 80, *90*
Leirer, V. O., 693, 694, 695, 705, 706, *718,* 746, 756, *761*
Leopold, F. F., *256*
Lesgold, A. M., 399, *417*
Levelt, W. J. M., 437, *456*
Levin, H., 396, 409, *416*
Lewis, C. H., 400, *416, 667, 669*
Lewis-Beck, M. S., 781, *800*
Liberman, A. M., 333, *345*
Lichtenstein, S., 694, *718,* 783, 793, 795, 797, *800*
Lieberman, K., 243, *254*
Liepa, P., 497, 508, 514, *519*
Light, L. L., 453, *456*
Lindblom, B. E. F., 476, 477, 478, *493*
Lindquist, E. G., 113, *125*
Lindsay, P. H., 243, *255, 257,* 320, *343*
Lindsley, D. B., 76, 79, 80, 87, 88, 89, *90, 91*
Lingo, W. M., 40, 43, *56,* 108, 124, *125*
Link, S. W., 356, *360*
Lockhart, R. S., 499, 516, *518, 519,* 660, *668*
Lockhead, F. R., 332, *343*
Lockhead, G. R., 179, 180, 181, 194, *196,* 335, *343*
Loftus, E. F., 596, 598, 599, 602, 604, *618, 619*
Loftus, G. R., 499, *519*
Logan, J., 243, *255*
Lohnes, P. R., 735, *743*
London, M., 720, *743*
Long, J. B., 161, 176, *178,* 241, 243, 253, *255,* 492, *494*
Lorch, R. F., 599, *619*
Lounsbury, F. G., 610, *619*
Loveless, N. E., 76, 79, 86, *90*
Low, M. C., 88, *90*
Luce, R. D., 129, 130, 132, 133, 141, *157,* 160, 166, *177, 178,* 181, 182, 189, 193, 194, *196,* 292, *295,* 363, *380,* 426, *433*

Subject Index

OC